Local Government Contracts and Procurement

LOCAL GOVERNMENT CONTRACTS AND PROCUREMENT

General Editor
Helen Randall, Partner, Nabarro Nathanson

Assistant Editor
Lianne Smith, Nabarro Nathanson

Editors
Ray Ambrose, Nabarro Nathanson
Rupert Battcock, Nabarro Nathanson
Rachel Bickler, Nabarro Nathanson
Mary Bonar, Nabarro Nathanson
Valda Brooks, Nabarro Nathanson
Ilyas Bulbulia, Nabarro Nathanson
Gerlando Butera, Nabarro Nathanson
Jess Connors, Barrister, 39 Essex Street
Michael Conroy Harris, Nabarro Nathanson
Elizabeth Cooper, Nabarro Nathanson
Alan Corcoran, Nabarro Nathanson
Nicola Greaney, Barrister, 39 Essex Street
Malcolm Iley, Nabarro Nathanson
David Lyon, Nabarro Nathanson
Chris Lee, Nabarro Nathanson
Paul McDermott, Nabarro Nathanson
Ashwin Maini, Barrister, 39 Essex Street
Rosemary Mulley, Nabarro Nathanson
Kath Nicholson, Head of Law, London Borough of Lewisham
Stephen Ravenscroft, Nabarro Nathanson
James Snape, Nabarro Nathanson
Colin Thomann, Barrister, 39 Essex Street
Mark Waring, Nabarro Nathanson

Members of the LexisNexis Group worldwide

United Kingdom	LexisNexis Butterworths Tolley, a Division of Reed Elsevier (UK) Ltd, Halsbury House, 35 Chancery Lane, LONDON, WC2A 1EL, and 4 Hill Street, EDINBURGH EH2 3JZ
Argentina	LexisNexis Argentina, BUENOS AIRES
Australia	LexisNexis Butterworths, CHATSWOOD, New South Wales
Austria	LexisNexis Verlag ARD Orac GmbH & Co KG, VIENNA
Canada	LexisNexis Butterworths, MARKHAM, Ontario
Chile	LexisNexis Chile Ltda, SANTIAGO DE CHILE
Czech Republic	Nakladatelství Orac sro, PRAGUE
France	Editions du Juris-Classeur SA, PARIS
Hong Kong	LexisNexis Butterworths, HONG KONG
Hungary	HVG-Orac, BUDAPEST
India	LexisNexis Butterworths, NEW DELHI
Ireland	Butterworths (Ireland) Ltd, DUBLIN
Italy	Giuffrè Editore, MILAN
Malaysia	Malayan Law Journal Sdn Bhd, KUALA LUMPUR
New Zealand	LexisNexis Butterworths, WELLINGTON
Poland	Wydawnictwo Prawnicze LexisNexis, WARSAW
Singapore	LexisNexis Butterworths, SINGAPORE
South Africa	LexisNexis Butterworths, DURBAN
Switzerland	Stämpfli Verlag AG, BERNE
USA	LexisNexis, DAYTON, Ohio

© Reed Elsevier (UK) Ltd 2002

A CIP Catalogue record for this book is available from the British Library.

ISBN 0 406 94897 6

Printed and bound in Great Britain by Clays Ltd, St Ives plc

Visit Butterworths LexisNexis *direct* at www.butterworths.com

PREFACE

Local government in the United Kingdom is a unique environment. It is highly regulated by both domestic and European legislation. Its constitution, structure and operation have been subject to almost continual change since the early 1970s and its members and officers work within a goldfish bowl, being open to a high degree of public scrutiny and constant audit. The culture of local government is quite different from other parts of the public sector, for example central government, health or education. Local government officers and members operate within a highly political environment that at the same time is subjected to criticism for its lack of democratic accountability. There is a strong sense of public service ethos while at the same time in pursuit of the Labour government's Third Way, the formerly clear cut division between the public and private sectors is becoming increasingly blurred.

Procurement is an important part of local government's functions. Local government purchases approximately £60 billion of goods, services and supplies in the United Kingdom each year. As such it is not only a huge market but engages in an enormous variety of procurements from small supply contracts, commissioning of personal care services to complex Public Private Partnerships and Private Finance Initiative schemes and e-government projects.

The importance of local government procurement in a policy context was recognised by the Thatcher government in the enactment of the compulsory competitive tendering regime and by our present government in its abolition of CCT and implementation of the Best Value legislation. The Byatt Report (covered in chapter 4 of this book) recognised that the delivery of better quality public services can only be achieved if procurement practice in local government is also improved. Furthermore, many authorities recognise that procurement can also be used as a means of implementing other policies and functions such as the power of economic, social and environmental well-being, sustainability, Local Agenda 21, regeneration and the encouragement of small and medium-sized enterprises in the local community.

Done badly, procurement in the public sector attracts negative press coverage at both national and local levels and it also decreases both the public and private sectors' confidence in doing business with each other.

Done well, procurement can achieve policy objectives, enhance public confidence and strengthen the economy and it is hoped that this work will go some way towards facilitating the achievement of those aims.

This volume has been written not just for lawyers and procurement professionals but also for both officers and members working with local government who are concerned with procurement and policy as well as those in the private, financial and voluntary sectors who do business with local government. My intention in collating and writing this book has been to clarify and demystify procurement law and practice in the particular context of local government. However, some sections will have application to other parts of the public sector. I hope the book provides detailed yet practical advice. It combines detailed explanation of areas of the law which affect local government procurement such as the European procurement rules, contractual interpretation, intellectual property rights and the Transfer of Undertakings Regulations. It also contains practical guidance for those wishing to engage in procurements at an operational level including a chapter on contract drafting and case studies on the new kinds of partnerships upon which local authorities are embarking including: construction, e-government, housing, leisure trusts, a library PFI, accommodation outsourcing, social services and health, education partnership and bus quality partnership schemes.

The lawyers I have chosen to contribute to this work are both experts in their specialist field of practice and also familiar with local government from their experience of advising both local authorities and private and voluntary sector parties who do business with local government. In this respect I have been fortunate to draw on colleagues in Nabarro Nathanson's Projects Group, where we advise over 180 local authorities and other statutory bodies as well as contractors and financiers, members of 39 Essex Street a set of chambers well known in the field of public law and Kath Nicholson, Head of London Borough of Lewisham's award winning legal services department.

It should of course be borne in mind that this book is intended to provide general guidance as to the topics covered within as at the date of publication and readers are reminded to seek specific professional advice in respect of particular contract or principles of procurement.

I would like to thank all the contributors to this book, who being busy transactional lawyers have in many cases sacrificed their weekends to write their chapters. In particular, I would like to thank my assistant editor, Lianne Smith, whose persistence and support have proved invaluable in achieving completion of this work.

Helen Randall
Partner, Nabarro Nathanson
Public Sector Group, Projects Department

October 2002

CONTENTS

ABBREVIATIONS AND ACRONYMS

4Ps	Public Private Partnership Programme Ltd
ADR	alternative dispute resolution
ALMO	arm's length management organisation
ARD	EC Acquired Rights Directive 77/187
BAFO	best and final offer
BCAs	basic credit approvals
BVPI	best value performance indicator
CCT	compulsory competitive tendering
CPC	central product classification codes
CPV	common procurement vocabulary
CRM	customer relationship management
C(RTP)A	Contracts (Rights of Third Parties) Act 1999
DCMS	Department for Culture, Media and Sport
DfES	Department for Education and Skills
DLO	direct labour organisation
DSO	direct services organisation
EAT	Employment Appeal Tribunal
EDI	electronic data interchange
EDP	Educational Development Plan
EMAS	eco-management and audit scheme
ERP	enterprise resource planning
ESCO	energy supply company
ETO	economic, technical or organisational
FBC	final business case
FM	facilities management
HRA	housing revenue account
ICT	information communications and technology
IEG	implementing electronic government
IPR	intellectual property rights
IPS	Industrial and Provident Society
IRR	internal rate of return
ITN	Invitation to Negotiate
ITT	Invitation to Tender
KPI	key performance indicator
LEA	local education authority
LGOL	Local Government Online Initiative

LSP	local strategic partnership
LSVT	large scale voluntary transfer
LTA	local transport authority
MEAT	most economically advantageous offer
NCA	notional credit approval
NCSC	National Care Standards Commission
NNDR	national non-domestic rates
NFPO	not for profit organisation
NRF	Neighbourhood Renewal Fund
OBC	outline business case
ODPM	Office of the Deputy Prime Minister
OGC	Office of Government Commerce
OJEC	Official Journal of the European Communities
PDA	principal development agreement
PFI	private finance initiative
PIN	prior information notice
PPP	public private partnership
PQQ	pre-qualification questionnaire
PRG	Project Review Group
PSA	public service agreement
PSBR	public sector borrowing requirement
REM	retention of employment model
RSL	registered social landlord
SCA	supplementing credit approvals
TTF	Treasury Task Force
TUPE	Transfer of Undertakings (Protection of Employment) Regulations 1981
UCTA	Unfair Contract Terms Act 1977

TABLE OF STATUTES

References in the right-hand column are to paragraph numbers. Paragraph references printed in **bold** type indicate where the Act is set out in part or in full.

TABLE OF STATUTORY INSTRUMENTS

References in the right-hand column are to paragraph number. Paragraph references printed in **bold** type indicate where the Statutory Instrument is set out in part or in full.

TABLE OF CASES

S

Z

Zephyr, The. See General Accident Fire and Life Assurance Corpn v Tanter, The
    Zephyr

PART I
PRINCIPLES OF PROCUREMENT

CHAPTER 1

Preparing for procurement*

Helen Randall

*   This chapter has been adapted and updated from an official annex which was prepared by Helen Randall for the Byatt Task Force (see para **4.23**).

1.01   Most procurement specialists (whether in-house or external) will tend to agree that thorough preparation by client officers for the commissioning or procurement of supplies, works and, in particular, services pays dividends. It enables the procuring authority to ascertain fully the nature of the works, supplies or services it wishes to buy and to what extent the market can deliver these, whether these will meet the needs of the authority, the community it serves, and to evaluate the nature of the obligations and liabilities that will form part of the contract.

1.02   Proper preparation minimises the scope for misunderstanding and consequent legal disputes between the procuring authority and the contractor as well as disappointment or even legal challenges by stakeholders. (The term stakeholder is used here to cover recipients of local authority services, tenants, community groups, local business, trade unions and employees.) This aspect assumes even more importance if the partnering principles recommended in the Egan report (see paras **4.13–4.22**) are to be adopted.

1.03   If an authority prepares well for a procurement the time spent in the early stages will be saved later on. The early ground-work will inevitably cut down the number and complexity of commercial, financial and legal issues to be negotiated between the procuring authority and the contractor. This in turn will tend to encourage and stimulate private sector interest in the transaction. Some potential providers of supplies, works or services are deterred from doing business with local government on the basis of a perception that negotiating with local government is too time consuming to be commercially attractive. Often the reason doing business with local government takes too long is because the officers have embarked on the procurement of a particular project at the members' behest without being sufficiently resourced to have carried out the necessary audits and consultation exercises first.

1.04   Thorough preparation for procurement helps prevent potential grounds for legal challenge under the European procurement Directives[1] which can arise, for example, by changes to specifications after publication of the OJEC advertisement or post-tender negotiation in the open or restricted procedures[2].

1   Council Directive (EEC) 50/92 of 18 June 1992 relating to the co-ordination of procedures for the award of public services contracts and implemented in the UK by the Public Services Contracts Regulations 1993, SI 1993/3228; Council Directive (EEC) 36/93 of 14 June 1993 co-ordinating of procedures for the award of public supply contracts and implemented in the UK by the Public Supply Contracts Regulations 1995, SI 1995/201; Council Directive (EEC) 37/93 of 14 June 1993 co-ordinating of procedures for the award of public works contracts

and implemented in the UK by the Public Works Contracts Regulations 1991, SI 1991/2680; Council Directive (EEC) 52/97 of 13 October 1997 amending Directives 92/50/EEC, 93/36/EEC and 93/37/EEC concerning the co-ordination of procedures for the award of public service contracts, public supply contracts and public works contracts respectively and implemented in the UK by the Public Contracts (Works, Services and Supply) (Amendment) Regulations 2000, SI 2000/2009.

2   See *R v Portsmouth City Council, ex p Coles and George Austin (Builders) Ltd* [1997] 1 CMLR 1135, CA (the *Bonaco Builders* case) for an example of a change to the nature of the procurement after the publication of the original specification, *Harmon CFEM Facades (UK) Ltd v Corporate Officer of the House of Commons* (1999) 67 Con LR 1 (the *Harmon* case) and *EC Commission v Belgium (Walloon Buses)* C-87/94 [1996] ECR I-2043, ECJ (the *Walloon Buses* case) for an example of unauthorised use of the negotiated procedure. The open procedure is found at reg 11 of each of the UK Regulations while the restricted procedure is found at reg 12.

1.05   Similarly, employment lawyers will probably endorse the view that many of the recent cases involving application of the Transfer of Undertakings (Protection of Employment) Regulations 1981[1] by aggrieved employees or unions might have been prevented if they had sufficient appreciation of the nature of the employees likely to be affected by the transfer being undertaken before the authority concerned had embarked on its procurement exercise.

1   SI 1981/1794, generally abbreviated to 'the TUPE Regulations'.

1.06   It is appreciated that within the local government context in particular, members will often be anxious to let the contract and secure service improvements within a limited timescale to accommodate the end or beginning of the authority's financial year or an electoral term. Training should, therefore, be made available to members to raise their awareness of the important benefits of allowing officers sufficient time to prepare for major procurements or commissionings.

1.07   Preparation for procurement can be categorised as follows:
(1)   external and internal consultation;
(2)   transfer of employees;
(3)   transfer of land;
(4)   transfer of assets and equipment (including ICT systems); and
(5)   preparation for the procurement process itself.

EXTERNAL AND INTERNAL CONSULTATION

External consultation

1.08   Consultation of relevant suppliers can help indicate how a contract can be packaged (for example in relation to the duration of the contract or the services/supplies/works to be included within the contract) to ensure the best competitive response from the market. It should be borne in mind, however, that over-consultation on every aspect of a proposed contract (with a resulting dissemination of responses from the market in general) can lead to 'consultation fatigue' within the proposed marketplace and failure to respect commercial confidentiality can compromise innovation.

1.09   If, as a local government officer, you intend to embark on a major procurement exercise without first consulting the market, consider the following examples where failure to carry out advance market consultation had a seriously detrimental impact on the procurement as follows :

— **Authority A** Authority A procured a joint accommodation and ICT systems contract only to find that its preferred partner was unable to take on a contract which risked complete termination on failure of ICT systems. Negotiations to close the transaction were delayed by several months. Market consultation before OJEC would have indicated that the two elements would have been more effectively let under separate contracts.

— **Authority B** Authority B advertised for a panel of suppliers under a call-off agreement with the aim of securing increased choice for stakeholders. Market consultation before OJEC would have revealed that few firms were willing to invest resources in bidding for a contract where they would have a relatively lower chance of winning work. The consequence was that the authority had to suspend and re-advertise its procurement, leading to several months' delay in contract start-up.

— **Authorities C, D and E** Authorities C, D and E all advertised contracts for large scale works and services in the same specialist sector at the same time. Market consultation would have shown that the relatively limited number of firms available to provide the works and services did not have sufficient resources to bid for all three contracts at the same time. Staggering the three contracts would have led to a better market response.

1.10   When feeding the results of a market consultation exercise into the procurement, however, the procurement officer should be aware that gearing of the specification to suit one particular supplier or group of suppliers could be deemed discriminatory under EC procurement rules. It is therefore advisable to keep an audit trail of all consultation exercises.

1.11   Under the duty of 'best value' (as a result of the Local Government Act 1999, s 3(2)) and other legislation (for example, the requirement to consult under the Housing Act 1985, s 105 in relation to housing management) and as a matter of ensuring that the procurement, of a service in particular, will meet the needs of its community, local authorities are obliged to undertake consultation of certain stakeholders.

1.12   Consultation with service users and proposed service users (as is required under best value) should be completed in advance of drawing up the specification and subsequent advertisement of a contract. If specific individuals within the community are consulted with regard to the content of any contract, suitable training should be offered to ensure that they understand issues of pricing against the specification and the need to maintain commercial confidentiality.

1.13   Consultation about the content or specification *after* the contract has been put out to tender, and particularly after bids have been received, will tend to raise false expectations within the community as to the extent that they can influence and subsequently change the specification, resulting in consequent disappointment.

1.14   Officers should be careful to keep an audit trail of all consultation carried out and ensure that the appropriate media are used for consultation. (For example, there is little point in advertising for comments in a local newspaper unless the newspaper is read by the particular section of the community from whom views are to be sought.)

Internal consultation

1.15   Unfortunately it is sometimes the case that part way through a procurement, and at worst after bids have been received, the department which is responsible for letting the contract will be notified by another department within that authority that the parameters for the contract should change in order to reflect a particular corporate or departmental requirement of that authority. Such changes compromise value for money and can give grounds for legal challenge if the specification needs to be amended after publication of the OJEC advertisement or if post-tender negotiations are required[1].

1   See *Bonaco Builders, Walloon Buses* and the *Harmon* cases.

1.16   To prevent this it is recommended that officers complete internal consultation with key departments in advance of completing the specification for the contract and certainly in advance of placing the OJEC advertisement. Key departments would include IT, human resources, financial and legal departments and any other parts of the authority which would be directly affected by the letting of the contract to an external organisation.

1.17   In all procurement exercises, particularly where complex procurements are involved, lack of preparation inevitably results in lack of effective risk-transfer from the local authority to its contractor. For example, a failure to audit base-line information will often lead to an insistence from the contractor on warranties from the local authority as to the accuracy of that information.

1.18   As part of internal consultation, local authorities also need to bear in mind that the consultation under Acquired Rights Directive ('ARD')[1] and the TUPE Regulations 1981, reg 10[2], should be undertaken by the authority as early as possible. Again, an audit trail for any consultation processes undertaken will help prevent later disputes and may be a crucial requirement of the contractor's due diligence process before the contract can be completed.

1   Council Directive (EEC) 187/77 relating to the safeguarding of employees' rights in the event of transfer of undertakings, recently replaced by Council Directive (EC) 23/2001.
2   SI 1981/1794.

PREPARATION FOR TRANSFER OF EMPLOYEES

1.19   Where a procuring authority has taken the time to ascertain not just the number and identities of the employees who may transfer to the external contractor, but has also obtained an up-to-date and accurate record of each employee's terms and conditions of employment, including the employee's employment history[1] (such as a record of any claims brought by that employee, the employee's entitlement to or membership of the Local Government Pension Scheme and the right to occupy any tied accommodation), then considerable time will be saved in negotiation. If this information is not gathered in a complete form before the contract is let, bid prices will not be accurate and value for money and probity will be affected detrimentally.

In addition, there is a possibility that aggrieved employees may bring a claim against the authority and/or the incoming contractor[2].

1 TUPE 1981, reg 10(2)(a)–(c).
2 TUPE 1981, reg 11.

TRANSFER OF LAND/PROPERTY

1.20 Occasionally a local authority will be transferring either the ownership or the right to occupy land or property to an incoming external contractor[1] (for example, a depot or surplus land which a contractor will develop in order to generate income to supplement payments by the authority). In these circumstances, before a procurement is embarked upon, the prudent officer will ensure that:

(1) the boundaries and nature of the legal or equitable title to the land have been confirmed;
(2) a survey to ascertain the extent of any environmental contamination or construction defects has been carried out; and
(3) the firm carrying out the survey is prepared to warrant its accuracy to the new contractor.

Steps should also be taken to secure vacant possession of any land to be transferred. Failure to do this will tend to delay the completion of the contract or lead to subsequent claims or disputes under the contract.

1 Eg using powers under the Local Government Act 1972, s 123 or the General Disposal Consent 1998.

TRANSFER OF ASSETS (INCLUDING ICT)

1.21 Many local authorities hold equipment and other assets under leasing agreements and will have a right to use ICT equipment by way of exclusive licence from the ICT supplier. If, as part of the procurement, the authority proposes that the incoming external contractor should use any of the equipment or ICT systems, the authority should ascertain the terms on which the equipment and ICT can be used before embarking on the procurement. The authority should also check whether the agreements (eg for the use of software) can be transferred or novated to the contractor. Again, failure to do this will tend to prolong negotiation of the transaction and/or lead to subsequent claims or disputes under the new contract or the existing contracts with the equipment/ICT supplier[1]. It is also advisable to undertake an audit or survey of all equipment and ICT systems (the ICT 'estate', as it is known) in order to produce an inventory that can be attached to any invitation to tender/invitation to negotiate. This is, of course, of particular relevance to procurement of electronic service delivery and the strategic partnerships for back-office services.

1 See for example *St Albans City and District Council v International Computers Ltd* [1996] 4 All ER 481, CA.

Audit of base-level data

1.22 The quality of base-level data supplied to prospective contractors will have a direct impact on contract price. Suppliers tend to price high those contingencies which they can not manage. For example, a local authority embarking on an outsourcing project should ascertain and check data provided to the contractor as to base levels of service currently delivered and the history of volume of supplies or services required. The data should be verifiable by the contractor, its sub-contractors, its insurers and any external funders. Otherwise, warranties will be sought and limits of liability will be lowered.

THE PROCUREMENT PROCESS

1.23   Officers initiating a major procurement or commissioning exercise should ensure that the specification for the works/services/supply is drafted before placing the OJEC advertisement. Otherwise, there is a risk that the specification may need to be changed following advertisement and the local authority will have the invidious choice of deciding whether to bear the risk of possible challenge under the European procurement Directives or to backtrack on the procurement process and to re-advertise the contract to avoid challenge[1].

1   See the *Bonaco Builders* case.

1.24   When setting tender evaluation criteria the authority should ask itself (if using the 'most economically advantageous tender' option[1]) why each tender evaluation criterion is important and what evidence it expects the tenderer to provide to demonstrate that it meets the particular criterion (which should be listed in order of importance[2]). The tender evaluation criteria should not of course be changed after the invitation to tender/invitation to negotiate has been sent out.

1   Council Directive (EEC) 50/92, art 36(1)(a) and SI 1993/3228, reg 21(1)(a) (services): Council Directive (EEC) 36/93, art 26(1)(b) and SI 1995/201, reg 21(1)(a) (supply): Council Directive (EEC) 37/93, art 30(1)(b) and SI 1991/2680, reg 20(1)(b) (works).
2   Council Directive (EEC) 50/92, art 36(2) and SI 1993/3228, reg 21(3) (services): Council Directive (EEC) 36/93, art 26(2) and SI 1995/201, reg 21(3) (supply): Council Directive (EEC) 37/93, art 30(2) and SI 1991/2680, reg 20(3) (works).

1.25   A thorough audit trail should be made of the entire procurement process and in particular the tender evaluation in order to fend off any complaints by tenderers before they become legal challenges. In a large procurement this will also cut down the time spent by the contractor or the contractor's financier in carrying out their due diligence process before the contract is signed.

CONCLUSION

1.26   If the above points are taken into account, the efficiency of procurement would be improved considerably, with the additional benefit of securing better value for money and an enhanced perception of local government by the commercial and voluntary sectors. Of course, the importance of ensuring the opportunity for taking into account the lessons learnt from any procurement by way of feedback, and the incorporation of those lessons within the next procurement undertaken by that authority, should not be underestimated. Nor should the importance of adequate project management skills.

Sufficient preparation for procurement may appear to be time-consuming at the outset but reaps dividends in time, cost and market perception in the long term.

CHAPTER 2

Why do we have public procurement rules?

Rachel Bickler

INTRODUCTION

2.01   There are basically two fundamental reasons why there are special rules governing public procurement. The first reason is an economic and budgetary one. Purchases by, or under the control of, government, represent a significant part of the gross domestic product (an estimated 14 per cent of the European Union's GDP and over €900 billion). There is therefore a strong incentive to ensure that the government gets the best value it can from the money it spends. One way of achieving this is to introduce competition for government-funded contracts by way of a tendering system.

2.02   The second reason is that the public procurement rules are derived from European Community law, which is aimed at creating a single market for goods and services within the territory of the European Union.

The EU context

2.03   It is fundamental to the objectives of EC law that nationality should not be grounds for discrimination (art 12) and that there should be free trade of goods and services within the Common Market. In particular, the EC Treaty prohibits restrictions on the free movement of goods and services between member states[1]. Article 28 of the EC Treaty provides that quantitative restrictions on imports and all measures having equivalent effect on trade between member states are prohibited. Similarly, art 43 prohibits restrictions on the freedom of establishment and art 49 prohibits restrictions on the freedom to provide services. These provisions are directly enforceable against a public authority which discriminates in its award procedures against goods or services offered by economic operators from other EU member states. An illustration of the importance of these provisions to the issue of public procurement is the judgment of the European Court of Justice (ECJ) in the *Dundalk* case[2] in which the court held that provisions in a public tender which discriminate against products from another member state breach art 28 of the EC Treaty (formerly art 30) concerning the free movement of goods.

1   EU member states: Austria, Belgium, Denmark, Finland, France, Germany, Greece, Ireland, Italy, Luxembourg, the Netherlands, Portugal, Spain, Sweden and the United Kingdom.
2   Case C-45/87 *EC Commission v Ireland* [1988] ECR 4929, ECJ. The case concerned a clause in a public works tender for a Dundalk Urban District Council water supply augmentation, which specified

that the water pipes must be certified as complying with a certain Irish standard. The District Council had refused to consider a tender from a Spanish undertaking with pipes which met international standards and had been the lowest priced tender submitted.

2.04   In addition to rules on free trade, the EC rules on competition can apply to public contracts. The most important of these provisions are the following: art 81(1) of the EC Treaty, which prohibits anti-competitive agreements, decisions by associations of undertakings and concerted practices which may affect trade between member states; art 82, which prohibits the abuse by one or more undertakings of a dominant position within the Common Market; art 86, which provides that public undertakings and undertakings which operate under special or exclusive rights should comply with the principles of art 81 and 82; art 87, which prohibits state aid which distorts or threatens to distort competition by favouring certain undertakings or the production of certain goods, in so far as this affects trade between member states.

2.05   These general provisions of the EC Treaty are applicable to public contracts regardless of the application or otherwise of the specific public procurement rules. Failure to comply with the provisions can lead to serious consequences. However, these general provisions do not by themselves create a single market for public procurement or ensure that this market operates in a competitive fashion[1]. While the Treaty rules described above prohibit certain discriminatory practices they do not impose any specific positive action in terms of the transparency and competition which would be required for contract award procedures. Legislation was therefore introduced at the EU level, from the early 1970s onwards, which was designed to ensure that firms from all member states would be eligible to tender for public contracts throughout the EU.

1   For a case pre-dating the application of EU legislation see for example *Blackpool and Flyde Aero Club v Blackpool Borough Council* [1990] 1 WLR 1195, CA where a local authority was sued for breach of contract and negligence for failing to consider a tender sent in before the expiry of the deadline.

2.06   These rules are based on the following principles:
(1)   that public contracts over a certain value should be advertised throughout the EU and be open to firms and other economic operators based in all member states;
(2)   the tendering system should be open and transparent;
(3)   the technical specifications should not discriminate against potential tenderers;
(4)   the criteria for the selection of candidates and the award of contracts should be fair and objective; and
(5)   in the event of a breach of the rules there should be an effective remedy.

Further background on the EC public procurement rules and their implementation into UK national law can be found at para **2.18**.

Geographic scope of the EC public procurement legislation

2.07   In applying the rules it is necessary to keep in mind that the geographic scope of the EC public procurement rules is being progressively increased by a number of factors, including the following:
(i)   the application of the rules on free movement and public procurement to the EEA countries, namely Iceland, Liechtenstein and Norway;

(ii) there are reciprocal provisions on procurement provided for in the 'Europe Agreements' signed with countries in Central and Eastern Europe and the Baltic countries, subject to transitional requirements[1];
(iii) limited provisions on procurement in the Euro-Mediterranean Agreements;
(iv) limited provisions on procurement in the Partnership and Co-operation Agreements with former Soviet Republics;
(v) the future enlargement of the EU by accession of new member states.

1   The EU has Europe Agreements extending the application of national treatment with the following countries: Bulgaria, the Czech Republic, Estonia, Hungary, Latvia, Lithuania, Poland, Romania, Slovakia and Slovenia.

The international context

2.08   In addition to the EC procurement rules, there are international trade rules on procurement drawn up by the World Trade Organisation (WTO). During the Uruguay round of trade negotiations, the WTO drew up a new Government Procurement Agreement (GPA) which entered into force on 1 January 1996 and replaced earlier agreements, the first of which was concluded in 1979. The GPA provides a framework for reciprocal open tendering among signatory countries. These rules are similar to those established by the EC Directives in the sense that they are also based on general principles of national treatment, non-discrimination and transparency. The GPA also has a system of thresholds which would trigger the application of the obligations, a prohibition on discriminatory technical specification, a requirement to publish tender notices and an obligation to use objective and non-discriminatory criteria to select candidates and award tenders. The EU has entered into bilateral agreements with a number of countries, the effect of which is to extend to undertakings from those countries the rights enshrined under the GPA[1]. The details of the GPA are not covered in depth within the scope of this text but contracting authorities should bear in mind that in some instances firms from signatory countries may be eligible tenderers.

1   Countries who are signatories to the GPA include: the EC, USA, Canada, Israel, Japan, South Korea, Liechtenstein, Singapore, Hong Kong, Norway and Switzerland.

THE LEGISLATIVE FRAMEWORK

The public procurement Directives

2.09   As discussed above, the EC Treaty imposes general rules on free movement of goods and services. In order to create a single market for public procurement within the EU, three principal Directives were adopted. The current Directives are:
—   the Public Works Directive 93/37/EEC[1] ('the works Directive');
—   the Public Supplies Directive 93/36/EEC[2] ('the supplies Directive');
—   the Public Services Directive 92/50/EEC[3] ('the services Directive').

These Directives apply to contracts for the award of works, supplies and services above certain financial thresholds awarded by public bodies.

1   Amended by Directive (EC) 52/97 (OJ L328 28.11.1997 p 1).
2   Amended by Directive (EC) 52/97 (OJ L328 28.11.1997 p 1).
3   Amended by Directive (EC) 52/97 (OJ L328 28.11.1997 p 1).

Remedies

2.10   In addition there are two remedies Directives[1]. Essentially, they set out the framework for seeking redress in the event that there is a breach of the procurement rules. Compliance requirements and redress are discussed in more detail at para **3.179**.

1   Directive (EEC) 665/89 (OJ L395 30.12.89 p 33) and Directive (EEC) 13/92 (OJ L076 13.3.92 p 14).

Utilities

2.11   The public procurement Directives apply to entities over which the state may exercise control. There is another category of entities, which tend, for the sake of convenience, to be referred to as 'utilities', and which are excluded from the scope of these Directives. Utilities which are involved in activities relating to the provision of water, energy, transport and telecommunications are instead governed by Directive (EC) 38/93[1] (the 'Utilities Directive').

1   As amended by Directive (EC) 4/98 (OJ L101 1.4.98 p 1).

2.12   The rationale for excluding utilities from the general rules on public procurement is that, within the EU, there are mixed systems of public and private ownership of such activities. The legal status of utilities varies from private companies, to purely government-owned entities through to concessions. There was therefore debate as to whether rules designed to regulate public bodies should, or could, be applicable. However, it was equally recognised that utilities, whether privately or publicly controlled, tend to operate under special or exclusive rights granted by law. As a result, governments continue to wield considerable financial influence over purchasing policy. Concerns over nationalistic and discriminatory purchasing were raised. Consequently, it was decided that so long as the purchasing policies of utilities are to some extent controlled or influenced by the state, then the utilities contracts should be regulated to ensure fair and non-discriminatory access.

2.13   As some of the regulated activities carried out by utilities are deregulated and are opened up to commercial market conditions, the need for regulatory intervention to provide incentives to go out to competitive tender are reduced. This is the reason why the rules are being gradually disapplied to certain sectors such as voice telephony[1] and to the oil and gas sectors in Austria, the UK and the Netherlands[2].

1   OJ C156 3.6.99 p 3.
2   Austria (OJ L068 131 12.03.02), the UK (OJ L156 155 13.06.97), the Netherlands (OJ L316/41 17.12.93).

2.14   The definition of a utility includes a public authority, a public undertaking or a 'relevant person' who carries out one of the defined activities in the water, energy, transport or telecommunications sector on the basis of a special or exclusive right. A non-exhaustive list of bodies covered by the Utilities Contracts Regulations 1996[1] is contained in Sch 1 to those Regulations.

1   SI 1996/2911.

Local authorities as utilities

2.15   Local authorities may fall under the definition of a 'utility' as far as they carry out any of the specified activities, and any contract relating to such activities will be governed by the Utilities Contracts Regulations rather that the public procurement regulations (conversely, any contracts which local authorities enter into which do not relate to the excluded activities would be governed by the public procurement regulations).

2.16   Among the bodies specifically listed in the Utilities Contracts Regulations 1996, Sch 1 are the following:
(1)   a water and sewerage authority established by the Local Government etc (Scotland) Act 1994, s 62;
(2)   a local authority engaged in the provision or operation of a fixed network which provides or will provide a service to the public in connection with the production, transport or distribution of heat;
(3)   a local authority engaged in the exploitation of a geographic area for the purpose of providing airport or other terminal facilities to carriers by air;
(4)   a local authority engaged in the exploitation of a geographic area for the purpose of providing maritime or inland port or other terminal facilities to carriers by sea or inland waterway;
(5)   regional Passenger Transport Executives (PTEs) including: Strathclyde PTE, Greater Manchester PTE, Tyne and Wear PTE, South Yorkshire PTE, South Yorkshire Super Tram Ltd, Blackpool Transport Services Ltd, Conwy County Borough Council and Transport for London;

2.17   The rules which apply to contracts entered into by utilities are based on the same basic principles to those relating to public authorities and there are similar rules with regard to the advertising of contracts. However, the rules are rather more flexible than those applying to public authorities. It should be noted that the specific rules under the Utilities Contracts Regulations 1996 are not covered by this book.

Direct effect of EU legislation

2.18   Under EU law, a Directive sets out the obligations which a member state has to achieve, but leaves to the national administration the form and method by which those obligations are implemented into national law, and sets a date by which this must be achieved.

2.19   The effectiveness of Directives is not necessarily dependent on the adoption of implementing measures in member states. According to the ECJ's case law on the concept of 'direct effect', once the time limit for transposing a Directive into national law has passed, a provision of a Directive which is capable of directly affecting the legal relationship between an individual and the member state can be enforced by that individual in the national courts. The member state cannot avoid the consequences of the provisions of the Directive because it has failed to implement that Directive by the due date or has failed to do so correctly[1]. The direct effect of the EC Directives was acknowledged by the Court of Appeal in *R v Portsmouth City Council, ex p Peter Coles and Colwick Builders Ltd and ex p George Austin Ltd*[2]. This means that government bodies need to be vigilant about compliance with new EC legislation even if there is a delay in the government timetable for implementation. This requirement applies not only to central government bodies and to national courts but also to regional and local bodies. The ECJ held in the *Fratelli* case[3] that when the conditions for direct effect are met, individuals may rely on the provisions of a Directive and that all organs of administration, including decentralised authorities such as municipalities are obliged to apply those provisions. In the *Hospital Ingenieure* case[4] the ECJ held that detailed rules in the public services Directive relating to the award of a contract could be relied upon by service providers in relation to a engineering service contract related to the construction of a paediatric clinic in a hospital. These provisions had not been properly implemented into national law at the time of the award of the contract. Service providers who wished to challenge the award sought to rely on the provisions of the Directive before the national courts. The ECJ held that the provisions in the Directive were sufficiently unconditional and precise to be relied upon by an individual against the state.

1   Eg Case C-76/97 *Walter Tögel v Niederösterreichische Gebietskrankenkasse* [1998] ECR I-5357, ECJ; Case 31/87 *Gebroeders Beentjes BV v Netherlands* [1988] ECR 4635, ECJ; Case C-258/97 *Hospital Ingenieure Krankenhaustechnik Planungs-Gesellschaft mbH (HI) v Landeskrankenstallen-Betriebsgesellschaft* [1999] ECR I-1405, ECJ.
2   *R v Portsmouth City Council, ex p Peter Coles and Colwick Builders Ltd and George Austin Ltd* [1997] 1 CMLR 1135, CA.
3   103/88 *Fratelli Costanzo SpA v Comune di Milano* [1989] ECR 1839, para 31, [1990] 3 CMLR 239, ECJ.
4   C-258/97 *Hospital Ingenieure Krankenhaustechnik*, paras 33–39.

Implementation in the UK

2.20   In the UK, the main EC public procurement Directives were transposed into national law in the form of Regulations drawn up by the Treasury. The four principal Regulations which establish the general framework for the advertising of government contracts are as follows:
—   Public Works Contracts Regulations 1991, SI 1991/2680[1];
—   Public Supply Contracts Regulations 1995, SI 1995/201[2];
—   Public Services Contracts Regulations 1993, SI 1993/3228[3].
—   Utilities Contracts Regulations 1996, SI 1996/2911[4].

The above Regulations are referred to in this text respectively as the Works Regulations, the Supplies Regulations and the Services Regulations (collectively these three are known as the public procurement regulations) and the Utilities Regulations.

1   Subsequently amended by SI 2000/2009.
2   Subsequently amended by SI 2000/2009.
3   Subsequently amended by SI 2000/2009.
4   These regulations revoked the Utilities Supply and Works Contracts Regulations 1992, which in turn implement Directive (EEC) 38/93 co-ordinating procedures of entities operating in the water, energy, transport and telecommunications sectors Directive (EEC) 13/92 on the review of procedures of entities operating in the water, energy transport and telecommunications sectors.

CHAPTER 3

UK procurement regulations

Rachel Bickler, Lianne Smith & Helen Randall

3.01 The public procurement regulations[1] apply whenever a 'contracting authority' whether by itself, or through a third party, seeks offers in relation to a proposed public 'works', 'supply' or 'service' contract, the value of which meets certain financial thresholds.

1   Ie the Public Works Contracts Regulations 1991, SI 1991/2680, Public Supply Contracts Regulations 1995, SI 1995/201, and the Public Services Contracts Regulations 1993, SI 1993/3228.

WHO IS A CONTRACTING AUTHORITY?

3.02 When determining whether a contract will be governed by the regulations, the starting point is to determine whether the authority entering into that contract is a 'contracting authority'. The rules apply to both state bodies and to other entities operating under public law in the general interest.

3.03 A contracting authority is defined in each of the public procurement regulations as:
(a)   the state;
(b)   Minister of the Crown;
(c)   a government department;
(d)   the House of Commons;
(e)   the House of Lords;
(f)   the Northern Ireland Assembly Commission;
(g)   the Scottish Parliamentary Body Corporate;
(h)   the National Assembly for Wales;
(i)   a local authority;
(j)   a fire authority constituted by a combination scheme under the Fire Services Act 1947;
(k)   the Fire Authority for Northern Ireland;
(l)   a police authority established under the Police Act 1996, s 3;
(m) a police authority established under the Police (Scotland) Act 1967, s 2;
(n)   the Police Authority for Northern Ireland;
(o)   an authority established under the Local Government Act 1985, s 10;
(p)   a joint authority established by Part IV of that Act;
(q)   any body established pursuant to an order under s 67 of that Act;
(r)   the Broads Authority;
(s)   any joint board the constituent members of which consist of any of the bodies specified in sub-paras (h), (i),(k), (l), (n), (o) and (p) and (q) above;

(t)   a National Park authority established by an Order under the Environment Act 1995, s 63;

(u)   the Receiver for the Metropolitan Police District.

3.04   There is a list of bodies to which the regulations apply in the Public Supplies Regulations, Sch 1. However, this list is not exhaustive but merely indicative. The requirement to comply with the rules, however, is not dependent on being listed in the legislation. A body which is listed may no longer be covered by the Directive if it no longer meets the criteria which defines it as a 'contracting authority'.

Definition of 'the state'

3.05   The definition in the regulation of state bodies generally covers the wide range of central, regional and local government bodies. For the sake of clarity, the regulations[1] clarify that in England, 'local authorities' include any county council, district council, London borough council, the Common Council of the City of London, parish council, a community council or the Council of the Isles of Scilly. Similarly in Wales, 'local authority' includes a county council or community council. In Scotland, the term 'local authority' is defined by reference to bodies referred to in the Local Government (Scotland) Act 1973, s 235(1) including any joint board or joint committee of such bodies. In Northern Ireland, it refers to a district council in the meaning of the Local Government Act (Northern Ireland) 1972.

1   Public Works Contracts Regulations 1991, SI 1991/2680, reg 3(2).

3.06   According to the case law, the notion of what constitutes 'the state' has to be interpreted in functional terms In the *Beentjes* case[1], the ECJ examined whether a local land consolidation committee with no legal personality of its own could be considered an emanation of the state for the purposes of the public procurement rules. The court concluded that a body such as this one, whose composition and functions were established by legislation and which was dependent on the authorities for the appointment of its members and was given the task of awarding works contracts, must be regarded as falling within the notion of 'the state' even though it was not formally part of the state administration.

1   Case 31/87 *Gebroeders Beentjes BV v Netherlands* [1988] ECR 4635, para 11.

3.07   It is not only the administrative organs of government which are covered by the procurement rules but also the legislature. This was confirmed by the ECJ in relation to a case concerning a contract involving the Vlaamse Raad (Flemish Regional Parliament in Belgium)[1]. In the UK, both the House of Commons[2] and the House of Lords are expressly named in the public procurement regulations.

1   C-323/96 *EC Commission v Belgium* [1998] ECR I-5063, ECJ.
2   Regulations 3(1)(c) and (d); see also *Harmons CFEM Facades (UK) Ltd v Corporate Officer of the House of Commons* (2000) 67 Con LR 1.

Bodies governed by public law

3.08   In addition to the specifically named government bodies outlined above, the regulations will also apply to a corporation established, or a group of individuals

appointed to act together, for the specific purpose of meeting needs in the general interest, not having an industrial or commercial character and:
(i)   financed wholly or mainly by another contracting authority; or
(ii)   subject to management supervision by another contracting authority; or
(iii) more than half of the board of directors or members of which, or, in the case of a group of individuals, more than half of those individuals, being appointed by another contracting authority, or
(iv)   an association of or formed by one or more of those bodies listed above in (i)–(iii).

Definition of bodies governed by public law

3.09   The identification of 'contracting authorities' who are bodies governed by public law can be more difficult. Such a body must:
(a)   have legal personality; and
(b)   be established for the specific purpose of meeting needs in the general interest, not having industrial or commercial character,
(c)   be state financed or managed by the state or have an administrative or management board more than half of whose members are appointed by the state or by other bodies governed by public law.

3.10   The only bodies which are established in the general interest and fulfil the other criteria which are not treated as 'contracting authorities' are those which are set up to meet needs of an industrial or commercial character. In other words they carry out a business which is the equivalent of a private operator. The distinction may not always be easy to determine, as some of the recent case law illustrates.

3.11   In some instances a body may be allocated certain tasks to be carried out in the general interest but may also derive financial benefits from commercial interests. For instance the Austrian State Printing office ('ÖS') was established to produce official administrative documents, some of which involved some degree of security (eg passports, driving licences and identity cards). However, it derived much of its income as a commercial printer. Where a dispute arose over its status as a 'contracting authority' in relation to a public works contract, the ECJ took the view[1] that since the ÖS was established for the specific purpose of meeting needs in the general interest, it was immaterial that it was free to carry out other tasks. Nevertheless, the court pointed out that a subsidiary undertaking which was established to carry out purely commercial activities and in which the contracting authority has a majority interest was not to be regarded as a body governed by public law.

1   Case C-44/96 *Mannesmann Anlagenbau Austria AG v Strohal Rotationsdruck GmbH* [1998] ECR I-73.

3.12   The term 'needs in the general interest not having an industrial or commercial character' does not exclude needs which are or could be satisfied by a private undertaking as well. An example of this is the *Arnhem* case[1]. Two Dutch municipalities established a new legal entity ('ARA') to carry out refuse collection, recycling and disposal. A dispute arose as to whether ARA was a 'contracting authority' under the procurement rules. The ECJ took the view that the removal and treatment of household refuse could be regarded as meeting a need in the general interest. The existence of competition from private operators was not conclusive evidence that the operations were of an industrial and commercial character. The court held that:

> 'the fact that there is competition is not sufficient to exclude the possibility that a body financed or controlled by the state ... or other bodies governed by public law may choose to be guided by other than economic considerations[2].'

A distinction was drawn in this regard between needs in the general interest not having an industrial character and needs in the general interest having an industrial or commercial character[3].

1   Case C-360/96 *Gemeente Arnhem and Gemeente Rheden v BFI Holding BV* [1998] ECR I-6821, ECJ.
2   [1998] ECR I-6821, para 43.
3   [1998] ECR I-6821, para 46, citing the *Mamesmann* case. See also *Agorà* joined cases C-223/99 and C-260/99 [2001] ECR I-3605, ECJ which concerned a non-profit making body responsible for organising fairs, exhibitions and conferences promoting trade relations.

3.13   The distinction between acting in the general interest or in the commercial interest is a question of function not form. Even a body established in the form of a private company may be a 'contracting authority'. The ECJ clarified this point in a case concerning the Coillte Teoranta (Irish Forestry Board)[1]. The Coillte Teoranta was set up as a private company under the Irish Forestry Act with specific tasks but otherwise operated independently on a daily basis. The court concluded that it was not an emanation of the state but it did carry out functions in the general interest and in other respects fulfilled the criteria establishing it as 'a body governed by public law'.

1   Case C-306/97 *Connemara Machine Turf Co Ltd v Coillte Teoranta* [1998] ECR I-8761, ECJ.

3.14   The issue of where public financing will carry with it the obligations to procure as a 'contracting authority' is proving to be particularly tricky for universities and other educational institutions in the UK which are financed from a range of sources, including not only state funds and student fees but also private sources of funds to support research work. The issue arose in one particular case involving the University of Cambridge and was referred to the ECJ for a ruling[1]. The court ruled that the requirement that a contracting authority be 'for the most part financed' by public funds, means that it receives more than half of all its income (including that which results from commercial activities) from public funds. Awards or grants to support research work and student grants paid by local education authorities for tuition of named students represent public funding, while contracts for research work, consultancy or the organisation of conferences do not. The decision as to whether a body in this position is a 'contracting authority' is one that must be made each year based on an assessment made at the beginning of the budgetary year in which the procurement procedure commences.

1   C-380/98 *R v HM Treasury, ex p University of Cambridge* [2000] ECR I-8035.

Government subsidised contracts

3.15   Contracting authorities are required to ensure that that the regulations are applied where they directly subsidise more than 50 per cent of a works contract valued at €5,000,000 (£3,093,491) which is awarded by a body other than themselves (whether public or private). This requirement, however, only applies to contracts for specialised engineering contracts as listed in Class 50.502 of NACE and contracts for building work for hospitals, facilities for sports, recreation and leisure, university buildings and administrative buildings. The Services Regulations apply to service contracts which are 50 per cent or more subsidised by public funds and valued at over €200,000 (£123,740).

Utilities

3.16   As discussed above (see para **2.11**), procurements by utilities are covered by a separate and parallel regime under the Utilities Regulations. Consequently, functions carried out by a utility are outside the scope of the public procurement Directives. A utility is defined as a public authority, public undertaking or any other relevant person (ie including private law bodies) which carries out activities in energy, transport, water or telecommunications operating on the basis of special or exclusive rights granted by a competent authority. A utility is therefore defined not in relation to ownership, control or financing but in relation to its function. These functions essentially are divided into several categories:
(i)   those which are related to the provision or operation of fixed networks intended to provide a service to the public in connection with production, transport or distribution of drinking water, electricity, gas, heat or to the supply of drinking water, electricity, electricity, gas or heat to such networks;
(ii)   those which relate to the exploration of a geographic area for the purpose of extracting oil, gas, coal or other solid fuels;
(iii)   those which relate to the provision of airport, maritime or inland port or other terminal facilities to carriers by air, sea or inland waterway;
(iv)   operation of networks providing a service to the public in the field of transport by railway, automated systems, tramway, trolley bus, bus or cable;
(v)   the provision of public telecommunications networks or the provision of one or more public telecommunications services.

Details relating to the definition of the utilities are set out in the Utilities Regulations[1].

1   Utilities Contracts Regulations 1996, SI 1996/2911, Sch 1.

THRESHOLDS

3.17   Once it is clear that the body concerned is a 'contracting authority' for the purposes of the regulations, it is then necessary to decide whether the contract itself is within the scope of the regulations. Only contracts over a specific value are subject to the EU-wide tendering requirements.

3.18   Threshold values are established in Euro. The national currency rate for the UK and other countries outside the Euro, is revised and published every two years in the OJEC. The values given in pounds sterling below apply from 1 January 2002[1].

1   OJ C222 27.11.01 p 5.

3.19   Table 1   Thresholds for public procurement contracts from 1/1/02–31/12/03

CONTRACT AUTHORITY	WORKS	SUPPLIES	SERVICES
Entities listed in SI 1995/201, Sch 1[1]	SDR 5,000.000[2] € 6,242,028 £3,861,932	SDR 130,000 €162,293 £100,410	SDR 130,000[3] € 162,293 £100,410
Other contracting authorities	SDR 5,000,000 €6,242,028 £3,861,932	SDR 200,000 €249,681 £154,477	SDR 200,000[3] €249,681 £154,477
Subsidised contracts	€ 5,000,000 £3,093,491	Not applicable	€200,000 £123,740.
Indicative notices	€ 6,242,028 £3,861,932	€750,000 £464,024	€750,000 £464,024
Small lots	€1,000,000 £618,698	Not applicable	€80,000 £49,496

1   Public Supply Contracts Regulations 1995, Sch 1 lists central government bodies subject to the WTO GPA.
2   Special Drawing Right equivalent of the Euro established at the international exchange rate for the purposes of the application of the WTO's GPA.
3   Except for Part B residual services, certain telecommunication services listed in category 5 of Annex 1A and research and development (category 8) services for which the threshold is €200,000 (£123,740)

3.20   Table 2   Utilities

CONTRACT AUTHORITY	WORKS	SUPPLIES	SERVICES
Water, electricity, urban transport (urban railway, trolleybus, bus services), airports and ports	SDR 5,000.000[1] €6,242,028 £3,861,932	SDR 400,000 €499,362 £308, 955	SDR 400,000 €499,362 £308, 955[2]
Oil, gas, coal and railway sectors	€5,000,000 £3,093,491	€400,000 £247,479	€400,000 £247,479
Telecommunications	€5,000,000 £3,093,491	€600,000 £371,219	€600,000 £371,219
Indicative notices	Works threshold	€750,000 £464,024	€750,000 £464,024
Small lots	€1,000,000 £618,698	Not applicable	Not applicable

1   Special Drawing Right equivalent of the Euro established at the international exchange rate for the purposes of the application of the WTO's GPA.
2   With the exception of Part B (residual services) research and development (Category 8), certain telecommunication services which have a threshold of €400,000 (£247,479)

Estimating contract value

3.21   The valuation rules for contracts can be somewhat complex. The general test for calculating the value of the contract is to estimate the total value of the consideration of the contract net of VAT at the time the contract goes out to tender. This value should include all aspects of consideration, whether it takes monetary form or the contribution by the contracting authority of other types of consideration such as goods or equipment. There is a general rule which prohibits the division or 'splitting' of contracts with the intention of evading the application of the procurement rules[1]. In addition, there are specific aggregation rules which apply where the contract is for an indefinite period or is a repetitive or 'regular' contract. However, there are some important exemptions to the 'aggregation' principle. The aggregation rules and the exceptions to them are discussed below with reference to works, supplies and services contracts.

1   Public Works Contracts Regulations 1991, SI 1991/2680, reg 7(8); Public Supply Contracts Regulations 1995, SI 1995/201, reg 7(10); Public Services Contracts Regulations 1993, SI 1993/3228, reg 7(11).

Aggregation rules

Works contracts

Estimating the total value

3.22   When assessing the value of a works contract it is necessary to include not only the value of the works themselves but all the related services, equipment (whether bought or hired) and materials which the contractor will be expected to provide under the contract. Sometimes, a contracting authority will provide the works contractor with some of the goods or equipment to use as part of the construction. The value of those goods should be included in the estimate as part of the consideration for the contract[1].

1   Public Works Contracts Regulations 1991, SI 1991/2680, reg 7(6).

3.23   If the contracting authority is granting a 'works concession'[1], the value of that contract should be based on the consideration which the contracting authority would have paid for the works to be executed if they had not granted a concession[2].

1   For a definition of a works concession see below at para **3.41**.
2   Public Works Contracts Regulations 1991, SI 1991/2680, reg 7(5).

Lots

3.24   When a works or construction project is divided into lots, each of which is the subject of a separate contract, then the value of all the lots must be taken into account when determining whether the threshold is reached. In other words, the threshold is based on the value of the project as a whole. If the threshold is met, the requirements of the Works Regulations must be applied to the award of each contract, regardless of the value of each individual lot. Contracting authorities may not circumvent the rules by splitting contracts or using special methods of calculating the value of the contract.

3.25 There is however a special exclusion for 'small lots'. Contracting authorities are free not to apply the regulations to lots whose estimated value (excluding VAT) is less than €1 million (£618,698). The aggregate value of lots which are freely awarded may not exceed 20 per cent of the total value of all the lots. The exception is therefore available only for larger projects where the lots which may be freely tendered without reference to the regulations represent a relatively small proportion of the value as a whole. All the other contract 'lots' will have to be tendered under the regulations. The fact that the project may involve several contracting authorities and the works cannot be carried out by a single undertaking will not prevent the application of the regulations[1].

1   Eg Case C-16/98 *EC Commission v France* [2000] ECR I-8315, concerning a project to the electrification and street lighting works for the Vendée region in France involving a syndicate of municipal authorities.

Supplies contracts

Estimating the total value

3.26 Where a supply contract is entered into, the estimated value of all the consideration which the contracting authority expects to give will be taken into account in determining the application of the threshold. There is a prohibition on the splitting of a procurement requirement with a view to circumventing the rules. Where the contracting authority has a requirement for goods and enters into a series of contracts for their supply, the total estimated value of the goods is taken into account[1]. This rule is intended to prevent contracting authorities from artificially splitting up their demand into separate lots to avoid the regulations.

1   Public Supply Contracts Regulations 1993, SI 1993/3228, reg 7(5).

Regular or renewable contracts

3.27 Where a contracting authority does have a requirement over a particular time for goods the question arises as to how to calculate the value. In a situation where the contracting authority will either:
(a) enter into a series of contracts; or
(b) enter into a renewable contract,
the contracting authority is free to make an estimate based on two possible alternative formulas so long as that choice is not intended to avoid the rules. The first allows the contracting authority to base estimates on pervious demand, while the second is based on future requirements.

3.28 The estimates are made based on either:
—   the aggregate value of contracts with similar characteristics awarded over the pervious 12 months or the last financial accounting period, adjusted to take into

account the expected changes in quantity and costs of the goods of that type in the next 12 months; or
— the estimated aggregate value of the successive contracts with similar characteristics concluded during the 12 months following the initial delivery or accounting period, where this exceeds 12 months.

3.29 'Similar contracts' refers to contracts involving supplies of the same type (which would include not necessarily just identical goods but also ones which are used for the same or similar purposes) and also assumes that other key elements of the contract are similar. In particular, where the purchases are made by an independent department, the contract may benefit from the exclusion relating to 'discrete operational units' (see below).

Lease, rental or hire-purchase

3.30 Supply contracts cover not only the outright purchase of goods but also the lease, rental or hire-purchase of goods or equipment. In these cases, the calculation of the value will vary in accordance with the length of the contract as follows:
— where the term of the contract is 12 months or less, the total value of the contract's duration;
— where the term exceeds 12 months, the total value of the contract's duration, including the estimated residual value of the products;
— where the contract is concluded for an indefinite period or where the term cannot be defined, the monthly value of the contract multiplied by 48.

Services contracts

Estimating the total value

3.31 For services contracts, the general rule is that total consideration (net of VAT) will apply. The nature of that consideration may vary depending on the type of contract involved. For instance, in addition to a lump sum payment, it could also include the following:
— the premium payable for insurance services;
— the fees, commissions or other remuneration payable for banking and financial services; and
— the fees or commissions payable for design services.

Indefinite, fixed, regular or renewable contracts

3.32 Where the contract does not specify a total price, the estimated contract value is calculated as follows:
— for fixed-term contracts of under 48 months, the estimate for total duration;
— for a fixed-term contract of more than four years or of indefinite duration, the estimate of the monthly payments multiplied by 48 months.

3.33 In the case of (a) regular contracts, or (b) renewable contracts, the contract values are estimated on the basis of the following test[1]:
— the aggregate value of contracts with similar characteristics awarded over the pervious 12 months or the last financial accounting period, adjusted to take into

account the expected changes in quantity and costs of the goods of that type in the next 12 months; or
— the estimated aggregate value of the successive contracts with similar characteristics concluded during the 12 months following the initial delivery or accounting period, where this exceeds 12 months.

If the contract provides for an option to extend or renew then the estimate should take into account the maximum value based on the assumption that this option is exercised[2].

1   Public Services Contracts Regulations 1993, SI 1993/3228, reg 7(6) and (7).
2   Public Services Contracts Regulations 1993, SI 1993/3228, reg 7(10).

Lots

3.34   There is a general prohibition against dividing a contract for the purposes of evading the application of the regulations[1]. Where services are made up of several 'lots', each of which is the subject of a contract, then the total value of all the lots should be taken into account in determining if the threshold is reached. There is however, an exception to the general rule on 'splitting'. The regulations will not apply to any lots worth less than € 80,000 (or £49,496) so long as the total value of such lots does not exceed 20 per cent of the aggregate value of all the lots. The lots which do not benefit from this exemption are still subject to the regulations.

1   Public Services Contracts Regulations 1993, SI 1993/3228, reg 7(11).

Discrete operational units (DOU)

3.35   Generally, where a contracting authority is made up of a number of departments or units which remain subject to a centralised administration, the requirements of the whole contracting authority must be taken into account when assessing the value or contracts. There is a limited exemption from the normal 'aggregation' rules where goods[1] or services[2] are purchased under a contract for a discrete operational unit within the organisation of a contracting authority where the decision to enter the contract has been devolved to the unit and that decision is taken independently of any part of the contracting authority. In those circumstances the DOU is treated as if it were an independent contracting authority and the aggregation rules only apply to the contracts which it enters into.

1   Public Supply Contracts Regulations 1993, SI 1993/3228, reg 7(7).
2   Public Services Contracts Regulations 1993, SI 1993/3228, reg 7(8).

WHAT IS A WORKS CONTRACT?

3.36   Contracting authorities may rely on a general contractor who takes care of the design and co-ordinates the project on their behalf, or else they may enter into a development or management contract which is financed and executed by the contractor and reimbursed by the contracting authority. In other words where the contractor is acting as an agent for the contracting authority the contract is covered.

A 'public works contract' is defined as a contract in writing for consideration (whatever the nature of the consideration[1]):

(a) for the carrying out of a work or works for a contracting authority, or
(b) under which a contracting authority engages a person to procure by any means the carrying out for the contracting authority of a work corresponding to specific requirements[2].

1   The pecuniary nature of the contract may take different forms. It does not necessarily have to refer to a cash payment. The consideration may take the form of an alternative financial benefit. See Case C-399/98 *Ordine degli Architetti delle province di Milano e Lodi, Piero De Amicis, Consiglio Nazionale degli Architetti and Leopoldo Freyrie v Comune di Milano, and Pirelli SpA, Milano Centrale Servizi SpA and Fondazione Teatro alla Scala* [2001] ECR I-5409 where the holder of a building permit carried out the certain construction works to provide community facilities at his own expense in return for an exemption to pay the contribution due to the municipality in respect of a building permit.
2   Works Contracts Regulations 1991, SI 1991/2680, reg 2.

3.37   The regulations make an important distinction between 'works' and 'a work'. 'Works' refers to particular activities, which are listed under Class 50 of the 'NACE'[1] industrial classification of activities and in Sch 1 to the regulations. 'A work', on the other hand refers to the outcome of any works which is sufficient of itself to fulfil an economic and technical function, eg a hospital, school or bridge. This definition is important in particular when calculating the value of the works contract. In most cases, a single contracting authority will be responsible for tendering a particular 'work'. This is not always the case. In some instances there may be a number of contracting authorities involved. This in itself will not call into question the existence of a single 'work' as defined by the regulations. In the *Vendée*[2] case, the ECJ clarified that 'a work' may in some cases be the preserve of several public bodies and may be awarded to more than one contractor. For instance, in the case of the construction of a road or electricity network, crossing the territory of several local authorities, each having responsibility for a different section, the work would not fall outside the application of the regulations because each section was below the relevant threshold. To do so would defeat the objectives of the regulations.

1   This classification system is in the process of being replaced by the more generalised common procurement vocabulary (CPV) classification system, COM (2001) 449 Final.
2   Case C-16/98 *EC Commission v France* [2000] ECR I-8315.

3.38   Where a contract involves the performance of works which are merely incidental or ancillary to the main object of the contract, it will not be considered a 'works contract'. This was confirmed in the *Gestion Hotelera International* case[1], in which a contracting authority advertised a mixed contract involving a service concession which included certain works to be carried out on a hotel and casino. The ECJ concluded that where such works were:

'....merely incidental to the main object of the award, the award, taken in its entirety, cannot be characterised as a public works contract...'[2].

The reasoning in this case was followed by the UK courts in *R v Brent London Borough Council, ex p O 'Malley*[3] in a case concerning a framework agreement entered into by the Brent London Borough Council for the redevelopment and refurbishment of two estates. The court in that instance concluded that the arrangement was a contract for development and did not fall within the ambit of the Works Regulations. This issue remains a grey area and whether any develpoment should be classified as a works contract or as a contract for the acquisition or disposal of a property interest needs careful examination on the facts.

1   Case C-331/92 *Gestion Hotelera Internacional SA v Comunidad Autonoma de Canarias, Ayuntamiento de Las Palmas de Gran Canaria and Gran Casino de Las Palmas SA* [1994] ECR I-1329, ECJ.
2   [1994] ECR I-1329, para 26.
3   (1997) 30 HLR 328.

3.39   A property management contract may involve some works but the contract as a whole would be regarded as a services contract[1].

1   See Directive (EEC) 50/92, Recital 16: 'Whereas public service contracts, particularly in the field of property management may from time to time include some works; whereas it results from Directive 71/305/EEC that, for a contract to be a works contract, its object must be the achievement of a work; whereas, in so far as these works are incidental rather than the object of the contract, they do not justified treating the contract as a public works contract'.

Works concessions

3.40   Over the past few years, there has been a growing tendency for public authorities to carry out large infrastructure projects in partnership with the private sector. This often takes the form of the grant of a concession. Concessions offer a number of advantages, not only in budgetary and financial terms but also as a means of maximising the specialist technical knowledge and experience which private companies can bring to a project.

3.41   A works concession is a contract where the right to exploit the construction is granted as the consideration for the execution of the work. A typical example of works concession is where a contracting authority grants a company the right to build a motorway or bridge and grants it the right to earn revenue by way of a toll on its use. It is therefore the users rather than the contracting authority who bear the cost of construction. A key to understanding the distinction between a public works contract and a works concession, is that with a works concession the risks involved in exploiting the construction fall on the concessionaire rather than the contracting authority. Nevertheless, the fact that the concessionaire receives payment for some of the work from the contracting authority in addition to the right of exploitation, would not prevent the contract from being classed as a 'works concession'[1]. This may be the case for instance where the contracting authority will pay the concessionaire a sum to reduce the fee paid by the users or to compensate the concessionaire for carrying out a construction which is in the social interest, but which may not be commercially viable. The European Commission has issued Guidelines on the definition of concessions under Community law[2] which elaborate on the distinctions between a 'public works contract' and a 'public works concession'.

1   The definition in the Works Regulations, reg 2(1) defines a public works concession contract as 'a public works contract under which the consideration given by the contracting authority consists of or includes the grant of a right to exploit the work or works to be carried out under the contract' the definition of a public works concession under art 1(d) of the Works Directive is even clearer on this point it refers to '...the consideration for the works to be carried out consists either solely in the right to exploit the construction or in this right together with payment'.
2   Commission interpretative communication on concessions under Community law, 12 April 2000 (OJ C121 2000 p 2).

3.42   Regulation 25 of the Works Regulations require that where a contracting authority seeks offers in relation to a public works concession, it must apply the rules on transparency and advertising[1]. There are also special rules applying to the subcontracts for works to be carried out under a public works concession contract. Contracting authorities should be aware that public services concessions are treated in a different manner from public works concessions. See para **3.65**.

1 See further para **3.124**.

How to distinguish a works contract from a supply or services contract

3.43 A contract for a works contract often involves elements requiring the supply of goods or the provision of services. Where a contract falls within the definition of a 'public works contract' (see above) it is covered by the Works Regulations regardless of whether the contract includes elements of works or services. The exception to this is where the works elements are merely incidental to some other arrangement, such as the assignment of property, in which case the contract may fall outside the scope of the Works Regulations[1]. In some instances, comparison with the definitions in the other Directive will assist in determining how a contract should be defined. For instance, building maintenance is defined in the Works Regulations, Sch 1 as a 'works contract'. However, property management is defined as a service under the Services Regulations even if it was to include the occasional works maintenance[2].

1 Case C-331/92 *Gestion Hotelera Internacional SA v Comunidad Autonoma de Canarias, Ayuntamiento de Las Palmas de Gran Canaria and Gran Casino de Las Palmas SA* [1994] ECR I-1329, ECJ.
2 Recital 16 to the Services Directive:
   'Whereas public services, contracts particularly in the field of property management may from time to time include some works, whereas it results from Directive 71/305/EEC that, for a contract to be a public works contract, its object must be the achievement of a work, whereas, in so far as these works are incidental rather than the object of the contract, they do not justify treating the contract as a public works contract.'

3.44 For a contract involving installation and siting of equipment or network systems it may be necessary to distinguish between works and supplies. The rule of thumb to apply is to distinguish between contracts which put into place what is essentially moveable property (which would be a supplies contract) and a contract which is intended to provide the contracting authority with the result of construction or civil engineering works which result in immovable property or which is incorporated into immovable property already in existence.

Exclusions

3.45 The Works Regulations cover a wide range of different contractual relationships. However, there are some important exclusions. The regulations do not, for example, cover the purchase of existing property, infrastructure or buildings unless they were built according to the requirements of the contracting authority under an arrangement whereby they would be purchased upon completion. This type of an arrangement would amount to property development and be caught by the regulations. In the same way, the lease or purchase of real estate will not be caught by the regulations if no element of construction is involved.

3.46   Other exclusions include:
— works classified as secret and security contracts for public interest reasons[1];
— contracts subject to international agreements involving joint implementation or exploitation of a project[2];
— international agreements relating to the stationing of troops[3];
— contracts subject to contract award procedures of international organisations (eg the United Nations)[4]; or
— works contracts covered by the Utilities Directive[5].

1   Works Contracts Regulations 1991, SI 1991/2680, reg 6(d).
2   Works Contracts Regulations 1991, SI 1991/2680, reg 6(e)(i).
3   Works Contracts Regulations 1991, SI 1991/2680, reg 6(e)(ii).
4   Works Contracts Regulations 1991, SI 1991/2680, reg 6(e)(iii).
5   Works Contracts Regulations 1991, SI 1991/2680, reg 6(a), (b) and (c).

3.47   These exclusions will be strictly interpreted. There is settled case law that the derogations in the public procurement legislation will be interpreted strictly[1]. To rely upon the argument of member state security, it would be generally be necessary to point towards some form of specific law, regulation, other administrative provision or facts which indicate that the works contract is rendered secret or is in some manner necessary to the protection of the essential interests of the state. Mere assertion of a public interest will be insufficient[2]. International organisations are not defined as 'contracting authorities' under the meaning of the Directives but many will operate their own procurement schemes.

1   Case 199/85 *EC Commission v Italy* [1987] ECR 1039, para 14; Case C-57/94 *EC Commission v Italy* [1995] ECR I-1249, para 23; and Case C-318/94 *EC Commission v Germany* [1996] ECR I-1949, para 13; on the temporal effect of a provision authorising derogations Case C-143/94 *Furlanis Costrozioni Generali SpA v Azienda Nazionale Autonoma Strade* [1995] ECR I-3633, ECJ.
2   See for example Case C-323/96 *EC Commission v Belgium* [1998] ECR I-5063, paras 36–39 where the ECJ dismissed a plea of reliance on the secrecy and security provision in relation to a contract for the building of the Flemish Parliament on the grounds of insufficient factual evidence.

WHAT IS A PUBLIC SUPPLIES CONTRACT?

3.48   A public supplies contract means:

'a contract in writing for consideration (whatever the nature of the consideration) –
(a) for the purchase of goods by a contracting authority (whether or not the consideration is given in instalments and whether or not the purchase is conditional upon the concurrence of any event) or
(b) for the hire of goods by a contracting authority (both where the contracting authority becomes the owner of the goods after the end of the period of hire and where it does not)...'[1]

In other words, a public supplies contract covers outright purchase of goods, purchase by instalments, hire-purchase and hire or lease of goods. This definition is wide enough to cover a wide range of purchasing practices, including open or standing contracts where the standard terms and conditions are agreed and supplies are ordered as and when required over a period of time[2]. Under the regulations 'goods' include electricity, substances (natural or artificial, whether in solid liquid or gaseous form), agricultural crops (where sold separately from the land) and any type of boat or ship, aircraft or vehicle. Generally, where the delivery of goods also includes siting and installation activities, this will be covered by the Supplies Directive. The exception is where the value of the siting and installation services is greater than that of the goods themselves, in which case, the contract would be regarded as a public services contract.

1   Public Supply Contracts Regulations 1995, SI 1995/201, reg 2.
2   European Commission Guide to the Community Rules on Public Supply Contracts, s 1.4.

3.49   The regulations will apply even where a contract for supply provides that the goods do not become the property of the contracting authority until the end of the contractual relationship and the consideration paid takes the form of an annual payment. This was confirmed in the *EC Commission v Italy*[1] case, which involved an Italian government body who had published a tender for an integrated computerised national lottery system.

1   C-272/91 *EC Commission v Italy* [1994] ECR I-1409, ECJ.

Mixed contracts

3.50   Where a contract involves both supply and service elements, it will be treated as a supply contract only where the consideration attributable to the goods is greater than the value attributable to the service elements[1]. The question arose in the *Teckal* case[2] in relation to a contract for the operation and maintenance of heating installations for municipal buildings, which included any necessary repairs and improvements and the supply of fuel. It was clear that the value of the fuel to be provided was worth almost twice as much as the maintenance and installation which were required. The ECJ held that where the goods exceed the value of the services it shall be treated as a supplies contract.

1   Public Supply Contracts Regulations 1995, SI 1995/201, reg 2(1).
2   Case C-107/98 *Teckal Srl v Comune di Viano and Azienda Gas- Acqua Consorziale (AGAC) di Reggio Emilia* [1999] ECR I-8121, ECJ.

3.51   In the *Italian data-processing* case[1], the Italian government tried to argue that a contract involving not only the purchase of hardware but also the design, planning and installation of the system, fell outside the definition of a 'supplies contract' on the grounds that the supply of hardware was simply ancillary to the creation of the data-processing system. The ECJ rejected that argument on the basis that the government could have approached companies specialised in software development for the design of the system and then purchased hardware which met the required technical specifications.

1   C-3/88 *EC Commission v Italy* [1989] ECR 4035, ECJ.

Exclusions

3.52   Exclusions to the above include:
—   contracts declared secret or accompanied by special security measures or security is required for public interest reasons;

— defence contracts as defined by the EC Treaty, art 296(1)(b) (formerly art 223(1)(b));
— contracts subject to contract award procedures of international organisations (eg the United Nations);
— supplies contracts covered by the Utilities Directive and therefore generally not likely to be relevant to local authorities (see above).

3.53   The exclusions to the regulations will be interpreted narrowly. For instance, in the *Italian data-processing* case (see para **3.51**), the Italian government attempted to rely upon the exclusion for contracts which are secret, in order to justify a requirement that data-processing systems for public authorities must only be granted to companies owned directly or indirectly by the state, their rationale being that the data involved would be used to fight against crime. The court rejected this argument. In his Opinion, Advocate-General Mischo explained that:

'…the development and technical operation of data-processing systems may unavoidably involve access to data of a confidential nature and of public importance, member states have, in the duty of official secrecy, a sufficiently effective means of guarding against disclosure without there being a need to restrict freedom of establishment or freedom to provide services for that purpose'[1].

1   C-3/88 *EC Commission v Italy* [1989] ECR 4035, Advocate-General's Opinion, para 31.

3.54   The 'defence' exclusion is similarly narrowly defined. In general, the regulations will apply to many types of contracts by the government bodies connected with the armed services except where these products fall within a list of arms, munitions and war materials as laid down in a Council Decision of 15 April 1958 and only where these are intended for military purposes[1].

1   Eg the Commission sent a Reasoned Opinion on 5 April 2001 to the German government in relation to the purchase of rubber protection pads designed for military vehicles such as tanks. The German government claimed that art 296 of the EC Treaty exempts materials for the production of or trade in arms, munitions and war materials. The Commission takes the view that since these pads are used in peace time for non-military purposes they cannot be regarded as war material and are covered by the rules applicable to public supplies contracts, IP/01/511. Reasoned Opinion dated 9 August 1999 in relation to a contract for the supply of operational leather belts with accessories for the Ministry of Development in Greece, IP/99/624.

3.55   As discussed above, where local authorities or other contracting authorities carry out functions relating to water, energy, transport or telecommunications, contracts related to these activities will be awarded under the Utilities Regulations. For example a local authority may act as a 'utility' in relation to provision of district heating. Where these activities become fully deregulated and open to competition (eg voice telephony), they can become exempt from the procurement rules on Community-wide tendering altogether.

WHAT IS A PUBLIC SERVICES CONTRACT?

3.56   A public services contract is a contract in writing for consideration (whatever the nature of the consideration) under which a contracting authority engages a person to provide services[1]. It is not relevant to the application of the public procurement rules whether those services are for the benefit of the contracting authorities or for the benefit of third parties. What constitutes a 'service' is not expressly defined in the regulations or the Directive. However, the EC Treaty, art 50, states that services include activities of an industrial or commercial character, activities of craftsmen and of the professions. In some instances (eg those involving some form of transfer of intellectual property rights) it may be difficult to identify whether a contract is a good or a service or indeed covered by the regulations at all[2].

1   Public Services Contracts Regulations 1993, SI 1993/3228, reg 2(1).
2   The distinction between 'goods' and 'services' has arisen regularly in the case law of the ECJ, particularly in relation to the doctrine of free movement of goods and services. Such definitions may be of assistance in cases where the distinction is not immediately clear.

Full application of the Services Regulation – Part A

3.57   The Services Regulations are different from the Works and Supplies Regulations in that they make a distinction between two categories of services. Schedule 1 to the Services Regulations contain two lists of categories services[1]. The first list, which appears in Part A and is set out below, contains the description of 16 types of services which are subject to the full application of the rules under the regulations. These services have been identified as of being of 'priority' interest to service providers from other member states of the European Union. In other words, they are the type of services which are most eligible for cross-border trade.

1   The categories of services are identified according to the Community classification of products activities known as the CPA (Council Regulation No 3696/93). This form of classification is being phased out and replaced by the Common Procurement Vocabulary (CPV) which at the time of writing was expected shortly to become the mandatory reference. A comparative table between the CPA and CPV for services can be found at http://simap.eu.int/EN/pub/src/welcome.htm

Part A services (full application)

3.58   Part A contains the following list:
(1) maintenance and repair of vehicles and equipment services;
(2) land transport services;
(3) air transport services;
(4) transport of mail by land and by air;
(5) telecommunications services;
(6) financial services (including insurance and investment services);
(7) computer and related services;
(8) research and development services;
(9) accounting, auditing and bookkeeping services;
(10) market research and public opinion polling services;
(11) management consultant services and related services;
(12) architectural, engineering, planning and related scientific and technical consulting services;
(13) advertising services;
(14) building cleaning services and property management services;
(15) publishing and printing services;
(16) sewage and refuse disposal services; sanitation and similar services.

Limited application of the Services Regulations – Part B

3.59   The services listed in Part B (sometimes referred to as 'non-priority' services) are subject to a more limited application of the rules (ie to the rules on technical qualification and the publication of a contract award notice). These services are not subject to the rules requiring publication of the tenders on a Community-wide basis because they would generally be of less interest to service providers from other member states for technical or practical reasons (eg legal, health and education services). While it is not mandatory to issue a Community-wide call for tender for Part B services, contracting authorities are of course free to do so if they wish. Bear in mind that once a contracting authority has opted to go down this route, however, it must apply all the rules under the regulations to the award of that contract (including for instance, deadlines, selection and award criteria etc).

Part B services (partial application)

3.60   Part B contains the following list:
(17) hotel and restaurant services;
(18) rail transport services;
(19) water transport services;
(20) supporting and auxiliary transport services;
(21) legal services;
(22) personnel placement and supply services;
(23) investigation and security services;
(24) education and vocational education services;
(25) health and social services;
(26) recreational, cultural and sporting services;
(27) other services.

Mixed contracts

3.61   Where the contracting authority is procuring both Annex A and Annex B services in a single contract then the determination of whether the full or partial application of the public procurement rules is appropriate will be decided according to which service comprises the greater value[1]. One such example might be the transport sector where certain services are categorised under Part A, while others would fall within Part B[2].

1   Public Services Contracts Regulations 1993, SI 1993/3228, reg 2(2).
2   Advocate General's Opinion in C-411/00 *Felix Swoboda GmbH v Österreichische Nationalbank* (18 April 2002, unreported), concerning a mixed contract containing elements of transport services listed both under Annex 1A ('priority' services) and Annex 1B ('non-priority' services) (case prending final judgment).

3.62   The same general rule of categorisation of a contract by reference to relative value is used to distinguish between a public service contract and a public supplies contract (see above)[1]. For example, if a contracting authority were to purchase certain computer services valued at £450,000 together with computer equipment valued at £150,000, the contract would be classed as a service contract. For the distinction between a works and services contract see para **3.43**.

1   See also the *Teckal* case C-107/98, paras 37 and 38.

Subsidised service contracts

3.63 Contracts which are put out to tender by a party which is not a contracting authority may nevertheless fall within the provisions of the regulations where a contracting authority will contribute more than 50 per cent of the value of the service contract and where the contract is awarded in connection with a works contract to which the Works Regulations, reg 23 applies. In other words, to specialised engineering contracts[1] and contracts for building work for hospitals, sports, recreation and leisure facilities, school and university buildings and administrative buildings. In those circumstances, the contracting authority must make it a condition of providing the contribution that the subsidised body will comply with the regulations and ensure that it does so. If the subsidised body fails to comply, the money should be recovered[2].

1 Listed in the Public Works Contracts Regulations 1991, SI 1991/2680, Sch 1, Group 502.
2 Public Services Contracts Regulations 1993, SI 1993/3228, reg 25(1).

Exclusions

3.64 There are a range of contracts which are excluded from the services contract because for public policy reasons it has been determined that it is inappropriate to subject them to the rules of competitive tendering under the Service Regulations. Contracts excluded from the regulation include those which are:

— declared secret or accompanied by special security measures or security is required for public interest reasons[1];
— defence contracts as defined by the EC Treaty, art 296(1)(b) (formerly art 223(1)(b))[2];
— subject to contract award procedures of international organisations (eg the United Nations);
— services contracts covered by the Utilities Directive (ie certain service contracts for water, energy, telecommunication and transport sector);
— for the acquisition of land or buildings or interest in land[3];
— for the acquisition, development, production or co-production of programme material for radio or television by a broadcaster or for the purchase of broadcasting time;
— for voice telephony, telex, radiotelephony, paging or satellite services;
— for arbitration or conciliation services;
— for financial services in connection with the issue, purchase, sale or transfer of securities or other financial instruments;
— for central banking services;
— for research and development services unless the benefits accrue exclusively to the contracting authority for the conduct of its own affairs and are wholly paid for by the contracting authority[4];
— contracts where services are provided by another contracting authority (including one which is an authority in another relevant state) because that contracting authority or person has an exclusive right under law to provide the services or which is necessary to provide the services under.

1 Only applies where services are declared to be secret or the execution of the services are accompanied by special security measures in accordance with the law or administrative provisions of the state or relate to the protection of the basic interests of state security. Eg the Commission took action against the Belgian authorities in respect of a contract awarded for the conduct of aerial surveys of the Belgian coast which was not put out to tender and was subsequently extended. The Belgian authorities argued

that the contract was covered by the exclusion in relation to national security. The Commission rejected the argument on the basis that as long as the contractor agreed to be bound by professional confidentiality, a military certificate necessary for aerial photography of the coast could be awarded to a non-Belgian company (IP//00/869) 27 July 2000. The case had not been decided by the ECJ at the time of writing.

2   Public service contracts will only fall within this exception if they are for the services in relation to a list of military products listed in Council Decision 15 April 1958 and are excluded only where the listed products are used exclusively for military purposes.

3   Only contracts for the purchase of land buildings or immovable property are excluded. Contracts to provide services in connection with such purposes eg real estate services, architectural services, property management and building cleaning services are all Part A services subject to the provisions of the Services Contract Regulations.

4   Research and development contracts intended to benefit third parties however are listed in Part A of the Regulations and should be put out to tender.

Services concessions

3.65   Unlike work concessions, contracts for services concessions are not covered by the public procurement regulations[1]. Service concessions are not defined by the Services Regulations. The Commission has, however, published an Interpretative Communication on Concessions which is intended to assist authorities. It describes a service concession as one:

> 'whereby a public authority entrusts to a third party—by means of a contractual act or a unilateral act with the prior consent of the third party—the total or partial management of services for which that authority would normally be responsible and for which the third party assumes the risk'[2].

1   When the Services Directive was being drafted, it was intended that there would be provision for services concessions but this provision was not adopted.

2   Commission interpretative Communications on concessions under Community law dated 12 April 2000 (OJ C121/2000 p 2).

3.66   The operator therefore establishes and operates the system and obtains a significant part of the revenue from the user, typically by charging some form of fees. A service concession is excluded from the ambit of the Services Directive by virtue of the fact that the concessionaire receives a right to exploit for payment its own services[1]. The grant of that right does not therefore come within the definition of a 'contract for pecuniary interest'.

1   See C-324/98 *Telaustria Verlags GmbH and Telefonadress GmbH v Telekom Austria AG* [2000] ECR I-10745 which concerned an analogous situation in respect of a services concession under the Utilities Directive.

3.67   Where the service provider is remunerated by a contracting authority, the contract is not a service concession but a public service contract. An illustration of this is the *Arnhem* case[1]. Two Dutch municipalities, Arnhem and Rheden, decided it would make economic sense to entrust, by way of a 'concession', their refuse disposal and municipal cleaning functions to a new legal entity, 'ARA', which they specifically created for this purpose. Both municipalities entered into framework agreements with the ARA to provide these services in consideration for remuneration based on an agreed price or on the basis of an invoice for the costs involved. The arrangement was challenged by a private waste disposal company who argued that the municipalities should have put the contract for the services out to tender. In defence of the municipalities, it was argued that the relationship between themselves and the

ARA was not a contract but a concession. The court rejected this argument on the basis that it was clear that the remuneration paid to ARA was a price and not the right to operate the service[2].

1   Case C-360/96 *Gemeente Arnhem and Gemeente Rheden v BFI Holding BV* [1998] ECR I-6821, ECJ.
2   [1998] ECR I-6821, para 25.

3.68   In addition to the matter of payment, for an arrangement to amount to a concession there must be a transfer of risk to the concessionaire. This was confirmed by the ECJ in the *Italian Lotto* case[1] which concerned a contract for the supply of an integrated computerised system for the conduct of the lottery. It was argued by the Italian government that the award of this contract amounted to a concession. The ECJ, however, found that the services to be provided were no different from technical services for the development of a public administration. The Italian government remained ultimately responsible for the operation of the system and therefore there had been no transfer of responsibility to the concessionaire for the various activities inherent in the lottery[2].

1   Case C-272/91 *EC Commission v Italy* [1994] ECR I-1409, ECJ.
2   [1994] ECR I-1409, paras 6–12.

3.69   It is worth recalling that although not covered by the procedures in the Services Regulations, the fundamental Treaty rules on non-discrimination on the grounds of nationality, transparency[1], free movement of services and competition law do apply to the grant of a service concession.

1   Case C-324/98 *Telaustria* paras 50 and 51.

WHICH PROCUREMENT ROUTE TO USE

3.70   Where a contract must be advertised in the Official Journal of the European Communities ('OJEC') in accordance with either the Public Works Contracts Regulations 1991, the Public Services Contracts Regulations 1993 or the Public Supply Contracts Regulations 1995, a local authority must decide which procedure it will use when carrying out the procurement process. Under the regulations the three main options are the open, restricted or negotiated procedure. An authority is free to choose whether it uses the open or restricted procedure. However, the wording of the regulations and ECJ case law has emphasised that the negotiated procedure can only be used where derogation from the open or restricted procedure is authorised.

3.71   Even where a contract does not have to be advertised under the regulations, a local authority may still of course choose to advertise the contract in order to demonstrate that the procurement process is open, transparent and non-discriminatory and to publicise its intention on the wider European marketplace. However, it should be noted that once a contract has been advertised in OJEC, the local authority must comply with the entire scope of the regulations as they apply to that contract, and should it wish to act outside of the scope of the regulations, it would have to terminate the procurement process and notify the OJEC and those contractors who expressed an interest in response to the original advertisement[1].

1   See for example the Public Supply Contracts Regulations 1995, reg 23.

Open procedure

3.72   Under the open procedure, any interested contractor may submit a tender for the contract in response to a notice placed by the authority in OJEC. As a consequence, an authority may be faced with a large number of tenders to evaluate and, depending on the nature of the contract, this may become a resource-intensive exercise. Therefore, use of the open procedure is suitable for the procurement of supplies or where there is a clear and comprehensive specification and the contract being procured is not complex and is well-known to the market place.

3.73   Where a contract is advertised under the open procedure, the authority must allow 52 days following the date of dispatch of the notice for tenders to be received. This timescale may be shorter, depending on the timing and extent of information contained in any prior information notice[1]. Generally, a timescale can be shortened to 36 days and should not be less than 22 days. Whichever timescale is chosen the authority must allow a sufficient period for contractors to prepare their tenders and for an effective tendering process to take place.

1   See for example, the Public Supply Contracts Regulations 1995, reg 11(3A).

3.74   The contract documents, for example the contract and specification, must be sent within six days of receipt of a request from any provider and the authority must supply any further information relating to the contract documents as may be reasonably requested by the provider. The relevant timescales are shown at para**3.153**.

3.75   Currently tenders may be submitted in writing either in person or by post unless the authority authorises another means, for example electronic submission. However, under the proposed changes to the European procurement Directives in future, authorities may be able to specify electronic tendering as the only means.

3.76   On receipt of tenders, the authority may exclude submissions by providers who are ineligible to tender on a ground specified in reg 14, or if the provider fails to satisfy the minimum requirements of economic and financial standing, ability and technical capacity required by the authority in accordance with the criteria set out in regs 15 and 16 of the relevant regulation (see paras **3.133–3.138**).

3.77   No negotiation is permitted and only compliant bids, ie those that meet all the requirements set out in the authority's tender documents, can be evaluated. Clarificatory questions and requests for further information are permitted as long as this does not distort competition.

3.78   The European Council has issued the following Communication[1]:

'The Council and the Commission state that in open and restricted procedures all negotiations with candidates or tenderers on fundamental aspects of contracts, variations in which are likely to distort competition, and in particular on prices, shall be ruled out; however, discussions with candidates or tenderers may be held but only for the purpose of clarifying or supplementing the content of their tenders or the requirements of the contracting authorities and provided this does not involve discrimination.'

1   OJ L199 9.8.1993 p 54.

3.79 The Commission and ECJ have emphasised that post-tender negotiations are a violation of the Directives unless the negotiated procedure has been justified, and are contrary to the principle of equal treatment.

3.80 On receipt of tenders the authority will need to evaluate bids on the basis of lowest price or most economically advantageous tender (see paras **3.142–3.145**)[1].

1 Public Works Contracts Regulations 1991, reg 20(1); Public Services Contracts Regulations 1993, reg 21(1) and Public Supply Contracts Regulations 1995, reg 21(1).

The restricted procedure

3.81 The restricted procedure is a two-stage process. Contractors are requested to express an interest in the contract following publication of a contract notice in OJEC. Following an assessment of those contractors who have expressed an interest, the authority must draw up a shortlist of those contractors it will invite to tender.

3.82 The restricted procedure continues to be widely used for works and services contracts in a local authority context and was the procedure required by the compulsory competitive tendering regime in the 1980s and 1990s.

3.83 The authority must allow 37 days following the date of the despatch of the notice for receipt of requests to be selected to tender. Under the restricted procedure, the authority must apply a two-stage process. At the first stage, contractors must be 'assessed' according to their economic and financial standing and ability and technical capacity, and can be excluded on the grounds set out under reg 14. Authorities may issue a pre-qualification questionnaire which sets out the information to be provided in order that the authority can assess the contractors' economic and financial standing and ability and technical capacity. Following assessment, the authority is then in a position to draw up a shortlist of contractors who it will invite to tender for the contract.

3.84 If the authority intends to predetermine the number of contractors it wishes to invite to tender, it must invite at least five (this has been emphasised by OGC Guidance issued in July 2001) and not more than 20 providers to tender. The range must be specified in the contract notice and must be sufficient to ensure genuine competition. Each contractor selected to tender must be notified at the same time as the other contractors and each invitation to tender ('ITT') must include the contract documents (or the address from where they can be requested). The ITT must set out the criteria for the award of the contract if this information was not included in the contract notice.

3.85 The authority must allow at least 40 days following the date of despatch of the ITT to receipt of tenders plus extra time if inspection of contract documents or site visits are needed. This timescale may be shortened, as with the open procedure, where a prior information notice has been published. The relevant timescales are set out at para **3.154**. Again, as with the open procedure, clarificatory questions or requests for further information relating to the contract documents is allowed but negotiation is ruled out (see para **3.78**) unless there are grounds to switch to the negotiatied procedure (for example, no compliant tenders have been received).

3.86 Where a prior information notice (see paras **3.128–3.132**) has been published at least 52 days before and no more than 12 months previously, the authority can require tenders to be submitted within 26 days of despatch of the ITT. When applying this shorter timescale, however, authorities should take into account how long it will realistically take a tenderer to compile a bid to the level of detail they require.

3.87   The chief feature associated with use of the restricted procedure is that no negotiation is allowed and therefore the authority must be able to pre-specify in detail all of its requirements before inviting tenders. In practical terms, this requires that the authority has certainty as to the precise scope of the contract and it will need to prepare the detailed specification and contract in advance of inviting tenders.

3.88   Some authorities address the constraints on dialogues with tenderers under the restricted procedure by requesting variant bids. If variants are to be considered, this information should be included in the contract notice and the alternative bases for the variants must be set out in the ITT.

3.89   The bids received for the contract cannot be treated by the authority as a basis for negotiation. This has been confirmed by a High Court case, *Harmon CFEM Facades (UK) Ltd v Corporate Officer of the House of Commons*[1]. An aggrieved contractor bought an action against the House of Commons in relation to an award of a contract for fenestration of Portcullis House, Westminster. In that case, the court found that the contracting authority had entered into post-tender discussions with one of the tenderers, as a result of which material changes had been made to the conditions of contract sent out with the ITT, and that the other tenderers had not been given the opportunity to submit bids against the same contract. This was held by the court to be a breach of the principle of equality of treatment which requires contracting authorities to afford equal opportunities for tendering and access to information to all prospective and actual tenders. In this case significant damages of £12 million were awarded.

1   (1999) 67 Con LR 1.

3.90   As with the open procedure, bids are evaluated on the basis of lowest price or most economically advantageous tender.

3.91   Use of the restricted procedure in respect of complex schemes or where innovation is required may cause commercial and practical difficulties to the authority. In such cases, the authority should consider whether it can establish sufficient grounds to justify use of the negotiated procedure (see para **3.95**).

Accelerated restricted procedure

3.92   Where the authority cannot comply with the normal deadlines for the restricted procedure for reasons of urgency, the restricted procedure may be accelerated in accordance with the time limits shown at para **3.154**. However, EC decisions have emphasised that the accelerated restricted procedure may only be used in circumstances where the authority is able to show that there are objective circumstances giving rise to urgency and a real impossibility of meeting the normal deadlines. For example, in 1998 the Commission considered in a reasoned opinion that an Italian Town Council which had used the accelerated restricted procedure to let a municipal waste collection contract had failed to demonstrate that there were urgent circumstances rendering impracticable meeting the normal time limits[1]. The reasons justifying recourse to the accelerated procedure must be set out in the contract notice published in the OJEC. It is therefore important when using this provision that the reasons are well expressed, transparent, objective and non-discriminatory since they may be more vulnerable to challenge by aggrieved parties. Where this procedure is used, the authority must send the ITT by the most rapid means possible.

1   European Commission press release (3 July 1998).

3.93   To date there have not been any cases relating to breach by a contracting authority for use of the restricted accelerated procedure. However, in *EC Commission v Spain*[1] which involved the construction of a new university building, the Spanish government was held to be in breach of the procurement rules for unjustifiable use of the negotiated procedure without prior advertisement (see para **3.112**), as the university could in the circumstances have used the accelerated procedure in order to meet the projected timetable. The ECJ held that the use of the negotiated procedure without a call for tender does not apply if 'sufficient time is available to the authorities awarding the contracts to organise an accelerated award procedure ...'.

1   C-24/91 *EC Commission v Spain* [1992] ECR I-1989, ECJ.

3.94   Before using the accelerated restricted procedure, the authority must be confident that it is able to provide concrete evidence as to why the normal time limits are not practical and why the contract must be urgently put out to tender. Each decision should be made considering the relevant justification on a case by case basis.

The negotiated procedure

3.95   The negotiated procedure allows the authority to enter into a dialogue with contractors and negotiate both the technical specification and conditions of contract. This can be particularly useful in complex contracts or where innovation is required.

3.96   At present the negotiated procedure may only be used as a derogation from the usual rules and the Works, Services and Supplies Regulations, regs 10 and 13 set out the circumstances under which use of the negotiated procedure is justified and procedure to be followed.

3.97   The negotiated procedure can be used either with or without the publication of a contract notice, depending on the appropriate justification.

Negotiated procedure with publication of a contract notice

3.98   As with the restricted procedure, this is a two-stage process whereby the authority carries out a shortlisting exercise following responses to the OJEC notice and then selects a number of contractors to be invited to negotiate. The authority must invite at least three bidders to negotiate the contract where there is a sufficient number of suitable contractors to select.

3.99   In addition, the negotiated procedure can be accelerated with prior publication of a notice where for reasons of urgency, contractors cannot be allowed the periods normally required under the negotiated procedure. In order to use the accelerated procedure the authority must indicate the grounds for justification in the contract notice. The timescale for use of the negotiated procedure with prior publication of a contract notice are set out at para **3.155**.

3.100   The following circumstances would allow an authority to use the negotiated procedure with prior publication of the contract notice.

Discontinuation of open or restricted award procedure[1]

3.101   The negotiated procedure with prior publication of a contract notice may be used where an authority has previously had to discontinue an award of contract either under the open or restricted procedure due to irregular tenders or unacceptable offers. This could happen where bids do not meet the technical specifications of the authority, variant bids are submitted which are not permitted in the ITT or where all the bids that come in are significantly over budget.

1   Services, Supplies and Works Regulations, reg 10(2)(a).

3.102   Under reg 10(3) of the Works, Services and Supplies Regulations, this ground can only be used where the terms of the contract are substantially unaltered. The Commission guidance states that changes to the financial arrangements, periods for execution of services and technical specifications do not allow recourse to the negotiated procedure.

3.103   A new contract notice must be published unless all the parties invited to negotiate include the bidders who submitted tenders in the previous tenders under the open or restricted procedure and they satisfy the authority's criteria for selection.

Where, due to exceptional circumstances, the nature of the services/ works or the risks attaching thereto are such as not to permit prior overall pricing[1]

3.104   An authority may decide to let a contract where contractors would not be able to submit a fixed-price tender. As a consequence, any tender price would incorporate a number of contingencies which would make a comparison of bids by the authority very difficult.

1   Public Services Contracts Regulations 1993, reg 10(2)(b) and Public Works Contracts Regulations 1991, reg 10(2)(c).

3.105   Justification for use of the negotiated procedure under this limb must be considered carefully and is not available under the Supplies Regulations. There is a considerable amount of case law from the ECJ and reasoned opinions which have been issued by the Advocate General, following complaints to the European Commission, which state that the exceptions allowing use of the negotiated procedure must be interpreted strictly and the burden of proving the actual existence of exceptional circumstances and justifying use of the negotiated procedure will fall upon the local authority.

3.106   The authority should note that ECJ case law and the reasoned opinions sent by the Commission in relation to the Ipswich airport and Pimlico School transactions have emphasised that this ground can only be used 'exceptionally' and a clear audit trail would need to be kept of reasons justifying use of this ground.

3.107   On 27 July 2000, the European Commission sent reasoned opinions to the United Kingdom government concerning decisions to award contracts for redevelopment of Ipswich airport for housing and the redevelopment of Pimlico School under the Private Finance Initiative ('PFI'). In both cases, the contracting authority had relied on the 'not capable of prior overall pricing' justification. The United Kingdom government has sent replies to the Commission and it is understood to have asserted that the complexities of the transaction meant that it was not possible to determine in advance the overall price of the project concerned. The Commission's view appears to be that the inability to estimate the value of those projects was essentially self-imposed by the open ended manner in which the contracting authority had gone out to tender. In particular, the Commission considered that the contracting authorities had left all the essential details (eg choice of site) to the discretion of the bidders. In the Commission's view, had the invitations to tender for the Ipswich and Pimlico contracts been more specific, the contracting authorities could have determined the price in advance and use of the negotiated procedure would not have been necessary.

3.108   It is likely that both of these references will be held in abeyance until the new legislative passage on the Consolidated Directives, in particular the use of the 'competitive dialogue' are adopted (see para **3.216**). In respect of PFI projects, Richard Footitt, Head of the former DTLR's Local Government and Competition and Quality Division, sent a clarification letter to Chief Executives of Local Authorities notifying them that the advice of the Office of Government Commerce in HM Treasury is that authorities should continue to use the negotiated procedure provided that they are able to demonstrate, if challenged, the need for doing so bearing in mind the exceptional nature of the procedure.

3.109   In the interim it is important that any authority using the negotiated procedure should carefully record in both the tender documentation and any reports compiled throughout the procurement process, the reasons why use of the negotiated procedure is justified. Use of the negotiated procedure should never be automatic, and even in PFI and PPP projects must be carefully considered with legal scrutiny of the justifications given to minimise vulnerability to challenge.

3.110   *R (Kathro) v Rhondda Cynon Taff County Borough Council*[1] is the first domestic decision on the application of the public procurement regulations to contract tenders pursuant to the PFI and use of the negotiated procedure. The contract was for a life-long learning facility in Wales, where the local authority had advertised for a service contract under the negotiated procedure. The judge held that whether the contract was a works or services contract the local authority would have been entitled to conclude that the circumstances justified the use of the negotiated procedure. However, it is important to note that this is an administrative court decision and as such other courts are not bound to follow it.

1   [2001] EWHC Admin 527, [2001] 4 PLR 83.

*Where the specification cannot be drawn up with sufficient certainty
to permit the award of the contract using the open or restricted
procedure[1]*

3.111   This ground is available for services contracts only. In long-term, high-value services contracts the authority may seek the private sector providers' knowledge and experience in developing the contract specification. The Services Regulations state that in particular, in the case of intellectual services or services specified in Sch 1, Pt A, category 6 this ground may be used.

1   Public Services Contracts Regulations 1993, reg 10(2).

Negotiated procedure without publication of a contract notice

3.112   The negotiated procedure without publication of a contract notice may be used in the following circumstances.

Absence of tenders[1]

3.113   Where the authority has begun a procurement process under either the open or restricted procedure to which there have been either no or inappropriate tenders in response, the negotiated procedure may be used without publication of a contract notice. The original terms of the contract must not be substantially altered and the original procurement process must be terminated.

1   Public Services Contracts Regulations and Public Works Contracts Regulations, reg 10(2)(d), Public Supply Contracts Regulations, reg 10(2)(b).

*When for technical or artistic reasons, or for reasons connected with
the protection of exclusive rights, the services, supplies or works may
be provided only by a particular provider[1]*

3.114   This is a very narrow exception and applies only in those cases where it can be said that to invite tenders or expressions of interest would be abusive because there is only one contractor who can provide the particular service, goods or works in question. The burden of proof in this exception lies with the authority and the authority should consider carefully implications of using this procedure. In *EC Commission v Italy*[2] the ECJ held that the authority is required to show that only one particular firm can produce what is required. In *EC Commission v Italy*[3] it was held that only when it is 'absolutely essential' that the contracts be awarded to one particular firm can this provision be relied upon.

1   Public Services Contracts Regulations and Public Works Contracts Regulations, reg 10(2)(e), Public Supply Contracts Regulations, reg 10(2)(d).
2   199/85 *EC Commission v Italy* [1987] ECR 1039, ECJ.
3   C-57/ 94 *EC Commission v Italy* [1995] ECR I-1249, ECJ.

Design contest[1]

3.115 Under the Services Regulations only the negotiated procedure can be used without prior publication of a notice when the rules of a design contest require the contract to be awarded to the successful contestant or to one of the successful contestants, provided that all successful contestants are invited to negotiate the contract.

1   Public Services Contracts Regulations, reg 10(2)(f).

Extreme urgency[1]

3.116 The regulations permit use of the negotiated procedure without prior publication of a contract notice insofar as it is strictly necessary when, for reasons of extreme urgency brought about by events which are unforeseeable by the contracting authority in question, the time limit for the open, restricted or negotiated procedures with publication of a contract notice cannot be kept. The circumstances invoked to justify extreme urgency must not, in any event, be attributable to the authority.

1   Public Services Contracts Regulations, reg 10(2)(g), Public Works Contracts Regulations, reg 10(2)(f) and Public Supply Contracts Regulations, reg 10(2)(e).

3.117 The *EC Guides to the Community Rules on Public Procurement of Services, Supplies and Works* explain that 'unforeseeable events' means events which fall outside the field of normal economic and social activity, for example, floods or earthquakes which necessitate urgent contracts to assist the victims. In addition, the recourse to this procedure is permitted only to the extent necessary to procure the relevant services, supplies and works necessary to deal with the immediate urgent situation.

3.118 The authority should consider whether it is able to demonstrate the factual circumstances giving rise to urgency as ECJ decisions have interpreted this justification very strictly. Cases concerning the award of contracts for the construction of an avalanche barrier[1], the supply of pharmaceutical products[2] and the construction of a new university faculty building[3] all held the contracting authorities in breach of the procurement rules for unjustifiable use of the urgency procedure.

1   C-107/92 *EC Commission v Italy* [1993] ECR I-4655, ECJ.
2   C-328/92 *EC Commission v Spain* [1994] ECR I-1569, ECJ.
3   C-24/94 *EC Commission v Spain* [1994] CMLR 621.

Additional works/services[1]

3.119 The negotiated procedure may be used without publication of a contract notice where an authority wishes an existing provider to provide additional services or works which were not included in the project initially or in the original contract, but which through unforeseeable circumstances have become necessary for the performance of the service or works.

1   Public Services Contracts Regulations, reg 10(2)(h), Public Works Contracts Regulations, reg 10(2)(g).

3.120   Three conditions must be satisfied:
(i)   the contract for the new services/works must be awarded to the provider who supplied the original services/works;
(ii)   the additional services/works must not be capable of being separated from the main contract without great inconvenience and must be necessary for the completion of the original contract;
(iii)   the aggregate estimated value of contracts awarded for additional services/works must not exceed 50 per cent of the amount of the main contract.

Repetition of services/works[1]

3.121   An authority may use the negotiated procedure without prior publication of a contract notice for services or works which are a repetition of similar works or services under the original contract which relates to the project for the purpose of which the original contract was made. This justification may only be used where the contract notice or the original contract expressly mentions the possibility of the additional works/services being awarded by negotiated procedures to the same provider. The new procedure must also commence within three years of the date of the original contract. It is helpful to bear this exemption in mind when drafting OJEC notices as it allows the authority flexibility.

1   Public Service Contracts Regulations, reg 10(2)(i) and Public Works Contracts Regulations, reg 10(2)(h).

3.122   The new services/works must be substantially similar to the previous services/works and the total estimated cost of the subsequent services/works must be taken into consideration in estimating the value of the contract for the purpose of determining the applicability of the procurement regulations.

Partial replacement or addition of supplies[1]

3.123   The negotiated procedure can be used without advertisement where the authority requires goods or supplies as a partial replacement for, or addition to, existing goods or an installation from an existing supplier. This ground can only be used where obtaining goods having different technical characteristics from another supplier would result in:
—   incompatibility between the existing goods or the installation and the goods to be purchased or hired; or
—   disproportionate technical difficulties in the operation and maintenance of the existing goods or the installation.
The contract must be for less than three years unless there is an unavoidable reason why the period should be exceeded[2].

1   Public Supply Contracts Regulations, reg 10(2)(f).
2   Public Supply Contracts Regulations, reg 10(4).

Advertising

3.124   An essential part of the EC procurement regime is to ensure that public contracts are advertised throughout the Community. The regulations provide for publication of contract notices to announce the various stages of the contract procedure and for notices announcing contract awards. Notices are published in the S series of the Official Journal, available online or on CD-ROM.

3.125 Directive 2001/78/EC, adopted in 2001, has introduced new standard form contract notices for public procurement from 1 May 2002. It is intended that the new forms will create uniformity across member states and facilitate electronic procurement.

3.126 The new standard forms are available on the Internet under the Simap website (www.simap.eu.int). Authorities should be aware that the drafting of notices is not simply a form-filling exercise. The notices alert the market to the possibility of a contract and should be drafted to give as much flexibility as possible so that if the scope, duration or other matters change, the authority will not have to terminate the current procurement process and re-advertise to include the additional or changed matters.

The new forms can be sent by e-mail to mp-ojs@opoce.cec.eu.int or by fax to 0352 29 29 44 619.

Common procurement vocabulary

3.127 Contract notices use codes in order to refer to the relevant services, supplies or works which an authority is procuring.

As part of the modernisation of the public procurement process, the Commission has put forward a proposal to make the use of the Common Procurement Vocabulary ('CPV') the mandatory standard classification system for procurement in the EU. Currently, it is one of several classification systems used and while the Commission issued a Recommendation in 1996 that it should be used as a matter of best practice it is not yet compulsory. With the introduction of the new law, which is expected to come into force in 2003, the CPV will replace other systems such as CPC, CN and CPA.

Prior information notices

3.128 Where an authority intends to award a works contract to a value which exceeds the threshold set out at para **3.19** it must publish a prior information notice (known as a 'PIN') as soon as it has approved the planning of the works.

3.129 In the case of supplies and services contracts, authorities should publish a PIN at the beginning of each financial year, indicating procurement plans for each product or priority service category where the value exceeds the relevant threshold in the forthcoming year. These notices are sometimes known as 'annual notices'.

3.130 The advantage of issuing a PIN is that it will generate market interest at an early stage. It should also demonstrate to the private sector that the authority has made the 'make or buy' decision at the beginning of the procurement process. Prospective bidders will have management board approval for a certain amount of expenditure which can be incurred in connection with any bid. If it is clear that the authority has made its 'make or buy' decision and intend to award a contract at the end of the procurement process, this will help bidders to obtain internal authorisation for expenditure on that basis.

3.131   Where an authority fails to issue a PIN it will be in breach of the requirements of the procurement regulations. However, it could be argued that non-publication of a PIN is not a serious breach as there is no effective remedy for failure to issue a PIN which would result in invalidity of any subsequent award procedure relating to the particular process.

Contract notices

3.132   A contract notice must be published in the OJEC in order to invite tenders for, or expressions of interest in, most contracts subject to the rules. There are exceptions with regard to contracts below the thresholds, framework contracts, Part 1B services and use of the negotiated procedure without prior publication of a notice.

Selection process

3.133   Where an authority wishes to exclude a tender under the open procedure or at the assessment stage under the restricted or negotiated procedures, it must do so in accordance with the criteria set out in the regulations. Candidates may be rejected where the candidate falls within one of the grounds specified under the Works, Services and Supplies Regulations, reg 14 and where the candidate fails to meet the minimum standards of economic and financial standing, in accordance with reg 15 criteria, or minimum standards of ability and technical capacity as provided for in reg 16. Under reg 17 of the Works, Services and Supplies Regulations, an authority may ask for supplementary information relating to matters specified in regs 14, 15 and 16[1].

1   See chapter 16 for the extent to which policy considerations can be considered during the selection process.

3.134   Under the Works, Services and Supplies Regulations, reg 14, an authority may exclude a candidate on the following grounds:
— bankruptcy;
— insolvency;
— where a company has passed a resolution or is a subject of an order by the court for the company winding up;
— where the candidate has been convicted of a criminal offence relating to the conduct of the candidate's business or profession;
— where the candidate has committed an act of grave misconduct in the course of the candidate's business or profession;
— where the candidate has not fulfilled obligations relating to payment of social security contributions under the law of any part of the United Kingdom or of the relevant state in which the candidate is established;
— where the candidate has not fulfilled obligations relating to the payment of taxes under the law of any part of the United Kingdom;

— where the candidate is guilty of serious misrepresentation in providing any information required of the candidate in respect of economic and financial standing and technical capacity;

— where the candidate if not licensed in the relevant state in which the candidate is established or is not a member of an organisation in that relevant state when the law of that relevant state prohibits the provision of the services or works to be provided under the contract by a person who is not so licensed or who is not such a member[1]; or

— the candidate is not registered on the professional or trade register of the relevant state in which the candidate is established under conditions laid down by that state.

An authority can request evidence in accordance with the regulations as proof that the candidate does not fall within the grounds specified above: in the UK this is usually sought in the form of statutory declarations.

1   This ground of exclusion does not apply to contracts under the Public Supply Contracts Regulations 1995.

Information as to economic and financial standing

3.135   At the assessment stage under the restricted and negotiated procedures, authorities frequently send out a pre-qualification questionnaire or equivalent document in which the authority requests the candidate to confirm that the candidate does not fall within any of the criteria stated under the Works, Services and Supplies Regulations, reg 14 and that the candidate meets any minimum standards of economic and financial standing and ability and technical capacity again, in accordance with criteria set out under regs 15 and 16. It should be noted that an authority can only take into account information prescribed by the regulations.

3.136   It is important to note the assessment stage is entirely separate from the evaluation of tenders and contract award stage set out at para **3.142** especially if there are any Requests for Information and ISOP stages where it is important to keep assessment distinct from evaluation see para **3.139**.

3.137   The type of information authorities are entitled to request at the assessment stage in relation to economic and financial standing includes statements from bankers, evidence of relevant professional risk indemnity insurance, a statement of accounts and a statement of the overall turnover for the last three financial years.

3.138   With regard to ability and technical capacity, under the Works, Services and Supplies Regulations, reg 16, authorities may request information relating to the candidate's ability (taking into account in particular the candidate's skills, efficiency, experience and reliability) and technical capacity, taking into account the candidate's educational and professional qualifications or the qualifications of the managerial staff where the candidate is not an individual and those of a person or persons who will be responsible for providing the contract; details of the principal contracts of a similar type provided by the candidate during the last three years; the providers' average annual manpower and the number of managerial staff over the past three years; tools, plant, technical equipment available to the provider for providing the contract and measures for ensuring quality.

Initial statement of proposals

3.139   Where an authority can justify use of the negotiated procedure, in some circumstances it could consider adding to the procurement process an Invitation to Submit Outline Proposals ('ISOP'). The ISOP is a two-stage evaluation process which takes place prior to the issue of the Invitation to Negotiate ('ITN'). It can be used where there is likely to be a large number of prospective tenderers and the authority is looking for innovative proposals from bidders. At this stage, the authority would ask short-listed tenderers to submit their outline proposals, which the authority would evaluate in accordance with the criteria set out in the ISOP. This would enable the authority to reduce the number of bidders to which it would then issue an ITN. As this is an additional stage in the procurement process additional time would need to be built into the project timetable if used.

Best and final offer stage

3.140   Following receipt of tender submissions in response to the ITN, the authority may wish to take forward negotiations with two or three bidders before appointment of a preferred bidder. This can assist the authority by requiring bidders to sign up to both commercial and legal issues while candidates are still within a competitive process. This stage is often referred to as the 'BAFO' (Best and Final Offer) stage whereby, following submission of responses to the ITN, the bidders are given the opportunity to discuss and amplify their responses with the authority and to revise their priced bids. Following submission of BAFOs, the authority will generally select a preferred bidder with whom it will continue to finalise the contract.

Post-tender discussions

3.141   Following the closing date for tenders, the contracting authority must evaluate bids with a view to selecting a contractor for the contract. While conducting its evaluation under any of the procedures, the authority is entitled to enter into discussions with tenderers for the purpose of clarifying or supplementing the tenders or the authority's specification. However, the authority is prohibited at this stage from negotiating the principal terms and conditions of the contract, including prices and specifications. The authority must be particularly wary of allowing individual tenderers to revise their bids in the light of post-tender discussions in case of compromise to the equality of treatment principle. Although, in effect the conduct of the negotiated procedure following advertisement and the proposed competitive dialogue procedure are based on iterative bids being submitted, the equality of treatment principle must still be respected. In practice, this means all tenderers remaining in the competition must be given the same chance to revise their bids and the scope of the contract and the specification should not be altered.

Contract award

3.142   Whichever procedure is used, tenders can only be evaluated and contracts awarded on the basis of lowest price or most economically advantageous offer

('MEAT'). The criteria used to determine the most economically advantageous offer include quality, technical merit, after-sale services, price and technical assistance and merit. Where a contracting authority intends to award a contract on the basis of MEAT it must state the criteria in the contract notice or contract documents and where possible in descending order of importance[1].

1   See also chapter 16 for the extent to which policy considerations can be considered at the contract award stage.

3.143   It is permissible for the authority to reject 'abnormally low' bids, provided that the contractor has an opportunity to offer an explanation for the bid and the explanation has been taken into account.

3.144   It is important that contract award criteria are carefully considered and clear. In *SIAC Construction v Mayo County Council*[1] the authority had sought tenders under the public works regulations for various public works, stating that 'the contract shall be awarded to the competent contractor submitting a tender which is judged to be the most advantageous to the council in respect of cost and technical merit'. The claimant brought a challenge arguing that the criterion of cost laid down by the council meant that it was obliged to award the contract to the lowest price tender (given equal technical merit), and not on the basis of the allegedly new criterion 'ultimate cost'.

1   C-19/00 [2001] ECR I-7725, ECJ.

3.145   The court laid down important principles with regard to the clarity of the contract award criteria but rejected the claim. It stated:

'The principle of the equality of treatment of tenderers implied an obligation of transparency in order to enable compliance with it to be verified, which in turn meant that award criteria must be formulated in such a way as to allow all reasonably well informed and normally diligent tenderers to interpret them in the same way.'

Contract award notice

3.146   The authority must send a contract award notice within 48 days of the date of award to the OJEC. Where an authority terminates the procurement process at any stage prior to contract award, it must inform the OJEC promptly and also inform any provider who submitted an offer or who applied to be included amongst those selected to tender or negotiate the contract of the reasons for its decision.

3.147   Under reg 22(2) of the Works Regulations and reg 23(2) of the Supplies and Services Regulations, where an unsuccessful tenderer requests reasons as to why it was unsuccessful, the authority must inform the provider of those reasons and of the relevant advantages of the successful tender as well as the name of the person awarded the contract.

3.148   Unsuccessful tenderers are entitled to a statement of the reasons why they were rejected within 15 days of making a written request. Any tenderer who has made an admissible tender is entitled to know the characteristics and relevant advantages of the tenderer selected as well as their name. However, the authority may withhold this information if its release will impede law enforcement, be contrary to the public interest or prejudice the legitimate commercial interest of a particular undertaking or prejudice fair competition between service providers.

3.149   The contracting authority must also prepare an internal record providing details of the contract award and the evaluation procedure. Great care needs to be taken with this record. It is likely to be discoverable in the course of any litigation and in addition both the Treasury and the EC Commission are entitled to call for a copy.

3.150   The authority is also required to compile periodic reports for the Treasury providing details of supplies, works and services contracts which have been awarded.

Technical specifications

3.151   In order to ensure equality of treatment between member states, standards and technical specifications cannot be used as barriers to trade. Under the regulations, standards which may legitimately be used in tender specifications are set out in the strict order of precedence. Wherever possible national standards implementing European standards must be used but in default, other recognised national or international standards can be accepted. An authority must also in many cases be prepared to consider products which do not comply with the technical specifications but have equivalent performance characteristics. An authority should only specify a particular trade mark, patent, type or origin if it is essential to do so and should add the words 'or equivalent'.

3.152   Discriminatory treatment between providers of different member states, including the technical specification used was one of the grievances claimed by the plaintiff in *Harmon Facades (UK) Ltd v Corporate Officer of the House of Commons*[1], where among other things, it was alleged that a British firm was treated more favourably than a European firm. The case of *Matra Communications SAS v Home Office*[2] involved a claim by Matra, a French company specialising in the design of mobile telephone systems. Matra claimed that the technical specifications issued by the Home Office for the supply of a mobile radio service were discriminatory and breached arts 30 and 59 of the EC Treaty because they favoured one type of technology ('TETRAPOL') over other equivalent technologies.

The Commission proposals for reform advocate that it should no longer be a requirement of contracting authorities to use EC standards to the exclusion of equivalents.

1   (1999) 67 Con LR 1.
2   [1999] 3 All ER 562, CA.

Public services/supply and works contracts

Open procedure

3.153

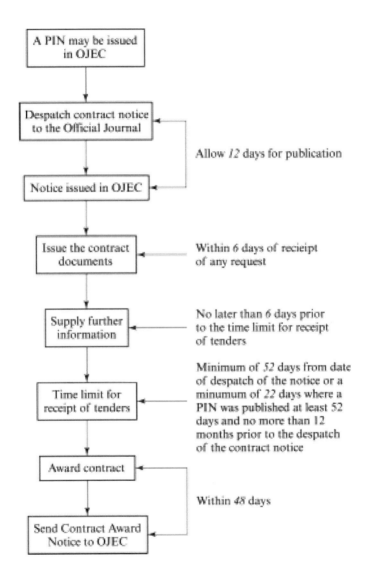

A PIN may be issued in OJEC

Despatch contract notice to the Official Journal

Allow *12* days for publication

Notice issued in OJEC

Issue the contract documents

Within *6* days of recieipt of any request

Supply further information

No later than *6* days prior to the time limit for receipt of tenders

Time limit for receipt of tenders

Minimum of *52* days from date of despatch of the notice or a minumum of *22* days where a PIN was published at least 52 days and no more than 12 months prior to the despatch of the contract notice

Award contract

Within *48* days

Send Contract Award Notice to OJEC

Note: Where the timescale stated ends in a non-working day it is extended to include the next working day (timescales exclude the date of despatch).

(This note applies to paras **3.153** to **3.155**.)

Restricted procedure

3.154

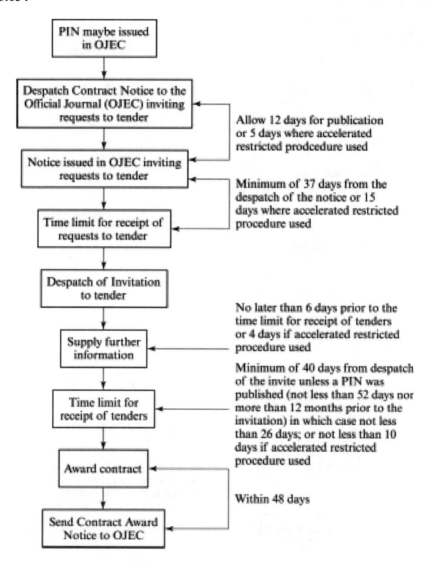

PIN maybe issued in OJEC

Despatch Contract Notice to the Official Journal (OJEC) inviting requests to tender

Allow 12 days for publication or 5 days where accelerated restricted prodcedure used

Notice issued in OJEC inviting requests to tender

Minimum of 37 days from the despatch of the notice or 15 days where accelerated restricted procedure used

Time limit for receipt of requests to tender

Despatch of Invitation to tender

No later than 6 days prior to the time limit for receipt of tenders or 4 days if accelerated restricted procedure used

Supply further information

Minimum of 40 days from despatch of the invite unless a PIN was published (not less than 52 days nor more than 12 months prior to the invitation) in which case not less than 26 days; or not less than 10 days if accelerated restricted procedure used

Time limit for receipt of tenders

Award contract

Within 48 days

Send Contract Award Notice to OJEC

Negotiated procedure with publication of a contract notice

3.155

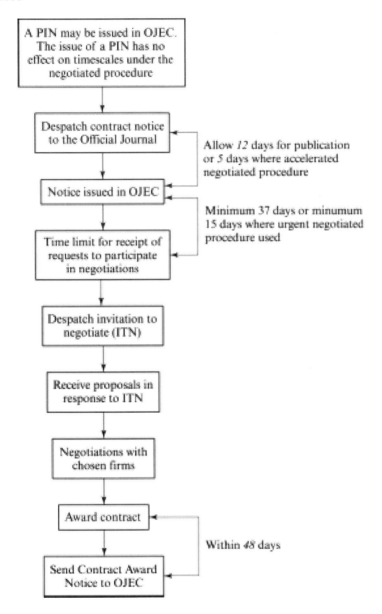

FRAMEWORK AGREEMENTS

3.156 At the time of writing the law relating to the use of framework agreements has been in a state of flux for over 10 years and will continue to be so until adoption of the new European Directive on the co-ordination of procedures for the award of public supply contracts, public service contracts and public works contracts.

3.157   This section explains what a framework agreement is, gives practical examples of where it can arise, and discusses the leading case law and European and domestic guidance on framework arrangements. Readers should also refer to para **3.214** which addresses the European Commission's proposals for the Consolidated Directive.

What is a framework agreement?

3.158   A framework agreement can consist of a framework arrangement, where a contracting authority sets up an arrangement with one or more suppliers on the understanding that the authority will call on the suppliers to provide works, services or supply as and when needed. A framework arrangement of this nature is not a legally binding contract under English law because there is no offer, acceptance or intention to create legally binding relationships. For example, if the contracting authority under a framework arrangement decided that in fact it had no requirement for the particular of works, services or supplies to be delivered, the framework supplier would not be able to sue the contracting authority.

3.159   The other type of framework agreement is a formal call-off contract where the contracting authority invites offers from suppliers on fixed terms and conditions which are then called off as and when necessary. If a legally binding contract is signed between the contracting authority and the framework suppliers and if the contracting authority were to procure its requirements for the particular supply from another supplier outside the framework arrangements there may, depending on the terms of the contract, be a right for the supplier to sue the contracting authority but in any event both parties will have a clear understanding as to the specification for the supplies to be made and the prices applicable for those supplies.

3.160   Framework agreements exist in a variety of different guises, they are sometimes called 'call-off contracts', umbrella agreements, panel arrangements and some approved lists are framework arrangements where the fundamental terms of the contract have been set in advance. The Office of Government Commerce (OGC) G-Cat and S-Cat are catalogues offering supplies of services and equipment which can be called off by government departments and other contracting authorities. G-Cat and S-Cat depend on the use of framework arrangements as do a number of electronic shopping malls and procurement hubs. For more information on the latter see chapter 4 on e-procurement.

Framework agreements under EC procurement rules

3.161   Framework agreements are envisaged under the Utilities Regulations 1996, reg 11 which provides that where a utility is procuring works, services or supplies that:

'(1) A utility which is proposing to enter into a framework agreement may choose to treat that agreement as a contract to which these Regulations apply; accordingly, in respect of such an agreement references in these Regulations to a contract shall include a reference to such a framework agreement.

(2) A utility which chooses to treat a framework agreement as a contract under paragraph (1) above shall not use the framework agreement to hinder, limit or distort competition.'

3.162   However at present there is no explicit reference to framework arrangements under the Works, Services or Supplies Regulations. This is now being addressed by the European Commission in its proposals for the Consolidated Directive where draft art 32 provides as follows:

'**Article 32**

Framework agreements
1   Member states may stipulate that contracting authorities may conclude framework agreements.
2   For the purpose of concluding a framework agreement, contracting authorities shall follow the rules of procedure referred to in this Directive for all phases up to the award of contracts based on that agreement. The parties to that agreement shall be chosen by applying the award criteria set in accordance with Article 53.

Contracts based on a framework agreement shall be awarded in accordance with the procedures laid down in paragraphs 3 and 4. Those procedures may be applied only between the contracting authorities and the economic operators originally party to the framework agreement.

When awarding contracts based on a framework agreement, the parties may under no circumstances make substantive amendments to the terms laid down in the agreement, *inter alia* in the case referred to in paragraph 3.

The term of a framework agreement may not exceed four years, save in exceptional cases duly justified, in particular by the subject of the framework agreement.

Contracting authorities may not use framework agreements improperly or in such a way as to hinder, restrict or distort competition.
3   Where a framework agreement is concluded with a single economic operator, contracts based on that agreement shall be awarded within the limits of the terms laid down in the agreement.

For the award of those contracts, contracting authority may consult the operator party to the framework agreement in writing, requesting it to supplement its offer as necessary. ·
4   Where a framework agreement is concluded with several economic operators, the latter must be at least three in number, insofar as there is a sufficient number of economic operators to satisfy the selection criteria and/or of admissible offers which meet the award criteria.

Contracts based on framework agreements concluded with several economic operators may be awarded either:
  — by application of the terms laid down in the agreement without reopening competition, or
  — where not all the terms are laid down in the agreement, when the parties are again in competition on the basis of the same and, if necessary, more precisely formulated terms, and, where appropriate, other terms

referred to in the specifications of the framework agreement, in accordance with the following procedure:

(a) for every contract to be awarded, contracting authorities shall consult in writing the economic operators capable of executing the subject of the contract;

(b) contracting authorities shall fix a time-limit which is sufficiently long to allow tenders for each specific contract to be submitted, taking into account factors such as the complexity of the subject of the contract and the time needed to send in tenders;

(c) tenders shall be submitted in writing, and their content shall remain confidential until the time-limit for reply has expired;

(d) contracting authorities shall award each contract to the tenderer who has submitted the best tender on the basis of the award criteria set out in the specifications of the framework agreement.'

3.163 The draft Consolidated Directive also allows for dynamic purchasing arrangement as follows:

'**Article 32a**

Dynamic purchasing systems

1 Member states may stipulate that contracting authorities may use dynamic purchasing systems.

2 In order to set up a dynamic purchasing system, contracting authorities shall follow the rules of the procedure opened in all its phases up to the award of the contracts to be concluded under this system. All the tenderers satisfying the selection criteria and having submitted an indicative tender which complies with the specification and any additional documents shall be admitted to the system; indicative tenders may be improved at any time provided that they continue to comply with the specification. With a view to setting up the system and to the award of contracts under that system, contracting authorities shall use solely electronic means in accordance with Article 42(2) to (5).

3 For the purposes of setting up the dynamic purchasing system, contracting authorities shall:

(a) publish a contract notice making it clear that a dynamic purchasing system is involved;

(b) indicate in the specification, inter alia, the nature of the purchases envisaged under that system, as well as all the necessary information concerning the purchasing system, the electronic equipment used and the technical connection arrangements and specifications;

(c) offer by electronic means, on publication of the notice and up to the expiry of the system, free, direct and full access to the specification and to any additional document and shall indicate in the notice the Internet address at which such documents may be consulted.

4 Contracting authorities shall give any economic operator, throughout the entire period of the dynamic purchasing system, the possibility of submitting an indicative tender and of being admitted to the system under the conditions referred to in the first subparagraph of paragraph 2. They shall complete evaluation within a maximum of 15 days from the date of submission of the indicative tender. However, they may extend evaluation provided that no invitation to tender is issued in the meantime.

The contracting authority shall inform the tenderer referred to in the first subparagraph at the earliest possible opportunity of its admittance to the dynamic purchasing system or of the rejection of its indicative tender.

5   Each specific contract must be the subject of an invitation to tender. Before issuing the invitation to tender, contracting authorities shall publish a simplified contract notice inviting all interested economic operators to submit an indicative tender, in accordance with paragraph 4, within a time-limit that may not be less than 15 days from the date on which the simplified notice was sent. Contracting authorities may not proceed with tendering until they have completed evaluation of all the indicative tenders received by that deadline.

6   Contracting authorities shall invite all tenderers admitted to the system to submit a tender for each specific contract to be awarded under the system. To that end they shall set a time-limit for the submission of tenders.

They shall award the contract to the tenderer which submitted the best tender on the basis of the award criteria set out in the contract notice setting up the dynamic purchasing system. Those criteria may, if appropriate, be formulated more precisely in the invitation referred to in the previous subparagraph.

7   A dynamic purchasing system may not last for more than four years, except in duly justified exceptional cases.

Contracting authorities may not resort to this system to prevent, restrict or distort competition.

No charges may be billed to the interest economic operators or to parties to the system.'

Case law on framework arrangements

3.164   The two leading cases on framework arrangements are the *DoE Northern Ireland* case and the *Greek Bandages* cases which are described in more detail below.

DoE Northern Ireland[1]

3.165   This case arose from a complaint to the European Commission concerning the use of a framework agreement by the Northern Ireland Department of the Environment. The Northern Ireland DoE had made widespread use of framework agreements for procuring architectural, engineering and other construction related services.

1   IP/97/1178.

3.166   In July 2000 the European Commission decided to take art 226 proceedings before the ECJ against the UK government as a result of the complaint. The Commission's initial opinion as set out in the Reasoned Opinion issued by the Advocate General was that the use of a frameworks agreement (outside the Utilities Directive) was non-compliant with the Services Directive. However, at the time of issuing its press release stating that it was taking the United Kingdom to the ECJ, the Commission indicated that it had modified its view with regard to the legality of framework arrangements under the Services Directive.

3.167   The press release stated that:

'The framework agreement itself must be awarded in accordance with the public procurement Directive. The Commission takes the view that if the frames of the framework agreement are sufficiently specific as to detail the key elements of any individual contracts to be awarded subsequently, and if these are set out in binding form, when those individual contracts are awarded it is not necessary to follow the detailed procedural requirements of the Directive. However, where the key terms and conditions of individual contracts are vague, or simply not specified at all, they must be advertised in the Official Journal and follow the detailed procedural requirements of the public procurement Directive.'

3.168   In the *DoE Northern Ireland* case, the Commission considered that the essential conditions of individual contracts were not specified in a binding manner in the framework agreement. Individual contracts awarded under the framework agreement in the Commission's view should therefore have followed the detailed procedural requirements of the public procurement Directives.

3.169   At the time of writing, this case has not yet been put before the ECJ and it is anticipated that it will be held in abeyance until adoption of the Consolidated Directive which will set out the firm view and parameters for the use of framework agreements under the European procurement rules.

The Greek Bandages *case*

3.170   The case of the *EC Commission v Greece*[1] concerned a framework agreement which was a legally binding contract where all hospitals and healthcare units, as well as the Greek army, were required to purchase certain types of medical dressing material from six Greek textile manufacturers for a period of three years, which could be extended for a further two years.

1   C-79/94 [1995] ECR I-1071, ECJ.

3.171   The Greek government had failed to advertise the contract in the OJEC both because the value of each of the individual orders under the framework arrangement did not exceed the value threshold of ECU 200,000 where the Supply Directive applies, and also because the Greek government argued that the dressing material in question could have been supplied only by the six producers which were party to the framework agreement since no producer in any other European member state had expressed an interest in the contract.

3.172   The ECJ took the view that the Greek government's framework agreement amounted to a supply contract within the meaning of the European public procurement rules, since it laid down all the main contractual elements on which orders would be called off, even though it did not specify the quantity to be supplied. Unfortunately, the judgment did not specify the details of the arrangements in place with the supplier but the case appears to indicate that a contracting authority is entitled to establish framework agreements provided they lay down the terms and conditions on which supplies may be ordered, even if the individual quantities are not specified until called off.

3.173 The OGC issued guidance on framework agreements in the context of correspondence between the UK government and the European Commission concerning the *DoE Northern Ireland* case.

3.174 The European Commission had been concerned that there should not be any potential for negotiation when calling-off a requirement under a framework agreement whether or not the framework agreement was legally binding. The OGC therefore advised that the approach to finalising the terms of any call-off contract under a framework agreement should be mechanistic not involving negotiation of the terms already established by the framework. The OGC further advised that contracting authorities should ensure that framework agreements set out the fundamental terms such as price upon which subsequent call-off contracts will be awarded and that framework agreements are awarded in accordance with the European public procurement rules. The OGC advice where the framework agreement involves a number of providers states that:

'... the basis for awarding the frameworks and then for deciding between [the providers] must be the application of the award criteria permitted under the Directive, ie lowest price or most economically advantageous tender.

When a specific need arises it may be necessary in some cases to complete the information available to the framework provider to enable it to complete its bid so that the contracting authority can decide whether to accept it or to go out to a fresh competition.

Where there is more than one framework provider this may have the effect that the ranking of the provider changes when the award criteria are applied.'

The OGC guidance then goes on to give the example of a supplier which had middle-rank cost rates but which was able to deliver the supplies within a shorter timescale might outrank another supplier with cheaper costs but only average delivery times.

DTLR advice on framework agreement

3.175 The Department of Transport, Local Government and the Regions (at the time of writing now the Office of the Deputy Prime Minister) on 5 November 2001 issued a Procurement Advice Note ('PAN') 13/2001 on the OGC guidance on framework agreements referred to above (among other matters) which reiterated that no negotiation of price or the pricing mechanism already established in a framework agreement can take place at call-off and that this restriction also applied to binding frameworks contracts including S-Cat and G-Cat.

3.176 The DTLR advice that where in either a framework agreement or a framework contract there is a panel of suppliers and the contracting authority intends to mount a mini-competition between two or more of the suppliers, the mini-competition must not involve negotiation on the prices and the pricing mechanism already established in the framework agreement. The DTLR suggested that the award criteria for the mini-competitions should be a combination of (i) quality/methodology and (ii) resources/costs. In the latter case, the calculation of (ii) must relate to the rates in the relevant framework that the contracting authority is allowed to take into account any price mechanism (eg discounts) established within the framework.

Summary of current law on framework arrangements

3.177   The current law on framework arrangements can be summarised as follows:
(1)   framework arrangements, whilst not expressly mentioned in the Works, Services or Supplies Regulations, are permissible providing the conditions set out below are complied with;
(2)   the contract awarded under the framework must be binding and clearly set out the main terms of the agreement, in particular the price or rates applicable;
(3)   framework arrangements must be advertised with due competition as if the public procurement rules applied;
(4)   where the contracting authority holds a mini-competition between suppliers under a framework, the main framework terms cannot be renegotiated but non-discriminatory criteria relating to lowest price or most economically advantageous can be applied (see para **3.142**) but the method of calling-off must be non-discriminatory;
(5)   once the framework has been entered into no renegotiation of its fundamental terms is allowed;
(6)   under the draft Consolidated Directive, framework agreements will be expressly permitted provided the above rules are complied with, the term of the framework agreement does not last for more than four years (save in exceptional and justified cases) and where a panel of suppliers is appointed, at least three suppliers must be appointed.

3.178   The OGC describes the distinction between framework agreements and framework contracts as follows:

'Framework agreements (sometimes known as "enabling agreements" or "standing offers") are not contractually binding until an order is formally "called-off" against them, whereas framework contracts are made contractually binding at the outset by the payment of consideration or by forming them as a deed.'

COMPLIANCE AND REMEDIES FOR BREACH

Introduction

3.179   Tendering procedures are highly complex and contracting authorities are aware that there are risks involved in the failure to comply with the law. Compliance procedures will often assist in raising awareness of the risks and the proper procedures to be taken to minimise such risks. When awarding contracts, contracting authorities will be subject to the requirements of administrative law, contractual law, EU law requirements on non-discrimination and free movement of goods and services, general common law principles and the specific rules on public procurement discussed below.

3.180   The public procurement remedies procedures are based upon the provisions of the so-called 'Remedies Directive' (Directive (EEC) 665/89), the provisions of which were implemented into UK law in the Works, Supplies and Services Regulations[1]. There is a general obligation under the regulations for contracting authorities to comply with the public procurement rules. There are specific provisions which establish the procedures for remedy where an aggrieved contractor, supplier or service provider suffers, or is at risk of suffering, some form of loss due to non-compliance by the contracting authority with the procurement rules. Enforcement of the procurement rules operate both at the EU and at the national level. The national courts or tribunals in each member state are empowered to take measures to remedy any violation of the law and to compensate for loss. At the EU level the Commission can commence proceedings against the national government concerned under the EC Treaty if any contracting authority breaches the rules. The remedies available under national law and EU law are quite distinct. Whereas an action in the courts permits a disadvantaged tenderer to seek a direct remedy, action under EU law is an enforcement action taken by the Commission against the member state concerned. It should be noted that action may be taken simultaneously at both the EU and the national level.

1   Public Works Contracts Regulations 1991, SI 1991/2680, the Public Supply Contracts Regulations 1995, SI 1995/201, the Public Services Contracts Regulations 1993, SI 1993/3228.

UK national courts

3.181   In the UK, the obligation to comply with the provisions of the Works, Supplies and Services Regulations in relation to contracts that fall within the ambit of those regulations is considered in law to be a 'duty' owed to providers. Non-compliance is not a criminal offence but it can give rise to a breach of statutory duty before the courts.

Obligation to notify contracting authority

3.182   Where a provider or potential provider considers that there is a breach of the duty owed to it under the regulations, it has an obligation to inform the relevant contracting authority of the precise nature of the breach or breaches and its intention to take action before the courts (this is sometimes referred to as the 'letter before action' stage).

3.183   This obligation is further supported up by a requirement in the regulations that an unsuccessful tenderer is entitled to request in writing from the contracting authority, the reasons why it was unsuccessful and, where the tenderer submitted an admissible tender, information about the characteristics and relative merits of the successful tender as well as the identity of the successful tenderer. The contracting authority has 15 days to respond to such a request.

3.184   Notification of the breach to the contracting authority provides the contracting authority with the opportunity to review the tender procedure and, if necessary, remedy the problem. For example, if a contract notice containing a discriminatory provision was notified to the contracting authority at the first stages of the process, that notice could be withdrawn and the notice republished with the appropriate amendments to the offending provision.

Three-month limitation period

3.185   Having notified the contracting authority, the aggrieved provider may bring an action before the High Court (in England, Wales and Northern Ireland) or before the Court of Session in Scotland. The aggrieved provider has only three months from the date when the grounds for bringing the proceedings arose, within which the action must be launched, unless the court considers that there is a good reason for extending that three-month deadline. The period of three months in which to bring action has been challenged in a number of recent cases. While the number of challenges before the courts is increasing there is still considerable initial reluctance to institute proceedings. Many suppliers unaware of the three-month time limit usually try to settle cases through negotiation and when those fail, find themselves starting proceedings outside the limitation period. They then have to seek the exercise of the court's discretion to allow the action to continue. The implications of the three-month time limit and the court's discretion to extend are considered in a number of cases, notably *Keymed Ltd v Forest Healthcare NHS Trust*[1]; *Matra Communications SAS v Home Office*[2] and *Resource Management Services v Westminster City Council*[3].

1   [1998] Eu LR 71. The case taken by Keymed involved the award of two contracts by the NHS trust for the supply of surgical equipment and furnishings on the basis that the tender did not comply with the procedures set out in the Supplies Regulations. The court found that the time begins to run from the moment that the regulations are breached and not the date of the breach being discovered. It was clear that Keymed had not brought an action within the specified three-month time period. Keymed took a preliminary case asking the court to use its discretion to extend the three-month time period. The court established that the test for using its discretion was: (i) the length and reasons for delay; (ii) the extent to which the plaintiff is to blame for the delay; (iii) the extent to which the defendant may have induced or contributed to the delay; and (iv) whether the defendant was or would be prejudiced by the delay or the grant of the extension.

2   (31 July 1998, unreported). The case involved a £1.8 billion emergency mobile radio contract for the UK Police. The Home Office published an OJ Notice and later the tender documents, which stipulated that the technical specification of the contract would be the proposed European Standard for mobile radio, TETRA. The specification excluded a rival form of technology (Tetrapol) offered by Matra. The court found that the date of the alleged breach was the date when TETRA was first specified in the contract documents. Proceedings before the court were not started until some 20 months after the OJ Notice's publication, during which time Matra had attempted to negotiate a settlement. The case came before the High Court on a preliminary issue relating to the limitation period. The court held that the grounds of the alleged breach first arose when the invitation to tender was published and accordingly the three month period had expired. The judge refused leave to extend time. An appeal before the Court of Appeal, *Matra Communications SAS v Home Office* [1999] 1 WLR 1646, failed.

3   (1999) 1 LGLR 893. The case concerned the award by a local authority of an audit contract to its own in-house organisation. The court found (applying the test in *Keymed*) that there had not been undue delay, that there were genuine practical difficulties in the plaintiff seeking concrete evidence to bring the case and that there was no prejudice to the local authority in allowing an extension.

3.186   It should be noted in the *Matra*[1] case, Judge Rattee confirmed that an action for damages may be capable of being brought for damages for breach of EC law (outside the scope of the UK Regulations) following the ECJ decisions in *Francovich*[2] and *Norbrook*[3]. The limitation period for these actions would be six years.

1   *Matra Communications SAS v Home Office* (31 July 1998, unreported) at p 33.
2   Cases C-6, 9/90 *Francovich and Bonifaci v Italy* [1991] ECR I-5357, [1993] 2 CMLR 66, ECJ.
3   Case C-127/95 *Norbrook Laboratories Ltd v Ministry of Agriculture, Fisheries and Food*[1998] ECR I-1531. ECJ.

Interim measures

3.187   Upon application, the High Court may, in appropriate circumstances, order the suspension of the award process or the implementation of a decision by the contracting authority pending a decision on the merits of the case. In seeking interim measures, the plaintiff must establish that it has a good arguable claim to the right it seeks. The test for granting interim relief in such cases follows guidelines established by the House of Lords in the case *American Cyanamid v Ethicon*[1]. It is necessary to show that there is a serious case to answer, whether damages would be an adequate remedy (in which case interim relief would not be granted) and the balance of interests between the parties. Interim measures to preserve the situation are also available under EU law (see below).

1 [1975] 2 WLR 316.

Remedies available

3.188 In proceedings brought under the Works, Supplies and Services Regulations the court has the power to take interim measures in the form of an order suspending the procedure leading to the award of the relevant contract or suspending the decision of a contracting authority. If the High Court does make a finding of breach of duty it may make an order setting aside the decision or action or require that any documentation be amended to cure the breach. A tenderer who can show that it has suffered loss or breach may also seek damages to remedy the breach. In a case where the contract has already been entered into, the remedy available to the provider will be damages. The type of remedy granted will depend on the nature of the breach in question.

Non-financial remedies

3.189 If the contract has not already been awarded, the plaintiff can seek the remedy of 'set aside'. In other words the wrongful act must be eliminated and the contractual authority is required to undertake the administrative process again, correcting its previous errors. What this means in practical terms will depend upon the point in the process when the error was made. For instance, the contracting authority may be required to advertise a contract previously tendered without recourse to an EU-wide tendering process or to re-advertise a contract which contained discriminatory specifications or revise contractual documentation which favoured a potential tenderer. It is, for instance, possible to seek injunctive relief to prevent a contracting authority from entering into a contract which would be made in breach of the procurement rules[1].

1 See for example *Severn Trent plc v Welsh Water Ltd, WPD Holdings UK & United Utilities* [2001] CLC 107, where injunctive relief was granted under equivalent provisions in the Utilities Regulations.

3.190 The remedy of 'set aside' is not available once a contract is concluded. In such circumstances, the plaintiff may only seek financial damages for any losses which it incurs as a result of the breach[1]. There is usually something of a time gap between the award of a contract (at which point the remedy of set aside is still available for breach) and the actual conclusion of that contract (from which point onwards only financial compensation will be available for any breach). Damages are generally regarded by tenderers seeking review as being a less attractive remedy than the opportunity for winning the contract itself which an injunction to set aside will provide. There is a potential danger that contracting authorities may minimise the chances of a successful claim by a disgruntled tenderer by entering into a contract immediately after the award. This issue arose on a preliminary question before the ECJ in the *Alcatel* case[2] on a reference from an Austrian court. The ECJ held that member states have an obligation to ensure that a contracting authority's decision to award a contract prior to the conclusion of that contract is open to a review process whereby an unsuccessful tenderer can have that decision set aside if the relevant conditions are met, even if, once the contract is concluded, it may only be able to obtain damages. Contracting authorities are still grappling with the full implications of this requirement.

1   Works Regulations 1991, reg 31(7), Supplies Regulations 1995, reg 29(6), Services Regulations 1993, reg 32(6).
2   C-81/98 *Alcatel Austria AG v Bundesministerium für Wissenschaft und Verkehr* [1999] ECR I-7671.

Damages

3.191   As discussed above, in an action involving a breach of the regulations, where the contract has already been entered into, the court is only able to award damages[1]. It is not open to the court to set aside the contract, although it has been suggested by some commentators[2] that under English law where both parties are aware of the breach when they enter into the contract, the enforceability of such a contract would be contrary to public policy. This proposition in a public procurement context remains untested in the courts.

1   See for example *R v Tower Hamlets London Borough Council, ex p Luck* [1999] COD 294. The Court of Appeal held that the applicant's complaint regarding its exclusion from the list of possible tenderers for a local government contract could only be based on the claim for damages and not by way of judicial review.
2   Eg Geddes *Public and Utility Procurement, A Practical Guide to the UK Regulations and Associated Community Rules* (2nd edn, 1997), p 102.

3.192   The calculation of damages for breach is a complex and technical issue is . In principle, the successful plaintiff is entitled to compensation for the loss suffered. There may in practice be a difficulty in quantifying such a loss in cases where it cannot show that it would have been awarded the contract but for the breach. There is nothing in the Works, Supplies and Services Regulations which assists. Regulation 32(7) of the Utilities Regulations provides that:

> 'Where ... the court is satisfied that a provider would have had a real chance of being awarded a contract if that chance had not been adversely affected by a breach of duty owned to him...the provider shall be entitled to damages amounting to his costs in preparing his tender and in participating in the procedure leading to the award of the contract'.

Relief in the form of damages for loss in preparing a tender does not exclude the possibility of the plaintiff from being entitled to other relief if it is able to establish loss, for instance for breach of contract[1] or the tort of misfeasance.

1   See for example a case outside the scope of the UK Regulations: *Blackpool and Fylde Aero Club Ltd v Blackpool Borough Council* [1990] 1 WLR 1195. The Court of Appeal upheld the decision of Judge Jolly in the QBD. A local authority put out to tender a concession for use of a local airport. The plaintiffs (a flight club) prepared a tender and posted it by hand in the local authority's post box before the expiry of the deadline for submission of tenders. The local authority omitted to clear the letterbox on time and did not consider the plaintiffs tender and granted the concession to another party. The plaintiffs successfully argued that there was a breach of the implied contract to consider timely and conforming tenders.

3.193 This is perhaps best illustrated by the *Harmon*[1] case. The background to this case was that Harmon, a European based company, tendered for a fenestration contract for a new parliamentary building for the House of Commons. The contract was ultimately awarded to a British competitor. Harmon brought an action claiming:

(i) breach of the EC Treaty provisions on non-discrimination and free movement of goods and services;

(ii) breach of the Public Works Regulations;

(iii) breach of implied contract in the request for tenders that tenderers would be treated equally and fairly;

(iv) for the tort of misfeasance.

The basis for its claim was that the House of Commons had sought tenders on the basis of 'best overall value for money' and should have awarded the contract only on the lowest price. They had failed to use the alternative of award based on 'economically most advantageous tender' or identified the relevant criteria for making such an assessment. Harmon was able to prove it had offered the lowest price and consequently should have been awarded the contract. The court upheld Harmon's claim and found that it was entitled to recover tender costs for all tenders, damages for breach of the EC Treaty, damages for breach of the Public Works Regulations, breach of contract and for misfeasance in public office. Following the award of interim damages, an out-of-court settlement was made for the level of damages amounting to £5.26 million[2].

1   *Harmon CFEM Facades (UK) Ltd v Corporate Officer of the House of Commons* (1999) 67 Con LR 1.

2   House of Commons Commission – Twenty Third Annual Report 2000–01.

Preliminary rulings

3.194 Where an issue arises before the national court which involves a point of EC law which the national courts are unable to clarify and which is essential to resolving the case, the courts can seek a preliminary ruling on that point from the ECJ under art 234 of the EC Treaty. The ECJ will rule on the matter of interpretation put before it and refer the matter back to the national courts for resolution on the facts of the case.

EU Remedies—complaint to the Commission and proceedings under art 226 of the EC Treaty

3.195 In addition to recourse before the national courts, it is open to an aggrieved tenderer to make a complaint to the Commission[1]. Under art 211 of the EC Treaty, the Commission is responsible for enforcing the rules established by the Treaty itself and any Directives or regulations made under it (including the public procurement Directives). The Commission is therefore empowered to bring proceedings against a government before the ECJ, either following its own monitoring process or in response to a complaint. Theoretically, one member state could bring an action for breach against another member state under art 227, but in practice this is highly unlikely.

1   An example of a case where action was taken simultaneously before both the UK courts and is a subject of a complaint to the Commission was the *Matra* case. While the case before the UK courts was found to have been out of time, the Commission has pursued the complaint

and on 20 July 2000 it announced its intention to take the matter before the ECJ (IP/00/813). The facts of the case have also influenced proposed amendments to the public procurement rules relating to technical standards which is the subject in dispute.

Advantages and disadvantages of a complaint to the Commission

3.196   As discussed above, an aggrieved tenderer may make a complaint to the Commission either as an alternative to, or in addition to, taking an action before the national courts. From the perspective of the aggrieved tenderer, the disadvantages of making a complaint to the Commission is that any action before the courts will be taken by the Commission itself against the government concerned. Unless the government is itself the contracting authority, the action is very indirect[1]. There is no direct involvement or direct remedy for the complainant, since any judgment is declaratory only. The legal process is generally very lengthy and drawn out and the complainant may feel out of control of the procedure.

1   If the ECJ finds that the government has breached art 226 and the government fails to comply, the Commission can take a further action against the government and the court can impose fines.

3.197   The advantages to the complainant is that making a complaint is a relatively easy process and the costs to him are relatively low, being principally those of putting together the complaint. The Commission will bear the costs of any litigation, as the complainant is not a party to any litigation. The commencement of the Commission's investigation will require the government concerned to look into the tendering procedures of the contracting authority. This in itself may be highly disruptive of the tendering process. Moreover, at some point the investigation will be brought into the public arena which, at a minimum, may cause embarrassment. The ECJ can, upon application by the Commission, take interim measures to prevent the award of a contract (discussed below). Although the final judgment is declaratory it can form the basis for a claim before the national courts (for instance in analogous cases).

The art 226 procedure

3.198   Following a complaint, there is a two-stage process. The first stage is an informal one and the second the formal process required by art 226 of the EC Treaty. The first and 'informal' stage commences with the Commission examining the merits of the complaint which has been made to decide whether there is a sufficient basis to take the matter forward. If, on the face of it, there appears to be a possible breach of the procurement Directives and/or of the EC Treaty rules (eg on non-discrimination or free movement of goods and/or services), the Commission will send a formal letter to the government in which it sets out the background to the case before it and asks the government to respond to certain questions. The letter will set out a deadline for response (the duration is not set down in the legislation but is generally around 1–2 months, although it may be longer and can be extended upon request). At this point the government will generally contact the contracting authority concerned to look into the matter and assist it in preparing a response. In some cases, the issue is resolved (eg by the contracting authority providing sufficient evidence to satisfy the Commission that there was no breach, by the contracting authority correcting the alleged breach or reaching a settlement with the complainant or the complainant agreeing to withdraw his complaint). The Commission will not, as a matter of practice, usually pursue a case where a resolution is reached between the parties at this early stage.

3.199 If the Commission receives no response from the government or the response is unsatisfactory and it wishes to take further action, it is required under art 226 to deliver a 'reasoned opinion' to the government setting out the details of the alleged failure to comply with EU law. The government is given a deadline to respond to the reasoned opinion (generally 1–2 months but it may be extended). The letter setting out the Commission's reasoned opinion is not made public, but as a matter of practice the Commission will usually issue press releases which indicates that it has sent such a reasoned opinion and giving a brief outline of the relevant facts and the alleged breach. Once again, there is a possibility for the parties to resolve the matter without further action. If a case on the same matter is pending before the national courts then the government should notify the Commission of that fact and any result.

3.200 Where there is no satisfactory resolution of the case or explanation following the reasoned opinion, the Commission may then bring the matter before the ECJ. It is a matter for the Commission's own discretion to decide what cases to take before the courts and many cases are filtered out at an earlier stage. In practice, the types of cases which the Commission are most likely to take forward are those involving either a blatant violation of the rules (eg the failure to publish a notice for a contract covered by the public procurement Directives) or where there is a particular point of law to be resolved which will provide useful guidance in other similar cases.

Interim measures

3.201 The Commission can, under art 243 of the EC Treaty, seek interim remedies before the ECJ (for instance to suspend the award of the contract). Interim measures may be granted where the Commission has been able to show that there is a prima facie case, urgency, the risk of serious and irreparable damage and the balance of interests between the parties. Purely pecuniary loss will not be regarded as comprising irreparable damage[1]. The system does not make interim measures particularly easy to obtain. For instance in the *Walloon Bus* case[2] the court found that the Commission had been tardy in pursuing the complaint and that the balance of interests in that case favoured the Belgian government and no interim measures were granted. In fact, delay in taking action is quite common since the Commission will have to go through the pre-litigation, fact-finding procedure first which generally takes some months, by which time the seeking of interim measures may no longer be a viable option. Notwithstanding these hurdles, there have been a few cases where interim measures suspending a decision of the Commission have been granted[3].

1   Case T-169/00R *Esedera SPRL v EC Commission* [2000] ECR II-2951, a case concerning the decision by the Commission not to award a contract relating to the management of a day nursery.
2   Case C-87/94R *EC Commission v Belgium* [1994] ECR I-1395, ECJ.
3   Case 194/88R *EC Commission v Italy* [1998] ECR 4559, concerning the suspension of the award of a works contract for the construction of an incinerator; C-272/91R *EC Commission v Italy* [1992] ECR I-3929, ECJ, concerning the tendering of a concession of a lottery computerisation system.

Action before the European Court of Justice

3.202   An action before the ECJ at present takes between two and three years on average, due to the time pressures on the court. Final judgment is preceded by an Opinion by an Advocate General whose job it is to advise the court. The Advocate General analyses the facts and the legal aspects of the case in detail and presents his resolution of the issues. The Advocate-General's Opinion is influential and is generally followed but the court is not bound by either its findings or the solution it presents. Where the Commission's case is successful, the court will issue a judgment requiring the infringement to be brought to an end.

3.203   Given the length of time involved in the legal proceedings, it is probably fair to say that often the more significant practical implications of an art 226 proceeding is felt at the earlier stages of the Commission's investigation and the success of any interim proceeding. However, this is not to say that the impact of the judgments themselves is not important. The ECJ has the final say in the interpretation of EC law and its judgments are therefore very significant in determining the law.

BREACH OF PROCUREMENT RULES—'OTHER CONSEQUENCES'

3.204   A breach of the EC procurement rules is not a criminal offence. This is expressly provided in the Public Services Contracts Regulations 1993, reg 32(2), the Public Works Contracts Regulations 1991, reg 31(3), the Public Supply Contracts Regulations 1995, reg 29(2) and the Utilities Supply and Works Contracts Regulations 1992, reg 30(2).

3.205   In order of severity, a local authority which is found to have breached the EC public procurement rules potentially faces one or more of the consequences set out below.

3.206   The breach of the European procurement rules could be regarded as an incidence of procedural impropriety or illegality giving grounds for judicial review as suggested by Lord Diplock in *Council of Civil Service Union v Minister for Civil Service*[1], which may render the local authority's decision to award the contract ultra vires and any associated contractual documentation being deemed to be void.

1   [1985] AC 374 at 410–411.

3.207   Expenditure under a contract which has been awarded in breach of the European procurement rules is likely to be challenged by the local authority's external auditor, who may regard it as unlawful expenditure and make an application to the court under the Audit Commission Act 1998, s 24, resulting in review and, until its repeal, potential surcharge of officers and members involved.

3.208   Most local authorities' standing orders require compliance with the EC public procurement rules in particular in relation to the advertisement and competitive tendering of contracts. A breach of an authority's contract standing orders is usually regarded as a disciplinary offence for the officer involved.

3.209 There are practical consequences which may arise where a breach of the European procurement rules has been discovered. Time and administrative costs may be wasted by the need to re-advertise the contract or, even worse, deal with the consequences of pending challenges. In the meantime, prospective contractors may lose confidence in the local authority's procurement process and withdraw or lose the support of their funders, whose due diligence check before contract signature will inevitably scrutinise compliance with the EC procurement Directives.

3.210 In PFI contracts, contractors tend to require that challenges to the contract or the implementation of interim measures as a result of a complaint of breach of the procurement rules are dealt with as a 'compensation event', which means that the private sector contractor is given relief from termination due to failure to meet timescales which would otherwise be of the essence (ie a fundamental term of the contract) as well as compensation for wasted costs.

3.211 Finally, the adverse impact on public relations resulting from a challenge brought on the basis of the breach of public procurement rules should never be disregarded in the local government context, where members may often be particularly sensitive as to reports in the national and local press in relation to the outsourcing or perceived privatisation of a public service. It should be borne in mind at all times that challenges to the procurement process can come from any direction, whether aggrieved contractors, land owners, school governors, community groups, disgruntled members of the same local authority, trade unions, auditors or stakeholders.

3.212 Where the authority takes the decision to re-advertise a contract in order to avoid breach of the procurement rules, the procurement officer should not forget to notify the OJEC and prospective tenderers who have expressed an interest in the contract that the procurement process has been withdrawn and will be re-advertised. The advertisement should be regarded as an opportunity to rectify errors in the previous procurement, taking into account any lessons that they have learnt from the market or stakeholders in relation to the procurement process to date.

THE FUTURE OF THE PUBLIC PROCUREMENT DIRECTIVES

Introduction

3.213 In May 2000 the Commission put forward a package of amendments designed to both simplify and consolidate the current legislation and at the same to modernise the regime to take into account liberalisation in the market place, new methods of procurement and the use of electronic tendering[1]. A similar proposal was put forward in respect of the Utilities Directive[2]. The legislation is expected to be adopted in 2003 and member states are expected to have 21 months to implement changes into national legislation. The major features of the proposal affecting the public procurement contracts are as follows.

1   Com (2000)275 final.
2   Com (2000)276 final.

Simplification

3.214   The aim is to consolidate the three present Directives on public works, supplies and services into one single text. This will also mean that certain inconsistencies and anomalies between the three regimes will be eliminated. The provisions will also be re-ordered to reflect the normal order of the award procedure. There will also be changes to the applicable thresholds to make them simpler to apply. The level of the thresholds will be changed and the current references to special drawing rights will be removed and references will be to the Euro alone.

Electronic purchasing

3.215   The first steps towards online electronic tendering were taken with the adoption of Directive 2001/78/EC which introduced, from 1 May 2002, new standard form contract notices which are published by the OJEC on their online Tenders Electronic Daily (TED) database. The new proposal is intended to make it easier for businesses to use electronic means for the submission of tenders. These changes will also permit the reduction of the publication deadlines. There is also a proposal which could allows contracting authorities to introduce an electronic award system under certain conditions. See also chapter 4 on e-procurement.

Competitive dialogue

3.216   One of the most important substantive changes proposed, is the introduction of a new and more flexible tendering procedure for complex contracts. The Commission recognises that for some types of purchasing, particular in high technology or complex financing arrangements, contracting authorities are not always aware of the best technical, legal or financial solutions for meeting their requirements. It is helpful therefore, to have some degree of dialogue with suppliers to ascertain what might best meet their needs. The current rules permit only a very limited form of 'technical dialogue' with suppliers and the open and restrictive procedures permit very little of this type of discussion. The negotiated procedure is permitted only in limited circumstances. The proposal is therefore to introduce a new form of 'competitive dialogue' negotiated procedure to deal with these types of situations. Use of the procedure will be limited to cases where there is a sufficient degree of complexity to objectively justify its use. Contracting authorities would be required to publish a notice setting out their needs and requirements and select candidates by using the usual selection criteria. The contracting authorities may then conduct a dialogue with selective candidates on a non-discriminatory basis until it can identify the solutions capable of meeting its needs. Equality must be maintained throughout, particularly in terms of provision of information which may provide an advantage to some tenderers over others. Once the solution is identified, the contracting authority can request final tenders to be made and award to the most economically advantageous tender based on its specified award criteria.

Framework agreements

3.217 Framework agreements (discussed at para **3.156** above) are agreements between contracting authorities and one or more economic operators and are used in the case of repeat orders to identify particular economic orders who will be able to meet the requirements of the contracting authority as and when required over a specified period. There is no provision for the award of framework contracts under the public procurement regulations as there is in the case of Utilities Regulations[1]. The Commission takes the view that framework agreements are not public contracts to the extent that they do not lay down specific terms and do not give rise to performance as a contract does. However, contracts with several economic operators (eg purchase order contracts) are public contracts and must be awarded in accordance with the public procurement rules where the thresholds are exceeded. In practice, it can be very difficult to comply with the strict letter of current rules and retain the flexibility which contracting authorities require when looking to establish such an arrangement. The proposal would introduce a provision permitting the use of a framework agreement and establish the mechanism, time limits and procedures for awarding such a contract.

1   Utilities Contracts Regulations 1996, SI 1996/2911, regs 2(1) and 11.

Clarification of technical specifications

3.218 The rules under the public procurement regulations on technical specifications are intended to ensure that references are made to specific sets of recognised standards and instruments to ensure that they are not biased towards national providers or specific operators. Where possible reference is made to harmonised standards or technical instruments exist at the European or International level, and family those at the national level or their equivalent. The objective of these provisions is to ensure fair competition. However, in practice there are sometimes situations where the standards are treated as mandatory requirements which would restrict the choice only to products which comply with the standard to the detriment of other products of equal merit in terms of performance standards and which would meet the same needs[1]. It is proposed that a clarification be made to indicate that specifications can be defined according to the performance to be achieved to ensure that products for equivalent use are not discriminated against. Another proposed change relates to the reference in specifications to environmental standards.

1   Eg in September 1999, the Commission sent a reasoned opinion to the UK government concerning a framework arrangement for a public safety communications project for the police and rescue services launched by the UK Home Office. The contract concerned the provision of telecommunication services and the supply of necessary equipment and made reference to the TETRA European technical standard for mobile radio services. A complaint had been made by the supplier of telecommunication systems which were equivalent for these purposes but were not manufactured according to the TETRA standard. The Commission gave its opinion that reference to European standards should:
'simply offer a common yardstick against which the solutions proposed by suppliers can be measured. If contracting authorities refuse to examine whether or not the products or services offered are genuinely equivalent to products or services manufactured in accordance with the European standards, this constitutes a violation of the public procurement Directives and of EC Treaty on the free movement of goods' (IP/49/664).

Clarification of selection and award criteria

3.219 A variety of problems were identified with respect to the current provisions relating to 'selection criteria' (ie the criteria used to check the suitability of candidates) and 'award criteria' (criteria used when awarding the contract) which the proposals are seeking to address. Clarifications are being considered in respect of both sets of criteria including those intended to reflect developments in recent case law¹. Another problem is the question of the weighting which the contracting authority will give to the different criteria it has identified in awarding a contract to the 'economically most advantageous tender.' There have been complaints that where the relative weighting given to the award criteria is not sufficiently transparent it can give rise to discrimination in awards. The Commission would like to see award criteria listed, not simply in descending order of importance but also given relative weighting. Changes are also proposed to recognise the reference to environmental management performance in selection criteria and the use of environment criteria in the award². A number of other changes are proposed.

1   Eg with reference to economic and financial standing, a clarification to reflect that an economic operator may rely on the capacity of other participants in the corporate group to which he belongs to indicate financial and economic capacity. This follows C-176/98 *Holst Italia SpA v Comune di Cagliari intervener: Ruhrwasser AG International Water Management* [1999] ECR I-8607.
2   Similar suggestions have been made in respect of social criteria but the treatment of these provisions are highly controversial at the time of writing.

Introduction of the mandatory common procurement vocabulary

3.220 A Recommendation was published in 1996¹ by the Commission about the use of the common procurement vocabulary (CPV) and this has now largely become standard practice. In August 2001 the Commission put forward a proposal for a regulation of the European Parliament and the Council which would establish the CPV as the only classification system used for public procurement in the EU (replacing all existing systems such as NACE, CPC and CPA). This regulation is expected to be adopted in autumn 2002 and come into force in autumn 2003. Use of the CPV is expected to become mandatory once the proposed amendments to the procurement Directives are adopted. The changeover to the CPV has the sole classification system is reflected in the draft revised public procurement Directive. All previous references to other codes have been replaced. In particular, the use of the detailed CPV codes for 'priority' and 'non-priority' public services should make distinguishing between the two categories of services considerably easier.

1   Commission Recommendation (EC) 527/96 on the use of the Common Procurement Vocabulary (CPV) for describing the subject matter of public contracts (OJL222 3.9.1996).

CHAPTER 4

Procurement methodologies

Helen Randall

THE EGAN REPORT AND PARTNERING

Context

4.01   The Egan Report *Rethinking Construction* was published in July 1998 by the Construction Task Force to Deputy Prime Minister, John Prescott, on the scope for improving the quality and efficiency of UK construction.

4.02   Sir John Egan (the Chief Executive of BAA plc) chaired the Task Force which consisted of Mike Reycraft (Property Services Director, Tesco Stores Ltd), Ian Gibson (Managing Director, Lithan Ltd), Sir Brian Moffatt (Chief Executive, British Steel plc), Alan Parker (Managing Director, Whitbread Hotels), Anthony Mayer (Chief Executive, Housing Corporation), Sir Nigel Mobbs (Chairman, Slough Estates and Chief Executive, Bovis Homes), Professor Daniel Jones (Director of the Lean Enterprise Centre, Cardiff Business School), David Gye (Director, Morgan Stanley & Co Ltd) and David Warburton (GMB Union).

4.03   The Construction Task Force was set up by John Prescott against a background of deep concern in the construction industry and amongst its clients that the construction industry was under-achieving, both in terms of meeting its own needs and those of its clients.

4.04   The terms of reference of the Construction Task Force were to advise, from the clients' perspective, on the opportunities to improve the efficiency and quality of delivery of UK construction, to reinforce the impetus for change and to make the industry more responsive to customer needs.

4.05   The Task Force's aims were to:
— qualify the scope for improving construction efficiency and derive relevant quality and efficiency targets and performance measures which might be adopted by UK construction;
— examine current practice and the scope for improving it by innovation in products and processes;
— identify specific actions and good practice which would help achieve more efficient construction in terms of quality and customer satisfaction, timeliness in delivery and value for money; and
— identify products to help demonstrate the improvements that could be achieved through the application of best practice.

4.06   The Task Force looked particularly at how to improve the quality and efficiency of house building. It believed that the main initial opportunities for improvement in house building performance existed in the social housing sector as most social housing is commissioned by a few major clients. The Task Force believed that housing associations and local authorities could work with the house building industry to improve processes and technologies and develop quality products. The Task Force also proposed that a forum be established for the improvement of performance in house building.

4.07   So far as procurement in local government is concerned, the main impact of the Egan Report has been to endorse the principles of partnering not only in construction projects but in other areas of local government procurement, in particular in the provision of professional services.

4.08   The Task Force recognised a number of weaknesses affecting the UK construction industry, namely:
—   the need to modernise;
—   growing client dissatisfaction;
—   fragmentation inhibiting performance improvement.

In this respect Egan developed the issues which had initially been explored by Sir Michael Latham in the Latham Report published in 1984.

1   Sir Michael Latham (HMSO, 1994) *Constructing the Team. Final Report of the Government Industry Review of Procurement and Contractual Arrangements in the UK Construction Industry.*

Key principles

4.09   The Egan Report established a number of key principles which are now being widely adopted across both the public and private sectors, in particular in local government in relation to contracts for works and services.

4.10   The Egan Task Force considered that there were a number of 'Drivers of Change' which could lead to achievement of performance improvement. Egan identified the key drivers of change as:
(i)   committed leadership;
(ii)   a focus on the customer;
(iii)   integration of the process and the team around the product;
(iv)   a quality driven agenda; and
(v)   commitment to people.

4.11   Integration of the project process focuses on continuously developing the product and the supply chain. The Egan Report considered that the supply chain was critical to driving innovation and to sustaining performance improvement.

4.12   From a local government point of view, where many contracts are required to be tendered under the EC procurement rules and/or a local authority's standing orders, one of the recommendations of the Egan Report is radical. Egan questioned the conventional wisdom that competitive tendering in itself produces quality. Egan considered that the repeated selection of new teams for construction projects inhibited learning, innovation and the development of skilled and experienced teams. Egan also considered that competitive tendering prevented the industry from developing products and a brand which could be understood by its clients.

4.13 Instead of competitive tendering, Egan recommended what is known as partnering the supply chain. This involved acquisition of new suppliers through value-based sourcing, organisation and management of the supply chain to maximise innovation, learning and efficiency, supply development and measurement of supplier's performance, managing work load to match capacity and to provide an incentive for suppliers to improve performance, and capturing suppliers' innovation in components and systems.

4.14 Partnering is perceived as more demanding than the traditional competitive tendering process and it involves establishing long-term relationships. Instead of suppliers being selected on the basis of lowest price, they are selected on the basis of attitude to team-working, ability to innovate and to offer efficient solutions. Demonstration of value for money is achieved through benchmarking and rigorous performance management.

4.15 As stated above, since the publication of the Egan Report many local authorities have endeavoured to adopt partnering principles in their relationships with suppliers. The establishment of long-term relationships has been achieved through letting contracts with a duration of 10 or more years, rather than 3–5 years as under compulsory competitive tendering. However, given the existence of the EC procurement rules, these long-term relationships have been for the most part put out to competitive tender. It is certainly possible, with care, to structure a long-term contractual relationship between a local authority and a supplier which incorporates partnering principles which are in any event complementary to the principles of best value under the Local Government Act 1999. For example, a contract for works, services or even in some cases supplies can include obligations on both parties to improve the performance against a pre-agreed mutual objective, and non-adversarial dispute resolution procedure and provisions for the sharing of gains. Considerable care needs to be taken, however, in relation to incorporation of partnering objectives which could be regarded as unenforceable. It will be remembered, for example, that an obligation on parties 'to agree' is not legally enforceable, nor are some partnering objectives which are more philosophical or aspirational than legal in their intention.

4.16 One of the Egan Report's recommendations is that there should be an 'an end to reliance on contracts'. The Task Force considered that effective partnering did not rest on contracts and that contracts added significantly to the cost of a project and did not add value for the client. The Task Force went on to state that it considered that if a relationship between a supplier and an employer was soundly based, the parties would recognise their mutual interdependence and formal contract documents would gradually become obsolete.

4.17 Whilst it is true that parties who recognise their interdependence on each other generally have an incentive to resolve disputes in a non-adversarial manner without resorting to litigation, unfortunately there is no guarantee that future changes having an impact on the relationship might not lead one or both parties to alter their attitude to each other. This risk could be perceived as more acute in the context of a particularly complex or innovative project, or where a contractual relationship changes over time because the parties' representatives change.

4.18   Given that in any event most local authorities' standing orders prohibit the setting up of long-term relationships without written contracts, local authorities adopting Egan principles have incorporated these within written contracts. It should also be borne in mind that at present under English law a valid contract for works, supplies or services can exist even where it has not been written down. A contract will inevitably arise where a local authority procures works, services or goods from a supplier in return for payment.

4.19   To address the difficulties mentioned above with regard to the incorporation of possibly non-legally enforceable partnering objectives within a document, it is recommended by the authors that such objectives are contained within a document such as a 'partnering protocol' which is specifically stated to be non-legally binding. The accompanying contractual documentation supporting the main relationship can provide that it should be construed in the light of the partnering protocol. This is a route that has been adopted by a number of local authorities including the London Borough of Islington, Liverpool City Council and Hertfordshire County Council.

4.20   In drafting such documents the use of the term of 'partnering' rather than 'partnership' should be used, as the latter bears a specific, narrow legal meaning as set out in the Partnership Act 1890.

4.21   One overwhelming advantage of a partnering approach to procurement is that it should do away with the formerly adversarial stance of local government contracting with the private sector which was prevalent under compulsory competitive tendering and which has still not entirely disappeared.

4.22   Where an adversarial approach to contracting with the private sector prevailed in the past, a local authority wishing to embark on a successful partnering arrangement with the private sector will need to secure real commitment to cultural and operational change from members, officers and trade unions within its own organisation before the procurement is embarked upon. A partnering arrangement grafted on to a local authority which is fundamentally hostile to the private sector is unlikely to achieve the hoped-for improvements in performance.

THE BYATT REPORT

Context

4.23   In Summer 2000, Hilary Armstrong, the Local Government Minister, and Sir Jeremy Beecham, Chairman of the Local Government Association asked Sir Ian Byatt, formerly the Water Industry Regulator, to chair a Task Force to review the state of procurement skills and practice in local government in England.

4.24   The members of the Task Force were drawn from across the public and private sectors and were chosen for their personal skill and expertise. The Task Force members were Sarah Wood (Director of Finance and Performance Review, Birmingham City Council), Neil Argyle (Associate Director, NHS Purchasing and Supply Agency), Iain Beaton (former Assistant Chief Executive, St Helens Metropolitan Borough Council), Jo Blundell (Marketing Director, SERCO Government Services), Gareth Davies (Regional Director of District Audit, Audit

Commission), Ian Elliott (Director of Engineering, Severn Trent Water Ltd), Richard Footitt (Head of Local Government Competition Quality Division, DTLR), Mike Grealy (Deputy Director of Local Government Finance, Local Government Association), Tony Wiltshire (Head of Procurement, Leeds City Council) and Helen Randall (Partner, Nabarro Nathanson).

4.25 Traditionally, there was a perception that local government procurement was concentrated on the purchase of low value items such as furniture and stationery and there was a lack of procurement skills within local government to enable it to engage in strategic procurement. Furthermore, the government was concerned that there appeared to be wide variations between procurement practices from one local authority to the next and lack of incentives to improve performance in procurement. In addition, improvement in procurement was regarded as inextricably linked to successful implementation of the government's best value policy in local government.

4.26 The Byatt Task Force sat for just under a year and took evidence from 90 organisations including 35 local authorities. The Procurement Task Force published its report, 'the Byatt Report', in June 2001 'Delivering Better Services for Citizens— a Review of Local Government Procurement in England' which was sponsored by the then Department for Transport, Local Government and the Regions and the Local Government Association.

Key recommendations

4.27 The Byatt Report made 39 recommendations. The recommendations and the reasoning behind them are set out below.

1 **'Procurement expertise should be integrated into best value reviews and represented in every local authority on the body which oversees best value'** As mentioned above, procurement traditionally had a low profile within local government seen as a backwater concerned with placing orders for low value items, whereas the private sector regards strategic procurement as a key tool to deliver value. The Byatt Task Force considered that the importance of procurement should be acknowledged within local government both at member and senior officer level.

2 **'Best value reviews should incorporate a wide-ranging approach to a local authority's key strategic objectives and be aligned to outcomes rather than the existing patterns of service provision'** The Byatt Report cited the government's best value policy, which made it clear that local authorities should consider all types of service delivery options and should choose the best delivery option based on a robust and challenging process which would deliver more flexible and economic services to its citizens. This procurement practice is regarded as being at the heart of best value.

3 **'Local authorities should adopt policies which ensure the effective involvement of staff in service reviews and in the procurement process'** It was noted that not only was there a shortage of officers with procurement skills within local government, but also it was difficult for local authorities to retain those who did have procurement skills. Byatt recommended that a training programme and a proper career path for procurement officers together with recognition within local government of the importance of procurement would help address this issue.

4   **'Local authorities should set out their procurement strategy in a document which includes principles and information on current and planned activities. This should be regularly reviewed and updated'** Byatt suggested that the information in an authority's procurement strategy should include the authority's strategic aims, details of current contracts with their renewal date, the performance of key suppliers and other matters. Local authorities are in any event required to develop a procurement strategy under the statutory guidance on best value published in DETR Circular 10/99. It was felt that the publication of a detailed procurement strategy would enable the private sector to plan more effectively for large-scale local authority procurement and engage more proactively with local government.

5   **'Local authorities should develop a corporate procurement function to collect management information, oversee dissolved buying, co-ordinate training and act as an internal source of expertise'** The background to this recommendation came from evidence which indicated that many local authorities engage with a proliferation of suppliers particularly for small value procurement, thus not taking advantage of economies of scale and savings in financial management and monitoring costs.

6   **'Smaller local authorities without resources to set up a corporate procurement function should work with others to share resources. The LGA should work with the private sector to build up centres of excellence available to such authorities'** This was suggested to encourage smaller local authorities to join together to share resources or obtain support from other larger organisations to enable sharing of knowledge and best practice.

7   **'Local authorities should review their procurement structures and processes as part of the best value review programme'** Procurement is a corporate function of a local authority and hence should be subject to the rigours of the best value process.

8   **'Local authorities should, at an early stage, map their procurement activities using techniques such as a low/high risk and low/high value matrices. They should identify the areas where procurement resources can have most impact and the appropriate skills and techniques for each type of procurement'** It was suggested that the procurement of low risk/low cost items could be carried out more efficiently by aggregation or buying through central contracts, consortia or framework arrangements to increase leverage through bulk buying to get better prices and reduce time. Instead procurement experts should focus their energies on high risk or complex procurements where their project management and other skills could be applied with more effect.

9   **'Local authorities should seek to aggregate demand and reduce costs by setting up central contract for commonly-used items and by requiring consolidated invoices'** This refers to the evidence mentioned above relating to proliferation of suppliers.

10 **'Elected members should take a strategic role in securing quality outcomes. This should include scrutinising the procurement processes and monitoring the outcome of procurement. There should be clear political responsibility for procurement with appropriate training'** Evidence presented to the Task Force indicated that elected members at some authorities tended to underestimate the importance of procurement or failed to understand the impact that procurement could have on the success or otherwise of a scheme.

11 **'Local authorities should review their standing orders to ensure they promote efficient and effective procurement whilst maintaining safeguards of probity and good governance. Standing orders should be used positively**

to encourage good practice. **Changes to standing orders should be accompanied by an effective education programme'** A number of local authorities had presented evidence that indicated that their standing orders inhibited modern methods of procurement including the use of partnering and negotiation with suppliers.

12 **'The Audit Commission should guide and train auditors and inspectors to support a strategic approach to procurement. This should emphasise a risk-based approach and aim to equip auditors and inspectors to deliver effective scrutiny in a mixed economy of service provision. The Audit Commission should continue to review its experiences of significant and large procurement exercises and disseminate the lessons learnt from the them'** Some local authorities have complained that they had had experiences of best value inspectors adopting an old fashioned and unimaginative approach to risk transfer with a tendency to discourage modern procurement methods. The Audit Commission has since implemented a training programme for its best value inspectors to address this perception.

13 **'To help local authorities, the Audit Commission should clarify the roles of inspectors and auditors in relation to procurement and seek to co-ordinate their activities locally'** Refer to comments in recommendation 12 above.

14 **'Each local authority should identify all those engaged in procurement within the organisation and identify the skills needed in each post across the authority. It should set out a strategy to meet these needs, including recruitment of suitable staff, training and ways of retaining trained staff'**

15 **'The Improvement and Development Agency (IDeA) and the Local Government Employers Organisation (EO) should lead on developing a suite of training programmes. This should particularly be developed in partnership with the Chartered Institute of Purchasing and Supply (CIPS) and the Society of Purchasing Officers in Local Government (SOPO). This should build on the work done by the Office of Government Commerce (OGC)'**

16 **'Pump-priming funding should be provided to support the development of training programmes and to subsidise cost of local government staff who use the courses. This could be provided through the IDeA or EO as part of the annual settlement or through government funding'** It was perceived that only a co-ordinated and comprehensive training programme would help to address the concerns identified with regard to lack of procurement skills within local government.

17 **'Local authorities should increase their use of simple forms of e-procurement such as purchasing cards and BACS payments. They should adopt a modular approach to the implementation of e-procurement solutions'** It was recognised that in local government there were two strands of e-procurement. The first consists of relatively commonly-used items such as BACS and electronic catalogues such as G-Cat and S-Cat. The second are more sophisticated solutions such as purchasing cards, electronic shopping malls and methods of electronic tendering, online contract management and electronic systems for gathering service users' feedback on contractor performance. At the time evidence was submitted to the Byatt Task Force, local authorities appeared to be nervous about engaging with the more sophisticated forms of electronic procurement. Since then, this reluctance has been partly addressed by the imposition of Best Value Performance Indicator 157 which requires local authorities to achieve 100 per cent of interacting between the public and the local

authority enabled for electronic delivery by 2005. For further discussion of this point please refer to para **4.29**ff on e-procurement.

18 **'The government should consolidate its funding for improvement in local government's capacity into single fund, designed to provide both revenue and capital support on a pump-priming basis for key priorities. Such a fund could usefully absorb the resources currently made available in support of PFI projects so as to allow a wider range of partnership options related to outcomes to be pursued'** In tandem with the government's proposed reforms to the local government finance system, it was considered that other innovative forms of contracting by local government, for example entering into strategic partnerships for the provision of back office services by the private sector, should be given an incentive by the provision of funding in the same way that private finance initiative projects attract subsidy in the form of PFI credit. The Task Force considered that specific financial incentives had the potential to distort the market and should be used with caution. For example, could it be said that some local authorities' choice of PFI to procure a project was motivated wholly or partly by the provision of PFI credit rather than by a decision that PFI was necessarily the best procurement route for that project.

19 **'Government funding for e-solutions (such as Local Government Online) should be used to support the development in a variety of different e-procurement models in local government. Projects should be designed to encourage joint working between local authorities'** This was inspired by evidence that many local authorities appeared reluctant to procure jointly with their neighbouring or higher tier authorities because of a history of distrust, lack of confidence or other differences. It was considered that although e-procurement should not be regarded as a panacea to problems in local government, e-procurement was particularly suited to controlling spending on low value and routine commodities and to reduce transactions costs.

20 **'Local authorities should identify the information they need about the markets for local authority goods, works and services. The LGA, together with the IDeA and the 4Ps, should lead in devising better systems of information exchanged on these markets, in consultation with the private sector'**

21 **'Each local authority should produce a prospectus for suppliers. This could usefully be adapted from its procurement strategy. It should include the significant items which a council expects to buy in the future, with an indication as to how and when it will procure them'** It was considered that a local authority could not carry out effective best value reviews or make good buying decisions without relevant, accessible and timely information about the range of suppliers and their markets. Conversely, it was also important that suppliers should understand the local government market better. Improvement on both sides would help develop a mixed economy of supplies to local government.

22 **'A joint national forum, convened by DTLR, the LGA and the CBI, should broker a dialogue between local authorities and suppliers. Matters affecting the wider local authority market should be raised and resolved in this forum. This should be underpinned by an open dialogue, conducted through a variety of media such as workshops, web-enabled discussed groups, training and development opportunities and case studies'** One example of an issue affecting the wider local authority market was the potential costs on a private sector supplier involved in obtaining admitted body status to the local government pension scheme.

23 **'Buying consortia should publish annual accounts and performance information which is sufficient to allow local authorities to make informed decisions'**

24 **'Buying consortia should review their services and their structures in the light of the need to retain and win new business in a competitive environment. They should pay particular attention to meeting the needs of smaller councils'** The Task Force had commissioned specific research on the operation and practices of local authority buying consortia. In general, this appeared to indicate that some local authority purchasing consortia were not operated transparently. Purchasing consortia tended to be used within local government for the procurement of large volume, low value commodities, and as such the Byatt Task Force considered there was considerable scope for consortia to obtain better value on behalf of their local authority client.

25 **'A project plan should be drawn up at the beginning of each procurement exercise, setting out all the strands of work, how they will be undertaken and the times for their completion'**

26 **'The LGA and DTLR should explore how a Gateway project review process can be developed to support local authorities who are involved in major, complex or high risk projects. It should include a strategy for providing high quality project review teams with an understanding and experience of commercial sector. It should take advantage of the work done by OGC'** Where a local authority is undertaking a complex major procurement there is evidence to show that in many cases the procurement could have been carried out more efficiently and effectively. The Office of Government Commerce, in particular Philip Gersham, has in the context of central government recommended the use of the Gateway process. This involved independent scrutiny of major procurement at five key stages to ensure that procurement is 'on track' and being carried out effectively to ensure the maximum chance of success. To be implemented within local government, the OGC Gateway process would need some adaptation but if adopted would tend to encourage better procurement practice, with the consequent knock-on advantage of enhanced market confidence.

27 **'Local authorities should, in conjunction with suppliers, rationalise their procurement processes, eg by using common documents and pre-qualification processes or by using websites to exchange information'** There has, even during the era of compulsory competitive tendering, been a proliferation of standard form contractual documentation used for local government contractors. For example, the Association of Metropolitan Authorities forms of contract, contracts used by the various professional procurement organisations, the Treasury Task Force and Office of Government Commerce's standard terms, for PFI projects as well the standard forms put out by the various professional organisations associated with the construction industry such as the Joint Contracts Tribunal, the Royal Institute of British Architects, the Institute of Civil Engineers. As with any model contract documentation, however, adaptations may be needed to suit the particular authority's specific circumstances. Although some standardisation of procurement documentation, such as pre-qualification questionnaires and basic tender documents, may be helpful to private sector suppliers, it was felt that universal standardisation of documentation would not necessarily be helpful.

28 **'Each local authority should develop a corporate strategy for managing risk which recognises the trade-offs between risk and reward. That strategy should be applied to individual procurement decisions'** Local authorities

needed to develop tools to identify and quantify risks correctly and to decide who should carry them. There generally appeared to be a reluctance amongst local authorities to recognise that risks passed on to contractors tended to carry a price and in some cases risks can be disproportionately expensive to pass on to a private sector contractor.

29   **'The Audit Commission should continue to develop good practice on risk management for auditors and inspectors which supports a balanced view of the risks and benefits of various procurement techniques'** See the comments under recommendations 11 to 13 above.

30   **'Local authorities, with the support of IDeA and other organisations, should develop evaluation criteria which incorporate quality and whole-life costs. The criteria chosen should not detract from the need for clear and prioritised objectives. They should be agreed in advance and should be published, transparent and auditable'** Several authorities gave evidence that even in procurements under best value, they had ended up taking into account price as the key factor in deciding whether to award a contract to a particular tenderer, despite intentions earlier in the procurement process to award on the basis of lifetime costs and quality. In other cases, local authorities had standing orders which prohibited award of contracts on anything other than the lowest cost, and in many authorities skill in assessing lifetime costs rather than short-term savings were either lacking or insufficiently developed.

31   **'The project plan for all major procurements should include a requirement for client managers to be recruited or receive training and development prior to contract awards. It should specify the skills needed by the client managers. Wherever possible, client managers should be party to the negotiation of a contract. The skills needed by managers should be discussed with potential service providers'** Most authorities giving evidence to the Task Force identified a lack of suitably experienced project managers within local government. Private sector organisations giving evidence also expressed frustration at dealing with local authority contract managers who lacked sufficient understanding as to the commercial operation of a contract.

32   **'Suppliers should provide managers who are experienced or trained to understand the local authority environment'**

33   **'Suppliers should be prepared to adopt an open-book approach to the contract in complex contracting environments where change is likely'**

34   **'Suppliers should help local authorities by publishing data to support performance measurements (though where they have legitimate commercial concerns about confidentiality, these should be respected and assured)'** The Byatt Task Force considered that the private sector should in some instances change to ensure improvement in local government procurement practice, particularly where a private sector organisation's business was focused on supplying local government.

35   **'Government should give a clear lead on how intelligent procurement might be achieved within the European public procurement rules'**

36   **'Changes are required to the European public procurement rules to simplify them and make them more flexible. Changes should support the setting up of framework arrangements and greater use of discussion negotiations'** However reluctantly, the Task Force had to recognise that in some cases the European procurement rules tended to hamper innovative forms of procurement and the establishment of long-term partnering arrangements without competitive tendering. However, at the time of writing its report, the Task Force was aware

of the forthcoming reforms to the European public procurement Directives. For more detail on this see paras **3.213–3.220.**

37 **'Central government should use the opportunity presented by the recent review of legislation on partnership working to relax restrictions which prevent effective joint delivery of goods, works and services'** The Task Force received relatively few examples of local authorities procuring jointly with each other, or local authority consortia taking the lead in bringing local authorities together to commission significant service contracts jointly.

38 **'Local authorities and contractors should understand and make best use of statutory and non-statutory arrangements to protect the legitimate interests of staff during transfers including TUPE Regulations, Cabinet Office statement of practice on staff transfers in the public sector and the provisions to allow admission to the local government pension schemes'**

39 **'Central government and the LGA should set up arrangements to monitor the effects of TUPE and Local Government Pension Scheme Regulations which particularly look at what happens on subsequent re-tender of contracts'** The Task Force recognised that a motivated and skilled workforce is crucial to the delivery of high quality services. The approach adopted in the public sector to TUPE had reduced concerns for staff transferring out and into the private sector, ie there is a presumption that TUPE will apply. Similarly, the ability for private contractors to seek admitted body status to the local government pension scheme had allayed other fears. However, there was evidence that some local authorities appeared less concerned with staff transfers on second generation of contract from one private sector contractor to its successor contractor than with initial transfers out. It was suggested that this discrepancy should be addressed at a national level.

4.28 In summary, the Byatt Report was intended to be practical and to build on previous reports and guidance issued in relation to procurement. If universally adopted, its recommendations would undoubtedly significantly improve the practice of procurement within local government. Without sufficient government funding or commitment and resources within local government, however, it may prove impossible to implement Byatt's recommendations fully.

ELECTRONIC PUBLIC PROCUREMENT

4.29 This section on electronic public procurement (e-procurement) looks at the forms of e-procurement currently used within local government and which may be used in the near future. It also examines the policy context to e-procurement, the use of electronic signatures, how e-procurement sits within the European rules relating to procurement and competition, and some of the commercial issues associated with e-procurement.

Introduction

4.30 One of the developments arising from the growth of the Internet and Internet-related business has been the increased focus upon the procurement activities of public bodies, with technological advances opening up a range of possibilities for the conduct of procurement transactions by electronic means. For some years now, the Internet has been used by local authorities primarily to exchange information. However, with the current focus on modernising government through use of technology, there is a shift from just simple use of the Internet and technology to more sophisticated approaches which could have far-reaching repercussions for the ways in which local authorities procure goods and services. This shift mirrors the growth in the private sector of business to business electronic commerce together with the ability for most citizens with access to the Internet to conduct a wide range of transactions, such as banking, booking holidays or bidding for particular goods, online. The technology currently exists to enable the entire procurement process—from product search, tendering, negotiation, ordering receipting and invoicing—to be conducted through electronic means. However, the extent and speed with which local authorities embrace a fully electronic procurement process must be viewed against a legal, policy and regulatory framework, which governs the way local authorities procure.

Drivers of electronic procurement—European and domestic dimensions

4.31   Since the mid-1990s, the European Commission has promoted the 'SIMAP' (Systeme d'Information pour les Marches Publics) project[1] with the objective of developing information systems infrastructure to support the delivery of an effective electronic public procurement policy in Europe. The project was originally focused upon the improvement of the quality and dissemination of information from contracting authorities to suppliers about EU procurement opportunities. Since then, however, the focus has broadened to address the use of ICT to make the entire procurement process more efficient.

1   See the SIMAP website at www.simap.eu.int.

4.32   Two important papers published by the European Commission set the stage for an understanding of the EC's approach towards electronic public procurement. The first of these was the Green Paper on Public Procurement[1] published on 27 November 1996, which focused on creating a statutory framework for electronic procurement which would contribute towards the broader objectives of the internal market in procurement, including widening the choice of value for money supplies for procuring entities, increasing the competitiveness of EU industry and increasing the accessibility and quality of information relating to current procurement opportunities. The Commission also expressed the view that electronic procurement would assist procuring authorities to describe their requirements more clearly and comprehensively (especially by using the common procurement vocabulary 'CPV' instead of central product classification codes 'CPC') and would also enable all suppliers (including small and medium sized enterprises) to identify and monitor procurement opportunities of interest to them.

1   See the SIMAP website at www.simap.eu.int.

4.33   The second of these papers was the European Commission's Communication of 11 March 1998[1] which, among other matters, stated a target of 25 per cent of all public procurement transactions in the EU to be handled electronically by 2003.

1   Public Procurement in the European Union COM(98)143.

4.34 The Commission has since identified three phases for the implementation of e-procurement. The first phase consists of processes for information transmission from contracting authorities to suppliers. Processes in this phase are of the lowest complexity and require the lowest degree of integration with back-end administrative systems and tend to consist of one way information database systems. The Green Paper mentioned above, and the subsequent report 'Technical Assistance for Electronic Tendering Development'[1] were concerned primarily with this first phase, and the OGC pilot project for the Government Supplier Information Database (GSID) was an example of such a database, accessible through a website which contains basic supplier information. The second phase consists of processes for the communication between contracting authorities and suppliers such as expressions of interest, tender submission, and clarification of technical specifications. The third phase consists of processes for the communication between contracting authorities and awarded suppliers such as debriefing of suppliers, closing of contract, invoicing and payment.

1   *Final Report: Technical Assistance in Electronic Procurement to EDI-EEG 12 Sub Group 1* (prepared by Peder Blomberg and Soren Lennartsson).

4.35 A recent study[1] published by the Commission found that very few pilot electronic procurement systems in Europe are fully established with respect to phases two and three, and concluded that the future focus of electronic procurement should be directed towards developing and implementing phase two and three solutions. This study looked at 39 pilot e-procurement projects throughout Europe, and the UK was involved in a more detailed interview round with respect to five of these pilot projects, several co-ordinated through the Office of Government Commerce[2]. These e-procurement projects related to the procurement of goods, works and services. The types of models studied included:

— infomediaries—third party organisations acting as intermediary between contracting authority and supplier;
— electronic notification systems—where suppliers are notified electronically of tenders;
— virtual procurer networks—where one contracting authority is linked to several suppliers;
— online auctions;
— EDI (Electronic Data Interchange) connected closed communities;
— procurer clubs, consisting of several cross-organisational linked purchasers.

1   *Analysis of Electronic Procurement Pilot Projects in the European Union: Report* (November 2000) carried out for the European Commission Internal Market DG (prepared by PLS Ramboll).
2   These five projects were: ELPRO, Government Supplier Information Database, Tender Trust, Local Lease and Delta Suite.

4.36 It was observed that establishing e-procurement systems which dealt with phase three processes was a technically complex task, involving the creation of two-way communication systems between contracting authorities and suppliers which shared common standards and which are compatible and capable of integration with systems already in use in both the public and private sectors. Nonetheless the report reaffirmed the EC's commitment to achieving its stated 2003 target by recommending:

— the yearly monitoring of the progress of e-procurement transactions at EU level;
— monitoring of the implementation in member states of the E-commerce and Electronic Signatures Directives as well as the proposed draft Consolidated Directive;
— the introduction of economic incentives for the use of e-procurement including making electronic submission of tenders a legitimate evaluation criterion;

— the development of best practice guidelines for communication standards including the development of XML standards defining content in communication and on the selection of general data formats; and

— monitoring the extent to which lack of common European standards poses a barrier to the development of e-procurement.

The domestic policy context

4.37 The White Paper on Modernising Government, published in March 1999, set out a programme to modernise the way government conducts its transactions with citizens and businesses, with a view to improving the efficiency, cost and effectiveness of government procurement. In the domestic context central government, led by the Office of Government Commerce, is strongly encouraging local authorities to embrace e-government (of which e-procurement is just a part) which it considers will make local services more accessible, more convenient, more responsive and more cost-effective and which it believes will make local government more open, accountable and inclusive and better able to lead its communities. Like the European Commission, the UK government has also set electronic government targets including 90 per cent of low value government procurement to be conducted electronically by April 2001 and 100 per cent of government services to be electronically available to citizens and businesses by 2005. A Best Value Performance Indicator (BVPI) 157 has also been introduced by the Audit Commission to measure the:

'... percentage of interactions with the public, by type, which are capable of electronic service delivery and which are being delivered using Internet protocols or other paperless methods.'

4.38 At the time of writing, the government's draft national strategy for implementing local e-government was set out in 'e-gov@local: Towards the National Strategy for Local e-government, a Consultation Paper' published by the former Department for Transport, Local Government and the Regions (now the Office of the Deputy Prime Minister) in conjunction with the Local Government Association. The objectives of this draft strategy are to provide a 'central-local vision of local e-government and a clear route map to promote its delivery' as well as setting out strategies for the use of funding earmarked for e-government initiatives (Government Online funding).

4.39 E-government is an area which will have a dramatic impact on the delivery of local services, which cannot be given full justice within this book. All local authorities have published IEG (Implementing Electronic Government) statements, many of which have addressed e-procurement. At the time of writing, Huntingdon, Leeds and Newham councils had been identified as implementing national Pathfinder projects for e-procurement.

Forms of e-procurement used by local authorities

Electronic payment systems

4.40 Electronic payments are often cited as an easy way for authorities to streamline and improve the efficiency of their procurement processes. For suppliers, electronic payment systems also promise faster completion of transactions and reduced costs associated with issuing manual invoices and follow-up procedures to obtain payment from the contracting authority. Most local authorities have been using Bank Automated Clearing Systems ('BACS') for several years now. BACS software systems allow local authorities to transfer sums electronically in payment for goods, works or services provided by suppliers. Its advantages are the increased security and speed with which funds can be transferred and, as far as local authorities are concerned, the fact that the transfer of funds can be easily tracked helps create a clear audit trail.

4.41 Some local authorities are also beginning to make use of purchasing cards, which act as a type of corporate credit card, to permit authorised users within the authority to make certain permitted purchases. Designated staff within the authority are given a card, which they can then use to order goods and services by telephone, fax, written order, or in person. There are usually restrictions attached to the cards limiting the types of goods they can purchase and the monetary value of such goods. The price of each item will then be charged to the card and at the end of an agreed period, the authority will receive a statement listing the products which have been purchased with the card. An invoice will then be sent to the authority for payment. In a research report carried out under the aegis of the Byatt Task Force, 13 per cent of local authorities said that they used procurement/purchasing cards.

4.42 The use of purchasing cards within an authority will also usually be governed by internal best practice guidance, which may sit within the authority's contract and financial standing orders. Such guidance would address matters such as purchasing procedures, security procedures, financial protocols and details of cardholders' personal responsibilities in the use of these cards. In addition there would be a need for the authority to formalise accounting procedures and audit trail protocols. Authorities need to be careful that purchases using purchasing cards do not in aggregate exceed the thresholds for application of the EC procurement regulations, if they are for a common purpose.

4.43 The government procurement card scheme was launched in October 1997 to allow central government to purchase low value items such as books, periodicals, small items of equipment and cleaning materials electronically. Currently, for example, the NHS Purchasing and Supply Agency makes use of purchasing cards for ward sisters and nurses to purchase low value items required for the efficient running of hospital wards. The advantages cited by the Office of Government Commerce in relation to the government procurement card include:

— reduced purchasing costs—staff go direct to suppliers and do not need to complete purchase request forms which then need to be checked and processed by procurement staff;
— speedier delivery of goods and services;
— ability to order goods and services when needed;
— suppliers receiving payment earlier (in 2–4 days);
— staff being in control of low-value purchasing;
— improved efficiency—less time is spent checking and authorising purchases and procurement staff are freed up to concentrate on strategic, higher value procurement.

Online catalogues

4.44   Local authorities have for many years been making use of the electronic G-Cat and S-Cat catalogues for the purchase of computer equipment and software. However, online or electronic catalogues are also being increasingly employed for a wider variety of purchases and have led to the development of electronic 'shopping malls' or 'e-market places'.

4.45   Electronic catalogues are simply electronic versions of traditional paper-based catalogues which local authorities can view over the Internet to see details of products or services offered by a particular firm. Some electronic catalogues may also involve a facility to order products or services through electronic means (see para **4.48** on electronic shopping malls below). The benefits of local authorities purchasing through electronic catalogues are basically the same as stated for the use of purchasing cards above, namely reduced purchasing costs, speedier delivery and improved efficiency of the procurement process, and greater individual staff control over low value purchases. The ability to exploit competition to exert downward pressure on prices is also enhanced in a highly visible way, with other suppliers being aware of the range of other services and products being offered by their competitors to local authorities. For suppliers, the benefits of electronic catalogues are the ability to provide information on products and services cost effectively and to be able to market their products to a wider range of potential purchasers.

4.46   Both G-Cat and S-Cat are set up as framework arrangements which local authorities can use to call off computer supplies and services as and when they are required. They are advertised to local authorities as being 'EC-compliant' because they have already been advertised in the OJEC and suppliers are appointed to the framework under a competitive tendering procedure. This is widely perceived by local authorities as an advantage because it saves the time and cost associated with a local authority advertising and tendering procurement itself (see also chapter 3 on framework arrangements and para **4.48** below).

4.47   The local authority wishing to use an electronic catalogue should, however, bear in mind that the fundamental terms of the contracts with suppliers will already have been set and subsequent negotiation to amend the standard terms of the frameworks arrangement will be regarded as a breach of the EC procurement rules according to the principles set out in the *Greek Bandages* case[1] and guidance from the Office of Government Commerce and the former DTLR (now Office of the Deputy Prime Minister). On the other hand, catalogue facilities for monitoring use and collecting order information can also assist the local authority to comply with the EC procurement rules. For example, the electronic catalogue may be able to provide information to determine whether, having aggregated the value of a local authority's procurement need for a particular supply, this value has reached the relevant threshold. The catalogue may also provide accurate information for the purposes of the statistical reporting requirements to HM Treasury.

1   C-79/94 *EC Commission v Greece* [1995] ECR I-1071, ECJ.

4.48   Local authorities may enter into catalogue arrangements with a single main contractor. It is more common, however, for authorities to use catalogue arrangements with more than one provider covering the same products or services as in G-Cat and S-Cat. Electronic shopping malls (also known as 'procurement hubs' or 'e-market places'), on the other hand, are websites which host a range of catalogues from which purchasers can actually order goods online. They tend to be suitable for large volume, low value and non-strategic purchasing. Shopping malls may be organised by either purchasers or suppliers and are enabled by software systems which use the Internet to conduct transactions. They take the traditional stages of the procurement process (product search and identification, tendering, negotiation, ordering, receipt, invoicing etc) and put that process online. At the time of writing, local authorities use electronic shopping malls less frequently. 'Fe-Online' is an example of a procurement hub set up by EDS with the Association of Colleges, which enables Further Education colleges to procure supplies online from a variety of different suppliers. 'Marketplace' is another example of a national procurement system for local government, which was launched by IDEA on 9 May 2002.

4.49 Despite the apparent ease of using purchasing cards and electronic catalogues, local authorities need to ensure both compliance with legal and regulatory requirements (such as EC procurement rules and internal standing orders) and that value for money is obtained. For example, negotiation of large value bulk purchase contracts to obtain price discounts may offer better value for money than the repetitive use of purchasing cards and electronic catalogues.

Online auctions

4.50 Online auctions can take a number of different forms. One form might be the notification of a purchasing requirement by a local authority on a website inviting supplier companies to submit an electronic quotation to meet that requirement, detailing the supplier's price and proposed range of goods. The local authority would then, depending on the prices offered, strike a deal with the supplier offering the best price. This type of auction is generally suitable where the authority wishes to purchase goods which do not require a detailed specification of requirements. For goods which exceed the relevant EC thresholds, the online auction would need to comply with the open or restrictive tendering procedures under the EC procurement rules.

4.51 Another alternative is the use of the 'reverse auction' whereby tenderers can electronically view the progress of the auction (including prices submitted by other tenderers) and are permitted to amend their own tenders on an ongoing basis in order to beat those other tenders. This type of purchasing also allows local authorities to exploit competitive market conditions by using the auction and bid model to exert downward pressure on prices. As with most procurement, suppliers will have been subject to a pre-qualification procedure to ensure that they are of sufficient financial, economic and technical standing to be able to fulfil the contract. Generally, the auction will be time-limited, with the authority keen to maximise competitive pressure in as short a period as possible.

4.52 Although at first sight it appears that reverse auctions only permit an authority to evaluate price (and thus not give it scope to evaluate for a 'most economically advantageous' bid which includes price and quality factors), the auction can be structured so that quality and price criteria are measured at different stages. At the first stage, the authority can ask bidders to submit information designed to measure pre-determined quality criteria and allocate a score. Thereafter, bidders can be asked to submit their prices and will be given an overall scoring which measures both price and quality. Tenderers will then be given information on how much their price bid needs to be reduced in order to improve the scored ranking of their bid. This scoring system can be done manually or by a software programme.

Electronic tendering

4.53   At the time of writing, dedicated websites for the conduct of public authority electronic tendering are in their infancy. The OGC 'TenderTrust' pilot project for electronic tendering is one such website offering a smartcard, Internet-based, electronic tendering system which is reliant on Public Key Infrastructure (for more details see para **4.78** below). To date, many of the advances in electronic tendering have focused on the improvement of communication exchange between the contracting authority and suppliers, from the point of issue of the invitation to tender to the point of notification of award of contract. Many local authorities continue to receive tenders in hard copy format pending the implementation of secure and reliable tender receipt systems. In many cases the contract standing orders of authorities also require amendment to permit the receipt of tenders in electronic form.

4.54   Electronic submission of contract notices to the Official Journal of the European Communities is now well established as the publication of OJEC notices in hard copy format ceased in 1996. Since 1 July 1998, published notices have only been available on CD-ROM and on Tenders Electronic Daily ('TED'). The current form of public procurement Directives requires contracting authorities to send their OJEC notices to the Office of Official Publications in Luxembourg as rapidly as possible, and new model term notices recently placed on the SIMAP website permit local authorities to email OJEC notices to the email address set out at the top of the model contract notices. These notices are then sent to the Office for Official Publications for publication in a CD-ROM version of the Official Journal and normally also in the TED database. In addition, some commercial suppliers offer software designed to assist local authorities in the automatic completion of OJEC notices, including generating the relevant CPC and CPV codes.

4.55   Many local authorities offer electronic versions of their procurement documents including pre-qualification questionnaires, invitations to tender, conditions of contract and specifications at dedicated web pages, providing further information for prospective tenderers as well as facilities for the acceptance of tenders submitted electronically.

4.56   The benefits of electronic tendering are perceived as including:
—   increased efficiency and effectiveness of local authorities in conducting procurement in terms of cost, quality, performance and time;
—   for the business sector, suppliers will experience reduced manpower costs, reduced administrative and transaction costs, improvements in tender quality and simplified public market access ; and
—   the provision of a clear indisputable audit trail.

4.57   At the European policy level, the benefits of electronic tendering are perceived as including:
—   the stimulation of increased European and global competition with the rise of new and more efficient market behaviours and structures adapted to the electronic way of conducting public business;

— a change in the techniques for supervision and review of national procurement operations enabling a quicker approach by supervisory bodies;
— the provision of procurement 'Services Centres' which make use of established databases and the Internet to provide information for the benefit of contracting authorities

4.58 Furthermore, it is argued that access to standardised electronic tendering documentation such as tender return and qualification documents for instance, would improve, speed up and facilitate the process for preparation and provision of tender documents, the process for preparation and submission of tenders and the process for the examination, evaluation of tenders and final award of contracts.

EC compliance

4.59 The issues relating to compliance with EC law in relation to electronic procurement can be broadly identified as including the following: the extent to which electronic communications are permitted under the existing EC Procurement Directives; framework arrangements and the extent to which post-tender negotiation is/is not permitted; the extent to which charging is permissible; competition law, in particular art 81(1) of the EC Treaty and the prevention, restriction or distortion of competition and art 82, abuse of dominant market position; and forthcoming proposals to amend the EC Procurement Directives.

Extent to which EC procurement Directives permit electronic tendering

OJEC advertisement

4.60 A local authority can draw up an advertisement for a procurement to be published in the Official Journal provided it is in the format required by the regulations (see para **3.126**) and complies with the requirements applicable to the relevant contract award procedure used as set out in the Services Regulations, Sch 2 or the Supply Regulations, Sch 3, respectively. The local authority may wish to include in the advertisement a reference to a website at which further information could be obtained. At present, the regulations do not allow contract documentation such as specifications to be made available exclusively by referencing a website. To comply with the current regulations, therefore, the local authority needs to make facilities available for prospective tenderers to be supplied with documentation in hard copy format, being careful to ensure that the information available on the website and in hard copy do not differ from each other in order to avoid breaching the equality of treatment principle.

Electronic submission of tenders

4.61 The Regulations have been amended to allow electronic submission of tenders to an authority provided:
— the local authority makes arrangements to ensure the confidentiality of tenders pending their evaluation; and
— the local authority makes arrangements for the tenders to be 'opened' only after the time limits for their submission has expired; and
— each tender contains all the information necessary for its evaluation.

4.62   The Regulations also allow contracting authorities to require tenders submitted electronically to be subsequently confirmed in writing, although, in the author's view, this would seem rather to defeat the point of carrying out an electronic tendering exercise in the first place.

Subscription and levying of charges

4.63   A local authority may be seeking to encourage as wide access as possible to its procurement, so it would be reasonable to expect that candidates should have direct free access to information which will enable the candidate to decide whether to express an interest in the procurement or not.

4.64   Similarly, it would appear reasonable that the contract documents at the pre-tender stage are directly accessible at nil cost to candidates. It is arguable, however, that as with paper tenders, if candidates request additional hard copies the authority could legitimately request a reasonable fee which reasonably covers its administration charges. Online competition following the invitation to tender stage, particularly in the case of a negotiated tendering procedure, would involve considerable security and data protection issues at a cost. It is a usual requirement of local authority procurement that candidates meet their own costs of tendering.

4.65   A question may arise as to whether it would be reasonable for candidates to be required to subscribe to a website operated by a third party agent for participation in the tender process. The website service costs involved could simply be picked up by the local authority. Alternatively, there could be an agreement as part of the tender process that the successful tenderer agrees to meet the cost. In effect, of course, the successful tenderer will simply add on these costs to its tender price. In particular, the issue arises as to whether requiring subscription or other pre-conditions as to membership of an electronic marketplace in order to participate in a contract award procedure, would be contrary to the EC Treaty or the Directive's equal treatment principle. The equal treatment principle applies to prospective tenderers as well as those tenderers who actually participate in an award procedure[1]. For example, a tenderer participating in an electronic tendering process, which involves an electronic marketplace, may incur costs and transaction fees which would deter a small or medium-sized enterprise. In relation to this it is likely that the court would consider whether the subscription or requirement to obtain membership before being allowed to participate in an electronic procurement exercise to be construed in the light of the likely commercial benefits that the tenderer will derive from obtaining membership and whether the controls achieved through subscription or membership would be achievable by other means, eg state control, ie the proportionality test would be applied[2].

1   Case C-16/98 *EC Commission v France* [2000] ECR I-8315.
2   See Case C-58/98 *Josef Corsten* (3 October 2000, unreported).

4.66   It should be noted that at the time of writing, art 32a of the proposed draft Consolidated Directive addressing dynamic purchasing systems would not allow charges to be billed to the interested economic operators or parties to the system.

Framework arrangements

4.67   Online catalogues and some electronic market places rely on the use of what are known as framework arrangements under the EC public procurement rules.

Framework arrangements, otherwise known as 'call-off contracts' or 'running contracts' raise particular complexities under the EC procurement rules which are dealt with in more detail in chapter 3.

Dynamic purchasing systems

4.68 At the time of writing, the draft proposed Consolidated Directive included suggested provisions relating to dynamic purchasing systems which could be applicable for electronic catalogues, procurement hubs and online auctions. The full text of the draft art 32a is set out at para **3.163**.

4.69 In summary the draft proposals in relation to dynamic purchasing systems provide as follows:
1   the dynamic purchasing system must be set up and run solely electronically;
2   the contracting authority must evaluate tenders within 15 days of submission;
3   tenderers can improve their bids provided they continue to comply with the specification;
4   the dynamic purchasing system has a maximum duration of four years;
5   authorities cannot charge parties to the dynamic purchasing system.

See also para **3.163**. For details as to how the EC Directives may be revised see para **3.213**.

EC competition law—arts 81 and 82 of the EC Treaty

4.70 Article 81(1) of the EC Treaty prohibits agreements between undertakings, decisions by associations of undertakings and concerted practices which have as their object or effect the prevention, restriction or distortion of competition within the Common Market.

4.71 The aim is to ensure that each undertaking determines its business policy and market conduct independently of others. No actual anti-competitive effect is necessary if the practices are intended to prevent, restrict or distort competition. It is the substance of the collaboration that matters, not the form that it takes, but it is necessary to demonstrate that any restriction of competition has an appreciable effect on intra-EC trade.

4.72 There may therefore be implications under art 81 for electronic procurement marketplaces. For example, if a number of local authorities were to set up a procurement marketplace this would be classifiable as an agreement between undertakings under art 81. If the local authorities were to use the market place as a means of exerting joint purchasing power to negotiate terms and conditions with suppliers, the local authority may as a quid pro quo commit itself to purchase the majority of its requirements for a certain product through the marketplace. If the particular supply being procured through the marketplace were an item where local authorities accounted for the majority of the demand (an example might be street lighting or domiciliary care services for the elderly) then the local authorities would have limited themselves to purchasing from members of the marketplace, thus depriving themselves of alternative sources of supply and depriving non-members of the marketplace of sales outlets. In that situation collective dominance in the marketplace might be construed as being restrictive of competition. In addition, it is important that conditions of access to the marketplace are objective and must not be discriminatory or impose unfair conditions on suppliers such as, for example, establishing facilities in the local authority's area.

4.73   Such a situation could also apply to a marketplace being operated by an independent entity, for example, where a commercial concern had established a marketplace which local authorities and their suppliers both use.

4.74   Article 82 of the Treaty prohibits any abuse of a dominant position by one or more firms. The existence of such a dominant or a joint dominant position is far more likely in a narrowly defined product market. A practical example might be the procurement of places in residential homes within a particular geographical region where local authorities with social services functions are likely to amount to a strong, if not dominant, share of the market. If, for example, local authorities through an electronic marketplace or other agreement were to use their dominant position to extract unfairly low prices or impose unfair trading conditions or unreasonable contract terms from suppliers, or the local authorities decided to boycott a supplier who refused to adhere to the authority's terms of contract, then this could be considered as an abuse by dominant suppliers contrary to art 82 especially if the suppliers who were excluded had no alternative purchasers whom they could supply.

4.75   It is possible for agreements which fall within the prohibitions contained in art 81(1) to obtain exemptions under art 81(3) provided the market place contributes to improving distribution and promoting technical or economic progress. Consumers (ie both suppliers and ultimately customers) are allowed a fair share of the resulting benefit, ie economic advantages, as long as the restrictions imposed are not indispensable to obtaining those objectives; and the agreement will not have the effect of eliminating competition in relation to a substantial part of the products in question.

4.76   There is no doubt that electronic marketplaces can offer quicker, better, cheaper and more efficient procurement within local government. However, where an electronic marketplace is manipulated by a number of local or private sector entities wishing to achieve anti-competitive purchases, the regulation of competition law will apply to check those abuses.

Commercial issues associated with e-procurement

4.77   The Byatt Report (see para **4.27** recommendations 17 and 19) highlighted that many local authorities had reservations about using e-procurement systems, including legal and commercial concerns such as data protection compliance, whether a particular form of e-procurement complies with the EC procurement regulations, and security and authenticity issues. The EC has also recognised the legal and policy barriers to e-procurement and has responded with the three major Directives on public procurement[1] which it claims will remove a number of the major legal obstacles to e-procurement. In addition to these there are a number of commercial issues arising out of e-procurement, which fundamentally affect the way local authorities procure, and the extent of business process change required of local authorities in order to maximise the effectiveness of e-procurement systems.

1   The proposed Consolidated Directive on the co-ordination of procedures for the award of public supply, service and works contracts; the E-commerce Directive; the Electronic Signatures Directive.

Security and encryption

4.78 Security is an issue of central importance to both contracting authorities and businesses involved in the e-procurement activities of the contracting authorities. Users of e-procurement systems need assurances in terms of confidentiality, integrity and authenticity of transactions, legitimate use and non-repudiation. Technically, all information over the Internet is insecure and capable of being intercepted, altered and viewed. For example, a local authority communicating with its supplier base over the Internet could involve the disclosure of financial information which, if received into the wrong hands, could have harmful business implications for the supplier and undermine any trust which the supplier base may have in a local authority's e-procurement system. It is a fundamental principle of competitive tendering, for instance, that tenders are kept private and confidential. In order to make e-procurement feasible, indeed e-commerce in general, the information needs to be kept private and this can be achieved through a range of cryptography or encryption techniques. It is essential that underlying public security infrastructure (such as authorised bodies and keys—see below) be made available before advanced e-procurement models can be implemented.

4.79 Encryption is a technique by which information can be transmitted in code form such that it cannot be read by individuals who do not have the right key or password to decode the information. Two main systems are used. The first is a symmetric key system whereby the same 'key' is used to encode and decode the message. For instance, information is encoded with a password and the recipient decodes the message using the same password. The key must be kept secret, but everyone to whom the information is transmitted must have access to the key. This of course renders the system vulnerable to a possible breakdown in security if a larger than permitted number of individuals know the key.

4.80 The second is a dual key system comprising public and private keys. To send an encrypted message, the sender locates the public key of the recipient and encrypts the message using the public key—the person with the corresponding private key can then read the message. To authenticate the sender of the message, the message will be encrypted with the private key and the recipient will decrypt the message with the public key knowing that only an individual with the private key could have sent the message. This system relies upon trusted third parties to hold the public keys in what are the equivalent of telephone directories.

Electronic signatures

4.81 Associated with the encryption techniques described above, are electronic signatures, which are defined in the Electronic Communications Act 2000, s 7(2) as:

'…anything in electronic form as-
(a) is incorporated into or otherwise logically associated with any electronic communication or electronic data; and
(b) purports to be so incorporated or associated for the purpose of being used in establishing the authenticity of the communication or data and the integrity of the communication of data or both.'

4.82 This definition is 'technology neutral' in that it does not prescribe the type of technology to be used for establishing authenticity or integrity. However most commonly used is the digital certificate, which makes use of the private and public keys discussed above and which is an electronic attestation which links signature verification data to a particular person and confirms the identity of that person. A major problem with transactions over the Internet is the possible repudiation of messages by an individual falsely denying that a message has been sent or received. This could, for instance, occur in business transactions such as online ordering and payment. Digital certificates can minimise risk of repudiation by identifying individuals in a secure way.

4.83   The Electronic Communications Act 2000 attempted to modernise the law and also to instil a degree of confidence in the use of electronic signatures. Section 7 of the Act gave an electronic signature the same legal effect as a handwritten signature (therefore capable of forming legally binding arrangements), creating certainty in what was previously an uncertain area of law. Other parts of the Act deal with the registration and certification of cryptography support service providers. Section 1 provides for the establishment of a register to be held by the Secretary of State, which contains details of approved providers of cryptography support services who will have been independently assessed in terms of quality.

4.84   The Electronic Signatures Regulations 2002[1], deal with the registration of certification service providers ('CSPs'). These regulations state, among other things, that a CSP will owe a duty of care to an individual and will be liable to an individual who relies on a 'qualified' certificate (which meets certain formal and technical requirements as set out in Sch 1) issued to the public and who suffers loss as a result of such reliance. The regulations also sets out a checklist of requirements which CSPs must adhere to when issuing qualified certificates. The Regulation of Investigatory Powers Act 2000 also deals with the regulation of encryption processes and provides new powers to law enforcement agencies to demand the release of keys for the purposes of carrying out certain law enforcement investigations.

1   SI 2002/318.

Business process re-engineering

4.85   The move towards electronic procurement by local authorities cannot take place without business process re-engineering (BPR) of existing procurement routines, practices and administrative systems. The general idea of BPR is to provide the means for optimising and enhancing business processes, and this can partly be done through the use of information technology. The focus is not to tailor the technology to fit the local authority, but rather to reorganise the local authority to fit the new processes and technologies. BPR questions existing procedures, rules and structures and replaces them with new procedures, rules and structures. The effects of BPR will be visible in many areas such as organisational design, role and functions of the authority's procurement unit/staff, staffing and competence requirements, establishment of new ways of working and contracting methods, and a redefinition of existing supplier relationships. It is hoped that the benefits of BPR will be expressed in terms of higher cost-effectiveness, improved quality in public services and performance and a higher degree of efficiency and reliability in procurement functions. At the time of writing, a number of local authorities are contemplating the outsourcing of their procurement activities as part of larger business process outsourcing projects which includes BPR activities.

4.86 Associated with BPR, is enterprise resource planning (or 'ERP'), which refers to highly complex software which attempts to integrate all departments and functions in an organisation into a single computer system with a common database, so that the single computer system can serve the particular needs of the different departments. The aim is to facilitate improved information-sharing and communication between the departments, as well as improving the efficiency of an organisation and streamlining processes. Within the context of procurement, ERP has the potential to take the procurement process, and automate the relevant stages along the procurement path. ERP can be used to manage purchasing activities, maintain inventories, interact with suppliers and track orders.

4.87 The successful deployment of an ERP system is an incredibly complex process and requires a significant degree of planning. Once deployed, however, the benefits of an ERP system are perceived to be:
— improved ability of the local authority to place and trace orders;
— easy access to product information;
— ability to put authority contracts can online, thus allowing suppliers to anticipate services and products required by the local authority;
— reduction in paperwork and resources required to approve and process purchases.

Systems and standards

4.88 The development of comprehensive technical and non-technical standards, together with an appropriate legal framework within which to develop local e-government, is a work in progress. Such standards might include the following:
— a common security framework which would provide a framework of functional security requirements for the delivery of services by and on behalf of government and which would deal with digital certificates and other authentication technologies;
— smartcard standards;
— privacy and data protection standards;
— interoperability framework ('E-GIF')—at the time of writing, Version 4 of E-GIF is the latest version of this framework. Basically the E-GIF framework prescribes the policies and technical specifications that aim to achieve information flow and integration across government. Version 4 utilises market-driven open standards to enable flow of information from back-end systems to citizen and businesses, and between government organisations. It is organised into two parts. Part 1 deals with high-level policy statements, management, implementation and compliance regimes, and Part 2 contains the technical policies and specifications. Adherence to E-GIF standards is mandatory for public sector bodies;
— XML schemas—concerns the adoption of XML/XSL as a core standard for data integration and management of presentational data;
— metadata—a metadata framework was published in May 2001 (www.schemas-forum.org/stds-framework/second), which provides a structure for standardising and tagging of information on websites and elsewhere, allowing dynamic links to be maintained between related information and services. The metadata standard will be incorporated into E-GIF Version 4;
— data standards property and people—the National Land and Property Gazetteer Project aims to use BS766 as the basis of a common local government address system and information service. BS766 is the standard that describes basic information;

— data sharing protocols[1]—need for a model framework for establishing such protocols;
— website guidelines—are in the pipeline. Current guidelines exist which are dated and apply only to central government;
— e-procurement interoperability—the government is in the process of consulting on the development of this standard. There appears to be support for the proposition that an e-procurement interoperability standard be developed for inclusion into the E-GIF Framework. However it is not settled exactly what these standards would be.

1   See *Privacy and Data Sharing—The Way Forward for Public Services* (Performance and Innovation Unit Report, April 2002).

4.89   The EC's recent study[1] of e-procurement pilots indicated a clear tendency towards the use of open access standards[2] which the EC welcomes as promoting easier access to procurement opportunities, increasing market transparency and competition, as well as being a solution which requires significantly less investment than other solutions such as Virtual Private Network solutions[3]. However the security of open access systems does promote some concern. The EC is of the view that in the early phases of the procurement process, open access systems are preferable, but that in the latter phases of procurement (for example stages involving communication between buyer and selected supplier) VPN or extranet solutions offering a higher level of security would also be acceptable.

1   *Analysis of Electronic Procurement Pilot Projects in the European Union* (November 2000) carried out for the European Commission Internal Market DG, prepared by PLS Ramboll.
2   Open access standards relate to e-procurement systems which are based on open access via an Internet web page. Access to special areas of the web page can be controlled by password if required.
3   Virtual private networks are Internet systems which use specific software applications incorporating security mechanisms such as encryption to ensure that only authorised users can enter a network.

PART II
CONTRACTS: CONTENTS AND PRINCIPLES

CHAPTER 5

Contracts: contents and principles

Jess Connors, Ashwin Maini, Nicola Greaney & Colin Thomann

POWERS TO CONTRACT, UNLAWFUL DELEGATION, UNLAWFUL FETTERS, ESTOPPEL

Capacity and authority to contract

5.01   The powers of a local authority to enter into contracts are limited to those which have been expressly conferred upon it by legislative provision or which are incidental to or consequential upon expressly conferred powers or purposes (see the Local Government Act 1972, s 111 and the Local Government (Contracts) Act 1997, s 1). If a local authority enters into a contract other than in furtherance of an activity expressly or impliedly authorised by statute, then that contract will be ultra vires and unlawful, and any interested party who can show locus standii or public law standing can seek a declaration to that effect[1].

1   *Hazell v Hammersmith and Fulham London Borough Council* [1992] 2 AC 1, HL.

5.02   If a contract is declared unlawful, then, as a general rule, neither party to the contract will be able to enforce the contract as against the other party. The legal consequences of entering into an unlawful contract are examined in the case of *Credit Suisse v Allerdale Borough Council*[1] and are addressed more fully in chapter 10 of this book[2]. In response to the issues raised by the *Credit Suisse v Allerdale* case, the Local Government (Contracts) Act 1997 was enacted and came into full force on 30 December 1997. The 1997 Act provides a mechanism whereby a local authority may 'certify' a contract, with the effect that, once certified, the contract has effect, and is deemed always to have had effect (subject to judicial and audit review) as if the authority had the power to enter into it and entered into it in proper exercise of that power (see s 2(1)). The provisions and effect of the 1997 Act are considered further in chapter 10 of this book[3].

1   [1997] QB 306, [1996] 4 All ER 129, CA.
2   See also Arrowsmith *The Law of Public and Utilities Procurement* (1996) and Craig *Administrative Law* (2001).
3   And also in Arden *Local Government Constitutional and Administrative Law* (1999).

5.03   Even where a local authority enjoys the legal power or capacity to enter into a particular contract, it must do so by the offices of an individual who has authority to contract on its behalf. Actual authority will exist where the agent (eg a local authority official) has actually been given, whether expressly, by statute, or by implication, because he has been appointed to a relevant office (eg head of purchasing), the power to bind his principal. Alternatively, a local authority's agent may enjoy ostensible authority only, because his principal has represented to the other party that the agent is empowered to bind it, when in fact he is not so empowered. In some cases, ostensible authority may be sufficient to bind a local authority to the same extent as actual authority[1]. However, ostensible authority cannot validate a transaction which is ultra vires the local authority's own powers or validate the delegation of authority to an agent where that is proscribed by the relevant statute[2].

1   See eg *Western Fish Products v Penwith District Council* (1978) 77 LGR 185, CA.
2   For a more detailed explanation of the relevant rules of agency see *Bowstead and Reynolds on Agency* (17th edn, 2001).

Unlawful delegation

5.04   It is a fundamental rule of public law that a discretionary power may only be exercised by the particular body which has been entrusted with the power, unless that body has been authorised, either expressly or by necessary implication, to delegate the exercise of the power to another body or individual. If a local authority is to take a decision by any body except the full authority, say a committee, sub-committee or officer of the authority, then the relevant committee, sub-committee or officer must be properly delegated to make that decision[1]. Section 101 of the Local Government Act 1972 substantially extended the power of local authorities to delegate their executive powers to committees, sub-committees and officers. When a valid delegation occurs, the local authority may be bound by decisions made by the delegate pursuant to the delegated power as if it had made the relevant decision itself[2]. The LGA 1972 ensures that the exercise of delegated powers remains open to public and democratic scrutiny, by requiring committees and sub-committees to give the public access to their meetings, agenda material and minutes. Decisions taken by a group of councillors and officers not amounting to a committee or sub-committee are not subject to equivalent supervision by the public, and therefore delegation to such groups is not permissible[3].

1   *Barnard v National Dock Labour Board* [1953] 2 QB 18, HL.
2   *Battelley v Finsbury London Borough Council* (1958) 56 LGR 165.
3   See Sedley J in *R v Tower Hamlets London Borough Council, ex p Khalique* (1994) 26 HLR 517 at 525.

5.05   In some cases, it is the extent of supervisory control exercised by the delegating local authority over the delegate committee, sub-committee or officer that is critical in determining whether the delegation is validly made or not. Generally speaking, the greater the extent of supervisory control retained by the local authority, the more likely that the delegation will be considered by the courts to have been validly made[1]. Other factors important in determining validity are the scope of the delegated power and the extent to which its exercise affects the rights of individuals. The greater the scope and effect of the power, the more difficult it will be to infer from the language and purpose of the relevant legislation an implied authority to delegate[2]. Sometimes, a local authority may validly 'delegate' the more limited power to make recommendations or to take decisions subject to final approval by the local authority. Properly speaking, this is not a delegation but a referral. In such cases, difficulties may arise when the delegate acts without first obtaining the necessary local authority approval, and the local authority then purports to ratify the action which has already been taken[3].

1   *Cohen v West Ham Corpn* [1933] Ch 814 at 826.

2   See *R v Conwy Borough Council, ex p Prytherch* [2001] EWHC Admin 869; *R v Secretary of State for Education and Science, ex p Birmingham City Council* (1984) 83 LGR 79.
3   *R v Heston and Isleworth Rating Area Authority and South Middlesex Assessment Committee, ex p Conti* [1941] 2 All ER 116.

5.06   In some such cases (where a decision is taken by a person to whom no delegation has been made) or in cases where a decision is taken by a person to whom an unlawful delegation has been made, ratification may be possible. However this requires as a minimum that the decision taken was one which was within the power of the authority to take for itself and also that it was a decision which was capable of being delegated to the person who purported to take it[1].

1   *Blackpool Corpn v Locker* [1948] 1 KB 349, CA; *Barnard v National Dock Labour Board* [1953] 2 QB 18, CA.

5.07   Where a local authority can delegate a particular function under the LGA 1972, s 101 it may, in some circumstances, be able to go one step further and devolve that function outside the authority altogether: see Part II of the Deregulation and Contracting Out Act 1994. However, not all activities which may be carried out by a public body such as a local authority 'in person' may lawfully be delegated to an independent contractor, or 'contracted out'. Rather some powers, for example the power to make subordinate legislation or judicial functions, are subject to an express or implied proviso that they are only to be exercised by the particular person, group or body specified by Parliament.

5.08   Another aspect of the duty owed by public bodies not to abdicate their powers is the duty not to act under dictation. This means that where a local authority has been entrusted with a discretionary power, it must not allow itself to be directed by any other body or person which has not been so entrusted, while purporting to decide for itself, but rather must truly exercise its own independent judgement[1]. Local authorities will normally be entitled, and indeed may sometimes be obliged, to take into account the views of other parties or stated government policies. However, absent express statutory provision to the contrary, they remain under an obligation to decide for themselves[2].

1   See eg *R v Board of Visitors of Dartmoor Prison, ex p Smith* [1987] QB 106, CA.
2   See eg *Laker Airways Ltd v Department of Trade* [1977] QB 643, CA.

5.09   A public body will also be considered to have abdicated its function if it fails to keep under review the question of whether or not to exercise the discretionary power which it has been given in light of the circumstances prevailing from time to time, for example by purporting to exclude its future exercise. This amounts to a surrender of the statutorily conferred powers and is unlawful[1].

1   *R v Secretary of State for the Home Department, ex p Fire Brigades Union* [1995] 2 AC 513 at 551.

Unlawful fetters

5.10   A decision-maker exercising public functions and entrusted with a discretionary power must not circumscribe or 'fetter' that discretion by adopting an inflexible policy which prevents it from considering individual cases on their particular facts and merits. If it does so, it will be vulnerable to challenge not only on the ground of illegality, because it has failed to use its powers as Parliament intended, but also on grounds of unfair procedure, because it has failed to give interested persons the opportunity to influence its exercise of the discretion[1].

1   See eg *R v Chief Constable of the North Wales Police, ex p AB* [1999] QB 396, CA; De Smith, Woolf and Jowell *Judicial Review of Administrative Action* (1995).

5.11   It is important to remember that the rule against fettering is not a rule against the adoption of policies as such, but a rule against the adoption of inflexible policies or the inflexible application of purportedly flexible policies. The rationale underlying the rule is that the need for an element of predictability and consistency in decision-making, which is served by the existence of legitimate policies (legitimate in the sense that they are based on relevant considerations and are not aimed at improper purposes), must not be given precedence over the need to recognise exceptional cases and treat them as such[1].

1   *British Oxygen Co Ltd v Minister of Technology* [1971] AC 610 at 625D; *R v Ministry of Agriculture, Fisheries and Food, ex p Hamble Fisheries (Offshore) Ltd* [1995] 2 All ER 714 at 722A.

5.12   The courts will, in appropriate cases, undertake a close examination of the decision-maker's behaviour in order to decide whether it has fettered its discretion, for example by looking at statistics on the number of applications of a particular class which it has granted[1].

1   *R v Warwickshire County Council, ex p Collymore* [1995] ELR 217; *R v North West Lancashire Health Authority, ex p A* [1999] Lloyd's Rep Med 399, CA.

5.13   The rule against fettering discretion also extends to the fettering of discretion by the giving of contractual undertakings. Since all contracts potentially limit, at least to some extent, the contracting parties' future ability to act freely as they choose, strictly speaking, the rule against fettering could prevent local authorities and other public bodies from entering into binding contracts at all. However, in light of the critical administrative importance of public bodies being able to conclude binding contracts, as early as the nineteenth century the courts set out the 'incompatibility' test of when a contractual obligation will constitute an unlawful fetter[1]. In essence, this test states that unless the contractual obligation is incompatible with the objects prescribed by the statute then it will be effective.

1   *R v Inhabitants of Leake* (1833) 5 B & Ad 469.

5.14   The test set out in *Leake* was confirmed by the House of Lords in *British Transport Commission v Westmorland County Council*[1]. The question in that case was whether the Council could dedicate a footpath across a railway bridge to the public, even though the railway authorities were statutorily empowered to remove the bridge if they so chose. The House of Lords, applying the *Leake* test, held that the footpath could be dedicated without incompatibility.

1   [1958] AC 126, HL.

5.15   In summary, whether a contractual fetter is lawful is determined by consideration of three factors: first, the likelihood that a conflict will arise between a contractual undertaking and the unfettered exercise of statutory discretion[1]; second, the nature and importance of the power so fettered[2]; and third, the advantages to be derived from permitting entry into contractual arrangements[3]. Contractual obligations which create a right of such duration that it is akin to a property right are more likely to be found to be incompatible with statutory objects than contractual rights which, generally speaking, create rights of a more limited duration[4]. Even where a local authority validly confers a proprietary right by contract under one piece of legislation, a subsequent enactment may render the contractual obligation incompatible[5]. For a recent case considering the question of unlawful fettering by contractual undertakings see *Alliance against the Birmingham Northern Relief Road v Secretary of State for the Environment, Transport and Regions*[6].

1   See *British Transport Commission* [1958] AC 126 per Lord Summer.
2   See *Rederiaktiebolaget Amphitrite v R* [1921] 3 KB 500.
3   *Birkdale District Electricity Supply v Southport Corpn* [1926] AC 355, HL.
4   See *Birkdale District Electricity Supply v Southport Corpn* [1926] AC 355, HL.
5   *Blake v Hendon Corpn* [1962] 1 QB 283, CA.
6   [1999] JPL 426, CO/1151/98.

5.16   An alternative formulation of the test for an unlawful fetter is whether entry into contractual arrangements is incidental to, or consequential upon, things which legislature has authorised. If so, it is unlikely to constitute an unlawful fetter[1].

1   *A-G v Great Eastern Rly Co* (1880) 5 App Cas 473 at 478, and see *Wade on Administrative Law* (8th edn, 2000).

5.17   In practice, both approaches are likely to give similar results. Powers located in the commercial sphere of a public authority's functions will usually permit contractual fetters, whereas those located towards the public law end of the spectrum rarely will.

5.18   If a private law contractual obligation is found to constitute an unlawful fetter on a decision-maker's public law discretion, or if the decision-maker, in the exercise of its public discretion, does something which is incompatible with its private law contractual obligations, no remedy is available to the other contracting party, unless the contract itself expressly so provides.

Legitimate expectations

5.19   Allegations of fettering of discretion often arise when an interested individual feels that a policy should not be applied to his particular case, because of its exceptional nature. In contrast, questions of legitimate expectation or estoppel arise when an affected individual argues that a published or established policy should be applied to his particular case because it is not exceptional. In such cases, the principle of predictability and consistency in decision-making suggests that the decision-maker should follow its own policy unless there are good reasons for departing from it, which are communicated to the affected party or parties. In some cases, fairness would seem to require that the decision-maker should give the affected parties an opportunity to attempt to persuade it to continue to adhere to the policy.

5.20   Legitimate expectations may be created if a public body makes a representation to an individual or group of individuals that it will follow a particular policy or that it will inform them before changing its policy[1]. Alternatively, legitimate expectations may arise when an individual has historically enjoyed a particular benefit in circumstances where he could legitimately expect to continue to receive that benefit[2].

1   See eg *R v Liverpool Corpn, ex p Liverpool Taxi Fleet Operators' Association* [1972] 2 QB 299, CA.
2   See eg *Council of Civil Service Unions v Minister for the Civil Service* [1985] AC 374 at 408.

5.21   Whether or not a legitimate expectation arises and the scope of any duty to consult which may thereby be created are matters to be construed by the courts in light of the facts of each particular case. Of particular importance are:
(i)   the nature of the policy or representation (eg how specific, clear and unqualified was it, and how often was it repeated, or over what period was it sustained);
(ii)   whether the affected person could be expected to foresee that the relevant policy was likely to change or would not be applied in his case;
(iii)   whether there was detrimental reliance (including but not limited to financial expenditure) by the affected person which means that it would be unfair if the public body were now allowed to resile from its previous representation; and
(iv)   whether the affected person fully disclosed all material issues to the public body[1].

1   See eg *R v IRC, ex p Matrix Securities Ltd* [1994] 1 WLR 334.

5.22   The Court of Appeal in the case of *R v North and East Devon Health Authority, ex p Coughlan*[1] identified three categories of legitimate expectation, giving rise to three different levels of judicial scrutiny:
—   first, there are cases in which the public body is simply required to take into account its previous policy or representation, giving it such weight as it thinks appropriate, before deciding whether to change its stance. In such cases[2] a decision to depart from the policy or representation may only be challenged on the *Wednesbury* grounds that no reasonable decision-maker could have made this decision;
—   the second type of case is where the applicant has a legitimate expectation of being consulted before a decision is taken. In such cases[3] the courts will require that an opportunity for consultation is given unless the decision-maker can show that there is an overriding reason why no such consultation should take place;
—   the third type of case is where the applicant claims that it has been given a legitimate expectation of a substantive benefit such as a licence or social security payment. In these cases[4], once the existence of the legitimate expectation has been demonstrated, the courts will themselves weigh the requirements of consistency and fairness on the one hand against the reason given by the decision-maker for the change in stance on the other, and will decide whether, in the circumstances, to defeat the expectation created by the policy or representation would be so unfair as to constitute an abuse of power, for example because there was in fact no overriding public interest justifying the change in stance.

1   [2001] QB 213, CA.
2   Eg *Re Findlay* [1985] AC 318, HL and *R v Secretary of State for the Home Department, ex p Briggs, Green and Hargreaves* [1997] 1 WLR 906, CA.
3   Eg *A-G for Hong Kong v Ng Yuen Shiu* [1983] 2 AC 629.
4   Eg *Re Preston* [1985] AC 835 and *R v IRC, ex p Unilever* [1996] STC 681.

CONTRACTUAL LIABILITY[1]

5.23   There are three essential requirements for the formation of a contract: an agreement (consisting of an offer and acceptance), contractual intention (otherwise known as an intention to create legal relations), and consideration. However, other matters relating to the form of the agreement are important including certainty of terms.

1   For more detailed discussion of this topic see *Chitty on Contracts* (28th edn, 1999) and Mckendrick *Contract Law* (2000).

The offer

5.24   An offer is a statement by one party that he or she is willing to enter into a contract with another party on stated terms, as soon as the other party to whom the offer is addressed, accepts those terms. Generally, the offer can be made in any particular form; orally, in writing or by conduct.

Objective test of intention

5.25   In deciding whether an agreement has been reached, as well as the scope of that agreement, the usual rule is that the courts apply an objective test of intention. Therefore, if the outward appearance of the party conduct is that an agreement has been reached, both parties are bound by that agreement. Usually neither party can escape by relying on an unexpressed reservation or qualification to show that he or she did not in fact reach an agreement.

5.26   Therefore, an offeror may be bound if a reasonable person would be lead to believe by his or her words or conduct that he or she intended to be bound[1]. As a result, a person can be bound by an apparent intention. Therefore, where a company offered to agree the current market rental value of a property at £65,000 (an offer which was accepted by the defendant company), it was bound by that sum, even though it had made a mistake and meant to propose £126,000[2].

1   *Smith v Hughes* (1871) LR 6 QB 597; *Bowerman v Association of British Travel Agents* [1996] CLC 451.
2   *Centrovincial Estates plc v Merchant Investors Assurance Co Ltd* [1983] Com LR 158, see also *OT Africa Line v Vickers plc* [1996] 1 Lloyd's Rep 700 at 702.

5.27   However, the objective test of intention is sometimes displaced by a test of subjective intention. Whether an offeror (A) will actually be bound by an apparent offer does depend on the state of mind of the offeree (B). If B knows that, in spite of A's apparent intention, A does not actually posses that intention, then A is not bound even though B has accepted A's offer. The reason for this is that B knows the truth about A's actual intention[1]. The subjective test of intention has also been applied in circumstances where the parties were genuinely at cross-purposes as to the subject-matter of the contract[2].

1   *Ignazio Messina & Co v Polskie Linie Oceaniczna* [1995] 2 Lloyd's Rep 566 at 571; *OT Africa Line v Vickers plc* [1996] 1 Lloyd's Rep 700.
2   *Scriven v Hindley* [1913] 3 KB 564.

Form of the offer

5.28   As stated above, an offer can be made orally, in writing or by conduct. An offer can be addressed either to an individual, to a specified group of persons or to the world at large. In some cases involving arbitration, it has been held that inactivity may amount to an offer to abandon the reference of a dispute to arbitration[1]. Usually, inactivity by one party is unlikely to amount to an offer because it is equivocal conduct which can be explained on other grounds. Therefore, it is unlikely to induce a reasonable person to believe that an offer has been made.

1   *The Hannah Blumenthal* [1983] 1 AC 854; *The Multibank Holsatia* [1988] 2 Lloyd's Rep 486.

Invitation to treat

5.29   It is important to distinguish between an offer and an invitation to treat. An invitation to treat is merely an expression of a willingness to enter into negotiations which it is hoped will lead to a concluded contract. The question is one of intention. Did the offeror, A, intend to be bound by the acceptance of the terms put forward, or was it envisaged that it was merely one step in the negotiating process? In *Gibson v Manchester City Council*[1] a council tenant, Mr Gibson, asked the council whether he could purchase his council house. The council replied that it 'may be prepared to sell' the house to him at a particular price and invited him to make a formal application. Mr Gibson sent of the application form. The House of Lords found that a contract had not been concluded between Mr Gibson and the council. The letter written to Mr Gibson from the council saying that it may be prepared to sell the house was merely an invitation to treat and not an offer, which was capable of being accepted[2].

1   [1979] 1 WLR 294, HL.
2   See further *Treherne v Amateur Boxing Association Ltd* [2002] EWCA Civ 381, [2002] All ER (D) 144 (Mar).

Invitation to tender

5.30   The general rule is that when a person invites tenders for a particular project, the invitation to tender is merely an invitation to treat. The offer is made by the person who puts in a tender which is accepted when and if the person inviting tenders accepts that particular tender. Although the preparation of a tender is often expensive, there is no contract until the person inviting tenders accepts the particular tender. However this primary rule can be displaced by evidence of contrary intention. If a person inviting tenders states that he or she will accept the highest offer to buy, the invitation to tender can be an offer, which is accepted as soon as the highest offer to buy is communicated. Alternatively, the invitation to tender could be regarded as an invitation to submit tenders with a promise to accept the highest offer[1]. The same rule would apply if the invitation stated that the lowest offer would be accepted[2].

1   *Harvela Investments Ltd v Royal Trust Co of Canada* [1986] AC 207, HL.
2   *William Lacey (Hounslow) Ltd v Davis* [1957] 1 WLR 932.

5.31   It has also been held by the Court of Appeal that if an invitation to tender states that tenders submitted after a particular deadline will not be considered, then the person inviting tenders is contractually obliged to consider a tender submitted before that date and a failure to do so leads to a claim in damages[1]. This should be borne in mind by all local authority officers engaged in procurement and it is therefore advisable that Invitations to Tender and Invitations to Negotiate clearly preserve the authority's right to discontinue a procurement process at any time at its absolute discretion. It should be remembered that the common law rules relating to tenders are modified by the public procurement legislation (see further chapter 3).

1   *Blackpool and Fylde Aero Club Ltd v Blackpool Borough Council* [1990] 1 WLR 1195, CA.

Termination of the offer

5.32   There are five main ways in which an offer can be terminated:
(i)   the offer may be withdrawn: this can take place any time before the offer has been accepted. It is necessary to bring notice of withdrawal to the attention of the offeree;
(ii)   by rejection of the offer by the offeree;
(iii) by lapse of time: for example an offer may state that it is only open for acceptance for a particular period of time if no specific period is stated, an offer is deemed to last for a reasonable period of time;
(iv)   an offer which states that it comes to an end when a certain event occurs, will come to an end if and when that event occurs;
(v)   by the death of the offeror.

The acceptance

5.33   An acceptance is an unqualified and final expression of assent to the terms of the offer. An acceptance can be made by word, as well as by conduct. The objective test of agreement applies to an acceptance as much as it does to an offer. In circumstances where there have been lengthy negotiations (for example in a PPP or PFI contract), it can sometimes be difficult to say whether an offer has been accepted or rejected. The task of the court, in those circumstances, is to look at the entirety of the correspondence and communications between the parties and decide whether the parties have agreed to the same terms.

Counter-offers

5.34   A purported acceptance which does not accept all the terms and conditions of the offer, but seeks to introduce new terms and conditions, is known as a counter-offer. A counter-offer operates as a new offer which is capable of being accepted or rejected. This happens where variant bids are submitted in response to Invitations to Tender or Invitations to Negotiate. The effect of a counter-offer is to kill off the original offer. In *Hyde v Wrench*[1], A offered to sell land to B for £1000. B replied by offering to buy the land for £950. A refused to sell it for £950. B then wrote to A agreeing to pay £1000 but A refused to sell the land. The court held that there was no contract between the parties because A's original offer had been killed off by B's counter-offer.

1   (1840) 3 Beav 334.

5.35   The rule that offer and acceptance must correspond is often referred to as the 'mirror image' formation. It can give rise to particular difficulty where one or both parties seek to contract by reference to standard terms of business. Whether it is A's or B's standard terms and conditions that prevail will depend upon a close analysis of whose terms were accepted by word or conduct of the other party[1]. These difficulties are often referred to the 'battle of the forms' and arise essentially because of the English law requirement of an unqualified acceptance.

1   *Butler v Ex-Cell-O Corpn (England) Ltd* [1979] 1 WLR 401, CA; *British Road Services Ltd v Arthur V Crutchley* [1968] 1 All ER 811, CA.

Communication of acceptance

5.36   The general rule is that acceptance must be communicated to the offeror. The acceptance is usually only valid once it is brought to the attention of the offeror[1]. If an offeror prescribes a particular mode of acceptance, the offeror will not be bound unless the offer is accepted in that way. However, it is necessary to use very clear words to achieve this purpose[2].

1   *Entores v Miles Far East Corpn* [1955] 2 QB 327, CA.
2   *Manchester Diocesan Council for Education v Commercial and General Investment* [1969] 3 All ER 1593.

5.37   The general rule is that an acceptance of an offer is not implied from silence on the part of the offeree[1], although the offeror may expressly or impliedly waive the requirement for the communication of acceptance.

1   *Felthouse v Bindley* (1862) 11 CBNS 869; *The Hannah Blumenthal* [1983] 1 AC 854.

5.38   The general rule in relation to the posting of an acceptance is that the acceptance takes effect when the letter is posted and not when it is received. This rule also applies to telegrams. It does not apply to instantaneous modes of communication such as the telephone. For this reason, it is usual for local authorities to confirm acceptance of bids by written letter.

Acceptance of a tender

5.39   As stated above, the submission of a tender normally amounts to an offer, and the effect of an acceptance of this tender depends on the construction of the acceptance and tender in each case. When a tender is submitted unless it expressly states that there is no contract between the parties until, for example, certain formal documents are executed, there will be a binding contract when the particular tender is accepted.

Certainty

5.40   The terms of the contract must be certain. If the terms of an agreement are uncertain, then a binding contract will not be formed[1]. In *Scammell*, the House of Lords held that an agreement to hire goods on hire purchase was too vague an agreement to satisfy the requirements of contractual certainty because there were many different types of hire purchase agreement and no particular type had been specified.

1   *G Scammell & Nephew Ltd v Ouston* [1941] AC 251, HL.

5.41 However there are some limitations to the requirements of certainty. It is not necessary that commercial documents are drafted with great precision. The courts are aware that if strict legal precision is required, many agreements would be struck down for failing to meet the requirements of certainty. Essentially the courts take a common sense view. Lord Wright stated in *Hillas & Co Ltd v Arcos*[1] that:

'Business men often record the most important agreements in a crude and summary fashion; modes of expression sufficient and clear to them in the course of their business may appear to those unfamiliar with the business far from complete or precise. It is accordingly the duty of the court to construe such documents fairly and broadly, without being too astute or subtle in finding defects …'

1   (1932) 147 LT 503 at 514.

5.42 In following this approach the courts have developed a number of principles to assist in the interpretation of uncertain or vague terms. If a term appears to be vague, the vagueness may be resolved by resorting to custom or trade usage. As long as the meaning of a particular term is known to those in that trade, then the court will not find that it is too uncertain[1].

1   *Shamrock Steamship Co v Story & Co* (1899) 81 LT 413, CA.

5.43 The courts also employ the concept of reasonableness in construing terms. This approach was followed in the case of *Hillas* (see above), where an agreement to sell timber 'of fair specification' was entered into between persons familiar with the timber trade. The House of Lords asked whether the clause was capable of a 'reasonable' meaning and found that it was. Accordingly, the clause was sufficiently certain[1].

1   See also *Hackney London Borough Council v Thompson* [2001] L & TR 7, CA.

5.44 Even if it is not possible to construe an uncertain or vague phrase in a meaningful way, it does not necessarily follow that the entire contract will be struck down as too uncertain. The court is able to sever the meaningless phrase from the contract, so that it can be ignored. However, if the parties considered a clause to be of great importance, its uncertainty will vitiate the whole agreement[1]. This principle is of particular relevance when drafting specifications and conditions of contract.

1   *Nicolene Ltd v Simmonds* [1953] 1 QB 543, CA.

Incomplete agreements

5.45 If the parties fail to reach agreement on important matters of principle, the agreement may be found to be incomplete with the effect that no contract was made[1]. However, the standard of reasonableness can often be applied to determine remaining details. Section 8(2) of the Sale of Goods Act 1979 provides that a reasonable price must be paid for goods if the contract does not set the price.

1   *Harvey v Pratt* [1965] 1 WLR 1025, CA; *Bushwall Properties Ltd v Vortex Properties* [1976] 1 WLR 591, CA.

Conditional agreements

5.46   A conditional agreement is one where the operation of the agreement depends upon an event which may or may not occur. The use of the word condition in this context refers to an event and must be distinguished from the use of the word condition to refer to a term of a contract (see para **5.135–5.136**). For example, if the river floods, A agrees to work for B, and B agrees to pay A £100 for that work. Unless the river does flood, neither party is under any obligation.

5.47   If a condition is precedent, a contract only becomes binding when a particular event occurs. A condition is subsequent if it provides that a previously binding contract determines on the occurrence of a particular event: for example, A agrees to provide accommodation to B until B marries.

5.48   When an agreement is subject to a condition precedent, there is no duty on either party to give performance under the contract until that particular event occurs. Although the principal obligations are not binding until that time, some other subsidiary obligations can be imposed on the party by that agreement. This depends on the construction of the terms of the particular agreement. For example, both parties may have an unrestricted right to withdraw before the event occurs[1] or one or both of the parties is/are not able to withdraw from the agreement before the event occurs, if the event is still capable of occurring[2].

1   *Pym v Campbell* (1856) 6 E & B 370.
2   *Smith v Butler* [1900] 1 QB 694, CA.

Contractual intention

5.49   An agreement between two parties supported by consideration (see para **5.55** below), may not be binding if it is found that there was no intention to create legal relations. For example, when agreements are made in a social or domestic setting, it will frequently be found that there was no intention to create legal relations.

Commercial transactions

5.50   In ordinary commercial transactions, it is not necessary to prove in an express contract that the parties intended to create legal relations. Rather the onus lies on the party who seeks to argue that there was no such intention, to prove that no legal effect was intended. In commercial transactions, the onus is a heavy one[1].

1   *Edwards v Skyways Ltd* [1964] 1 WLR 349 at 355; *General Accident Fire and Life Assurance Corpn v Tanter (The Zephyr)* [1985] 2 Lloyd's Rep 529 at 537.

Agreements construed from conduct

5.51   If it is argued that an agreement should be inferred from conduct of the parties, the person who alleges that a contract has been formed has also to prove an intention to create legal relations. The courts have made it clear that a contract will not lightly be implied from conduct[1].

1   *Blackpool and Fylde Aero Club v Blackpool Borough Council* [1990] 1 WLR 1195 at 1202.

Objective test of intention

5.52 In ascertaining the intention of the parties as to whether legal relations were intended, the courts also apply an objective test[1].

1   *Bowerman v Association of British Travel Agents* [1996] CLC 451; *Edmunds v Lawson* [2000] QB 501.

Express negation of contractual intention

5.53 In certain cases, a particular express clause may negate contractual intention. A common example is where land is sold 'subject to contract'. Until the contract is concluded, the parties do not intend to create binding legal relations. Whether or not a particular phrase negates contractual intention depends upon the construction of the individual phrase[1]. The conduct of the parties can also negate contractual intention[2].

1   See *Edwards v Skyways Ltd* [1964] 1 WLR 349.
2   *Baird Textile Holdings Ltd v Marks and Spencer plc* [2001] EWCA Civ 274, [2002] 1 All ER (Comm) 737.

Other agreements

5.54 Many social or domestic agreements do not amount to contractual arrangements because they were not intended by the parties to be legally binding[1]. If a promise is extremely vague, the courts are more likely to find that such vagueness negates contractual intention[2].

1   *Lens v Devonshire Social Club* (1914) Times, 4 December; *Hadley v Kemp* [1999] EMLR 589; *Jones v Padavatton* [1969] 1 WLR 328, CA.
2   See also *Baird Textile Holdings Ltd v Marks and Spencer plc* [2001] EWCA Civ 274, [2002] 1 All ER (Comm) 737.

Consideration

5.55 In order to be binding, a promise must be either contained in a deed or supported by consideration. The requirement of consideration serves to put a legal limit on the sorts of promises that are legally binding. The basic requirement of the doctrine of consideration is that 'something of value in the eyes of the law' must be given for a promise, or a contract has not been made[1]. If a gratuitous gift is given to someone for charitable or sentimental motives, no value is given and such a promise is not legally binding unless contained in a deed. Deeds no longer have to be sealed as long as they are expressed as a deed. However, many local authorities' standing orders require deeds to be sealed with the official seal of the authority, particularly if the contract is above a value specified in its standing orders.

1   *Thomas v Thomas* (1842) 2 QB 851, 849.

Benefit and detriment

5.56 The law requires that there be consideration for a promise, as opposed to consideration for a contract. Each promise has to be looked at separately. If A promises to pay B a sum of £x to buy B's goods, payment by A is consideration for B's promise to deliver and can be seen as a detriment to A or a benefit to B. Delivery by B is consideration for A's payment and can be seen as a detriment to B or a benefit to A. In this example, the consideration for each promise involves both detriment to the promisee and benefit to the promisor. However, it is sufficient if there is either a detriment to the promisee or benefit to the promisor.

Adequacy and reality

5.57   The courts require some value to be given for a promise but do not concern themselves with whether adequate value has been given. It does not matter whether, objectively judged, someone has paid too much or too little for a promise[1]. Very trivial acts have been held to amount to consideration (eg the provision of chocolate wrappers in *Chappell & Co v Nestle*[2]). Consideration must be real in the sense that it is judged of some value in the eyes of the law[3] .

1   *Newbold v Leicester County Council* [2000] LGR 58.
2   [1960] AC 87.
3   *Tweddle v Atkinson* (1861) 1 B & S 393; *R v Pembrokeshire County Council, ex p Coker* [1999] 4 All ER 1007 (considering the Local Government Act 1972, s 123).

Past consideration

5.58   If the consideration for a promise consists of acts or forbearances which had already been done before the promise was made, they are past consideration and do not amount in law to consideration for the promise[1]. The courts do not necessarily apply a strict chronological test and if the acts form part of the same transaction, the precise timing does not matter[2].

1   *Roscorla v Thomas* (1842) 3 QB 234.
2   *Thornton v Jenyns* (1840) 1 Man & G 166.

Consideration must move from the promisee

5.59   A person can only enforce a promise if he or she has provided consideration for that promise. If the consideration was provided by a third party, the promisee cannot enforce that promise. Under the Contracts (Rights of Third Parties) Act 1999, a term in a contract between A (the promisor) and B (the promisee) can be enforced by C, a third party, in certain situations. It does not matter that no consideration for A's promise moved from C. This is a quasi-exception to the principle, but not a true exception because B is the promisee and not C[1]. It is not necessary that the promisee suffers a detriment because it suffices if benefit is conferred on the promisor[2]. Conversely, consideration need not move to the promisor, if the promisee has suffered detriment at the promisor's request[3].

1   See further paras **5.168–5.176**.
2   *Edmunds v Lawson* [2000] QB 501, CA.
3   *Re Wyvern Developments Ltd* [1974] 1 WLR 1097; *Lloyd's Bank plc v Independent Insurance Co Ltd* [2000] QB 110.

Forbearance to sue

5.60   A promise by a creditor not to sue on a valid claim can be consideration for a promise given in return[1].

1   *Pullin v Stokes* (1794) 2 Hy Bl 312; *GN Angelakis Co SA v Cie Algerienne de Navigation (The Attika Hope)* [1988] 1 Lloyd's Rep 439.

Performance of existing duties

5.61   A promise to perform a duty that one is already under a duty imposed by law to perform is not good consideration[1].

1   *Collins v Godefroy* (1831) 1 B & Ad 950.

5.62   The position used to be that a promise to perform an existing contractual duty owed to the promisor was no consideration for a fresh promise from the promisor. The rule was traced back to the case of *Stilk v Myrick*[1]. The reasoning is based on the need to protect the party to whom the duty is owed from extortion, as well as idea that the promisee suffered no detriment in performing an obligation that was already due from him or her. However, it has now been held that where there is no risk of extortion and a performance of an existing duty provides a practical benefit to the promisor, the promisee can enforce the promisor's new promise[2]. In *Williams*, A promised to make extra payments to B for works which B was already obliged to perform under the contract and B undertook no new obligations in return. A recognised that the originally agreed sum was too low and obtained a 'practical benefit' by obtaining B's performance under the original contract which was otherwise at risk. Actual performance of a contractual duty owed to a third party (C) can constitute consideration for a promise between A and B[3].

1   (1809) 2 Camp 317.
2   *Williams v Roffey Bros & Nicholls (Contractors) Ltd* [1991] 1 QB 1; *Simon Container Machinery Ltd v Embra Machinery AB* [1998] 2 Lloyd's Rep 429 at 435.
3   *Shadwell v Shadwell* (1860) 9 CBNS 159.

Estoppel

5.63   If a court finds that there is no consideration for a promise, limited effects to the promise may be given under the estoppel doctrines (see paras **5.193–5.194** for further discussion).

CONTRACTUAL INTERPRETATION

The purpose and process of interpretation

5.64   The term 'contractual interpretation' is invariably used interchangeably with the term 'contractual construction'. Both these terms refer to ascertaining the legal meaning (and effect) of the words used by parties to a contract.

5.65   The purpose of interpreting—or construing—a contract is to determine the parties' mutual intention regarding their respective rights and obligations under the relevant agreement. That exercise must be done primarily by reference to the parties' intentions at the time the contract was entered into. In interpreting a contract, one adopts the perspective that a court would ultimately take, should an authoritative judicial view ever have to be given on the meaning and effect of the contract.

5.66   The parties' mutual intention under a contract must be ascertained by using an objective (not a subjective) approach to interpretation[1]. That is to say, a court will adopt the interpretation that a reasonable person would intend the words used to carry. The policy reason for an objective approach is principally that it achieves commercial and legal certainty: '... otherwise all certainty would be taken from the words in which the parties had recorded their agreement or their dispossessions of property'[2]. The modern approach to interpretation is that the court will look for:

> 'the meaning which the document would convey to a reasonable person having all the background knowledge which would reasonably have been available to the parties in the situation they were at the time of the contract'[3].

1   *Mannai Investment Co Ltd v Eagle Star Life Assurance Co Ltd* [1997] AC 749, HL.
2   *IRC v Raphael* [1935] AC 96 per Lord Wright.
3   *Investors Compensation Scheme Ltd v West Bromwich Building Society* [1998] 1 WLR 896, HL per Lord Hoffmann at 912.

5.67   As will be seen from para **5.71**ff, a court may in certain circumstances validly make reference to the circumstances surrounding the execution of a contract. It is also entitled to take certain account of, and to give effect to, any underlying purpose of an agreement. The latter approach is sometimes referred to as adopting a 'purposive' or 'expansive' (as opposed to a 'literal') method of interpretation or construction. This use of commercial common sense has its limits, however. Even if a contract fails to disclose a commercial purpose, a court is still obliged to give effect to the particular words used in that document, having construed them objectively.

5.68   A court will generally presume that contracting parties intend the words they have used to bear their natural meaning. In interpreting a contract, the question to be answered is 'From an objectively reasonable standpoint, how would the words used by the parties be interpreted?', not 'What did the parties actually mean to say?'. In other words, whilst the court seeks to give effect to the parties' intention, it can only do so by reference to the intention as expressed. The court achieves this by ascertaining the meaning of the words actually used.

5.69   A court would be entitled to draw upon its own experience of contracts generically similar to the particular contract before it, if an issue of interpretation is raised.

5.70   Where the parties intend all the terms of their contract (apart from any implied by law) to be contained exclusively in a document or documents, then the interpretation of those instruments is solely a question of law, not a question of fact. That legal rule dates from the eighteenth century. It was maintained because it was essential to the development of English commercial law. If questions of contractual interpretation had been left to juries (which were far more widely used in civil matters at that time and which gave no reasons for their decisions), 'there could have been no precedent and no certainty in the construction of standard commercial documents'.

However, the rule does not apply when the parties' intention, objectively ascertained, has to be gathered partly from documents but also from oral exchanges and conduct. In the latter case, the terms of the contract are a question of fact. Furthermore, whether the parties intended the document(s) to be the exclusive record of their agreement is also a question of fact[1].

1   *Carmichael v National Power plc* [1999] 1 WLR 2042 per Lord Hoffmann at 2049, citing *Moore v Garwood* (1849) 4 Exch 681.

Available materials and the 'factual matrix'

5.71   Traditionally, the 'material available' for contractual interpretation was always confined to the written document to which the parties had reduced their commercial bargain. Absent fraud or mistake, that document would be binding upon the parties. Documents characterised as 'supplemental' to the original document could (and still can) also be referred to when construing the original document[1].

1   Law of Property Act 1925, s 58.

5.72   The law on 'material available' has been the subject of much judicial controversy and development within the past five years. Over that very recent period, the House of Lords has considered the subject in various contexts. Historically, the 'parol evidence rule' provided that oral evidence was not admissible to add to, vary or contradict the terms of a bargain reduced to writing. The rule was not confined to the exclusion of oral evidence, despite the word 'parol'. It amounted to a prohibition on interpreting contracts using any form of extrinsic evidence. Sometimes, the rule led to harshness. For example, potential beneficiaries under a will were deprived of their inheritance (because extrinsic evidence could not be adduced to clarify the intention of the creator of the relevant instrument).

5.73   Over the years, the courts developed limited exceptions to the rule. Examples include evidence indicating that the parties had not intended to create a contract or that the agreement was subject to fulfilment of outstanding conditions precedent.

5.74   The modern legal approach to interpretation has significantly eroded the parol evidence rule, if not dispensed with it entirely. A document does not nowadays necessarily have to be ambiguous or uncertain before extrinsic evidence can be admitted. The court must consider the factual circumstances prevailing at the time that the relevant contract was entered into. Effectively, a court will place itself in the equivalent 'factual matrix' to that within which the contracting parties were operating when they executed their agreement. The matter has been judicially summarised in this way:

> 'No contracts are made in a vacuum; there is always a setting in which they have to be placed. The nature of what is legitimate to have regard to is usually described as "the surrounding circumstances" but this phrase is imprecise: it can be illustrated but hardly defined. In a commercial contract it is certainly right that the court should know the commercial purpose of the contract and this in turn presupposes knowledge of the genesis of the transaction, the background, the context, the market in which the parties are operating'[1].

1   *Reardon Smith Line Ltd v Yngvar Hansen-Tangen ('The Diana Prosperity')* [1976] 1 WLR 989 per Lord Wilberforce.

5.75 Generally, drafts of the ultimate version of a contract, minutes of pre-contractual negotiations and correspondence from the pre-contractual stage cannot be relied upon, when interpreting a contract. This principle is sometimes regarded as an aspect of the parol evidence rule. It must, however, be read subject to what is said below about the surrounding 'factual matrix' of a contact. The policy reason for not generally admitting evidence of pre-contractual negotiations or exchanges is not one of convenience or technicality. It is merely that such evidence is frequently unhelpful. As the House of Lords has stated:

> 'By the nature of things, where negotiations are difficult, the parties' positions, with each passing letter, are changing and until the final agreement, though converging, still different. It is only the final document which records a consensus'[1].

1   *Prenn v Simmonds* [1971] 1 WLR 1381 per Lord Wilberforce.

5.76 The judiciary has gradually admitted extrinsic evidence about the objective 'factual matrix'—or surrounding factual backdrop—known to the parties at the time of contracting, where it establishes that the parties did not intend words used in a contract to have their natural (or literal) meaning[1]. Put another way, there are circumstances in which the courts will adopt the 'purposive' judicial approach to interpretation (referred to under the previous sub-heading). This approach stems from a series of legal decisions. These culminated in two fairly recent—and controversial—decisions of the House of Lords. Their Lordships construed contracts in a manner that was, on the face of it, inconsistent with the plain meaning of the words used by the parties themselves[2]. There is a body of legal opinion that considers those two decisions to have created undue uncertainty about what extrinsic evidence of contractual intention may be adduced. However, the balance of judicial opinion at the highest level has tipped in favour of opposing that conservative view. The English courts have concluded that it is illogical and unnecessary for a court to give words a meaning that is contrary to their demonstrably intended meaning, on an objective appraisal of the evidence.

1   *Shore v Wilson* (1842) 9 Cl & Fin 355.
2   *Mannai Investment Co Ltd v Eagle Star Life Assurance Co* [1997] AC 749; *Investors Compensation Scheme Ltd v West Bromwich Building Society* [1998] 1 WLR 896. Compare Staughton LJ's critical comments on *Investors Compensation* in the Court of Appeal decision in *Scottish Power plc v Britoil (Exploration) Ltd* [1997] 47 LS Gaz R 30, which took a more restrictive view of the factual matrix. See also Staughton LJ's views in *New Hampshire Insurance Co v MGN Ltd* [1997] LRLR 24.

5.77 The *Mannai Investment* case provides a tangible example of the modern approach to construction. A tenant gave notice of termination to its landlord under an office lease. The lease contained a break clause entitling the tenant to terminate early, upon six months' written notice, 'such notice to expire on the third anniversary of the term commencement date'. The relevant anniversary date was 13 January 1995, but the notice given referred to 12 January. The landlord claimed that the notice was patently defective and could not, therefore, terminate the lease. By a majority, the House of Lords found in favour of the tenant. It held that the tenant's notice complied with the lease requirements (albeit that it gave an incorrect date). This was because the notice (properly construed against the factual matrix and context) would have been understood by a reasonable recipient as being intended to be effective on 13 January. This was despite it being expressed to take effect on 12 January.

5.78 Lord Hoffmann in *Mannai Investment* cited an amusing example of how such an 'understanding' can arise even in an everyday context:

'If one meets an acquaintance and he says "And how is Mary?", it may be obvious that he is referring to one's wife, even if she is in fact called Jane. One may even, to avoid embarrassment, answer "Very well, thank you", without drawing attention to his mistake. The message has been unambiguously received and understood.'

5.79 Facts almost identical to those in *Mannai Investment* arose in a House of Lords case decided 60 years ago[1]. A notice of termination was served by a landlord in relation to a lease dated 25 December 1934, under which six months' notice was required in order to determine the arrangement. The notice (given as of 21 June 1941) purported to determine the lease on 21 December 1941. The notice was acknowledged by the tenant's representative, but the tenant subsequently argued that it was ineffective. It was held that the landlord's notice was indeed ineffective, despite it being apparent to the court that (viewed objectively) a reasonable person would have understood the notice as being intended to terminate the lease on the correct date (that is, 25 December 1941). Lord Greene MR took a strict approach:

'... the whole thing was obviously a slip on [the landlord's] part and there is a natural temptation to put a strained construction on language in aid of people who have been unfortunate enough to make slips. That is a temptation which must be resisted because documents are not to be strained and principles of construction are not to be outraged in order to do what may appear to be fair in an individual case...'[2]

1   *Hankey v Clavering* [1942] 2 KB 326.
2   [1942] 2 KB 326 at 328.

5.80 By the time of the decision in *Mannai Investment*, English law had simply evolved. The approach in *Hankey v Clavering* was deemed (by a 3:2 majority of the House of Lords) to be too rigid and formalistic. The notice to determine the relevant lease had to be interpreted in accordance with business common sense. It remains the case, however, that the subjective (undisclosed) intention of a party is not admissible to assist in interpreting an agreement.

5.81 Leaving aside the legal controversy caused by the above cases, the following guidelines emerge from the various modern authorities concerning the 'factual matrix':

—   interpretation is the ascertainment of the meaning which a document would convey to a reasonable person, with all the background knowledge which would reasonably have been available to the parties (principally, at the time of contracting);
—   subject to the requirement that the factual matrix should have been reasonably available to the parties (and to the inadmissibility of evidence of previous negotiations and declarations of subjective intent), there is no conceptual limit to what can be regarded as factual background. The factual matrix theoretically includes 'absolutely anything which would have affected the way in which the language of the document would have been understood by a reasonable man'[1];
—   however, the term 'absolutely anything' only encompasses anything that a reasonable man would regard as relevant to interpreting the contract. It is not a mandate to trawl through background documents in the hope of adducing something relevant[2];
—   the factual background may enable the reasonable man to choose between the possible meanings of words which are ambiguous (or even to conclude that the

parties have used the wrong syntax or words). The law does not require the courts to attribute to the parties an intention they plainly could not have had;

— evidence of subsequent conduct is inadmissible to interpret a purely written contract, except where it is argued that a variation by conduct or an estoppel has arisen[3]. However, evidence of subsequent conduct may be admissible where a contract has not been recorded exclusively in writing[4]. In the former case, what the parties thought they had agreed is of no consequence. In the latter, where the contractual terms may be based upon conduct and conversations also, what the parties thought they had agreed may be relevant.

1   *Investors Compensation Scheme Ltd v West Bromwich Building Society* [1998] 1 WLR 896 per Lord Hoffmann at 913.
2   See Lord Hoffmann's own qualification (of his comments in Investors Compensation) in *BCCI v Ali* [2002] 1 AC 251 at 269. In *Reliance Industries Ltd v Enron Oil and Gas India Ltd* [2002] 1 Lloyd's Rep 645, Aikens J gave judgment in proceedings concerning a contract governed by Indian law and an arbitration agreement governed by English law. Aikens J noted that the parties had expressly agreed at the relevant arbitration hearing that the English law principles on the construction of contracts were those set out by Lord Hoffmann in *Investors Compensation* as 'explained and expanded' by his Lordship in *BCCI v Ali*. Aikens J further observed that the arbitration award rendered by the 'distinguished' panel (chaired by Arthur Marriott QC) expressly noted that the parties had asked the panel to take Lord Hoffmann's statements on this area of English law as 'authoritative'.
3   *James Miller & Partners Ltd v Whitworth Street Estates (Manchester) Ltd* [1970] AC 583, HL; *Wates Ltd v Greater London Council* (1983) 25 BLR 1; *Schuler AG v Wickman Machine Tool Sales Ltd* [1974] AC 235, HL.
4   *Carmichael v National Power plc* [1999] 1 WLR 2042 per Lord Hoffmann at 2051.

5.82   The Court of Appeal in *The 'Tychy' (No 2)*[1] has recently considered Lord Hoffmann's statements of principle in *Investors Compensation* and in *BCCI v Ali*. In delivering the judgment, Lord Phillips, MR (sitting in the Court of Appeal with Lord Mustill and Jonathan Parker LJ) reviewed the relevant authorities. The court respectfully distanced itself from Lord Hoffmann's view in *Investors Compensation* that 'almost all the old intellectual baggage of "legal" interpretation has been discarded'. Lord Phillips made the tongue-in-cheek observation that the Court of Appeal was 'inclined to think that a little intellectual hand luggage is no bad thing when approaching the task of construing a contract'. The Master of the Rolls suggested the following refinements to Lord Hoffmann's guidance. Before taking extrinsic evidence into account, it is important to consider precisely why it is said to assist in deciding the meaning of what was subsequently agreed and to consider whether its relevance is sufficiently cogent (to the determination of the joint intention of the parties) to have regard to it. It is also important, though not always easy, to identify what is extrinsic to the agreement and what forms an intrinsic part of it. When a formal contract is drawn up and signed, care must be taken to distinguish between admissible background evidence relating to the nature and object of the contractual venture, and inadmissible evidence of the terms for which each party was contending in the course of negotiations. Where an agreement is alleged to have been reached in the course of dealings which do not culminate in the drawing up of a formal contract, the task is to identify whether, and if so which, terms proposed in the course of negotiations have become the subject of a joint agreement.

1   [2001] EWCA Civ 1198, [2001] 2 Lloyd's Rep 403.

5.83   There is a tension between the 'expansive' approach adopted in *Investors Compensation* and the tendency of the English courts invariably to hold commercial parties to the strict letter of the written contractual bargain they have struck. If it is a bad bargain, it is nonetheless a binding one. The underlying legal rationale for this approach is that 'agreements are to be observed'. The principle is derived from the Latin legal maxim *pacta sunt servanda*, an ancient doctrine intended to yield commercial and legal certainty. The courts have adhered to this principle, even if it led to a result that the court suspected was not anticipated by the parties themselves, or yielded an otherwise unwarranted contractual benefit or consequence.

5.84 As can be seen, traditionally, the courts were inclined to interpret the intention of contracting parties solely from the natural meaning of the words they used. Despite the decision in *Investors Compensation*, the principle of 'agreements are to be observed' has been reinforced by the House of Lords as recently as in 1998 in *Total Gas Marketing Ltd v ARCO British Ltd*[1]. Perhaps oddly, this decision was handed down almost simultaneously with that in the *Investors Compensation* case.

1   [1998] 2 Lloyd's Rep 209, HL.

5.85 An overview of the facts in the *Total* case may illustrate the important practical consequences of upholding agreements in accordance with their express terms. It may also serve to demonstrate that it is relatively exceptional for the courts to have recourse to extrinsic evidence of the surrounding context. Briefly, the facts in *Total* were as follows. Total (in the capacity of buyer) had entered in to identical long-term commercial contracts for the purchase of North Sea gas from three sellers (including ARCO). The purchase contracts were expressly made conditional upon three matters. The express contractual consequence of the non-fulfilment of two of these conditions precedent was that Total would be entitled to terminate the agreements. Those conditions were duly fulfilled. However, the consequence of non-fulfilment of the remaining condition was not expressly addressed. This became highly relevant, since Total purported to terminate the purchase contracts for non-fulfilment of the remaining condition. By the time of the first contractual delivery date (and subsequently), the market price for gas was substantially lower than the contract price. Total could, therefore, obtain gas more cheaply elsewhere than under the purchase contracts with ARCO. Their Lordships were fully aware of this commercial dynamic.

5.86 The question at issue was whether the contracts terminated for non-fulfilment of the outstanding condition (in circumstances where the remaining condition gave no fixed date by which it had to be fulfilled and the contract was silent as to the consequence of non-fulfilment of that particular condition).

5.87 On appeal, the House of Lords in *Total* held the following factors to be relevant, in determining how the disputed condition operated:
(a) the contractual language;
(b) the contractual scheme;
(c) the surrounding commercial and factual matrix; and
(d) the reasonable expectation of the parties at the time the contracts were entered into.

5.88 Although some of their Lordships were reluctant to release Total entirely from its conditional purchase commitment, it was held that Total could regard itself as effectively discharged from the contracts. Lord Hope stated:

'Commercial contracts should, so far as is possible, be upheld ... It is disappointing to find that, in this case, it has not been possible to construe the agreement in such a way as to provide the seller with the protection which it was designed to achieve.'

5.89   The most recent House of Lords' decision[1] on contractual interpretation has reinforced the pragmatic, purposive approach applied in *Investors Compensation*. Their Lordships found it possible, on the facts, to interpret the agreement at issue in a manner consistent with its commercial purpose and the context in which it was entered into. Accordingly, the bargain could be upheld. This decision stands in stark contrast, therefore, to the *Total* case where the result ostensibly stood at odds with the commercial purpose of the contract.

1   *Amoco (UK) Exploration Co v Teesside Gas Transportation Ltd* [2001] UKHL 18, [2001] 1 All ER (Comm) 865, often referred to as 'the Enron case' because the defendant was an Enron joint venture company.

The meaning of words

5.90   In the first instance, a court will apply the ordinary and natural meaning to words used in a contract. The assumption is that the parties used wording in the manner that a reasonable person would do. Exceptions to this starting point include terms that have a particular meaning within trade usage or where the context points to some special or unusual meaning.

5.91   It follows that one need not necessarily interpret a contract using the dictionary meaning of words. However, a court will make reference to such materials if it is necessary in order to identify the meaning of words. A dictionary may be referred to in order to show not only the meaning of a word but also its application or use. Nonetheless, even dictionary terms must be interpreted 'in the way in which business men would interpret them, when used in relation to a business matter of this description'[1].

1   *Southland Frozen Meat and Produce Export Co Ltd v Nelson Bros Ltd* [1898] AC 442 per Lord Herschell.

5.92   There is a considerable range of judicial opinion on the discretionary scope enjoyed by a court in construing the meaning of words. As noted earlier, a high watermark in the 'purposive' judicial approach to eliciting the meaning of contractual words was reached in the *Investors Compensation* case, when Lord Hoffmann stated:

'The meaning which a document (or any other utterance) would convey to a reasonable man is not the same thing as the meaning of its words. The meaning of words is a matter of dictionaries and grammars; the meaning of the document is what the parties using those words against the relevant background would reasonably have been understood to mean'[1].

1   *Investors Compensation Scheme Ltd v West Bromwich Building Society* [1998] 1 WLR 896 at 913.

5.93   If parties choose to use technical words, then the primary rule is that the technical meaning will be given to them. It is only if the meaning of the term itself is in dispute that a court will hear evidence about that term. A court will be entitled to refer to its own linguistic knowledge, in construing foreign words. However, the same is not true of scientific terms. As the Court of Appeal has itself noted, if a judge ventures beyond dictionaries or other works into highly technical matters, then 'he may easily go astray'[1].

1   *R v Patents Appeal Tribunal, ex p Baldwin & Francis Ltd* [1959] 1 QB 105, per Lord Reid.

5.94 If a word bears both an ordinary meaning and a more specialised meaning, then a court will not admit evidence of the specialised meaning, unless it is demonstrated that the parties themselves intended to use the word in its specialised sense. For example, two parties may enter into an insurance contract. If they are not engaged in the insurance business, then the agreement will not be interpreted in the manner that would have been applied to a contract formed by parties who were engaged in that market.

5.95 In drafting or amending legally-binding documents, for example conditions of contract and specifications, there is an overriding need for clarity of expression. This is because of the close scrutiny applied by the courts, when interpreting contracts. Where a draftsman uses legal terms of art, the need for absolute clarity of expression is reinforced. There is a presumption in favour of interpreting a legal term of art with its technical meaning (unless it is apparent from the context that the technical meaning should be displaced). For example, if one uses the term 'grant a bare licence over the property', that has a fixed legal meaning—namely, conceding a permission to do something that creates no permanent or irrevocable interest in the land affected. The policy reason for this strict approach to legal terms of art is that individual judges, when interpreting a contractual term, are inevitably influenced by:

> 'personal idosyncracies of sentiment and upbringing, not to speak of age. [Contracts] would fail in their object if the rights and duties which could be enforced depended on the personal idiosyncracies of the individual judge or judges upon whom the task of construing them chanced to fall[1].'

1   *Sydall v Castings Ltd* [1967] 1 QB 302 per Lord Diplock.

Implied terms

5.96 Where a bargain is not expressed in sufficient detail, or where implying a term into a contract would leave obligations suspended in a way which the parties did not intend, a contract will not be upheld. However, as the *Total* and *Enron* cases show[1], the English courts will also be slow to 're-write' an agreement freely arrived at between commercial contracting parties, whatever its consequences.

1   See paras **5.84** and **5.89** respectively.

5.97 Implied terms are those that may legitimately be inferred from (or implied into) a contract, even though the parties have omitted expressly to address the issue in the contract. Terms may need to be implied either where an unexpected contingency arises that the parties simply failed to foresee or where the parties neglected to record their mutual intention in sufficient detail.

5.98 Terms may only be implied into contracts as a matter of law by a court. There is a rebuttable presumption against implying terms into written contracts. This presumption becomes exponentially stronger the more detailed the terms of a contract are. Terms will be implied in the following two situations:
(a)   if it is necessary to give 'business efficacy' to the relevant contract; and
(b)   if the term is so obvious that it did not need to be expressly stated.

5.99 These are regarded by some commentators as cumulative requirements, by others merely as alternative requirements. Additional considerations are that the term to be implied must not contradict an express term of the contract, should be reasonable/ equitable and may be implied from conduct. Furthermore, a term will not be implied merely because it would improve a contract or make its performance more convenient[1].

1   See *Lewison on Interpretation of Contracts* (2nd edn), Chapter 5, for a fuller exposition of conditions for implying terms.

5.100   The 'business efficacy' test was first formulated as long ago as 1889[1]. It has evolved over subsequent years. It may be now reduced to a test of business necessity, not one of mere reasonableness. In summary:

'it must be such a term that both parties must have intended that it should be a term of the contract, and have only not expressed it because its necessity was so obvious that it was taken for granted'[2].

5.101   Examples of terms that have been implied include: in an agency contract, that the principal would not deprive the agent of commission by breaching the contract between himself and a purchaser, thereby releasing the purchaser from his obligation to pay the purchase price; in a contract of bailment, that the bailee had authority to do all things reasonably incidental to the reasonable use of the bailed goods; and in a contract for the use of a wharf, that it was safe for a ship to berth there.

1   *The Moorcock* (1889) 14 PD 64.
2   *Re Comptoir Commercial Anversois and Power Son & Co* [1920] 1 KB 868, CA per Scrutton LJ.

5.102   The 'obvious inference' test for implying a term is as follows:

'... something so obvious it goes without saying; so that if, while the parties were making their bargain, an officious bystander were to suggest some express provision for it in their agreement, they would testily suppress him with a common "Of course"'[1].

An example is a case in which a contract between two local authorities and a company prohibited either local authority from operating public transport services for a 99-year period. The company was obliged to pay a percentage of its profits in return. A successor entity to the company contended for an implied term that the agreement should end if Parliament should make it unlawful for the company to operate public transport services. It was held that it was by no means obvious that the parties would have agreed such a term[2].

1   *Shirlaw v Southern Foundries (1926) Ltd* [1939] 2 KB 206 per MacKinnon LJ.
2   *Kirklees Metropolitan Borough Council v Yorkshire Woollen District Transport Co Ltd* (1978) 77 LGR 448.

5.103   If a term is something more than a mere trade practice, but represents a general usage or custom of a trade or place, then such a term may be implied into a contract. The term must, however, be certain, reasonable and 'notorious' in the sector concerned. A term may also be implied from a previous course of dealing, where parties have consistently adopted a particular approach. For example, a covenant for interest for late payment could be implied from a previous course of dealings. Interest on late payment of commercial debts is now the subject of a statutorily-implied term. The relevant statute implies a term for statutory interest into contracts for the supply of goods and services on qualifying debts[1].

1   See the Late Payment of Commercial Debts (Interest) Act 1998.

5.104 One important term that may be implied into a contract is a duty to co-operate. The existence and extent of any duty to co-operate will be determined by reference to the express and implied obligations on the parties (not from what is reasonable in the circumstances). The parties may be under an implied obligation not to prevent the fulfilment of a condition or an obligation by a counter-party under a contract. The duty can even extend to taking positive steps to enable the other side to discharge its obligation. However, each case turns on its own facts and the wording of the particular contract[1]. In the context of IT procurement/supply contracts, parties operate under an implied duty of active co-operation (including, as a customer, accepting reasonable solutions to issues that have arisen and working with a supplier to resolve technical problems)[2].

1   *Scottish Power plc v Kvaerner Construction (Regions) Ltd* 1999 SLT 721, a Scottish decision of the Outer House.
2   *Anglo Group plc v Winther Browne & Co Ltd* [2000] ITCLR 559.

5.105 In considering whether words have to be read into a contract, in order to give effect to a given term, the question is not whether some sensible commercial purpose could be put forward for the words used by the parties. Before a court may 'do violence to the language used', the court must be satisfied that:
(a)   the words used produce a result so commercially nonsensical that the parties could not have so intended; and
(b)   by adapting the term, a construction exists which gives a commercially sensible purpose which the parties must have intended[1].

1   *City Alliance Ltd v (1) Oxford Forecasting Services Ltd, (2) Advanced Transaction Systems Ltd* [2001] 1 All ER (Comm) 233 per Chadwick LJ.

5.106 If a contract is silent as to its duration, as to the price for the benefit to be conferred or as to time of performance, then a term may be implied as to reasonable notice, a reasonable price or performance within a reasonable period. Various terms (as to title to goods, quality, fitness for purpose and so forth) are specifically implied by statute into certain types of contract.

Guidelines (or canons) of construction

5.107 The courts have evolved various guidelines (or canons) of construction over the years. The salient guidelines may be summarised as follows[1].

1   The guidelines summarised in this section are essentially based upon (and are to be found in greater detail in) *Chitty on Contracts* (28th edn) and *Lewison on Interpretation of Contracts* (2nd edn).

5.108 A clause must be considered in the context of the entire document in which it appears, not construed in isolation. Every part of the document may be brought into play in order to obtain a 'uniform and consistent' sense from the whole. That does not mean to say, however, that undefined expressions appearing more than once in the same contract must automatically be given the same meaning wherever they appear. Sometimes, the same word might even appear in the same clause, but in a different sense. For example, the term 'payable' in a lease containing review dates may mean 'accruing from time to time' or 'falling due for payment', depending on the context[1]. However, there is a presumption in favour of consistent meaning, where ambiguity arises.

1   *Tea Trade Properties Ltd v CIN Properties Ltd* [1990] 1 EGLR 155.

5.109   The *ejusdem generis* rule states that if words of a particular class (or genus) are followed by general words, then the general words will be interpreted as being limited to the particular class (or genus). An example of the application of this rule is: a lease with a covenant to yield up to the landlord all doors, locks, keys, and all other buildings, fixtures and things on the rented property would validly be interpreted as being limited to only items in the generic nature of landlord's fixtures. Accordingly, machinery affixed to the property by a tenant, for the purpose of his trade, would not be included[1].

1   The statement of principle and the illustration at para **5.109** are drawn from *Lewison on Interpretation of Contracts* (2nd edn).

5.110   The *contra proferentem* rule states that, in cases of ambiguity concerning a document or instrument, the doubt will be resolved against the grantor or creator of the document. A particular application of the rule is that exemption or exclusion clauses are construed against the person for whose benefit they are inserted[1]. The policy reason for the rule has been stated as follows:

> '... a person who puts forward the wording of a proposed agreement may be assumed to have looked after his own interests so that if the words leave room for doubt about whether he is intended to have a particular benefit there is reason to suppose that he is not'[2].

This is of particular relevance to local authorities using their standard terms and conditions to procure contracts.

1   See para **5.118**.
2   *Tam Wing Chuen v Bank of Credit and Commerce Hong Kong Ltd* [1996] 2 BCLC 69 per Lord Mustill.

5.111   The rule in favour of 'saving the document' states that if words used in a contract are capable of two meanings, one of which would validate the instrument but the other would render it invalid or meaningless or void, then the court should favour the meaning that would validate it.

5.112   So far as possible, a contract will be interpreted so as not to allow a party to take advantage of his own breach (in order to avoid his obligations or to terminate the contract or to obtain some benefit pursuant to it).

Exclusion clauses

5.113   In the context of local government contracts, a wide variety of types of exclusion clauses (or 'exemption clauses') may be encountered. Leading commentators regard such provisions as broadly comprising:
(a)   clauses purporting to limit a party's substantive contractual obligations;
(b)   clauses purporting to exclude or restrict a party's liability for breach of contract; and
(c)   clauses purporting to exclude or restrict a defaulting party's liability to indemnify the counter-party (for example, in terms of the level of damages payable in respect of the breach or the time limit within which a claim must be brought)[1].

1   This 'tri-partite classification' derives from Donaldson J's comments in *Kenyon Son and Craven Ltd v Baxter Hoare & Co Ltd* [1971] 1 WLR 519 and is cited in *Lewison on Interpretation of Contracts* (2nd edn).

5.114 In relation to consumer contracts or those based on written standard terms, an exclusion or limitation of liability must satisfy a requirement of reasonableness under the Unfair Contract Terms Act 1977. However, the UCTA 1977 does not regulate the remaining field of contracts. As the House of Lords noted in the leading case on interpretation of exclusion clauses:

'… in commercial matters generally, when the parties are not of unequal bargaining power, and when risks are normally borne by insurers, not only is the case for judicial intervention undemonstrated, but there is everything to be said, and this seems to be Parliament's intention, for leaving the parties free to apportion the risks as they think fit and for respecting their decisions[1].'

1   *Photo Production v Securicor Transport* [1980] AC 827 per Lord Wilberforce.

5.115 In a commercial (or non-consumer) context, contracting parties are deemed by the courts to be capable of looking after their own interests. They are also considered to be capable of deciding how risks inherent in the performance of various kinds of contract can be most economically borne. This is generally by insurance. The courts have traditionally been hostile to exclusion clauses in a non-commercial context. They have, therefore, developed various rules of interpretation for such clauses. However, when interpreting exclusion clauses that arise in a contract between well-advised parties, where neither deals as a consumer or on the other's written standard terms of business, the courts will refrain from an interventionist approach.

5.116 In view of the foregoing, the UCTA 1977 is likely to have relatively limited application in the context of local government contracts. The Act has some relevance to attempts to exclude or limit liability arising in contract. As mentioned above, aside from contracts where one party deals as a consumer, the 1977 Act also regulates situations where one contracting party deals on the other's written standard terms of business. In that situation, UCTA 1977 provides that the other party cannot, by reference to any contract term, exclude or restrict any liability of his for breach of contract, except insofar as the contract term satisfies the requirement of reasonableness (as defined under UCTA 1977)[1].

1   For a more detailed exposition on UCTA 1977 in the context of interpretation, see *Keating on Building Contracts* (7th edn).

5.117 Contract terms and notices purporting to exclude liability for negligence are regulated by UCTA 1977. A person cannot by reference to any such term or notice, whether the latter is given generally or to particular persons, exclude or restrict liability for death or personal injury arising from negligence. As regards other loss or damage, a person cannot so exclude or restrict his liability for negligence except insofar as the term or notice satisfies the statutorily-defined requirement of reasonableness.

5.118 Various rules of construction apply to exclusion clauses. The principal rules are summarised below[1]:
(i)   any ambiguity in an exclusion clause will be resolved *contra proferentem* (that is, against the party seeking to rely upon it). The rule has already been referred to in para **5.110**. The language of an exclusion clause must be sufficiently explicit to disclose the parties' common intention, without straining the language. If a party wishes to relieve itself of liability, it must do so in clear words;
(ii) exclusion clauses are construed strictly. They must cover precisely the nature of the liability at issue. Accordingly, a clause excluding liability for breach of

implied terms will not exclude liability for breach of express terms. However, the degree of strictness may be qualified according to the extent of the exclusion that the clause purports to confer;

(iii)   an exclusion clause will not relieve a party from liability for negligence, unless it does so expressly or by necessary implication. If the only liability of the party pleading an exclusion is a liability for negligence, the exclusion clause will more readily operate to exempt that party. A party will not be exempted from liability for negligence of its employees or servants unless adequate words are used;

(iv)   it is a question of construction of the particular contract as to whether or not a contractual provision excludes or limits a party's liability for fundamental breach. There is no rule of law prohibiting an exclusion clause from applying in such circumstances. There is, however, a rebuttable presumption that an exclusion clause is not intended to apply to a fundamental breach. It would seem that especially clear words must be used before the court will allow an exclusion clause to relieve a party from the consequences of a fundamental breach;

(v)   the courts do not regard limitation clauses with the same hostility as exclusion clauses[2]. This is because limitation clauses must be related to other contractual provisions (governing matters such as risks to which a party may be exposed, the remuneration to be received and any opportunity to insure)[3].

1   Chapter 11 of *Lewison on Interpretation of Contracts* (2nd edn) sets out a fuller account of the standard rules.
2   *Ailsa Craig Fishing Co Ltd v Malvern Fishing Co Ltd* [1983] 1 WLR 964, HL.
3   For further reading on the subject of interpretation generally, the reader is referred to three standard reference works (*Chitty on Contracts* (28th edn), *Lewison on Interpretation of Contracts* (2nd edn) and *Keating on Building Contracts* (7th edn)), to the 2nd Keating Lecture given by Lord Phillips of Worth Matravers MR on the subject of interpretation of contracts and statutes, and to two articles by Gearoid Carey in the Irish Law Times Nos 16 and 17, 2001. The author gratefully wishes to acknowledge the general assistance derived, in the preparation of this chapter, from these sources.

PERFORMANCE AND BREACH

Performance

The general rule

5.119   The starting point in evaluating whether contractual obligations have been fulfilled is that performance must match the requirements spelt out in the contract document exactly. Only discrepancies which are no more than trivial ('microscopic' according to Lord Atkin, below) will be excused.

5.120   The strictness of this rule is best illustrated by contracts for sale of goods. A seller is not able to argue that goods supplied, whilst deviating from the contractual specifications, are entirely suitable for the buyer's purposes, and can even be regarded as commercially superior. This is illustrated by the seminal decision of *Arcos Ltd v Ronaasen & Son*[1]. The seller supplied Russian timber. When goods arrived in London, prices had fallen. However, the contract specified a stave thickness of half and inch. Some staves varied from this measure. The discrepancy rendered the staves no less valuable, and they remained fit for their envisaged purpose. Lord Atkin confirmed the basic rule:

'If a condition is not performed the buyer has a right to reject. No doubt, in business, men often find it unnecessary or inexpedient to insist on their strict legal rights ... But in a falling market I find that buyers are often as eager to insist on their legal rights as courts of law are ready to maintain them'[2].

1 [1933] AC 470.
2 [1933] AC 470 at 480.

5.121 A crucial distinction is drawn between (a) promises to achieve a result, and (b) promises to use one's best endeavours. Obligations falling within limb (a) include promises to supply goods, construct buildings and, of course, pay sums of money. Limb (b) comprises contracts to supply services. Even the most skilful doctor, lawyer or teacher is not usually expected to guarantee a particular result. The test becomes whether efforts to achieve the hoped for outcome are in keeping with the general standards of the professional body in question.

5.122 It is not always easy to determine whether a party has promised to achieve a result, or merely to use its best endeavours. The court will look at the contractual wording, the intentions of the parties and the surrounding practicalities. This task is simplified by the following statutory provisions.
(a) supply of goods: these must be of satisfactory quality[1] and where a buyer makes known the purpose for which goods are required, they must be reasonably fit for this purpose[2];
(b) supply of services: these must be carried out with reasonable care and skill[3].

1 Sale of Goods Act 1979, s 14.
2 Supply of Goods and Services Act 1982, s 4(5).
3 Supply of Goods and Services Act 1982, s 13.

5.123 There are several ways of mitigating the strictness of results based contractual requirements.
— first, the parties may provide for slight variations within the contractual terms. This had, in fact, been done in the contract reviewed by the House of Lords in *Arcos Ltd v Ronaasen & Son*[1]. The terms permitted variations relating to length and breadth of staves. Fatally, no such terms were incorporated relating to thickness. This illustrates the importance of considering potential discrepancies in performance, and consequences arising, prior to entering an agreement;
— second, less serious deviations from the contractually specified norm may sound in damages only. A promissee will thus remain obliged to perform his or her own side of the bargain (see para **5.177** below);
— third, failure by a recipient to voice an objection within a reasonable time period may lead the courts to conclude that the discrepancy has been overlooked/ accepted, and the contract affirmed.

1 [1933] AC 470.

Time for performance

5.124 In commercial contracts, the parties will usually stipulate the time at, or within which, performance is to take place. Where the parties have omitted to do this, the courts will imply an obligation to perform each side of the bargain within a reasonable time. Again, regard is had to all the circumstances of the case, as well as general commercial practice. In some fields, such as major construction projects, anything short of a fixed time for completion has been perceived impractical. It follows that, unless a fixed time for completion can be implied, agreements may be deemed void for uncertainty.

5.125 If the parties have stipulated a fixed time for completion, the general rule is that a failure to meet this deadline will not entitle the innocent party to terminate the agreement[1] . However, a right to terminate may arise in the following cases:

— where the parties have expressly stipulated that 'time shall be of the essence' in relation to a particular term. The precise wording need not be followed. The contract term must make it clear that delay will invalidate the parties' mutual obligations;
— where the parties have by implication stipulated that time shall be of the essence. The test to be applied is whether 'the nature of breach, its subject matter or the surrounding circumstances make it inequitable not to treat the failure of one party to comply exactly with the stipulation as relieving the other party from the duty to perform his obligations under the contract' (per Lord Diplock in *United Scientific Holdings v Burnley*[2]). Whilst the courts have frequently been ready to imply such a term in the commercial sphere, each contract must be considered in its own factual matrix. A useful example is a contract to arrange the purchase of shares. Since share values are liable to fluctuate following delay, purchasers cannot be compelled to accept late transfers[3];
— where one party is already in delay, and the other gives notice of (a) a further reasonable period for performance and (b) that henceforth, time will be of the essence. The editors of *Chitty on Contracts* highlight two practical considerations to be borne in mind before giving such a notice. First, it is advisable to be 'cautious' (ie generous) in stipulating the further time for performance. This is due to the fact that one party is effectively varying the nature of the contractual term. Hence a court may jealously guard the breaching party's right to be given a proper opportunity of complying with the revised timetable[4]. Second, the consequences of making 'time of the essence' in relation to a particular term or part of the contract will work both ways. Should the party giving such notice not be ready to perform its side of the bargain at the date envisaged, the other party, too, will be entitled to terminate[5];
— where delayed performance deprives one party of substantially the whole of the benefit envisaged under the contract. A useful example is provision of music/ catering at a village fete. Delayed performance of a couple of hours may deprive the organiser of the benefit bargained for[6].

1   Law of Property Act 1925, s 41.
2   [1978] AC 904 at 927.
3   See *Hare v Nicol* [1966] 2 QB 130.
4   See the remarks of Purchas LJ in *Behzadi v Shaftesbury Hotels Ltd* [1992] Ch 1 at 24, CA.
5   See *Chitty on Contracts* (28th edn, 1999) at § 22-014 to 22-015.
6   See generally *Hong Kong Fir Shipping Co v Kawasaki* [1962] 2 QB 26.

5.126 A subsequent extension of time by the parties will not affect the consequences of late performance. Time will remain of the essence. However, a party may forfeit the right to terminate the agreement if, following breach, it continues to treat the contract as binding.

Partial performance

5.127 Does anything short of complete performance of an obligation entitle the defaulting party to payment? The answer is to be deduced, initially, from the terms of the contract, which may expressly provide that nothing short completion will trigger an entitlement to be remunerated. If this is done, the courts will, in all but extreme cases (see paras **5.139–5.146**) respect the bargain struck.

5.128 Absent such express provision, the courts are left to determine for themselves whether a particular obligation is 'entire' or 'divisible'. In straightforward exchange contracts the answer will be clear. For example, patrons will not expect to pay for transport to a theatre, if it emerges the organiser has omitted to secure tickets. In more complex transactions provision for payment by instalments, as commonly found under a fixed-term employment contract, or a major construction project, indicates that obligations are intended to be divisible.

5.129 It will be observed that a finding that particular obligations are 'entire' may result in the innocent party securing a windfall. The effects upon the defaulting party can appear harsh. The courts have developed three tools for mitigating such effects:
— first, under the controversial doctrine of 'substantial performance', innocent parties may be compensated by way of a price reduction or damages for minor failures to complete entire obligations[1];
— second, the fact that an innocent party has chosen to accept a benefit provided will render the perfuming party entitled to a 'quantum meruit' payment. The measure of damages here is not governed by the terms of the contract. A reasonable sum is awarded, by reference to the benefit bestowed. Since the basis for recovery is *free* acceptance of such benefits, the doctrine cannot operate where the innocent party has no real choice as to acceptance[2];
— finally, in cases of doubt, the courts will err on the side of classifying obligations as divisible and hence avoid the above contortions.

1   See *H Dakin & Sons v Lee* [1916] 1 KB 566.
2   See *Sumpter v Hedges* [1898] 1 QB 673.

Tender and performance obstructed by a contracting party

5.130 On occasion, the promissor will be impeded in performing one side of the bargain by failure to co-operate on the part of the promissee. In such cases, it may suffice for the promissor to demonstrate he has 'tendered' performance, only for it to be refused. The significance of the doctrine is evident in two situations:
— first, provision of money due under a contract, provided money is actually forwarded, will bar any claim for interest in subsequent court proceedings following refusal to accept payment. The debt itself will not, of course, be discharged following such a refusal[1];
— second, the fact that goods have been offered to a buyer and refused, may discharge the obligation due. The seller will be entitled to payment, having discharged its side of the bargain. The latter will, of course, remain under an obligation to resell the goods if he can, and hence mitigate his loss.

1   For the technical rules on this subject see *Chitty on Contracts* (28th edn, 1999) at para 22-083 ff.

Breach

Renunciation/anticipatory breach and frustration

5.131 At the time one party informs the other that it is either no longer able, or no longer willing, to perform its side of the bargain a fundamental ('repudiatory') breach will have been committed. Such anticipatory breaches leave the other party with a choice of whether to accept termination, and rescind the contract (see para **5.161**) or affirm and insist upon continuing performance.

5.132 To permit the innocent party to treat itself as discharged, the renunciation must be clear. Three difficulties arise. First, whilst renunciation need not be by way of express statement, words or conduct must be sufficiently clear. A refusal to perform premised upon one party's genuine, albeit mistaken, view of its legal entitlement, will probably not bring contractual obligations at an end. The leading case of *Woodar Investment Development v Wimpey Construction*[1] illustrates the difficulties faced in judging a response. It was not in issue that the innocent party had been faced with a refusal to perform. However, this refusal had emanated from the breaching party's mistaken view that the contract itself entitled it to cease performance. Absent bad faith, such an assertion did not amount to a refusal to be bound. What is more, in purporting to accept the renunciation, the innocent party itself was held in fundamental breach.

1   [1980] 1 WLR 277.

5.133 Second, the contractual obligation renounced must be sufficiently fundamental. The test is whether the obligation was an essential part of the contract. Breach of lesser elements ('warranties') or of distinct parts of a divisible contract will not prevent the parties remaining bound by the remainder. See para **5.135**.

5.134 Third, in very limited circumstances, the court will excuse inability to perform. This is not done lightly, as commercial operators are taken to have foreseen potential changes of circumstance, and allocated responsibility accordingly. However, if the change is such that performance becomes wholly impossible, or radically different from that envisaged at the time of entry, the contract may be brought to an end. See para **5.151**.

Classification of terms, consequences of breach

5.135 In determining the consequences of breach, it is essential to distinguish between three types of obligations:
(1) conditions: breaches of these terms entitle the innocent party to treat the contract as at an end;
(2) warranties: breaches of such terms sound in damages only;
(3) intermediate terms: a term the breach of which may sound in damages, or rescission, depending on the circumstances.

5.136 Classification is in accordance with the intentions of the parties. The act of labelling a term 'condition' or 'warranty' will not be decisive, unless it appears the parties actually intended this label to prescribe the specific legal effects outlined above.

Absent an express indication from the parties, the test for ascertaining a condition has been formulated 'whether breach will deprive the innocent party of substantially the whole of the benefit sought to be derived from the contract'[1]. The courts will thus look at all the circumstances of the case to determine whether the contractual purpose will be frustrated by a failure to meet the term's requirements in full. If so, any breach, however significant, of the term will provide the innocent party with the option of rescinding the contract.

1   See generally *Hong Kong Fir Shipping Co v Kawasaki* [1962] 2 QB 26.

5.137   By contrast, breach of an intermediate, or innominate, term will not invariably give rise to a right to terminate. In determining the consequences of breach, regard will be had to the actual consequences following. If the result is that the innocent party retains the substance of benefits bargained for, and may adequately be compensated by way of damages, the contract will survive. The best example of an intermediate term is a time clause (see paras **5.124–5.126**).

5.138   In some commercial contexts the need for certainty is all pervasive, and courts will be reluctant to classify terms 'intermediate'. Hence the House of Lords has held, in the context of large charter parties, that any failure to meet notification time periods will rescind the contract[1].

1   *Bunge Corpn v Tradax Export South Africa* [1981] 1 WLR 711, HL.

Liquidated damages, penalties and forfeiture clauses

5.139   A variety of benefits may be derived by stipulating, at the outset, that in the event of breach a certain fixed sum will be payable. Upon breach, 'liquidated damages clauses' permit the costs consequences to be dealt with swiftly. Complex computations of actual damages are avoided. The breaching party is able to assess the risk of non-performance at the outset, and obtain insurance accordingly. Further, provided a contracting party is able to point to a fixed sum owed by the breaching party, it is able to set such sums off against other claims made by the latter, even under unrelated contracts.

5.140   Liquidated damages clauses have proved particularly attractive in large scale building contracts, when a multitude of parties are working simultaneously, and the effects of delay by a single contractor upon the overall progress of the project (the 'critical path' to completion) may be impossible to ascertain. A stipulation that £X shall be paid per week of delay avoids the costs and uncertainties of such an analysis.

5.141   The courts have in modern times approved and enforced such terms, subject to two considerations. First, any failure to follow the precise mechanism, and notification periods, for claiming under a liquidated damages clauses will render the latter inapplicable. The parties are thus left to determine damages under general contract principles. Second, if the amount of money to be paid upon breach is disproportionate or oppressive, the courts may strike down the clause as constituting a 'penalty'. The test to apply is whether the parties have made a genuine pre-estimate, at the time of entering the agreement, of likely costs consequences of breach.

5.142   Clauses under which a single sum is stipulated to cover a multitude of breaches, ranging from the trivial to the more serious, have thus been struck down. Likewise, the fact that the penalty payment would vary greatly by reference to extraneous factors indicates that no genuine pre-estimate was undertaken. This is illustrated by the Privy Council's decision in *Public Works Comr v Hills*[1]. The penalty stipulated consisted of forfeit of whatever sum happened to be retained, at the time of breach, by the client to cover for defective work. The extent of fluctuation this fund was subjected to persuaded the Privy Council that this could not be not be viewed a genuine pre-estimate of likely damage.

1   [1906] AC 368.

5.143   Some uncertainty will remain, given that classification turns on all the circumstances of the particular contract. For example, the issue as to whether deductions under a payment mechanism from a unitary charge in a PFI contract have not been before a court to determine whether it is a penalty clause or a genuine calculation of liquidated damages. However, provided the sum stipulated is not wholly disproportionate, or fixed capriciously, liquidated damages clauses may be taken to be valid. The courts have proved particularly generous in upholding sums fixed by parties under contracts where the extraneous factors were unpredictable, and accurate assessment of consequences would have proved all but impossible[1].

1   See *Philips Hong Kong Ltd v A-G for Hong Kong* (1993) 61 BLR 41 (Privy Council), Lord Woolf deemed it insufficient for one party to point to *particular circumstances* where a liquidated damages clause worked in an 'objectionably penal' way. The parties agreement should be upheld, unless, looked at broadly, liquidated damages were 'out of all proportion' to likely loss.

5.144   A similar test has recently been developed in relation to clauses which provide, in the event of breach, for the breaching party to:
(i)   forfeit money/other benefits (forfeiture clauses)[1];
(ii)   become liable to increased payment obligations under a continuing, executory contract[2].

1   See *Workers Trust and Merchant Bank Ltd v Dojap Investments Ltd* [1993] AC 573, PC.
2   See *Lordsvale Finance plc v Bank of Zambia* [1996] QB 752, in this case a default interest increase of 1 per cent.

5.145   The courts have stated themselves ready to examine the 'effects' of penalty clauses rather than the substance they take[1]. Nonetheless, the expanding application of this jurisprudence has yet to achieve comprehensive coverage.

1   See *Lordsvale Finance*, above per Coleman J at 760–763.

5.146   This is illustrated by the present position on 'termination clauses' (or conditions, see above). The Court of Appeal in *Lombard North Central plc v Butterworth*[1] considered a clause providing the innocent party with an option to terminate upon late payment of instalments. This was deemed immune from 'penalty clause' scrutiny. The court did not go on to examine whether entitlement to termination, however slight the delay, could be considered proportionate. It thus appears that penalty clause scrutiny is limited to clauses directly stipulating that sums of money be paid/forfeited, rather than ones indirectly achieving this result. The ruling has been criticised, and may yet be revisited[2].

1   [1987] QB 527.
2   See *Chitty on Contracts* (28th edn, 1999) para 27-116.

Waiver

5.147   One of the fundamental principles of contract law is that a party is not permitted to blow hot and cold in communicating its intentions. It follows that a promise, representation or statement of intention may affect the parties' rights under the contract, albeit that no consideration is provided in return. The fact that one party has relied to its detriment upon a representation may render inconsistent conduct inequitable. This is discussed at para **5.193–5.194**.

5.148   Even without detrimental reliance, the parties may be taken to have waived their rights to insist upon strict compliance with the contract in the following circumstances:

1   election of one of several inconsistent remedies flowing from breach: the most common example here is where breach entitles an innocent party to choose either to repudiate the agreement or affirm, and thus continue to insist upon performance. Once this option has been exercised, the choice will be binding;
2   prospective waiver: communication that a party will excuse the other from future performance under the contract. Any subsequent attempt by the representor to enforce performance, or withhold its own side of the bargain will be unsuccessful;
3   waiver of all remedies: upon breach, a party may evince an intention neither to affirm the contract, nor to pursue a remedy in damages *Wilken and Villiers* label this 'total waiver'[1];
4   'waiver clauses': it is, of course, always open for the parties to specify within the contractual terms that certain remedies will be unavailable, or certain breaches excused. Such terms will be upheld, subject to scrutiny as to the reasonableness, in the case of consumer and standard term contracts[2].

1   Classification of types 1 to 3 follow that outlined by the editors of this monograph, see Wilken and Villiers *Waiver, Variation and Estoppel* (2nd edn, 2001) chapter 3 ff.
2   See the Unfair Contract Terms Act 1977, and the Unfair Terms in Consumer Contracts Regulations 1999, SI 1999/2083.

5.149   Two essential conditions must be present to found a waiver. First, the waiving party must be fully apprised of its entitlements, as well as the facts underlying its rights. Second, an unequivocal intention to waive its rights must have been communicated. In cases of election, such a choice may easily be deduced by the acts of a party continuing or withdrawing from the contract. The courts will, however, treat claims by the breaching party that there has been a prospective waiver, or a waiver of all remedies, unsupported by consideration, with more scepticism. A clear intention to waive the specific right in question must be evident[1].

1   See *Ets Soules & Cie v International Trade Development Co Ltd* [1980] 1 Lloyd's Rep 129, CA.

TERMINATION

5.150   A contract may be terminated or discharged in one of four ways: by frustration, by breach, by agreement or by performance. The last of these is dealt with at paras **5.119–5.130**. The first three are dealt with immediately below.

Termination by frustration

5.151   The doctrine of frustration provides that a contract may automatically be terminated if, during the term of the contract and without either party being at fault, some event takes place which renders further performance impossible or illegal, or so radically changes the circumstances that it becomes something objectively fundamentally different from what was originally contemplated by the parties[1].

1   *Davis Contractors Ltd v Fareham UDC* [1956] AC 696, HL.

5.152   One obvious example of an event which renders further performance impossible is the destruction of the subject matter of the contract, as in the case of *Taylor v Caldwell*[1], in which a music hall which the claimant had agreed to hire from the defendant was destroyed by fire through no fault of either party. Similarly, contracts for personal services, such as contracts of employment, are frustrated by the death or permanent ill-health of either party to the contract.

1   (1863) 3 B & S 826.

5.153   Alternatively, the subject matter of the contract may, again for reasons which cannot be blamed upon either party to the contract, continue to exist but nonetheless become unavailable, as, for example, when a ship is requisitioned[1]. Where a contract has a fixed term and the subject matter is only temporarily unavailable, the courts will consider the length of the likely interruption as a proportion of the length of the contract. The higher the ratio, the more likely that the contract will be found to have been frustrated. Where it is only a particular method of performance which becomes impossible, the contract will only be frustrated if that particular method was essential to the performance of the contract and was specified, either expressly or by necessary implication, in the contract itself[2].

1   *Bank Line Ltd v Arthur Capel & Co Ltd* [1919] AC 435, HL.
2   *Tsakiroglou & Co v Noblee Thorl GmbH* [1962] AC 93, HL.

5.154   If a change in the law renders further performance of a contract illegal, the contract will be frustrated. So, for example, the outbreak of war may render further performance of a supply contract illegal as 'trading with the enemy'[1]. Where the illegality is only temporary or partial, it is only if the illegality substantially or fundamentally affects the performance of the contract that the contract will be frustrated[2].

1   *Fibrosa Spolka Akcyjna v Fairbairn Lawson Combe Barbour Ltd* [1943] AC 32, HL.
2   *Cricklewood Property Investment Trust Ltd v Leighton's Investment Trust Ltd* [1945] AC 221, HL.

5.155   In exceptional circumstances, a contract may be frustrated because of the occurrence of some extraneous event which means that although further performance is both legal and technically possible, it is radically different in nature from what was originally contemplated by the parties. The most famous example of such a case is *Krell v Henry*[1], where the defendant hired a flat in Pall Mall from the claimant during the daytime only for two days for the sole purpose of watching the coronation of Edward VII. This was postponed due to the King's illness, and the contract was found to be frustrated. However, the case of *Krell v Henry* has subsequently been very narrowly construed as applying only to cases where the particular purpose (eg in *Krell v Henry* the happening of the coronation) was the 'common foundation' of the contract[2]. A contract will not be frustrated where a change of circumstances makes it more difficult or less profitable to perform but not radically different in nature[3].

1   [1903] 2 KB 740, CA.
2   *Amalgamated Investment and Property Co Ltd v John Walker & Sons Ltd* [1977] 1 WLR 164, CA.
3   *Davis Contractors Ltd v Fareham UDC* [1956] AC 696, HL.

5.156   The courts have placed a number of limits on the doctrine of frustration. First, the alleged frustrating event must not be 'self-induced', that is to say brought about by the fault of one of the parties. If it is, it will constitute a breach of contract by the defaulting party. The burden of proving that the frustration is self-induced lies on the party which so alleges[1].

1   See eg *J Lauritzen AS v Wijsmuller BV (The 'Super Servant Two')* [1989] 1 Lloyd's Rep 148.

5.157   Second, the relevant contract may contain express terms which deal with the potential occurrence of a frustrating event. If that event (illegality excepted) then occurs, then the doctrine of frustration does not apply, and the risks will fall as specified by the contract. The courts will interpret provisions of this type narrowly[1].

1   *Metropolitan Water Board v Dick Kerr & Co Ltd* [1918] AC 119.

5.158   Third, there is authority to the effect that if one party to the contract had special knowledge which meant that it did in fact foresee or should reasonably have foreseen that the alleged frustrating event would occur, then that party will be liable for breach of contract and the doctrine of frustration will not apply[1]. However, this decision was thrown into doubt by Lord Denning in the case of *The Eugenia*[2], which suggested that even a foreseeable event might frustrate a contract. In still another case, *WJ Tatem Ltd v Gamboa*[3], it was held that if both parties foresaw or should have foreseen the frustrating event but failed to make contractual provision to deal with it, then the contract may be frustrated. Accordingly, the status of the law in this area is unclear.

1   *Walton Harvey Ltd v Walker and Homfrays Ltd* [1931] 1 Ch 274, CA.
2   [1964] 2 QB 226, CA.
3   [1939] 1 KB 132.

5.159   The legal consequences of a finding that a contract is frustrated are set out in the Law Reform (Frustrated Contracts) Act 1943. In summary, any sums paid before the occurrence of the frustrating event and termination of the contract are recoverable and any money payable before that date ceases to be payable (s 1(2)). However, if the party to whom sums are paid or are payable had already incurred expenses in performance of the contract at the date of termination, then the court may order that that party be compensated for such expenses up to a maximum of the amount of money paid or payable before termination (s 1(2)).

5.160   Alternatively, if one party has, as a result of anything done by the other party in performance of the contract and notwithstanding the occurrence of the frustrating event, obtained any valuable benefit other than money before termination, that party may be ordered to pay a just sum in respect of that benefit. The sum is to be determined by taking into account all the circumstances of the case, including whether the party receiving the benefit has incurred expenses in performance of the contract before termination in respect of which no award has been made under s 1(2) (s 1(3)).

Termination by acceptance of repudiatory breach

5.161 Breach of contract is considered at paras **5.131–5.138**. In summary, it occurs when a party to a contract fails to perform (actual breach), or indicates that it does not intend to perform (anticipatory breach), its obligations under the contract.

5.162 As discussed above, obligations may be classified into those less important obligations whose breach entitles the innocent party to sue for damages only (known as warranties) and those more important obligations whose breach entitles the innocent party to terminate the contract as well as suing for damages (known as conditions). For a third type of obligation, the innominate term, the remedy for breach will depend upon the nature and extent of the breach.

5.163 All breaches of a condition and serious breaches of innominate terms will be repudiatory breaches, which entitle the innocent party to treat itself as discharged from further performance of the contract if it so chooses. If it elects to accept the repudiatory breach and terminate the contract, the innocent party must communicate that fact to the repudiating party. If it fails to do so within a reasonable time, then it may be deemed to have waived the breach.

Termination by agreement

5.164 Parties to a contract may agree between them to terminate the contract. However, consideration (see paras **5.55–5.63** above) will be necessary to support such an agreement. Where neither party to a contract has completely performed its obligations under the contract, the contract is wholly executory, and consideration can be found in the promise of each party to forego the right to compel the other to perform. By contrast, where a contract has been completely performed or executed by one party, then the other party's promise to abandon the contract will not, on the face of it, be supported by consideration. Such an agreement to terminate will only be enforceable by the party who has not completely performed if he provides fresh consideration ('accord and satisfaction', see eg *British Russian Gazette and Trade Outlook v Associated Newspapers Ltd*[1]) or if the agreement is made in the form of a deed (see eg *Foster v Dawber*[2]).

1 [1933] 2 KB 616 at 643.
2 (1851) 6 Exch 839 at 851.

5.165 Even without the execution of a deed or accord and satisfaction, the party who has not completely performed may be able to resist enforcement of the original contract by the other party (who has completely performed) if it can show that the other party is estopped from resiling from his representation that he would not enforce performance by the other party or alternatively has waived his rights to demand performance. In exceptional circumstances, the court will infer the abandonment of a contract from a long period of delay or inactivity on both sides[1].

1 *Andre et Cie SA v Marine Transocean Ltd* [1981] QB 694, CA.

5.166 Where a contract is executory on both sides, it may be possible to 'unravel' it completely by means of an agreement to rescind[1]. Where a contract has been fully executed on one side, it may still be rescinded so long as the party which has not fully performed returns the performance that it has received, in exchange for which it is released from its own obligation to perform[2]. The consequence of an agreement to rescind is that the previous contract is completely discharged and cannot be revived[3].

1 *Davis v Street* (1823) 1 C & P 18.
2 *Raggow v Scougall & Co* (1915) 31 TLR 564.
3 *Andre et Cie SA v Marine Transocean Ltd* [1981] QB 694.

5.167 Alternatively, a contract may be terminated by a provision (known as a condition subsequent) in the contract itself which specifies that a previously binding contract will terminate on the occurrence of a specified event. One obvious example is the elapse of a certain period of time from the conclusion of the contract. Another is a contractual notice provision in an employment or other contract.

CONTRACTS (RIGHTS OF THIRD PARTIES) ACT 1999

5.168 The Contracts (Rights of Third Parties) Act 1999 reforms the rule of privity of contract which provides that a person can only enforce a contract if he or she is a party to it, even if the contract was made for his or her benefit[1]. The Act received the Royal Assent on 11 November 1999, however, unless stated otherwise in the contract, it does not apply to contracts entered into within six months of that date[2]. The C(RTP)A 1999 enables a third party (C) to acquire rights under a contract, in so far as that is the intention of the parties to the contract (A and B). To date, there is no case law on the Act. The C(RTP)A 1999 is of particular relevance to local authorities where procuring on behalf of other entities, for example school governing bodies.

1 For judicial statements about the effect of the C(RTP)A 1999 on the doctrine of privity see *Alfred McAlpine Ltd v Panatown Ltd* [2001] 1 AC 518, HL.
2 C(RTP)A 1999, s 10(2), (3).

Circumstances when a third party can enforce a contract under the C(RTP)A 1999

5.169 There are essentially two circumstances in which C can acquire rights under a contract. The first is where the contract expressly provides that C may enforce a term of the contract[1]. The second is where the contract 'purports to confer a benefit' on C unless, on a proper construction of the contract, it appears that the parties did not intend the term to be enforced by C[2]. It is not sufficient if the contract happens to benefit C, it must 'purport' to confer a benefit. This will be a matter of construction. There is no definition of 'benefit' in the Act. It would appear that benefit can include any performance due under the contract between A (the promisor) and B (the promisee). It can also include the benefit of an exemption or limitation clause[3]. C must be expressly identified in the contract by name, as a member of a class or as answering a particular description but need not be in existence when the contract is entered into[4]. It is insufficient for C to argue that the contract refers to him by implication.

1 C(RTP)A 1999, s 1(1)(a).
2 C(RTP)A 1999, s 1(1)(b) and (2).
3 C(RTP)A 1999, s 1(6).
4 C(RTP)A 1999, s 1(3).

5.170   The Court of Appeal has stated that local authorities who perform their statutory functions by contracting out to the voluntary sector, should bear in mind that the contract between the local authority and voluntary sector should contain provisions which fully protects the rights of recipients of the services under the Human Rights Act 1998[1]. An action could then be brought for breach of contract by the service recipient relying on the C(RTP)A 1999, on the basis that the contract purported to confer a benefit on him or her, provided that the other conditions for enforcement in the Act are satisfied.

1   *Heather v (1) Leonard Cheshire Foundation (2) A-G* (2002) Times, 8 April at para 34.

Remedies

5.171   When C has a right to enforce a term of a contract between A and B, he or she has the same remedies available for breach of contract as if he or she were a party to the contract, including damages, injunctions and specific performance[1].

1   C(RTP)A 1999, s 1(5).

Right to rescind or vary the contract

5.172   The C(RTP)A 1999 restricts the circumstances in which A and B may rescind or vary the contract so as to affect C's rights under the contract by virtue of the Act, without C's consent[1]. The details of the rules are not set out here. However, it should be remembered that the restrictions laid down by the Act can be overridden by express terms in the contract to the contrary[2].

1   C(RTP)A 1999, s 2.
2   C(RTP)A 1999, s 2(3).

Defences of the promisor

5.173   The C(RTP)A 1999 contains detailed provisions which set out what matters A can rely upon by way of defence, set-off or counterclaim in an action brought by C for enforcement of the contract between A and B pursuant to s 1[1].

1   C(RTP)A 1999, s 3.

Position of promisee

5.174   The C(RTP)A 1999 does not affect B's rights to enforce any term of the contract[1], although, there are provisions to protect A, the promisor, from double liability[2].

1   C(RTP)A 1999, s 4.
2   C(RTP)A 1999, s 5.

Other rights of third party

5.175   The C(RTP)A 1999 does not affect C's ability to enforce any rights arising from the contract between A and B which existed before the Act but restricts rights under the Unfair Contract Terms Act 1977[1].

1   C(RTP)A 1999, s 7.

Exceptions

5.176 The C(RTP)A 1999 sets out a number of situations where it does not apply, including contracts for bills of exchange and certain contracts for the carriage of goods[1].

1 See further C(RTP)A 1999, s 6.

REMEDIES

Damages

5.177 In order to recover damages, a party must show three things:
(a) the contract has been breached;
(b) this breach has caused loss to itself; and
(c) this loss was foreseeable at the time of entry into the contract.
Limb (a) is considered at para **5.131**.

5.178 The courts have approached the ascertainment of limb (b)'s causal link as a common sense question of fact. Two further issues need to be considered. First, the claimant himself may bear a share of the damages if it is shown that he or she did not take reasonable steps to mitigate the loss. The crucial test is whether the claimant has acted reasonably. Provided he has done so, even an increase in loss resulting from attempted mitigation will be recoverable. Second, an intervening act of a third party which can be said to be a 'truly independent', or unforeseeable cause of the loss, will break the chain of causation. A mere breach of contract, or common law duty by a third party will not suffice, unless the claimant is in law responsible for the third party.

5.179 This is illustrated by the recent decision of the Court of Appeal in *Clark v Ardington*[1]. The claimant had placed his vehicle, damaged by the defendant's negligence, with a repair company. The repair took 12 days, which was considered to be seven days longer than was reasonable. The claimant was held entitled to recover the cost of hiring a substitute vehicle for the full 12 days. The Court of Appeal found he had 'acted reasonably in placing the car in hands of respectable repairers', and was not in law responsible for their default. Any perceived injustice could be remedied by the defendant seeking a contribution from the repairers themselves[2].

1 [2002] EWCA Civ 510, [2002] 3 WLR 762.
2 See para 121 of the judgment.

Measure of damage

5.180 The general measure of damage is the cost of placing the claimant in the position he would have been had the breach not occurred. In cases of fundamental breach, the claimant may, in the alternative, repudiate the contract and seek to be put in the position he would have been had the contract not been entered.

5.181 If measures necessary to achieve the precise contractual specifications are wholly disproportionate, the courts may limit a claimant to the difference in value (including, in the case of consumer awards, a modest disappointment award) between the performance contracted for and performance actually provided Thus in *Ruxley Electronics v Forsyth*[1], the £21,000 costs of deepening a swimming pool diving area by 18 inches was deemed unreasonable, given the built pool's equality of value. A disappointment award of £2,500 was allowed.

1   [1996] AC 344.

Remoteness

5.182   The general rule in contract is that for damages to be recoverable, they must either be likely to occur in the usual course of things, or constitute risks which have specifically been drawn to the contracting parties'attention prior to entry. Given each party's opportunity of notifying any unusual risks prior to entry, it will be seen that the remoteness test is relatively strict. Thus failure, in *Hadley v Baxendale*[1], to notify a repairer that a shaft delivered was urgently required for use in the claimant's mill barred the latter from recovering loss of business due to its late return.

1   (1854) 9 Exch 341.

Contribution

5.183   Under the Law Reform (Contributory Negligence) Act 1945, the courts apportion responsibility on a just and equitable basis, in accordance with each party's share of blame and causation. Recourse to the Act is available where contractual duty is concurrent with a tortious one[1]. In addition, Part 20 of the Civil Procedure Rules allows the courts a wide discretion to join cases conveniently managed together. The Court of Appeal's indication in *Clark v Ardington*[2] is that third parties who have contributed to damage should be joined as parties to proceedings and responsibility apportioned accordingly.

1   See *Forsikrings Vesta v Butcher* [1989] AC 852.
2   [2002] EWCA Civ 510, [2002] 3 WLR 762.

Limitation

5.184   Claims in contract must, in general, be brought within the six-year time period specified under the Limitation Act 1980, s 5. Time starts to run from the time the cause of action accrues. A contractual claim is complete when the breach in question has occurred. Unlike in tort, it is unnecessary that damage has resulted therefrom. There are several further special rules:
(a)   where the breach of contract results in personal injury, claims must be brought within three years from accrual of the cause of action, or the date of the claimant's knowledge of injury[1];
(b)   actions for negligence, where there is concurrent contract/common law duty furnish the claimant with a six-year period from cause of action to institute proceedings, or three years from the date on which the claimant was in a position to know the cause of action accrued[2]. The overall cut off point is 15 years from the act or omission causing damage[3];
(c)   defective products, the cut off point three years from the date of knowledge[4];

(d)   actions brought under a deed, the claimant has 12 years from the date on which the cause of action accrued to start proceedings[5].

1   See Limitation Act, s 11.
2   Limitation Act, s 14A.
3   Limitation Act, s 15.
4   Limitation Act, s 11A.
5   Limitation Act, s 8.

Specific performance

5.185   A party may only insist upon specific performance if:
(a)   it has a legitimate interest in such performance; and
(b)   the contract is of a type amenable to such an order.

5.186   In determining whether the claimant has a legitimate interest, the test applied is whether damages would provide an adequate alternative remedy. Contracts for the purchase of unique items, such as land, antiques and works of art will readily satisfy this criterion.

5.187   A justice-based approach has been developed in considering adequacy of damages, the courts on occasion considering the fact that damages would merely be nominal, and leave the claimant unjustly enriched[1] as justifying specific performance. Likewise, of course, the claimant's own conduct may render it inequitable to order specific performance, as will hardship resulting for the defendant.

1   *Beswick v Beswick* [1968] AC 58, HL.

5.188   Contractual terms that will never be specifically enforceable are those entailing personal service, or extensive, continuing dealings between the parties. The rule is based on the impracticality of the courts compelling parties who object to further dealings with each other to co-operate. On the borderline lie building contracts where, provided the courts will not be embroiled in an undue amount of supervision, specific performance may be ordered.

5.189   Of particular interest is *Wolverhampton Corpn v Emmons*[1]. There, the Court of Appeal ordered the defendant who had obtained land from the local authority in consideration, inter alia, of erecting a specified number of houses thereupon to carry out works stipulated. Damages would clearly have proved an inadequate remedy.

1   [1901] 1 KB 515.

5.190   When faced with a negative obligation to desist from a particular type of conduct, the courts have proved less reticent. Unless the consequences would result in particular hardship (such as a restriction de factor compelling a defendant to continue personal service) or run contrary to public policy (such as an unreasonable restraints of trade clause) injunctions are granted as of course.

Declaration

5.191   A final remedy of particular interest to parties awaiting payment of contested sums of money under a contract is the action for a declaration. This remedy permits a party, following an allegation of breach, to seek the court's assistance in resolving the matter without having to await the claimant's institution of proceedings.

Public interest

5.192   One further point should be borne in mind. The public interest may, on occasion, influence the range of relief available. Thus in *R v Ministry of Agriculture, Fisheries and Food, ex p Monsanto plc*[1] the Divisional Court refused an application for interim relief, here suspension of the Pesticide Safety Directorate's approval of sale and advertisement of a herbicide, on the grounds that such relief could frustrate the public interest. Free competition would have been restricted unduly.

1   [1999] QB 1161.

ESTOPPEL

5.193   The doctrine of estoppel is a flexible tool which may, in a range of specific circumstances, render communications by a contracting party ('the representor') relied upon by the other contracting party ('the representee') binding even absent supporting consideration. The main instances of relevance for present purposes comprise:
(a)   estoppel by representation—the representor has induced the representee to rely to its detriment upon a *representation of fact*. The representor may be estopped from denying the truth of the state of affairs it has communicated;
(b)   estoppel by conduct—the parties under the contract have engaged in a continuing course of dealings, which is only consistent with a certain state of affairs being true. Each may be estopped from denying the existence of the state of affairs thus presumed;
(c)   promissory estoppel—the representee relies, to its detriment, upon the representor's assurance that it will not enforce a particular contractual right. The latter may only resile from this promise in so far as it is just and equitable to do so;
(d)   proprietary estoppel—the representor indicates that it intends to demise a piece of personal or real property upon the representee. The latter relies upon this promise to its detriment. The former may only resile from its promise in so far as it is just and equitable to do so.

5.194   Three points should be noted. First, the above provides but a rudimentary summary of the main types of estoppel, and the reader is referred to specialist textbooks on this evolving and controversial area of the law[1]. Second, the courts continue to be reluctant to submit public authorities to the full rigour of these doctrines. Given the need to preserve flexibility in policy-making, and keep decisions within the bounds of statutory powers, the scope for enforcing extra-contractual promises is limited. Third, the courts have held the line in refusing, regardless of reliance, to enforce performance of positive obligations flowing from gratuitous promises of future intent.

1   See Wilken & Villiers *Waiver Variation and Estoppel* (2nd edn, 2002) chapter 7 ff.

MISREPRESENTATION

5.195 If a party can show that it was induced to enter a contract by the other party's misrepresentation of fact, it may invoke one of the following remedies:

(1) rescission—this remedy is always available following a fraudulent representation, and may follow from a negligent/innocent representation provided it is sufficiently significant. As discussed above, the option to treat contractual obligations at an end may be lost upon failure to exercise this option promptly;

(2) damages—in cases of negligent/innocent misstatements, the Misrepresentation Act 1967, s 2(2) gives the courts a discretion to award damages in lieu of rescission. Damages are further available following negligent, but not innocent, misstatements, even outside the ambit of s 2(2).

CHAPTER 6

Drafting techniques

Elizabeth Cooper

DRAFTING SKILLS

6.01   The aim of contract drafting is to set down wording which will ensure that the document reflects accurately the contractual agreement between the parties. This means that an understanding of the detail and scope of the contract is paramount.

6.02   Contract drafting is a written word skill and, as with other forms of drafting, it is an acquired skill which develops through practice. Drafting contracts is a specialist area of law and although local authority officers can benefit from a good precedent bank, legal advice is recommended for any contract other than very straightforward contracts, and in particular PFI and PPP contracts. The reason for this is that more technical, legal and financial considerations are present in these type of contracts and if they are not precisely drafted then the consequences for the local authority can be considerable.

6.03   Drafting is an ongoing process and it is unlikely that a contract can be drafted without further amendment at first attempt, particularly where the terms are to be negotiated. There are some basic principles to remember:
— try to use plain English;
— be precise;
— be clear;
— avoid ambiguity;
— avoid too many cross references;
— avoid over-use of definitions;
— use spell checks but always proof read as well;
— check for grammatical errors;
— draft in the present tense;
— use document control—always know which version of document you are working on;
— be aware of your timescales and draft accordingly.

6.04   Local authority contracts can range from the simple to the complex depending on the contractual relationship which is being entered into. A PFI contract, for example, may easily be 80 pages long without any appendices but a straightforward consultancy agreement for management consultancy services may easily be as few as eight pages. However, the skills required for drafting contracts of any length or complexity and general drafting rules are basically the same.

WHAT IS THE CONTRACT FOR AND WHAT STAGE HAS BEEN REACHED?

6.05   Before getting started it is essential to understand what is being contracted for and what stage has been reached in the process. Understand the purpose of the contract and the drafting can follow. Too often local authority officers, and in some cases contract lawyers, simply change the title and commencement date of a contract negotiated for a previous agreement when preparing a first draft. Whilst this may save time and effort it may have serious implications. At the very least the local authority will look unprofessional and it could reduce its bargaining power, particularly if the terms are still to be negotiated.

6.06   Contracts are usually entered into following a procurement, also known as a tendering process, and many are subject to European procurement rules. For contracts which are being procured through a restricted or open procedure a draft contract should be sent out with the invitation to tender. For contracts which are subject to a negotiated procedure it is advisable to prepare, at the very least, a set of heads of terms to be negotiated and these may be as detailed as the contract demands. For example, what is the local authority's starting position, ie minimum requirements and points open for negotiation?

6.07   It is not uncommon for contractual arrangements to be agreed through negotiations without a draft contract and then for contract lawyers to be asked to reflect what has been agreed in a written contract post-negotiations. This can cause confusion and lengthy follow-up negotiations whilst the parties trawl through minutes of meetings to try and recall what was actually agreed. It is therefore always advisable to have a starting point and as mentioned above, this could be in the form of heads of terms. If negotiations have already taken place then it is important to gather together details of what has been agreed; this may be in the form of notes from meetings, correspondence or records of telephone conversations.

CHECKING THE BASICS

6.08   Once you ascertain the stage the contract has reached, the next step is to consider the following basic details:
— What is the contract for?
— Who are the parties?
— What is the term of the contract?
— What is the expected commencement date?
— What is the estimated contract price?
— What has already been agreed? For example, a payment mechanism based on performance.

6.09   The final contract will usually comprise a number of different contract documents together with and appended to the contract conditions. Typically these documents may include:
— specification;
— contract drawings;

— pricing document/payment mechanism;
— service delivery plans;
— forms of warranties.

6.10   The various supporting contract documents usually sit as appendices to the contract conditions. Alternatively articles of agreement are drafted which incorporate the various contract documents and the contract conditions and articles of agreement are executed simultaneously. Whichever method is chosen, the aim is to ensure that all relevant contract provisions are incorporated and are legally binding on the parties.

6.11   The contract conditions are generally referred to as the contract and this can cause confusion. For example, an officer may be asked to draft a contract but what is really required is the contract specification. Officers sometimes mistakenly believe that their lawyer will draft all the contract documents whereas in practice the specifications, pricing documents and performance measurement systems are best drafted by an officer or adviser with appropriate knowledge and expertise, particularly when the contract is for something highly technical, for example systems software and support. Of course, the lawyer will need to ensure the contract documents accurately reflect, and are consistent with, the contract as a whole.

DOCUMENT CONTROL

6.12   Document control is essential. It is always useful to have discussions about simple matters such as font type and size and document control before anyone involved with the drafting of the contract documents starts any detailed work. At the beginning of any tender exercise:
— establish who has responsibility for drafting the contract and each of the other contract documents;
— agree who will have access to read and/or amend the draft documents;
— agree how documents will be amended, for example, new versions of each document or documents which highlight changes made;
— agree how documents will be distributed, for example hard copies or electronically by email;
— check IT systems compatibility with internal and external recipients of documents;
— consider whether an intranet can be used;
— agree a confidentiality/data protection strategy.

LEGAL POWERS

6.13   Ensure that the local authority has the relevant powers to enter into the contract. This may appear obvious but hard lessons have been learnt in previous court challenges and even though the well-being powers included in the Local Government Act 2000 introduced new contracting powers it is always worth double checking at the start. The various powers used can be inserted in the recitals which sit at the beginning of the contract, so it is clear from the outset to tenderers or bidders that the local authority can lawfully enter into the contract. Further comfort will be given in the form of a certificate under the Local Government (Contracts) Act 1997 where applicable.

STARTING FROM SCRATCH OR CLEAN SHEET DRAFTING

6.14   It is very unusual for a contract to be drawn up which is not in some way similar to other contracts. There are many developing areas, particularly in ITC, which require new forms of contract but it still remains rare to be asked to draft something completely unique. However, drafting is, after all, recording what the agreement is for, how it will be performed, how it will be paid for and monitored and how and when it may end. Specifications and supporting technical documentation may become more and more complex but the fundamental basis of the contract conditions will still seek to fulfil these primary objectives. It can be daunting being asked to draft a contract for a pilot project, but the best way is to have a go and seek appropriate specialist advice. Provided the project team involved understands what end result they are aiming to achieve then drafting the contract will become easier over time by amending the draft as required as the project progresses. If clean sheet drafting is required then precedent clauses from comparable types of contracts can be useful as a starting point.

SETTING OUT THE FRAMEWORK

6.15   A typical contract will include:
(i)   a front sheet naming the contract and the parties;
(ii)   recitals;
(iii)   definitions;
(iv)   conditions of contract;
(v)   execution page;
(vi)   schedules/appendices.

6.16   Recitals are commonly used at the beginning of the contract and these can be useful for three reasons:
(1)   for listing the legal powers which the local authority is entering into this contract;
(2)   for stating the offer and acceptance of the parties to enter into the contract;
(3)   as a lead in to the conditions of contract.

6.17   Before drafting commences a skeleton of the contract conditions should be drawn up. Plan each clause carefully and think about the order of clauses required. It is then easier to identify those areas which may be tricky and as each clause is drafted a tick-sheet can be used to monitor progress. Always remember the overriding purpose of the contract being drafted, as this can help the drafter remain focused. Drafting each clause may take time. Words and phrases may need changing or grammatical changes may be required. Each clause should be precise, concise, grammatically correct, easily understandable and unambiguous. Any contract should follow a sequence; for example chronological, ie the pre-conditions near the beginning and the termination provisions near the end. It is a useful exercise to ask another person to read the draft to see if it makes sense. When drafting a long document it is easy to get too lost in the minor detail and lose track of the whole picture.

USE OF PRECEDENTS

6.18 Precedents can either be invaluable or create headaches in different scenarios. Precedents should always be used with forethought. Over-use of precedents as a shortcut to drafting can result in a contract which looks more like a jigsaw puzzle than a coherent document. The contract being drafted must accurately represent the contractual agreement.

6.19 Precedents are useful for providing a framework, ideas on layout of clauses and clause structure and in some cases a near complete contract which can be used. Confidence may be gained from knowing that the contract has been tried and tested.

Industry precedents

6.20 Precedent forms of contract are particularly useful for construction, also known as 'works contracts'. The construction industry is well used to these forms of contract and using them as a basis for a local authority works' contract can save time and effort; which means contractors may start on site more speedily. There are numerous industry standard contracts (*Emden's Construction Law* is a useful source of information and guidance) and contract precedents. However, where local authorities tender their works' contracts using the standard forms of industry contract they still need to consider whether any amendments are required to the industry standard to reflect the authorities' standing orders or other requirements. Any amendments can be set out in the preliminaries to the contract documents. In addition, the various professional consultants involved in delivering works contracts, including chartered surveyors, architects and engineers have precedent forms of contract. More recently the construction industry has produced partnering documents which can provide a framework agreement (for example, the ACA Standard Form of Contract for Project Partnering).

In-house precedents

6.21 Local authorities will have copies of previous contracts entered into and individual lawyers often have a set of contracts which they use and adapt for new contracts. Some local authorities have a bank of precedent contracts for straightforward contracts such as consultancy agreements for management services, which can be adapted easily for new contractual arrangements. Although this can save time, it is important to check whether there have been any legal developments since the precedent was last used. If the precedent contracts are updated regularly then this should not be a problem but it is not uncommon to see contracts which still refer to the Data Protection Act 1984 and not the more recent 1998 Act.

6.22 There are potential problems with using in-house precedents. Quite often the precedent contracts have been used, so that the specific details have been completed, for example the parties, term of contract, the contract price. If this is the case it is essential to remove all trace of the previous contract specific details and include the new details as appropriate. Also, cutting and pasting from different contracts can be useful but will inevitably result in changes to font, clause and page numbering. There is the added risk that confidential commercial details from a previous contract find their way into the new contract.

Commercial precedents

6.23   Published commercial precedents can be very useful, particularly when asked to draft a contract which is new to the person drafting and possibly to the local authority. In particular they can be useful for looking at drafting of specific clauses. If the exact type of contract is not included it is worth looking at comparable types of contract for ideas on wording.

6.24   A number of different precedents may be useful but if the content does not accurately reflect the requirements of the agreement to be drafted they will require adapting, particularly where precedents were drafted by different authors. Different drafting styles may have been used which look inconsistent when placed in the same document.

6.25   Standardisation guidance for PFI contracts produced by the Treasury Task Force and now updated by the OGC which includes specimen contract drafting, has been the subject of consultation with the public and private sectors and should therefore contain clauses commercially acceptable to both sectors. For PFI contracts the guidance should be followed unless there are justifiable reasons why a local authority should depart from it, for example where there are special project features. The guidance is also useful for similar types of PPP or complex contracts, particularly where the parties have agreed that payment will be based on key performance criteria. The local authorities specific guidance contained in the *Standardisation of Local Authority PFI Contracts*[1] is useful for best value provisions which can be included in contracts, particularly medium to long-term contracts where best value reviews will take place during the contract term.

1   Produced by OGC and published by Butterworths.

SUPPLIERS TERMS AND CONDITIONS

6.26   Suppliers often submit their own terms and conditions when tendering for local authority contracts. Usually the instructions to tenderers will prohibit these terms on the basis they may represent irregular tenders. However where a contract is not subject to tendering requirements, usually because the estimate value is below the EU or contract standing order thresholds, then they can provide a useful starting point. Where used, the local authority should ensure that the terms do not contradict its own contractual requirements, for example payment may be required within a certain number of days which would be administratively impossible for the local authority to deliver.

ACCURACY IN DRAFTING: ENGLISH GRAMMAR

6.27   Practice in drafting contracts usually results in good grammatical use but the precise nature of drafting requires thought on appropriate grammatical contract. The need for certainty in drafting cannot be over-emphasised. If a party is being obligated to do something then the wording must state this in clear terms. The use of the auxiliary verbs 'shall' and 'will' provide this certainty whereas using 'should' and 'would' are less certain and imply that the obligation is discretionary. For example 'The contractor shall provide the service in accordance with the requirements of the specification'. Compare with 'The contractor should provide the service in accordance with the specification'. What happens if the contractor fails to comply with this obligation? In the first example if the contractor fails to meet the obligation it will be in breach of a contractual obligation which may lead to a default and rectification procedure coming into play. In the second example it would be difficult to say for certain that the contractor is in breach as it only states that the contractor should do something, not that it must.

6.28   'When' and 'where' are also words of significance in drafting. Use 'where' when referring to a contractual event which may occur more than once, for example 'Where the contractor is in breach of any of the conditions of this sub-clause 25.3 then the Council shall be entitled to deduct an amount from the monthly payment in accordance with the payment mechanism'. Use 'when' where there is only one such possible occurrence: for example 'When the contractor has delivered the goods to the location, the Council will pay the delivery payment in accordance with clause 6'.

6.29   Where possible statements in contracts should be drafted using an active as opposed to a passive voice, for example:

'If the contractor fails to remedy the specified default within 14 days of the default notice being delivered, the Council shall be entitled to deduct an amount from the monthly payment in accordance with the payment mechanism'.

The same term using the passive voice would be:

'If the specified default is not remedied by the contractor within 14 days of the default notice being delivered, an amount shall be deducted by the Council from the monthly payment in accordance with the payment mechanism'.

6.30   It is not uncommon to see drafting which links a number of possibilities together by the use of and/or. However, linking more than two possibilities together within the same paragraph can cause ambiguity. The use of separately drafted sub-clauses will provide greater clarity.

6.31   Capital letters are often used to emphasise words but this practice should be avoided. Defined words and expressions should have capital letters at the start of each word to indicate that those particular words have been defined and the reader can refer to the definitions section for meaning.

PUNCTUATION

6.32   Punctuation makes a document easier to read. Leases are commonly drafted without punctuation. However, for contract drafting punctuation is recommended as it can assist in certainty of terms and avoid ambiguities. Contract clauses can often be lengthy and without punctuation be difficult to understand. Where long sentences have been used, consider breaking them down into sub-clauses or new sentences.

6.33 Careful consideration should be given to the use of punctuation, particularly the use of commas and semi-colons. A comma used incorrectly can totally change the meaning of a sentence. Brackets are commonly used to surround a subsidiary phrase to include an explanation or addition which is an aside to assist the understanding of the sentence but over-use should be avoided.

TYPES OF CONDITIONS

6.34   The conditions of contract will contain a mix of boilerplate clauses, ie clauses so commonly used as to be considered standard in the type of contract being drafted, and conditions specific to a particular contract. Boilerplate clauses are ready made and can be inserted into contracts as appropriate, whereas contract specific clauses require more work and should be appropriate to the specific contract being drafted.

6.35   Typically, the boilerplate clauses may include:
— definitions and interpretations;
— data protection;
— the contract manager;
— confidentiality;
— contractor's staff;
— taxes;
— waiver;
— compliance with statute and good practice;
— invalidity and severance;
— health and safety and environmental protection;
— Contracts (Rights of Third Parties) Act 1999;
— assignment and sub-contracting;
— notices;
— force majeure;
— law and jurisdiction;
— operational and financial records.

The clause headings are illustrative only but they do show that time spent drafting boilerplate clauses will save time on drafting future contracts. It is still essential to check each contract thoroughly as the individual boilerplate clauses may need to be adapted to suit particular contract requirements, for example some social service contracts may place an obligation on the contractor to carry out police checks on its employees.

DRAFTING SPECIFIC CONDITIONS

6.36   More time will be spent on drafting conditions which are contract specific but it will be time well spent as the contract conditions should then accurately set out the intentions of the parties. Guidance on drafting some of the main contract specific conditions in relation to local authority contracts is set out below.

6.37 Contract specific clauses set out obligations and rights of the parties which are specific to the contract being entered into and will typically include:
— pre-conditions;
— the service;
— equipment;
— licence to use the premises;
— payment and price review;
— warranties and indemnities;
— change procedure;
— best value;
— service user surveys;
— complaints;
— TUPE;
— insurance;
— dispute resolution;
— defective service;
— liquidated damages;
— termination;
— break option.

There may be additional clauses which are required and these can be added in as appropriate to where the clause will best fit in the document. Other clauses may not be required; for example a continuous improvement obligation within a best value clause where the contract term is only for one year. Using the skeleton framework will assist the drafter in ensuring all the appropriate clauses are included.

APPROPRIATE CONDITIONS

6.38 It is essential that the conditions accurately mirror the contractual agreement between the parties. Conflicting conditions will create uncertainty and even where the contract contains a clause which deals with ambiguities or conflicts between the various documents, it is preferable to ensure the document is drafted correctly before the contract is executed. Disputes may arise over contract interpretation once the contract is underway. Time spent proof reading the contract can help avoid disputes and any subsequent knock-on effects in service delivery.

6.39 It is not uncommon to see contract clauses which refer to events outside the scope of the contract, such as terms and conditions which the parties contract to perform before the services commencement date. For example a clause may state that the contractor is required to provide a performance bond. These clauses should not be confused with pre-conditions which state the circumstances which must be achieved before the contract can be enforced or performed, for example a pre-condition that the contractor must by a certain date have obtained planning permission to carry out works.

6.40 If the contract is being negotiated then as part of the invitation to negotiate the local authority should require that the other party seek legal advice on the draft contract at an early stage in the process. In addition, the instructions should require the bidder to mark up the draft contract by agreeing each clause separately or providing alternative proposed drafting. The contentious clauses will then focus the parties contract negotiations.

REFERRING TO CONTRACT DOCUMENTS IN DRAFTING

6.41   Throughout the contract conditions cross-references will be made to other contract documents, for example the specification. The documents which make up the contract must be incorporated and this is usually achieved by appending the documents as schedules or appendices to the contract conditions. Once the contract drafting is finalised and the parties agree the final documentation the contract and schedules or appendices can be bound into the contract document which may comprise a number of volumes depending on the size of the final document.

DEFINITIONS

6.42   Definitions can assist in creating a coherent document. As a general rule definitions should be listed together in alphabetical order without additional definitions being included in the body of the contract. In some cases it may be appropriate to include definitions which are only used for a specific clause in the clause concerned. As with precedent clauses there are precedent definitions which can save time on drafting, for example where there are cross-references to statutory or regulatory indices or regulations. One of the most important definitions is the definition of Contract or Agreement. Once defined ensure the same term is used throughout the document. After each re-draft revisit the definitions section to check whether definitions are still applicable or not.

6.43   Avoid over-using a number of definitions within the same clause, if possible and cross referring back to a clause which included the defined word, for example 'RPI' means the indices referred to in clause 5. If clause 5 states that the indices to be applied is the RPI then the reader is still not clear as to the meaning of RPI.

6.44   Be as precise as possible in the definition and cross-refer to appendices and clause number as appropriate. For example:

> '"Services" means the services to be provided by the contractor in accordance with clause 3 of this contract and with the requirements of the Specification annexed hereto as Appendix 1'.

VARIATIONS TO THE CONTRACT

6.45   One of the most common omissions from contracts are clauses which deal with changes to the provision of services and changes to the contract conditions. 'Variations to contract' is a term which is often mistakenly used to cover both scenarios. One alternative is to divide the clause into 'variation procedures for changes to services' and 'variations to the contract conditions'.

6.46 Changes to the services may include additional service requirements, omissions of services contract may include an amendment to a specific term, for example an extension to the contract period.

BEST VALUE

6.47 Best value clauses should be drafted as appropriate to the nature and term of the contract. Consideration must be given to the following:
— how this particular contract will assist the local authority in meeting its best value duty under the Local Government Act 1999;
— the level of input required from the contractor;
— the number of reports and the timing of such reports;
— any key performance indicators which the contractor's performance will be measured against;
— any customer survey satisfaction monitoring requirements;
— whether any services will be benchmarked;
— whether benchmarking may lead to parts of the service being retendered.

PAYMENT PROVISIONS

6.48 For straightforward contracts the payment provisions will usually be included in the contract conditions. These will deal with submission, checking of and payment of invoices. In addition, reference may be made to referral to dispute resolution where disputes arise about the amounts payable.

6.49 The payment provisions may cross-refer to a separate document which forms part of the contract documents. This may be a pricing document completed by the contractor which details prices and rates against specified items. For more complex contracts, including PPP/PFI contracts, a payment mechanism schedule will form part of the contract documents. This document, usually drafted by financial advisers, sets out how payments under the contract will be calculated and details any arrangements for deductions for poor performance and/or non-availability of services. The contract conditions will refer to the payment mechanism in various clauses dealing with adjustments to the contract price.

DISPUTE RESOLUTION

6.50 Dispute resolution clauses are increasingly important, particularly as they are more commonly seen by courts and practitioners as a prerequisite to court action. Blanket referrals to arbitration are commonly used in contract drafting, often without forethought on the appropriate dispute resolution procedure for a specific contract. It is important to consider:

(i)   the nature of the contract;
(ii) the term of the contract, for a short-term contract referral to external dispute resolution may be inappropriate;
(iii) whether there is a recognised or statutory scheme which deals with disputes for this type of contract;
(iv) whether there will be an informal dispute resolution procedure followed by a referral to an adjudicator or expert;
(v)   whether it is appropriate to refer to different experts on particular disputes, for example for disputes relating to calculation of estimates or disputes relating to performance levels.

6.51   One of the best ways to determine which is the appropriate dispute resolution procedure is to look at recent comparable contracts. Which dispute resolution procedure is applicable will also depend upon the relationship between the parties; partnering or longer-term contracts may require a sophisticated mediation procedure, whereas a fast track procedure, for example, may be more suitable for a one-year services agreement.

TERMINATION PROVISIONS

6.52   Termination clauses are one of the most important provisions of a contract. Termination should always be seen as a last resort and where dispute resolution procedures are included, the two clauses should be linked provided it is appropriate to the nature of the dispute.

6.53   Termination can arise through fault or no-fault of either party. The drafting should accurately reflect:
—   which incidences will lead to termination;
—   which incidences may lead to termination;
—   whether any compensation is payable by either party should such incidence arise;
—   any obligations on the parties for service continuance.

6.54   Termination clauses are often copied from previous contracts but this is not recommended. For example, a previous contract may contain a break provision which permits either party to terminate on three month's notice. If the new contract is for a term of 15 years leaving in the three-month's break provision may lead bidders to price their bid higher on the basis that the contract may be terminated early. Termination for default is an area which is frequently ignored in drafting. It is not uncommon to see a condition that the contract may be terminated for any breach of any of the conditions. This is not only too widely drafted, it is not necessarily legally enforceable. Termination for breach would need to be justified as a substantial breach. For each contract the events which may constitute a substantial breach should be considered and included as appropriate. The case of *Rice (t/a the Garden Guardian) v Great Yarmouth Borough Council*[1] is useful for considering termination for persistent breach provisions and what amounts to a substantial breach justifying termination.

1   (2001) 32 GLR 4.

6.55 Insolvency events should be included in the termination provisions. Boilerplate provisions are commonly included to allow for any insolvency event regardless of the contractor's status. Taking out any irrelevant provisions will assist in creating contractual certainty and make the clause easier to read and understand.

CONTRACT EXECUTION PROVISIONS

6.56 The layout of the contract document should indicate how the contract will be executed, ie as a deed or underhand. If the contract is to be executed as a deed the articles of agreement may sit at the beginning of the contract or at the end of the contract conditions. In both cases it is essential to state which documents are incorporated into the contract. Separate articles of agreement are commonly used where there are several volumes of contract documents. Before contracts are prepared for execution the contact should be proof read one last time and this should include checking all numbering, cross-referencing, spelling and grammar and consistency in the contract documents. Parties should execute each contract document and contract drawings as well as the articles of agreement.

CHAPTER 7

Managing contracts

Chris Lee

INTRODUCTION

7.01 In the good old days under compulsory competitive tendering ('CCT') (c 1981–1999) local authority contract management was a reasonably straightforward affair. A detailed specification was written, setting out what the contractor was to do, when they were to do it and how they were to do it.

7.02 Things have changed quite dramatically since then with the introduction of best value, PFI and the development of public private partnerships. The growing pressure on local authorities to be 'enablers' rather than 'providers' of services has made it increasingly important for local authorities to be aware of what they need to do 'in-house' and what can be undertaken by a third party. Contract management is now an issue that prudent local authorities are addressing at a very early stage of the procurement process. They have recognised that it is not solely a matter of ensuring that there is a budget in place for a contract management team once the contract has been completed; it is also about making an assessment at the start of the process as to what the private sector partner (PSP) is being required to do, how its performance will be monitored, the relationship between it and the local authority, how the contract will develop over time and what the benefits to the parties will be.

7.03 Contract management therefore is not something that arises at the end of the contract. It is becoming an increasingly important aspect of the procurement process and is often tested and evaluated as part of the procurement phase (eg the PSP's approach to 'partnering'). There is an increased awareness from those that use the services about what they can do if they are not satisfied and, as a result, local authorities now need to be far more knowledgeable about what a PSP is doing on their behalf. In addition, although service provision is effectively removed from a local authority's direct control, that local authority, because of its continuing statutory duties in relation to that service, must be in a position to not only make sure that those duties are not being compromised, but that the service is being delivered in line with the contract.

7.04 The contract manager (the client) should be in a position to know not only the business that has been outsourced but also the measures and controls within the contract, to have expert input from client departments and to be able to address issues as and when they arise in a proactive and knowledgeable manner. In other words, there will be an 'intelligent client'.

7.05 Failure properly to address contract management issues can lead to a number of difficult scenarios for a local authority. In particular, it might not be able to ascertain whether what is being provided is value for money, is an improvement over previous provision or is what its customers require.

THE BASIS FOR MANAGING THE CONTRACT

Specification

7.06   In order for the PSP to be able to provide the service it needs to know at an early stage what it will be required to do. One of the major changes local authorities currently face is the shift away from an 'input' specification, where the methodology of undertaking and providing a service together with those who were to undertake the work was set out in the contract, to an 'output' based specification, where the local authority states the outcomes it expects to see together with corresponding standards for measuring performance, and it is for the PSP to work out within its own organisation how the outcomes will be met.

7.07   The specification will detail the areas of work to be undertaken by the PSP. It needs to be sufficiently detailed to not only provide those bidding for the work with the information to properly price their bids, but also to provide the information as to what the successful bidder will be doing. Ideally, the full specification should form part of the invitation to tender, and should provide comprehensive information about each service that is to be procured.

7.08   If the local authority wants a PSP that can provide the services as seamlessly as possible, the provision of a detailed specification will provide a greater possibility of that occurring[1]. A contract that does not start off on the right foot inevitably means that both parties are chasing to catch up; service provision might suffer, monitoring of performance is more difficult, tensions arise and far more remedial work needs to be done than should otherwise be necessary.

1   A checklist for a sample specification is set out at para **7.103**.

7.09   The PSP should also be required to provide method statements as to how it will, or proposes to, undertake those services. Although these might change over the life of the contract (and will be updated accordingly), it is necessary for the local authority to have them at as early a stage as possible. The local authority will retain the method statements for information if it needs to 'step in' during the life of the contract and provide the services, or for any subsequent provider who will be taking over at the end of the contract.

Example of information found in a method statement

7.10   A method statement will set out the guiding principles for delivery of the service by the PSP. The local authority should however be aware that a generic method statement might not be sufficient if a number of services are being outsourced. It is not usual for 'one size' to fit all, and in general method statements will be developed as the PSP gets to grips with the local authority's operating requirements and develops its own way of delivering the service. The following, however, should all be included in a method statement to some degree although the exact details will obviously depend on the nature of the services and the relationship between the local authority and the PSP:

— arrangements for producing a client manual to be prepared by the PSP and contain frequently requested information about procedures, addresses and telephone numbers and, where appropriate, proformas in respect of letters, order forms etc. It can also be useful if a brief structure chart is provided showing the relationship of the PSP to local authority officers together with the arrangements for democratic accountability;
— arrangements for identifying names of those in the PSP who will be the contact points for orders, contract information and liaison between the parties;
— arrangements for issuing orders and those personnel able to issue and receive them;
— arrangements for acknowledging orders issued;
— arrangements for reporting the information required in the terms and conditions of contract;
— arrangements for providing progress reports;
— arrangements for overview meetings;
— steps to be undertaken in respect of the particulr piece of work (ie explaining the process);
— arrangements for any estimates on costs for a particular order (this is more usual in an administrative services outsourcing rather than the more blue collar oriented contracts);
— arrangements for orders on non-routine/non-standard transactions including procedures for dealing with such issues;
— arrangements for identifying when the work has been completed (eg completion of record sheets; memo to instructing officer etc);
— arrangements for dealing with complaints and disputes.

MANAGING PERFORMANCE

Measuring performance

7.11   The introduction of the duty of best value in the Local Government Act 1999 also brought with it a statutory definition of 'performance indicators' and 'performance standards'[1]. 'Performance indicators' are defined as factors by reference to which a best value authority's performance in exercising functions can be measured[2]. 'Performance standards' are defined as standards to be met by best value authorities in relation to 'performance indicators'[3].

1   Local Government Act 1999, s 4(1).
2   Local Government Act 1999, s 4(1)(a).
3   Local Government Act 1999, s 4(1)(b).

7.12   The duty of best value and the local authority's general requirement to exercise its functions with regard to a combination of economy, efficiency and effectiveness has therefore meant the adoption of formalised methods of measurement of performance. The performance indicators and performance standards applied will, to an extent, be based on central government targets, Audit Commission criteria and standards of performance, and those additionally set by a local authority to meet particular conditions in its area.

7.13   Once the local authority has determined which outputs will be measured, it will need to consider how the PSP's performance will be assessed during the life of the contract. Being able to analyse performance means that the local authority will also be able to incorporate into the contract a number of management controls that will allow it and the PSP to ensure that service delivery is under continual review.

7.14   The local authority therefore needs to have a number of 'markers' against which it can identify whether the service is being provided as required, is falling below those requirements, or indeed being delivered beyond them. From these the local authority will be able to: compare how the PSP is faring against other similar public or private services; benchmark (to identify progress against other local authorities), review performance (to identify changing requirements) and, perhaps in the case of over achievement, award bonuses and incentive payments to the PSP.

7.15   In order to manage properly the PSP's performance the local authority will need base information of its own performance in delivering the services that it wants to outsource. The local authority should not put itself in a position whereby it is not in control of the process or of the outcomes of the contract. Thus, in preparing the tender documentation, it will need to have information available about current levels of performance, the strategic aims and statutory obligations of the local authority in terms of improvements sought and how the performance, upon which improvements will be based, is going to be measured. This will apply as much as if the service is currently performed by a PSP as it would if the local authority had remained as the provider.

7.16   To be in a position to collate that information, the local authority will have to decide the areas of work that it requires to be undertaken in the contract. This exercise should dovetail with the work that it is doing in preparing the specification.

7.17   Collating the information can be a time-consuming, and at times, problematical process. The earlier it commences the easier it will be to identify the areas of concern. It is in everyone's interests at an early stage to determine what the local authority's current levels of performance are and how they would be expected to improve during the life of the contract. It also enables any prospective PSP to assess the likely resources required to meet the local authority's aims and objectives and the period over which they can be achieved. It might be that the local authority is being over-optimistic in its aims. For example, low standards in-house coupled with a short contract period might not provide sufficient time for the PSP to achieve the wished-for outcomes. In such circumstances, therefore, it is in the interests of both parties to be realistic and practical in their aims and objectives. It is of no use to a prospective PSP to contract to meet the local authority's objectives when it is quite clear that it is not going to be feasible. In such circumstances, tensions will inevitably arise within the relationship, aided by pressure from elected members and service users who are frustrated that promises which have been made are not going to be kept and levels of expectation are therefore not met.

7.18   This does not mean that the performance targets should be so easy that they do not incentivise the PSP to meet targets that the local authority might not be able to achieve. Performance targets should be realistic but challenging and there is nothing wrong with a local authority setting goals higher than those currently set re the in-house team. However, authorities should accept that the PSP must be able to fulfil the contract and make a profit over the period.

7.19   Thus it is imperative that at the earlier stages of the procurement process officers and members of a local authority (and external stakeholders where relevant) fully discuss what the contract to be let is intended to do, how it is intended to do it and why it is being done.

7.20 Once that has been determined, the levels of performance that the PSP is expected to reach in any contract year will have to be thoroughly considered. Although the requirements will usually start with a base level that represents current performance, it is common for incremental increases to be provided for throughout the life of the contract such that by the end the local authority is receiving a service that is significantly better than the one at the beginning. However, it might be that in some circumstances the services are already being provided in-house at a level that cannot be improved, although there might be the opportunity for them to be provided more cost effectively. As such, service provision might require some reorganisation (for example the provision of new or alternative methods of delivery) which will make its provision no more efficient but more 'user friendly', or 'customer-centric'. To enable this to be the case the performance regime will need to contain a means of identifying where and when new technologies or investment will be required (for example, creation of a 'one stop shop' for customer services, or investment of new ICT).

7.21 The central issue, however, will be the delivery of the service, in accordance with identifiable targets, to the local authority's customers. The methods the PSP uses to deliver it is perhaps not as important for the local authority as ensuring that agreed and identified performance targets are met. For example, if missed bin collections are not reducing, or housing benefit payments are not being made within the agreed timescales, then the local authority might have cause for concern.

7.22 Performance will be linked to targets and targets will be based, as far as possible, on objective and identifiable criteria. The PSP has to be as certain as it can be that what it is being required to do is identifiable and achievable.

7.23 An example of how the performance targets might be set out in a contract is set out below.

Table 1

Indicator	PI Ref	Current Standard	Year 1	Year 2	Year 3	Year 4	Year 5	Monitoring frequency
Customer satisfaction	KPI 1	Not measured	Set baseline (not less than X %)	Baseline + 2% (max of 80%)	Baseline + 4% (max of 80%)	Baseline + 6% (max of 80%)	86%	Quarterly
Average number of days to register planning applications	PI 6	4 days	4 days	3 days	3 days	2 days	2 days	Quarterly
To answer telephone calls within 15 seconds	PI 7	95%	95%	96%	96%	97%	97%	Quarterly

7.24 In the above table, local authority standards have not been provided for the first year of the contract for 'customer satisfaction'. This situation should be avoided if at all possible. It means that there is no more than an 'agreement to agree'. There will also be considerable debate between the local authority and the PSP as to what the base level should be and it will be very difficult to argue that the level should be any higher than the PSP's performance in that first year. This in turn might mean the PSP is happy not to concentrate on that area because they are in a position of strength regarding setting (or renegotiating) the performance levels for the coming years. If the first year performance was not as good as the local authority was expecting, this might impact on the ability (or willingness) of the PSP to meet the aspirational targets during the remainder of the contract.

The performance mechanism

7.25   The performance mechanism will provide the base levels for acceptable and unacceptable performance over the life of the contract.

Performance indicators

7.26   Performance indicators derive from the level of performance by the PSP that the local authority consider to be acceptable, or which it is required to meet.

7.27   The local authority needs to make sure that it does not create too many performance indicators. There needs to be a balance between key performance indicators (KPI), which clearly affect the strategic direction of the local authority, and lower level indicators which reflect the PSP's general ability to provide services to the local authority's customers. KPI's are likely to be the matters that will be most closely monitored and be of the greatest concern to the local authority. They might be cross-cutting, in the sense that they are not service- or function-specific, but they will as a whole affect the local authority's position in the market place in terms of ranking against other local authorities and its ability to deliver particular services.

7.28   Therefore, the local authority needs to think long and hard as to the issues that are strategically the most important, as it will be these that it will need to address within the KPIs. Again, these will need to be considered at a very early stage and be part of the planning process for the whole contract. That is not to say that during the life of the contract there is not a change mechanism in place which will enable the local authority, in consultation with its PSP, to amend the targets to reflect changing priorities nationally and/or locally.

7.29   Underpinning these 'strategic' KPIs can be any number of lower level, managerial, performance indicators (PIs). These will identify particular service areas and feed into the 'strategic' KPIs. The relationship between the two will need to be carefully considered, but a PI is likely to involve the production of regular management information which the local authority would normally have provided if it had been undertaking the service in-house, to enable it to identify weak spots or improvements. Although PIs might be far greater in number, they should only be included if they are relevant to the contract. Collecting information for the sake of it is a waste of time for everybody involved. It can also mean an inordinate amount of time is spent on the minutiae of the contract, which might inhibit the PSP getting on with the job.

7.30 A PI will not usually (on its own) attract any of the more stringent default criteria which will apply for failure to perform, but could, for example, have a cumulative effect in causing a bonus payment not to be awarded, or for a rectification plan to be produced and implemented by a PSP. Failure to rectify the fault could lead to possible performance deductions by the local authority (ie payment of damages to the local authority as a result of a continued failure to provide a particular level of service).

7.31 There will need to be a linkage between these two levels of performance indicators to ensure that:
(a) the PSP will be addressing all the issues under the contract and not focus on one or two which might provide it with quick wins against the overall strategic aims of the local authority; and
(b) the PIs are relevant to the strategic KPIs.

Performance standards

7.32 During the life of the contract the levels of performance might well change and become more, or less, onerous. Therefore the contract should provide an element of flexibility to try and meet the changing obligations upon the local authority and PSP. Changes in service delivery could arise from a number of factors: from a system of best value reviews, performance benchmarking with other like services, and performance review of the PSP as well as changes in legislation, volumes of work or technology. They should not arise from incorrect performance data provided by the local authority during the procurement process!

7.33 It is therefore vital that the local authority is able to respond and involve itself very quickly in what the PSP is doing. Failure to do so can damage the reputation of the local authority, lead to court action by those affected (for example, a breach of the local authority's statutory duty), perhaps affect its funding from central government (particularly as more and more of it is tied to performance) and lead to a lack of trust between it and the PSP.

7.34 When a PSP is not providing the service required there should be within the contract an escalating range of remedies available to the local authority:eg a mechanism whereby the PSP is required to rectify the poor performance. If the PSP continues to under-perform following an initial 'warning', the contract should contain a provision for performance deductions and in the very worst case, the opportunity for the local authority to either step in itself to either provide the service (or those parts that are not acceptable) or appoint a substitute contractor to undertake part or all of the service provision, or terminate the contract. This procedure will be reasonably lengthy and should be undertaken at the same time as negotiations between the parties regarding the perceived failings.

7.35 One of the most common methods of identifying the PSP's level of performance is by the use of 'traffic lights'. Green will be an acceptable standard, amber will be a failure at a level slightly below green and red will be either a substantial failure or be a cumulative failure of a number of amber warnings.

7.36 An example of performance monitoring in a waste management contract is shown at Table 2:

For each contract task that is measured, three performance levels are identified as follows:

— **Green**: at this standard the PSP is performing to the contract standard;
— **Amber**: at this standard the PSP is not meeting the contract standard and the provisions of the performance monitoring clause will apply to improve performance to the geen standard;
— **Red**: at this standard the PSP is performing below the contract standard and the provisions of the performance monitoring clause will apply.

7.37

Table 2 Performance standards

Description	Green	Amber	Red	Frequency of monitoring report	Strategic deduction
Number of missed collections (as defined in Part X of Schedule) per [X00,000] collections of household waste:				Weekly and per calendar month	Yes
(a) from the services commencement date until 31 March 2004 (Year 1)	Below 100	100–500	More than 500		
(b) from 1 April 2004 until 31 March 2005 (Year 2)	Below 75	75–400	More than 400		
(c) from 1 April 2005 onwards (Year 3 +)	Below 50	50–300	More than 300		
Percentage of people satisfied with cleanliness standards:				Annual	Yes
(a) from the services commencement date until 31 March 2004 (Year 1)	Greater than 48%	43–48%	Less than 43%		
(b) from 1 April 2004 until 31 March 2005 (Year 2)	Greater than 56%	49–56%	Less than 49%		
(c) from 1 April 2005 onwards (Year 3 +)	Greater than 65%	55–65%	Less than 55%		

7.38 Finally, where there are difficulties in maintaining performance, the local authority might wish to consider increasing the level of monitoring within the particular service area until such time as the service delivery is back on track.

7.39 It is also necessary to remember that performance is not only performance of the services under the contract. It should also address issues of how the PSP conducts itself generally. For example, a notifiable health and safety incident might mean that the amber 'traffic light' is triggered.

Incentivisation

7.40 Although incentivisation can arise through the possibility of performance deductions for under-performance, the local authority might wish to consider using a carrot as well as a stick. Successful delivery of services might be a reason to make 'bonus' payments to the PSP for over-achievement in a particular area of the contract. This needs to be carefully addressed in the performance mechanism to ensure that concentration by the PSP in one or two areas that attract bonuses is not to the detriment of other areas of the service where the PSP takes a commercial view that failures in those are outweighed by success in others. The local authority needs to be sure that all the services are being delivered as required and not just some.

Again, robust information will enable the local authority to identify those areas which are succeeding, as well as those that are not.

Best value review

7.41   Section 3 of the Local Government Act 1999 places a duty on every local authority to consider how their services are to be provided having regard to economy, efficiency and effectiveness. A contract should be subject to the best value duty and impose a requirement upon the PSP to assist the local authority with any best value review of the services provided by it.

Customer satisfaction survey

7.42   The local authority will also want to ensure that the people receiving the service are satisfied with it. The contract should provide for an annual customer satisfaction survey which will help inform the local authority and PSP as to how the PSP's performance is perceived by its users.

Annual service review

7.43   This is based upon the monitoring information provided over a contract year and will flag up to the local authority and the PSP:
(i)   any sticking points or areas which are not succeeding as they had hoped; or
(ii)   any areas of success.

7.44   In addition, as the contract and relationships develop, the PSP might well wish to change the way it delivers a service and these review periods give both parties the opportunity to discuss how that can be done.

Performance benchmarking

7.45   Performance benchmarking is a useful tool to measure the ongoing delivery of services or works against other, similar, service providers in the public and private sectors. It provides an 'independent' measure of how the PSP is addressing the service delivery issues against those of similar authorities and service providers and provides valuable information for the local authority and its PSP in respect of the future development of the contract.

Changes to the contract

7.46   Where as a result of a service review, a rectification procedure or changes in legislation, the local authority or PSP wish to change how part (or all) of a service is delivered, the contract should provide a mechanism to permit changes to terms and conditions. Such a provision should allow for the initiative to be taken by a co-operative rather than confrontational method of addressing the issue at hand.

7.47   As for all other aspects of the contract it is important that where issues (positive or negative) arise which might require a change to the way a service, or part of a service, is delivered, they are dealt with as soon as possible. Therefore tight deadlines should be placed on dealing with changes to ensure that:
(i)   they are raised as soon as one party realises that a change might be required; and
(ii)   the issue is properly addressed by the parties as quickly and as effectively as possible to ensure as little disruption to service provision as possible.

MANAGING RISK

7.48   The local authority also needs to consider whether the contract is transferring sufficient risk from it to the PSP. One of the main aims of the local authority will be for a service (or services) to be provided more effectively, more efficiently and, in some cases, more cheaply than is currently the case. To enable this to happen the PSP will need to be in a position whereby it is incentivised to deliver and this can partly be achieved by requiring it to carry a significant amount of risk in the contract. If all the risks under a contract remain with the local authority there is very little incentive for an external provider to maximise its efficiency, its ability to deliver services or control its costs if it knows that it is going to be paid in any event.

7.49   The local authority, however, will need to balance the level of risk that it transfers. The PSP will price its bid according to the level of risk to which it considers itself open. A risk that is unacceptable or extremely high will be reflected in the contract price. For the division of risks to be balanced, and for the local authority to be able to know what and how these risks should be managed internally, early identification must be a priority.

7.50   The local authority will therefore need to consider which risks each party should bear under the terms of the contract. A helpful way of visualising this is to draw up a risk matrix which will identify as many of the issues as possible that will arise under the contract, allocate a level of risk (for example low, medium and high) and then allocate them to either the local authority or the PSP or, in some cases, share them. From that there will no doubt be a debate as to whether the risks have been properly allocated, and the local authority will need to bear in mind that the greater the risk being placed on the PSP the higher the price that the local authority will be required to pay for that service.

7.51   For example, in respect of a high risk with little likelihood of it occurring the local authority would no doubt want to ensure that such a risk is not transferred so that the costs in the contract are not unduly skewed. If that risk is transferred the PSP will be pricing for a risk which, if it occurs, will be very costly but is very unlikely to occur in the circumstances of that particular relationship. The local authority will be paying a premium price which may not represent best value for money and which will, to all intents and purposes, be 'dead money'.

7.52 An example of a risk matrix with some of the issues that might be considered for an outsourcing contract is set out in Table 3.

7.53

Table 3 Termination risks

No.	Risk Heading	Definition	Public Sector	Private Sector	Shared
	Termination due to default by the local authority	There is a risk that the local authority defaults leading to contract termination and compensation for the PSP	X		
	Default by the PSP leading to step in by guarantor	The risk that the PSP defaults and the guarantor steps in. This leads to higher costs than agreed in the contract.		X	
	Termination due to default by the PSP	The risk that the PSP defaults and step in rights are exercised by the guarantor. They are unsuccessful, leading to contract termination.		X	
	Part termination – for PSP's non performance	There is a risk that PSP defaults and guarantor steps in – contract terminated		X	
	Part termination – voluntarily by local authority	Risk that the local authority defaults leading to part or whole contract termination and compensation for PSP	X		
	Termination as a result of a force majeure event	There is a risk that an event of force majeure will mean the parties are no longer able to perform the contract			X

FINANCIAL MANAGEMENT

7.54 Management of the contract is not limited to ensuring that services are delivered in accordance with the agreed standards. The local authority will also want to make sure that it is paying for what it is getting. Therefore, an integral part of the management of a contract will be the level of financial control that the local authority has over the service delivery. This is a further reason to ensure that the local authority has a properly resourced and skilled client function so that when it pays the PSP's invoices these have been properly ratified and agreed as being acceptable.

7.55 Payment might be linked to how the contractor is performing the contract. There might be service deductions because of low service delivery and these need to be identified and calculated accordingly. The performance information will need to feed into the payment mechanism to ensure there is a consistent approach to the issues.

7.56 Similarly where there is any variation to a contract the local authority needs to be sure that the costs incurred by that variation are acceptable and that the local authority can afford them[1]. Failure to do so might mean the budget increasing without proper consideration, such that the local authority has to rely on the PSP resolving the increased costs issue and loses effective control of how the contract is run. An additional danger is that the contract costs increase such that the local authority's budget is constantly under pressure, with ramifications for other parts of the local authority's service. As one of the expected advantages to the local authority is likely to be the provision of services more efficiently and more economically than it can provide them, this is going to be an important issue particularly with respect to how the local authority sets its budget for that contract.

1   For more detail on variations to a contract, see para **7.105**.

7.57   On a practical level, the terms and conditions of the contract will have provisions for payment (including timescales), set off and challenging invoices. The local authority needs to make sure that its internal systems are sufficiently robust to meet the agreed time periods. There is little point in agreeing to pay invoices (which will have to be approved and any queries resolved) in a timescale that will never be achieved. It is increasingly the case that a lot of PSP's will be special purpose vehicles ('SPV') which have been set up specifically to deliver the contract. It is likely that the SPV will not have any cash reserves and will be reliant on the payment of invoices to pay its workforce and other overheads. The PSP might be basing its cash flow projections on timely receipt of monies and if this is not forthcoming it might get into financial difficulties with knock-on effects on its performance. Constant failure by the local authority to pay promptly might also mean that the PSP has the right to terminate the contract and receive compensation.

7.58   In addition, it would not be helpful to the developing relationship between the parties if one was constantly failing to meet its obligations. There is also likely to be provision in the contract for interest on late payment of invoices, which will increase the costs to the local authority.

7.59   Therefore, the local authority should make sure payment provisions are realistic and it has systems and procedures in place to ensure timely payment of invoices. This includes ensuring that the parties' banking, payroll and financial systems can 'talk' to each other. At the same time, the local authority needs to ensure that the payment provisions are robust and that only money properly due and owing is remitted. It is far harder to get money back once it has been paid!

Implementing the contract

7.60   Entering into a major contract with a PSP will inevitably lead to upheavals in the local authority, whether it is transferring staff, acquiring information and communication technology (ICT) or passing the delivery of a particular service to the private sector.

7.61   To enable the transition to take place as painlessly and as seamlessly as possible, the local authority should prepare and plan for the event prior to commencing the procurement process. It is often the case that the PSP will be keen to commence the contract as soon as possible after signing, if only for the reason that it will need the income!

7.62 Although the contract might allow for a mobilisation period during which staff are inducted, systems set up (for example payroll) and offices prepared, in reality these often happen at the same time as the procurement process.

7.63 The potential for upset is immense. Staff might be concerned for their jobs, systems might not operate correctly first time and offices might not be ready. All these situations (and plenty of others!) can be avoided if there is proper planning by the parties. Again this requires resources and time, but if properly done will allow for a much less stressful transitional phase than might otherwise be the case.

7.64 Assets too have the potential to be a sticking point. A proper inventory of assets used in the particular service, taken early on in the process, will provide the local authority with information about its resources and what can and cannot be made available to the PSP. It will assist the PSP in knowing what it can utilise in the local authority and what it will need to bring in which in turn will have an impact on the cost of the contract.

7.65 If the local authority has a number of contractors providing services or equipment for a particular service, those contracts might have to be either terminated or transferred to the PSP. Leaving issues such as these until late on in the procurement process might mean additional cost to the local authority because the contractor might either demand a payment to agree to the transfer, or the PSP will have to make more costly alternative arrangements.

7.66 The local authority needs to provide as much certainty as possible in the mind of the PSP about its ability properly to deliver what is needed to provide the services.

Change management

7.67 During the life of a contract there are inevitably going to be changes in the circumstances of either the local authority or the PSP. These might arise because of internal decisions, or as a result of external intervention (for example, a change in legislation), but whatever the origin they might have dramatic effects on the eventual costs of, or ability of the PSP to deliver, the services (or indeed, the services that are to be delivered).

7.68 The ability of the local authority to manage the contract in such circumstances will be dependant to a large extent on the information that it has available. Any proposals for change from the PSP will have to be analysed against the current situation and estimates as to costs and benefits made. Timely responses might be necessary to deal with urgent situations and a failure to address them in a limited timescale might lead to cost and performance consequences which do not benefit anyone.

7.69 Long term, planned for change will still require information to be provided and made available to the PSP. If, for example, the PSP has agreed to undertake major ICT investment, the local authority will perhaps need to plan for the installation of cabling and equipment with the minimum of disruption. By the same token the PSP will need information as to the current systems, what needs to be replaced and when and what the local authority's needs will be in respect of the new technology.

Terminating the contract

7.70   Managing a contract is not going to be all plain sailing, but arriving at a position whereby a decision has to be made by the local authority as to whether it should terminate it is, fortunately, a rare occurrence.

7.71   Provisions for termination by the local authority are likely to be based primarily on failing performance, and usually termination will only be possible if it has the necessary audit trail of information to back up such a drastic act. If it cannot support its contention, it might be faced with a claim for substantial compensation or damages from the PSP.

7.72   It is important to note that termination will also be available to the PSP should the local authority fail to meets its obligations under the terms of the contract. Thus a further important aspect of contract management is to ensure that the obligations placed on the local authority are being met. For example, as has been discussed above, the failure to pay the PSP in accordance with the terms of the contract might well lead to a situation whereby the PSP has the right to terminate the contract and seek damages from the local authority. These could be quite substantial if the PSP has invested a lot of money under the terms of the contract and has not received a return on that investment.

7.73   Proper management of the relationship should hopefully ensure that termination will not occur. It is a matter of last resort and if the situation has got to a point where that sanction is pursued it is likely that the relationship is of such poor quality there is little that can be done to repair it.

The end of the contract

7.74   This period is going to be as vital as any of the contract periods. Whenever the contract ends, whether by expiry of the contract or through early termination, the local authority will need to be sure that it has all the necessary information available to it to enable either it, or a third party, to be able to continue to undertake the services required. Similarly, if the contract is going to be extended to the existing provider the same requirements will be necessary.

7.75   Failure to monitor properly performance over the life of a contract will be exceedingly detrimental to the ability of the local authority to renew it on its own terms. Lack of information and lack of management control will mean that the local authority is increasingly driven into the hands of the PSP in terms of what will be required for the future, how it will be provided and the cost of providing it. Thus, a comprehensive record of information should be available to the local authority at every stage of the contract period (see also paras **7.15–7.17**).

7.76   The above are all matters that will need to be managed during the life of the contract. They are not easy to identify initially and can involve a great deal of work within the organisation prior to the procurement of a PSP. They are, however, vital steps along the way to enable a successful contractual relationship to develop. Failure to address these issues might mean unnecessary extra work during the life of the contract and the increased likelihood of a contract that cannot be properly managed because of the lack of, or provision of incorrect, information. This in turn will shift the balance of power away from the local authority to the PSP, making it (the local authority) reactive to situations rather than proactive.

The intelligent client function

7.77 It is self-evident from the above, but proper contract management requires a well resourced client. A well resourced client will be an 'intelligent client', and the development of the intelligent client should begin, as with all aspects of contract management, at the start of the procurement process.

Development of the intelligent client

7.78 During the procurement of the contract it is vital that those who will be engaged in its day to day management and those that will be required to have input during it are appraised of its aims and objectives and, more fundamentally, its terms and conditions.

7.79 It is good practice to have the person who will be the day to day contract manager involved in the contract negotiations so that he/she is aware of the various issues and have a ready grasp of the matters that need to be dealt with at an early stage. Similarly, heads of service departments that will be using the contract should also be kept 'in the loop' as regards contract negotiations so that they too are aware of how things will develop once the contract is completed. They have a vested interest in ensuring that their services do not suffer on the introduction of the new contract and therefore should be willing and able to be involved in the process from the beginning.

7.80 Often, however, because of a lack of resources and time this is not possible and it is necessary to arrange a series of meetings to discuss the terms of the contract and what it means for each service area. In addition, the elected members of a local authority will also wish to be appraised of the contract's contents because there is often a degree of publicity in respect of it. Members will usually be keen to know the benchmarking provisions, default provisions and performance/payment provisions of the contract. A series of seminars held shortly after the completion of the contract is especially useful together with the production of an 'English language' summary of the main contract terms. This provides a dual purpose, in that it cascades the information throughout the organisation and can help to put peoples' minds at rest over what is required and by whom. Public eyes will also be on the contract to ensure that service delivery does not suffer.

7.81 In some cases there might be a 'TUPE' transfer of staff[1]. In order to ensure as smooth a transition as possible, which will be of benefit to the PSP at the beginning of the contract and also reduce the chances of service provision being disrupted, all staff affected by the contract should be given regular updates as to progress.

1   TUPE transfers are discussed in detail in chapter 15.

7.82   In addition issues of internal communication and explanation of procedures and monitoring requirements should be discussed at all stages of the procurement process. It is important that all parties on the local authority side are aware of their general strategic monitoring role of the contract and are able to identify at an early stage issues that might need addressing. Although there will be a contract manager, that person will not be able to deal with everything and not have an all-seeing eye. They will rely to an extent on the service departments to provide information of good or not so good performance or any other issues that they might wish to raise with the PSP.

7.83   The development of the performance mechanisms, payment mechanisms and specification of service provision should leave the local authority with a contract that is robust for the local authority's purposes. It will, however, mean nothing if the local authority has not addressed the issue of a well-resourced and competent contract management/monitoring team to undertake the necessary work once the contract is up and running.

7.84   There is a tendency for local authorities to consider that once services are being provided externally and, for example, the PSP has guaranteed efficiency savings and an increase in overall service delivery performance, the local authority does not need to bother any further. Having spent a lot of time accumulating data and negotiating the performance mechanism and monitoring regime, the failure to invest in a resource that can help deliver what the local authority requires would be short sighted. A robust, intelligent client, supported by officers who are knowledgeable about the service provision will enable proper and effective monitoring to take place. This does not mean that there has to be a mirror service provider within the local authority, but there does also need to be a facility (whether in-house or brought in from outside) that can advise the local authority on issues that need to be addressed.

7.85   There will be a cost to the local authority for this resource and this should be built into calculations for the overall cost of the contract at the beginning of the procurement process. It is something that is vital to enable the contract to be properly managed and for it to succeed. It also enables the local authority to properly retain control of the contract without being entirely dependent on the PSP which will be providing much of the information to it.

7.86   In essence, the ICF functions will be:
— strategic service planning: ie what sort of local authority do members wish to see over the period of the contract?
— strategic relationship management: how does the local authority's vision 'fit' with what the PSP is being required to do?
— monitoring of control and performance: ie are the aims and objectives (the outputs) of the local authority being met?
— financial control: is the local authority getting what it pays for?
— contract management: is the PSP doing what it says it will?

7.87   It is essential that there is independent monitoring of the PSP's plans and performance and the existence of checks and balances, particularly in terms of financial processes and service delivery. There is no conflict between sound governance arrangements and a degree of close co-operation necessary to effect a successful contractual relationship. The old adversarial nature of CCT is eroding and by any degree practical working, co-operation and good governance are ultimately necessary. They also provide certainty to the parties about what is required of them.

7.88   Proper resourcing and skilling of the management function means that the local authority is far better placed to manage effectively its relationship with its PSP. The local authority does not wish to be in a position whereby it is always being led by the PSP because it does not have the necessary skills or intelligence within its own organisation to query or question the route being suggested by the PSP. In addition, the local authority needs to be able to maintain a level of authority which will provide the PSP with confirmation that it is taking the relationship seriously.

7.89   Therefore, to increase or ensure leverage and the strength of its intelligent client the local authority should consider the following:

1   **Levels of management**: To keep the PSP's senior management involved in the contract it is prudent to ensure a similar level of senior staff involved on the local authority side. Such high level investment in senior staff demonstrates to all those with an interest in the local authority service delivery that the relationship is a serious one and that the aims and objectives (outputs) of the local authority are going to be delivered. This does not mean that senior management involvement is required on a day to day level, but that where serious strategic or managerial issues have to be addressed there is a mechanism whereby they can be dealt with quickly and effectively. For example, in partnering arrangements for outsourcing services there are usually a number of relationships within the contract structure. The day to day management will be undertaken by a contract manager or administrator but above him/her there will be senior officers of the local authority and of the PSP who will determine disputed and strategic issues such as re-engineering of KPIs or payment mechanisms. Above them might be a further layer, perhaps in the form of a partnership board or similar organisation, which might comprise senior elected members, the chief executive of the local authority and the managing director or chief executive of the PSP whereby strategic issues of a long-term nature, performance reviews and developments to the service to be provided by the PSP will be discussed.

2   **Physical proximity**: One of the major issues in letting contracts post-CCT is how to change the 'culture' between the parties. Originally, adversarial positions were adopted, but now the emphasis is very much on partnership working. This will require a change in culture on both sides and is something which the present generation of contractual relationships is seeking to address. There are practical measures that can be undertaken to assist in this shift and also to assist in identifying the common sense of purpose that the relationship is intended to produce. Although this is not practical for every contract, one such measure is to place the local authority and PSP contract managers as near to each other as possible. Although they do not need to be in the same room it would be advisable to have them in the same building if at all possible. This enables easy dialogue between them, meetings can be arranged far more successfully and a good working relationship on a daily basis can be developed. Remote working can lead to blockages in the system which might mean situations that could be easily resolved otherwise becoming exacerbated, which in turn has the potential to produce a 'bunker' mentality in both parties.

3   **Devote time to the contractual relationship**: There will be a number of contractual requirements in terms of meetings and reviews of the contract and it will be a matter for the parties to determine how best these can be dealt with.

As a general guide, day to day issues should be dealt with at a lower level and might be spread amongst a number of individuals depending on the extent of the contract and the level of services provided. In some circumstances, for example in a PFI school, the 'contract administrator' might be the head teacher or an authorised member of staff at the school. The contract does need to enable a constant dialogue to ensure issues are dealt with as soon as possible at as lower level as possible. Failure to address or deal with issues or allowing long periods of time between identification and resolution could lead to an escalation of problems rather than resolution, and so to the breakdown in the relationship. By the same token, decision-making in respect of matters raised must be tightly controlled to ensure the integrity of the contract.

4   **Development of good personal relationships between the parties**: Although the contract will set out targets there will be times when they might not be reached. The reasons might be varied, but the ability to raise them as soon as possible in a non-defensive manner is extremely beneficial. It is a question of balance in all cases but the contract should, to a degree, run itself and matters should not have to be continually referred 'up the chain' before decisions can be made. It might be inevitable in major situations, but for day to day issues these should be resolved on the ground.

7.90   It is worth noting, however, that whatever the relationship is between the local authority and the PSP, all discussions and matters raised in respect of the contract should be noted and confirmed in writing by either side. There is a real danger of 'slack' procedures whereby matters are agreed but not written down which leads in turn to confusion as to what has and has not been agreed as the contract progresses. Part of the monitoring regime has to be a robust and agreed method of recording discussions and any agreed changes to the contract.

7.91   Thus, in light of the above, the in-house management team must be of sufficient strength and seniority to be able to deal with issues as and when they arise. Under-resourced, under-staffed and under-skilled contract management will lead to blockages and an imbalance of power towards the PSP. As this is the local authority's contract and it is its services that are provided, it needs to be in a position whereby it retains control of the process. Without these, a healthy partnering/contractual relationship will be far more difficult to promote.

Retained strategic planning capability

7.92   The local authority needs, throughout the life of the contract, to be able to assess critically a PSP's strategic direction in relation to its service delivery. Without this the local authority will inevitably be in a position whereby it is being dictated to by the PSP as regards those strategies and the direction for service development.

7.93   An even worse scenario would be one where the PSP does not address strategic issues at all and simply continues to deliver the contracted service without anticipation of future development. Thus, when new initiatives/requirements do arise (for example, perhaps in the form of new legislation) they come as a surprise and any changes suffer from inadequate planning. This in turn might mean serious deterioration in the service or an increased cost that otherwise would not have been incurred.

7.94 In order for the local authority's strategic aims and objectives to be met the local authority needs to be able to draw upon skills that will enable it to draw up a strategy, monitor its progress and change and adapt it as the contract progresses. These could be either 'in-house' or bought in through external provision.

7.95 In addition, part of the local authority's role will be to critically appraise the PSP's plans, work with the PSP to develop and improve on their ideas and, where necessary, guide the PSP to address strategic issues and keep them high on the agenda. This will be done at a senior level and should not be considered as one of the day to day issues. It is therefore imperative that the arrangements between the parties allows for sufficient strategic meetings and ongoing dialogue.

Retained operational capability—monitoring and control

7.96 From the above it will be seen that it is extremely important to hold the PSP to its obligations from the outset and for the local authority to be consistent in its purpose. Monitoring is overseeing the PSP's compliance with contractual service obligations, and control is used to get the PSP back on track if monitoring exposes deviation from the agreed service.

7.97 The local authority will need to be aware that in most cases it will be reliant upon the PSP to provide the information. This places the local authority in a difficult position in terms of relying on that information. Another example of the advantage of retaining knowledge will be that the information provided can be analysed and tested against inspections of the service at any time.

Effective control

7.98 Control means discovering, investigating, devising a solution for and finally implementing the solution to a problem in service delivery. The local authority therefore needs to be able to address issues as to how that control is to be exercised. Will it be through deductions, or through a partnering ethos whereby the principal aim of the parties is to achieve the output, or a combination of the two? Whichever solution is chosen, the local authority needs a well-resourced and knowledgeable core of staff that are able to understand and address the issues as they arise, or who can call ipon trusted external advisers for specialist advice. What the local authority does not want is a role that is merely to point out that problems might, or do, exist and place all the responsibility on the PSP to resolve them. Such a situation would lead to further loss of control.

Contract flexibility

7.99 Where contracts are for a lengthy period (for example a PFI contract of 20–25 years or a partnering arrangement of 10–15 years) it is inevitable that changes to legislation, the role of local authorities and perhaps even the ownership of the PSP will change over that period. Therefore the contract manager needs to be aware of changes and build in sufficient advance warning and notice of how these will affect the contract. A properly drawn contract will provide for flexibility over that period as far as possible to enable changes to be addressed within the contract mechanism itself. Appropriate contractual change mechanisms in the contract should be followed and, as mentioned at para **7.90**, properly annotated and agreed. That information then will need to be properly dispersed throughout the organisation to ensure that all parties who need to be aware of it are aware of it and that any changes are properly synchronised.

Required resources

7.100   An example of the local authority's contract management team might be:
(i)   an experienced contract manager with overall responsibility for managing the relationship. This person will need general management skills;
(ii)   distributed, local liaison at each location where the service will be delivered. These people will report on a 'dotted line' basis to the contract manager;
(iii)   someone with expertise in the relative function area being undertaken by the PSP. For example, ICT, finance, human resources etc. This retained expertise must be sufficient to enable the local authority to translate its service needs, and for clear, complete measurable requirements to be addressed by the service provider;
(iv)   someone responsible for contract monitoring, negotiation and communication skills to oversee the contract itself;
(v)   someone with financial skills to measure the requisition and payment process.
In addition, it is usual that regular monitoring meetings will take place between representatives of the local authority and its PSP at various levels of seniority.

Organisational development

7.101   When a PSP is contracted to work with the local authority this usually means that there will need to be organisational change within the local authority itself. This might be because staff are transferring across to the PSP or that as a result of the service provision by the PSP there is an opportunity to restructure within the local authority. These new organisational structures and relationships with the PSP will create new challenges for retained staff and it will be important for a communications strategy to be implemented to appraise staff of what is happening.

CONCLUSION

7.102   Successful management of contracts starts at the beginning of the procurement process. Much of the information that a local authority will require to set performance standards and monitor that performance will need to be collated at that stage. Performance will largely determine the success or otherwise of the contract. It will influence service provision, payment and ultimately whether the contract should continue. To ensure that the local authority is able properly to manage the contract, a well-resourced, intelligent client needs to be in place. Without the necessary information and someone to effectively interpret it, the local authority will be in danger of losing control of its ability to provide services to its residents and businesses on its terms and to their expectations.

APPENDICES

Checklist for a sample specification

7.103   The specification will set out as accurately as possible the nature of the work required. It should contain the following matters:

(i)   **Scope**: this will set out the broad areas of work which will be incorporated within the specification;

(ii)   **Definitions**: this will include any definitions used specifically within the specification which are not contained in the main terms and conditions of the contract;

(iii)   **Service description**: this will describe as accurately and in as much detail as possible the various services that are undertaken within the scope of the specification;

(iv)   **Service exclusions**: this will set out those areas of the service (if any) which are not to be included in the specification;

(v)   **Current service standards**: these will set out the current level of performance of the various services being undertaken against identified targets. Thus, the only performance data that should be included is that which will be measured as part of the performance management regime. That information will be normally used as a benchmark for calculating any improvements required and performance generally by the PSP;

(vi)   **Service volumes**: where there are provisions within the contract for payment to the PSP to be varied depending on the volume of work being undertaken, it is necessary to identify what the current volume of work is and the increases which would trigger any volumetric change mechanism. The volume can be either up or down such that if the amount of work undertaken drops the price might increase because the level of investment would still need to be paid for. Alternatively, it might reduce according to the reduction in volume if the PSP can make the necessary cost efficiency savings. The same might apply for any increase in volume. Up to an agreed level an increase might be capable of being contained within current numbers of staff and type of technical support (eg software). If there was a consistent increase more staff might be required or an upgrade in the software needed which would have to be paid for. It is therefore important that at an early stage in the process the volume of work for each of the processes to be outsourced is identified and monitored to see if there are any noticeable fluctuations throughout a period in the year. In some circumstances the work will not vary (eg street cleaning) except in defined circumstances which will be addressed specifically in the specification and payment mechanism;

(vii)   **Service investments**: if the PSP has agreed to invest in one or other of the services that are to be provided by it, the type of investment and the date by which that investment should have been implemented should be included in this paragraph;

(viii)   **Performance indicators**: these should set out in a table the form of performance indicator that is being measured (ie whether it is a KPI or a PI) and will list the performance indicator reference and the improvement targets that are expected throughout the period of the contract. The current standard will be the baseline and the years of the contract will then show an increase (if an increase is desired) or a continues level of performance from the PSP. For example, if the current standard is 100 per cent, the improvement targets would be to maintain it at 100 per cent. Other measures might commence at a level which is below, for example, a best value performance indicator (BVPI) and the improvement targets would require it to either meet or exceed that BVPI. Also included in this paragraph would be the definitions of each of the performance indicators. For example one of the performance indicators might be the percentage of invoices processed and ready for payment within seven working days. The definition might be that the percentage is calculated by the percentage of invoices that are processed and made ready for payment within seven days. It would not necessarily mean that the invoices had been processed for payment but that they are ready for processing;

(ix)   **Dependencies**: this would detail the external factors which would impinge upon the ability of the PSP to deliver the services to the standards required. It might mean that information is required from another department to ascertain the reasons for service failure before any action can be taken.

7.104   Drawing up the specification will be a time-consuming and detailed business. It is something that should be started at the beginning of the procurement process. Considerable time should be given to all those areas of the local authority that are going to be part of the outsourcing to be able to produce the necessary information regarding current volumes of work, time taken to deal with the various types of work and the various performance indicators that the PSP is required to adhere to. In addition, the sheer volume of the services and the need to detail what is comprised in each one can be quite overwhelming. Sufficient time should be given to properly consider what is proposed to be outsourced, how that service is provided and what details the PSP will need to enable it to consider whether what is being asked of it is acceptable.

Variations to the contract: specimen clauses

7.105   Depending on the nature of the contract, changes can be immensely complicated or fairly straightforward. To some extent the method chosen will depend on the type of service being delivered (for example if the contract is for blue collar services the functions are often fairly straightforward and easily definable; in the case of white collar services they might be far more intricate and volume-based, which could mean fluctuations in the type and nature of the service provided) and will therefore be quite different in their approach.

7.106   Set out below are specimen clauses for a fairly straightforward change in variation which will deal with changes to the service but not to volumes provided.

1   Variations for change in service

1.1   Local Authority changes

1.1.1   The Local Authority has the right to propose changes in Service in accordance with this Clause. If the local authority requires a change in Service, it must serve a notice (a **'Local Authority Notice of Change'**) on the Contractor.

1.1.2   The Local Authority Notice of Change shall:

(a)   set out the change in Service required in sufficient detail to enable the Contractor to calculate and provide an Estimated Revised Costs in accordance with **sub-Clause** 1.1.3 below;

(b) require the Contractor to provide the Local Authority within fifteen (15) Working Days of receipt of the local authority Notice of Change with the Estimate (the **'Estimate'**).

1.1.3 As soon as practicable and in any event within fifteen (15) Working Days after having received the Local Authority Notice of Change, the Contractor shall deliver to the Local Authority the Estimate. The Estimate shall include the opinion of the Contractor on:

(a) any impact on any Service Commencement Date;

(b) any impact on the provision of the Service;

(c) any amendment required to this Contract and/or any Contract Document as a result of the change in Service;

(d) any Estimated Revised Costs that result from the change in Service; and

(e) the proposed method of certification of any construction or operational aspects of the Service required by the change in Service.

1.1.4 As soon as practicable after the Local Authority receives the Estimate, the parties shall discuss and agree the issues set out in the Estimate. In such discussions the Local Authority may modify the local authority Notice of Change, in which case the Contractor shall, as soon as practicable, and in any event not more than ten (10) Working Days after receipt of such modification, notify the Local Authority of any consequential changes to the Estimate.

1.1.5 If the parties cannot agree on the contents of the Estimate then the dispute will be determined in accordance with **Clause** [ ] (Dispute Resolution).

1.1.6 As soon as practicable after the contents of the Estimate have been agreed or otherwise determined pursuant to **Clause** [ ] (Dispute Resolution), the Local Authority shall:

(a) confirm in writing the Estimate (as modified); or

(b) withdraw the Local Authority Notice of Change.

1.1.7 If the Local Authority does not confirm in writing the Estimate (as modified) within twenty (20) Working Days of the contents of the Estimate having been agreed in accordance with **sub-Clause** 1.1.4 above or determined pursuant to **sub-Clause** 1.1.5 above, then the Local Authority Notice of Change shall be deemed to have been withdrawn.

1.1.8 In the event that the Estimate has been confirmed by the Local Authority, then the adjustment to the Contract Payment shall be determined in accordance with this Clause.

1.2 **Contractor Changes in Service**

1.2.1 If the Contractor wishes to introduce a change in Service, it must serve a notice (a) **'Contractor Notice of Change'**) on the Local Authority.

1.2.2 The Contractor Notice of Change must:

(a) set out the proposed change in Service in sufficient detail to enable the Local Authority to evaluate it in full;

(b) specify the Contractor's reasons for proposing the change in Service;

(c) request the Local Authority to consult with the Contractor with a view to deciding whether to agree to the change in Service and, if so, what consequential changes the Local Authority requires as a result;

(d) indicate any implications of the change in Service;

(e) indicate, in particular, whether a variation to the Contract Payment is proposed (and, if so, give a detailed cost estimate of such proposed change); and

(f) indicate if there are any dates by which a decision by the Local Authority is critical.

1.2.3   The Local Authority shall evaluate the Contractor's proposed change in Service in good faith, taking into account all relevant issues, including whether:
    (a)   a change in the Contract Payment will occur;
    (b)   the change affects the quality of the Service or the likelihood of successful delivery of the Service;
    (c)   the change will interfere with the relationship of the Local Authority with third parties;
    (d)   the financial strength of the Contractor is sufficient to perform the changed Service;
    (e)   the change materially affects the risks or costs to which the Local Authority is exposed.

1.2.4   As soon as practicable after receiving the Contractor Notice of Change, the parties shall meet and discuss the matter(s) referred to in it. During their discussions the Local Authority may propose modifications or accept or reject the Contractor Notice of Change.

1.2.5   If the Local Authority accepts the Contractor Notice of Change (with or without modification), the relevant change in Service shall be implemented within twenty (20) Working Days of the Local Authority's acceptance. Within this period, the parties shall consult and agree the remaining details as soon as practicable and shall enter into any documents to amend this Contract or any relevant Contract Document which are necessary to give effect to the Change in Service.

1.2.6   If the Local Authority rejects the Contractor Notice of Change, it shall not be obliged to give its reasons for such a rejection.

1.2.7   Unless the Local Authority's acceptance specifically agrees to an increase in the Contract Payment there shall be no increase in the Contract Payment as a result of a change in Service proposed by the Contractor.

1.2.8   If the change in Service proposed by the Contractor causes or will cause the Contractor's costs or those of a Sub-Contractor to decrease, there shall be a decrease in the Contract Payment in accordance with **Schedule** [ ] (Payment Mechanism).

1.2.9   The Local Authority cannot reject a change in Service which is unavoidably required in order to conform to a Change in Law at no cost to the Local Authority.

Note: A number of terms in the clause will be defined (eg Service Commencement Date, Contract, Contract Document Service and Contract Payment).

The local authority might wish to give its reasons (clause 1.2.6) in order to maintain a partnering ethos.

It should always be borne in mind that the 'dry' details of the contract will be complemented with ongoing dialogue between the parties in respect of issues raised.

CHAPTER 8

Intellectual property rights

Rupert Battcock

BACKGROUND AND TYPES OF INTELLECTUAL PROPERTY

Importance of intellectual property

8.01   Intellectual property is important to a whole range of commercial contracts and, while not traditionally thought of as a major issue for local authorities, is increasingly significant for local government contracts as well as for contracts and procurement in the private sector. One key area where intellectual property can be critical for local authorities is in contracts for information and communications technology (or ICT, the acronym used in the public sector). Of more recent development, intellectual property is similarly key to 'e-government' contracts, but it can also be important in many more traditional types of agreement, for instance in the provision of design, architectural or other creative services. Probably the central contractual issue to do with intellectual property is that of ownership (or scope of use, where intellectual property is being licensed). There is no single global answer to the question of who should own intellectual property rights generated in the course of a contract, and no single set of licence provisions which can necessarily be taken as appropriate for local authority agreements. Although there are some standard approaches which may be appropriate, these are issues which need to be judged on a case-by-case basis for each contract. Treatment of some other intellectual property issues, such as infringement risk and indemnities, will tend to vary less from contract to contract, but may still require different approaches in different situations.

8.02   If there is a single message to be conveyed in this chapter, it is the value and importance of considering intellectual property issues early in the procurement process, and giving proper thought to how they should be dealt with for the specific procurement in question. Intellectual property is not always a matter of truly central strategic importance to local government contracts, but in some cases it genuinely may be, and in others it can still be an important subsidiary issue. It is certainly a mistake to assume that intellectual property can be left to be considered along with the boilerplate provisions needing little detailed scrutiny. Leaving the contract silent on intellectual property issues can be even more fatal. Some authorities' contract standing orders specifically require it to be confirmed that intellectual property issues have been properly considered and addressed (at least for certain types of contract), and whether or not it is mentioned in standing orders, this places a proper importance on the treatment of intellectual property in local authority contracts.

8.03   This chapter will look first at the different types of intellectual property likely to be relevant in local authority contracts, and will then look at ownership, licensing and other matters. Some ancillary issues which tend to be regarded as intellectual property concerns will also be briefly mentioned.

Nature and types of intellectual property

8.04   Intellectual property rights are rights protecting creative effort, reputation and goodwill. Most types of intellectual property exist in law as formal property rights which can be assigned, mortgaged or otherwise dealt with, as can more tangible property. Variously abbreviated as 'IPR' or 'IPRs', a distinction is sometimes made (for instance in contract definitions sections) between IPRs and 'intellectual property'—the former referring to the rights as such, and the latter referring to manifestations of intellectual property in specific items owned by a party. For most purposes however, the abbreviations are used fairly interchangeably.

8.05   The main types of IPR likely to be relevant to local authorities are the classic quartet of copyright (and its close relation, database right), trade marks, patents, and design rights. Rights in confidential information do not strictly amount to 'property' rights as such, but they are generally considered to be a type of intellectual property and will also be relevant. Of these IPRs, the most likely to be of importance in local authority contracts are copyright and database right, followed closely by confidential information (or 'know-how') and then trade marks. Patents and design rights may be relevant to certain types of local authority contract, but are less frequently encountered. A number of other more 'exotic' types of IPR also exist (for instance plant variety rights and semi-conductor topography rights) but they are likely to be only very rarely relevant to local authorities and are not discussed in this chapter. For a general introduction to these and also the more mainstream types of IPR, readers are referred to Philips and Firth[1] or other general intellectual property textbooks.

1   Philips and Firth *An Introduction to Intellectual Property Law* (4th edn, 2001, Butterworths).

Copyright

8.06   Copyright is probably the most familiar of intellectual property rights. It is a right that subsists in certain types of work as provided for in the Copyright, Designs and Patents Act 1988. Literary works, films, sound recordings, photographs, architectural drawings and other types of artistic work are all types of material potentially protected by copyright. The owner of a copyright work will, under s 16 of the Act, have the exclusive right to do or permit certain types of act relating to that work, including copying, distributing or making other use of it (subject to certain 'fair dealing' and other exemptions).

8.07   Copyright does not require to be registered or formally applied for in order to come into existence. There are advantages in indicating or marking that a work is subject to copyright protection (by use of the © symbol, the name of the creator or owner and date of publication), but this is not strictly a requirement for the existence of copyright. The main requirement for copyright to exist in an item is simply that it should be an original work. This 'originality' test however does not mean that there needs to be any particular level of artistic merit or innovation in a work. The requirement means just that the work should not be a slavish copy of an existing item.

In practice a requirement of substantiality also exists—thus for instance a single word will be unlikely to have the benefit of copyright[1], but this requirement will usually be fairly easily met even for quite short works.

1 *Exxon Corpn v Exxon Insurance Consultants International Ltd* [1982] Ch 119, CA.

8.08 Examples of works created by or for a local authority in which copyright would exist include reports written by authority employees, council publications and newsletters, architectural drawings, websites and other artistic and design materials. Technical specifications and even contractual documents themselves are also likely to be subject to copyright. Another important category of material in which copyright may exist is computer software, which for historical reasons is treated as a 'literary work' for the purposes of the Copyright, Designs and Patents Act 1988. Copyright may also exist in compilations, collections and anthologies of material (ie in addition to the copyright in the individual items within the compilation), however there is an overlap here with database right as discussed at para **8.12**.

8.09 A major difference between copyright and patent protection is that copyright does not create a complete monopoly. If another person creates a similar, or even an exactly identical work, independently of and without reliance on the original work, then they are fully entitled to make use of that new work. What copyright is concerned with is the *copying* (or possibly the adaptation) of the original work. A party may also create a work which is an expression of a similar idea on which another work is based, since it is a generally accepted rule that copyright protects the particular form of *expression* of ideas rather than ideas as such. Needless to say, the distinction between the two may not always be easy to draw, and a certain amount may depend on how detailed the 'idea' is, but the idea /expression distinction is still meaningful as a general rule of thumb.

8.10 An illustration of these principles in a case involving a local authority may be found in *Jones v Tower Hamlets London Borough Council*[1]. In that case Mr Jones, an architect, alleged that Tower Hamlets Council had copied his site plans for a housing development which the council had taken over in a partially completed state. There were indeed a number of similarities between Mr Jones' plans and the house layouts as implemented by the council. However, the High Court held that in relation to a number of the similarities there was no infringement because there was a common stock of architectural ideas and the council had simply drawn on those (in which Mr Jones could not claim copyright) rather than copying Mr Jones' specific plans. Some of the constraints of the site also contributed to the similarities. In respect of one specific feature however, which involved a clever solution to locating a bathroom in a very small two floor house, it was held that the council had done more than just implement a general idea—it had copied the specific form of Mr Jones' plans, which were protected by copyright. The case is an interesting example in the architectural field; others may be cited in relation to literary, artistic and other types of work. For further discussion of these issues and other matters to do with subsistence and scope of copyright, readers are referred to relevant specialist copyright texts[2].

1 [2001] RPC 23.
2 Laddie, Prescott and Vitoria *The Modern Law of Copyright and Designs* (3rd edn 2000, Butterworths). is recommended. Or for a briefer practical text, Flint, Fitzpatrick and Thorne *A User's Guide to Copyright* (5th edn, 2000, Butterworths).

8.11   Copyright is not a perpetual right. The general rule is that it subsists for a period of 70 years from the date of death of the author (or last-surviving author, in the case of jointly-created works), although some different durations apply for certain types of work. For a local authority the issue of duration may need to be considered in the context of using material from council archives or other historical collections, but for most day-to-day purposes it is not an issue which requires very detailed consideration.

Database right

8.12   Until fairly recently databases were protected in the UK (provided that the originality and other tests were met) solely by copyright. As from 1998 however, the Copyright and Rights in Databases Regulations 1997[1] have introduced a separate form of intellectual property protection for databases. This right was introduced in order to harmonise protection for databases in EU Member States (some of which did not provide protection for such materials at all) and is generally referred to as 'database right'. In many respects database right is similar to copyright, and indeed in casual discussion or correspondence a reference to copyright may probably be assumed to include database right, but legally it is a distinct and separate right and in contractual documentation care should be taken to include reference to database right if it is intended to be dealt with.

1   SI 1997/3032.

8.13   Database right will exist in collections of materials (in the collection itself, as distinct from the component items which in theory may have their own separate protection) if arranged in a systematic and methodical way, with the individual elements accessible by some means, and there has been a 'substantial investment in obtaining, verifying or presenting the contents of the database'. Thus a collection of items of information not now capable of protection by copyright may be protected by database right if a sufficient degree of investment (of time or resources) has gone into its collection or organisation. A large number of listings and other collections of information maintained by local authorities (or contractors on their behalf) may therefore have the benefit of database right protection.

8.14   In practice there remains a significant, and sometimes confusing, overlap with copyright, as the Copyright, Designs and Patents Act 1988 provides that databases in the development of which there has also been a degree of 'intellectual creation' will qualify for the stronger protection of copyright. A database created by pure rote activity (or 'sweat of the brow', as the phrase has it) may therefore be protected by database right, but one which has had some more creative input to its organisation or structure may be protected by copyright.

8.15   Database right is a lesser protection than copyright primarily because it lasts for a shorter period of time: for 15 years from the date of creation (as opposed to life of the author plus 70 years for copyright), although there are ways in which database right can be 'refreshed' if the database is updated. There are also differences in the precise rights of owners and in certain other technical legal matters and terminology used (the right is said to be infringed by the 'extraction' of contents of a database, rather than by *copying* of such contents).

Registered trade marks

8.16   There are two main forms of intellectual property protection for trade marks or trade names in the UK: registered protection through the Trade Marks Registry, and common law protection for unregistered marks via the remedy of 'passing off'. The registered right, as one would expect, provides the stronger protection and it is registered rights which are most likely to present significant issues in local authority contracts, but both types of right are relevant.

8.17   A system of registered trade mark protection has existed in the UK since 1875. The current governing legislation is the Trade Marks Act 1994, which defines a trade mark as 'any sign capable of being represented graphically which is capable of distinguishing goods or services of one undertaking from those of other undertakings'. Marks need to be registered in respect of certain 'classes' of goods or services (there are currently 34 classes relating to goods and 11 relating to services). If granted, they provide what is effectively a monopoly right for use of the registered mark in the classes and for the types of goods or services for which they are registered. Both words and logos (and some other types of signifier) may be registered as trade marks, although there are some qualifying requirements and some types of mark which may not be capable of registration[1].

---

1   For discussion of such matters see Morcom, Roughton and Graham *The Modern Law of Trade Marks* (2000, Butterworths), or Gyngell and Poulter *A User's Guide to Trade Marks and Passing Off* (2nd edn, 1998, Butterworths).

8.18   Trade mark protection can be of enormous value to commercial enterprises, and brands protected by registration can be amongst the most valuable assets owned by a business. It might be thought less immediately obvious as to why local authorities should wish to obtain registered trade mark protection, but as of July 2002 around 110 UK local authorities owned some 300 or so registered trade marks (not counting marks in the name of local authority companies or other associated bodies). Of these, some larger city authorities own portfolios of a dozen or more marks, others own just one or two. Two common classes in which marks are registered are class 41 (leisure and education services) and class 39 (transportation services), but there are many registrations in other classes as well. The number of marks is low in relation to the number of authorities, and the real value and benefit derived from some of these registrations (especially some of the more whimsical) may be open to question. However, in principle trade mark registrations can be of significant value to local authorities, and contractual control of how they should be used can be a matter of importance. Where citizen-interfacing services are contracted out, private sector partners may also devise trade marks to be used in relation to such services, and it may be important to decide who has actual ownership of trade marks devised for such purposes.

8.19   Registered trade marks require renewal on a regular basis, but may continue to exist indefinitely, for as long as they are being used in relation to relevant goods and services. Ownership of a trade mark may be assigned, but there are certain formalities which need to be observed. Use of a trade mark may also be licensed but there are certain formal provisions it is advisable to include in any such licence. It is possible to envisage local authority contracts in which there may need to be trade mark licences going both ways—from authority to contractor and vice versa.

Unregistered trade marks/passing off

8.20   Unregistered trade marks may have the benefit of a lesser form of protection through the law of passing off. This is a common law right which can be used to protect the unauthorised use of a name or get-up by a person so as to 'pass off' their goods or services as being those of another. The scope of passing off is not restricted just to trade marks, but may also encompass other forms of appropriation of reputation. The requirements for an action in passing off have been classically formulated[1] as consisting of:

(i)   a misrepresentation;
(ii)   which is made in the course of trade or business;
(iii)   which is calculated to injure the goodwill or business of another; and
(iv)   which causes actual damage to the other.

Use of another's unregistered trade mark might amount to passing off because it would constitute a form of misrepresentation as to the origin of goods and services to which the mark is applied. It is, however, much more difficult to succeed in an action for passing off than for infringement of a registered trade mark, which is why trade mark registration is so popular.

1   The leading case is probably *Erven Warnink BV v Townend & Sons* [1979] AC 731 (the *'Advocaat'* case).

8.21   Applying the formulation set out above, passing off has generally been seen as a right available to *traders* in goods and services, and so it might be queried as to whether it is a right applicable to local authorities, but case law involving non-trading bodies such as charities, and the changing nature of local authority activities suggest it is perfectly capable of application in a local authority context.

8.22   Strictly speaking, unregistered marks cannot be assigned or licensed in quite the same way as registered marks, but in practice it can still be meaningful to talk of their assignment or licensing (together with accompanying goodwill) in relevant local authority contracts.

Patents

8.23   Patents are sometimes seen as the ultimate form of intellectual property protection, in that once granted a patent provides monopoly protection over an invention for a potential maximum period of 20 years (subject to some limited restraints). Patents are granted by the UK Patent Office in relation to invented products or processes that:

(a)   are new;
(b)   involve an inventive step;
(c)   are capable of industrial application; and
(d)   do not fall within any relevant excluded category (excluded categories include computer software, although some software-related inventions are capable of patent protection).

8.24 To be granted, the Patent Office must be satisfied that the invention is a new addition to the previous state of the technical art and is not something that would be obvious to a large number of people.

8.25 Central government agencies, particularly those in technical and defence-related sectors, own a very large number of patents, but the number owned by local authorities is small. Some authorities do own patents, as is clear from a search at the Patent Office, but they are limited to a few larger city authorities, some counties and just a handful of others. In theory, ownership of a workable patent could be a very valuable 'windfall' source of revenue for an authority (although the commercial activity in exploiting it would be likely to present vires and other issues). These benefits certainly exist for universities and similar institutions which devote considerable effort to the exploitation of their patent portfolios, but local authorities (with perhaps just a few exceptions) are probably not particularly well placed or organised so as to carry out effective exploitation of patents.

8.26 More likely to be relevant in local authority contracts is authority use of others' patented products or processes, or the use by a contractor working for an authority of such products or processes. Certain technical activities in municipal treatment plants, for instance, might make extensive use of patented processes, and if so it would be important to make sure that appropriate licences are in place to allow this. Licences may need to continue for longer than the term of appointment of any particular contractor. It may also be appropriate to seek indemnities from a contractor that its delivery of services or goods will not involve the authority in any infringement of relevant patents.

Designs

8.27 There are two types of intellectual property protection for designs in the UK: one under the registered design right provided for by the Registered Designs Act 1949, and the other being an unregistered right, similar to copyright, which exists under Part III of the Copyright, Designs and Patents Act 1988. These two types of protection are generally referred to as 'registered designs' and 'design right', although a great deal of confusion exists among non-intellectual property lawyers as to the difference between the two.

8.28 Broadly speaking, aside from one being a registered and the other being an unregistered right, registered designs create a monopoly right for features of shape, configuration, pattern or ornament in the appearance of a product, where these features are novel and have some individual character. If granted by the Designs Registry, protection can last for a maximum of 25 years. Significant changes in registered designs law have recently been introduced by the Registered Designs Regulations 2001[1]. Design right (unregistered), on the other hand, is a right similar to copyright, relating primarily to three-dimensional functional designs, providing protection just against the *copying* of the design. It lasts for a period of 15 years from the end of the year of creation, or 10 years from the date when articles based on it were first made available with the consent of the owner, whichever is the longer.

1   SI 2001/3949.

8.29   Items registrable as registered designs or qualifying for design right protection are perfectly capable of being generated in the course of local authority contracts, and ownership of or the right to use such designs are matters which may need to be dealt with in similar manner to the use of copyright or patents.

Confidential information

8.30   Confidential information is commonly referred to as a type of intellectual property, although it is debateable whether strictly speaking it constitutes 'property' as such. Leaving such arguments aside, the legal basis for asserting rights of ownership in confidential information is based on the law of breach of confidence, and it is well established that an action for breach of confidence can be sustained in respect of confidential information generated or disclosed in the course of a contract.

8.31   The requirements for a breach of confidence action to be successful were famously set out in *Coco v AN Clark (Engineers) Ltd*[1] as being:
(a)   that the information must have the necessary 'quality of confidence' about it;
(b)   that the information was disclosed in a situation suggesting confidentiality; and
(c)   that there has been unauthorised use or disclosure of the information to the detriment of the party communicating it.
As well as these common law rules, most types of contract will also include specific confidentiality provisions and a breach of confidence under such a contract may be both a common law breach and also a breach of relevant contractual undertaking.

1   [1969] RPC 41.

8.32   For the purposes of local authority and indeed other types of contracts, a useful distinction may be made between two types of confidentiality provision. The first, typically included in the boilerplate clauses, is concerned with imposing relevant confidentiality restrictions—and is usually most directed towards confidential aspects of the deal structure or the parties' internal operations. Issues to do with this type of provision are discussed in para **8.72** below. The second type of provision relates more to the *ownership* of confidential information—or of trade secrets or 'know how'— as items of intellectual property.

8.33   As an item of ownable intellectual property, confidential information is commonly seen as ancillary to other rights. Thus, for instance, a trade secret which is potentially protectable by patent may be protected before a patent is granted by virtue of its status as confidential information (and indeed it may be necessary to keep the information confidential in order for the patent to be successfully obtained). Some confidential information may also be protected by copyright, but where the information is on the margins of qualifying for copyright then confidentiality provides a 'back-up' form of protection for it.

8.34   Some providers contracting with local authorities may place greater reliance on ownership provisions relating to copyright and other statutory rights rather than on confidential information. For others however, the question of who owns confidential information and know-how generated during performance of the contract may be of considerable significance. In any event, appropriate consideration will need to be given to how is to be treated. In practice, confidential information is generally subsumed into a general definition of IPR, ownership and use of which is then dealt with according to the general chosen scheme of the contract.

Other rights

8.35 Mention has already been made of some slightly more esoteric types of IPR such as plant variety rights. Other variant types of right include performers' rights— although this is essentially just a form of copyright, and unlikely to be of significance in mainstream local authority contracts. Some local authorities own or have applied for 'certification marks', a specific type of trade mark which may be used to authenticate the local origin or other relevant features of third parties' goods or services (for instance the 'Pembrokeshire Produce' mark which identifies produce originating from the historical county of Pembrokeshire). Reference should be made to the trade mark texts cited above for further details on this type of right.

8.36 One important additional type of IPR is what is referred to as 'moral rights'. These exist under the Copyright, Designs and Patents Act 1988 to provide protection for authors and creators of works (as opposed to owners) against unfair treatment. In the UK there are three main moral rights:
(i) the right to be identified as the author of a work (provided assertion of the right has been made);
(ii) the right to protect a work from derogatory treatment (eg distortion of a written text or cinematic work); and
(iii) a right not to be wrongly identified as the author of a work.

8.37 These rights cannot be assigned except by death—by their nature they are rights which are intended to vest in the author or creator of a work—but they can be waived. Moral rights do not exist in relation to computer programs. When dealing with most types of provider, moral rights are likely to have fairly limited impact upon local authority contracts, but on some occasions it may be relevant to give consideration to their existence.

Infringements of intellectual property: types and consequences

8.38 The rules relating to what constitutes infringement of IPR vary from case to case. For reasons of space it is not intended to set these out here for each type of right. Suffice to say that as the law recognises the existence of such property rights, it also provides for action to be taken against those who make use of them without lawful authority. Infringement may be committed directly, by use of the right without authority, or indirectly—for instance by the importation of or other commercial dealing in infringing goods (referred to as 'secondary' infringement in the case of copyright, or 'contributory' infringement in the case of patents).

8.39 Infringement of copyright may also be committed where a person 'authorises' another to do an act restricted by copyright. A case of particular relevance to local authorities in this regard is *Pensher Security Door Co Ltd v Sunderland City Council*[1]. In this case Pensher owned the copyright in drawings for security doors which it called the Pensher PS1000. Sunderland Council issued an invitation to tender which specified the doors required for a building contract as being 'type Pensher PS1000'. The tender was circulated and the contract awarded to a company other than Pensher. The successful company then produced doors similar to Pensher's and which infringed its copyright. The main infringing party here was the contractor that produced the infringing doors, but Pensher sued the council as well, which was found also to be liable on the basis that it had effectively authorised and was clearly aware of the infringement. Even though the tender had not mandated that the doors should be so closely similar as to be infringing (merely that they should be '*type* Pensher PS1000'), the council's subsequent sight and approval of the design was enough for it to be found that it had committed an infringement. The case has obvious lessons for the drafting of tender documents as well as contracts.

1   [2000] RPC 249, CA.

8.40   Remedies for infringement vary depending on the right involved but may include injunction, delivery up of infringing materials, award of damages or an account of profits deriving from the infringement. There are also criminal offences relating to certain types of infringement, but in practice, notwithstanding recent extension to their scope, these are primarily used against traders engaged in active piracy or counterfeiting. Interestingly, it is local authority trading standards departments who often take the lead in pursuance of such infringement.

8.41   Local authorities may from to time wish to enforce ownership of, or rights in, intellectual property themselves, but otherwise the main infringement issues arising out of local government contracts relate to the dangers of the authority itself being unauthorised to use IPR, or outside the scope of licence.

Permitted acts and exemptions to infringement

8.42   A number of tightly-drawn 'permitted acts' and exemptions from infringement exist in relation to various of the statutory IPRs (for instance certain limited 'fair dealing' provisions in relation to copyright). It is not intended to set all of these out here, but it may be worth mentioning one particular exemption sometimes raised by those seeking to use local authority copyright materials. Section 47 of the Copyright, Designs and Patents Act 1988 provides an exemption from copyright infringement where use is made of copyright works which are required to be open to public inspection or on an official register (a similar exemption also applies in relation to database right). This exemption has been interpreted by some commercial information providers as giving them a broad right to reproduce public register materials maintained by local authorities. The precise scope of the exemption is subject to some debate however, and it is unclear how far it may be used by commercial providers seeking to derive revenue from the re-publication of such material. Other exemptions, including those applying to local authority libraries and educational institutions, are outside the scope of this chapter.

OWNERSHIP AND USE OF INTELLECTUAL PROPERTY

Ownership: basic rules

8.43   To understand properly IPR ownership issues in contracts, it is necessary first of all to appreciate certain basic rules regarding 'first ownership' of IPR. For copyright, the Copyright, Designs and Patents Act 1988, s 11(1) provides that the first owner of the copyright in a work will be the *author* of the work (or the joint authors if it is a work of genuine joint authorship). There is a well-known exception to this rule, under s 11(2), where a work is created by an employee in the course of his or her employment. In such cases, ownership will be vested in the employer. Where a council official or other employee creates copyright work in the course of their employment, ownership of the copyright will therefore vest automatically in the council[1]. However, no such equivalent rule applies in the case of an independent contractor (either a company or non-employee individual) engaged by an authority to provide services, or commissioned by it to produce relevant materials. Thus, where a contractor company is providing services to an authority, ownership of copyright in works created by the contractor's employees under that contract will vest in the contracting company—notwithstanding that the works may be specifically intended for the sole use of the authority, or may have been specifically commissioned by the authority.

1   The same is not necessarily true for elected members, but thankfully that issue rarely needs to be dealt with.

8.44   The above rule sometimes comes as a surprise to those unfamiliar with copyright law, but it is avoidable only by express contractual agreement to the contrary. Very occasionally a court may be willing to imply a term into a contract such that 'equitable' ownership of copyright will be deemed to vest in a commissioning party, but the circumstances in which a court will do so are very limited indeed, and this rare possibility is not one that should be relied upon. Courts are somewhat more willing to imply a *licence* to make use of copyright into a contract, where such licence is not expressly provided for, but implied licences are generally of very limited scope and it is similarly ill-advised to rely on the generosity of a court in finding that one should be implied.

8.45   Differing rules on ownership apply to other types of intellectual property. For database right the position is broadly the same as for copyright, notwithstanding some potentially different interpretations of ownership provisions in the Database Regulations[1]. For design right (unregistered) there is a contrary rule as regards commissioned works, such that the person who commissioned the work shall own the design right in it. In practice however, given the overlap between copyright and design right, it will always be sensible for a commissioning party to make express contractual provision for ownership of IPRs in a design if it wishes to have them. For patents and other registered rights the issue of ownership is one sense less problematic, since a common sense view of the matter is that the owner is the person who actually makes the application for registration. There is a real issue however as to who should be *entitled* to make such application. The ability to make the application and to use it may also depend on ownership of ancillary rights, and of related confidential information or know-how. In practice these are matters which should be dealt with by express provision in the contract.

1   Particularly reg 14(1), which may make it advisable for a contractor to expressly reserve ownership
     if it needs to have it.

8.46   It is worth clarifying one matter in relation to local authority IPRs, which is that local authorities are perfectly capable of owning IPR entirely in their own right. For central government departments, and certain government agencies, ownership of copyright and other IPRs is formally vested in the Crown rather than in the department or agency as such (though control of use may effectively be delegated back to the department or agency in question). Some differing legislative rules also apply to Crown copyright materials (for instance on the duration of protection). Local authorities however, having independent constitutional status, fall outside the scope of Crown copyright—although there may be occasions, such as under relevant funding agreements, where a government department may seek contractually for ownership of local authority IPRs to be vested in the Crown.

The 'fight for the rights'—who should own?

8.47   Given the background set out above, the issue then arises of what the contract should say about ownership of IPR, since the rules may be varied by express contractual provision. Where there is disagreement as to who should own, the issue has been characterised as sometimes taking on the nature of a 'fight for the rights'. However, a realistic approach to ownership by both authority and contractor can usually help avoid disputes. It will also be particularly important for an authority to take a realistic approach when drafting terms and conditions to be used (where procurement rules apply) under the restricted procedure. Failure to do so may result either in contractors refusing to bid against such terms or in the terms having to be varied, which may present difficulties under the procedure.

8.48   The approach to be taken will depend on the background and nature of the contract, but some general guidance may nevertheless be ventured. At one end of the scale, where an authority is commissioning creation of a specific 'one-off' piece of work, it may be simplest and also quite justifiable for the authority simply to require for ownership of IPR in the work to vest in the authority. Even with one-off commissions, however, this approach will sometimes run up against the contrary requirements of relevant contractors. Bodies such as the Royal Institute of British Architects for instance—representing just one type of provider with whom authorities may deal—publish standard form agreements which generally provide for ownership to vest in the commissioned party (subject to appropriate licences to the client). Similar approaches are taken by other professional bodies, and while such bodies are clearly not neutral observers, they may nevertheless reflect prevailing industry practice which it will be relevant at least to take into account. Moreoever, in many such cases where ownership is retained by a contractor, a licence in sufficiently broad terms may well be sufficient for an authority. A judgement needs to be made based on each particular set of circumstances.

8.49   In relation to larger services or development agreements (for instance such as might be entered into under the PFI), the approach taken by public sector bodies, including local authorities, is one that has evolved over time. Traditionally, there used to be an approach that all IPR created during the contract should be assigned to the authority. Standard contracts used both in the public and private sector (for instance those published by the Chartered Institute of Purchasing and Supply) also typically took such an approach. Over time, however, it has been realised that this approach to ownership of IPR is not always the most effective for public sector bodies. Contractors who are required to assign over ownership of developed IPR will often factor this into their charges for a contract, making it much more expensive. Contractors have an obvious interest in seeking to make further commercial use of IPR developed in a project (IPR being their life-blood in many cases), and denying them the ability to do so may simply deter efficient contractors from bidding, or cause them to bid at much increased cost. Within central government the 1999 Baker Report[1] (although concerned primarily with public sector science projects) also suggested that, subject to revenue sharing and other considerations, there should as a matter of public policy generally be a presumption towards IPR being vested in the contractual party best able to further use or exploit it. In most local government contracts it is probably fair to say that the authority is not usually likely to be the party best placed to do this.

1 *Creating knowledge, creating wealth* Report by John Baker to the Minister of Science and Financial Secretary to the Treasury (August 1999).

8.50   The current state of thinking on ownership of IPR in these types of contract is now perhaps best set out in the OGC guidance on *Standardisation of PFI Contracts* ('the PFI Guidance')[1]. This states as a general presumption that it is not necessarily required for authorities to own the IPR in relevant materials as long as appropriate licences are available. Division II of the guidance goes into particular detail on the issue of ownership of IPR in software (but is applicable to other IPR) and states that 'the authority does not need to own all IPR used in the services, but there may be circumstances where ownership is appropriate'. One example given of such circumstances is in relation to defence contracts, obviously not of great relevance to local authorities. Another may be summarised as being where

(i)   there is 'a large amount of bespoke software development which represents the major value of the project'; and
(ii)   there is a good argument that rights of commercial exploitation should belong to the authority.

1 *Standardisation of PFI Contracts* (revised 1 August 2002, OGC) (Butterworths).

8.51   Authorities sometimes argue this line on the ground that in the circumstances it would be an 'unjust enrichment' for the contractor to retain all IPR (and hence all exploitation rights) in the developed materials. This can be a valid argument, but if they make it authorities should generally be able to point to the specific reasons why contractor ownership would be unjust in the particular circumstances. It is also worth noting that other mechanisms can be adopted in response to this enrichment argument—for instance some form of agreement by the contractor to share commercial exploitation revenues[1]. As against the PFI Guidance, a number of high-profile public sector contracts have been criticised on account of the 'lock-in' to the initial provider caused by that provider's ownership of IPR. In truth however, it is not necessarily the lack of ownership which has caused these problems. More often it is the failure to agree licence provisions (and particularly post-termination licences) of appropriate scope.

1 Although such revenue sharing schemes do not always work very well in practice.

8.52   One solution to the question of ownership which may seem superficially attractive is to agree for IPR to be jointly owned. A fundamental problem with this 'solution' however is that subsequent use of or dealings in the IPR will generally need the consent of both or all joint owners (a point not always well appreciated). Intellectual property lawyers therefore have a well-grounded prejudice against joint ownership as an easy solution—although there may be cases where for specific reasons it is an option to be considered. On occasion joint ownership may arise because the very creation of the IPR was a joint act (eg where there is significant collaboration between employees of each party). Where this might happen, then the default ownership position can become very complicated, and express contractual provision comes into its own as a means of clarifying the lines of ownership.

Assignment

8.53   Where ownership is to be assigned or similarly dealt with by way of contractual provision, it will be important to make sure the assignment is made in proper form. The assignee should generally require for ownership to be transferred with 'full title guarantee', and with other appropriate indemnities and warranties. It may also be useful to provide for the assignor to carry out any acts necessary in order to comply with patent office or other ownership formalities, and occasionally it may be appropriate to consider provision for waiver of moral rights.

8.54   Assignment provisions included in contracts will frequently take one of two forms:
(i)   the assignment of IPR in already-existing materials (eg existing software or databases); and/or
(ii)   assignment of *future* IPR, in materials not yet created but which will come into existence during performance of the contract.

8.55   It is perfectly possible to assign ownership of IPR in both types of material, although for not yet existing intellectual property there may be particular issues in ensuring that it is correctly identified and defined. Assignment of already-existing intellectual property may take place by way of assignment from the authority to contractor (for materials the use of which is to be taken over by the contractor on commencement) or from contractor to authority (for materials assigned back to the authority on expiry) although in either case it is just as likely that use of such IPR will be dealt with by way of licence rather than assignment.

Licensing

8.56   If IPRs are to be licensed to the authority as an alternative (in some ways as a 'second best') to them being assigned, it will obviously be particularly important to ensure that the scope of the licence is sufficiently broad. There are two aspects to the scope of licence which will need to be addressed:
(i)   to make sure the licence covers IPR in all relevant materials, and
(ii)   to make sure that it allows for all relevant *uses* by all relevant parties (including, for services contracts, both during and after termination of the contract).

8.57   The first aspect is one that needs to be addressed primarily as a practical issue—making sure for instance that definitions cover all relevant items. The second aspect however is one that requires more careful strategic consideration, as a number of potential licensing requirements may come into play. For a procurement of pure deliverables the position may be relatively straightforward (although some issues, like assignment or sub-licence to outsourcing providers will need to be considered), but for services contracts it can be more complex. One useful way of thinking about the possible requirements is by picturing them as a matrix of different possibilities, relating to different parties, categories of intellectual property and time periods. Various of these may be represented (for a services contract) as in Figure 1.

Figure 1

		For authority	For replacement contractor	For consortia parties	For ancillary parties / end-users
Rights during contract term	'Contractor's IPR' (pre-existing materials)	The authority might require a licence but may just be interested in receiving the services not in using the IPR itself	A licence or right to assign may be required if provision of services may be split during the term	Required rights will depend on nature of project	A right to sub-license may be required in certain circumstances. Consideration should also be given to an authority's internal end-users
	'Specially Written IPR' (IPR created for the contract)	See above, but it may be appropriate to take a licence in any event (any licence should cover sub-contractor IPR)	Will depend on circumstances		Will depend on circumstances
	'Third Party IPR'	Licence may or may not be required (NB: authority's licence(s) may be direct with the third parties)			
Rights after contract	'Contractor's IPR'	A continuing licence may be required to avoid 'lock-in' (subject if necessary to appropriate ongoing fees)	The authority will certainly wish to allow a replacement provider to step-in	Will depend on circumstances	Will depend on circumstances
	'Specially Written IPR'	Continuing licence should generally be free of charge (if IPR not owned by authority)	Licence should generally be free of charge		
	'Third Party IPR'	Contractor may not be able to guarantee ongoing licence (alternatively, may be required to use best endeavours to procure one)	NB: third party may veto certain replacement contractors		

The table is illustrative only, and should not necessarily be taken as an exhaustive statement of all possible requirements. Certain comments however are made below about various elements represented in the table.

Licensing—categories of IPR

8.58   A distinction is commonly made between IPR in existence and owned by the contractor prior to the commencement of provision of the services, usually defined as 'Contractor's IPR', and IPR created by the contractor in the course of performance or specifically for the contract, defined as 'Specially Written IPR' (these definitions are so commonly used that they are adopted in the text which follows). Distinguishing between the two is useful, as the way in which they are treated may differ. Contracts for the provision of a service will not necessarily require the authority to have a licence of Contractor's IPR during the active lifetime of the contract at all, seeing as the authority's primary interest may be in receiving the services rather than in making its own use of the IPR. Negotiation of a licence for during the term may therefore be a task and expense which can be saved by the authority (subject to 'step-in' and authority end-user considerations as commented on below). For Specially Written IPR the same considerations may apply during the term, but to provide for a licence would probably not have the same cost impact as for Contractor's IPR, and a licence in fairly broad terms is therefore often included in any event (other than in cases where the IPR is owned outright by authority). Also, where the contract provides for revenue sharing on commercial exploitation of IPR, it is in respect of the Specially Written IPR that such provisions would apply. Specially Written IPR may comprise IPR created by the contractor itself, and also by sub-contractors, and indeed it is good practice to oblige the contractor to ensure that it properly mirrors the IPR arrangements in the head-contract within each of its sub-contracts with subsidiary providers.

8.59   The other category illustrated in Figure 1 is Third Party IPR[1], which may constitute materials that the contractor needs to have (to provide the service) or that the authority needs to use (to receive them). In respect of any use by the authority, the licence to make use of such IPR may come either directly from the third party or from the contractor by way of a sub-licence. It may depend on the circumstances, but it will generally be more convenient for the authority to deal with a single party and for any licence to be routed through the contractor. In some cases however there may be collateral arrangements that need to be handled with the third party owner or intermediate distributor.

1   Although see the separate discussion at para **8.64** for an additional category of IPR.

Licensing—post-contract use and step-in rights

8.60   One of the most important considerations in long term services contracts is to preserve a reasonable degree of freedom for the authority to change direction in how it decides to receive services, and to avoid lock-in whereby an incumbent contractor is able to perpetuate its position purely through control of the relevant IPR—use of which may have become integral to the authority's way of doing business. Contractors ought to be entitled to a fair commercial return for use of their IPR, but in particularly egregious cases contractors have been described as effectively holding authorities to ransom at the time of contract renewal on the basis of their ownership of critical IPR. The main way to avoid this sort of problem (short of outright authority ownership), is for the contract to expressly set out the rights of use which the authority will have after termination. For Specially Written IPR a perpetual and royalty-free licence may be agreed fairly easily. For Contractor's IPR it is normally possible to agree some form of post-termination licence, but it is likely in many circumstances that the contractor may require some form of royalty to be paid if the authority is to make continued use of it. A prudent authority will wish to obtain some assurance as to what the level of such royalty will be. For Third Party IPR the position may be more complicated, as the contractor will not necessarily be able to easily guarantee that relevant third parties will agree to a licence at any specific royalty. A judgement will need to be made on how to deal with Third Party IPR depending on the importance of that IPR to the ongoing service provision.

8.61 In many contracts it may be sensible to provide for such licences to commence, at the authority's option, before formal termination of the contract. If the contractor's performance is poor, if the authority wishes for policy reasons to take back a part of the services, or just if it is difficult to provide for a quick termination of the contract, an earlier 'step-in' right to obtain the benefit of an ongoing licence may be appropriate. Such a right may exist independently or, more often, may exist as a part of more general step-in rights within the contract as whole. Sometimes the right will be subject to ongoing royalty fees; sometimes a lump sum payment is sufficient to trigger a perpetual or periodic royalty-free licence. In cases where the step-in is triggered by contractor default then obviously there may be a case for setting such payment at a fairly nominal level or at nil.

Licensing—rights for different parties

8.62 The main party requiring to be licensed will obviously be the authority itself. If step-in or post contract licences are utilised however, it is likely (unless services are taken back in-house) that it will be a replacement contractor or contractors who will eventually need to be licensed to make use of relevant IPR. This should be expressly allowed for in the contract. Sometimes with Third Party IPR there can be difficulty in obtaining consent to such use when the replacement contractor might be a competitor of the third party owner. Authorities should however seek to retain as much freedom of choice as possible over who the potential replacement might be.

8.63 Occasionally issues may arise as to who is comprised within the contracting authority. In the context of consortia or multi-authority procurements, the consortia members obviously need to be clearly identified as beneficiaries of the licence[1]. There may also be other ancillary parties who need to make use of relevant IPR. Sometimes an authority may perceive that (during the contract term) it does not need to take a licence of IPR, but specific authority employees may in fact have a requirement to do so—for instance perhaps to receive terminal-based services provided by the contractor. It is sometimes useful to consider such individuals as ancillary parties, although in fact the licence which would need to be granted for them to use IPR would be a licence granted to the authority. Members of the public might also on occasion need to be granted sub-licences to make use of terminal-based or other similar services, and the ability to grant such licence should be expressly reserved to the authority.

1   Including bodies that the authority may wish to have added at a later date.

Licences to contractor

8.64 The discussion above has dealt solely with licences by the contractor to the authority (or to related parties of the authority). However it may also be required for the contractor to have the benefit of certain licences from the authority. For instance in an outsourcing the contractor may need to use software hitherto used just by the authority's internal personnel, and may also need to use certain data or other IPR resources owned by the authority. In theory an option exists for such IPRs to be outright assigned to the contractor, but unless there are special circumstances it will generally be preferable for authorities to grant a licence or other form of permission. In services contracts two additional definitions therefore typically appear, of 'Authority's IPR' (or 'Authority's Software') and 'Authority's Data'—with appropriate licence of such items to the contractor during the period of the contract. It will be useful at an early stage of the procurement for the authority to identify those items which may need to be licensed in this way. For materials which may be subject to amendment or enhancement during the period of services (eg a database which may be added to or refined by the contractor) it will also be sensible to clarify that ownership of the material as a whole, including amendments, will remain with the authority or related authority party.

8.65   Complications arise in respect of materials used by an authority, but in which it does not own the IPR. Typically for instance, an authority may use a number of items on the basis of licences granted by other commercial providers. These may include software licences, and database or information access agreements. In this situation an authority will need to procure an assignment or novation of the licence, or some other permission from the third party provider (perhaps by way of authority sub-licence) so as to enable the contractor to make such use. This is by no means always a simple matter, and in some cases it may be found that existing licences with third parties prohibit assignment, sub-licensing or other equivalent arrangements (at least without prior consent). Sophisticated contractors are likely to address these issues in their contractual due diligence exercises (and/or request appropriate warranties as to the ability to make such use); authorities should be sure that they make appropriate investigations into their capacity to make such assignment or to grant such other permission. Obtaining appropriate consents can sometimes be a major administrative exercise. Any assignment or other permission for the contractor to use IPR should also provide for use to revert to the authority on termination of the contract or in other appropriate circumstances.

Usage risk issues

8.66   Use of IPR materials from another party brings with it certain risks, particularly in relation to infringement of third parties' intellectual property rights. Contracts should therefore include appropriate IPR indemnity undertakings, from the contractor to the authority. Under such undertakings, the contractor will indemnify the authority in respect of damages or costs incurred due to IPR infringement proceedings or allegations brought by a third party against the authority, arising out of the authority's use of IPR provided by the contractor. There is also a case for including an indemnity even in circumstances where no licences of IPR are formally granted within the contract at all, since there is a risk of suit from a third party in respect of other activities carried out by a contractor[1].

1   See the *Pensher* case discussed at para **8.39**.

8.67   Contractors are or should generally be willing to give such indemnities, but particular issues will arise as to their exact scope and nature. One issue in particular is whether the indemnity may be subject to some form of monetary cap—contractors obviously preferring to limit their liability. No settled practice can be said to prevail, but in many cases authorities do appear willing to agree for a cap to apply, based either on the value of the contract or on insurance available to the contractor. Contractors will also typically wish to place certain conditions on the indemnity (for example that they should receive prompt notification, be entitled to conduct defence of the suit, and receive assistance in relation to such defence). They may also wish to specify certain exceptions—for instance if the authority is making use of the IPR outside the scope of its licence, or making use of versions of IPR materials which should be regarded as having been superseded. An additional right that contractors commonly wish to retain in relation to software is to be able to make replacements or modifications of software if the contractor has a reasonable belief that an infringement risk may exist. Such a right should usually be acceptable to an authority, subject to provisos that the replacement or modification should not cause any decrease in functionality or level of services, and not cause undue inconvenience or cost to the authority.

8.68   Where IPR licences are granted by an authority to the contractor, then a contractor will typically request a cross-indemnity from the authority to the contractor in respect of the use of relevant IPR materials by it. Other forms of cross-indemnity are sometimes also requested. With ancillary parties possibly to be taken into account, indemnity clauses can become quite complicated (sometimes, it seems, unduly complicated) and will require careful crafting and scrutiny.

Specific issues relating to software

8.69   Some other particular issues arise with licences of software. In a complex agreement different types of software may need to be defined and dealt with separately, quite apart from the general treatment of IPR. Thus in relevant services contracts there may be at least four different defined types of software involved: 'Contractor's Software', 'Specially Written Software', 'Third Party Software' and 'Authority's Software', all dealt with on principles similar to those set out above for IPR generally. (Indeed, in some contracts it may be software alone that needs to be dealt with according to this sort of scheme, and other IPR can be dealt with more simply.) Similar indemnity and due diligence issues will also exist in the same way as set out above for other IPR.

8.70   One additional issue that will need to be dealt with for software is that of software maintenance, and the related issues of access to source code and escrow. Software maintenance is important, as during any period of use bugs and problems are likely to arise with software which will require specialist expertise, knowledge— and access to source code—to resolve. During the period of services provision under a services contract, this maintenance should generally be the responsibility of the contractor (albeit that for certain software, performance of these obligations may be sub-contracted to the third party software owner or other specialist maintenance provider[1]). However, in circumstances where a post-contract licence of software is to be provided (perhaps so that the software may be used for performance of services by a replacement contractor) consideration will need to be given to the maintenance arrangements on which the authority will be able to rely during this period. Post-contract licence provisions therefore need to deal with the ongoing maintenance of the software as well as the simple continued right to use it.

1   And note that in some cases the authority may need to have maintenance arranged directly between itself and the actual maintenance provider.

8.71   In respect of maintenance during any period, attention also needs to be paid to the arrangements which will exist in case the maintenance provider becomes insolvent, ceases to trade, or materially defaults on its maintenance obligations. In any of these cases the authority may be left in a position where it is unable to obtain maintenance for the software if arrangements have not been made to provide for the 'source code' of the software to become available[1]. For certain software, an authority may be able to insist that it is provided with relevant source code on request and/or at the time of creation of the software (typically this may apply to Specially Written Software, whether or not the contract also provides for the IPR in such software to vest in the authority). In other cases however, the authority will need to rely on an appropriate escrow agreement to ensure that it, or a replacement contractor, has access to source code when required. Escrow agreements are tri-partite contracts, ancillary to the main contract, which provide for source code to software to be deposited with a third party 'escrow agent' (typically, in the UK, the National Computing Centre) with provisions allowing for release of the code by the agent on the occurrence of relevant insolvency or default events. Where software from many different parties is involved, escrow arrangements may become quite complex, but they are an essential form of insurance if an authority is not to be left stranded without the means of effectively maintaining software. Authorities should therefore ensure that appropriate escrow provisions are included in the contract. Equally importantly, they should ensure as matter of good contract management that escrow provisions are actually invoked and followed at relevant times during contract performance (it is a sad fact that authorities sometimes have adequate provisions in the contract, but nevertheless encounter difficulties because the escrow provisions were allowed to lie quiescent and unused until too late a stage).

1   Computer software exists in two forms: in 'object code' or executable form (the form in which it is commonly provided by suppliers to licensees but which does not facilitate ongoing maintenance), and in 'source code' form (which should enable maintenance but which licensors are generally reluctant to make available).

ANCILLARY ISSUES

Confidentiality and access to information

8.72   Issues relating to the ownership of confidential information have already been discussed above[1]. Distinct from the question of ownership however, local authority contracts will also include standard provisions imposing confidentiality restrictions upon the parties. Such provisions are common in many types of commercial contract, and it is not proposed to analyse them in any great depth here. It is however worth noting certain exceptions distinctive to local authority circumstances which may need to be included in contracts. It will generally be appropriate for instance to include exceptions allowing for disclosure of information to the District Auditor and others exercising similar functions, and perhaps (in relevant cases) to sponsoring government departments. Authorities also need to give consideration to the application of the Freedom of Information Act 2000 which is expected to be fully in force for local authorities by January 2005.

1   See para **8.30**.

8.73 It is recognised in the Freedom of Information Act 2000 that there will be information disclosed by private sector contractors which is of a genuinely commercial confidential nature, or which may amount to trade secret information, and exemptions relating to the required disclosure of such information therefore exist under the Freedom of Information Act 2000, ss 41 and 43. At the same time however, authorities should be careful of accepting overly-extensive confidentiality provisions in their contracts. Draft guidance from the Lord Chancellor's Department[1] (being the department with responsibility for the Act) states that:

'When entering into contracts with non-public authority contractors, public authorities may be under pressure to accept confidentiality clauses so that information relating to the terms of the contract, its value and performance will be exempt from disclosure. Public authorities should reject such clauses wherever possible.'

This is guidance which may present some difficulties in practical compliance, but however the issue is dealt with, it is something that ought to be considered by local authorities in advance of the Freedom of Information Act 2000 access right coming into force.

1 Draft Code of Practice on the Discharge of the Functions of Public Authorities under Part I of the Freedom of Information Act 2000 (LCD, July 2002) to be issued under the Freedom of Information Act 2000, s 45.

8.74 Confidentiality obligations may also be imposed at the pre-contract stage of procurements. Indeed, bidders disclosing details of proposed solutions may, in some cases, require that these take place subject to appropriate confidentiality undertakings—and careful scrutiny should be given to these undertakings just as to final contract provisions. (Authorities should also take care to honour the terms of such undertakings, as unsuccessful contractors may complain of breach if IPR elements of their unsuccessful proposed solutions are 'cherry-picked' by authorities so as to find their way into solutions delivered by other contractors.) There will also of course be cases where the authority needs to obtain appropriate pre-contract undertakings from contractors or bidders.

Data protection

8.75 Data protection law relates to the privacy of individuals in their personal data. This is not strictly speaking a matter of intellectual property law, but treatment of data protection issues is nevertheless commonly seen as an adjunct to confidentiality and intellectual property issues. The main piece of UK legislation in this area is the Data Protection Act 1998, at the heart of which lie eight 'data protection principles' which need to be followed in order for processing of personal data to be lawful[1]. A general survey of the Data Protection Act 1998 is outside the scope of this chapter, but one set of requirements which should be noted here are the contractual requirements under the seventh data protection principle (relating to security of processing) where an authority or other body appoints a contractor to act as a 'data processor' for it within the meaning of the Act.

1 The principles are set out in the Data Protection Act 1998, Sch 1.

8.76 A 'data processor', as defined in the Data Protection Act 1998, is any person or body that processes personal data on behalf of another organisation (that organisation being, in Data Protection Act terminology, the 'data controller' for such personal data). There are a wide number of local authority contracts where an external contractor may effectively be in the position of a data processor for an authority. These will include, for instance, strategic partnering or outsourcing contracts where the contractor has access to personal data, but may also many other types of contract. Even a contract for the operation of a CCTV system will probably fall within this category, since images captured on CCTV will be likely to constitute personal data within the scope of the Act.

8.77   The contractual requirements which a data controller must comply with are set out in the Data Protection Act 1998, Sch 1, paras 11 and 12. The requirements are as follows:

1   when choosing a data processor, the data controller (ie the authority) must choose a processor providing 'sufficient guarantees in respect of the technical and organisational security measures governing the processing to be carried out' (para 11(a));

2   the data controller must include provisions in the contract which:
   (i)   require the data processor to act only in accordance with the instructions of the authority as data controller; and
   (ii)   oblige the data processor to comply with obligations equivalent to those imposed on the data controller under the seventh data protection principle (ie on security); and

3   the authority must take reasonable steps to ensure the data processor's compliance with the measures (para 11(b)).

8.78   These requirements mean that data protection needs to be addressed not just in the contract, with appropriate wording, but also at the tender and selection stage of contracts (probably with appropriate questions in the invitation to tender), and also as a matter of ongoing contract management. It may also be appropriate to include additional data protection provisions and indemnities in the contract, depending on the nature of the procurement and services to be performed. Many current local authority contracts tend not to deal with data protection requirements particularly effectively.

CHAPTER 9

Dispute resolution

Gerlando Butera

INTRODUCTION

9.01   Despite the best intentions of parties at the outset of a contractual relationship, they should anticipate that disputes or differences may well (and on a complex project, almost certainly will) arise between them at some point during the course of the relationship. The management of disputes that do arise can be extremely costly and time consuming, diverting valuable management time from more productive activities, and potentially causing acrimony that may fatally damage an ongoing relationship. The selection of appropriate procedures for the resolution of disputes is therefore a matter of some importance.

9.02   When a difference or potential dispute does arise, the first resort should invariably for the parties to discuss the matter to try to resolve the issue by agreement. A well-managed project will have inbuilt systems (eg regular reviews and escalation procedures) to ensure that issues are addressed effectively at an early stage, preventing them from turning into disputes so far as possible. After this, the possible procedures for dispute resolution that might be selected range from those which give rise to final and binding decisions made by a tribunal (court proceedings, arbitration and expert determination); through those where the tribunal's decision has temporary finality (adjudication); to others still where the procedure does not involve a person making a decision as such, but rather the facilitation of a settlement agreement between the parties themselves (alternative dispute resolution, or 'ADR'). For more complex contracts, it may be that a combination of certain of these methods may be appropriate.

9.03   For example, the OGC guidance on *Standardisation of PFI Contracts*[1] puts forward a three-stage process for the resolution of disputes under PFI contracts:
(1)   in the first instance, the authority and contractor are to consult for a fixed period in an attempt to come to an agreement in relation to the disputed matter;
(2)   if the parties are unable to agree through consultation, either party may refer the matter to an adjudicator who is appointed from a panel of independent experts;
(3)   if either party is dissatisfied with the adjudicator's decision, it may refer the matter to arbitration for a final and binding decision.
Possible variations on the model in the TTF guidance are to make the expert's decision final and binding for certain types of dispute, or to stipulate for court proceedings instead of arbitration as the final stage in the process.

[1]   OGC Guidance, Issue 3 (revised 2002).

COURT PROCEEDINGS

9.04   Court proceedings are effectively the 'default procedure' for the resolution of contractual disputes. In other words, if a contract does not stipulate any other method of dispute resolution or is silent on the matter, it will be open for an aggrieved party to seek redress by pursuing a claim in the civil courts. The claim may be, for example, a claim for damages for breach of the contract by another party, or a claim for a declaration as to the respective rights and obligations of the parties on a matter that is in issue between them. The process then results in a determination of the dispute that is binding and enforceable between the parties.

9.05   For many, court proceedings also represent the mechanism of choice for dispute resolution, favoured over all other available options, and it is not uncommon for commercial contracts to provide expressly that disputes between the parties are to be dealt with by the courts. This is perhaps increasingly the case following the radical changes to the civil court procedures that were brought about by the introduction of the Civil Procedure Rules 1998[1] in April 1999.

1   SI 1998/3132.

9.06   The CPR 1998 are a product of the review of the civil justice systems that was led by Lord Woolf, and are designed to sweep away the arcane features of the previous system at the same time as rendering it more accessible and less prone to abuse. The overall tone of the new approach is set by Part 1 of the Rules, which identifies that they are 'a new procedural code with the overriding objective of enabling the court to deal with cases justly'. The CPR then clarify what is meant by 'dealing with a case justly', namely as including

'... so far as is practicable –
(a) ensuring that the parties are on an equal footing;
(b) saving expense;
(c) dealing with the case in ways which are proportionate:
    (i)   to the amount of money involved;
    (ii) to the importance of the case;
    (iii) to the complexity of the issues; and
    (iv) to the financial position of each party;
(d) ensuring that it is dealt with expeditiously and fairly; and
(e) allotting to it an appropriate share of the court's resources, while taking into account the need to allot resources to other cases'[1].

1   CPR 1.1(2).

9.07   These are not just words to which lip-service is to be paid. The rules direct that the court 'must' seek to give effect to this overriding objective when it exercises any power under the rules or interprets any rules[1], and that the court must further the overriding objective by actively managing cases[2]. They also expressly provide that parties 'are required' to help the court to further the overriding objective[3]. This statement of the fundamental purpose of the rules permeates their entire content and strongly influences how they are operated in practice.

1   CPR 1.2.
2   CPR 1.4.
3   CPR 1.3.

9.08 The most dramatic of all changes brought about by the CPR 1998 is how they have affected the behaviour of disputing parties before proceedings are commenced, and coupled with this the emphasis on the pursuit of court proceedings as being a measure of last resort. This has been achieved by the introduction of 'pre-action protocols' which outline the steps which parties should take to exchange information about a prospective legal claim. Separate detailed protocols are to be approved by Practice Directions of the court in respect of different types of claim. So far, six pre-action protocols have been approved (including protocols for construction and engineering disputes, and for claims for professional negligence), with others currently in development.

9.09 A common feature of all of the approved protocols is to establish a timetable for the parties to provide to each other full and detailed information with respect to the prospective claim. This enables the issues to be identified clearly at an early stage, and allows each party to make a realistic assessment of the merits of the case on an informed basis. This 'cards on the table' approach in turn increases the likelihood that the parties will be able to negotiate a settlement of the dispute. Indeed one of the stated objectives of the protocols is to enable parties to avoid litigation by agreeing a settlement of the claim before the commencement of proceedings.

9.10 Compliance in substance with the terms of a pre-action protocol is backed by sanctions for failure to comply. In particular, if in the opinion of the court non-compliance has led to the commencement of proceedings which might otherwise not have needed to be commenced, or has led to costs being incurred in the proceedings that might otherwise not have been incurred, then the court may order the party at fault to pay part or all of the costs of the proceedings. Alternatively (or even additionally), where the claim results in an award of damages, the court may penalise the claimant who has been at fault by depriving it of interest on damages; or where it is the defendant which has been at fault, it may be penalised by a direction to pay interest at a higher rate than the rate at which interest would otherwise have been awarded[1].

1   Practice Direction—Protocols, para 2.3.

9.11 Similarly, in cases that are not for the time being covered by an approved protocol, the court expects the parties likewise to act reasonably in exchanging information and documents relevant to the claim and generally in trying to avoid the necessity for the start of proceedings[1]. In all cases, the conduct of the parties, before as well as during the proceedings, is a factor that the court is specifically required to have regard to in deciding what order to make about the costs of the proceedings.

1   Practice Direction—Protocols, para 4.

9.12 Under the CPR 1998, once proceedings are commenced on a commercial claim, they typically follow a pattern of steps that is broadly similar to how a case would have run under the old rules, but in many respects more efficiently and with a greater level of control by the court over the management of the process:
(1)   Proceedings are commenced by the issue of a claim form either in the High Court or a county court (the CPR 1998 provide a unified code covering proceedings in both courts). Generally, proceedings may only be commenced in the High Court where the claim is for damages or a sum of money exceeding £15,000.
(2)   A claimant may join more than one defendant in the proceedings, and a claim by a defendant against a third party for a contribution or indemnity or some other

relief may also be joined into the same proceedings (for example, where proceedings are brought by an authority against a contractor, the contractor may join in a claim against its sub-contractor).

(3) Cases are allocated by the court to one of three 'tracks' which dictates how they will be managed through the court system. The small claims track is the normal track for any claim which has financial value of up to £5,000; the fast track applies to claims valued between £5,000 and £15,000, where the trial is expected to last no longer than one day with limited expert evidence; and the multi-track is the normal track for all other claims, which will cover most claims under commercial contracts.

(4) The issues in the action are identified by 'statements of case' that are served by the parties. These broadly correspond to 'pleadings' under the old rules, but are now expected to be more concise and focused on the facts relied on in support of a party's case, and they must be verified by a statement of truth signed by the party or its legal representative. Proceedings for contempt of court may be brought against any person who makes, or causes to be made, a false statement in a statement in case without an honest belief in its truth.

(5) Where a case is allocated to the multi-track, the court at an early stage gives directions for the management of the case and sets a timetable for the steps to be taken by the parties up to the trial. These directions will normally be given at a case management conference, and the court will also fix a trial date or trial window as soon as practicable. Parties are now expected to observe the timetable dates fixed by the court, and they are not permitted even to agree amongst themselves to extend the date fixed for any step if this would necessitate a variation of the date fixed for a case management conference or the trial or trial window. This effectively outlaws the interminable delays in the period up to trial that were commonplace before the CPR 1998 were implemented.

(6) In most types of proceedings, summary judgment may now be sought at any stage by either claimant or defendant, or may be given by the court on its own initiative. The court may give summary judgment if a claim or defence or a particular issue has 'no realistic prospect of success', and there is no other reason why the case or issue should be disposed of at trial.

(7) As before, there is provision for parties to disclose to each other documents that relate to the case. However, the procedure under the CPR 1998 (termed 'disclosure') is quite different from the former 'discovery', which entitled the parties to see all documents relating to the issues in the action however tangential their relevance. Discovery involved the routine wastage of thousands of pounds of clients' money on the management of piles of documents, few of which would ultimately be relied on by either party. Now, the disclosure obligation is subject to the overriding objectives of dealing with cases justly, including the concept of proportionality having regard to (amongst other things) the amounts at stake and the financial position of each party. The court may now dispense with disclosure altogether; and, where disclosure is ordered, it will normally be for 'standard disclosure' requiring only the disclosure of documents on which the party relies, which adversely affect its or another party's case, which support another party's case, or which must be disclosed pursuant to a relevant Practice Direction. Additionally, when giving 'standard disclosure', a party's duty to search for documents is limited to making a 'reasonable search', having regard to (amongst other things) the ease and expense of retrieval of any particular document, and the significance of any document which is likely to be located in the search.

(8) As regards witness evidence, the court will normally order a party to serve in advance written statements containing the evidence to be given by witnesses

which the party intends to rely on at the trial. The court's extensive powers of case management include the ability to control such evidence by giving directions as to the issues on which it requires evidence, the nature of the evidence required, and the way in which it is to be placed before the court.

(9) Likewise, in relation to expert evidence, the new rules require that it be 'restricted to that which is reasonably required to resolve the proceedings', and no party may tender expert evidence without the court's permission. Further, where two or more parties wish to submit expert evidence on a particular issue, the court may direct that the evidence on that issue is to be given by a single joint expert.

(10) The proceedings culminate in a trial before a judge. The trial must generally be heard in public, but the court may direct that the trial or any part of it should be heard in private in appropriate circumstances, for example, if it involves confidential information and publicity would damage that confidentiality.

9.13   As regards costs, the CPR 1998 preserve the general rule that the unsuccessful party will be ordered to pay the costs of the successful party. The order will normally be for the costs to be assessed on 'the standard basis', in which case costs are only allowed which are proportionate to the matter in issue, and which have been reasonably incurred for a reasonable amount. However, in support of the overriding objective, the court now has a very wide discretion as to whether costs should be payable by one party to another and as to the amount of those costs, and in particular regard is to be had to the conduct of the parties and the degree of success attained.

9.14   There is also now greater scope for a party to acquire a measure of costs protection by making a payment into court or an admissible offer to settle. Notably, a claimant as well as a defendant can now make an offer to settle the claim on the basis that, if the offer is not accepted but the other party fails to do better at trial, then the other party will be penalised (by way of costs and/or interest on the sum awarded) unless the court considers it unjust to direct this.

9.15   A particular area in which the court has demonstrated its willingness to exercise its discretion on costs is with respect to the resolution of disputes by alternative means if possible. The duty of the court to further the overriding objective by active case management includes a duty to encourage the parties to use an ADR procedure if the court considers that appropriate, and to facilitate the use of such procedure. A graphic display of how far the court will go to fulfil that duty was given in *Dunnett v Railtrack plc*[1]. In that case, no order for costs of an appeal was made in favour of the defendant, even though it had been completely successful in the appeal, because the defendant had declined to pursue the court's suggestion that the case was suitable for ADR. Following this case, and having regard to the effect of the CPR 1998 on pre-action behaviour of the parties, it may fairly be said that a decision by contracting parties to opt for court proceedings as their chosen method of dispute resolution entails also a commitment by them to explore ADR wherever appropriate.

1   [2002] EWCA Civ 303, [2002] 2 All ER 850.

ARBITRATION

9.16   Arbitration is a private method of achieving the final and binding determination of a dispute that is enforceable, if necessary, through execution against the assets of the losing party. It is similar in effect to court proceedings, in the sense of producing a decision which is final, binding and enforceable, but differs because the jurisdiction of the arbitral tribunal is founded on the agreement of the parties, albeit (in England and Wales or Northern Ireland) constrained by a statutory framework which is now the Arbitration Act 1996 ('AA 1996'). Hence, arbitration is necessarily consensual: a person cannot be forced to take part in arbitration proceedings unless it has agreed to submit disputes to arbitration (whether that agreement be an agreement in advance to submit disputes that may arise, or an agreement after the event with respect to a dispute which has arisen).

9.17   The direct enforceability of an arbitration award is important, and distinguishes arbitration from 'expert determination' (see para **9.29** below). Under the AA 1996, s 66, an arbitration award may be enforced in the same way as a judgment or order of the court. This is subject to the need to obtain the leave of the court, but leave is given as a matter of course unless it is shown that the tribunal lacked substantive jurisdiction to make the award.

9.18   The key features that distinguish arbitration from court proceedings are, first, that arbitration proceedings are conducted in private, enabling the parties to limit the extent to which details of their affairs (more especially, of their disputes) are publicised to strangers; and second, the tribunal in an arbitration is ultimately selected by the parties, who are thus free, for example, to chose a technical person whom they may consider to be more suited to resolve their dispute than would be a judge of the courts. Other differences that might lead to a preference for arbitration over court proceedings are that an arbitration is less formal, is less heavily regulated by procedural rules, and there is greater flexibility for the tribunal to adopt procedures tailored to the particular dispute. Psychologically, resort to court proceedings might also be perceived as a signal that the relationship between the parties has broken down, whereas this may be less so if they proceed by way of arbitration.

9.19   Just as civil court procedures were radically changed by the CPR 1998, the laws governing the conduct of arbitrations were extensively modernised by the AA 1996; and, in a similar fashion, s 1 of the Act sets out a mission statement which encapsulates the intended spirit of the process:

> 'the object of arbitration is to obtain the fair resolution of disputes by an impartial tribunal without unnecessary delay or expense'.

9.20   In furtherance of that objective, the AA 1996 imposes upon the arbitral tribunal duties 'to act fairly and impartially as between the parties, giving each party a reasonable opportunity of putting his case and dealing with that of his opponent'; and 'to adopt procedures suitable to the circumstances of the case, avoiding unnecessary delays or expense, so as to provide a fair means for the resolution of the matters falling to be determined'[1]. The parties for their part are enjoined 'to do all things necessary for the proper and expeditious conduct of the arbitral proceedings'[2].

1   AA 1996, s 33(1).
2   AA 1996, s 40(1).

9.21   An arbitration clause will normally provide for the number of arbitrators who are to form the tribunal, and the procedure for selection and appointment of the arbitrator(s) (if not named in the contract). A typical provision is the appointment of a sole arbitrator whose identity is to be agreed between the parties within a short period from either party inviting the other's agreement, and in default of agreement for the arbitrator to be appointed by a nominating person or body (such as the President of the Law Society or the President of the Chartered Institute of Arbitrators). Another common provision (more so where the contract has an international element) is for the appointment of a panel of three arbitrators, with each party nominating an arbitrator, and the third being selected by the two so appointed. In the latter case, the party-nominated arbitrators do not in any sense act for the parties by whom they were respectively nominated: each arbitrator owes the duty to act fairly and impartially as between the parties. The AA 1996 contains default provisions that apply where the arbitration clause is silent as to the number of arbitrators and their appointment.

9.22 The arbitration clause may also provide that the proceedings are to be conducted in accordance with one or other of the many sets of procedural rules for arbitration that have been published by various institutions, such as the Chartered Institute of Arbitrators Arbitration Rules or the ICC Rules of Arbitration. Each of those published sets of rules has its own particular characteristics and particular advantages which parties may find attractive. However, where no such rules are specified in the arbitration clause, the AA 1996 itself contains sufficient provisions to enable the arbitration proceedings to be conducted expeditiously. In particular, the Act confers extensive powers on the arbitral tribunal to decide all procedural and evidential matters, subject to the rights of the parties to agree any matter, including[1]:

— whether and if so what form of written statements of claim and defence are to be used and when these should be supplied;
— whether any and if so which documents or classes of documents should be disclosed between the parties and at what stage;
— whether to apply strict rules of evidence;
— whether and to what extent that there should be oral or written evidence or submissions;
— whether and to what extent the tribunal should itself take the initiative in ascertaining the facts and the law.

The tribunal also has power to direct that the recoverable costs of the arbitration (or any part of the proceedings) are to be limited to a specified amount[2].

1   AA 1996, s 34(2).
1   AA 1996, s 65.

9.23 One important power that is lacking to the arbitrator (and which may be regarded as a significant disadvantage compared with court proceedings) is the ability to join into the proceedings persons who are not party to the arbitration agreement. An arbitrator may not even consolidate the proceedings with other arbitral proceedings on the same subject matter, or order that concurrent hearings be held, unless the parties so agree. This can give rise to problems: for example, where an authority has suffered a loss which may be attributable to two or more other parties, not all of whom are parties to the same arbitration agreement with the authority. In that case, the authority may face the prospect of having to pursue separate proceedings against them and the risk of inconsistent findings in those separate proceedings. The authority could not then overcome this by simply starting court proceedings against all of the other parties contrary to their wishes, as any party with whom the authority has an applicable arbitration agreement would be entitled as of right to a stay of the court proceedings against it[1].

1   AA 1996, s 9.

9.24   The culmination of arbitration proceedings (unless, of course, they are settled) is an award by the arbitral tribunal determining the issues that have been submitted for its decision. Unless the parties otherwise agree, the tribunal must decide the dispute in accordance with the law applicable to the substance of the dispute: in other words, it is not for the tribunal to decide in accordance with what it considers to be 'fair' or 'reasonable' if the applicable law dictates a different result.

9.25   As regards finality, the arbitral tribunal's decisions on matters of fact are always conclusive, but (unless excluded by the parties' agreement) there are limited rights of appeal under the AA 1996 on questions of law. Specifically, an appeal on a question of law may only be brought with the agreement of all parties to the proceedings or with the leave of the court. The court has the discretion as to whether it will grant leave, and it will only do so if satisfied that the determination of the question will substantially effect the rights of a party, and either that decision of the tribunal is obviously wrong, or that the question is one of general public importance and the decision is at least open to serious doubt[1]. Apart from the possibility of appeal, an award may also be challenged on the grounds that the tribunal did not have substantive jurisdiction[2], or on the ground of serious irregularity (such as failure by the tribunal to deal with all the issues that were put to it)[3].

1   AA 1996, s 69.
2   AA 1996, s 67.
3   AA 1996, s 68.

9.26   In relation to costs, unless the parties otherwise agree, the tribunal has power under the AA 1996 to make an award allocating the costs of the arbitration between the parties. The award of costs is to follow the general principal that costs should follow the event except where it appears to the tribunal that this is not appropriate in the circumstances in relation to the whole or part of the costs[1].

1   AA 1996, s 61.

EXPERT DETERMINATION

9.27   Contracts often provide for the reference of disputes to an independent person who is to act 'as an expert and not as an arbitrator', and whose decision is agreed to be 'final and binding on the parties'. Such provisions are generally known as 'expert determination' clauses.

9.28   The salient characteristics of expert determination are that:
—   it is an entirely private, contractual mode of dispute resolution; and
—   subject to the parties' agreement, it results in a conclusive decision on the matter in dispute, with no rights of appeal or other judicial review.

9.29   Whilst expert determination proceedings result in a decision that is final and binding on the parties (if they have so agreed), the decision is not directly enforceable in the same way as an arbitration award. An expert's decision can only be enforced by commencing court proceedings on the basis of the decision and obtaining judgment in those proceedings.

9.30 The fact that expert determination is founded entirely on the parties' agreement also distinguishes it from arbitration. True, arbitration only applies where the parties have agreed to resolve their disputes in that fashion. However, arbitration operates within a statutory framework that regulates the process, which is not the case with expert determination proceedings.

9.31 For expert determination, this has both advantages and disadvantages. The advantages derive from the fact that, in the absence of a controlling framework for the procedures, the parties have the greatest possible flexibility to agree how their disputes are to be resolved. However, without a statutory framework, there are no 'fall-back' provisions regulating what is to happen if there are any gaps in what the parties have agreed, or if there is a breakdown of the procedure—for example, in the event of the death or incapacity of the appointed expert, or where one party is unwilling to co-operate with the expert determination process. There is not even a set of conventional procedures that are recognised by the common law as applicable to such proceedings. In terms of the common law, the most that can be said is that expert determination proceedings should, no doubt, be conducted in accordance with the general principles of natural justice, and that the parties have implied obligations to co-operate so as not to prevent the expert from arriving at his/her decision. These general principles would require, for example, that the independent expert should act neutrally between the parties. However, the precise requirements of these general principles can vary from case to case, and are necessarily tinged with some uncertainty. Hence, expert determination clauses need to be drafted with particular care, as nothing can be taken for granted; and if a desired feature is not spelt out in the parties' agreement (such as the power for the expert to award costs between the parties), then it is likely not to apply to the procedure at all.

9.32 As regards finality, an expert's decision as a result of expert determination is, in fact, even more impregnable than an arbitrator's award. Specifically, in the absence of fraud or collusion (or, no doubt, failure to observe the principles natural justice), an expert's decision cannot be challenged on the grounds of any mistake, whether of fact or law, unless it can be shown that the expert has not performed the task assigned to him/her.

9.33 Broadly, what this means is that so long as the expert has answered the right question, then his/her decision will be binding on the parties; but if the expert answers the wrong question (ie not the question that the parties have referred), then the expert's decision will be a nullity. The limits of the possibility of challenge were underlined in a case in 1992, where the judge commented as follows:

> 'The true construction of this expression was a matter with which the expert was required to grapple. The fact that he may have placed upon it a particular construction and sought to justify it with reasoning which is flawed—or even incomprehensible—would simply mean that he had answered the right question wrongly. I would go further … The fact that he may be patently wrong does not mean that he has not done what he was appointed to do nor that he has asked himself the wrong questions'.[1]

1   *Pontsaru Investments Ltd v Kansallis Osaka Pankki* [1992] 1 EGLR 148.

9.34 This again has its advantages and disadvantages. On the positive side, one of the main reasons why expert determination is selected for the resolution of disputes is the parties' desire to obtain a conclusive decision once and for all. The downside is that the losing party may be stuck with a perverse decision brought about by the incompetence of the expert, or perhaps a simple mistake on his or her part. Hence, care in the selection in the expert, and ensuring that the issues in the dispute truly lie in his/her area of expertise, become matters of the greatest importance.

9.35   As noted above, the contractual basis of expert determination allows the parties effectively unrestricted flexibility to decide what procedures are to apply to the resolution of their disputes. As a result, expert determination provisions sometimes set out elaborate provisions covering such matters as the exchange of written statements of case between the parties and the mutual disclosure of documents etc. More often, however, the contract will say little or nothing at all about the procedures that are to be followed by the expert in arriving at his/her decisions, for example as to whether the expert should hear submissions and evidence from both sides to the dispute.

9.36   Where the contract is silent in this respect, the expert is left free to adopt such procedures as he/she considers appropriate in the circumstances, and these may or may not involve the hearing of evidence and contentions brought forward by the parties. He will be entitled to rely on his own judgment and opinion, giving any evidence or submissions that he receives from the parties only such weight as he thinks proper (if any).

9.37   In practice, where the contract is silent as to the procedures to be followed, the expert will typically invite the parties to submit any relevant factual information that is known to them and will give the parties the opportunity to put forward their contentions in writing or orally according to their preference. Depending on the subject matter of the dispute, the expert will also typically want to carry out a site visit, and he may wish to carry out other tests and investigations or (if the parties agree) consult specialists on areas that lie outside the scope of his expertise.

9.38   It might be said that allowing the expert to conduct the proceedings in the manner he sees fit is preferable to attempting to stipulate in advance precisely what procedures are to be followed. Otherwise, the parties and the expert may find themselves constrained by a procedure that is really inappropriate for the dispute that has arisen, although the value of leaving the procedure to the expert's discretion very much depends on the capabilities of the appointed person to devise an appropriate procedure. Additionally, parties should particularly resist the temptation to prescribe a period within which the expert is required to arrive at his decision unless the issue referred is within well-defined and narrow confines. The desire to impose a time limit on the procedure is understandable, but extremely complex issues may be raised in an expert determination and time limits that are imposed in advance are all too often found to be wholly unrealistic.

9.39   There is no limit on the types of disputes that parties might agree to remit to an expert, and some contracts do provide that any and all manner of disputes arising under or in relation to the contract are to be resolved in that way. Some contracts provide for all disputes to be referred to a single named individual, while others provide for the selection of the expert to depend on the nature of the particular dispute that has arisen (eg disputes on contract interpretation to be referred to a lawyer, technical disputes to be referred to an engineer etc). Other contracts provide for only certain types of dispute to be referred to an expert (eg disputes relating to technical issues).

9.40 Where the over-riding desire of the parties is so far as possible to achieve absolute finality in the resolution of a dispute, then expert determination remains a valid mode of dispute resolution. To a large extent, however, the same degree of finality can be achieved through arbitration proceedings by agreeing to exclude all rights of appeal. With the modernisation of arbitration procedures that have been introduced by the AA 1996, the other reasons that have led parties to select expert determination in preference to arbitration are less compelling than in the past, and the relative certainty of the statutory framework for arbitration will be seen by many as making it a better option for the private binding resolution of most types of dispute.

ADJUDICATION

9.41 Since May 1998, a system of statutory adjudication has applied to disputes under construction contracts by virtue of the Housing Grants, Construction and Regeneration Act 1996 ('HGCRA 1996').

9.42 The essence of adjudication under the HGCRA 1996 is that either party to a construction contract has a statutory right (which cannot be excluded) to invoke the adjudication procedure at any time. The adjudicator (who may be named in the contract, or appointed by an adjudicator nominating body) must then reach a decision on the matter referred to him/her within 28 days of referral (extendable by 14 days with the consent of the referring party, or for a longer period with the agreement of both parties). The adjudicator's decision is then binding until the dispute is finally determined by court proceedings or arbitration.

9.43 The scope of application of HGCRA 1996 adjudication is wide, extending for example to professional appointments for the provision of services relating to construction works. However, there are a number of specific exclusions: notably PFI agreements that would otherwise fall within the HGCRA 1996 are excluded so long as certain formalities are complied with.

9.44 Although HGCRA 1996 adjudication is only applicable to construction contracts, the scheme and procedures adopted under that legislation can be (and are, as in the model in the OGC guidance for PFI contracts) replicated for other types of contract where it may be considered appropriate to have a 'fast track' decision on a dispute with temporary finality.

ALTERNATIVE DISPUTE RESOLUTION

9.45 In the eyes of many, arbitration, expert determination and adjudication are all species of 'alternative dispute resolution' in its widest sense. However, for the purposes of this section, the expression is used to refer to non-binding methods of dispute resolution, which are all private and voluntary processes.

9.46   The use of non-binding ADR to facilitate the settlement of disputes has grown rapidly over the last decade, reflecting parties' disenchantment with the cost, delays and damage to business relationships associated with court and arbitration proceedings. Considerable further impetus has been given to this trend by the approach of the courts to alternative dispute resolution (in its widest sense) following the introduction of the CPR 1998. Not surprisingly, with the growing take-up of ADR procedures, they are reputed to enjoy a high success rate in terms of settlements achieved.

9.47   The best known and most widely-used ADR procedure is mediation. In a mediation, the parties select a neutral person to assist them in reaching an acceptable agreement. Typically, the procedure involves the parties first exchanging summaries of their positions on the matters in dispute. They will then meet together with the mediator, when the parties will be invited to make informal presentations in joint sessions, and there then follows a series of 'caucuses' between each party and the mediator alone, with open and frank discussions about the merits and demerits of each party's case. The role of the mediator is to persuade the parties to focus on their underlying interests and concerns and move away from fixed positions that often cloud the real issues; it is his or her function to act as the facilitator or honest broker. The success of the process depends to a very large extent on the quality of the mediator. It is also vital that the parties' representatives at the mediation have authority to negotiate a settlement.

9.48   Another well-tried form of ADR is a 'mini-trial'. This is a process whereby each party makes a truncated presentation of its best case before a mini-trial panel. Typically, the panel consists of one member of management from each party and a neutral adviser. Ideally, the managers should not have been directly involved in the dispute before, and they must have settlement authority and sufficient seniority to participate actively in forging creative solutions. The function of the neutral is to advise and give an objective view on matters of fact and applicable law. The procedure is tailored to the parties' requirements, but typically the parties will have provided each other with limited disclosure of documents and information in order to define issues and learn the weaknesses and strengths of each other's case. The presentations then provide an opportunity for the managers to focus on the essential issues in the dispute. At the conclusion of the presentations, the managers enter into negotiations in an attempt to settle the dispute, assisted by the neutral adviser. If settlement is not reached immediately following the presentations, then the parties can require the neutral adviser to provide a non-binding opinion as to the probable outcome of litigation, and this can then be used as a basis for further negotiation.

PART III
SPECIAL FEATURES RELEVANT TO
LOCAL GOVERNMENT
PROCUREMENT

CHAPTER 10

Statutory powers of local authorities and ultra vires

Ray Ambrose

INTRODUCTION

10.01 There are a number of special features that affect local authorities in their procurement of contracted services, etc. These features generally arise from the specific statutory position of local authorities and the way in which the court has supervised the exercise of statutory functions by such authorities. This chapter deals particularly with these aspects of local government procurement, of which the procurement practitioner should be aware.

THE LEGAL CAPACITY OF LOCAL AUTHORITIES— THE 'ULTRA VIRES' RULE

Judicial control of local authorities

10.02 Probably the most important special feature of local authorities in relation to procurement arises from the fact that they are corporate bodies created by statute, which are subject to the judicial control of the court in relation to their administrative actions and decisions. This jurisdiction of the court became established because such corporate bodies are the creations of Parliament, formed for the purpose of the performance of public duties and functions for the benefit of the public or a section of the public funded by taxation levied upon the public.

10.03 The courts have long enjoyed a supervisory role over the administrative actions of such bodies to ensure that they do not abuse the power granted to them by Parliament (eg by straying beyond their statutory purposes and limitations, do not reach perverse decisions and do not misapply their taxation powers). This jurisdiction of the courts exists so that the interests of the public are protected from any abuse of the powers granted to such bodies.

10.04 Originally the supervisory jurisdiction of the court was exercised by means of 'prerogative writs' which enabled the court either:
(i) to correct perverse decisions or refer them back to the body for proper consideration (a writ of certiorari);
(ii) to grant a positive injunction requiring the body to perform its statutory functions (a writ of mandamus); or

(iii) to prohibit the body from taking a decision anticipated to be perverse (a writ of prohibition).

In addition 'relator' actions could be initiated by the Attorney General at the behest of an aggrieved member of the public challenging the legality of actions or decisions of such bodies.

10.05   In the 1960s these actions were grouped together into a legal process termed judicial review, under which the court could issue orders with similar effect to the former prerogative writs. In addition an aggrieved member of the public could take an action against a statutory body in his own name without being required to involve the Attorney General. More recently an Administrative Court has been created to administer what is now termed 'administrative law' under similar general principles under which the names of the orders have been updated – certorari becoming a 'quashing order', mandamus becoming a 'mandatory order' and prohibition a 'prohibiting order'.

10.06   In addition, it is open to an authority and/or an interested person, provided there is a real dispute between them as to their legal rights or powers, to seek a declaration in which the court states the legal relationship between the parties.

10.07   Another potent means of judicial control affecting local authorities, in particular, is that their accounts are subject to statutory audit which, in addition to the audit of the financial aspects, includes scrutiny by the auditor of the legality of all expenditure incurred. The audit process also provides the ability for local taxpayers to object to any expenditure on the basis that it is unlawful, thus requiring the auditor to examine the legality of such expenditure.

10.08   If the auditor considers any expenditure to be unlawful, an application can be made to the court for an order determining whether or not it is lawful. Until 27 July 2002 if the court found the expenditure unlawful, it could also order that the members or officers of the local authority responsible for it be surcharged the amount of the unlawful expenditure. Whilst the power of surcharge has now been abolished, the auditor's power to seek an order of the court on the legality of local authority's expenditure remains in force.

10.09   In addition the auditor has a power to seek judicial review of any decision of the authority he considers unlawful as though the auditor were a 'person aggrieved' at that decision. Many of the notable decisions of the court on ultra vires issues relating to local authorities emanate from this audit process.

10.10   The court's judicial control of the administrative action of local authorities (and other public and governmental bodies) described above has given rise to a large body of case law which now governs the legal status of such bodies and the discharge of their statutory powers and duties. The case law has important legal consequences and effects governing the activities of local authorities, and has important implications for their procurement as discussed in this chapter.

The ultra vires doctrine

10.11   The courts have, since the growth of corporations created by or under statute during the nineteenth century, applied what is known as the ultra vires rule to corporations. Ultra vires means 'beyond the powers'. Its effect is that the court regards the powers of such corporations to be limited strictly to those matters which Parliament has by statute authorised them to perform and anything necessarily inferred thereby.

10.12 Thus this rule creates a distinction between the legal capacity of an individual under the law and that of a statutory corporation. An individual has the freedom and capacity to do anything that is not forbidden by the law. A statutory corporation may, in contrast, only do those things which Parliament has specifically authorised it to do by the terms of the Act or Acts of Parliament that confer duties and functions upon it or anything necessarily inferred from those statutes. Anything not specifically so authorised is, in principle, regarded as beyond the powers of the corporate body and of no effect in law.

10.13 The ultra vires doctrine applies to all statutory corporations (including government bodies created by statute, eg non-departmental government bodies (ie quangos)) and 'functional bodies' created under the legislation that established the Mayor and Assembly in Greater London and to bodies such as the National Assembly for Wales. It also formerly applied to companies registered under the various Companies Acts, but this has now been virtually negated by subsequent legislation. However, whilst early case law on ultra vires arose in relation to limited companies, local authorities are now the largest group of corporations to which the rule applies and much of the recent case law emanates from local authorities and from the special legislation that governs their establishment and operations.

10.14 It should be noted that the ultra vires doctrine in its strictest form applies specifically to statutory corporations only. Other types of corporations, eg common law corporations (ie those created by Royal Charter, including the City of London Corporation, other ancient cities and boroughs, and certain charitable and public bodies) and corporations sole (ie government ministers and bishops, etc) are not constrained by the doctrine in the same way as statutory corporations, although they must act for the purposes for which they were established and must not abuse their charter or other powers.

Features of the ultra vires doctrine

10.15 In interpreting and applying the ultra vires doctrine it is necessary to consider a number of different aspects and features of the doctrine as established by the courts. These features may be grouped under the following headings:
(a) illegality (ie breach of the terms or scope of the relevant legislation or an abuse of the purpose of the legislation);
(b) irrationality (ie breach of the principles required for a proper and rational application of statutory powers);
(c) procedural impropriety (ie abuse of the statutory or other requirements applicable to action under the legislation or the process required by its terms);
(d) fiduciary duty (ie the duty to have regard to conflicting interests especially the interests of those who will be required to fund the related expenditure).

10.16 In *Council of Civil Service Unions v Minister for the Civil Service*[1], Lord Diplock set out the following classification of breaches of the ultra vires doctrine which are subject to the control of the court by means of judicial review:

'Judicial review has I think developed to a stage today when without reiterating any analysis of the steps by which the development has come about, one can conveniently classify under three heads the grounds upon which administrative action is subject to control by judicial review. The first ground I would call "illegality", the second "irrationality" and the third "procedural impropriety".

By "illegality" as a ground for judicial review I mean the decision-maker understanding correctly the law that regulates his decision-making power and must give effect to it.

By "irrationality" I mean what can now be succinctly referred to as "*Wednesbury* unreasonableness"[2]. It applies to a decision which is so outrageous in its defiance of logic or of accepted moral standards that no sensible person who had applied his mind to the question to be decided could have arrived at it.

I have described the third head as "procedural impropriety" rather than failure to observe basic rules of natural justice or failure to act with procedural fairness towards the person who will be affected by the decision.'

The following paras examine the principles applied by the courts under these three broad labels. To these has been added a further label of 'fiduciary duty' which is relevant to local authorities in particular because of their recourse to local taxation (council tax and non-domestic rates) to fund their expenditure.

1   [1985] AC 374, [1984] 3 All ER 935, HL.
2   *Associated Provincial Picture Houses Ltd v Wednesbury Corpn* [1948] 1 KB 223, CA.

Illegality

10.17   A cardinal principle of the ultra vires doctrine is that any action or expenditure undertaken by a statutory corporation must be within the terms of the authorising legislation. This requires a careful examination of any proposal in terms of the relevant statutory provisions to establish that what is proposed falls within the terms of the Act or is something necessarily to be inferred from its terms, and that the intended purpose of the proposed action is within the purpose of the enactment.

10.18   A degree of relaxation of this strict rule of interpretation of the scope of statutory powers is provided by the decision in the case of *A-G v Great Eastern Rly Co Ltd*[1], in which the court held that a statutory corporation may not only do those things for which there is express or implied authority, but also anything that is incidental to the doing of those things. Whilst this decision remains of effect at common law, the position in this respect in relation to local authorities and many other statutory corporations created in more recent years has been codified by statute law. The relevant statutory provision relating to local authorities is the Local Government Act 1972, s 111(1), which provides that (subject to certain important exceptions and restrictions)[2] '... a local authority shall have power to do anything ... which is calculated to facilitate, or is conducive or incidental to, the discharge of any of their functions'. This apparently wide power is, however, regarded by the courts to be merely a statutory re-expression of the principle in *A-G v Great Eastern Rly Co Ltd*[3] and is regarded as limited in scope to minor matters that are strictly incidental to the exercise of the 'parent' statutory power.

There are a number of important decisions of the courts relating to s 111 which are discussed in greater detail below.

1   (1880) 5 App Cas 473.
2   These exceptions are set out in sub-s (1): 'Without prejudice to any powers exercisable apart from this enactment but subject to the provisions of this Act, and any other enactment passed before or after this Act', which means that the subsection cannot be relied upon to circumvent or override the specific provisions of other relevant legislation.
3   (1880) 5 App Cas 473.

10.19   Accordingly local authorities and those contracting with them need to be extremely cautious in placing any reliance upon s 111(1) for the authorisation of action that goes beyond the scope of the specific statutory powers of the local authority, except in so far as the section is merely relied upon for minor matters that are truly incidental to the 'parent' statutory power.

10.20   The scope and terms of the legislation are paramount and the courts are reluctant to read more into the words of a statute than is strictly required to give the legislation's words their ordinary or natural meaning (in accordance with the normal principles of statutory interpretation). Thus it is very important for the practitioner to examine the words of the statute and to consider whether the proposed action falls squarely within the meaning of those words or must necessarily infer that the proposed action is required to give effect to the statutory purpose.

10.21   Examples of cases considered by the courts of the scope of legislation include the following:
(1)   *A-G v Manchester Corpn*[1] where the court held that the corporation could not carry out a general parcels delivery service on the basis of a power to carry and deliver parcels, etc under its private Act to run tramways.
(2)   *A-G v Fulham Corpn*[2] where the court held that the corporation was not empowered to provide a laundry service for residents under its power under the Baths and Washhouses Acts 1846 and 1878, which empowered it to provide facilities for residents to wash their own clothes.
(3)   *Hazell v Hammersmith and Fulham London Borough Council*[3] where the House of Lords held that the undertaking of interest rate swaps by the council for the purpose of profit was outside the express statutory powers of the council with regard to the conduct of its financial affairs as set out in the Local Government Acts.
(4)   *Credit Suisse v Allerdale Borough Council*[4] where the council established a company to construct a swimming pool and timeshare apartments, it was held that a guarantee to the company for sums borrowed by the company was not within the council's spending and borrowing powers.

1   [1906] 1 Ch 643.
2   [1921] 1 Ch 440.
3   [1992] 2 AC 1, HL.
4   [1997] QB 306, [1996] 4 All ER 129, CA.

10.22   Another aspect of 'illegality' is that statutory powers must be operated for the purpose for which they are enacted. For example in the *Allerdale* case the court held that the intention of the council in establishing the company and guaranteeing the bank loan was to avoid central government controls on its capital expenditure. This was an abuse of the statutory purpose of the legislation governing the provision of recreational facilities and a breach of the trust provided by Parliament through the terms of the statutory controls on the council's expenditure.

10.23   More recently, the House of Lords has held that the sale of council housing for an ulterior motive (ie for the purpose of gaining of additional votes for a council's majority party) was an abuse of the statutory powers of the council to sell its housing stock and was unlawful, giving rise to the surcharging of the persons responsible[1].

1   *Porter v Magill* [2002] LGR 51.

10.24   Thus it will be seen that in relation to any procurement or other decision of a local authority, it is of vital importance that full consideration is given at an early stage to the statutory powers upon which the authority is to rely for that procurement or decision. It is important to ensure that the authority and its officers are clear that the statutory purpose for which the procurement or decision is being made falls squarely within the relevant powers of the authority or is necessarily inferred thereby. In addition it is necessary to ensure that the proposed procurement or decision is to be made to fulfil the purpose of the statutory scheme and no other ancillary or alternative purpose, in order to avoid the possibility of an accusation that the statutory powers of the authority are being abused and that the relevant decision of the authority is therefore susceptible to challenge as being ultra vires.

Irrationality

10.25   The head of irrationality is concerned with the examination of the nature of the decision making process undertaken by the statutory body and with ensuring that the decision-maker applied its collective mind to the proper matters to be considered in reaching the decision. The leading case in relation to this area of the law is *Associated Provincial Picture Houses Ltd v Wednesbury Corpn*[1] in which Lord Greene MR said:

> 'It is true the discretion must be exercised reasonably. Now what does that mean? Lawyers familiar with the phraseology commonly used in relation to the exercise of statutory discretions often use the word "unreasonable" in a rather comprehensive sense. It has frequently been used and is frequently used as a general description of the things that must not be done. For instance a person entrusted with a discretion must, so to speak, direct himself properly in law. He must call his own attention to the matters which he is bound to consider. He must exclude from his consideration matters which are irrelevant to what he has to consider. If he does not obey those rules, he may truly be said, and often is said, to be acting unreasonably. Similarly, there may be something so absurd that no sensible person could ever dream that it lay within the powers of the authority. Warrington J in *Short v Poole Corpn*[2] gave the example of a red-haired teacher dismissed because she had red hair. That is unreasonable in one sense. In another sense it is taking into consideration extraneous matters. It is so unreasonable that it might also be described as being done in bad faith; and in fact, all these things run into one another.'

1   [1948] 1 KB 223, CA.
2   [1926] Ch 66, CA.

10.26   The principle is that the decision-maker must apply his mind properly to the matters in hand, must reach a real decision based upon the consideration of all of the factors that are relevant, disregarding extraneous matters, and reach a decision which is not so absurd that no sensible decision-maker would reach it.

10.27   These principles may be distilled into the following rules:
(a)   that the decision-maker must take into account all of the relevant considerations;
(b)   that the decision-maker must disregard irrelevant considerations;
(c)   that the decision must not be so unreasonable that no reasonable decision-maker would come to that decision.

10.28   The courts have always held that the burden of proof of unreasonableness is a heavy one and that in considering that question the court cannot substitute its own decision for the decision of the person entrusted by Parliament with the responsibility of taking the decision.

10.29   The court's role is limited to examining the process by which the decision was reached and of intervening only if the proper principles of reasonable decision-taking have not been observed. The standard of unreasonableness is, therefore, pitched at a high level so that the test of unreasonableness is a stringent one only met where a defect in the process has taken place (covering illegitimate motives, irrelevant considerations and mistakes and misunderstandings and misdirections) or an absurd decision has been taken. The overriding principle and purpose is to ensure that the exercise of powers must be confined within the scope and policy of the relevant enactment.

10.30   Examples of irrationality are:
(1)   *R v Ealing London Borough Council, ex p Times Newspapers Ltd*[1] where a local authority refused to provide certain newspapers in its public libraries because the newspapers were perceived to be politically hostile to the authority. It was held that the political motive of the local authority was irrelevant to its statutory duty to provide a comprehensive and efficient library service;
(2)   *Wheeler v Leicester City Council*[2] in which the decision of the council to ban a local rugby club from using the council's sports grounds because of the failure of the club to condemn a tour of South Africa was held to be unreasonable in that it sought to punish a club that had done no wrong;
(3)   *R v Somerset County Council, ex p Fewings*[3] where the council's decision to ban deer hunting on its landholding was held to have been irrational because the attention of the councillors had not been drawn to the relevant statutory provisions (as to the holding and management of its land) and that the council had come to the decision on grounds of 'ethics, animal welfare and social considerations' which reflected a failure to appreciate the overriding statutory constraints.

1   (1986) 85 LGR 316.
2   [1985] AC 1054.
3   [1995] 1 All ER 513.

10.31   In view of the above discussion of W*ednesbury* reasonableness, consideration needs to be given in each relevant case to the information that should be placed before the decision-making body of a local authority or other statutory corporation in order to ensure that all of the relevant considerations, and no irrelevant ones, are being taken into account. Thus the report should address all relevant considerations, both for and against the proposed decision, and must not contain any irrelevant factors. It is, of course, for the decision-making body itself to decide the weight to be given to each of these factors and whether any other factors are relevant to its consideration of the matter. In addition the duty of the decision maker to take into account all relevant factors, disregard irrelevant ones and not come to a decision that no reasonable body would come to, may with advantage be restated in the report.

Procedural impropriety

10.32   The third head of ultra vires relates to the meeting of prerequisites or requirements arising both from the relevant statute or from the common law. These requirements must be complied with by the local authority or other decision-maker before exercising a statutory discretion, or in connection with the exercise of a statutory discretion.

Express procedural requirements

10.33   These requirements often arise from the express provisions of a relevant statute which prescribe the taking of specific steps with regard to consultation or the decision-making processes. A difficulty that arises is whether or not a court will, in any particular instance, treat these stipulations as mandatory or directory.

10.34   The breach of a mandatory requirement will render the decision a nullity, whereas the breach of a directory requirement will not. There is no clear or simple test to ascertain whether any particular statutory requirement is mandatory or directory. The court will look at the general purpose and context of the enactment, the particular purpose of the requirement itself within that general context and the nature of the prejudice that would be caused by non-compliance. The public interest reposing upon the performance of the requirement is a major factor taken into account by the court in determining whether or not it will be treated as mandatory.

10.35   The courts have in recent times expressed in a number of ways the principles involved in determining whether or not a requirement is mandatory or directory. In *Wang v IRC*[1], Lord Slynn of Hadley posed the question 'did the legislature intend that a failure to comply with [the requirement] would deprive the decision maker of jurisdiction and render any decision which he purported to make null and void?'.

1   [1995] 1 All ER 367.

10.36   In *R v Stoke City Council, ex p Highgate Projects*[1] Sedley J posed two questions as follows:

'Was there a breach of a procedural requirement?'

'Was the harm done by that breach serious enough that the decision so reached ought to be set aside?'

1   (1994) 26 HLR 551.

10.37   The likelihood is that neglecting a requirement which has the effect of preventing or restricting the ability of interested persons from having their voices heard, will be held to be mandatory. In other cases the position is more uncertain and there is little that can be offered in the way of clear advice as to whether or not a requirement is likely to be held to be mandatory rather than merely directory.

10.38   Whilst the present state of the law may appear to be rather unsatisfactory and uncertain, there are clear risks involved in a failure by an authority to observe statutory requirements which could be held to be mandatory. It is therefore clear that local authorities and those contracting with them should ensure that all statutory requirements are complied with in order to avoid the possibility of a successful challenge to the authority's decision on the ground of breach of a mandatory requirement.

Legitimate expectation

10.39 The position becomes yet more difficult at common law, where the principle of 'legitimate expectation' may arise from four possible circumstances, as follows:
(1) there may be a substantive right to the relevant right or benefit;
(2) there may be an expectation that a right or benefit will not be withdrawn without adoption of a fair procedure;
(3) there may be an expectation that that a procedure followed in the past or that has been promised will be followed; and
(4) there may be an expectation that a fair procedure will be followed.

10.40 A legitimate expectation may arise either from a promise given by a public authority or from the existence of a regular practice which the claimant may reasonably expect would be continued. The intrinsic importance of the subject matter of the decision or its context will not of itself give rise to a legitimate expectation. However, a legitimate expectation cannot bind an authority or body to action that would be ultra vires (ie beyond their power to adopt).

10.41 To constitute a legitimate expectation by way of a promise, the terms of the promise must be clear and unambiguous and without any relevant qualification or reservation. It must also be given by an officer of the authority who is authorised to give it. If the promise is of benefit to a person, that person has a legitimate expectation that he will be consulted (with an opportunity to express his views) before the authority takes a decision to change its policy.

10.42 In *R v Liverpool Corpn, ex p Taxi Fleet Operators' Association*[1] a public undertaking given by a member of the relevant sub-committee of the corporation, that no new licences would be issued until new legislation was in force, was held to constitute a legitimate expectation that the association would be consulted on any change of policy. In *R v Brent London Borough Council, ex p MacDonagh*[2] a promise that gypsies would not be evicted from a site until alternative sites were found was held to constitute a 'legitimate expectation'.

1   [1972] 2 QB 299.
2   [1990] COD 3.

10.43 Equally if a promise is made that a particular procedure would be followed in reaching a decision, the authority will not be allowed to retract from that promise unless it has been validly revoked. Thus in *R v Devon County Council, ex p Baker*[1] the council was held to an undertaking promising the 'fullest possible consultation'.

1   [1995] 1 All ER 73.

10.44 It is, however, important to establish in precise terms what it is that the authority has promised. For example a promise to keep someone informed is not a promise to consult. It is also necessary to ensure that the person claiming a legitimate expectation is a person to whom the promise was made or a member of a class of persons to whom it was made.

10.45   Legitimate expectations based upon past practices may arise from an established practice of an authority consulting in a particular way. Provided that the practice has not been validly revoked, the authority will be treated as acting unfairly if it fails to follow that practice. By way of example, in *R v Birmingham City Council, ex p Dredger & Paget*[1] where a council had previously consulted on fees to be charged for market stall pitches but failed to consult the market traders on a new method of assessment and scale of fees, the new fees were quashed because of a breach of consultation practice. In *R v Brent London Borough Council, ex p Gunning*[2] a legitimate expectation was held to have arisen from a past practice of the council in consulting affected parents about its school closure programme.

1   [1993] COD 276.
2   (1985) 84 LGR 168.

10.46   A legitimate expectation based upon past practice is not limited to the right to be consulted. It may extend to other benefits granted by the authority, so that a person may legitimately expect to be given rational grounds for the removal of the benefit and an opportunity to state his case. By way of example in *R v Enfield London Borough Council, ex p F Unwin (Rodton) Ltd*[1] an approved contractor was held to have the legitimate expectation that the council would give reasons for the removal of the contractor from its approved list of contractors, and the opportunity to respond and a reasonable time in which to consider its response.

1   [1989] 1 Admin LR 50.

10.47   An authority is free to change its policy or revoke its promises and practices provide those changes are carried out fairly and in accordance with any legitimate expectations existing at the time. Once a valid change has been made to a policy or practice, any legitimate expectations that may have existed die with those policies and practices.

Natural justice

10.48   A further element in the head of procedural impropriety is the requirement that decision-makers act fairly and in accordance with the rules of 'natural justice'. It was long considered that this requirement applied only to decision-makers acting in a judicial or quasi judicial capacity and did not apply to administrative decisions. It is now clear, however, that this distinction is not valid and that the duty to act fairly to those affected by their decisions applies to all decision-makers.

10.49   The principle enunciated in *Hillingdon London Borough Council v Commission for Racial Equality*[1] is as follows:

> 'When an Act of Parliament confers on an administrative body functions which involve it in making decisions which affect the rights of other persons or curtail their liberty to do as they please, there is a presumption that Parliament intended that the administrative body should act fairly towards those who will be affected by their decision.'

1   [1982] AC 779.

10.50 The rules of natural justice are twofold:
(1) a right to a fair hearing; and
(2) the rule against bias.

10.51 The right to a fair hearing does not necessarily mean that the decision-maker must invite the person involved to appear physically before it to put his case. In most cases it is sufficient that the applicant's views are made known to the decision-maker and this may be done in written submission, by means of a letter or other appropriate means. The basic requirement is that the applicant's views must be heard and considered by the decision-maker. However this right often gives rise to ancillary rights, such as the right to have sufficient time to consider, prepare and put forward views, a right to have those representations genuinely taken into account and in some cases a right to have access to documents, representations made by other parties and post decision reasons.

10.52 The extent to which these ancillary rights may arise depends entirely upon the circumstances. and context of the decision to be made. In *R v Devon County Council, ex p Baker*[1] (see above) it was held:

'First, that consultation must be at a time when proposals are still at a formative stage. Second, that the proposer must give sufficient reasons for any proposal to permit of intelligent consideration and response. Third, … that adequate time must be given for consideration and response and finally, fourth, that the product of consultation must be conscientiously taken into account in finalising any statutory proposals.'

1   [1995] 1 All ER 73.

10.53 The second rule of natural justice is that there should be no bias. If bias is present it means that the decision has been taken in bad faith and should be quashed. The test adopted by the House of Lords in *R v Gough*[1] was not so much whether bias in fact was present but whether there was a real risk or a real possibility of such bias.

1   [1993] AC 646.

10.54 Thus where a member of a local authority had an interest in a development and voted on the decision to grant planning permission it was held that bias was present[1]. Whether the interest of the decision-maker is a pecuniary interest or a non-pecuniary interest makes no real difference, although the existence of pecuniary interest (even an indirect one) is usually sufficient to establish bias.

1   *R v Hendon RDC, ex p Chorley* [1933] 2 KB 696.

Summary

10.55 By way of summary, it needs to remembered that the various rules as to procedural considerations are not unimportant and if breached will give rise to a risk of a finding of ultra vires even where there is no hint of illegality or irrationality. It is therefore incumbent upon local authorities and those contracting with them to ensure that any procedural requirements, whether of an express statutory nature or which amount to a legitimate expectation, are observed and that the rules of natural justice are complied with where any decision affects the rights of any person or persons.

Fiduciary duty

10.56   A fiduciary duty is a duty owed by a local authority and its councillors to their council tax payers and ratepayers which is analogous to the duty owed by trustees to their beneficiaries. The courts have held that local authorities are under such a duty in the making of decisions that incur expenditure which is to be funded from the council tax or the rates. It is a duty to act prudently and in good faith in the interests of those to whom the duty is owed.

10.57   It is as matter of opinion whether this fiduciary duty is a separate duty placed upon those bodies who raise their expenditure from taxation or rates, or whether it is merely an aspect of the duty to act without irrationality under the *Wednesbury* reasonableness principles. It seems, in view of relevant cases, that this is a sufficiently important principle, applying in particular to local authorities, that it requires separate consideration.

10.58   The leading case on the question of the fiduciary duty of local authorities is *Roberts v Hopwood*[1]. In that case a local authority decided that it would pay a minimum wage of £4 to all of its employees. That sum was in excess of the market rate for many of its staff. It was held that the authority was under a duty to act in a fairly business-like manner with reasonable skill, care and caution and had breached that duty in expending ratepayers money thriftlessly and for philanthropic reasons.

1   [1925] AC 578.

10.59   In *Bromley London Borough Council v Greater London Council*[1] the GLC took a decision to reduce fares on London Transport services, the cost of which was to be met from a supplementary precept upon the ratepayers of Greater London. An effect of this increase in the GLC's precept was the loss of some £50m of government grant thereby almost doubling the cost of the fare reduction to the ratepayers. It was held that the GLC was in breach of its fiduciary duty to the ratepayers in that it had failed to balance its duty to the ratepayers against the benefits to transport users. Lord Diplock said that 'the fiduciary duty includes a duty not to expend [ratepayers] moneys thriftlessly but to deploy the full financial resources available to it to the best advantage'.

1   [1983] 1 AC 768.

10.60   It should be noted that this decision of the GLC was also held to be subject to illegality as a breach of the scope of the relevant statute (which required London Transport to operate so far as possible on a 'break even' basis) and irrational because the GLC councillors had misdirected themselves by regarding the GLC as irrevocably committed to the reduction by the majority party's election manifesto in which the fares reduction was a major policy.

10.61   It is, therefore, necessary for local authorities taking decisions that involve the expenditure of money raised from, or to be raised by, taxation to be seen to balance the interests of the council tax payers and ratepayers against the interests of those who would benefit from the expenditure and to do so in a business-like manner with reasonable skill, care and caution.

Importance of the ultra vires doctrine in procurement by local authorities

10.62   It will be appreciated, not least from the *Bromley v Greater London Council* fares case referred to above, that many of the principles that make up the ultra vires doctrine cross over each other and sometimes merge together. However, a single breach of one of these principles may be enough to lead to a decision that the relevant decision was ultra vires.

10.63   It will be appreciated from this brief exposition of the ultra vires doctrine, that the doctrine is a most important aspect of the law, applying to the decisions and actions of local authorities in all spheres in which they operate, not least the procurement of contracts. As will be seen from the discussion below[1] on the effect and implications of a breach of the ultra vires doctrine, it is vital that appropriate notice is taken of the need for the authorities to avoid acting unlawfully and in excess of their statutory powers.

1   See paras **10.64–10.73**.

10.64   The effect of a ruling by the court that a decision of a local authority is ultra vires may in many cases result in a finding that the relevant decision is void and of no effect in law. However, it should be borne in mind that the court has a discretion in any case where it decides that a decision of a local authority or of a similar body is ultra vires, whether or not to hold that the decision is void and of no effect in law. Indeed it is open to the court, even though it finds that a decision is ultra vires, to order that legal effect should be given to the decision and that any contract or other legal documentation reliant upon that decision should be regarded as having effect in law.

10.65   Formerly the court, in dealing with a judicial review, could exercise its discretion whether or not to hold that a contract based upon an ultra vires decision should have effect in law. Section 5(3) of the Local Government (Contracts) Act 1997 now provides that where the court, when dealing with both applications for judicial review or applications for audit review (initiated by the auditor of a local authority under the provisions of the Audit Commission Act 1998), is of the opinion that the local authority did not have power to enter into the contract, it should also have regard to the likely consequences for the financial provision of the authority and the provision of services to the public. The court should then decide whether or not to exercise its discretion to determine that, nonetheless, the contract should have (and always have had) effect as though the local authority had power to enter into the relevant contract and exercised that power properly.

10.66   Subject to the exercise of discretion, where a court finds that the local authority was acting ultra vires in entering into a contract, and the court orders that the decision of the authority be quashed, the consequences of this decision will be that anything dependent upon it (eg any contract or other legal transaction entered into by the authority in reliance upon that decision) will be of no effect in law.

10.67   The general principle arising from a ruling of the court that a decision of a local authority or similar body should be quashed, is that the decision and all legal transactions reliant upon it are to be treated as though they had not taken place and that the parties, so far as is practicable, be restored to the positions they enjoyed immediately before the ultra vires decision and the related transactions. It will be appreciated that the consequences of such a decision can be uncertain and unexpected, may leave the parties to an ultra vires contract bereft of any anticipated consideration and may render them unable to recover any payments made to the other party or to receive payment or other consideration for obligations already fulfilled.

10.68   An example of this is *Credit Suisse v Allerdale Borough Council*[1]. In that case Allerdale Borough Council established a company (wholly owned by the council) for the purposes of constructing a swimming pool and timeshare apartments. The bank made a loan to the company to cover the capital cost of the construction and the loan was guaranteed by the council. The company went into liquidation and the bank sought to call in the guarantee. The court held that the scheme initiated by the council and in particular the guarantee provided by the council to the bank, were ultra vires and of no effect in law. The result was that the bank was unable to recover the loan from the company and unable to recover under the guarantee.

1   [1997] QB 306, [1996] 4 All ER 129. See also para **10.21**.

10.69   In *Burgoine v Waltham Forest London Borough Council*[1] a similar situation occurred in relation to a company established by the council to develop a water leisure park. The bank loaned the requisite capital to the company on the security of the council's guarantee which was (following the court's ruling in *Allerdale)* accepted by all of the parties to have been ultra vires. The directors of the company were council officers who enjoyed the benefit of an indemnity from the council in respect of relevant legal claims against them in the course of their duties for the council. The bank again could not recover the loan either from the company or from the council and claimed its loss from the directors of the company on the basis that they were in breach of their duties to the company and to its creditors in their conduct of the company's affairs. The court held that as the formation of the company and all related transactions were ultra vires the council and of no effect in law, the directors were not entitled to recover under the indemnity from the council. This decision left the directors potentially liable to the bank for the amount of the loan.

1   [1997] BCC 347.

10.70   In the case of *Hazell v London Borough of Hammersmith and Fulham*[1] the council had undertaken interest rate swaps on its behalf and on behalf of other local authorities. The interest rates swaps were held to be ultra vires with the effect that the transactions between the banks and the local authorities were held to be void and of no effect in law. Accordingly the banks were unable to recover the sums advanced to the councils under the interest rate swap transactions. However the banks claimed against the authorities in equity for 'money had and received'[2]. The court held that the banks were able to recover the amount transferred to the council as money had and received together with simple interest at the statutory rate of interest applying to court debts, but could not recover compound interest at a higher rate.

1   [1992] 2 AC 1.
2   See *Westdeutche Landesbanke Girozentrale v Islington London Borough Council* [1996] AC 669, [1996] 2 All ER 961.

10.71   It will be seen from the cases cited above that the outcome of a finding of ultra vires in relation to a decision of a local authority to enter into contractual relationships with another party or parties is capable of giving rise to unexpected results. Indeed the effects of the above cases (in particular *Hazell v London Borough of Hammersmith & Fulham)* severely prejudiced the view of the banking fraternity as to the credit rating of local authorities generally and a number of banks became extremely cautious about financing some transactions with local authorities, especially long-term contracts for the provision of services by a private sector partner requiring bank finance to support its performance of the contract under the PFI or in the form of a PPP.

10.72   As a result of these cases legislation has been enacted, in the Local Government (Contracts) Act 1997, to enable those contracting for the provision of services to local authorities and those who provide funding in support of such contracts, to have greater confidence in the power of the local authority to enter into and perform its obligations under such contracts. It is also the case that private sector bodies contracting with local authorities and their funders are acutely aware of the possible pitfalls for them arising from the possibility that the local authority's decision to enter into contract with them might be impugned as being ultra vires the authority. These legislative measures are discussed at paras **10.82–10.91**.

10.73   In consequence it is now common for those contracting with local authorities and their funders to carry out extensive 'due diligence' examination of the authority's decision making process and the procedures under which it purports to act, in order to assure themselves that the risk of the decision to enter into the contracts being held at some future time to have been ultra vires the authority is reduced to the absolute minimum.

STATUTORY POWERS AND FUNCTIONS RELEVANT TO LOCAL AUTHORITY CONTRACTS

10.74   In a sense all of the powers and functions of a local authority are capable of being relevant to contracts entered into by the authority. This is because whenever a local authority enters into a contract it does so in order to perform one or more of its statutory powers or duties. Whilst those statutory functions generally do not in specific terms permit or authorise the authority to enter into a contract, it may be inferred from those statutes that Parliament intended that the authorisation provided to an authority to perform a function must necessarily include the authorisation of action required to carry that function into effect.

10.75   In addition if the power to contract could not be implied from the terms of the enactment authorising the statutory function, then the courts have historically extended the scope of the statute to include anything that is incidental to the performance of the statutory function[1]. In relation to local authorities this principle has been given statutory force by the Local Government Act 1972, s 111(1).

1   *A-G v Great Eastern Rly Co Ltd* (1880) 5 App Cas 473.

10.76   However, as mentioned above, in recent years Parliament has enacted specific legislation to provide a means whereby the authority may be able to give assurance as to its powers to enter into a particular contract and to provide some protection for private sector contractors contracting with local authorities against the effects of a finding of the court that the local authority entered into the contract acted ultra vires. These enactments, together with s 111, are discussed in the following paras.

Local Government (Contracts) Act 1997

10.77   This Act was specifically designed to deal with the effects of a series of court decisions on ultra vires handed down in the 1990s (principally *Hazell v London Borough of Hammersmith and Fulham* and *Credit Suisse v Allerdale Borough Council* together with the related decisions in *Credit Suisse v Waltham Forest London Borough Council*; *Morgan Grenfell v London Borough of Sutton* and *Burgoyne v Waltham Forest London Borough Council*) and to provide confidence and security for those persons funding such contracts.

Section 1: specific power to contract

10.78   Section 1 of the LG(C)A 1997 provides for the first time a specific statutory power for local authorities to enter into contracts. Sub-s (1) states:

'(1) Every statutory provision conferring or imposing a function on a local authority confers power on the local authority to enter into a contract with another person for the provision or making available of assets or services or both (whether or not together with goods) for the purposes of, or in connection with, the discharge of the function by the local authority.'

10.79   This section thus provides a clear statutory power for all local authorities to enter into contracts for the provision of assets, services or goods that are required for, or in connection with, the performance of any of their statutory functions. The term 'assets' is defined in sub-s (4) as meaning 'assets of any description (whether tangible or intangible) including, (in particular) land, buildings, roads, works, plant, machinery, vehicles, vessels, apparatus, equipment, and computer software'.

10.80   It is of course necessary, in relying on this power, to ascertain and consider the statutory function that is to be performed by the local authority for, or in connection with, which the contract is to be entered into. The power is only available for, or in connection with, the discharge of a statutory function by the local authority. It does not otherwise authorise a local authority to enter into a contract for any other purpose. It is therefore necessary for procurers of contracts on behalf of local authorities and those entering into contracts with local authorities to be clear as to the statutory function or functions of the local authority for or in connection with which the contract is to be entered into.

10.81   Section 1(2) also specifically authorises a local authority entering into a contract under sub-s (1) (the 'provision contract') to enter into a contract with the financier, or insurer or trustee for the financier, where, in connection with the provision contract, the financier makes a loan or provides any form of finance for a party to the provision contract other than the local authority. This subsection therefore widens the scope of the contracts that fall within the specific authority of the Act, and enables the local authority to enter into contracts with the funders of their provision contractors. This makes clear that where, for example, the provision contractor is prepared to invest in the provision of assets or services to the authority in order to improve the quality of the services it is able to provide, then the authority is able to enter into a direct contract with the financier of the provision contractor in order to regulate the position with regard to early termination and step in by the financier or the authority and to provide appropriate assurances to the financier. This is especially useful in connection with longer term contracts involving considerable investment by the contractor for which it requires outside funding, as is the case with contracts under the PFI or longer term contracts for service provision and improvement in partnership with a contractor (PPP) which enable the local authority to perform its relevant functions in accordance with the statutory best value duty under the Local Government Act 1999, Pt I.

Sections 2–7: certified contracts

10.82   The LG(C)A 1997 goes further, by making provision for the certification of certain types of local authority contracts, to provide partial protection against proceedings alleging that the contract is ultra vires the local authority and to provide other protections where a finding of ultra vires is nonetheless made which has the effect of rendering the contract of no effect in law.

10.83   These protections apply only to contracts that are 'certified contracts' under the provisions of the LG(C)A 1997. To be capable of being a certified contract, a contract entered into by a local authority with another person must be a contract for the provision or making available of services (whether or not together with assets or goods) for the purposes of, or in connection with, the discharge by the local authority of any of its functions and must operate or be intended to operate for a period of at least five years (see s 4(3)).

10.84   In addition, s 4(4) also provides that a contract entered into by a local authority with a person who, in connection with a contract falling within sub-s (3), makes a loan or provides any other form of finance for a party to that contract, other than the local authority, or with an insurer or trustee of such a person, is capable of being a certified contract under the Act.

10.85   It should be noted that the certification provisions of the LG(C)A 1997 do not, like the contracts within s 1, extend to all contracts entered into by a local authority for the purpose its functions, but are limited only to contracts for the provision of services (with or without assets and/or goods), which operate for five years or more.

10.86   The possible statutory 'protections' offered in respect of certified contracts are as follows:
(a)   subject to s 5 (which preserves the possibility that a certified contract may be held to be ultra vires and of no effect in law as a result of a judicial review or an audit review: see (c) below), a certified contract has effect (and is deemed always to have had effect) as if the local authority had the power to enter into it and had exercised that power properly in entering into it;
(b)   notwithstanding a finding (as a result of a judicial review or an audit review) that the local authority did not have power to enter into the certified contract, the court may nonetheless hold that having regard to the likely consequences for the financial position of the local authority and for the provision of services

to the public it should have (and be deemed always to have had) effect as if the local authority had power to enter into it and had exercised that power properly in entering into it;

(c)   if, as a result of a judicial review or an audit review the contract is held to have been ultra vires the local authority and not to have effect in law, such a finding shall have no effect on the enforceability of any 'relevant discharge terms' in relation to the contract. These are terms agreed by the local authority and any person with whom the local authority entered into the contract which form part of the contract or of another agreement entered into no later than the date of the certified contract and which provide for the consequences of such a finding. The relevant discharge terms may provide for the payment of compensatory damages (measured by reference to loss incurred or any other circumstances) by one party to the other and/or the adjustment between the parties of rights and liabilities relating to assets or goods provided under the contract; and

(d)   if the contract is held to be of no effect in law and there are no relevant discharge terms, or the court has ordered that the relevant discharge terms shall have no effect, the other party is entitled to be paid by the local authority such sums (if any) as the contractor would be entitled to be paid if the contract had had effect until the time of the court's determination or order but had terminated at that time by the acceptance by the contractor of a repudiatory breach of the contract by the local authority.

10.87   The LG(C)A 1997 specifies in some detail the certification requirements that have to be fulfilled in order that a contract capable of certification may enjoy the status of a 'certified contract' under the Act. In brief these requirements are that the local authority must have issued a certificate (whether before or after the contract operates or is to operate):

(a)   describing the purpose of the contract;

(b)   containing a statement that the contract falls within s 4(3) or (4) (ie, is a contract for services operating or intended to operate for at least five years or is a contract with a financier of a person who has entered into such a contract);

(c)   stating that the local authority has the power to enter into the contract and specifying the statutory provision or each of the statutory provisions conferring the power;

(d)   stating that a copy of the certificate has been or is to be given to the persons required to be given copies by regulations made under the Act;

(e)   complying with the requirements of the regulations;

(f)   signed by a person who is required by the regulations to sign it.

10.88   A certificate must be issued by the local authority within the certification period. The certification period commences on the day on which the local authority entered into the contract and expires six weeks after that date.

10.89   A replacement contract (ie one which replaces a certified contract but which is entered into with a different contractor), is also a certified contract if the period for which it operates ends at the same time as the period for which the original contract was intended to operate and, apart from that, its provisions are the same as the original contract.

10.90   Regulations made under the LG(C)A 1997[1] make further provision by way of requirements for certification including the specification of the officers of local authorities of different types who are capable of being authorised to sign certificates, and requiring that where the Local Government Act 1972, s 111 is the statutory power relied upon by the local authority in entering into the contract, the certificate shall also state the statutory power conferring the main relevant function or functions (ie the function or functions the discharge of which is calculated to be facilitated by the contract or to which the contract is incidental or conducive).

1   Local Authorities (Contracts) Regulations 1997, SI 1997/2862.

Effective certification

10.91   It should be noted that the statutory requirements for the effective certification of relevant contracts under the LG(C)A 1997, should be strictly adhered to. Great care is required in determining the relevant statutory power or powers to be stated in the certificate. This is something for the local authority to determine at an early stage (rather than be left until later) in order that any contracting parties and financiers may be aware of the powers concerned. Also, the local authority must obtain the consent to the issue of a certificate under the Act from each of the persons with whom it has entered, or is to enter, into contract.

10.92   The contracting parties will wish to carry out 'due diligence' testing of the processes adopted by the authority to be assured that the certificates are accurate, state the correct powers and that its issue is authorised by the authority. They will also wish to be assured that the officer signing the certificate is one of the officers specified in the Regulations and has been authorised by the authority to sign the certificate. They will also be keen to establish that the authority has acted in accordance with its standing orders and that the executive or committee authorising the completion of the contract has the delegated authority to do so.

10.93   It will be noted that the authority itself (acting through the appropriate channel, be it the council meeting (comprising all elected members) or through the executive (eg leader and cabinet or mayor and cabinet) or through a committee (comprising a selection of elected members with appropriate delegated power) or an officer (with appropriate delegated power) will make the decision to enter into the contract. However, the certificate under the Local Government (Contracts) Act 1997 is to be signed by a designated officer of the authority in his/her own name. Having regard to the reliance placed upon such certificates by the other contracting parties, it is not unusual for the officer concerned to seek an indemnity from the authority in respect of any claims that may be made against him or her personally should that eventuality occur.

Delegation

10.94   At this point it may be appropriate to consider the question of delegation of powers by the authority either to an executive, committees or its officers. A distinction needs to be made between the exercise of a statutory discretion by the authority itself (acting through its elected members in plenary session) and the exercise of those powers by others on behalf of the authority.

10.95   The principle is that the legal maxim *delegatis non potest delegare* (a delegate has no power to sub-delegate) applies. Since Parliament has delegated powers to the authority itself by statute, those powers cannot be further delegated by the authority except as specifically authorised by statute. There are a number of statutory provisions that permit delegation of powers to an executive and to committees and officers and indeed to other local authorities. Principal among these provisions is the Local Government Act 1972, s 101(1), which specifically permits the authority to delegate its powers (other than a power relating to the raising of a rate or council tax or the borrowing of money) to a committee, sub-committee or officer of the authority and permits a committee or sub-committee also to sub-delegate to an officer. Under Part II of the Local Government Act 2000, where an authority has appointed an executive most day-to-day decisions are by the statutory provisions delegated to the executive who may sub-delegate to officers of the authority. An authority's standing orders will normally provide for such officer delegations or, alternatively, they may be given by individual decisions of the authority or its executive or relevant committee or sub-committee. A specific delegation is often required to enable an officer to agree last-minute amendments to the legal documentation before completion of a contract.

10.96   Where the authority is relying on delegation of power to an executive, committee or officer the other contracting parties will wish to satisfy themselves that the authority has the power to delegate these matters and has effectively done so.

Other 'safe harbour' provisions

10.97   In addition to the Local Government (Contracts) Act 1997, there are two further 'safe harbour' protections for persons dealing with local authorities that are worth mentioning.

Local Government Act 1972, s 128(2)

10.98   This subsection provides protection to persons dealing with local authorities in relation to land transactions against any failure of the local authority to obtain a requisite consent under the LGA 1972 or any other enactment.

10.99   It provides that where a local authority purports to acquire, or dispose of land, then in favour of any person whose title is derived from the local authority or is claiming under the authority, the acquisition or disposal shall not be invalid by reason that any consent of a Minister that is required has not been given or that any requirement as to advertisement or consideration of objections has not been complied with. Further, a person dealing with the authority or claiming under the authority shall not be concerned to see or enquire whether any such consent has been given or whether any such requirement has been complied with.

10.100   The most relevant requirements are probably those contained in the LGA 1972, s 123(2) and (2A). Section 123(2) provides that except with the consent of the Secretary of State, a local authority shall not dispose of land otherwise than by way of a short tenancy (ie one for up to seven years) for a consideration less than the best that can reasonably be obtained. There is a considerable body of case law on the duty of a local authority under this provision and what measures it should carry out to ensure compliance with the duty. A local authority disposing of land in connection with a contract (eg a depot or other accommodation to be made available to the contractor) will need to ensure that the terms on which the disposal takes place complies with the duty to obtain the best consideration that can reasonably be obtained, unless consent is to be sought.

10.101 However, the contractor or other person dealing with the local authority is absolved from any duty to enquire whether or not the duty has been complied with, or a consent has been obtained, and their title to the acquired property will not be affected in any detrimental way if the local authority has failed, or is accused of having failed, to comply with the duty.

10.102 Section 123(2A) requires a local authority proposing to dispose of open space land or land which is a pleasure ground or a burial ground, to advertise their intention to do so and before confirming the proposed disposal, to consider any objections received by it. Again purchasers are not concerned to enquire whether the subsection has been complied with and their title will not be invalidated by any failure of the local authority to comply with the provision.

Local Government and Housing Act 1989, s 44(6)

10.103 Section 44(6) provides that a person lending money to a local authority shall not be bound to enquire whether the authority have power to borrow the money and shall not be prejudiced by the absence of any such power.

10.104 This provision is intended to absolve a lender of money to a local authority from investigating the authority's position under the complicated provisions of the LGHA 1989, Pt IV and the Local Authorities (Capital Finance) Regulations 1997[1] to ascertain whether or not the authority has the necessary power under the enactments to borrow the money.

1 SI 1997/319.

10.105 It is, however, necessary for any person dealing with a local authority seeking protection under this provision to make sure that it is applicable. It applies only to persons lending money to the authority. It does not apply in other types of transaction. For example in *Credit Suisse v Allerdale Borough Council*[1] the bank sought protection under s 44(6) but the court rejected this application on the basis that the bank lent money not to the authority but to the limited company set up by the authority (a different entity in law) and that the guarantee given to the bank by the council in respect of the company's loan was not a lending of money to the authority.

1 [1997] QB 306, [1996] 4 All ER 129.

Local Government Act 1972, s 111

10.106 This section provides a general power of competence to local authorities in the terms set out in sub-s (1) which are as follows:

'Without prejudice to any powers exercisable apart from this section, and subject to the provisions of this Act and any other enactment passed before or after this Act, a local authority shall have power to do anything (whether or not involving the expenditure, borrowing or lending of money or the acquisition or disposal of any property or rights) which is calculated to facilitate, or is conducive or incidental to, the discharge of any of their functions.'

10.107   As mentioned above[1], at first sight the section appears to provide a wide general power for local authorities to do anything related to the performance of their functions (including a combination of several different statutory functions, see *R v Eden District Council, ex p Moffatt*[2]). However, having regard to a number of court decisions on the use of s 111 by local authorities, it appears that the courts regard the section as no more than a statutory expression of the principle established by the court in the case of *A-G v Great Eastern Rly Co Ltd*[3]. Accordingly it is important that extreme caution is applied in placing reliance upon the use of the section for any widening of the powers of local authorities beyond those minor and restricted matters directly incidental to another statutory power. In *Hazell v London Borough of Hammersmith & Fulham*[4] the House of Lords held that the interest rate swap transactions entered into by the council were not authorised by s 111 because they did not assist the council to borrow and did not facilitate the management of the function of borrowing but only assisted the consequences of borrowing.

1   See paras **10.18** and **10.19**.
2   (1988) Times, 24 November.
3   (1880) 5 App Cas 473.
4   [1992] 2 AC 1, HL.

10.108   It is also important to give effect to the opening words of the section, particularly the words '… subject to the provisions of this Act and any other enactment passed either before or after this Act…'. These words make it clear that the section cannot be used to override any provisions of another enactment which places limits or restrictions upon the powers of the authority in relation to any particular subject matter of a statutory power.

10.109   In *Alsop v North Tyneside Metropolitan Borough Council*[1] the council sought to rely upon s 111 (inter alia) for the payment, to certain of its staff accepting voluntary severance, of redundancy terms more generous than those payable under the redundancy and early retirement regulations relating to local authority staff made under the Superannuation Act 1972. The Court of Appeal held that since the regulations set out a code of redundancy and early retirement terms payable to its staff, the council was not authorised by s 111 to make payments in excess of the amounts prescribed by the regulations. The court regarded the regulations as 'another enactment' to which the use of s 111 is subject.

1   (1992) 90 LGR 462.

10.110   However, the section remains a valid power available to local authorities within the above constraints. This is borne out by the reference to its potential use in the certification of contracts under the Local Authorities (Contracts) Regulations 1997[1]. As indicated by those regulations the power is available to facilitate the discharge of another (or main) statutory power provided the court's approach to its scope and use is complied with. One example of its valid use might be where an authority is entering into a contract for the provision to it of serviced accommodation in which to perform its various statutory functions. The relevant 'main' powers are likely to be the various statutory duties and powers performed by the officers of the authority who are housed in that accommodation. It is a valid application of s 111 for the authority to acquire the necessary accommodation in which to house those officers since to do so is clearly calculated to facilitate the discharge of those functions. Since the enactment of the Local Government (Contracts) Act 1997, s 1 such a contract is likely also to be authorised by that section also.

1   SI 1997/2862.

Local Government Act 2000, Pt I

10.111   This Act introduced a new power for local authorities to do anything which they consider is likely to achieve the promotion or improvement of the economic, social and/or environmental well-being of their area (s 2(1)). This useful power may be available on its own or in conjunction with other powers of the authority. For example, where a proposed contract, in addition to being for the performance of services in connection with the authority's functions with regard to housing, education, etc, is also calculated to bring some benefit to the area of the authority in economic, social or environmental terms, then the latter power may also be utilised alongside the other powers (where if, say, increased employment opportunities or regeneration may result) and may provide additional powers to those available in the specific powers otherwise available to the authority.

10.112   Thus where a partnership contract is likely to bring such benefits, the well-being power may enable the authority to enter into a joint venture or joint venture company with the partner to secure the well-being benefits for the area, which action might not be within the terms of the other powers relied upon (whether or not used in conjunction with the LGA 1972, s 111).

10.113   The use of the well-being power may be exercised in relation to or for the benefit of the whole or part of the local authority's area, or all or any of the persons resident or present in that area. The well-being power includes a power to incur expenditure, give financial assistance to any person, enter into arrangements with any person, exercise any functions on behalf of another person and provide staff, goods, services and accommodation to any person, and can be exercised outside the authority's area if it is likely to achieve one or more of the objects of the power.

10.114   The limits to the power are set out in s 3, which includes a restriction on the use of the well-being power to do anything which the local authority is unable to do by virtue of any prohibition, restriction or limitation on its powers contained in any other enactment. The power does not enable the local authority to raise money (whether by precepts, borrowing or otherwise). The authority must also have regard to any guidance issued by the government and orders may be issued preventing the performance of specified actions under s 2.

10.115   In exercising any of the well-being powers under s 2, the local authority is required to have regard to its strategy under s 4 of the Act. That section requires every local authority to prepare a community strategy for promoting the economic, social and environmental well-being of its area and for contributing to the sustainable development of the United Kingdom.

10.116   The well-being power is likely to prove to be a useful additional power in the hands of local authorities which will be likely to enable them to achieve significant additional benefits for their areas which they could not achieve by other means. It may be used as a 'stand alone' power for the contracting of services, etc to provide the well-being benefits or, as mentioned above, a useful additional power for use alongside other powers to increase the benefits available from a partnership approach with a contracting partner.

Human Rights Act 1998

10.117   The HRA 1998 brought into legal effect in the United Kingdom the basic rights and freedoms contained in the European Convention on Human Rights and Fundamental Freedoms and those contained in the First and Sixth Protocols thereto. The Act sets out in Sch 1 the Articles of the Convention and Protocols brought into effect.

10.118   Section 6 provides that it is unlawful for a public authority to act in a way which is incompatible with a Convention right, unless required to do so by legislation. It is clear a local authority falls within the scope of this section as a 'public authority' and is therefore amendable to actions brought under the Act in relation to alleged breaches of Convention rights. This opens up an additional route of challenge to local authority decisions and actions over and above the administrative law route, although there is likely to be considerable overlap and common ground on the grounds for challenge and the approach adopted by the courts under both regimes.

10.119   Section 6(3)(b) applies the s 6 duty to 'any person certain of whose functions are functions of a public nature'. It is at present uncertain whether, and to what extent, this section could be applied to persons contracting with local authorities for the performance of public functions. The distinction appears to be whether or not the person concerned is exercising public or private functions. However, in a climate where it is becoming possible under current legislation for statutory functions and related discretions to be delegated by local authorities to contractors, it is not beyond the realm of possibility that the law may develop in the direction of bringing such contractors within the definition of a 'hybrid body' under s 6(3)(b).

CHAPTER 11

Statutory best value duty

Mark Waring

INTRODUCTION

11.01   The enactment of the Local Government Act 1999 has made local government contracting and procurement subject to the fulfilment of an overriding duty to secure 'best value'. This duty requires local government (and other determined public bodies) to observe and achieve statutory obligations in the procurement process (including consultation with service users, fundamental performance reviews and inspections by external auditors) and, fundamentally, to ensure that the procurement adds to and secures continuous improvement of the quality of services a local authority provides to its local community. Best value's introduction was designed to promote and foster high quality performance, innovation and continuous improvement and it has introduced by its application numerous factors which must be met in the procurement process.

11.02   Best value replaced the former compulsory competitive tendering regime (CCT), introduced primarily by the Local Government Act 1988 which could only be dismantled by primary legislation. Best value, however, is much broader in its scope, covering all functions of a local authority and without the limitations of the CCT approach which classified functions subject to CCT by way of defined activities. The concept of best value under the Local Government Act 1999 embodies the familiar procurement principles of the three 'es' of economy, efficiency and effectiveness which had long been a key component of performance management in public authorities[1]. However, best value's purpose is to ensure local authorities review the fundamental aspects of their service provision and assess the underlying objectives and priorities of their work particularly in relation to other organisations in the public, private and voluntary sectors.

1   Consolidated into the Audit Commission Act 1998.

11.03   The basis for the Local Government Act 1999 was established in the Labour manifesto prepared for the General Election of May 1997. Following this election victory the then Local Government Minister, Hilary Armstrong, announced the new government's intention to press ahead with its manifesto promise to place upon local government a new duty to promote continuous improvement in the economy, efficiency and effectiveness of local services. Clearly indicated as well was the fact that the legislative process would provide the means with which to sweep away the restrictive CCT regime.

11.04   The best value regime came into force when the LGA 1999 received Royal Assent on 27 July 1999. Part I of the 1999 Act deals with best value and the general duty is contained in s 3(1) which requires a best value authority to:

'Make arrangements to secure continuous improvement in the way in which its functions are exercised, having regard to a combination of economy, efficiency and effectiveness'[1].

1   The Local Government Act 1999 (Commencement No 1) Order 1999, SI 1999/2169 brought s 3(1) into effect in England on 1 April 2000. Fire and police authorities in Wales were subject to the duty from 1 April 2000 by virtue of SI 1999/216. The full general duty of best value in Wales came into effect by the Local Government Act 1999 (Commencement) (Wales) Order 1999, SI 1999/2185 which was made on 28 September 1999 and brought the general duty into effect from 1 April 2000.

11.05   The LGA 1999 brought into force the most radical shake up of local government performance management approach to service delivery since the previous Conservative administration's unpopular CCT regime. CCT's legacy had been the statutory requirement upon authorities to advertise and tender services before being allowed to use their own staff to carry out such works in-house. Critics argued that the restraints of CCT created an atmosphere of suspicion and mistrust between contracting authorities and through the stipulation that contracts had to be let under the 'restrictive procedure', innovation and value were stifled.

Best value and local government—what is best value?

11.06   Local government is subject to the duty as it falls within the definition of a best value authority in s 1(1)(a) of the LGA 1999 as a 'local authority'. A 'local authority' in England is defined by s 1(2) as:
   '(a) a county council, a district council, a London Borough council, a parish council or a parish meeting of a parish which does not have a separate parish council;
   (b) the Council of the Isles of Scilly;
   (c) the Common Council of the City of London in its capacity as a local authority;
   (d) the Greater London Authority so far as it exercises its functions through the Mayor.'

In relation to Wales the term 'local authority' as defined by s 1(3) means a 'county council, a county borough council or a community council'[1]. Under the provisions of the LGA 1999, s 2(1), powers were reserved to the Secretary of State to provide by order that certain other authorities would be subject to the extension of the application of best value in relation to those functions set out in the order[2].

1   Other best value authorities defined in s 1 of the Act are: National Park Authorities; The Broads Authority; police authorities; fire authorities constituted by a combination scheme and metropolitan county fire and civil defence authorities, the London Fire and Emergency Planning Authority, waste disposal authorities, metropolitan county passenger transport authorities, Transport for London and the London Development Agency.
2   The Local Government Act 1999, s 2(2) sets out that these authorities and bodies are (a) the local precipitating authority within the meaning of s 39(2) of the Local Government Finance Act 1992; (b) a levying body within the meaning of s 74(1) of the Local Government Finance Act 1988 (these include Passenger Transport and certain National Park Authorities) and (c) a body to which s 75 of that Act applies (special levies) (example of such a body includes an internal drainage board).

11.07   Section 3 of the LGA 1999 requires that best value authorities are to make arrangements to secure continuous improvement in the way in which its functions are exercised, having regard to a combination of economy, efficiency and effectiveness. Section 3 deliberately lays down a general duty of best value which is not described exhaustively, but which is wide in its ambit by its relation to all of a local authority's 'functions'. The use of the terms 'functions' is no accident and was employed as a term to set out the all-encompassing nature of best value, rather than the more restrictive 'services'[1]. A broad interpretation as to what best value really is was initially set out in the *Modernising Local Government: Improving Local Services Through Best Value* White Paper which contained the principles of best value. This stated that best value authorities must procure and deliver services:

— ensuring that public services are responsive to the needs of citizens, not the convenience of service providers;
— ensuring that public services are efficient and of high quality;
— ensuring that policy making is joined up and strategic, forward-looking and not reactive to short-term pressures;
— using information technology to tailor services to the needs of users;
— valuing public services and tackling the under-representation of minority groups.

1 See Woolf J's comments in *Hazell v Hammersmith and Fulham London Borough Council* [1992] 2 AC 1.

11.08   The accompanying guidance to the LGA 1999 contained in DTLR Circular 10/99 states that best value is about best value authorities delivering these commitments at local level in a way which makes life better for people and for business. Additional to this is the requirement that best value authorities should command a leadership role in the local community and develop in partnership with other public bodies, quality public services. Guidance states that key to the development of the leadership role is the establishment of the community strategy which sets out the broad objectives and vision for the local community and reflects the way in which the authority and its partners are expected to make and improve the economic and environmental well-being, both in the immediate and in the longer term[1].

1 The community strategy obligation is placed upon a local authority by the Local Government Act 2000.

11.09   At the heart of the regime lies the performance management framework which requires local authorities to establish strategic objectives and corporate priorities. Section 4 of the LGA 1999 gives the Secretary of State (or the National Assembly for Wales) the power to specify performance indicators and performance standards in respect of the way in which the best value authorities exercise their function. The Act provides that in specifying the performance indicators and standards, the Secretary of State (or the National Assembly for Wales) aims to promote improvement in the way in which functions are exercised having a regard to a combination of economy, efficiency and effectiveness. Best value performance indicators are specified by order of parliament under s 4. The performance management framework sets in context the best value review and performance plans. Section 4 makes it clear that both performance indicators and performance standards will be essential tools for measuring performance and thus evidencing compliance within the best value duty. However, this alone will not provide a mechanism for securing continuous improvement. To measure this an authority will be judged against its own performance on a year by year basis.

Extent of the duty

11.10   The primary duty at the heart of best value contained in the LGA 1999, s 3(1) is not expressed in specific terms, rather, a best value authority is compelled to:

'... make arrangements to secure continuous improvement in the way in which its functions are exercised, having regard to a combination of economy, efficiency and effectiveness'.

This statement of a general duty was carefully avoided as an absolute obligation as it could:

'...make decisions vulnerable to challenge by anyone claiming that they see a better or less costly way to provide any service'[1].

1   *Modernising Local Government—Improving Local Services through Best Value* (Green Paper, March 1998), para 3.4.

11.11   Best value differs from CCT[1] as best value's application lies in respect of all an authorities' functions. What best value is in practice can be seen as the decisions taken at the local level which must aim to secure the duty of continuous improvement and the three 'e's' of economy, efficiency and effectiveness. Commentators have described best value broadly as the requirement to achieve the balance of cost, quality of service and assessment improvement under delivery of services.

1   CCT required authorities to expose to competition only those services within the definition of activities set out in the Local Government Act 1988, s 2(2).

11.12   The LGA 1999 requires the best value authority to examine, consider, have regard to and make accountable its manner of delivering services in a way in which seeks to secure the 'holy grail' of continuous improvement. Whilst, as mentioned, the duty is not expressed absolutely in the Act its anchor is that the duty will embrace a framework (including targets) which are policed. This framework which is embodied in the 'best value performance management framework' allows central government to put into place a means of measurement and standards required by ensuring that authorities are compared against nationally-imposed performance indicators and standards.

To whom is the duty of best value owed?

11.13   Both the Green Paper and the White Paper made it clear that accountability to the local electorate was core to the fulfilment of best value. Whilst a local authority's responsibility to central government is established through the best value performance management framework and the measurement of performance indicators and performance standards (which arguably establishes that the key duty is to central government, as the yardsticks as to success and failure are determined by these objective forms of measurement), local authorities have placed upon them a mandatory duty to consult widely amongst those who have a financial, service delivery or other interest in the functions of the best value authority in question.

11.14   Though the LGA 1999 itself is not prescriptive on the manner of consultation (the government recognised that many authorities have well-established methods of consultation which did not require prescription), the Secretary of State (or the National Assembly for Wales) may issue guidance on consultation process by virtue of s 3(4) including the form, contents and timing of the consultation[1].

1   Section 26(1) and (2): the Secretary of State or the National Assembly for Wales may issue different guidance to or in respect of different authorities or groups of authorities.

11.15 The practical outcome for consultation and the review process is the best value performance plan, the statutory requirement which is set out in the LGA 1999, s 6(1).

BACKGROUND TO THE LOCAL GOVERNMENT ACT

Compulsory competitive tendering

11.16 Prior to 'best value', local authority services were subject to the CCT regime which was held by the former Conservative government (1992–1997) as core to the securing of economy, efficiency and effectiveness and as a principal mechanism in holding local government accountable[1]. The statutory obligations of CCT required local and certain other authorities to subject certain defined activities to compulsory tendering before such work could be undertaken in-house. In essence, a local authority could only carry out certain defined activities in-house, through its own direct labour organisation (DLO) or direct services organisation (DSO) if the work had first gone out to tender and had been won by the in-house organisation in a process of open competition. Additionally, following the process of advertisement of the competitive tendering, the DLO or DSO was required to meet certain financial criteria and objectives which were designed to prevent anti-competitive practices by requiring self-sufficiency in the contractual organisation and stipulation that the contracting organisation would not operate at a loss.

1   CCT was embodied in the Local Government, Planning and Land Act 1980, Pt 3 and the LGA 1998, Pt 1. These were repealed on 2 January 2000 by the LGA 1999, s 21.

11.17 CCT was universally unpopular and was held by the then Opposition as 'inflexible, bureaucratic and inefficient'[1] and also considered by many to be an unnecessary cause of antagonism between local government and the private sector. CCT's progress had begun with the blue collar services of construction, maintenance and highways works services which were applied, by virtue of Part III of the Local Government Planning and Land Act 1980. CCT was further extended by the Local Government Act 1988, initially to waste, building cleaning, grounds maintenance and catering and then further on to leisure management. Finally much of white collar services were subject to the requirement in 1996.

1   Address by the then Leader of the Opposition, Tony Blair, to the Shadow Assembly of the Local Government Association on 23 July 1996.

11.18 CCT imposed requirements upon contracting authorities which many of its critics felt were obstructive to service provision. Not least was the stipulation that all contracts let under CCT had to be done so by the issuing of a contract under the restrictive procedure. The restrictive procedure placed an obligation upon the contracting authority to employ a two stage process to tendering based upon the assessment of tenders according to financial standing and technical ability and then subsequent evaluation of the tenders in accordance with pre-published criteria. Such a procedure prevented negotiation and dialogue between contracting parties (save for clarificatory queries) and, coupled with the CCT requirement to let contracts on a local authority's standard terms and conditions, there was little scope for negotiation of a specification between the parties. The result of these restrictions were contracts which were overly proscriptive, based upon detailed 'inputs' rather 'outputs' which stifled innovative service delivery from private sector providers.

The development of best value

The 12 principles of best value

11.19   The government published a provisional list of 12 'key principles of best value' in June 1997 which were later reproduced in its Green Paper *Modernising Local Government: Improving Local Services Through Best Value*[1]. At the time of publishing, the aim was to promote discussion into the nature of the best value framework and ways in which local authorities, the private sector and community could contribute to the delivery of high quality services seen as vital to the quality of peoples' lives. Discussions particularly focused not just on best value achieving economy and efficiency but also the effectiveness and quality of public services in setting out the best value principles. Ministers stressed that government kept an open mind as to whether or not services were better delivered by either the public private sector or directly within the public sector. Emphasis was particularly placed upon best value's ability to present an opportunity for innovative and efficient partnership working.

1   Published by DETR in March 1998.

11.20   The principles are:
1   The duty of best value is one that local authorities will owe to local people, both as taxpayers and the customers of local authority services. Performance plans should support the process of local accountability to the electorate.
2   Achieving best value is not just about economy and efficiency, but also about effectiveness and the quality of local services—the setting of targets and performance against these should therefore underpin the new regime.
3   The duty should apply to a wider range of services than those now covered by CCT. Details will be worked up jointly with Departments, the Audit Commission and the LGA.
4   There is no presumption that services must be privatised, and once the regime is in place there will be no general requirements for councils to put their services out to tender, but there is no reason why services should be delivered directly if other more efficient means are available. What matters is what works.
5   Competition will continue to be an important management tool, a test of best value and an important feature in performance plans. But it will not be the only management tool and is not in itself enough to demonstrate that best value is being achieved.
6   Central government will continue to set the basic framework for service provision, which will in some areas now include national standards.
7   Detailed local targets should have regard to any national targets, and to performance indicators and targets set by the Audit Commission in order to support comparative competition between authorities and groups of authorities.
8   Both national and local targets should be built on the performance information that is in any case needed by good managers.
9   Audit processes should confirm the integrity and comparability of performance information.
10   Auditors will report publicly on whether best value has been achieved, and should contribute constructively to plans for remedial action. This will include agreeing measurable targets for improvement and reporting on progress against an agreed plan.

11 There should be provision for intervention at the direction of the Secretary of State on the advice of the Audit Commission when an authority has failed to take agreed remedial action, or has failed to achieve realistic targets for improvement.

12 The form of intervention should be appropriate to the nature of failure. Where an authority has made limited use of competition, and as an exception to the usual rule, intervention may include a requirement that a service or services should be put to competition. Intervention might also take the form of a requirement that an authority should accept external management support, and may relate either to specific services, or to the core management of the council.

Further best value principles

11.21   The original 12 principles of best value set out above were revisited again in the DETR circular letter dated 25 July 1997 which as well as establishing the framework for the selection of local authority best value projects also produced five further key features of best value.

1 Establishing a corporate view of what an authority wishes to achieve and how it performs against both objective indicators and the views of the local community.

2 Reviewing the proportion of an authority's service activity each year.

3 Reviews to establish improved performance and efficiency targets and how these are to be achieved, using open competition, unless authorities are able to demonstrate why this is inappropriate in the circumstances.

4 Requiring publication reporting back on all authorities performance against targets and requiring participation with other authorities in sharing performance information and experience.

5 An audit process to ensure that the integrity of the reviews and certification of the monitoring of information with intervention by the Secretary of State as a last resort.

OPERATIVE ELEMENTS OF BEST VALUE

Introduction

11.22   The essence of best value has been described as the continuous improvement of service quality. The government in its determination of the best value regime held key that an authority should be provided with a comprehensive base line of performance against which assessment by the relevant authority and its services consumers could be made. The LGA 1999, s 4 gives power to the Secretary of State (or the National Assembly of Wales) to create performance indicators and standards to be met by the best value authorities. The duty to meet the performance standards set by the Secretary of State (or the National Assembly for Wales) is imposed upon best value authorities by s 4(5), and the recently published White Paper, *Strong Local Leadership—Quality Public Services* sets out the national framework of standards. The government intends to put in place a comprehensive framework for a continuous improvement in the quality of local government services which will streamline and form the best value framework.

Performance indicators and standards

11.23   Core to the measurement of continuous improvement and the duty of best value is the tool of comparison, primarily involving the use of performance indicators[1]. The introduction to the BVPIs and Audit Commission Performance Indicators for 2000/2001 states that at the heart of best value is the statutory performance management framework which provides for a set of national performance indicators and standards set by the government.

1   With the aim of improving comparability between authorities CIPFA have co-defined proper accounting practice in 'Best Value Accounting – Code of Practice' which was published in Spring 2000. The government expects authorities to follow this code to ensure that performance information is reported in a consistent manner.

11.24   Section 4 of the LGA 1999 enables the Secretary of State to specify performance indicators and performance standards. Particularly, s 4(1)(a) gives the Secretary of State power to specify by orders factors (referred to as performance indicators) by reference to which an authorities' functions can be measured. Further, by s 4(1)(b) the Secretary of State may by order set standards (performance standards) to be met by best value authorities in relation to the performance indicators specified[1].

1   Terminology was set out by DETR and the Audit Commission in *Performance Indicators for 2000– 2001—A Joint Consultation Document* CDETR and the Audit Commission on Best Value and Local Authority Indicators:
    (a) performance indicators – the measure of an authority's performance in exercising specified functions;
    (b) performance standard – the minimum acceptable level of service measured by reference to a performance indicator. Failure to meet a performance standard will be judged as failing the test of best value;
    (c) performance target – the level of performance that a best value authority is expected to achieve over a minimum period of a year, measured by reference to a performance indicator.

11.25   The provisions of the LGA 1999 give the Secretary of State flexibility over the making of an order. However, there is a duty of the Secretary of State to consult (only with 'such persons as he thinks fit'). The Audit Commission has the power to make recommendations to the Secretary of State which must be taken into account in specifying performance indicators and standards[1].

1   A new role for the Audit Commission was outlined in the Best Value Performance Indicators for 2001/2002. Instead of specifying performance indicators as they had in the past the Audit Commission were to consult local authorities on the set of voluntary quality of life and cross cutting indicators measuring performance across traditional service boundaries and in partnership with other state corporates. This is similar to the Audit Commission's previous practice under the Local Government Act 1992.

11.26   The distinction between a performance indicator and a performance standard is set out at para **11.24**. However, it is important that authorities note the provisions of s 4(5), which states that 'a best value authority must meet any applicable performance standards specified'. The essence of this is that meeting the performance standard is a mandatory obligation and that an authority which fails to meet a relevant performance standard will be deemed a 'failing' authority and subject to the powers contained in the LGA 1999, s 16.

The application of performance indicators, standards and targets

11.27 Best value authorities are required to publish performance information as illustrated by performance indicators, standards targets, in their annual best value performance plan.

Best value performance indicators

11.28 Best value performance indicators (BVPIs) are the first element of the performance management framework which provide the tools to measure the level of performance which a best value authority is achieving in the performance of its services. Between years 1993/1994 and 1999/2000 it was the Audit Commission which specified performance indicators through the mechanism of the Audit Commission Performance Indicator. With the advent of best value, these indicators are now specified by government as BVPIs.

11.29 BVPIs are consulted on annually prior to the issuing of a direction, which lists all the indicators to be reported. The current BVPIs for 2002/2003 have been reduced in number by government on the basis that authorities were over burdened with a variety of performance management obligations. The government intends to put in place a comprehensive framework of performance management and its intentions have been announced in the local government White Paper, *Strong Local Leadership—Quality Public Services*. The intention of this framework is to include:

— clearly defined priorities and exacting performance standards;
— a framework for performance assessment (including a proportionate and co-ordinated inspection) and regular and comprehensive assessment of accounts performance;
— local public service agreements (PSAs) to deliver accelerated improvements in priorities services supported by additional freedoms;
— a streamlined and reformed best value framework to help councils manage improvement across all services.

11.30 The BVPIs are of two types[1]. The first, the Best Value Corporate Health Indicator is designed to enable comparisons to be made between performance against different authorities. By far, however, the greatest proportion of performance indicators were intended to be developed locally and local authorities are encouraged to develop and use local performance indicators to achieve an important measure of local performance and of the responsiveness of the authority to meet local needs[2].

1 Best Value Performance Indicators for 2002/2003 (DTLR).
2 The Audit Commission has published guides to devising sets of performance indicators and to the setting and monitoring of local performance targets in its publication *Aiming to Improve: the Principles of Performance Measurement* (Audit Commission, 2000). Further the Audit Commission together with the Improvement and Development Agency (IDeA), established a library of definitions of local performance indicators where local authorities can select and use quality approved performance indicators appropriate to local circumstances.

11.31 BVPIs are to be published in best value authorities' annual best value performance plans which are required to contain details of performance against all

BVPIs relevant to an authority's function combined with improvement targets and goals.

Performance targets

11.32 The second element of the performance framework is that of performance targets, which is essentially the level of performance that a best value authority is expected to achieve over a minimum period of a year, measured by reference to a performance indicator. Performance targets will provide an indication to local people as to how an authority intends to improve its performance in future. The framework for assessing performance targets against BVPIs for 2002/2003 is that all targets will continue to be set locally by authorities. However, government guidance[1] must be adhered to as to the factors which authorities should take into account when setting targets. Local authorities, as best value authorities, are required to take account of all nationally specified performance indicators and attach targets where possible and these should take account of any relevant priorities and targets. In particular, authorities should take into account the relevant public service agreement ('PSA') targets under the national PSA for local government. For some indicators, the government is keen for authorities to set targets that are consistent with reaching, over five years, the performance level of the top 25 per cent of authorities at the time the targets were set. This approach is intended to highlight those authorities that are performing poorly, standards that others are achieving and to facilitate the narrowing of the gap between the range of performance.

1   Best Value Performance Indicators for 2002/2003 (DTLR), ch 4.

11.33   It is noted, though, by government that national comparisons will not always be appropriate and therefore groupings of local authorities are done according to type (eg district council, metropolitan borough) for the purpose of the establishment of top quartile targets for cost efficiency indicators. This is adapted in accordance with the traditional Audit Commission approach to group and comparison and performance of authorities.

Performance standards

11.34   The third element of the performance management framework is the performance standard which is defined as the minimum acceptable level of service measured by reference to a performance indicator. Failure to meet a performance standard is normally judged as a failure to achieve best value for a particular service. Assurance has been given that standards would be set for only a small proportion of services and recent guidance has provided that the government will use them sparingly and where there is a legitimate national interest in doing so. The essential difference, however, is that the 'default' situation with standards is even stronger than that for performance indicators and targets. An authority's performance in respect of performance indicators and targets is essentially a matter for the best value performance plan. The sanction for failure to attain for 'standards', however, is quite clear and stated in s 4(5) and any local authority 'must meet any applicable performance standard' or it will be in breach of the Act and thus deemed to be 'failing'[1].

1   This was confirmed by the Minister in Parliament who stated 'an authority that fails to meet a standard will be judged to have failed the test of best value for that service' (Hillary Armstrong, HC Official Report (6th series) col 114, 28 January 1999).

Consequences of performance indicators, standards and targets

11.35   The essential consequence of establishing performance indicators is that they are an integral part of the best value review process under the LGA 1999, s 5. In the undertaking of the best value performance review a local authority has to produce a best value performance plan. Within this plan the Secretary of State has the power to specify matters which an authority must include and the Secretary may require a local authority to:
—   state any performance indicators, standards and targets specified or set in relation to the local authority's functions;
—   summarise the performance of the council in the previous financial year with regard to performance indicators;
—   summarise its assessment of success in meeting any performance standard which was relevant;
—   summarise its assessment of progress towards meeting any performance target;
—   summarise any plan of action to be taken in the financial year to which the plan relates for the purposes of meeting a performance target.

11.36   The main consequence of the establishment of performance indicators is that through the LGA 1999, s 5 there is a link into the best value review process. Under s 5, the Secretary of State may by order specify matters which a best value authority should include within its best value review. Section 5(4) enables the provision of the requirement for a local authority to assess its performance by reference to:
—   any performance indicator (sub-s (4)(d));
—   its success in meeting any performance standard which applies in relation to the function (sub-s (4)(g)); and
—   its progress to meeting any relevant performance target (sub-s (4)(i)).

The best value review

11.37   The best value review is the central procedural element of the regime under the LGA 1999. Section 5 of the Act requires authorities to conduct a best value review in accordance with any order that the Secretary of State may issue in respect of time table, procedures, forms and content of such reviews[1]. The aim of a best value review is to help an authority fundamentally to review its service delivery and to deliver targets to facilitate continuous improvement. A best value authority trust in the undertaking of a review of functions[2], will need to:
—   consider whether it should be exercising this function;
—   consider the level at which and the way it should be exercising the function;
—   consider its objectives in relation to the exercise of the function;
—   consider its performance in exercising a function by reference to any performance indicators specified for the function;
—   assess the competitiveness of its performance in exercising the function by reference to the exercising of this function or similar functions by other best value authorities and/or commercial or other business organisations;

— consult other best value authorities, commercial and other businesses, including voluntary sector organisations about the exercise of this function;

— assess its success in meeting any performance standard which applies in relation to the function;

— assess its progress towards meeting any relevant performance standard which was been specified but which does not yet apply.

1   SI 1999/3251. The duties specifically laid down in s 5(1) provide that 'a best value authority must conduct best value reviews of its functions in accordance with the provisions of any order made under this section'. The first statutory instrument (SI 1999/3251) was issued in December 1999.

2   Best value performance relates to an authority's 'functions' rather than 'services'. The use of the word 'functions' refers to the 'multiplicity of specific statutory activities [the council] is expressly or impliedly under a duty to perform or have power to perform' per Woolf LJ in *Hazell v Hammersmith and Fulham London Borough Council* [1992] 2 AC 1.

'Review elements'

11.38   Broadly the best value review is the principal means by which an authority should consider new approaches to service delivery and to ensure that challenging but realistic targets are set for all services which take account of national and local requirements. The legal duty within the LGA 1999, s 5(3)(a) requires the local authority to 'aim to improve the way in which its functions are exercised, having regard to a combination of economy, efficiency and effectiveness' and it is this aim which must be kept at the heart of the review process.

11.39   The best value review has several functions, and indeed one major function will be to identify a programme for performance review. From the inception of best value it was clearly stated that authorities will need to develop a programme approach to service review which would 'be firmly routed in the corporate planning process through which the authority identifies its objectives and priorities and the values that underpin them'[1].

1   Green Paper *Modernising Local Government—Improving Local Services Through Best Value* (1998), para 4.3.

11.40   Guidance[1] contains advice on the corporate elements of the review programme at paras 15–27. Paragraph 17 states that in order to realise the potential of best value to make a real difference to performance of the authorities' functions, the reviews will need to:

— take a sufficiently long term perspective;
— involve elected members;
— seek advice from outside the authority;
— involve those currently delivering a service;
— question existing commitments;
— engage with users and potential users for services;
— address equity considerations;
— give effect to the principles of sustainable development.

1   DETR Circular 10/1999.

11.41   These matters will need to be considered along with other duties, particularly with respect to an authority's community strategy (introduced under the Local Government Act 2000). Authorities are expected to demonstrate that the programme follows the community strategy and is based upon a comparison using best value and other indicators as well as from consultation with local people, business and employees.

The four C's

11.42 The main tool for assessing the overall performance of the best value authority will be the comparison of a range of different performance indicators and standards. A further useful diagnostic tool has been set out in the Guidance which details the practical four elements of review being the four 'Cs' of challenge, comparison, consultation and competition[1].

1 Circular DETR 10/1999, para 16.

Challenge

11.43 Why, how and by whom are services provided? Authorities are required to undertake a fundamental rethink asking basic questions about the basis each service is intended to address and the method of procurement. Authorities are expected to show evidence that they have considered the underlying rationale for services under review and any alternative ways in which the services may be provided. The potential for utilising new technology and services provision must be explored and capacity developed whereby authorities analyse the effects of demographic, social and economic changes on local service needs.

Compare

11.44 Authorities are required to compare their performance to that of others over a range of relevant indicators, taking into account the views of users and suppliers. Comparison should be made of an authority's current and prospective performance against other public sector bodies, and those in the private and voluntary sectors. This should be an intelligent exploration of analogous services and identification of improvements required over a review period. Comparison of BVPIs must be used for this purpose, as well as selective and informed benchmarking which can be useful in identifying escape proficiency improvements, by analysing processes which help to deliver better performance and outcomes.

Consultation

11.45 Section 3 of the LGA 1999 requires authorities to consult a wide range of local and other interests as to the way in which they fulfil their duties to secure best value. Section 5 and SI 1999/3251 provide specific requirements in respect of the carrying out of reviews. However, Guidance[1] noted that the government had no current plans to issue guidance under the LGA 1999, s 3(4), taking the view that authorities are best placed to decide whom to consult and in what way, taking account of other statutory requirements as well as good practice.

1 *Implementing Best Value—A Consultation Paper on Draft Guidance* (DETR, 1999).

11.46 Authorities should take a strategic approach to consultation and should ensure that adequate arrangements are in place to meet responsibilities to consult both on the general requirements for best value under s 3 and also for the specific purposes of the review processes required under s 5.

Compete

11.47   One of the key elements of best value and process of review is the assessment of the competitiveness of different functions by reference to the performance of other bodies, including best value authorities and private and voluntary sector providers. Whilst the LGA 1999 does not require authorities to subject functions to competition in the same manner as the previous regime of CCT, the government held that a fair and open competition is essential in demonstrating that a function is being carried out competitively and meeting the full requirements of best value.

Best value reviews conclusions

11.48   At each review authorities will be expected to demonstrate that they have explored the full range of practical alternatives and selected the options most likely to deliver best value to the public. A clear audit trail is necessary and external auditors will also expect clear and proper justifications for any conclusions reached. The core outcome of a review which gives full consideration to the four C's of challenge, comparison, consultation and competition is the establishment of demanding targets for service improvement, and action plans to deliver these to a realistic timetable, including the key decisions on the best value option for future service delivery. Following the review authorities should explore and select one of the core options which are as follows:

— the cessation of the service, in whole or in part;
— the transfer or externalisation of the service to another provider (with no in-house bid);
— the creation of a private partnership, through a strategic contract or a joint venture company (linked as above);
— the market testing of all or part of the services (where the in-house provider bids in open competition against the private or voluntary sector);
— the re-negotiation of existing arrangements with current providers where this is permissible;
— the restructuring or repositioning of the in-house services;
— the joint commissioning or delivery of the service.

11.49   The choices amongst these options will depend upon on an objective analysis of what has emerged from the review itself. These should emerge from a corporate perspective which embraces both a clear procurement strategy and the written policy on evaluation and appraisal. Authorities have, and should frequently re-visit their, standing orders and procurement and tendering to ensure that they are consistent with the statutory provisions of the LGA 1999 and the requirements of guidance.

Review and its outcomes

11.50   The government, in the formulation of best value, envisaged the review as the fundamental mechanism for accountability by the authority to its service users and wider community. The legislation establishes a system of audit of an authority's performance and provides auditors with extensive powers to make recommendations for remedial action. The message from the then Local Government Minister[1] was that the focus would not be on the review process itself but the action taken as result of that process. In essence the outcome of the review process is the development and publication of the best value performance plan (see para **11.53**).

1   HC Official Report col 191, 2 February 1999.

The best value review programme

11.51   Section 5(2) of the LGA 1999 provides that Secretary of State may by order specify a period within which authorities must review all of their functions. The original explanatory notes to the LGA 1999 state that initially all authorities are likely to be required to conduct best value reviews for all of their functions over a five year period. A five year timescale was specifically introduced by SI 1999/3251 which required all best value authorities to undertake reviews in anticipation of the best value resume and that service areas would be required to be reviewed again before 31 March 2005. Authorities have now been released from this stringent requirement and reviews will now be carried out at such intervals as each best value authority considers fit unless directed by the Secretary of State under the provisions of the Act[1].

1   SI 20002/305 at art 5 removes the requirement for authorities to review all of their functions within a five year period.

11.52   Local authorities are required to agree and publish a program of best value reviews in their local best value performance plan. The program should cover all local authority services and functions and should be reviewed using a mix of service specific and cost cutting reviews which should cross traditional department and service boundaries. These cost cutting reviews should provide a local authority with the means to tackle issues beyond the scope of single department services and to insure a unified and joined up approach to the changing issues of the social exclusion, regeneration and community safety.

Best value performance plans

11.53   Best value authorities are required under the LGA 1999, s 6(1) to prepare best value performance plans in each financial year in accordance with any order made or guidance issued by the Secretary of State. These plans, sometimes referred to as 'local performance plans', are a point of reference to auditors in the determination of an authority's performance in relation to its best value duties. Best value performance plans are corporate documents that bring together information about performance and expenditure across all services. Performance is measured against performance targets, which enables comparisons to be made with other authorities and to compare performance with previous years. Once the plans are prepared, they are audited in accordance with the LGA 1999, s 7 (discussed further in para **11.59**) and an auditor's report could recommend follow up action by the best value inspector or by the Secretary of State (intervention powers are discussed further in para **11.71**).

11.54   Whilst the best value review is a tool for identifying targets for service improvements, the requirement to prepare an annual performance plan establishes the goals and yardsticks against which continuous improvement can be measured and is the 'principal means by which authorities are held accountable for the quality and efficiency of their services'[1].

1   Green Paper *Modernising Local Government—Improving Local Services Through Best Value* (1998), para 4.22.

11.55   Guidance provides that performance plans are an opportunity for authorities to undertake their duties as to consultation and engage with local people and others with an interest in the delivery of local services. Particularly, performance plans should reflect the strategic objectives and corporate priorities in authority and should engender a genuine dialogue with local people and local priorities and the delivery opportunities that best value provides.

11.56   Section 6 of the LGA 1999 and SI 1999/3251 established the matters which must be included in the performance plan. This amounts to a clear statement about:
—   what sections an authority will deliver to local people;
—   how it will deliver them;
—   to what levels services are currently delivered;
—   what levels of service the public should expect in the future;
—   what action it would take to deliver such levels of service and over what timescale[1].

1   *Implementing Best Value—A Consultation Paper on Draft Guidance* (DETR, 1999).

11.57   In order to achieve the key objective of the performance plan in the demonstration of effectiveness against performance indicators and targets for the previous year, a performance plan should include:
—   a summary of the objectives for services;
—   a resumé of current performance and a comparison with performance in previous financial years;
—   a summary of an authority's approach to efficiency improvement;
—   a statement describing the review programme;
—   the key results of completed reviews;
—   a plan of action;
—   a response to audit and inspection reports;
—   a consultation statement;
—   financial information.

11.58   Authorities were required to publish their first performance plans no later than 31 March 2000 and then no later than 31 March in each subsequent year. This provision ensures that plans are published before local elections in May and before an authority has finalised the accounts for the previous year.

The role of audit

11.59   The external scrutiny of an authority's best value processes by external auditors is core to establishing whether best value has been achieved and what possible constructive plans or remedial action can be arrived at. The legal framework relating to audit is provided by the LGA 1999, ss 7–9, which builds upon and supports the general auditor provisions already established in respect of local government under the Audit Commission Act 1998.

11.60   All best value performance plans which are published by an authority must be audited in accordance with the provisions of the LGA 1999, s 7(1). The auditor's brief is to ensure that the local performance plan was prepared and published in accordance with the statutory requirements of s 6 and any further order or guidance issued by the Secretary of State (under s 7(2)). Inspections are vital to assess how best value is being delivered and in helping to guide and support the process. The key to this is the Audit Commission, which has now adopted a differentiated regime for audit inspection based upon an inspection of both present and past performance. Best value authorities are responsible for ensuring that their best value performance plans and the performance information that they contain are accurate and targets established are both realistic and realisable. The auditor's role is to review the key elements assessed, to ascertain whether or not the plan is being prepared and published in accordance with statutory guidance and to ensure that the systems employed are adequate for providing accurate information.

11.61   Once the plan has been audited, the auditor must issue a report certifying that the plan is being audited[1] and stating whether he believes it to have been prepared and published in accordance with s 6[2]. If the auditor is not satisfied that the plan complies with s 6, he may make recommendations, if appropriate, as to how it should be amended[3]. The auditor may also recommend procedures to be followed by the authority in relation to the plan[4] . The auditor also has power to recommend that the Audit Commission carry out a best value inspection under s 10[5] or that the Secretary of State intervene directly by giving a direction under s 15[6].

1   In accordance with s 7(4)(a).
2   LGA 1999, s 7(4)(b).
3   LGA 1999, s 7(4)(c).
4   LGA 1999, s 7(4)(d).
5   LGA 1999, s 7(4)(e).
6   LGA 1999, s 7(4)(f).

11.62   Under s 7(5), six copies of the auditor's report must be sent to the authority and to the Audit Commission by 30 June of the financial year to which the plan relates, or such other date as the Secretary of State may specify by order. If the auditor recommends intervention by the Secretary of State then a copy of the report must also be sent to the Secretary of State by the same date.

Response to the auditor's report

11.63   The best value authority is under an obligation to publish the auditor's report. However the LGA 1999 itself is silent upon any prescription as to method of publication or the time in which it must be published[1]. Further, under the provisions of s 9(2) and (3) where the report recommends that:
(a)   the plan be amended;
(b)   certain procedures be followed in relation to the plan;
(c)   the Audit Commission carry out a best value inspection, or
(d)   the Secretary of State intervenes directly,
then the authority must prepare a statement of any action which it intends to take and as a result of the report propose a timetable for doing so.

1   LGA 1999, s 9(1).

11.64 This statement must be prepared within 30 working days of receipt of the auditor's report or within such time as the auditor report requires under the provisions of s 9(4). If the report recommends that:

(a) the local performance plan be amended;

(b) procedures be followed in relation to it; or

(c) there should be an intervention by the Audit Commission or the Secretary of State,

then the authority must include its response to the auditor's report in the next performance plan[1]. If intervention by the Secretary of State is recommended by the report, the authority's response must also be sent to the Secretary of State within 30 days or within such time as required by the auditor's report[2].

1   LGA 1999, s 9(5).
2   LGA 1999, s 9(6).

Best value inspection

11.65 Under best value all functions will be subject to inspection, with many already being scrutinised by existing specialist inspectorates, for example the Office for Standards in Education (OFSTED). However, the LGA 1999 provides that the Audit Commission will inspect those services that are not already the responsibility of an existing inspectorate. Section 10 of the LGA 1999 gives the Audit Commission the right to carry out detailed inspections of an authority's compliance with any requirements of Part I of the Act. These may either be conducted at will by the Audit Commission or, if directed to do so, by the Secretary of State.

11.66 Section 7(3) provides an auditor with a wide-ranging right of inspection of documents and access to information[1] which are wide-ranging including not only access to any documents which are apparently necessary for the purpose of functions under the Act but also to require any person holding documents to give such information and explanation as the inspector deems necessary, and to attend before the inspector if required to do so.

1   Similar to the rights under the Audit Commission Act 1998, s 6.

11.67 The LGA 1999 further provides, under s 11(1)(a), for inspectors to act for access to any premises of the authority at reasonable times[1]. Under the Audit Commission Act 1998, s 6(5) an authority is already obliged to ensure that there is suitable provision of accommodation in which the auditor can exercise his functions and that all information and facilities are provided to secure the commission of the auditor's duties. Individuals who fail to comply (without reasonable excuse) with the auditor's requests can be liable to prosecution and fine and the costs of bringing action can be recovered from the authority under inspection.

1   Arguably going beyond the provisions of the Audit Commission Act 1998.

11.68 The authority under inspection is responsible for the payment of the inspection fee and can be held either to a fee which is larger (or smaller) than the standard fee according to the LGA 1999, s 12(3) than that envisaged by the standard scale.

The auditor's report

11.69 The Audit Commission is required to publish a report in respect of the best value inspection which must be sent to the authority concerned and then published. Should a best value inspector, following an inspection, deem that the authority's compliance with its best value duty under the LGA 1999 is not satisfactory then the report must refer to the matter in which the authority is deemed to be failing. If the findings of a report engender cause for concern a report may recommend that the Secretary of State should intervene directly, in accordance with s 15. If such a recommendation appears in the report, as soon as is reasonably practicable the Audit Commission must arrange for the recommendation to be published and send a copy of the report to the Secretary of State[1].

1   LGA 1999, s 13(4).

Tackling service failure

11.70 Prior to best value the government already had powers to intervene where there were serious failures in the delivery of certain local services. However, the LGA 1999 enables the Secretary of State to intervene if there is deemed to be a best value default. Section 15(1) sets out the Secretary of State's interventionary powers where he is satisfied that there is a failure to comply with the requirements of Part I of the Act. Where the Secretary of State is so satisfied he may direct the authority to:
(a)   prepare or mend a performance plan;
(b)   follow specified procedures in relation to a performance plan;
(c)   carry out a review of its exercise of specified functions.

Where there is a best value default the Secretary of State may also, under s 15(3), direct a local enquiry to be held into the exercise by the authority of the specified function[1].

1   Section 15(4) of the LGA 1999 ensures that the Local Government Act 1972, s 250(2)–(5) shall apply in relation to the enquiry which the Secretary of State directs to be held under the section. This in essence insures that there is power of summons by the enquiry to any person, and sanction of summary conviction to a fine not exceeding level three on the standard scale or to imprisonment for a term not exceeding six months (or to both) for deliberate non co-operation. Further costs incurred by the Secretary of State in relation to the enquiry have to be paid by such local authority or party to the enquiry as the Secretary of State may direct.

11.71 Section 15(5) provides that the Secretary of State may also direct the authority to take any action which it considers necessary or expedience to secure compliance with requirements of Part I of the LGA 1999.

11.72 Section 15(6) enables the Secretary of State, in the event of a best value default, to direct that the specified authority function will be exercised by himself or his nominee for a period specified in direction or for so long as the Secretary of State considers appropriate. Further, the Secretary of State can also direct that the authority should comply with any instructions from either the Secretary of State or a nominee.

11.73 The protocol[1] indicates that in addition to the holding of the local enquiry intervention, the Secretary of State may also include the direction to:
—   prepare or amend a performance plan;
—   follow specified procedures in relation to a performance plan;

— carry out a review of its exercise of specified functions;
— take such other action as in the Secretary of State's opinion is necessary or expedient to secure compliance the requirements of Part I of the LGA 1999;
— make sure a function is carried out so as to achieve specified objectives;
— secure advice/consultancy on the performance of that function;
— secure the function from a specified provider or put the function out to tender to expose a particular service or work of a particular description to competition (with or without an in-house bid to carry out the work);
— accept external advice from a specified source relating to the performance of a management function;
— obtain a function from a specified provider;
— transfer responsibility to another authority or third party.

1   The protocol is set out in DETR Circular 10/1999, Annex D.

11.74   The protocol process is underpinned by the LGA 1999, s 15(9)–(13). The authority in question will be notified in writing of the improvements that the Secretary of State considers to be necessary, and will be given an opportunity to make representations and to produce and publish an action plan to make the necessary improvements, including costs, intended outcomes and other details required. If the statement of action prepared by the authorities is deemed acceptable by the Secretary of State then the authority will be given a deadline to secure improvements. If however, it is unacceptable the Secretary of State will inform the authority and the Local Government Association of his decision to exercise his intervention powers. Representations may be made by the authority about the direction proposed. If monitoring shows that the authority is not implementing its statement of action or achieving the outcomes on time then the Secretary of State may intervene. However, the Secretary of State may (by virtue of s 15(11)) give a direction without complying with the duties set out above (s 15(9) representations and s 15(10) statement) if he considers that the making of a direction is sufficiently urgent. If this is done, then under s 15(12) the Secretary of State is required to inform the authority concerned and such persons appearing to represent the best value authority as deemed appropriate[1].

1   A section 15 direction is enforceable by order of mandamus on the application of the Secretary of State.

Events of default under the protocol

11.75   In chapter 5 of the consultation paper, *Modern Local Government Improving Local Services Through Better Value*[1] the government catalogued best value default into failure of substance and failures of process. These have been refined and are included as follows in Appendix A to the protocol.

1   March 1998.

Failures of process

11.76   Failures of process are as follows:
— failure to consult or to consult adequately as identified by the external auditor;

— failure to produce a best value performance plan, or a failure to include any of the prescribed elements within it;

— a failure to agree, publish, or carry out a program of fundamental performance reviews in compliance with the statutory framework;

— unreasonable neglect of alternative options for service provision when conducting performance reviews;

— failure to set performance targets or publish details of performance against them;

— a failure to set performance targets, which, in the opinion of the external auditor, are sufficiently challenging;

— a failure to publish details of how performance compares with that of others;

— a failure to publish performance information as prescribed (in respect of content, form or timing);

— a failure to make adequate information available to local people about the comparative performance of the bodies.

Failures of substance

11.77 Failures of substance include:

— failure to meet any single nationally prescribed standard of performance;

— persistently high unit costs (by comparison with other councils or, where appropriate, with private and voluntary sector providers) which are not satisfactorily accounted for by higher quality service or greater level of need;

— failure to improve service standards or a deterioration in standards;

— failure to draw up and implement an action plan following a critical inspection report.

11.78 The opening paragraph of Appendix 8 of the protocol makes the statement of intent quite clear that the Secretary of State is prepared to intervene. However, this is tempered by the declaration that the Secretary of State's:

'intention is to intervene proportionately to the seriousness of the failure. The single failure process, for example, is unlikely to trigger intervention by the Secretary of State, whereas a failure of substance is more likely to attract intervention'.

CONTRACTING TO SECURE BEST VALUE

11.79 As has been noted the enactment of the LGA 1999 has made local government contracting and procurement subject to the overriding duty to secure 'best value'. Best value has provided performance management a framework within which local authorities are required to deliver improvements and performance to match the very best services available. Best value lies at the heart of procurement whether outsourcing a major service area or sourcing supplies. As part of the duty of best value the contract process is required to demonstrably aim to secure continuous improvement in the way in which the contracting authority's functions are exercised. Contract documentation, particularly long term or PFI contracts, should have specific provisions which allow flexibility to react to changes arising through the best value process. The key approach is that all procurement should have due regard to the combination of economy, efficiency and effectiveness and should seek to further the continued improvement of the contracting organisation.

11.80   The best value regime has established a national framework which is made up of the three constituent parts of plans, reviews and performance information. Local authorities' performance management arrangements will primarily be reviewed by external auditors in respect of compliance with the best value regime and best value inspection service when reviews are inspected. Auditors will focus upon the adequacy of arrangements the authority has made in general when contracting to ensure that resources are employed to the best of their use. Particularly auditors will review how a contracting authority and its contractual process has achieved the following:
—   established strategic aims and objectives;
—   implemented effective service and business planning;
—   carried out service and performance reviews;
—   set performance targets and monitored performance against these targets.

Planning an approach

11.81   Core to the achievement of best value are the underlying key principles first established in the Green Paper *Modernising Local Government: Improving Local Government Services Through Best Value*[1]. First port of call for any procurement process would be a revisiting of these principles to establish the aims and objectives in the procurement process and the achievement of the securement of economy, efficiency and effectiveness of provision of services. DTLR Circular N/99 reminds us the central purpose of best value is to make a real positive difference to the services local people receive from a contracting authority. This aim will not work unless the strategic objectives, targets and standards ascertained and set at a corporate level within the contracting organisation are actually implemented in practice.

1   Published in June 1997.

11.82   These key strategic objectives and the duty of best value must lie at the heart of the framework of the contractual process. The contractual documentation itself should ensure that the process is set out to enable both parties over the contract term to review performance with regard to the provision of the services and to ensure that goals are achieved. Furthermore, a contracting authority should ensure that contractual documentation sets performance standards and ensures monitoring of compliance with those standards. Processes should also be implemented through which reasonable flexibility to meet changing needs is ensured. This is the practical essence of best value!

Starting off

11.83   Procurement specialists state that thorough preparation by client officers for the commissioning or procurement of the supplies, works and, in particular, services pays dividends. Such a focused approach by the procuring authority allows the ascertainment of the nature of works, supplies or services and the extent that the market can provide with the aim of meeting the needs of the community.

11.84   The principles of best value must lie at the heart of this investigation of the procurement process, including decisions as to whether services should be provided internally within the contracting organisation or outsourced. Each case must be examined on its own merits. However, wide strategic objectives can be established to achieve best value and ultimately the provision of high quality services to local people. A core requirement of best value is that contracts must set out processes which enable the parties over the contract term to review performance against the existing needs and demands of the service which exist at the time of such review. Each procurement process and framework of the individual contract relating to this must achieve the widest strategic aim to secure:
—   continuous improvement;
—   innovation;
—   effective service delivery arising from technological developments;
—   cost efficiencies;
—   service performance improvement;
—   swift response to changing local and national priorities;
—   adaptation to factors and circumstances which should arise through the life of the contract.

11.85   In the case of local government, the benchmarking and management of the performance required to track whether or not best value is being achieved should stem from the local authorities' community strategy. At the apex of this should be the corporate strategy of the contracting authorities which can be underpinned with departmental or service plans.

11.86   Contracting authorities will undoubtedly have undertaken an annual corporate review process which provides a framework of the contracting authority's overall corporate objective. This process will determine the strategic direction of the contractual authority, coupled with the employment of resources to enable achievement of goals and also an opportunity to provide adjustment as to any previous direction undertaken. The overall effect of this should be to provide, in the specific contract, for clear and concise mechanisms for the facilitation and delivery of performance information to ensure that an effective system of performance management is established.

Sketching the procurement process

11.87   Set out below is a quick overview of the key elements of the procurement process. At each stage best value requires the contracting authority to establish within the constituent elements set out below mechanisms for ensuring the achievement of the overall objective. Procurement covers the complete chain of action, for determining what is to be achieved through pre-tender enquiries and purchasing to managing the relationship during the contract. Broadly four stages regarding the achievement of best value in the procurement process can be set out:
—   approval of the process, service consultation and user involvement in service standards;
—   designing and setting the specification of outcomes sought;
—   structuring the contract;
—   managing performance.

Approval of the process, service consultation and user involvement in service standards

11.88   To achieve best value, contracting authorities must establish a required performance level for the service by reference to outputs or the service standards that are required to achieve the contract aim. When setting a performance level the contracting authority should focus on the level of service it decides is appropriate. This can only be effectively established with prior consultation with users, interested parties and other key stakeholders and is vital to secure the statutory objective of consultation set out in the LGA 1999. Clever and correct consultation should result in a performance management system which should focus on the agreed outcomes for the local community and which will establish the right indicators to measure contractual achievement.

11.89   Consultation at this point in the procurement should ensure sufficient dialogue with any and all stakeholders, which will assist in the establishment of effective service standards. Consultation with stakeholders can also assist in the wider aim of packaging and establishing key elements of the contract such as a contract term or the services/ supplies/works to be included. The LGA 1999 includes two references to consultation with the first duty set out in s 3(2)[1].

1   Section 3(2) of the LGA 1999 provides 'For the purpose of deciding how to fulfil the duty arising under sub-section (1) [ie the general duty] an authority must consult—
    (a) representatives of persons liable to pay any tax, precept or levy to or in respect of the authority;
    (b) representatives of persons liable to pay non domestic rates in respect of any area within which the authority carries out functions;
    (c) representatives of persons who use or are likely to use services provided by the authority; and
    (d) representatives of persons appearing to the authority to have an interest in any area within which the authority carries out functions'.

11.90   The consultation process should also occur as a form of good procurement practice. The contracting authority should approach the exercise with the aim of producing a tool to formulate and tailor contract specification and to ensure that the subsequent advertising of a contract (if relevant) ensures maximum flexibility in order to guarantee that procurement delays are not caused and grounds for legal challenge do not arise. Legal challenge can occur if the specification needs to be amended after the publication of the OJEC advertisement or if post tender negotiations are required.

11.91   Consultation before the procurement process commences, as well as forming a basis of a contracting authority's decision to commence a project leading to the procurement, provides also an opportunity to consider procurement problems, standards and output performances to be included. Consideration should also be given as to what BVPIs and local performance indicators are relevant and linked to the contract for performance purposes.

11.92   Where there is outsourcing involved the application of the Transfer of Undertakings (Protection of Employment) Regulations 1981[1] is essential to the achievement of best value. Coupled with the best value duty of consultation, TUPE, reg 10 requires authorities to consult their employees and recognise trade unions or staff representatives throughout the process, with full disclosure of information on all matters affecting the workforce[2]. It has been acknowledged by government[3] that best value cannot be delivered without a well-trained and motivated workforce.

1   SI 1981/1794.
2   The Treasury Taskforce Private Finance, Policy Statement number 4, *Disclosure of Information and Consultation with Staff and other Interested Parties,* sets out the central government strategy for the disclosure of information and consultation at various stages in the procurement process this does not explicitly cover local government. However the 4 P's published on the 21 July 2000 specific guidance for local governments setting out disclosure of information and consultation procedure with staff and other interested parties.
3   Draft Circular on Best Value and Performance Improvement—consultation paper (Office of the Deputy Prime Minister).

11.93   Consultation can not be underestimated as the principal tool in a successful procurement. As well as being used as a mechanism to anticipate outcomes, standards and objectives consultation must be undertaken to fulfil the statutory duty, particularly 'to seek out views of all potential users especially those who have been particularly unrepresented'[1]. Consultation should not cease at the pre-procurement stage: it is a further useful tool to measure and monitor performance and to ensure feed back on whether performance standards set under the contract standards have been met. Whilst user consultation is a contracting authority responsibility, the contracting authority will need to explore within its procurement process and contractual matrix how the contractor proposes and will be held to ensuring that a local authority meets it consultation objectives in respect of the services.

1   DTLR Circular 10/99.

11.94   In summary, pre-procurement service consultation and user involvement in service standards should achieve the following:
—   form the basis of a local authority's decision to commence a project leading to procurement;
—   decide what services, standards and outputs for performance are to be included;
—   decide the range, design and functionality of the services to be provided; and
—   decide the key BVPIs and LPIs which the contract might be linked to for performance purposes.

Designing and setting the specification of outcomes sought

11.95   Following a successful consultation exercise the next priority for a local authority embarking on a procurement process designed to secure a long-term contract, resulting in the provision of services, must be the identification and establishment of the key outcomes sought. The service requirements to be achieved and the contract should take into account not only the local authority's current requirements (as ascertained from the analysis of users and other stakeholders achieved in the consultation process above) but also anticipated future requirements, in so far as these can be identified and indeed quantified.

11.96   Key to the establishment of a successful contract and its performance is the establishment of an 'output' based specification. This, essentially, is where a local authority states the outcomes it expects to see in the performance of a contract, together with corresponding standards for measuring performance. The onus is placed upon the potential service provider to work out within its own organisation how the outcomes will be met. In determining the nature of the outputs when drafting the service specification the local authority should remember that the statutory duty of best value requires measurement of outputs against 'performance indicators' and 'performance standards'. Remember, DTLR Circular 10/99 states that best value will not work unless the strategic objectives, targets and standards ascertained and set at the corporate level are actually implemented by local authorities in contracts and procurement. The performance indicators should be reviewed at regular intervals and should also be linked into the payment provisions with the contract conditions, so that poor performance will lead to a deduction of monies or indeed even non-payment of the full contract sum. In particular, the local authority's objectives, targets and standards identified through the corporate best value review and best value performance plan, following consultation with users, council tax payers, local business, councillors and other stakeholders, should be enshrined or reflected in the contracts.

11.97 Establishing processes within the document is crucial in the structuring of the contract. This will enable the parties to review performance against the existing needs and demands of the services over the contract term.

Structuring the contract

11.98 The effect of local authority procurement is to create an arrangement whereby the contracting authority makes payments to a contractor provided the contractor meets a specified contract standard. Since performance standards are often agreed at the outset of a contract following the competitive negotiation process, it is essential that the far reaching proposals, often on very long term contracts, are based on the proper assessment of long-term need and the best possible performance from the service supplier throughout the life of the contract. The contracting authority therefore needs a number of performance standards or markers against which it can identify whether or not the service is being provided as required.

Setting performance standards

11.99 Performance standards can often be formulated from the preparation of the local authority's best value performance plan and also making use of performance information supplied by bodies such as the Audit Commission, as well as BVPIs set and guidance issued by central government. Such information can be used to formulate performance standards within a particular contract and will enable a contractor who is engaged in the provision of services to a local authority to perform the contractual functions and to ensure that the local authority achieves its best value duty. It is core, and indeed set out in guidance[1], that the criteria used to set performance standards of contract signature must look far enough ahead to anticipate prospective changes to the demand for services and the means by which they might be delivered.

1   *Standardisation of Local Authority PFI Contracts* Contracting To Achieve Best Value (OGC, 2002).

The essential requirements

11.100 Contracts should be structured to ensure that these aims are met and it is crucial that the approach to achieving best value in a contract is carefully thought through. Particularly, contracts should seek to:

— involve contractors in the annual local authority best value performance plan in the cycle of best value reviews at suitable stages over the life of the contract;
— co-ordinate the planning of approaches to use consultation and feedback within the best value performance plan and best value review cycle between the authority and the contractor to best effect;
— reflect those obligations placed on local authorities within the best value legislation in contracts relating to the whole of the service or part of the service (as the case may be) for which the contractor has operational responsibility;
— where appropriate, consolidate any soft service cost benchmarking and market testing opportunities with whole service performance reviews and continuous improvement obligations;
— where appropriate, benchmark the contractor's performance against the performance of a comparative group.
— ensure adequate change mechanisms to implement the outcomes of any best value review;
— link performance with pricing!

11.101 The contract should be structured and the contractor encouraged, to assist the local authority to achieve its best value duties by meeting performance standards and performance targets set by the local authority and/or by government and/or the audit commission and by securing continuous improvement throughout the life of the contract[1]. The most appropriate starting point for addressing these issues arising from the structure of the contract is for the local authority to invite bidders initially to submit method statements setting out how the bidder proposes to assist the local authority in meeting and indeed continuing to meet its best value duty of continuous improvement.

1 Performance standards are discussed at chapter 7.

11.102 The method statement should include specific references to the following issues:
— how the bidder will enable the authority to demonstrate continuous improvement in service delivery over the duration of the contract term;
— how flexibility is to be introduced into service delivery arrangements to meet changing local and national priorities;
— the process the bidder will adopt to engage key stakeholders in consultation about service provision[1].

1 For further detail on the method statements reference should be made to *Standardisation of Local Authority PFI Contracts – Contracting to Achieve Best Value* which states that method statements should include specific references to:
   (a) performance indicators;
   (b) change to BPVIs;
   (c) new BPVIs;
   (d) annual service report;
   (e) continuous improvement;
   (f) changes to standards/targets;
   (g) consultation;
   (h) best value performance plans and best value reviews;
   (i) flexibility.

11.103 In particular, a local authority should be clear in its identification of appropriate contract performance standards at the earliest possible stage. Useful starting points for the identification of performance standards are the outcomes of any existing best value reviews and/or best value performance plans. Further proposals as to performance standards could also be developed following any consultation or soft market testing exercise with potential bidders at an early stages of a best value review and indeed at contractual invitation to negotiate stage. Procurement officers should at all times consider very carefully the valuation of the market reality and also the commerciality of service delivery in terms of the identification and establishment of performance standards and targets as well as local performance indicators. This will certainly ensure that the local authority is clear as to which proposed contract performance standards are likely to be commercially acceptable and to achieve value for money, which is essentially one of the driving aims of the best value process itself.

Drafting the contract

11.104   Highly recommended for sample drafting for both the tender (including the output specification) and contract drafting is *Standardisation of Local Authority PFI Contracts – Contracting to Achieve Best Value*[1] which can be adapted (with careful legal advice) to form a useful basis for most long term contracts. Any contract officer should consider including core points in the contract documents. A summary is set out below for illustration.

1   OGC 2002 (Butterworths).

Contractual obligations

11.105   The project agreement should ensure that the contractor undertakes to assist the contracting authority in its obligations under the LGA 1999 which include (but are not limited to) the following:
(i)   the preparation of a best value performance plan;
(ii)   the assistance of an authority during a best value review;
(iii)   assistance and facilitation to an auditor in respect of the audit of an authority's best value performance plan further to the LGA 1999, s 7;
(iv)   assisting the authority in any responses it requires to an auditor's report further to the LGA 1999, s 9;
(v)   assistance in any inspection further to the LGA 1999, ss 10 and 11;
(vi)   assisting the authority with any intervention or action undertaken by the Secretary of State further to the LGA 1999, s 15;
(vii) ensuring an open book and fully co-operative approach in the facilitation to the best value inspector of any facilities documents, data or agent or employee of the contractor.

Specific performance review obligations

11.106   It is recommended that provisions are included in the project agreement to ensure that the contractor undertakes to provide regular end user or customer satisfaction surveys, as well as the requirement to provide more frequent progress reports. The substance of the clause relating to an end user or customer satisfaction survey should ensure that the contractor undertakes to provide such a survey on the anniversary of the commencement date of the contract and, say, every 12 months thereafter throughout the services period.

11.107 The clause could detail the nature of the survey itself, which could be a test of customer opinion by either the employment of a written questionnaire (the specific aims of the questionnaire itself can be set out in the schedule to the project agreement) or in a form otherwise agreed between the council and the contractor. The purpose of the customer satisfaction survey can be set out in the clause which should achieve the following:

— assess the level of satisfaction amongst customers and service users;
— assist in the preparation of the contractor's annual service report;
— monitor the compliance by the contractor with the output specification; and
— assist the authority in the preparation of its best value performance plans and conduct of its best value reviews.

11.108 A summary of the results of the customer satisfaction survey should be provided to the authority within a specified time set out in the clause with perhaps the proviso that if the customer satisfaction survey discloses dissatisfaction with service levels (or that the quality of the services has declined since the last survey) then the parties shall meet to implement a service plan. The clause could include that such a plan should be implemented by the contractor at its own cost or can result in a change to contract specification or the contract's method statement.

Annual service report

11.109 It is suggested that the project agreement should include a clause which provides that the contractor undertakes to produce an annual service report on the performance and delivery of the services over the last 12 months. It is suggested that the provision and review of an annual service report by the contracting authority should be linked into the service of a change notice under the contract. This will enable swift action to ensure that actions identified can be quickly implemented into the contract by a change notice which states the nature and time of the changes to the performance and provision of the services.

11.110 This can be a useful tool in the incentivisation of a contractor and it should be considered and added into the clause dealing with the provision of an annual service report, linked into the implementation of the proposals of the annual service plan and the result in a decrease in the cost of the contracting which can be shared between the authority and the contractor.

Best value reviews

11.111 The project agreement should contain a clause which reflects the proposals determined by the contracting authority for best value reviews. This will also be outlined in the tender documents in the output specification. It should be noted also for long term and PFI contracts that additional capital investment may be required from the service provider as a result of any changes or suggested improvements that result from a best value review. A best value review clause could include the following:

— the ability of the authority to serve a change notice if in its reasonable opinion as a result of the best value review, it is necessary to ensure effective, efficient and/or economic delivery of service by reviewing and revising the service. The change notice should state the nature and timing of the changes of the provision that the authority desires;

— a mechanism for the parties to meet and discuss the proposed service change;
— provision that if agreement cannot be reached then determination may be made in accordance with the contract's dispute resolution procedure;
— provision to ensure that action of the change notice and the best value review plan can be implemented;
— incentivisation through cost sharing.

Benchmarking

11.112   The clause referring to performance standard benchmarking is only relevant if performance standards are linked to the performance of a comparator group. It is recommended that specific drafting should include that the contractor should participate in a performance standard benchmarking exercise (carried out by the authority at its own cost) to undertake an objective comparison in accordance with the chosen comparator.

11.113   Furthermore, drafting should again link into any findings arising from such a benchmarking exercise to be instigated by the service of a change notice. Contract performance standards should be adjusted in accordance with the findings of the performance standard benchmarking exercise.

Managing performance

11.114   Effective reporting, monitoring the performance of the services procured and taking action when indicators show that targets may not be met, are essential aspects of managing the services and delivering improvement. Monitoring itself, however, should not be treated as the sole aim of the exercise in itself. However, that is not to underestimate the fact that performance management is a vital component in the drive to improve services. A detailed and thorough discussion as to the requirements for managing the performance of the contract are contained in chapter 7.

CHAPTER 12

Partnership arrangements including joint ventures and joint venture companies

Ray Ambrose

12.01   In recent years there has been a significant move by local authorities away from the relatively simple contracting arrangements formerly employed by them under the compulsory competitive tendering process, to longer term and more complicated contractual arrangements (often involving considerable investment by the contractor sometimes with funding from financiers) to enable real improvements in the local authorities services to be secured in partnership between the authority and the contractor. These arrangements may be merely contractual in nature or may go further into joint ventures and participation by the authority in a joint venture limited company with the sharing of profits and joint action not only to improve the services provided under the contract but also to bring wider benefits through regeneration activities or the attraction of additional business through the joint venture vehicle.

CONTRACTUAL PARTNERSHIP ARRANGEMENTS AND JOINT VENTURES

12.02   The simplest form of joint venture arrangement is one based on contractual relationships between the authority and the contractor for co-operation in the provision of improved services to the authority and its customers. Such arrangements may simply be included within the contract document and may comprise regular consultation meetings to discuss the services, any problems encountered and how they may be rectified, and the future improvement of efficiency and economy in the provision of the services. These arrangements may also include consultation with the customer base, satisfaction surveys, and incentives to the contractor to improve the services. They may also include a sharing of any savings in costs achieved by the contractor from greater efficiency or other means.

12.03   These types of arrangement carry little or no risk of the local authority exceeding its statutory powers, provided the purpose of the contract falls within its powers and the contractual terms do not allow the authority to stray outside the scope of its powers.

12.04   However, these arrangements may require a specific business transfer agreement (to provide for the transfer of staff, assets and sub-contracts from the authority to the contractor on appropriate terms). Also a joint venture agreement may be required to regulate the consultation and co-operation between the authority and the contractor and the sharing of savings.

THE USE OF JOINT VENTURE VEHICLES (EG COMPANIES)

12.05   There is, however, an increasing tendency for these sorts of arrangements to use a special vehicle (eg a limited company) to achieve the co-operation and sharing arrangements negotiated between the parties. Greater care is necessary where there is any proposal that the local authority should establish or participate in a limited company or an industrial and provident society in order to achieve these benefits.

Powers to participate in companies etc

12.06   The first consideration is the question of the power of the local authority to participate in a company or similar separate legal entity. This is a vexed question in itself. The Court of Appeal in *Manchester City Council v Greater Manchester Metropolitan County Council*[1] approved the establishment of a trust by the county council under the Local Government Act 1972, s 137 (as then enacted) for the purpose of allocating and investing a fund provided by the county council for the purpose of enabling children to be educated at privately funded schools. However, more recently the power of local authorities to establish or participate in separate vehicles (in particular limited companies) has been doubted unless they are able to rely upon a specific power to participate in the company.

1   (1980) 78 LGR 560.

12.07   Formerly, it was considered that the LGA 1972, s 111[1] might provide such a power where to establish or participate in a company would facilitate or be incidental or conducive to the discharge of a function, but this proposition is doubted because the intrinsically distinct nature of the establishment of a separate legal vehicle could not in most circumstances be regarded as merely incidental to the discharge of a statutory function. A further difficulty is that the company must be regarded as a separate entity from the local authority and cannot perform the authority's functions because for it to do so would be an unlawful delegation of those functions to the company. Accordingly the applicability of s 111 in this instance is severely doubted.

1   See paras **10.106–10.110**.

12.08   With the enactment of the well-being power in the Local Government Act 2000[1] it is generally considered that the power would enable local authorities to establish and participate in companies, etc for the purposes of the performance of the well-being power. The guidance issued by the former Department of Transport, Local Government and the Regions makes clear its view that the well-being power includes a power to establish or participate in companies for those purposes. However it should be noted that a specific power to establish or participate in a company is absent from the Act (in distinction to s 33 of the Local Government and Housing Act 1989 which it in part replaced) and the proposition has not yet been tested in the courts.

1   See paras **10.111–10.118**.

12.09   In any event it should be appreciated that any reliance upon the well-being power for the establishment of, or participation in a company, by a local authority must be for the purpose of the use of the well-being power, and unless a well-being element is present, that power cannot be relied upon.

Local authority companies

12.10   In addition the provisions of Part V of the Local Government and Housing Act 1989 (classification of local authority companies) and the Local Authorities (Companies) Order 1995[1] require consideration. The LGHA 1989 classifies local authority companies into three types, as follows:

1   first there is the 'controlled company' where the local authority has a majority of the votes at a general meeting or a directors' meeting or has the right to appoint or remove a majority of the directors;

2   second there is the 'influenced company' where the local authority has a right to between 20 per cent and 50 per cent of the votes at general meetings or directors' meetings or the right to appoint and remove between 20 per cent and 50 per cent of the directors, and the company enjoys a 'business relationship' with the authority which provides it with advantageous benefits from the public funds of the authority;

3   finally there is the 'minority interest' company which is a company which does not have a 'business relationship' with the authority but would be an 'influenced company' if it had, or a company in which the authority's voting rights and director appointment and removal rights amount to less than 20 per cent of the total.

1   SI 1995/849.

12.11   The Local Authorities (Companies) Order 1995 provides that any controlled company and an influenced company in which the local authority has actual control or a 'dominant influence' (such that if the local authority were a company it would be required to issue joint accounts) shall be a 'regulated company'. A 'dominant influence' exists where the authority has the power either under a shareholders agreement or by other means to give directions to the directors of the company which they are obliged to comply with whether or not they are for the benefit of the company.

12.12   The order requires regulated companies to comply with certain requirements such as notifying publicly its connection with the local authority, limiting the payment of remuneration to directors who are local authority councillors and ensuring the provision of information to the authority's auditor, and to members of the local authority and of financial information to the authority. Also, under the order, the capital expenditure and receipts of a regulated company must be aggregated with those of the local authority and be met from within the capital provision available to the authority under the capital finance legislation.

12.13   In view of these provisions, local authorities usually need to ensure that any joint venture (or other) company in which they participate is not a regulated company and will not become a regulated company by default (eg by virtue of the resignation of one or more members or directors resulting in the authority having more than the requisite percentage level of votes or director appointments required to render it a regulated company). For this reason it is common practice for local authorities participating in companies to restrict their voting or appointment rights to less than 20 per cent of the total to avoid any suggestion of effective control or dominant influence over the company by the local authority.

The position of local authority appointed directors

12.14   Often the local authority participating in a company insists that it must be free to appoint one or more of its members or officers to be directors of the company. It is, therefore, necessary to consider the legal position of these directors.

12.15   A local authority member or officer appointed as a company director is subject to the same duties and responsibilities as any other company director to act in the best interests of the company and its shareholders, and not to engage in fraudulent trading, etc. It is not inconceivable that at times the duties of a local authority appointed director to the company and its shareholders may conflict with that person's duties to the local authority. If that occurs the conflict should immediately be resolved, probably by the director resigning from one or other appointment.

12.16   In addition it is necessary to consider the potential personal liability a company director may incur as a result of his activities as a director. It is not unusual for local authority appointed directors to seek and be granted an indemnity from the authority to protect them from such an eventuality. However, such an indemnity may not always protect such directors, as was the case in *Burgoyne v Waltham Forest London Borough Council*[1] where the court held that whilst the council had the power to provide such an indemnity to its appointed directors of a local authority company, the indemnity could not, in that case, be relied upon by the two local authority officer directors because the council's decision to establish the company was ultra vires the council.

1   See para **10.69**.

Local authorities and shadow directors

12.17   It is also necessary for local authorities involved in companies to beware of the possibility that the measures sought by it to control the company and its operation of these controls in certain circumstances, might lead to the authority being treated as a 'shadow director' of the company. If this were to occur the authority could be held to liable for the debts and liabilities of the company in the event of its insolvency.

CHAPTER 13

The Private Finance Initiative

Helen Randall

13.01   The Private Finance Initiative ('PFI') was initially a policy launched by the Conservative government, which has since been adopted by the present Labour Government and given legislative support. The PFI was launched in 1992 by the then Chancellor of the Exchequer, Norman Lamont, but it was not until the following year and the publication by HM Treasury (under Kenneth Clarke) of the booklet *Breaking New Ground* that the PFI began to be adopted.

13.02   The incentive for introducing the PFI was the need to upgrade public infrastructure and improve the quality of public services without having to increase the public sector borrowing requirement ('PSBR') or to increase taxation. The increasing tension between limited opportunity for government to increase public sector income and increasing demands on public expenditure lies behind the creation of the PFI concept.

13.03   The key objectives of the PFI are:
— to take government procurement back to the *fundamental provision of services* with the assets acting purely as 'enablers';
— to take advantage of the private sector's financial resources, innovation, business and management skills and to apply them to areas which have traditionally been managed by the public sector;
— to achieve value for money;
— to achieve the optimum allocation of risks between the public and private sectors to the party best able to manage the risks thereby improving value for money;
— to transfer the design, building, financing, operation ('DBFO') and maintenance risks of public sector assets to the private sector;
— to encourage the upgrading and rationalisation of public sector assets;
— to release the public sector from the burdens associated with maintenance of those assets to enable the public sector to focus more on service provision with the assets acting purely as 'enablers'.

13.04   Most PFI contracts have a long-term duration of between 25 and 60 years to enable the private sector's initial investment in the assets to be fully amortised and to enable the private sector to realise its return on its investment. In local government, PFI contracts (apart from those relating to the provision of ICT assets alone) tend to have a 25–30 year duration.

WHAT TRIGGERED THE CREATION OF THE PRIVATE FINANCE INITIATIVE?

Cash constraints

13.05   In the second half of the twentieth century, the rise in living standards produced higher demands on public expenditure; the UK government currently spends about 40 per cent of its GDP on the provision of public services. As inflation increased in the 1970s and 1980s, public expenditure had to be curtailed. By the early 1990s, the government's petroleum revenue taxes and the privatisation proceeds from the years of the Thatcher government began to decrease.

13.06   There are also increasing demands on public expenditure in the twenty first century arising from requirements:
—   for pensions/social services; and
—   for infrastructure maintenance/renewal.

Procurement failures

13.07   Traditionally, the best method of conducting business under public sector contracts was to bid aggressively against a tightly defined specification. Both parties would realise that the eventual outcome would differ sufficiently from that envisaged by the contract and that change orders or variations would be used. Therefore, the tendency has been for many public sector contracts to overrun both monetary and time budgets.

Cash-driven management

13.08   The government's finances, in common with those of many other governments in the developed world, have until recently been virtually entirely driven by cash accounting. All the primary tools of government management, such as the Public Sector Borrowing Requirement and the Public Expenditure Surveys, are essentially measures of *cash expenditure* in the current year. This produces one of a number of biases away from the normal processes of private sector contracting and does not take into account long-term liabilities.

Long-term liabilities

13.09   The management processes in both central and local government do not record, manage or control the *long-term consequences* of policy decisions as part of day to day management. This is partly a function of the cash driven approach to management. If, for example, a school's governing body decides to postpone the roof repairs for a building in order to release funds to pay for additional books; there is no mechanism in the public accounting system to record the ongoing liability which has increased not only due to inflation, but as a result of the incremental dilapidation caused by the deferral of the maintenance.

WHAT ARE THE IMPLICATIONS OF THE PFI?

From the government's point of view

13.10 PFI represents a radical change in the approach to capital investment in public services and most importantly a departure from the assumption of government that most infrastructure and many public services are inherently public and have to be financed and managed by the public sector.

13.11 PFI redefines the role of the civil service and effects the change from government being the 'primary provider of services' (eg in education, health, transport, prisons) towards the government using departments as 'facilitators' rather than primary providers of services.

13.12 Another way of looking at this is that at the start of the twenty first century, the role of government can be summarised as having the following three functions:
— to establish policies;
— to regulate those policies; and
— to procure services to implement those policies.

From industry's point of view

13.13 Over £22 billion of PFI deals have been signed so far. Research in 1996 indicated that the bank debt raised for UK infrastructure represented 75 per cent of the total bank debt raised for infrastructure spending in Europe as a whole.

13.14 The creation of new businesses is a fundamental aim of the PFI. The PFI concept is now being 'exported' to other countries. Accordingly, the PFI has resulted in a dramatic rethink by many of the UK's major companies of their strategic plans, and the scale and breadth of its application in the UK and in many other countries means that PFI can not be ignored. Construction companies, starved of major contracts for several years, seized the opportunity thinking it to be a return to business as usual but with a PFI stamp.

13.15 However, PFI is about long-term service delivery contracts; the only businesses which will succeed are those whose shareholders and management are driven by the creation of value in the long term. There have recently been a number of announcements in the press regarding the withdrawal of some companies from involvement in the PFI due to the high costs of bidding.

A THREE STAGE PROCESS

13.16 The PFI is, arguably, the third stage of a process which began with privatisation:
— privatisation: adopted by the Thatcher government as one of its key strategies, the funds raised helped defer the need for increases in public sector income, but

the primary effect was intended to be the improvement in the quality of services provided (eg the utility companies);

— 'contracting-out': the transfer of entire businesses from state control to the private sector was followed by an examination of those parts of government which were not standalone businesses but which existed to supply services to or for the tax-payer. The outsourcing of services, particularly in local government, was initially enforced in the first Thatcher government through the introduction of the Compulsory Competitive Tendering ('CCT') regime through the Local Government (Planning and Land) Act 1980 and the Local Government Acts 1988 and 1992 which compelled local government to put out to competitive tender first blue collar, and then white collar, services;

— PFI: the PFI, therefore, represents the extension of contracting out of public sector assets and services where no private sector operator/provider previously existed, eg road, hospital and school infrastructure operators.

PFI in central government

13.17   PFI has been used in central government to procure a variety of large infrastructure projects including roads, office accommodation, museums, ICT systems and more controversially, prisons. In the health sector, PFI has been embraced by the Department of Health and is now the primary means of procurement for new hospitals and the LIFT programme is applying PFI-style procurement to new primary health care facilities in the community.

13.18   In local government, PFI has been applied primarily to schools but also to roads, libraries, magistrates' courts, police stations, sea defences, civic accommodation, libraries, street lighting, social housing, residential homes for the elderly, waste management and leisure centres and the application of the PFI to new types of local government infrastructure continues unabated.

The financial background to PFI in local government

13.19   The starting point for understanding how PFI operates in local government is the general statutory financial regime which governs local authorities' capital and revenue expenditure. The government facilitated the implementation of PFI in local government by making amendments to the Local Authorities (Capital Finance) Regulations 1997[1].

1   SI 1997/319 (as subsequently amended), referred to as the 'Capital Finance Regulations'.

13.20   Central government imposes controls on local authorities' expenditure as a means of regulating the public sector borrowing requirements. The current legislative framework governing capital expenditure by local authorities is set out in the Local Government and Housing Act 1989, Pt IV, reforms to which were announced in a DTLR Green Paper[1].

1   *Modernising Local Government Finance* (19 September 2000).

13.21   The current key features of the financial controls on local government can be summarised as follows:

(1) local authorities must charge all expenditure to a revenue account. The controls on revenue arise from the requirement on the local authority to prepare a balanced revenue budget each year and from the rule on capping revenue expenditure (these rules have now been replaced under the Local Government Act 1999 by certain reserve powers of the Secretary of State);

(2) local authorities may either fund capital expenditure out of revenue or in one of the ways permitted by the capital finance system and described below:

    (a) in order not to be charged to the revenue account, expenditure must be of a capital nature and fall into one of the following categories:

        — expenditure funded from capital grant paid by a central government department towards some types of specified local authority expenditure (eg transport);

        — expenditure funded from usable capital receipts after the disposal of a capital asset (some assets, principally council housing and assets within the council's housing revenue account ('HRA') must be set aside to repay outstanding debt but for most non-housing assets set aside was abolished as from 1 September 1998);

        — expenditure undertaken on the strength of a credit approval which is issued by a central government department. A credit approval is a permission to borrow. There are two types of credit approval: basic credit approvals ('BCAs') which are issued to cover general capital expenditure and supplementing credit approvals ('SCAs') which the government issues to local authorities for specific projects and purposes. A PFI Scheme gets special revenue support from central government which is given by the issue of notional credit approvals ('NCA');

    (b) local authorities may also obtain the use of capital assets on credit, for example, through a finance lease or a deferred purchase agreement. The difficulty with this is that under the capital finance system, they count as 'credit arrangements' under the Local Government and Housing Act 1989, s 49 and the local authority has to provide credit cover either by earmarking credit approvals, usable capital receipts or revenue. The full value of expenditure under a credit arrangement scores against the local authority's capital resources in the year that the contract begins (just as if money had been borrowed to buy the assets outright). This has deterred local authorities from entering into credit arrangements. For reasons which are explained below (see para **13.22**) credit arrangements which are classified as 'private finance transactions' have nil initial cost and hence the local authority does not need to earmark credit cover when entering into a PFI contract.

Capital Finance Regulations

13.22 The key principles of PFI contracts in local government are defined in the Capital Finance Regulations 1997. Regulation 16 defines a private finance transaction by identifying key features of a PFI contract which, if satisfied, allow the contract, as a credit arrangement, to be rated as having nil value. (It should be noted that all private finance transactions by their nature involve the deferred acquisition of assets over their life and hence will be classified as credit arrangements. It is not correct to say that a PFI transaction is not a credit arrangement.)

13.23   Regulation 40 sets out a test requiring transfer of risk from the local authority to the private sector which, if satisfied, will allow the local authority to claim the notional credit approval (ie. the subsidy from the central government department which is also known as a 'PFI credit'). This will need to have been pre-approved by the Project Review Group ('PRG') which is an inter-departmental group held under the auspices of HM Treasury's Office of Government Commerce and which oversees the approval process for local government PFI projects requiring central government revenue support. The full text of regs 16 and 40 is set out at paras **13.57** and **13.60**.

What is the difference between PFI and PPP?

13.24   'PPP' stands for Public Private Partnership. It tends to be used interchangeably with the term 'PFI'. In the local government context, however, contracts which satisfy the tests set out in reg 16 but which do not seek revenue support from central government are often referred to as PPP's rather than PFI's. Although the term 'private finance transaction' is defined in the Capital Finance Regulations, neither PFI nor PPP have legal definitions.

Process for procuring a PFI project in local government

13.25   If a local authority wishes to enter into a PFI transaction benefiting from PFI credits from the relevant government department, it needs to plan ahead. The current approval process does not allow for the existing contracts to be converted into PFI transactions attracting revenue support.

A local authority intending to enter into a PFI transaction will need to allow for the following stages in the process.
(1)   Central government, as part of the comprehensive spending review, announces the overall value of local authority PFI contracts that it is willing to support over the next financial year and an indicative split between services.
(2)   Each sponsoring government department decides and publishes its priorities for deciding what sort of local authority PFI projects it wishes to support from its indicative allocations.

13.26   The local authority identifies and develops projects which would be suitable for procuring through the private finance initiative. The relevant sponsoring government department's criteria for PFI projects should be checked (as published on that department's website). At this early stage, the relevant service department should work with the authority's finance and legal departments and may wish to involve the Public Private Partnerships Programme Ltd ('4P's') which is a unit set up in April 1996 by the local authority associations to support PFI. It should be borne in mind that in the present market, projects with a net present value of under £10 million may find it difficult to attract private sector funding and hence it may be advisable to bundle a small scheme with another PFI scheme which is being procured, whether in a different service area or by a neighbouring local authority.

13.27   The local authority should make informal contact with the government department which will be sponsoring the project to take initial soundings as to feasibility, timetabling, etc.

13.28   If the authority intends to pursue the PFI route, it should appoint its financial, legal and technical advisers at this stage as their assistance will be needed with the preparation of the outline business case ('OBC') which will require the authority to set out the relevant advantages and disadvantages of the following options:

1   the 'do nothing' approach;
2   a traditional procurement;
3   using the PFI; or
4   any other viable options which could improve the service and related infrastructure.

13.29   The local authority then submits its OBC to the sponsoring department and the project will be considered by that department and at the next meeting of the PRG. (At the time of writing, PRG meetings are held approximately monthly. It is therefore prudent to check both the time of the meeting and the timescale before the meeting before which the government department will require the OBC to be submitted.)

Outline of process after OBC

13.30   The following is an outline of the stages in a procurement of a standard PFI project:

(a)   preparation of draft prior indicative notice ('PIN') and draft skeleton output specification, carry out user consultation;

(b)   once PRG indicative approval to proceed is obtained, publish PIN draft OJEC notices. Consider whether the contract should be classified as a contract for works or services (see para **3.50**). Ensure maximum flexibility is allowed for in the OJEC notice;

(c)   prepare prospectus and pre-qualification questionnaire. The PQQ may need to be adapted to take notice of the fact that members of consortia will be applying for inclusion on the short list rather than single organisations as is the case in conventional procurements;

(d)   carry out survey and assemble base information relating to transfer of staff and/ or assets (see chapter 1);

(e)   carry out soft market testing;

(f)   refine OJEC and PQQ and accompanying documentation;

(g)   publish OJEC having taken into account soft market testing results;

(h)   technical advisers to work with service managers to draw up list of output for each service area to be included within the output specification. Public sector comparator (PSC) to be drawn up with assistance from financial advisers;

(i)   HR department to commence TUPE consultation exercise having prepared full list of potentially transferring employees and terms and conditions of employment (see chapter 15);

(j)   deadline for expressions of interest to be no earlier than 37 calendar days following despatch of the OJEC notice. Responses to PQQ's to be checked for financial and economic standing and technical capacity and ability. Chase up incomplete replies and information missing such as copies of accounts or references to be chased up;

(k)   depending upon the number of expressions of interest, consider requesting prospective bidders to respond with an initial statement of proposals to be evaluated against pre-published tender evaluation criteria to cut down and refine shortlist further;

(l)   prepare invitation to negotiate ('ITN'), including instructions to bidders. Draft project agreement to be based on TTF/OGC standard terms and conditions adapted to take into account local circumstances as necessary. Base level information, confidentiality undertakings in respect of TUPE and other commercially confidential information to be passed to bidders to be used in preparation of bids;

(m)   circulate ITN to bidders remaining on the short list. As negotiated procedure is being used, at least three bidders should be sent the ITN or, if less than three remain, all bidders. Allow bidders at least 5-6 weeks as a minimum for preparation of their responses;

(n)   evaluate bidders' responses to ITN against pre-determined tender evaluation criteria;

(o)   reduce list of bidders to two or three and, if further evaluation is necessary, issue invitation to submit best and final offers ('BAFO');

(p)   evaluate BAFOs against the same tender evaluation criteria allowing time for queries to be clarified or answered and incomplete or ambiguous information to be chased up,

(q)   select preferred bidder—seek member approval if required by scheme of delegation. Depending upon quality of other BAFOs nominate a reserve bidder in the event negotiations with the preferred bidder fail,

(r)   revise output specification, conditions of contract, public sector comparator (if necessary) and related documentation and issue to preferred bidder;

(s)   undertake negotiations with preferred bidder to finalise output specification, project agreement, financier direct agreement, payment mechanism and related documentation. This usually takes several months. The precise timescale will depend upon the nature and extent of the issues that remain to be agreed not just between the local authority and the preferred bidder but also the preferred bidder and its funders and sub-contractors;

(t)   obtain internal auditor's opinion that the transaction is 'off balance sheet';

(u)   submit final business case ('FBC') to sponsoring government department to obtain notional credit approval ('NCA');

(v)   contractual/commercial close: preferred bidder and local authority sign project agreement. This can be simultaneous with or succeeded by financial close where the preferred bidder finalises the terms of its funding with its financiers a pre-requisite of which will be the satisfaction of any conditions precedent in the project agreement and the signature of the financier direct agreement, all sub-contracts and property agreements;

(w)   publish contract award notice in OJEC within 48 days;

(x)   the private sector will then build and commission the facility and services will start on the service commencement date which will trigger liability of the local authority to pay the unitary charge.

Detail of structure of typical PFI transaction (including guarantee and step-in arrangements)

13.31

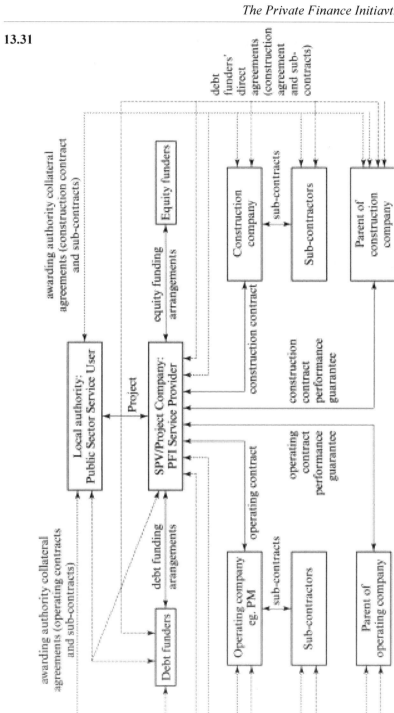

Powers to contract for long-term service provision

13.32   At the outset of PFI many local authorities were nervous that the long-term duration of PFI contracts would fetter the authority's discretion because the authority would be tying itself into a legally binding agreement for a long period which may stretch across several political administrations, and which may subsequently conflict with the authority's later changes of policy, changes in government policy or practical and legal restrictions on the authority's budget. The phrase most often used to express this concern is 'mortgaging the future'.

13.33   It is true that the early termination of PFI contracts before the end of the contractual term will involve the local authority paying a significant amount of compensation to reimburse the private sector's investment and inability to make a return on its investment. The precise amount depends on the nature of the investment the private sector has made, the terms on which it is has secured finance, the contractual terms agreed between the authority and the private sector, the cause of the early termination and the point at which early termination occurs in the duration of the contract. Often, the authority may regard early termination as an option which has no financial viability given the sums involved.

13.34   It should be borne in mind, however, that if a local authority were procuring an asset under a conventional building contract, the sums which it repays as compensation in a PFI contract would have been paid up-front in stages and on completion of the building contract. In effect, the compensation paid will cover the purchase and financing of the assets.

13.35   There is also a question whether a long-term contract amounts, from a legal point of view, to an invalid fetter on the authority's discretion. It has long been established that a local authority does not have the power to enter into a contract which is incompatible with the exercise of its powers or the discharge of its duties or which would divest the authority of its statutory powers or which would oblige the authority not to exercise its powers[1]. However, the length of the term of a contract does not in itself bind or fetter the authority. As long as the PFI contract is not incompatible with the authority's powers or duties, it should not amount to a fetter on the authority's discretion.

1   *Birkdale District Electric Supply Co v Southport Corpn* [1926] AC 355 at 364; *Dowty Boulton Paul Ltd v Wolverhampton Corpn* [1971] 1 WLR 204 and *William Cory & Son Ltd v City of London Corpn* [1951] 2 KB 476.

13.36   The next question is what happens where a change in central government legislation or policy would appear to be incompatible with the provisions of a PFI contract. The best value policy requiring continuous improvement and regular performance reviews under the Local Government Act 1999, is usually specifically catered for within local authority PFI contracts. Similarly, the OGC Guidance on standardisation of PFI contracts contains standard provisions in relation to the sharing of risk on a change in law.

13.37   Future adjustments to the capital finance regime affecting local authorities will need to take into account the potential ramifications on local authorities which have entered into PFI contracts under the current regime.

Standard contract terms

13.38   A number of standard contract terms have been published in relation to PFI contracts. The Government's Treasury Task Force first issued guidance on the *Standardisation of PFI Contracts* in July 1999. This has now been superseded by guidance produced by the OCG[1] , drafts of which were sent out for consultation with the public and private sectors respectively. The aims of the guidance are to:
(i)   promote a common understanding as to some of the risks which are encountered in a standard PFI contract;
(ii)   allow consistency of approach and price across a range of similar products; and
(iii) reduce the time and costs of negotiation by enabling all parties concerned to agree a range of areas that can follow the standard approach set out in the guidance without extended negotiations.

1   *Standardisation of PFI Contracts* published by Butterworths in July 2002.

13.39   In addition, further guidance building on TTF has been published in relation to specific areas as follows:
—   DfES guidance for the standardisation of schools PFI contracts;
—   guidance for leisure projects published by 4Ps;
—   guidance of standardisation of PFI contracts in the National Health Service published by the Department of Health in December 1999; and
—   4Ps guidance for standardisation of housing PFI contracts.

13.40   Judging by experience of negotiation of the earliest PFI contracts, it is certainly true that the standard position set out in guidance has advanced debate on common issues such as termination, compensation payable on termination, force majeure, change in law and some other areas which were previously subject to extensive negotiation between the public sector, private sector consortia and their funders. Sponsoring government departments and Partnerships UK ('PUK') are keen to discourage significant departures from standard terms for public policy reasons.

13.41   The OGC guidance also discourages parties negotiating a PFI contract from 'cherry picking' certain terms from OGC. That said, however, it would be naïve in the extreme to assume that a PFI contract could be completed entirely on standard terms, as inevitably the local authority's own circumstances, the funding and sub-contracting arrangements of the private sector, changes to prevailing market conditions and, not least, the operational details of the particular scheme, will require some adaptation and expansion of the standard terms. The local authority will need to bear in mind, however, that in submitting its final business case to the sponsoring government department and PRG, departures from standard terms will need to be explained and justified. In particular, PUK has emphasised that its standard guidance on the issue of refinancing should be followed unless approval has been obtained from 4Ps, PUK or OGC.

13.42   It should also be borne in mind that the OGC guidance on the standardisation of PFI contracts is intended to cover PFI contracts in all parts of the public sector including central government and the National Health Service. As a result, there are some incidences where the standard terms require adaptation to suit local authority circumstances—the inclusion of 'relevant discharge terms', for example, to take into account the Local Government (Contracts) Act 1997.

Output specification

13.43   PFI contracts depend on specifications which are expressed in terms of their outputs rather than their inputs. For example, a specification for an accommodation PFI contract will set out the following: the type of accommodation to be provided in the form of a schedule of rooms and other spaces, and the minimum requirements for that accommodation in terms of fixtures and fittings, furniture, temperature, lighting, cleanliness etc. A failure by the contractor to meet one of the specified outputs will result in a deduction from the contract payment (usually called the 'unitary charge' in a PFI context) either for the reason that the required space is not available or because the relevant performance standards have not been met. Often output specifications for PFI projects are divided into a specification for the building or accommodation to be provided and a separate specification for the standard of services (for example, cleaning, maintenance, catering) to be provided. Deductions for unavailability of accommodation are usually more stringent than deductions for failure to meet performance standards and the level of deductions applicable will be set out in a separate payment mechanism attached to the project agreement. If the contractor exceeds a specified threshold of deductions for unavailability or performance failures, the local authority will have a right to terminate the PFI contract for what is known as 'contractor default'. The output specification is an important contractual document which is linked to the authority's ability to enforce its 'instant' remedy of making deductions from the unitary charge.

13.44   Given their importance to the success or otherwise of a PFI project, local authorities often fail to allocate sufficient time or resources to the preparation and refinement of the output specification. Local authorities who devote time at an early stage to articulate their service requirements clearly in the output specification reduce negotiation time and tend to experience fewer disputes.

13.45   If the PFI transaction is to involve a private sector partner taking over services that are currently provided by the local authority, it is essential that the authority spends time before embarking on the procurement collecting and auditing accurate information about the authority's current levels of performance in relevant service areas. The authority should also formulate a clear view on the improvements to be sought from the private sector partner and how these improvements will be measured. Before embarking on drafting an output specification the local authority should assemble the following information:
—   a clear view as to the proposed service boundaries between the local authority and the contractor;
—   a clear view of what the users of the service and other relevant stakeholders expect and require (for example other council departments, housing tenants, school governors, staff);
—   a clear view of existing levels of performance and costs of current service delivery—for example, has the relevant council department been underspending on repairs and maintenance?
—   the relevant standards and performance measures;
—   likely future requirements and needs for flexibility to reflect demographic or policy changes;
—   the extent to which some factors potentially impacting on availability or performance may lie outside the control of the private sector, for example, fluctuations in school pupil numbers and exercise of a tenant's right to buy.

13.46 The aim of a good output specification should be to define the outcome required by the local authority without specifying the means of delivering that outcome. Ideally the output specification should:

— provide corporate and departmental policies objectives;
— be clear, precise, unambiguous and objective in its outputs—the output specification is not the place for aspirational language;
— provide potential bidders with sufficient information to cost the services to be included in their bid to the authority;
— take into account the need for compliance with statutory or other legal requirements such as health and safety, the Disability Discrimination Act 1995, the Human Rights Act 1998;
— be sufficiently objective to form the basis of the payment mechanism;
— only contain requirements which the local authority will be able to afford;
— contain references to technical standards which are non-discriminatory and comply with the EC procurement rules (see para 13.47).

13.47 Given that the value of PFI contracts means that they are governed by the EC procurement rules and in any event the local authority has a duty under the EC Treaty not to discriminate between potential service providers from different EC member states, the EC rules on technical specifications must be complied with. Under the regulations, standards which may legitimately be used in technical specifications are set out in strict order of precedence. Wherever possible national standards implementing European standards must be used, but in default, other recognised national or international standards can be accepted. An authority must also be prepared to consider products which do not comply with the technical specifications but have equivalent performance characteristics. Only if it is absolutely essential should an authority set aside a particular type of goods and in that event should add the words 'or equivalent'. The standards in an output specification are likely to be formulated on the basis of a combination of the following:

— national standards implementing European standards or, if none exist, recognised national or international standards;
— statutory or regulatory standards (eg health and safety);
— best value performance indicators;
— local performance indicators or local authority standards;
— standards established as 'best practice' by benchmarking;
— standards required to satisfy the expectations of service users following consultation;
— good industry practice.

13.48 Collation of baseline performance information can be a time-consuming and, at times, frustrating process. The earlier it is begun, the easier it will be to identify the areas of concern. It is in all parties' interests at an early stage to determine what the local authority's current levels of performance are and how they should be expected to improve during the life of the PFI contract. This also enables bidders to assess more accurately the likely resources that will be required to meet the local authority's aims and objectives and the period over which any improved standards can be achieved. Doubt as to the accuracy of baseline performance information tends to result in the preferred bidder seeking warranties from the local authority as to the information it has supplied as well as the right to claim relief events or compensation events if the contractor fails to meet a baseline which cannot be verified.

13.49   It is also usual, particularly in PFI transactions which comprise a combination of refurbished and new accommodation, for the contactor to be allowed some latitude through the payment mechanism in achieving performance levels (ie a bedding-in period) in the first few months of the contract. This is only reasonable where disruption to performance levels could arise as a result of incomplete or misleading information as to previous performance levels, building works being carried out, difficulties with transfer of staff or other factors which tend to arise during the early transitional phase of any large contract.

13.50   There are no hard and fast rules as to how a local authority should prepare its output specification for a PFI contract. Many local authorities tend to seek external technical advice in preparing the output specification and this can save valuable time, and in the long run costs, especially if there are insufficient resources or expertise available in-house to undertake such tasks. The authority may, in drafting the output specification, wish to involve its own PFI project team, use working groups from departments affected by the PFI project and stakeholders. It is generally helpful for aspects of the output specification to be dealt with by specialist sub-groups and, in involving stakeholders and service users, the officer responsible for managing the projects should be careful to manage expectations within the affordability envelope.

13.51   Readers may wish to refer to the following useful guide in relation to drafting output specifications: *4Ps Guidance and Case Studies—Output Specifications for PFI Projects*. The 4Ps recommend the following standard headings for an output specification:
— required outcome—this summarises the key results that the local authority expects from the project;
— scope;
— general quality standards;
— performance requirements;
— additional information.

13.52   Once the output specification has been produced it is recommended that it is reviewed by legal advisers to ensure that does not contain any terms which are legally ambiguous, unenforceable or which contradict the other contractual documentation or the commercial deal struck by the parties. Terms in the output specification which are vague, ambiguous or aspirational may in contract law be held to be void due to uncertainty. Similarly, the common law principle of 'contra proferentem' means that where a term is uncertain or ambiguous the courts will construe that term against the party which seeks to rely on it: see para 5.110.

13.53   It is also important for the purposes of both affordability and value for money that where any amendments to the output specification are negotiated with the local authority's preferred bidder, that the local authority updates its public sector comparator to reflect the revised output specification.

Capital Finance Regulations: regs 16 and 40

13.54   The provisions of the Local Authorities (Capital Finance) Regulations 1997[1] are important for PFI transactions in local government because they set out the tests which a transaction has to meet in order to qualify as a 'nil-rated' credit arrangement.

1   SI 1997/319.

13.55 The provisions of reg 16 and reg 40 have been amended several times since 1997. The measures provide for complete or partial abatement of credit cover for credit arrangements meeting certain criteria. A credit arrangement is defined in the Local Government and Housing Act 1989, s 48 as follows:

'(1) Subject to the following provisions of this section, a local authority shall be taken for the purposes of this Part to have entered into a credit arrangement—

(a) in any case where they become the lessees of any property (whether land or goods); and

(b) in any case (not following within paragraph (a) above) where, under a single contract or two more contracts taken together, it is estimated by the authority that the value of the consideration which the authority have still to give at the end of the relevant financial year for or in connection with the provision to the authority of any land, goods or services or any kind of benefit is greater than the value of the consideration (if any) which the authority were still to receive immediately before the beginning of that financial year; and

(c) in any case where the authority enter into a transaction of a description for the time being prescribed for the purposes for this section by regulations made by the Secretary of State;

and, in any case, the "credit arrangement" is the lease, the single contract or, as the case may be, the two or more contracts taken together.'

13.56 To summarise briefly, a credit arrangement is a lease or form of deferred purchase agreement. Under normal rules the local authority would have calculate the 'initial cost' of the credit arrangement by means of the formulaic mechanism set out in the Local Government and Housing Act 1989, s 49 and earmark an amount of credit cover which is equal to the initial cost of the credit arrangement. Credit cover can come from a credit approval (in effect permission to borrow), capital receipts or provision from revenue accounts for meeting credit liabilities. However, if a credit arrangement satisfies the tests set out in regs 16 and 40 this has the advantage of being regarded as having 'nil initial cost' and hence no credit cover is required.

13.57 At the date of publication, reg 16 of the Local Authorities (Capital Finance) Regulations 1997 provides as follows:

(1) In this regulation—
'assets' means—
(a) any tangible asset, including (in particular) any land, house or other building, plant, machinery, vehicle, vessel, apparatus or equipment; or
(b) any computer software;
'relevant asset' means any asset apart from housing land; and
'works' means any works consisting of the construction, enhancement, replacement or installation of an asset, apart from works consisting of the construction of a house or other dwelling on housing land.

(2) For the purpose of this Part a transaction is a private finance transaction if—
(a) the consideration received by the authority under the transaction includes—
(i) the provision or making available of a relevant asset or the carrying out of works for the purposes of, or in connection with, the discharge of a function of the authority; and

(ii) the provision of services for the purposes of, or in connection with, the discharge of the same function;

(b) the authority do not give to any other person any indemnity or guarantee in respect of any liabilities of the person with whom they enter into the transaction (whether those liabilities are incurred in respect of the transaction or otherwise);

(c) the consideration given by the authority under the transaction includes the payment of fees by instalments at annual or more frequent intervals;

(d) the fees are determined in accordance with factors which in every case include—

(i) standards attained in the performance of the services; or

(ii) the extent, rate or intensity of use of the relevant asset, or, as the case may be, of the asset which is constructed, enhanced, replaced or installed under the transaction; and

(e) the first instalment of fees to be paid after the services started to be provided.

13.58   In the light of the above, during negotiation of PFI transactions particular care must be taken to avoid terms which would be tantamount to guarantees or indemnities to those who are not direct parties to the contract with the local authority (such third parties might include sub-contractors, financiers or insurers). In addition, structuring of payments under the contract will need to comply with the provisions of reg 16(2)(c) and, in particular, reg 16(2)(d) and (e). This needs careful thought, particularly where the local authority intends to pay lump sums (for example, capital receipts on the sale of land or National Lottery grants) early in the contract.

13.59   Regulation 40 was simplified in 1999 to replace what was formerly known as the 'contract structure test' with the requirement that private finance transactions wishing to benefit from the nil initial cost provision must demonstrate sufficient risk transfer so as not to fall on the local authority's balance sheet.

13.60   Regulation 40 provides as follows:

'(1) A credit arrangement which is a private finance transaction shall be excluded from section 49(2), and the initial costs and the cost at any time of the arrangement shall be nil, if the authority determine that in accordance with proper practices no item, other an item specified in paragraph (2) is required to be recognised as an asset in any balance sheet they are required to prepare in accordance with such practices for any financial year during the term of the credit arrangement with respect to property which is either:

(a) provided or made available under the transaction; or

(b) constructed, enhanced, replaced or installed under the transaction.

(2) The following items are specified for the purposes of paragraph (1):

(a) any item relating to a contribution by the authority of an asset to any person with whom they enter into the private finance transaction in return for a reduction in the consideration payable by the authority to that person under the transaction; or

(b) any item relating to an asset to be provided or made available under the private finance transaction by any person which is transferred into the ownership of the authority, whether or not upon payment of any consideration by the authority, at the end of the contract term relating to the transaction'.

13.61 Sub-paragraph (2) means, in effect, that if the contract reduces its unitary charge to the local authority because the authority has provided an asset (for example land) or the asset provided under the PFI transaction (for example a school) is transferred to local authority ownership at the end of the contract this would not adversely affect the assessment of transfer of risk. More information on the accounting treatment of PFI transactions can be found in TFG Guide on How to Account for PFI Transactions and Financial Reporting Standard No 5.

13.62 In addition, there are further concessions under the Local Authorities (Capital Finance) Regulations 1997, regs 41–45 relating to replacement or enhancement of buildings and provision of heating services, arrangements for improving the heating or lighting of buildings and arrangements for improving street lighting respectively.

13.63 Throughout the negotiation of the PFI transaction it is important that the local authority section 151 Officer or Chief Finance Office retains an overview of the transaction in order to enable him or her to assess whether the provisions of reg 40 will be met by ensuring sufficient risk transfer to the private sector so that the assets to be provided under the PFI transaction will not fall on the local authority's balance sheet.

ALLOCATION OF RISKS

13.64 As mentioned at para **13.03**, one of the objectives of the PFI is to achieve the optimum allocation of risks between the public and private sectors to the party best able to manage the risks, thereby improving value for money. It is therefore helpful for an authority at the outset of procuring a PFI transaction to seek to identify, categorise and provisionally allocate all the risks inherent in the project. In broad terms, the private sector can be expected to bear the chief risks of designing, financing, building, managing and operating the facility, but assumption of these risks is in itself dependent on the authority taking on board other risks.

13.65 Authorities should appreciate that the financiers who fund PFI transactions will be banks and institutional investors who will be seeking to ensure a return on their capital investment and the ability to recover their investment should the project fail. Equally, a PFI contractor, as a special purpose vehicle whose only asset will be the contract payments it receives, will not be prepared to take on risks under the project agreement which it cannot pass down to its sub-contractors. Similarly, the PFI contractor's sub-contractors will each have relatively lower value contracts and as such cannot reasonably be expected to assume financial risks which would exceed the value of their own sub-contracts. None of the parties on the private sector side, whether they are contractors, sub-contractors or funders, will be prepared to accept the risk for matters which fall outside their control (for example, fluctuations in volume due to demographic factors or changes in central or local government policy).

13.66 To assist in early allocation of risk, most authorities include a draft risk matrix into their invitation to negotiate and update the risk matrix throughout contract negotiations to reflect changes in risk allocation in order to maintain an overview as to the extent of transfer of risks.

13.67   It is often helpful to hold a workshop or brainstorming session early in the process to endeavour to identify all potential risks associated with a project and to debate whether each of those risks should lie with the private sector, the public sector or be shared, and if shared, in what proportion.

13.68   Risks might be categorised as follows:
— design risks (encompassing design development, changes in requirements, failure to build to design);
— construction and development risks (encompassing cost and time estimate, on-site safety and security, relief and compensation events, changes in tax, industrial acts, planning);
— availability and performance risks (encompassing latent defects, sub-contractors' performance, failure to meet standards);
— volume or demand risks (including demographic and community factors);
— operating cost risks (including cost estimate, changes in insurance premiums);
— variability of revenue risks (encompassing non-availability and non-performance, volume changes, third party income);
— termination risks (whether by local authority or private sector);
— technology and obsolescence risks; .
— control risks;
— residual value risks (ie, what will happen to the assets at the end of the contract?).

However, there will be many other risks potentially affecting a PFI contract which will need to be categorised and allocated in a way that represents value for money.

13.69   The eventual allocation of risk will be reflected in a number of ways, including the items which are categorised as relief events or compensation events in the project agreement, provision of indemnities, the provision allowing one party to terminate the contract and the operation of a payment mechanism in conjunction with the standards in the output specification. As mentioned above, the overall allocation of risk will need to be reviewed in order to ensure that the transaction complies with reg 40. In addition, at the early stages of procurement it is important that the local authority probes bidders thoroughly with regard to their proposed arrangements for allocation of risk within the members of their consortium in order to ensure both that the risk transfer is sustainable and will represent value for money. (For example, it is not always the best value for money to obtain insurance against a potential risk such as third party challenge to planning permission which may be better value for money if retained by the local authority.)

CHANGES IN WORKS OR SERVICES

13.70   Given the changes that have affected local government over the past 20 years, mainly as a result of central government policy, it is essential that any PFI contract which is intended to remain in place for a long period, say 10, 25 or 30 years, should be flexible enough to provide for change. Furthermore, local authorities are required to comply with the best value performance management framework and the duties set out in the Local Government Act 1999 and to achieve continuous improvement in the provision of their services. In addition, changes to the PFI contract may also be necessary to cater for changes in the authority's requirements which could not have been anticipated or quantified at contract signature. The contractor may also wish to propose changes either to the accommodation which is being provided or to the services which are being provided with the accommodation.

13.71   A proposed change may involve the changes to the building and/or changes to the way in which the asset is operated. A substantial change to the accommodation or the operating cost may require capital investment by the contractor. In that situation the contractor will either need to obtain supplementary financing or obtain the funding from the local authority itself. Other changes may involve the contractor having to change its sub-contractor who in turn may have to recruit staff or make staff redundant. In any change, the local authority will need to appreciate that the contractor's financiers are unlikely to allow the contractor to agree to any change which would increase the project risk, financing risk or reduce the rate of return. The standard drafting PFI contract envisages the following change procedure:

(1)   either the local authority or the contractor suggests a change to the works and/ or the services;

(2)   the contractor prepares an estimate showing how much the change would cost, in particular whether it would involve any additional capital costs. The estimate will take into account all the factors which are likely to lead to increased or decreased costs including the costs of obtaining consents (eg, planning permission), resulting loss of revenue and effect on current service level. The contractor usually has a right to veto changes which would adversely change its risk profile or be incompatible with health and safety or other legislation or good industry practice;

(3)   the parties then discuss the amount of the estimate and the notice of change may be modified. If the parties fail to agree the changes are referred to the dispute resolution procedure. If the contractor is unable to fund the change, the local authority may have an option to fund the change itself, although in practice this may be difficult to implement if the local authority does not have capital funding available. The local authority may also require the contractor to obtain competitive tenders for carrying out the change to the works;

(4)   the OGC guidance also recommends drafting contracts to cover small changes (for example, changes with a value under £1,000) which are priced according to a schedule of rates. The contract may also provide for mandatory changes which are changes that the other party cannot refuse, for example, where a change has to be made because it arises from a factor over which the other party has no control. From a local authority's point of view, it is usually helpful to negotiate payment for changes by means of an increase to the unitary charge rather than by lump sums, both for affordability reasons and in the case of mandatory changes, to prevent breach of the local authority's fiduciary duty not to place an undue burden on the tax payer.

CHANGES IN LAW

13.72   An understandable concern often expressed by local authority members when contemplating entering a PFI transaction is whether the contract will be flexible enough to address changes in the law when they arise at any time throughout the entire life of the contract. Local authorities, being creatures of statute and bound by the doctrine of vires (see chapter 10), are required to comply with all applicable legislation. Equally, a PFI contract will require a contractor to comply with legislation otherwise giving the local authority the right to terminate the contract for contractor default. The OGC guidance recommends that the cost of complying with current or foreseeable legislation should be built into the contractor's bid price. However, neither party will be able to ascertain the potential effects and costs arising from changes in law which are unforeseeable at contract signature. Under conventional procurement, in particular shorter term contracts, the change in law is less of an issue because it is more likely to be foreseeable over the shorter term, although the costs of compliance can be passed through as a price increase. However, PFI contracts in local government tend to last for 25–30 years and the contract price or unitary charge is usually fixed at the outset.

13.73 The impact of a change in law will, of course, depend on the nature of the PFI project. For example, changes in environmental law are likely to have a significant impact on waste disposal and waste. Any changes in employment law are likely to have the most impact on projects which are service intensive, such as catering, cleaning, grounds or building maintenance.

13.74 The OGC guidance broadly recommends that contractors should bear the cost of complying with a 'general change in law' or that the costs should be shared with the authority. However, where the change in law is either 'discriminatory' or 'specific' the authority should bear the entire cost of compliance with that change. A discriminatory change in law is defined as the terms of which apply expressly to:
(1)   the project and not similar projects procured under the PFI;
(2)   the contractor and not to other persons; and/or
(3)   PFI contractors and not to other persons.

13.75 A 'specific change in law' is defined as a change in law which specifically refers to the provision of services the same as or similar to the service or to the holding of shares in companies whose main business is providing services the same as or similar to the service. Often the risk sharing for general change in law is expressed in the contract in terms of sharing the cost of compliance on a progressive scale so that, for example, the contractor takes 100 per cent of the first £X of expenditure, 75 per cent of the next £Y, 50 per cent of the next £Z, and so on. Once a certain amount is reached, the local authority bears the full cost of any amount above that threshold. Again, in a local authority context, lump sum payment for a change in law may cause budgetary difficulties as far as the authority is concerned, in which case it is to be hoped that central government would subsidise the authority's capital expenditure required in order to comply with the change in law. It should, in any event, at all times, be appreciated that the change in law provision in PFI contracts are intended to address unforeseeable changes in law and hence recent or forthcoming changes in law which have wide-reaching implications, such as compliance with the Disability Discrimination Act 1995, will not be covered by the change in law provisions.

TERMINATION PROVISIONS

13.76 Give that some local authorities embark on the PFI route only reluctantly after exhausting other potential means of obtaining funds to improve services, the termination provisions of PFI contracts, whereby in all cases of early termination a local authority has to compensate, can prove controversial, especially with local authority members and officers more accustomed to contracts let under the CCT regime. Particularly controversial is the requirement that the local authority will be required to pay the contractor compensation where the local authority has had to terminate the contract early because the contractor has failed to meet the required performance standards ('contractor default').

13.77 In this context it is helpful to understand that at the end of the PFI contract, whether on early termination or expiry, the local authority will be getting an asset (eg, a building or an ICT system). A bank or institutional investor will have lent funds to the contractor to build the asset and the bank would not have been prepared to lend the funds unless it was certain that it would be repaid, preferably with interest. The contractor, therefore, needs to be compensated by the local authority in order to pay back its investors. The amount of compensation payable will vary depending on the reasons why the contract has been terminated early. Broadly speaking, the more the cause of early termination is attributable to the local authority, the more compensation the local authority will have to pay the contractor.

13.78 PFI contracts generally provide for early termination in the following circumstances:
(1)   failure by the contractor (contractor default);
(2)   failure by the authority (authority default);
(3)   force majeure;
(4)   the contractor has committed fraud or corruption ('corrupt gifts or fraud');
(5)   a court declaring the PFI contract to be outside the authority's power ('ultra vires');
(6)   voluntary termination by the authority;
(7)   termination for the breach of the refinancing provisions.

13.79 The amount of compensation payable, detailed provisions as to how compensation should be calculated and methods of payment of compensation are covered in OGC *Guidance on Standardisation of PFI Contracts*[1]. Therefore, a summary of the standard termination provisions for PFI contract follows, and readers should refer to that publication for more detail.

1   Sections 20 and 21, published by Butterworths.

13.80 In the early days of PFI, the private sector was concerned that local authorities would either have insufficient means to pay compensation in the event of early termination of a PFI contract or would lack the powers to do. The latter point was addressed by the enactment of the Local Government Contracts Act 1997 and the inclusion of relevant discharge terms in PFI contracts which are covered by a certificate issued under the 1997 Act (for more detail see para **10.77** on safe-harbour provisions and certification, relevant discharge terms and compensatory damages). In its publication 'Local Government and the Private Finance Initiative' the then Department of Environment Transport and the Regions (now ODPM) cited the following facts as relevant to a local authority's ability to pay compensation on termination:
(1)   local authorities' access to many sources of funds, including transfers from central government of unhypothecated grants as part of the annual local government finance settlement and receipts from their own tax raising powers;

(2)   the revenue support made available each year as part of the annual local government finance settlement;

(3)   local authorities' statutory obligation to set a balanced budget which takes account of all their liabilities of payment;

(4)   the fact that in past local government reorganisations, pre-existing obligations and liabilities were taken fully into account;

(5)   the fact that where a local authority had been found by the courts to have a liability it had met the liability in full;

(6)   a local authority's ability to address financial difficulty by realising assets and by being granted additional borrowing powers or consent to use balances or set aside proceeds of sale.

13.81   The booklet also indicated that:

'the government would look sympathetically at the case for continued support for steps taken by the authority to put in place alternative arrangements in the event of early termination of a PFI contract, provided that those steps were consistent with the general principles governing PFI projects'.[1]

Additionally, qualms expressed by local authority Chief Finance Officers in early PFI projects that the compensation on termination provisions on PFI contracts may be incompatible with common law fiduciary duties have now been eased by the above and the negotiation of local authority's ability to pay by instalments in the event of early termination for contractor default and some other instances of early termination.

1   See *Local Government and the Private Finance Initiative—an Explanatory Note on PFI and Public/ Private Partnerships in Local Government* (DETR, September 1998), paras 5.11 and 5.15.

Compensation on early termination for contractor default

13.82   The Treasury Task Force and now the OGC have recommended that the 'market value approach' is adopted in relation to the provision compensating on early termination of a PFI contract due to contractor default. The market value approach is basically that the contractor will be paid an amount considered to represent the value that would be paid for the remaining part of the PFI contract on the market. The policy behind the market value approach is that the government considers that it would encourage the senior lender (banks and providers of senior debt) on a project to step in to the project and find a substitute contract in the event that the local authority has served notice to terminate the contract because the incumbent contractor has defaulted. Not surprisingly, the market value approach has not proved popular with the private sector both because the method of calculation is regarded as hypothetical and, more significantly, compensation paid to reflect the market value may not cover the amount of funds required to pay back the project's funders.

13.83   Broadly, the market value approach gives the local authority a choice of re-tendering the unexpired term of the contract in the circumstances that there is a liquid market for similar contracts at the time, in which case the authority pays the outgoing contractor the highest price that has been tendered for the contract less the costs of the tendering exercise. Alternatively, if the local authority chooses, or there is no liquid market, the local authority pays the outgoing contract the 'estimated fair value of the contract' which is based on a forecast cashflow for the project.

Compensation on early termination for local authority default

13.84 The most likely and serious form of default by a local authority under a PFI contract would be failure to pay the unitary charge to the contractor. The principle here is that the contractor therefore should receive compensation which leaves the contractor in the position it would have been in had the contract run its full course and to ensure that the contractor and its financiers are no worse off than if the contract had proceeded as expected. As a result, compensation on termination for authority default usually covers the amount of outstanding senior debt, redundancy payment and costs of breaking sub-contracts, as well as repaying to the contractor's equity investors. Again, in a local authority context, to satisfy both the common law fiduciary duties and requirements to take into account all relevant consideration, it is important that the potential amount of compensation payable on early termination can be ascertained before the contract is signed by reference to the contractor's financial model which should either be incorporated within the contract documentation or kept in safe custody for the duration of the agreement.

Compensation on early termination for force majeure

13.85 Unlike conventional contracts, force majeure is defined very narrowly in PFI contracts. The OGC guidance defines a 'force majeure event' as:

'the occurrence after the date of the contract of:
(a) war, civil war, armed conflict or terrorism; or
(b) nuclear, chemical or biological contamination unless the source or cause of the contamination is as a result of actions of the contractor; or
(c) pressure waves caused by devices travelling at supersonic speeds,

which directly causes either party to be unable to comply with all or a material part of its obligations under this contract.'

13.86 OGC guidance recommends that on the occurrence of a force majeure event, both parties should endeavour to find a way through the event to ensure survival of the project. However, if this proves impossible the contract will have to be terminated early. OGC guidance recommends that the contract should give the authority the right to prevent termination for force majeure by paying the contractor as if the services were being fully provided for a fixed period. However, if the contract terminates on force majeure the principle is that the local authority compensates the contractor on the basis that force majeure is neither party's fault and both parties should therefore share the financial consequences. The OGC guidance therefore recommends that compensation payable in the event of force majeure by the local authority to the contractor should be an aggregate of the amount of senior debt outstanding at the date of termination of the contract plus junior debt (less payments of interest and principle), amount paid for shares, redundancy payments and sub-contract breakage costs.

Early termination on corrupt gifts and fraud

13.87 Here, the OGC guidance suggests that a balance needs to be struck between the authority's desire to free itself from a fraudulent or corrupt partner and the PFI financiers' fear that they will lose their investment for reasons which may be caused by the corrupt actions of a contractor, sub-contractor or a third party outside their own control. The government's approach is that the only compensation that should be paid to the contractor in the circumstances of the local authority terminating the PFI early because of a fraudulent act or a corrupt gift, is the amount of senior debt outstanding on the termination date, but the equity investors do not have any right to be compensated because it is perceived that their relationship to the contractor means that they are more responsible for the contractor's acts. However, some regard this approach as not entirely justifiable in the case of equity providers who are purely institutional investors who, as such, have no direct involvement in the operation of the project.

Early voluntary termination

13.88   There are circumstances where a local authority may wish to terminate a PFI contract voluntarily where neither party is in default. This may arise, for example, where a local authority changes its policy with regard to provision of the service or the function is transferred to another public body. In such circumstances, the local authority needs to be aware that the consequences of voluntary termination will be extremely costly, as the standard contractual terms provide that, in such circumstances, the authority would have to pay full compensation to the contractor on the same basis as if authority default had occurred.

Compensation on termination for breach of the refinancing provisions

13.89   It is first helpful to explain what is regarded as 'a refinancing'. Given the long duration of PFI contracts, the contractor may, during the life of a PFI contract, wish to replace or change the terms of the funding as obtained before the contract was signed. This may, for example, involve an increase or a decrease in the amount of debt, extending the debt term or reducing the interest margin—all of these can be classified as 'refinancing'. A few years ago some controversy arose as a result of reports by the National Audit Office into some PFI projects where refinancing had taken place, resulting in an increase of return to the contractor's investors in which the public sector could not share[1]. As a result, it has become government policy to include provisions addressing refinancing in all PFI contracts[2].

1   See *The Refinancing of the Fazakerley PFI Prison Contract* (NAO, June 2000) and subsequent recommendations of the House of Commons Public Accounts Select Committee.
2   The provisions are set out in detail in the OGC *Guidance on the Standardisation of PFI Contracts* (Butterworths), section 35. Therefore, only a summary of these provisions has been set out below.

13.90   The standard terms require a contractor to keep the local authority fully informed of any refinancing and to approve refinancing which was not planned when the contract was signed at financial close or which will lead to a higher than anticipated gain for investors. PFI contractors are therefore required to allow a local authority to share half of any gain realised as a result of a refinancing.

13.91 The negotiation of refinancing provisions in PFI contracts has proved controversial and in some cases it can be challenging to tailor the provisions to meet the particular funding circumstances of a contractor.

13.92 In the event that the contractor breaches the refinancing provisions of the contract, the local authority is entitled to terminate the contract early, and in such circumstances the compensation due from the local authority to the contractor would be the same as provided on early termination for corrupt gifts or fraud, ie the element of equity investment is not reimbursed.

CHAPTER 14

Trading and profit

Ray Ambrose

INTRODUCTION

14.01   The power for local authorities to trade has long been a source of debate. 'Trading' in this context covers not only true commercial activities undertaken by local authorities, but also the mere provision of services to other bodies even where there is no profit motive involved.

14.02   Over the years local authority trading has been limited by the courts who found, on the basis of the ultra vires principle, that a local authority, without express statutory authority for it to do so, would not have the power to engage in the supply of goods and services to others by way of trade.

14.03   In the early years of municipal government the question as to what was 'trading' perhaps did not matter too much. All the energies of a local authority were aimed at improving and developing the borough for its citizens, and the aims of the local authority were understood to be for those purposes only. Sometimes a local authority would be seen to be going too far in trying to improve the life of its residents and that would be when the courts would step in to determine whether that local authority had the power to do what it was purporting to do.

14.04   Statutory restrictions (or liberations, depending upon how one looked at it) on a local authority's ability to trade arrived in 1970 in the form of the Local Authorities (Goods and Services) Act 1970 which operated quite well until the introduction of compulsory competitive tendering ('CCT'), which required local authorities, where they had an in-house provision, to make a return (6 per cent) on those services which were subject to the CCT process. There was therefore an incentive on local authorities to seek to increase income streams by either undertaking additional work in house, or looking to the wider world for work.

14.05   With the increasing requirement for local authorities to manage their budgets ever more carefully, caps on expenditure and the introduction of 'business' practises and attitudes into the town hall, it is perhaps inevitable that local authorities are seeking to become more like businesses themselves, to the extent that the role of a local authority is becoming increasingly blurred as we enter the twenty-first century. The introduction of the 'well-being' powers contained in the Local Government Act 2000 have perhaps created greater opportunities for local authorities to trade.

14.06   The fact remains, however, that no matter what the local authority wishes to do for others, it is not allowed to be driven by the profit motive (although the making of a profit might be an incidental benefit arising from the trading that is undertaken), and that is perhaps the biggest restraint on a local authority ever being able to develop a proper presence in the market place.

LOCAL AUTHORITY TRADING POWERS

The ultra vires principle

14.07   As will be seen from the cases described below, the ultra vires doctrine applies to the provision by local authorities of goods, works or services to others (ie 'trading') as it applies to anything else that local authorities carry out.

14.08   A detailed discussion of the ultra vires doctrine in relation to local authorities generally is set out at paras **10.02–10.71**. The powers of a local authority to enter into 'trading' activities must, therefore, be considered in the light of these principles.

14.09   The basic principle is that a local authority may only do those things it is authorised to do by Parliament and those things reasonably inferred therefrom[1]. Thus whenever a local authority wishes to undertake the provision of goods, works or services for any other person or body, whether or not for payment, the question must be asked, 'Is the proposed activity within its statutory powers (or to be inferred from them) or is it incidental to those statutory powers (in the terms set out in the section relating to s 111 of the Local Government Act 1972[2])'?

1   *Ashbury Railway Carriage and Iron Co v Riche* (1875) 7 HL 653.
2   See paras **10.106–10.110**.

The early cases

14.10   Local authorities in particular were not slow to get involved in trading, and as a result a number of cases came before the courts. The following are the principal examples:
— *A-G v Manchester Corpn*[1] The council ran tramway services under local Act powers that also permitted them to carry animals, goods and parcels. It introduced a service for a general parcels delivery service within and beyond its area not confined to the carriage of parcels on its trams. The council argued that the general service was ancillary or incidental to its tramway powers. It was held that it had no power to carry parcels except by means of its trams.
— *A-G v Fulham Corpn*[2] The council had a power to provide facilities under the Baths and Washhouses Acts for residents to wash their clothes. The council introduced a new service whereby residents could bring their washing to the washhouse and have it washed by the staff. A collection and delivery service was also offered, at a small extra charge. The court said that the council did not have the necessary powers; the statutory provisions did not extend to washing clothes for others but were restricted to the provision of facilities for persons to wash their own clothes. Nor could the washing of clothes be said to be incidental or consequential to the mere provision of washing facilities.
— *A-G v Smethwick Corpn*[3] The council established a printing works to produce printed books and other material for, or in connection with, its statutory purposes.

It was held that this was incidental to the performance of its functions and was within the council's powers to establish such an operation.

1   [1906] 1 Ch 643. See para **10.21**.
2   [1921] 1 Ch 440 . See para **10.21**.
3   [1932] 1 Ch 562.

Limited specific statutory provisions

14.11   However, over many years many local authorities have been involved in supplying goods, works and services. Many of them ran (and some still run) tramway and bus services. For example Blackpool Borough Council still runs trams. Kingston-upon-Hull ran its own telephone service for many years. Others provided electricity supply, district heating systems available to the public and the London County Council ('LCC') used to provide 'civic restaurants'. They were able to do this because the services that they provided were specifically authorised by local Acts of Parliament.

14.12   More recently Parliament has provided statutory relaxations of the strict rules to specifically enable local authorities to provide services to other people and bodies. One of the earliest examples of a general power to enable the operation of a 'supplies organisation' was a power in the London Government Act of 1936 for the London County Council to provide goods and services to the old Metropolitan Boroughs in London. It was an obvious means of securing increased purchasing power for the authorities and eliminating duplication of effort and costs between these local authorities.

The Local Authorities (Goods and Services) Act 1970

14.13   This led to the enactment of the Local Authorities (Goods and Services) Act 1970 which provides a general statutory power specifically permitting local authorities to provide goods, etc, and services to any 'public body'. The LA(GS)A 1970 covers (s 1(1)):
(i)   the supply of any goods or materials;
(ii)   the provision of professional, technical, administrative services;
(iii)   the use of any vehicle, plant or apparatus with the services of personnel employed in connection therewith;
(iv)   the carrying out of maintenance work (but not construction) to land or buildings for which the public body is responsible; and
(v)   the purchase and storage of goods and materials which may be required in pursuance of (i) above.

14.14   The LA(GS)A 1970 allows the parties to agree terms as to payment they consider appropriate (s 1(3)). There is also a restriction that any property or service supplied to the local authority must be supplied to the other public body for purposes for functions which that body has power to undertake (s 1(2)(b)).

14.15   A 'public body' is defined by the LA(GS)A 1970 to include any local authority (including a police authority and certain national police bodies) or housing action trust, and other person or body designated as a 'public body' by order under s 1(5).

That sub-section empowers the appropriate government minister to designate by statutory instrument as a 'public body' any person, or description of persons, which he considers appear to be exercising functions of a public nature.

14.16   A great number of such orders have been made but care is needed in applying them. Some are unrestricted in the scope of the authorities and services but others are restricted to a greater or lesser degree by limiting the authorities who can provide services, the purposes for which services may be provided and the nature of the services themselves.

14.17   Other bodies have been added by virtue of provisions within their specific legislation, eg health authorities and the Secretary of State for Health[1], regional development agencies[2] and further and higher education corporations[3]. It is, therefore, always worth checking the relevant legislation for possible specific instances of powers for local authorities to provide services. There might be more possibilities than are immediately apparent!

1   National Health Service Act 1977, s 28.
2   Regional Development Agencies Act 1998, Sch 7, para 3.
3   Further and Higher Education Act 1992.

YORKSHIRE PURCHASING CASE: CROSS-BOUNDARY TENDERING AND SPARE CAPACITY

14.18   With the introduction in 1988 of CCT in respect of local authority contracts, there was a move by a number of local authorities to promote the use of the LA(GS)A 1970 powers for 'cross boundary tendering' (ie tendering for work required to be put out to tender by another local authorities). This practice was frowned upon by the government of the day, which wished to see local authority works and services contracted out to private contractors.

14.19   As a consequence the Audit Commission (by a technical release) and Department of Environment issued guidance to the effect that the LA(GS)A 1970, s 1(2)(b) should be interpreted so that authorities could only use 'spare capacity' in the provision of goods, works or services to other bodies under the Act. Under this view, authorities were said to be unable to engage staff or stockpile goods or materials specifically for use for the purposes of providing such goods, materials, services or works to other bodies under the 1970 Act, with the result that their ability to bid for cross-boundary tenders was limited. There was considerable debate as to whether the guidance issued was accurate, and in a letter sent by the then DoE to the various local authority associations in 1995, there appeared to be a change of heart, in that the view was expressed that local authorities were in fact permitted to use the LA(GS)A 1970 to undertake trading activities as provided by that Act, and that such trading activities were not limited to the use of 'spare capacity'.

14.20   In *R v Yorkshire Purchasing Organisation, ex p British Educational Suppliers Association*[1] a local authority purchasing organisation was challenged on the grounds that it could not purchase goods in advance of firm commitments for them from its customers and that it could not arrange and profit from 'call-off' sales to its customers.

The first challenge was dismissed on the grounds that the LA(GS)A 1970, s 1(1), which specifically allowed the purchase and storage of goods, had no such restriction. The second challenge was upheld on the basis that such 'call-off' arrangements are not within the scope of the 1970 Act.

1   (1997) 95 LGR 727, CA.

14.21   As a result of the *Yorkshire Purchasing Organisation* case and the DoE change of heart, the 'spare capacity' argument is no longer valid and would not provide a restriction for a local authority tendering for the provision of goods, materials, works or services to other public bodies (as defined in the LA(GS)A 1970).

LOCAL GOVERNMENT ACT 2000 AND OTHER STATUTORY POWERS RELATING TO TRADING

14.22   Other statutory provisions exist which are more restricted in scope but are worth considering in particular cases. Some examples are as follows:

—   **London Government Act 1963, s 5(2)**: powers for London Boroughs and other London bodies, *for the better performance of their functions*, to provide services for each other in generally similar terms to the LA(GS)A 1970. This section also applies to local authorities whose areas are contiguous with Greater London and to certain bodies established under the Local Government Act 1985 to inherit functions of the Greater London Council and the Inner London Education Authority after their abolition;

—   **Local Government (Miscellaneous Provisions) Act 1976, s 38**: power to allow use by any person of computers provided for the purposes of a local authority's functions and to provide services in connection therewith;

—   **Control of Pollution Act 1974, s 22(3)**: power to clean any land in the open air that is situated in the local authority's area by agreement with the owner;

—   **Local Authorities (Land) Act 1963, s 3**: power for the benefit or improvement of the local authority's area to erect any building or works on land and repair, maintain and insure such building or works;

—   **Local Government Act 1972, s 111**: power to do anything that is calculated to facilitate or is incidental or conducive to the discharge of any of the local authority's functions. It might also be possible to argue that s 111 of the 1972 Act would be available to authorise the provision of services or goods to third parties. The use of this section would need to be limited strictly to the provision of services, or the supply of goods etc directly related to the performance of a statutory function. However, reference is made to the discussion relating to the general use of s 111 of the 1972 Act (see paras **10.106–10.110**). In these circumstances great caution should be observed in the use of this section as authorising trading activities.

Local Government Act 2000, s 2

14.23   Section 2(1) provides another significant statutory relaxation of the ultra vires rule. That section empowers a local authority to promote the economic, social or environmental well-being of its area (ie all or part of its area of for the benefit of all or some of persons there present or resident). Section 2(4)(f) specifically provides that the power in sub-s (1) includes power for the authority to 'provide staff, goods, services or accommodation to any person' and s 2(4)(e) allows the authority to 'exercise on behalf of any person any functions of that person' (see also the Health Act 1999)[1]. The DETR (now Office of the Deputy Prime Minister) has issued guidance[2] under the Act which gives some useful information on the operation in practice of this power.

1   See paras **10.111–10.116**.
2   *Power to Promote or Improve Economic, Social or Environmental Well-Being* (March 2001).

14.24   As mentioned above (see para **10.114**), the s 2 power is subject to a number of restrictions, which in relation to trading activities may be summarised as follows:
(i)   in exercising it regard must be had to the strategy under s 4, although the guidance advises that if the strategy is not in place, that should not prevent local authorities from exercising their well-being powers (para 25);
(ii)   it does not permit a local authority to do anything contrary to any prohibition, restriction or limitation on their powers which is contained in any enactment;
(iii)   it does not extend to the raising of money (whether by precepts, borrowing or otherwise): the guidance acknowledges that local authorities should not use the well-being powers *primarily* to raise money, but it acknowledges that where the power is used for a different purpose but incidentally the local authority receives income as a result, that does not, in the government's view, amount to raising money. Thus, as long as the local authority is providing service or goods and the primary intention is not to raise money, the implication is that if, in providing those services, income is received as a result, the local authority will not be acting ultra vires. As an alternative, provision of services can be made 'in kind', which would, perhaps, obviate the need to charge. However, local authorities will also need to bear in mind the government's intention to make regulations under the Local Government and Housing Act 1989, s 150 to provide local authorities with powers to charge for certain discretionary services, including those provided by virtue of the well-being power. As at August 2002, the regulations are still awaited!
(iv)   the Secretary of State may by order prevent authorities taking specified actions under the well-being power. No such orders have to date been issued under this power.

14.25   In using the s 2 power to trade or provide services, the local authority will need to satisfy itself that its actions will benefit all or some of the 'persons present' in its area and will improve or promote the social, economic or environmental well being of some or all of those persons. If it is intending to trade outside of its boundaries, the local authority will need to consult with the authority(ies) within whose boundaries it will be seeking to operate, and also consider the impact of any such proposal (Guidance, para 56). It will also need to consider that the action it is proposing to take will achieve or contribute to the economic, social or environmental well-being in its *own* area.

14.26   The Guidance poses a number of questions that a local authority should ask itself in order to determine whether the well-being power is appropriate;
(i)   is the proposed action likely to promote or improve the well-being of its area?
(ii)   is the primary purpose to raise money?

(iii) is it expressly prohibited on the face of other legislation?
(iv) are there any other explicit limitations and restrictions on the face of other legislation?

If the answer to the first question is 'yes', and the answers to the next two questions is 'no', the local authority can proceed, subject to answering the fourth question.

14.27 Thus a local authority will still need to consider very carefully the reasons why it is seeking to use the well-being powers for the purpose of trading. Failure to do so might well mean that an action for judicial review is launched on the basis that the action is ultra vires the powers contained in the legislation. It does seem clear, however, that the statutory relaxation of the effects of the ultra vires rule by the well-being power could prove significant, assuming that authorities have the staff and/or finance to use it adequately.

14.28 The LGA 2000 does provide a reasonably untrammelled power to provide goods and services to any person (whether a public body or a commercial organisation or a voluntary body or individuals) when compared with the LA(GS)A 1970. It remains to be seen what use will be made of it and what challenges arise to its use in this way.

DIRECT SERVICE ORGANISATIONS AND THE PROVISION OF SERVICES TO OUTSOURCING CONTRACTORS

14.29 A further aspect of trading by local authorities relates to circumstances in which the local authority may wish to provide that its own in-house organisation should continue to provide services in circumstances where the main service provision activity is to be outsourced to a private contractor. There may be good reasons for such a proposal (eg that the in-house organisation has the expertise and technical knowledge which is not available (at reasonable cost or at all) in the private sector).

14.30 The difficulty with such a proposition is that in any such arrangement the in-house organisation (which in legal terms is a part of the local authority itself) would be providing goods, materials or services to the outsourcing contractor which in all probability would not be a 'public body' within the LA(GS)A 1970. Of course, it might in contrast be argued that in doing so, the in-house organisation is in fact providing the services, etc to the authority (albeit via the contractor).

14.31 In practicable terms it is difficult to see how a transfer of the risk of the provision of the services can be effectively transferred to the outsourcing contractor when the authority is itself providing part of those services by means of its in-house organisation.

14.32 In legal terms it is necessary in each case to examine whether or not what is proposed falls within the terms of one of more of the enactments that permit local authorities to undertake trading activities or whether or not the services, etc, are in fact being provided to the authority rather than to the contractor. The determination of the position is likely to depend upon the precise legal and practical contractual arrangements put in place between the authority and the contractor in relation to the relevant services and the method of their control, management and supervision and who takes responsibility for any breach of, or defect in, the service provision requirements.

CONCLUSION

14.33   The basic point is that the ultra vires rule still applies (although much relaxed by statute). Thus it remains necessary to examine the 'small print' of the legislation to ascertain whether or not any particular use of the powers is appropriate.

14.34   The LA(GS)A 1970 provides a limited ability for local authorities to trade or provide services. Despite the plethora of orders made under the Act, the range of bodies to whom provision of goods and services may be made is severely restricted in practice. However, the Act does allow bulk purchasing organisations for the public sector and other important opportunities for the public benefit.

14.35   Other statutes, whilst limited, may also provide a useful power in particular circumstances. In particular the Local Government Act 2000 may provide wider and less constrained opportunities for local authorities to provide services if to do so is for the 'well-being' of the authority's area in social, economic or environmental terms, but the charging and other restrictions may limit its use in practice and will need to be carefully treated if the allegation of a profit motive is to be avoided.

14.36   It therefore needs to be emphasised that the principle is that the relevant Act is designed to achieve benefits in public administration or services and must be operated for those purposes. The enactments do not, and should not be utilised to, allow authorities to trade with a view to making a profit. Thus it is necessary for local authorities to eschew a profit motive in deciding to undertake trading activities (although arguments related to greater efficiencies and economy for the public benefit arising from such activities are valid considerations) and to base any decision to undertake such activities clearly on the public benefits arising both for the supplier of the activities as well as the receiver of them. There is a risk that any divergence from these principles may lead an authority's auditors to take the view that the power is being exercised for an improper purpose or give rise to a legal challenge to the authority's operation of the power for that purpose.

14.37   Whatever route is to be adopted, however, the clear message is that precision in interpretation of the statutory provisions and a careful and proper application of them is paramount, along with a healthy caution for anything that might indicate that the activity is being undertaken purely for the making of a trading profit for its own sake.

CHAPTER 15

Affected staff, TUPE and pensions

Ilyas Bulbulia

15.01   In this chapter, we consider the protection afforded to employees by the Transfer of Undertakings (Protection of Employment) Regulations 1981, generally referred to as 'TUPE'[1]. TUPE gives effect to the EC Acquired Rights Directive 77/187 (known as 'the ARD') and is intended to protect an employee's employment in the event that the undertaking for which he or she works is transferred by the employer to a new owner.

1   SI 1981/1794.

15.02   At common law, the transfer of an undertaking from one employer to another automatically terminates the employee's contract of employment. There is therefore a dismissal and the reason for the dismissal will usually be redundancy as the employer's requirement for employees to do work of a particular kind will have ceased or diminished. If the transferred undertaking's new employer requires the old employees' services, it can offer them a new contract of employment on whatever terms it likes.

15.03   Where TUPE applies, the transfer of the undertaking will not terminate the employees' contracts of employment. Therefore there will not be a dismissal. The employees will transfer with the undertaking and will be employed by the new owner under the original contract. If there are any dismissals, whether before or after the transfer, and if those dismissals are connected with the transfer they may be automatically unfair.

WHERE DO THE REGULATIONS APPLY?

15.04   TUPE applies 'to a transfer from one person to another of an undertaking ... or part of one ...'. In seeking to identify whether or not there is a relevant transfer for the purposes of TUPE , two principal issues have to be considered, namely:
(i)   the mechanism of transfer; and
(ii)   whether there was an economic entity capable of transfer in the hands of the transferor that has maintained sufficient of its identity in the hands of the transferee.

Mechanism of transfer

15.05   TUPE applies whenever there is a change in the natural legal person who is responsible for carrying on the business. A typical situation where TUPE applies is the sale of a business as a going concern. However, TUPE has been held to apply to a variety of other situations, such as contracting out of services by an organisation. TUPE has been applied even where there is no contract between the transferor and transferee, eg 'second generation contracting out'. TUPE would not, however, apply to a transfer of shares, as there is no change in the natural legal person that carries on the business.

Whether there was an economic entity capable of transfer

15.06   The European Court of Justice has propounded various tests and guidelines as to the existence of a relevant transfer. In *Spijkers v Gebroeders Benedik Abattoir CV*[1], the ECJ outlined the general test to be applied in determining whether there has been a relevant transfer. According to the decision of the ECJ the decisive criterion for establishing whether there is a transfer for the purposes of the ARD is whether the business in question retains its identity upon transfer. A transfer of an undertaking, or part of an undertaking, does not occur merely because the assets of the undertaking are disposed of. It is necessary to consider whether the business was disposed of as a going concern. This would be indicated, inter alia, by the fact that its operation was actually continued or resumed by the new employer, with the same or similar activities.

1   24/85 [1986] ECR 1119, [1986] 2 CMLR 296.

15.07   In order to determine whether those conditions are met the court stated that it is necessary to consider all the facts characterising the transaction in question, including:
—   the type of undertaking or business;
—   whether or not the business's tangible assets, such as buildings and movable property, are transferred;
—   the value of its intangible assets at the time of transfer;
—   whether or not the majority of its employees are taken over by the new employer;
—   the degree of similarity between the activities carried on before and after the transfer; and
—   the period, if any, for which those activities were suspended.

15.08   According to the ECJ, all the above circumstances are merely single factors in the overall assessment, which must be made and cannot therefore be considered in isolation. It is for the national court to make the necessary factual appraisal, in the light of the criteria for interpretation set out above, in order to establish whether or not there is a transfer for the purpose of the ARD.

15.09   In *Christel Schmidt v Spar und Leihkasse der Fruheren Amter*[1], the ECJ held that when a bank which employed one part-time cleaner contracted out its cleaning operations to a third party there was a relevant transfer of an undertaking.

1   C-392/92 [1994] IRLR 302, ECJ.

15.10   In the light of such ECJ decisions the UK courts and tribunals had little difficulty in deciding that in most cases there was a relevant transfer and that this applied to first and second generation contracting out and on contracting in (return of the service in-house).

15.11   However, in *Ayse Suzen v Zehnacker Gebaudereinigung GmbH*[1], the ECJ upset the previous certainties. The ECJ reaffirmed that the decisive criterion is 'whether the entity in question retains its identity'. However, the ECJ went on to state that it is necessary to consider all the facts of the transaction and held that the mere fact that the service provided by the old and new contractors is similar does not support the conclusion that an economic entity has been transferred if there is no accompanying transfer from one undertaking to another of significant tangible assets, or taking over by the new employer of a major part of the workforce.

1   [1997] IRLR 255, ECJ.

15.12   An example of how the UK courts interpret the legislation in the light of *Spijkers* and *Ayse Suzen* can be found in *RCO Support Services and Aintree Hospital Trust v UNISON*[1]. In this case, the EAT upheld the decision of the employment tribunal that there had been a relevant transfer under TUPE because the cleaning and catering activities carried out by the contractors in question (who supplied such services to an NHS Trust) had in itself formed an economic entity which had been transferred even though there had been no transfer of staff at all. This decision appears to favour the broad interpretation of the decision of the ECJ in *Spijkers*. In *RCO Support Services*, Lindsay J said that a literal application of *Ayse Suzen* would leave unprotected precisely those, such as cleaning and catering staff and others in labour-intensive employment markets, prone to contracting out, whose vulnerability the ARD had been implemented to protect.

1   [2000] IRLR 624.

15.13   In the light of the confusion surrounding the application of *Ayse Suzen* in the UK, the EAT, in *Cheesman v R Brewer Contracts Ltd*[1], tried to give some guidance concerning the application of the transfer rules to contracting-out scenarios. In the EAT's view, it was necessary to consider the question of whether there had been a transfer in two stages:
(i)   whether there was an undertaking capable of being transferred; and
(ii)   whether that undertaking had been transferred.

1   [2001] IRLR 144.

15.14   On the issue of whether there is an undertaking, the EAT observed that:
(i)   there needs to be a stable economic entity whose activity is not limited to performing one specific works contract—ie an organised grouping of persons and of assets enabling (or facilitating) the exercise of an economic activity which pursues a specific objective;
(ii)   in order to be such an undertaking it must be sufficiently structured and autonomous, but it will not necessarily have significant tangible or intangible assets;
(iii) in certain sectors such as cleaning and surveillance the assets are often reduced to their most basic and the activity is essentially based on manpower;
(iv)   an organised grouping of wage-earners who are specifically and permanently assigned to a common task may, in the absence of other factors of production, amount to an economic entity;
(v)   an activity of itself is not an entity: the identity of an entity emerges from other factors such as its workforce, management staff, the way in which its work is organised, its operating methods and, where appropriate, the operational resources available to it.

15.15   As to whether there has been a transfer, the EAT acknowledged that the decisive criterion for establishing the existence of a transfer is whether the entity in question retains its identity, as indicated, amongst other things, by the fact that its operation is actually continued or resumed. In a labour-intensive sector an entity is capable of maintaining its identity after it has been transferred, where the new employer does not merely pursue the activity in question but also takes over a major part, in terms of their numbers and skills, of the employees specially assigned by his predecessors to that task. That follows from the fact that in certain labour-intensive sectors a group of workers engaged in the joint activity on a permanent basis may constitute an economic entity.

15.16   In considering whether the decisive criterion had been satisfied, the EAT made the following observations:
(i)   it is necessary to consider all the factors characterising the transaction in question— but each is a single factor and none is to be considered in isolation. However, whilst there is no legal authority on the point, it is presumably not an error of law to consider 'the decisive criterion' in isolation because that is an aspect of its being 'decisive', although, when considering 'the decisive criterion' it is necessary to have regard to the fact that it is not itself dependent on a single factor;
(ii)   where an economic entity is able to function without any significant tangible or intangible assets, the maintenance of its identity following the transaction cannot logically depend on the transfer of such assets;
(iii)   even where assets are owned and are required to run the undertaking, the fact that they do not pass does not preclude a transfer;
(iv)   the mere fact that the service provided by the old and new undertaking providing a contracted-out service or the old and new contract-holder is similar does not justify the conclusion that there has been a transfer of an economic entity between predecessor and successor;
(v)   the absence of any contractual link between transferor and transferee may be evidence that there has been no relevant transfer but it is not conclusive as there is no need for any such direct contractual relationship;
(vi)   where no employees are transferred, the reasons why can be relevant to determine whether or not there was a transfer;
(vii)   the fact that the work is performed continuously with no interruption or change in the manner or performance is a normal feature of transfers of undertakings, but no particular importance should be attached to a gap between the end of the work by one sub-contractor and the start by the successor.

15.17   Whilst the above list is helpful in deciding whether or not TUPE applies, the uncertainties still remain. This is well illustrated by the recent decision of the ECJ in *Oy Liikenne Ab v Liskojärvi and Juntunen*[1]. In this case, the Greater Helsinki Council tendered for the right to run seven local bus routes. The outgoing contractor lost the contract, and it was awarded to Oy Liikenne Ab (the incoming contractor). The outgoing contractor owned 26 buses and dismissed 45 people. The incoming contractor bought its own buses, ie not taking over the outgoing contractor's buses, and re-engaged 33 of the 45 drivers who applied (hiring another 18 of its own) on less favourable terms. The incoming contractor therefore took over a majority of the workforce but no assets. On the facts, the ECJ held that despite the majority of the workforce moving over, the lack of the transfer of the main assets (ie the buses) 'must lead to the conclusion that the entity does not retain its identity' and therefore held that there was no transfer.

---

1   C 172/99 [2001] IRLR 171.

15.18 In the public sector, in addition to TUPE, organisations must have regard to the statement of practice on staff transfers in the public sector[1]. The aim of the statement of practice is to ensure that the protection afforded by TUPE will apply to employees unless there are genuinely exceptional reasons why this should not be the case. The statement of practice sets out a framework to be followed by public sector organisations in order to implement the government's policy on treatment of staff transfers where the public sector is the employer when contracting out or the client in a subsequent re-tendering situation. The statement of practice applies directly to central government departments and agencies under the NHS. However, the government expects other public sector organisations such as local authorities to follow it.

1   January 2000 issued by the Cabinet Office.

15.19 The statement of practice covers public private partnerships including PFI transactions. The overriding principle is that TUPE should apply to these transactions save where there are genuinely exceptional reasons why this should not be the case. Such exceptional reasons are, broadly:

(i)   where a contract is for the provision of both goods and services, but the provision of services is ancillary to the provision of the goods; or
(ii)   where the activity for which the public sector organisation is contracting is new or is a one-off project; or
(iii) where services or goods are essentially a commodity bought 'off the shelf' and no grouping of staff are specifically and permanently assigned to a common task; or
(iv)   where the features of the service or function, subject to the contracted exercise, are significantly different from the features of the function previously performed within the public sector or by an existing contractor, eg a function to be delivered electronically, and in such a way that it requires radically different skills, experience and equipment.

15.20 The statement of practice goes on to state that where a public sector organisation believes such genuinely exceptional circumstances exist then it should be prepared to explain them. In central government departments, the agreement of the relevant ministers may need to be obtained before such an exception is made.

15.21 The statement of practice further states that in such exceptional cases where staff do not transfer and TUPE does not apply, the public sector organisation should, in the case of first generation contracts, seek to identify as soon as possible with the contractor any staff that will be taken on voluntarily by the contractor; and then, where possible, re-deploy those members of staff remaining within the public sector organisation.

WHO TRANSFERS UNDER THE REGULATIONS

15.22 As a general rule, TUPE applies to individuals who were employed under a contract of employment with the transferor and who were still employed immediately before the transfer took place.

Employees

15.23   It should generally be clear from the terms of engagement whether or not somebody is or is not an employee (as opposed to a self-employed contractor) of the transferor. If there is no written contract but the employer has complied with its obligation to give employees a written statement of particulars, then these will be taken as forming the basis of the contract.

15.24   It is sometimes the case that individuals are engaged on a fairly informal basis, with only a short-form letter of offer indicating not much more than the start date, salary, notice periods and holiday entitlement. In the absence of any other written terms, this letter similarly would be taken to form the basis of the contract, and should help clarify whether the individual is an employee or not.

15.25   If, for whatever reason, there is nothing in writing to suggest what the nature of the relationship is, it will be necessary to look at other indicators, such as whether the employer deducts PAYE and pays employer's National Insurance contributions on behalf of the individual. As a general rule, those individuals who are self-employed and working for the transferor under a contract for services will not be covered by TUPE, although whether their relationship with the transferor amounts to a contract for services or a contract of service will be up to the courts or tribunals to decide.

Assigned to the undertaking or part of undertaking transferring

15.26   Where part of a business is transferred employees will not be affected by TUPE if they did not work in the part transferred. Even employees who perform duties in relation to the part transferred, eg administrative duties, will not be covered unless they are wholly or mainly assigned to the part transferred.

15.27   In *Botzen v Rotterdamsche Droogdok Maatschappi BV*[1], the ECJ stated that in these situations the test to be applied is whether there is a transfer of the part of the undertaking to which the employees 'were assigned and which formed the organisational framework within which their employment took effect'.

1   186/83 [1985] ECR 519, [1986] 2 CMLR 50, ECJ.

15.28   Useful guidance on the *Botzen* test was given by the EAT in *Duncan Web Offset (Maidstone) Ltd v Cooper*[1]. In this case, the EAT set out three possible factual situations which might arise under TUPE, reg 5:
1   X has a business in which he employs a number of people. X transfers part of his business to Y. In order to determine which employees were employed in the part transferred, it is necessary to ask which employees were assigned to the part transferred. In determining to which part of the employer's business the employee was assigned, a tribunal may consider matters such as:
    (i)   the amount of time spent on one part of the business or the other;
    (ii)   the amount of value given to each part by the employee;
    (iii) the terms of the contract of employment showing what the employee could be required to do; and
    (iv)   how the cost to the employer of the employee's services was allocated between different parts of the business;

2   a person is employed by X to work on Y's business and Y transfers that business to Z. Prima facie, TUPE would not apply, since the employee must be employed by the transferor (Y) for TUPE to apply. However, the tribunals will be astute to ensure that TUPE is not evaded by devices such as service companies, or by complicated group structures which conceal the true position;

3   X, which is part of a group of companies, employs a number of people on X's sole business. The whole of X's undertaking is transferred by X to Y. Some of X's employees worked partly for X and partly for other parts of the group. Almost certainly, X's employees will be transferred, but there may be cases where it could be said that, despite being employed by X, they were in reality assigned to the business of another part of the group. This recognises that the contract of employment test is not the only matter for consideration, and that an employee might be employed by one company but assigned to the business of the other. Tribunals will keep in mind the purpose of the ARD and the need to avoid complicated corporate structures from getting in the way of a result which gives effect to that purpose.

1   [1995] IRLR 633.

Employment immediately before the transfer

15.29   Employees have to be employed by the transferor immediately prior to the transfer. On a strict interpretation of TUPE, reg 5, employees who are dismissed shortly before completion are not employed immediately before the transfer and, consequently, would not come within the regulation, ie their contracts would not be transferred to the transferee and they would have to pursue claims for the termination of their contracts against the transferor. This was the approach which the Court of Appeal took in *Secretary of State for Employment v Spence*[1], when it held that the contract must subsist at the moment of transfer. The contracts of employees who were dismissed several hours before completion were held not to be transferred to the transferee.

1   [1987] QB 179, [1986] IRLR 248.

15.30   On this interpretation, a transferee would be able to circumvent reg 5 by insisting that the transferor dismisses some or all of the workforce prior to completion. The House of Lords, however, in *Litster v Forth Dry Dock and Engineering Co Ltd*[1] added a significant gloss to the wording of reg 5. The House of Lords held that reg 5 applies not only to a person who is employed immediately before the transfer but also to a person who would have been so employed if he had not been unfairly dismissed in the circumstances described in reg 8(1). Regulation 8(1) provides that the dismissal is automatically unfair unless the employer can show that the dismissal was for an economic, technical or organisational reason ('ETO reason') entailing a change in the workforce.

1   [1989] 1 All ER 1134, [1989] IRLR 161.

15.31   As a result of the *Litster* decision, reg 5 now applies to two groups of employees:

1   to those employees actually employed by the transferor at the time of the transfer. Their contracts of employment transfer to the transferee and they will work for the transferee under the terms of those contracts;

2   to those employees who were dismissed for a reason connected with the transfer where no ETO reason exists. Although their dismissals will be effective and therefore their contracts of employment will not be transferred, all rights, duties and liabilities relating to their previous employment will transfer, including any rights they may have had with regard to unfair or wrongful dismissal, together with any claim for a redundancy payment.

Secondments

15.32   The usual practice is for employees engaged in the provision of transferring services to themselves transfer to the new service provider. The Cabinet Office statement of practice states that all parties should usually proceed as if TUPE applies. However, the government has recently introduced the Retention of Employment Model ('REM') in the NHS. According to the REM, employees engaged in the provision of the service or services being outsourced to the private sector remain in the employment of the NHS Trust. The employees are then temporarily seconded to the project company or its contractors. The REM scheme is currently undergoing a trial period in the provision of 'soft' services at three NHS hospitals.

15.33   The REM, or 'secondment model' as it is sometimes known, gives rise to a number of difficult legal issues. The ARD envisages an automatic transfer from the transferor to the transferee. This does not sit easily with the concept of seconding employees to the transferor. There is unfortunately little or no direct UK or European case law on whether seconding employees to a contractor is compatible with the provisions of the ARD and/or TUPE. However where employees are seconded a number of practical issues have to be considered. Some of the main issues have been highlighted below.

15.34   The reality will undoubtedly be that the contractor will have day-to-day control of the work to be undertaken by the seconded employees and the manner in which it is to be performed. This will require the degree of management control by the contractor to be clearly defined and understood between all parties especially the affected employees. Matters such as to sickness absence and reporting procedures will have to be defined.

15.35   A decision will have to be made as to whether the client organisation or the contractor will be responsible for the operation of disciplinary, grievance, capability and dismissal procedures. The client organisation will remain the employer, so it will be necessary for the client organisation to retain responsibility for the dismissal of employees. However, the management of the employees will undoubtedly have transferred to the contractor and therefore the parties will need to decide who will have responsibility for the conduct of disciplinary procedures.

15.36   It should be noted that as the employer, the client organisation will be the named respondent in any unfair dismissal proceedings issued in the employment tribunal. Any compensation award will be made against the client organisation and not the contractor, although the secondment agreement could require the contractor to indemnify the client organisation in appropriate circumstances.

15.37   The discrimination legislation provides for the potential liability of both the employer and the beneficiary of a seconded employee's services. For example, if an employee seconded by the client organisation was subjected to harassment by a manager of the contractor, this could result in the contractor incurring liability. However, the possibility also exists of the client organisation as the employer being held liable under discrimination legislation.

15.38 It is likely to be harder for the contractor, not being the employer, to have the same degree of control over the seconded employees as it would if it employed them. If, therefore, contractually agreed service levels are dependent on changes to working practices being effected, the contractor may have to rely on the client organisation, as the employer, to achieve this. If the client organisation fails, for any reason, to achieve service levels the contractor is likely to want some sort of limitation or deduction from any penalties imposed on it, if that failure leads to service levels falling below the specification.

15.39 The assessment of the value for money of the secondment arrangement compared to the transfer of staff under TUPE will also be important. The contractor may reflect the perceived risk associated with the split in employment and management control of the seconded staff in the bid price. On the other hand the client organisation may have to continue incurring costs such as salaries for human resources staff and managers who are retained by the client organisation to manage the seconded employees. The client organisation would not have incurred these costs if those staff had transferred to the contractor under TUPE.

15.40 The parties will need to be clear about the period of secondment and what will happen at the end of the secondment period. It should be noted that if, at the end of the secondment period, seconded employees decide to enter into a contract of employment with the contractor they may not necessarily transfer to the contractor by virtue of TUPE at that stage. This would mean that the would not be able to claim continuous service. It should also be noted that at the end of the secondment period the employees may return to the client organisation and the client organisation may have to make the employees redundant if no work is available for them.

EMPLOYEES RIGHT TO OBJECT TO THE TRANSFER

15.41 Those employees who are assigned to the transferring undertaking are not, however, obliged to transfer. In *Katsikas v Konstantinidis*[1], the ECJ held that employees were entitled to object to the transfer of their employment contracts. The legal effect of this objection is a matter for each Member State to determine. Therefore domestic law determines what happens in the event of an objection by the employee to the transfer.

1   C-132/91 [1993] IRLR 179.

15.42 Regulation 5(4A) of TUPE provides that if an employee informs the transferor or the transferee that he objects to becoming employed by the transferee, TUPE shall not transfer his contract of employment or the rights, powers, duties and liabilities under or in connection with it. Regulation 5(4B) goes on to state that:

> 'where an employee so objects the transfer of the undertaking or part in which he is employed shall operate so as to terminate his contract of employment

with the transferor but he shall not be treated for any purpose, as having been dismissed by the transferor'.

15.43   It had been thought that the effect of these provisions was to absolve both the transferor and the transferee of any liability for the employee, in terms of any liabilities under the contract or any claim for unfair dismissal. However, this will not always be the case. In *University of Oxford v Humphreys*[1], the Court of Appeal held that where an employee objects to the transfer of his or her contract of employment because he or she knows the transferee intends to make substantial and detrimental changes in terms and conditions, the exercise of the right to object can be regarded as a constructive dismissal by the transferor. The court also held that liability for the relevant dismissal rests with the transferor and does not transfer to the transferee under TUPE, reg 5(2).

1   [2000] IRLR 183.

15.44   A particularly perplexing feature of this decision is the Court of Appeal's refusal to accept that liability for a constructive dismissal which occurs before the transferee is threatening to change terms and conditions passes to the transferee in accordance with the principle set out in *Litster*. The practical consequences of this is that the transferor may incur substantial liabilities as a result of matters which are entirely outside its control, ie the transferee's intentions in relation to terms and conditions.

WHICH RIGHTS TRANSFER WITH THE EMPLOYEES?

15.45   According to TUPE, reg 5, where a relevant transfer takes place, the transferring employees transfer from the transferor to the transferee under their existing terms and conditions of employment and with their continuity of service intact. In effect, the transferee steps into the shoes of the transferor.

15.46   The transferee inherits all accrued rights and liabilities connected with the contract of employment of the transferred employee. If, for example, the transferor was in arrears with wages at the time of the transfer, the employee can sue the transferee as if the original liability had been with it. The transferee also inherits all statutory rights and liabilities which are connected with the individual contract of employment, eg unfair dismissal, redundancy and discrimination. TUPE does not, however, have the effect of assigning criminal liability and rights and liabilities relating to the provisions of occupational pension schemes which relate to benefits for old age, invalidity or survivors (this is dealt with at para **15.54**).

Collective agreements

15.47   Under TUPE, reg 6, any collective agreements made with a union by the transferor are deemed to have been made by the transferee. However, the agreements apply only in relation to the transferred employees and not those subsequently hired. It should be noted that many of the substantive terms, eg wages, are incorporated expressly or by custom into individual contracts of employment and will transfer anyway under reg 5.

15.48   Two cases illustrate the effect of reg 6 and how collective agreements transfer to the transferor. In *BET Catering Services Ltd v Ball*[1], the provision of schools meals were contracted out to a contractor. According to the transferred employees' contract of employment, pay rises would be those agreed by the NJC. The contractor continued to recognise the union concerned but refused to apply an NJC-negotiated pay rise to the transferred employees. The EAT held that pay rises for transferred employees would be those agreed by the NJC as stated in the collective agreement and that there was no reason why the employer's conditions could not be regulated by a third party, ie the NJC.

1   EAT 637/96, unreported.

15.49   The case of *Whent v T Cartledge Ltd*[1] concerned employees of a local authority street lighting department. Their contracts of employment stated that their pay would be in accordance with the NJC agreement. The local authority contracted out its street lighting function to a private sector contractor who ceased to recognise the relevant union 10 days after the transfer and refused to pay its employees the pay increase agreed under the NJC collective bargaining process. The EAT held that the relevant part of the NJC agreement had been incorporated into the individual contracts of employment. The incorporated terms included not only the rate of pay in general terms which existed at the time of transfer, but also the terms providing for the collective bargaining mechanism itself. In the circumstances, the NJC and not the contractor would set the level of pay. The EAT went on to state that the fact that the contractor had ceased to recognise the union was irrelevant.

1   [1997] IRLR 153.

Transfer of union recognition

15.50   If the undertaking or part of undertaking which is transferring retains its distinct identity after the transfer then according to reg 9, union recognition is treated as automatically transferred. Therefore, certain rights which are afforded only to recognised trade unions, such as the right to disclosure of information for collective bargaining, the right to be consulted on certain matters and the right to have paid time off for union officials to carry out duties related to collective bargaining or for union training are treated as transferred. It may be possible for the contractor to derecognise the union but there are, of course, substantial industrial relations implications involved in doing so. Furthermore the contractor may be prevented from derecognising the union unless the provisions governing derecognition in the Trade Union and Labour Relations (Consolidation) Act 1992, are complied with.

Problematical terms and conditions

15.51   It may be difficult for contractors to replicate some of the benefits previously enjoyed by the transferring employees. For example, transferring employees may have had the right to participate in their employer's share option scheme before the transfer. On a strict interpretation of TUPE, this right to participate in the scheme transfers to the contractor. There is very little case law on this point. However, the EAT recently had to consider this matter in *Mitie Managed Services v French*[1]. In this case, the employees had transferred from Sainsburys to PBMS and then finally to Mitie. A term in their contracts made with Sainsburys entitled them to participate in the profit-sharing scheme which provided employees with Sainsburys' shares annually. Mitie could not operate this scheme as it did not have the power to award shares in a unrelated company and it did not have access to confidential figures on which the allocation was based. The employment tribunal found in favour of the employees, stating that TUPE applied so as to render the term contractually enforceable. The EAT, however, overturned the employment tribunal's decision on the basis that the term would be impossible to perform. The EAT stated that employees in these circumstances were entitled to participate in a scheme of substantial equivalence but which was free from unjust, absurd or impossible features. Although this decision makes practical sense, it does not follow the strict interpretation of TUPE. The decision is being appealed to the Court of Appeal and the case is due to be heard in December 2002.

1   [2002] IRLR 512.

PENSIONS AND TUPE

15.52   Rights and liabilities relating to provisions of occupational pension schemes which by their very nature relate to benefits for old age, invalidity or survivors do not transfer to the transferee. These rights are excluded by virtue of TUPE, reg 7. Notwithstanding the apparently clear wording of reg 7, the question of whether pension rights may transfer has been subject to a considerable amount of litigation over the past few years.

15.53   In *Adams v (1) Lancashire County Council (2) BET Catering Services Ltd*[1], the Court of Appeal confirmed that a transferee does not have to replicate or set up an occupational pension scheme for a transferring employee under TUPE. It should be noted that the exclusion is only in relation to an occupational pension scheme as defined by the Pensions Scheme Act 1993, s 1. An employer's contribution to, for example, an employee's personal pension plan should transfer to the transferee. It should also be noted that the exclusion under reg 7 only relates to old age, survivors and invalidity benefits. If the scheme deals with other matters, these may transfer.

1   [1996] IRLR 154, Ch D; affd [1997] IRLR 436, CA.

15.54   The ECJ has also recently delivered its long awaited judgment in *Beckmann v Dynamco Whicheloe Macfarlane Ltd*[1]. The case deals with the scope of the pension exclusion under the ARD, art 3(3) and TUPE, reg 7. The central question in the case was whether certain early retirement and lump sum payments which were payable by the transferor on an employee's early retirement due to redundancy fell within the scope of the pension exclusion. Referring to the general objective of the legislation to safeguard the rights of employees on a transfer, the ECJ ruled that the exception provided by art 3(3) must be interpreted strictly so as to apply only to the benefits listed exhaustively in the article (old age, invalidity or survivors benefits). These benefits must, in themselves, be construed in a narrow sense. The ECJ went on to state that only benefits which are paid when an employee reaches the 'end of his normal working life', as laid down by the general structure of the pension scheme in question, can be classified as old age benefits. Benefits paid in circumstances such as those in the present case (eg on early retirement) could not be regarded as old age benefits, even if they are calculated by reference to the rules for calculating normal pension benefits.

1   [2002] IRLR 578, ECJ.

15.55   The government's policy however goes beyond the requirements of TUPE. It states that former public sector employees transferring to the private sector should continue to have pension provision made for them. The government considers that there is a risk of claims of constructive dismissal where the transferor does not require the transferee to provide broadly comparable pension rights after the transfer.

15.56   There are two methods of dealing with the pension rights of employees transferring to an external employer. These are:
(i)   that the external employer will itself provide a pension scheme for transferring employees which is 'broadly comparable' with the pension scheme of which the transferring employers were members at the date of transfer (the 'broadly comparable' route); or
(ii)   in relation to local authority employees the local authority will support the external employers application to join the existing local authority pension scheme as a participating employer within the scheme with effect from the date of transfer (the 'admission' route).

15.57   Until January 2000 it was not possible for a contractor or sub-contractor in a PFI project involving a local authority to deal with the pension rights of transferring employees, other than by transferring them to a pension scheme which was broadly comparable with their existing local authority scheme. Whether or not a new scheme was 'broadly comparable' was decided by the government actuaries department. The broadly comparable approach used in local authority PFI transactions is not unlike the requirement to provide a 'mirror image' scheme in private sector transactions, eg where a large long-established industrial group hives off a small subsidiary, which seeks to maintain the benefits of the group pension scheme.

15.58   With effect from 13 January 2000 the Local Government Pension Scheme Regulations 1997[1], by which local authority pension schemes are governed, were amended to allow external employers to enter into an admission agreement with a local authority in relation to the outsourcing of that authority's functions. The effect of such an agreement is to allow the external employer to be admitted to the relevant local government pension scheme in respect of those (former local authority) employees who are concerned with delivery of the outsourced functions. Such admission agreements may be 'open' or 'closed', ie 'open' to the external employer's future employees concerned with delivery of the same service, or 'closed' to all but those employees nominated at the date of transfer. Employers admitted to a local authority pension scheme in this way will pay an employers contribution (for future service) assessed by the scheme actuary and employees will continue to make the same contribution as previously. However, the external employer will, in addition, be required to provide the local authority with an indemnity or bond to cover the pension risk of the early termination of the agreement between itself and the local. The amount of the bond is set by the local authority scheme actuary.

1   SI 1997/ 1612.

THE PROVISION OF INFORMATION AND CONSULTATION UNDER TUPE

The obligation to inform

15.59   Regulation 10 of TUPE imposes twin obligations to both inform and consult in respect of 'affected employees'. These are employees of the transferor or the transferee (whether or not employed in the undertaking or the part of the undertaking to be transferred) who may be affected by the transfer or may be affected by measures taken in connection with it.

15.60   The transferor must inform all the appropriate employee representatives of the following:
(i)   the fact that a relevant transfer is to take place;
(ii)   when it is to take place (approximately);
(iii) the reasons for it;
(iv)   the legal, economic and social implications of the transfer for the affected employees;
(v)   whether the transferor envisages taking any 'measures' in connection with the transfer which will affect the employees, and if so, what action is envisaged;
(vi)   the 'measures' which the transferee envisages he will take in relation to those employees who are to be automatically assigned to him on the transfer (the transferee must provide this information to the transferor).

15.61   There is no firm guidance on when the information under reg 10 has to be provided to the appropriate representatives. However, it should be provided 'long enough before the transfer' to enable the transferor to consult the representatives properly.

The duty to consult

15.62   Where it is envisaged that 'measures' will be taken in connection with the transfer there is a duty not only to inform but to consult in relation to the 'measures'. The term 'measures' was considered by Millett J in *Institution of Professional Civil Servants v The Secretary of State for Defence*[1], where he said it was:

> '... a word of the widest import, and includes any action, step or arrangement, while "envisages" simply means "visualises" or "foresees". Despite the width of these words it is clear that manpower reductions are not measures at all; though positive steps to achieve planned reduction in manpower levels otherwise than through natural wastage would be.'

1   [1987] IRLR 373.

15.63   The learned judge was also of the view that for the need to consult to arise the employer must have formulated some definite plan or proposal which it has in its mind to implement. 'Measures' would therefore include matters such as reorganisations, redundancies, changes in the way a particular job is to be performed, changes in employees duties, changes to policies etc. According to reg 10(5) consultation must be undertaken 'with a view to seeking [the trade union representatives'] agreement to measures to be taken'.

The special circumstances defence

15.64 Regulations 10(7) and 11(2)(a) provide a defence where there has been a failure to inform and/or consult in certain circumstances:

1   it is a defence (to a claim of failing to inform or to consult) for a transferor to say that the information was not provided by the transferee. However, notice must be given to the transferee of this and the transferee may then be liable;

2   it is a defence to say that it was not reasonably practicable to comply because of special circumstances and the transferor took all reasonably practicable steps to comply in the circumstances.

Who is a representative?

15.65 Appropriate representatives are:

(i)   trade union representatives where the affected employees are of a description for which the union is recognised for collective bargaining (TUPE, reg 10(2A)(a));

(ii)   employee representative who are:

(a)   employees appointed or elected otherwise than for that specific purpose of TUPE but, given the purpose and method of their appointment or election, they have authority from the employees to receive information and to be consulted (reg 10(2A)(b)); or

(b)   employees elected for the specific purpose of being given information or being consulted by the employer under TUPE, in an election satisfying the regulations (reg 10(2A)(b)).

15.66 Where there is a trade union, the employer must consult it. But where there is no union, the representatives are whichever of the employee representatives the employer chooses to deal with. In other words, even when a workforce has elected its own representatives in accordance with the regulations, the employer may still decline to inform and consult them, if there is another group of representatives in place for another purpose.

15.67 If there are no representatives in the above definitions the employer is not excused the duties to inform and consult. But the practical effect of the enforcement mechanism is that the employer is excused if it has (reg 10(8)) invited any of the affected employees to elect representatives; and issued the invitation long enough before the time it is required to give information to enable them to elect representatives; and given information and consulted as soon as is reasonably practicable after the election.

15.68 According to reg 10(8A) if no one comes forward to be a representative or the affected employees fail to elect representatives within a reasonable time after the employer has invited them to do so, the employer must give the relevant information to (but not necessarily consult) all the affected workforce.

What will failure to comply cost?

15.69 An appropriate representative may make a complaint (no later than three months after the date of the transfer) to an employment tribunal. If that complaint is upheld, the tribunal must make a declaration in those terms and the tribunal has a discretion to award compensation of up to 13 weeks' actual pay in respect of each affected employee. It should also be noted that, following the decision of the EAT in *Transport and General Workers Union v James McKinnon, JR (Haulage) Ltd*[1], where a transferor fails to comply with his duty to inform and consult employee representatives prior to transfer, liability for that failure does not pass to the transferee but remains with the transferor.

1   [2001] ICR 1281.

DISMISSAL

15.70   The effect of TUPE, reg 8(1) is that any dismissal, where the principal reason is connected with the TUPE transfer, is automatically an unfair dismissal. However, the automatic unfairness rule will not apply where the dismissal is shown to be for an economic, technical or organisational reason ('ETO reason') entailing changes in the workforce of either the transferor or the transferee. The key factors are therefore to determine when a dismissal will be treated as connected with a TUPE transfer and what will amount to an ETO reason.

Is the dismissal connected with the transfer?

15.71   Whether or not any particular dismissal is connected to the TUPE transfer is a question of fact. Although it will be for the employee to prove his dismissal was so connected, in practice this will be a reasonably easy burden for the employee to discharge where his dismissal is at least proximate in time to the TUPE transfer. The employer will normally produce evidence that, notwithstanding the proximity of the dismissal to the TUPE transfer, there is no connection between the two. This means showing, effectively, that the dismissal was going to take place anyway, for example because of performance, misconduct, or a decision to reduce the workforce which has nothing to do with the TUPE transfer.

15.72   The importance of the automatic unfairness rule is that a dismissal which falls within the rule and for which there is no ETO reason is automatically unfair. This means that the employer cannot argue about how reasonably it has acted in all the circumstances.

An ETO reason

15.73   Where a dismissal is potentially automatically unfair, the employer may be able to escape liability if it can show that the reason for dismissal was an economic, technical or organisational reason entailing changes of workforce of the transferor or the transferee. The ETO reason exception has two limbs, both of which must be satisfied in order for an employer to be able to rely on it:
1   the dismissal must be an economic, technical or organisational in nature. This means that it must be to do with the day-to-day running of the business. A dismissal which is effected in order for the sale to go through (for example,

because the purchaser says he will not buy the business unless the vendor gets rid of X number of employees, where such request has nothing to do with the running of the business) may not fall within the scope of an ETO reason[1];

2   the reason must also entail changes in the workforce. This means that it must be to do with the numbers, functions and levels of employees. Dismissal following an attempt to harmonise terms and conditions of employment will not satisfy this second limb because it has nothing to do with the numbers, functions and levels of employees[2]. This is particularly important to note, because quite often a purchaser wishes to assimilate the employees into his existing human resources policies and structures and thereby harmonise the terms and conditions of employment.

1   *Wheeler v Patel and J Golding Group of Companies* [1987] IRLR 211, EAT.
2   *Berriman v Delabole Slate Co Ltd* [1984] IRLR 394, EAT; affd [1985] IRLR 305, CA.

15.74   The upshot of the restrictive definition of an ETO reason is that genuine redundancies, reorganisations, relocations, changing of working arrangements, changing of working times, changing of job functions and duties are likely to fall within its scope. Dismissals caused by changes of the financial aspect of a contract of employment, for example salary, commission schemes and other emolument benefits, are very unlikely to fall within the scope of an ETO reason. It should be noted that even if a dismissal is for an ETO reason, the employer must still satisfy the tribunal that it has acted reasonably in all the circumstances.

POST-TRANSFER VARIATIONS TO TERMS AND CONDITIONS

15.75   Pre-transfer terms and conditions may not easily translate into terms applicable in transferee's business or the terms may simply not be acceptable to the transferee, for example because they cost too much. Most transferees will want to make some variations to terms and conditions. The extent to which this is possible has been the subject of considerable legal debate. According to recent case law a transferee may not be able to change the terms and conditions of employment of transferred employees if the reason for changing the terms is connected with the transfer.

15.76   In *Wilson v St Helens Borough Council* and *British Fuels Ltd v Baxendale*[1], Lord Slynn gave his opinion, obiter, on the question of post-termination variations to contracts of employment. He stated that:

'But I add that, although on a transfer, the employees' rights previously existing against the transferor are enforceable against the transferee and cannot be amended by the transfer itself, it does not follow there cannot be a variation of the terms of contract for reasons which are not due to the transfer either on or after the transfer of the undertaking.'

1   [1998] IRLR 706, HL.

15.77   In two cases decided before *Wilson* and *Meade*, but which are consistent with it, the Court of Appeal considered the impact of post-transfer contractual variations.

In *Credit Suisse First Boston (Europe) Ltd v Padiachy*[1] the High Court refused to enforce a non-competition covenant which had been agreed to by an employee post-transfer as part of an overall package of contractual changes, notwithstanding that the employees were said to be in a better overall position as a result of the changes. In *Credit Suisse First Boston (Europe) Ltd v Lister*[2] the court stated that a restrictive covenant entered into by an employee post-transfer was unenforceable because the variation was made by reason of the transfer.

1   [1998] IRLR 504.
2   [1998] IRLR 700.

PRACTICAL CONSIDERATIONS WHEN DRAFTING THE PROJECT AGREEMENT

Information relating to transferring employees

15.78   Where TUPE applies, the effect is that employees wholly or mainly engaged in the provision of the services which transfer to the contractor will transfer to the contractor. The contractor would also inherit all accrued rights and liabilities connected with the contract of employment of the transferred employee.

15.79   A contractor will therefore want to know exactly who will be transferring to it. This is usually dealt with by listing the names of transferring employees in a schedule to the agreement relating to the services/business to be transferred. The contractor will normally require a warranty that the only employees transferring to it are those listed in the schedule.

15.80   The contractor will have priced its bid on the basis of information provided by the client organisation and will therefore require the client organisation to indemnify it if more employees transfer to it by virtue of TUPE than those listed in the schedule. This poses a problem for client organisations where some of the transferring employees are not employed by it, for example where the employees of a current contractor transfer to the PFI contractor along with the client organisation's own employees. The client organisation may therefore be reluctant to confirm that any list of transferring employees provided by the existing contractor is accurate.

15.81   Contractors will also normally require the client organisation to warrant the accuracy of all details of transferring employees, for example, names, start dates, notice periods, salary and benefit details, details of all standard terms and conditions of employment. Again, in relation to the client organisation's own employees, this will not pose a problem. However, where some/all of the information relates to the employees of an existing contractor, the client organisation may be reluctant to warrant the information as being accurate as the client organisation may have no way of verifying the information

Indemnities

15.82   As discussed above[1], the effect of TUPE is that the contractor inherits all accrued rights and liabilities connected with the contract of employment of the transferring employees. Therefore, the contractor will want an indemnity from the client organisation in relation to pre-transfer liabilities.

1   See para **15.46**.

15.83   The client organisation will normally be required to indemnify the contractor for and against all claims, demands, awards, penalties, fines, damages, rights of action, interests, costs, expenses and all other liabilities, the material fact of which occurred prior to the completion date in respect of any of the transferring employees or any trade unions, staff associations or worker representatives of such transferring employees.

15.84   Similarly, the contractor will be required to fully indemnify the client organisation against all claims, rights of action compensation, awards, damages, fines, penalties, costs, expenses, interests and all other liabilities which affect the client organisation after the completion date in respect of any transferring employees or any trade union, staff association and worker representatives of such employees.

During the contract

15.85   Client organisations will also need to consider at the outset what controls they will want to have over the employees during the period of the contract. Client organisations will want to have in mind the possibility that they may inherit the employees back at the end of the contract. They may, therefore, wish to have some control over changes in the terms and conditions of the employees who work for the contractor.

15.86   Client organisations may wish to include a requirement that the contractor does not make any material changes to the employees' terms and conditions of employment, or increase the salaries over and above a reasonable level without the client organisation's prior consent. A requirement to notify the client organisation of the dismissal of any employee by the contractor (including a requirement that the contractor identify replacement employees and obtain the client organisation's consent to the replacement) is also an option. The client organisation may also want to place an obligation on the contractor to keep the client organisation informed of which employees are working on the contract.

Restrictions during notice period

15.87   Once client organisations have given notice of their intention to terminate the contract with the original contractor, they will clearly want some control over the way in which employees are dealt with. For example, they may want a prohibition against the contractor cherry-picking the good employees away from the contract and replacing them with less able employees. They will also want controls over any increases in salaries and any changes to terms and conditions as such changes will be binding on them when they get the employees back at the end of the contract.

15.88   Similarly, incoming contractors will want information on terms and conditions and may seek assurances that no material changes will be made prior to their succession to the contract. In view of this, an obligation should therefore be put on the contractor to provide information on numbers of employees and details of their terms and conditions of employment. Ideally, the contractor should be required to warrant that the information being provided is complete and accurate.

Termination of the contract

15.89   If the client organisation appoints another contractor, it will be asked to give the incoming contractor an indemnity in respect of employee liabilities. Similarly, if the client organisation takes the service back in-house the client organisation is likely to want similar protection from the outgoing contractor. The client organisation should therefore include either an indemnity by the contractor to the client organisation or an obligation for the contractor to give an indemnity to any incoming contractor in respect of employee liabilities relating to the period the employees were employed by the outgoing contractor.

15.90   It is also difficult to assess if TUPE will apply at the end of the contract, particularly in the case of long contracts. For example, if the legal test for deciding whether TUPE applies changes between now and the end of the contract, the contractor may find itself liable for redundancy costs if, at the end of the contract, the employees, in fact, do not transfer to the second contractor or go back in-house.

15.91   In this situation, contractors will be left without a contract, but with the employees who used to service the contract, and they may not be able to relocate them elsewhere. Contractors may therefore ask for an indemnity from the client organisation in respect of any redundancy costs which may accrue to them. Alternatively, the contractor could require the client organisation to either offer employment to the employees, or to obtain agreement that any incoming contractor does so. Although the employees may still be entitled to statutory redundancy payments, the offer of new employment will reduce any contractual claims by the employees, and may increase the likelihood of TUPE applying in any event.

REFORMS

15.92   On 1 October 2001 Stephen Byers, Secretary of State for Transport, Local Government and the Regions announced a review of the best value regime for local authorities. The key terms of reference for the review were to identify practical ways in which best value can deliver high quality services efficiently and effectively whilst ensuring fair treatment for employees charged with delivering the services. The review was undertaken by a group chaired by the minister for Local Government and the Regions, Nick Raynsford, and included representatives of trade unions, private and voluntary sector service providers, local authorities and the Audit Commission.

15.93   On 26 March 2002 Stephen Byers released the text of a letter which he sent to Nick Raynsford in which he set out a package which the government believes will achieve the twin aims of high quality services and fair treatment of employees. The details of the package are:

(i)   the government will give statutory force, within local government, to the provisions of the Cabinet Office statement of practice on staff transfers in the public sector and the annex to it entitled 'A Fair Deal for Staff Pensions';

(ii)   the Department will draw up a Code of Practice on the treatment of *new recruits* working on local authority contracts alongside transferred staff. The code will oblige contractors to offer employment to new staff on fair and reasonable terms and conditions which are, overall, broadly comparable to those of transferred employees;

(iii)   the above Code of Practice will include a requirement on contractors to offer *new recruits* working on local authority contracts alongside transferred staff, one of the following pension arrangements: membership of the local government pension scheme, membership of a good quality employer pension scheme (this will require employers to match employee contributions up to a maximum of 6 per cent for the employer's own defined contribution scheme, or membership of a contracted out, final salary-based defined benefit pension scheme) or employer contribution to stakeholder pensions matching those of the employee up to a maximum of 6 per cent.

15.94   The code will also include a requirement to consult recognised trade unions on the terms and conditions, including pensions, of new recruits to these contracts. The code will be incorporated into contracts between local authorities and contractors; and its application will be included as part of the best value inspection and enforcement regime. The current best value guidance will be revised in order to ensure that staff and recognised trade unions have a role in the contracting out process carried out by local authorities. The government has confirmed that nothing in the package will apply retrospectively to any existing local authority contracts or to the terms and conditions of staff currently employed under them.

15.95   On 10 September 2001 the Department of Trade and Industry published a long-awaited consultation document outlining its proposals for reform of TUPE. The proposals relate to occupational pensions, requirement on transferors to notify transferees of all rights and obligations in relation employees who will be transferred, dismissal, changes to terms and conditions of employment and trade union recognition. Responses were sought by the Department of Trade and Industry by 15 December 2001. However, as yet the Department of Trade and Industry has not indicated how it intends to amend TUPE.

CHAPTER 16

'Non-commercial considerations' and workforce matters

Lianne Smith

16.01 When procuring a contract, a local authority may wish to include certain policy considerations, such as workforce, environmental or social matters either in the scope of the goods, works or services which are being procured, the selection of the contractor, the award of the contract or in the execution of the contract. Local authorities can only take into account policy considerations to the extent that these are permitted by both domestic and European law, the key provisions of which are set out below.

NON COMMERCIAL CONSIDERATIONS AND DOMESTIC LEGISLATION

16.02 In the era of compulsory competitive tendering the Local Government Act 1988, s 17 set out a number of policy matters which it designated as non-commercial and as such local authorities were prohibited from taking into account when they exercise their contracting functions, eg the inclusion of contractors in the local authority's select list or the award of a contract, as follows:

(a) the terms and conditions of employment by contractors of their workers, or the composition of, the arrangements for the promotion, transfer or training of or the other opportunities afforded to, their work forces;

(b) whether the terms on which contractors contract with their sub-contractors constitute, in the case of contracts with individuals, contracts for the provision by them as self-employed persons of their services only;

(c) any involvement of the business activities or interests of contractors within irrelevant fields of government policy;

(d) the conduct of contractors or workers in industrial disputes between them or any involvement of the business activities of contractors in industrial disputes between other persons;

(e) the country or territory of origin of supplies to or the location in any country or territory of the business activities or interests of, contractors;

(f) any political, industrial or sectarian affiliations or interests of contractors or their directors, partners, or employees;

(g) financial support or lack of financial support by contractors for any institution to or from which the authority gives or withholds support;

(h) use or non-use by contractors of technical or professional services provided by the authority under the Building Act 1984 or the Building (Scotland) Act 1959.

16.03   Section 17(6) makes it clear that the matters referred to above include matters which occurred in the past as well as matters which subsist when the contract function in question falls to be exercised. In addition, the non-commercial matters set out above cannot be considered in respect of suppliers, sub-contractors and associated bodies of the contractor.

16.04   The prohibition of non-commercial considerations, except to the extent excluded in relation to best value contracts or where the TUPE regulations apply, as set out in para **16.06**, means that local authorities cannot, for example, consider the contractor's record in relation to disputes with trade unions or any financial support given by contractors to institutions.

16.05   However, in response to lobbying by the trades unions and the Confederation of British Industry, the restrictions on the inclusion of non-commercial considerations were relaxed by the Labour government in accordance with the Local Government Act 1999, s 19 which confers power on the Secretary of State to make an order providing that certain matters will cease to be 'non-commercial' under the Local Government Act 1988, s 17.

16.06   The Local Government Best Value (Exclusion of Non-Commercial Considerations) Order 2001[1] came into force on 13 March 2001. This confirms the Secretary of State exercising the power under the Local Government Act 1999, s 19 to exclude the following non-commercial considerations in relation to best value authorities (which includes all local authorities) in England and Wales and to police and fire authorities in Wales:
— the terms and conditions of employment by contractors of their workers or the compositions of, the arrangements for promotion, transfer or training of or the opportunities offered to, their workforce[2]; and
— the conduct of contractors or workers in industrial disputes between them or any involvement of the business activities of contractors in industrial disputes between other persons[3].

1   SI 2001/909.
2   LGA 1988, s 17(5)(a).
3   LGA 1988, s 17(5)(d).

16.07   As a result, under the order, the above matters cease to be non-commercial considerations only in relation to best value requirements under the Local Government Act 1999, Pt I or where there is a transfer of staff to which the Transfer of Undertakings (Protection of Employment) Regulations 1981 may apply[1].

1   For more detail on TUPE, see chapter 15.

16.08   The effect of the order means that local authorities are now able to consider issues such as staff training, rates of pay and other terms and conditions on which a contractor employs its workforce and are able to look at a contractor's track record in relation to industrial disputes provided that the contract is a best value contract or where TUPE may apply. The Department of the Environment Transport and the Regions (now ODPM) issued guidance by way of a circular, 'Local Government Act 1999: Section 19: Best Value and Procurement: Handling of Workforce Matters in Contracting'[1].

1   April 2001.

16.09   The guidance sets out how workforce issues should be taken into account in local government tendering. Local authorities must have regard to the guidance[1], which explains how, in the view of the Secretary of State, workforce issues should be taken into account in contracting under best value and in circumstances where TUPE applies. It is important to note the provisos in the guidance which state that workforce matters can only be taken into consideration where they are 'directly relevant to the delivery of the service in question' and 'affect directly the cost and quality of the services'.

1   Local Government Act 1999, s 19(4).

16.10   The guidance confirms that authorities will still need to comply with the requirements of the EC Treaty regarding openness, transparency and non-discrimination and the requirements of the European public procurement legislation where applicable.

16.11   The guidance notes that workforce matters will come into consideration at the pre-qualification, service specification, invitation to tender and tender evaluation stages of the procurement process and provides examples of where workforce matters could be considered. These include, for example, the consideration of training policies at the tender evaluation stage where they are relevant to the delivery of the contract, such as where it will be necessary for staff employed to keep abreast of any technical or other developments during its term. In addition, authorities should, during the pre-qualification stage, seek information as to the general competence, track record, details of criminal offences and acts of grave misconduct (as set out in the European public procurement rules) in relation to legislation on gender, race and disability. Contractors can then be excluded from the procurement process where they have been convicted of a criminal offence or have committed an act of grave misconduct.

16.12   When drawing up the service specification, the guidance reminds authorities that sometimes service contracts which involve regular contact between providers and users of a service or the wider community, may require providers to have specific attributes with regard to fair treatment and equality of opportunities. Where the service requires particular qualities in the staff, contracting authorities should address these matters in the output specification, ie how the bidder would meet the needs of a particular community group. In terms of health and safety, the local authority cannot delegate its duty under the Health and Safety at Work etc Act 1974, which requires authorities to take reasonable steps to satisfy themselves that contractors have the ability and resources for managing health and safety in relation to the work being carried out. In assisting with such arrangements, the guidance confirms that authorities may request details of a contractor's health and safety policy in respect of the work concerned but that additional, non-statutory requirements should not be placed on external providers where they are not placed on in-house providers supplying the same or comparable service.

16.13   The Local Government Act 1988, s 18 still allows a limited exemption relating to race relations in order to enable local authorities to comply with the general duty placed on them under the Race Relations Act 1976, s 71(1)[1] and any duty imposed by an order under s 71(2)[2], to make appropriate arrangements with a view to securing that their various functions are carried out with due regard to the need:
(a)   to eliminate unlawful racial discrimination; and

(b)   to promote equality of opportunity and good relations between persons of different racial groups.

1   As amended by the Race Relations (Amendment) Act 2000.
2   Race Relations Act 1976 (Statutory Duties) Order 2001, SI 2001/3458.

16.14   Section 18(2) provides that a local authority should not be excluded from:
—   asking approved questions seeking information or undertakings relating to workforce matters and considering the responses to them; or
—   including in a draft contract or draft tender for contract terms or provisions relating to workforce matters and considering the responses to them,

if this is necessary to secure compliance with the s 71(1) duty or any duty imposed by an order under s 71(2).

16.15   Therefore, local authorities are permitted to ask six approved written questions (which have been specified by the Secretary of State) and include terms in a draft contract which relate to workforce matters if it is necessary to secure compliance with s 71.

16.16   While local authorities cannot divest themselves of their ultimate legal responsibility to comply with the s 71 duty, they can in practical terms pass down their obligations. The exemption contained within the Local Government Act 1988, s 18(2) together with the provisions of the Local Government Best Value (Exclusion of Non-Commercial Considerations) Order 2001, mean that it would be entirely legitimate for local authorities to request tenderers to submit proposals for meeting s 71 in their bids, provided that these relate specifically to service user's requirements. Some examples of areas where this may be possible include community care services, economic development services, dealing with public enquiries, schools and welfare and staff catering. Authorities could also ask referees to comment on a contractor's record on addressing racial equality issues in its service delivery. Local authorities could require tenderers to submit method statements outlining how they propose to comply with the requirements of the Race Relations Act 1976 (Statutory Duties) Order 2001[1], for example how the contractor proposes to implement arrangements set out in the authority's race equality scheme in its delivery of services. Method statements should cover operational matters, and issues such as supply and access to information. Method statements can be evaluated and incorporated as obligations within the final contract.

1   SI 2001/3458.

16.17   It is important to note that the legislation does not prevent a local authority making stipulations about equal opportunities in relation to service delivery. On the contrary, the requirement for a local authority to provide services to residents on an equal basis is not negated by procuring a service from a private sector employer. It is proper that a contractor is required to comply with a local authority's equal opportunity and diversity policies in delivering the service and in dealing with members of the public, authority staff and other contractors. For example, it is perfectly lawful for local authorities to stipulate that a contractor must provide a service to certain disadvantaged target groups within the local authority's area or that a contractor's staff must treat all customers equally.

16.18   Where a local authority is permitted to consider a 'non-commercial' matter it must ensure that this does not conflict with its duty under the EC Treaty of the need to ensure transparency, openness and non-discrimination and any further requirements under the European public procurement regime which may apply to a contract.

EUROPEAN CASE LAW

16.19   There have been several cases that have challenged a contracting authority's ability to consider social and environmental issues by way of criteria applied either at the assessment stage or the contract award stage. In *Gebroders Beentjes BV v Netherlands*[1] the ECJ held that the ability of a potential contractor to employ the long-term unemployed was not a relevant criteria to apply when assessing contractors. In *Beentjes* it was held, however, that a condition relating to the employment to the long-term unemployed is compatible with the Works Directive, provided that the contracting authority alerted potential contractors to this point in either the contract notice or contract and that there was no direct or indirect discriminatory effect on tenderers from other member states.

1   Case 31/87 [1988] ECR 4635, ECJ.

16.20   It had been thought by many that in *Beentjes* the court was confirming the ability of a contracting authority to include a condition relating to the employment to the long-term unemployed in the execution of the contract. The court's judgment in *Beentjes* does not appear to address explicitly whether it is legitimate to include social issues amongst permitted tender award evaluation criteria. However, in the European Commission's interpretative communications on incorporating social and environmental considerations into public procurement[1], the *Beentjes* decision is referred to in the 'Award of the Contract' sections under the heading 'Additional Criteria' which was explicitly referred to in the *Nord-Pas-de-Calais* case below.

1   Paras **16.24–16.70**.

16.21   In *EC Commission v French Republic – Nord-pas-de-Calais School*[1] the contract award criteria referred to a condition relating to employment linked to a local project to combat unemployment. The ECJ rejected the European Commission's complaint that this was not legitimate criteria and held that authorities could consider employment matters provided the criteria is listed in a contract document, that the criteria is non-discriminatory and related to the nature of the contract. The ECJ found that this was 'additional criteria' which could be applied where the authority could not decide between two equal bids having been evaluated in respect of the most economically advantageous option.

1   Case C-225/98 [2000] ECR I-7445, ECJ.

16.22   The ECJ has recently held in *Stagecoach Finland Oy AB v City of Helsinki & HKL Bussiliikenne*[1] that where a contract is awarded on the basis of most economically advantageous tender, it is not necessary for each award criterion used by a contracting authority to be of a purely economic nature. In addition, it is acknowledged by the court that factors which are not purely economic may influence the value of a tender from the point of view of a contracting authority. The contract involved the provision of urban bus services and the contracting authority decided to award the contract to the tenderer who submitted the most economically advantageous tender, where the award criteria took into account the level of nitrogen oxide omissions and noise levels of the bus fleet. The ECJ held that environmental criteria could be considered, provided that they are linked to the subject matter of the contract, do not confer an unrestricted freedom of choice on the authority, are expressly mentioned in the contract documents or OJEC notice and comply with all the fundamental aspects of Community law, in particular the principle of non-discrimination.

1   Case C-513/99.

16.23   In practice, provided that local authorities can comply with the conditions set out in the case decisions above, there are opportunities to incorporate non-commercial matters into the award stage and conditions relating to the execution of a contract. However, authorities are reminded that where contracts fall within the ambit of the public procurement rules, they are extremely limited in what can be taken into account at the assessment, ie selection stage.

EUROPEAN COMMISSION INTERPRETIVE COMMUNICATIONS

16.24   The EC have issued two interpretive communications on the possibilities of incorporating environmental and social considerations into the public procurement process. Both documents provide useful guidance to authorities and provide practical examples[1].

1   'Interpretive communication on the Community Law applicable to public procurement and the possibilities for integrating social considerations into public procurement' (October 2001) and 'a Commission interpretive communication on the Community Law applicable to public procurement and the possibilities for integrating environmental considerations into public procurement' (July 2001).

Interpretation on environmental considerations

16.25   The purpose of the communication is to explain the possibilities for taking into account environmental considerations in public purchases under the existing procurement regime. It is worth noting that the Commission intends to produce a practical handbook on green public procurement, aimed principally at local authorities, which will contain best practice throughout the EU and practical guidance on the incorporation of environmental issues into day to day purchasing. In addition, the proposals for the reform of the public procurement Directives explicitly list environmental characteristics amongst the criteria which may be used to identify the most economically advantageous tender.

Scope of the contract

16.26   The communication acknowledges that at the stage where a contracting authority decides what it is that it wishes to construct or purchase there is a wide opportunity to take into account environmental considerations. It provides useful examples of the possibilities for different contracts.

Works contracts

16.27 Local authorities should be aware that in respect of works contracts opportunities exist at the design stage for incorporating environmental considerations, for example specifying low energy consuming buildings and the requirement to keep the necessity of lifts to a limited extent. Also in respect of the overall execution of the works, requirements can be put in place, for example, in relation to energy and water use or waste management on and around the construction site.

Service contracts

16.28 In the performance of contracts methods can be prescribed, for example, with regard to a contract for building cleaning, requiring environmentally friendly cleaning products to be used. Another example given is waste contracts where the method of collecting household waste can be prescribed. This can give a local authority the opportunity to incorporate recycling requirements into the scope of the contract.

Supply contracts

16.29 The communication acknowledges that the possibilities to incorporate environmental considerations is not as extensive as with works or services contracts, the main opportunity being the choice of the subject matter of the contract.

16.30 Provided that a local authority complies with both domestic and EC law (including EC Treaty principles in respect of free movement of goods and services) it has the freedom to define the subject matter of the contract in the way that it considers the most environmentally sound, even through the use of variant bids.

Contracts covered by the public procurement directives

Technical specifications

16.31 As referred to elsewhere in this publication, under the public procurement regime there is an obligation to refer to standards within a hierarchy where preference is given to European standards and in the absence of these national or other compliant standards. Where European standards are not used the term 'or equivalent' must be inserted. The communication makes it clear that the obligation to refer to standards (including European standards) does not imply that contracting authorities are bound to purchase only goods and services in conformity with these. The obligation is only to to refer to these instruments as a benchmark, leaving the possibility for suppliers to offer equivalent solutions. As very few European and national standards exist for dealing with the environmental performance of products and services, until environmental performance attributes can be integrated into standards, contracting authorities can define the required level of performance provided this does not lead to discrimination.

16.32 The communication provides examples of possibilities of incorporating environmental considerations into technical specifications by prescribing the primary materials to be used eg recycled materials and in the absence of mandatory references, by referring to eco-labels which certify that products are deemed to be more environmentally friendly than similar products. The communication confirms that variants may be used, for example, to provide for a higher environmental performance.

16.33 When drawing up technical specifications, local authorities could review their Local Agenda 21 policies and ensure that any requirements under such policies which are compatible with the European procurement rules are included in the specification.

Selection of the candidates

16.34 The communication sets out the means by which potential contactors may be selected to tender for a contract, ie an assessment of financial and economic standing, technical capacity and exclusions from participation.

16.35 Examples are given of grounds for exclusion of candidates which includes cases where legislation qualifies non-compliance with environmental legislation as an offence concerning professional misconduct. In addition, the Commission has proposed a Community Directive defining a minimum set of criminal offences to the detriment of the environment.

16.36 In respect of technical capacity, the communication reminds contracting authorities that the objective of the selection process is to identify those candidates who are considered by the contracting authority to be capable of executing the contract in the best way. The different requirements must therefore have a direct link to the subject matter or the execution of the contract in question.

16.37 The communication provides examples of including environmental considerations into the assessment of technical capacity. These include the possibility of requiring potential contractors to have specific environmental experience, if the contract justifies such requirement eg the construction of a waste treatment plant and the possibility of requiring contractors to operate an environmental management scheme, such as the eco-management and audit scheme (EMAS) where the system would have an impact on the quality of the supply or the capacity of the company to execute a contract with environmental requirements.

Award of the contract

16.38 Contracting authorities are reminded that where tenders are evaluated according to the most economically advantageous tender, the criteria applied must concern the nature of the works or services and linked to the subject matter of the contract, as confirmed in the *Beentjes* case. While environmental considerations are not currently listed in the current public procurement legislation, contracting authorities could take into account the 'environmental soundness' of products or services by translating the environmental objective into a specific product related and economically measurable criteria, eg by requiring a rate of energy consumption.

16.39 The communication refers to the case of *Beentjes* and *Nord -Pas-de-Calais* (see paras **16.19–16.21**) and states that 'additional criteria' could be equally applicable to environmental protection or performance.

16.40   The communication was issued prior to the *Stagecoach* decision referred to at para **16.22** and therefore does not consider the implications of that decision. In *Stagecoach* it was held that environmental criteria could be considered, provided they are limited to the subject matter of the contract, are expressly mentioned in the contract documents or OJEC notice and comply with all aspects of EC law, including non-discrimination.

Execution of the contract

16.41   The communication gives a number of examples of contract clauses which have a bearing on the performance or execution of the contract and which meet environmental objectives:
— delivery/packaging of goods in bulk rather than by single unit;
— re-use of packaging materials by the supplier;
— delivery of goods in reusable containers;
— collection, take back, recycling or re-use of waste produced during or after use or consumption of a product by a supplier;
— transport and delivery of chemicals (for example, cleaning products) in concentrate and dilution at the place of use.

16.42   In order to comply with the principles of transparency and non-discrimination the contract provisions should be notified in advance to all applicants and all applicants should be in a position to execute the clauses.

16.43   Local authorities could therefore consider building up a precedent base of standard contractual conditions to ensure that an authority's environmental policies are incorporated within contracts. Authorities must be careful to ensure that only those elements of policy which are compliant with the European procurement rules are adopted.

Contracts not covered by the procurement directives

16.44   Contracts not covered by the procurement directives do not have to comply with the detailed rules set out in the earlier parts of the communication. As a consequence authorities can choose a broad range of requirements and conditions, selection and award criteria as long as they are permitted by national legislation and the Treaty rules and EC law principles are observed.

Interpretation on social considerations

16.45   The aim of the communication is to clarify the range of possibilities under the existing EC legal framework for integrating social considerations into public procurement. The communication notes that domestic legislation in so far as it is compatible with community law is binding on contracting authorities, ie legislation relating to worker's rights and on working conditions.

16.46   The communication gives guidance on the integration of social considerations at each stage of the procurement process in relation to contracts which are within the ambit of the European procurement directives and also those which are not.

16.47   It is confirmed that in the proposals for modification of the public procurement directives, specific mention is made of the possibility to use contractual conditions regarding execution of a contract that have as their goal the promotion or employment of disadvantaged or excluded persons, or the combating of unemployment.

Contracts covered by the public procurement directive

Definition of the subject-matter of the contract

16.48   As with the communication in respect of integrating environmental considerations into public procurement, the Commission states that contracting authorities have a great deal of scope for taking social considerations into account and choosing a product or service that corresponds to their social objectives when defining the subject matter of the contract, although the possibilities will vary depending on the type of contract let.

16.49   A contracting authority can, for example, choose to buy goods or services which meet the specific needs of a given category of person, such as the socially disadvantaged or excluded. The Commission reminds authorities that service contracts which have a social objective relate in most cases to services within the meaning of Annex 1B of Directive 92/50/EEC or Annex XVIB of Directive 93/38/EEC and are therefore not subject to the detailed procedures of the Directive.

16.50   The communication states that generally, contracting authorities are free to choose to buy goods, services or works which correspond to its concerns as regards social policy, including through the use of variants, provided that the choice does not result in restricted access to the contract in question which would breach the EC Treaty principle of non-discrimination.

Technical specifications

16.51   The provisions of the public procurement directives on technical specifications apply without prejudice to legally binding national technical rules that are compatible with EC law. These national rules include requirements for people with disabilities to have access to certain buildings, as is the case in England and Wales under the requirements of the Disability Discrimination Act 1995. In addition, specifications may integrate social considerations and which therefore characterise their product or service and therefore relate to the subject matter of the contract eg purchase of computer equipment or services adapted to the needs of the visually impaired.

16.52   As with the environmental communication, the Commission confirms that contracting authorities may take account of variant bids which may allow authorities to choose the option which best meets their needs in financial and social terms, while fulfilling the minimum conditions set out in the contract documents. An example is given of variants which concern different technical solutions intended to ensure access for disabled persons to equipment or services. Local authorities may want to incorporate precise specifications which enable persons of different physical and mental capabilities to access technical equipment.

Selection of candidates or tenderers

16.53   The Commission reminds authorities that the directives set out grounds for exclusion of candidates and those criteria on which candidates may be assessed relating to economic, financial or technical capacity. Only the selection criteria set out in the Directives can be applied, and must be confined to the subject matter of a contract. The Commission refers to the *Beentjes* case[1] and notes that contracting authorities can include a condition relating to the employment of long term unemployed when setting conditions relating to the execution of a contract. Under the directives, the information required as evidence of a contractor's financial and economic standing and technical capacity must be confined to the subject matter of a contract.

1   See paras **16.19–16.20**.

16.54   The Commission confirms that the public procurement directives permit the exclusion of a candidate who has not fulfilled obligations relating to the payment of social security contributions in accordance with the legal provisions of the country in which the candidate is established or those of the country of the contracting authority. In addition, the directives permit the exclusion of the tenderer who has been convicted of an offence concerning the candidate's professional conduct or who has been guilty of gross professional misconduct, for example non-compliance with provisions on equality of treatment or on health and safety, providing non-compliance is deemed to constitute grave professional misconduct or an offence having a bearing on the candidate's professional conduct.

16.55   With regard to the assessment of candidates, the communication provides that if a contract requires specific know how in the 'social' field, specific experience may be used as a criteria as regards technical capability and knowledge in proving the suitability of candidates eg specific experience of management of a crèche, or of training services for the long term unemployed.

Award of the contract

16.56   As with the communication on environmental considerations, where contracts are awarded on the basis of most economically advantageous tender, criteria must be stated in the contract documents and must be linked to the subject matter of the contract or the manner in which it is carried out.

16.57   Social criteria are not included among the examples given in the directives. If criteria are used which make it possible to evaluate, for example, the quality of the service intended for a given category of disadvantaged persons, such a criterion may legitimately be used if it assists in the choice of the most economically advantageous tender. An example is given of a contract to provide computer services to all employees of a local authority (services under Annex 1A). A criteria relating to the methods proposed by the tenderer to ensure, at all times and in a satisfactory fashion, a quality service which meets the needs of any person with disabilities, may, in principle, be one of the criteria to be taken into account in determining the most economically advantageous tender.

16.58   In effect if a contractor has failed to meet the local authority's technical specification to provide equipment accessible to persons of different capabilities, then the contractor has failed to provide an economically advantageous bid.

16.59   Criteria relating to whether tenderers employ a certain category of persons, or have set up a program for the promotion of equal opportunities, would be incompatible with the current public procurement directives as they will be considered criteria which are unrelated to the subject matter of a given contract or to the manner in which the contract is executed. Such criteria, which do not assist in the choice of the most economically advantageous tender, are not permitted under the public procurement directives.

16.60   The communication confirms that criteria involving social considerations may be used to determine the most economically advantageous tender where they provide an economic advantage for the contracting authority which is linked to the product or service which is the subject matter of the contract.

16.61   There is the question as to whether each individual criterion has to provide an economic advantage which directly benefits the contracting authority or if it is sufficient that each individual criterion has to be measurable in economic terms without requiring that it directly provides the economic advantage for the contracting authority.

16.62   The communication refers to the case of *Beentjes* and *Nord -Pas-de-Calais*[1] and referring to 'additional criteria' acknowledges that these might also be the case for other conditions in the social field. As with the communication in respect of environmental considerations, the communication was issued prior to the *Stagecoach* decision referred to at para **16.22** above and therefore does not consider the implications of the decision.

1   See paras **16.19–16.21**.

Execution of contract

16.63   The communication reminds authorities that one way to encourage the pursuit of social objectives is in the application of contractual clauses or of conditions for execution of contract, provided that they are implemented in compliance with EC law and in particular, do not discriminate directly or indirectly against tenderers from other member states. The clauses or conditions must be implemented in compliance with all of the procedural rules in the directives, in particular the rules on advertising tenders. Transparency must also be ensured by mentioning such conditions in the contract notice so they are known to all candidates or tenderers.

16.64   The communication lists examples of specific conditions which a contracting authority might impose on a successful tenderer and which allow social objectives to be taken into account:
—   the obligation to recruit unemployed persons, and in particular long-term unemployed persons, or to set up training programs for the unemployed or for young people during the performance of a contract;
—   the obligation to implement, during execution of the contract, measures that are designed to promote equality particularly between men and women or ethnic or racial diversity;

— the obligation to comply with the substance of the provisions of the ILO court conventions during the execution of the contract, in so far as these provisions have not already been implemented in national law;
— the obligation to recruit, for the execution of the contract, a number of disabled persons over and above what is laid down by the national legislation in the member state where the contract is executed or in the member state of the successful tenderer.

16.65 The communication acknowledges that it is more difficult to envisage contractual clauses relating to the manner in which supply contracts are executed, since the imposition of clauses requiring changes to the organisation, structure or policy of an undertaking established on the territory of another member state might be considered discriminatory or to constitute and unjustified restriction of trade.

16.66 Policies on employment opportunities for local persons, such as advertising jobs in the local authority's area, must therefore be specified in the contract notice and such policies must enable a contractor from any other member state to comply with the condition. In practice, this means that such local employment opportunities are proportional and linked to the actual service or works project; advertised in the OJEC notice or contract documents and exclude any attempt to require the contractor to provide employment in other areas of their business.

Public procurement contracts not covered by the Directives

16.67 The communication confirms that subject to domestic legislation, contracting authorities remain free to define and apply in their procurement procedures, selection and award of criteria of a social nature, provided that they comply with the general rules and principles of the EC Treaty.

16.68 Practices that reserve contracts to certain categories of persons, for example to disabled persons or to the unemployed, are permitted. Such practices must not, however, constitute direct or indirect discrimination as regards tenderers from other member states.

Social provisions applicable to public procurement

16.69 The Commission confirms that even if the public procurement directives do not contain a specific provision, all EC, international and national regulations, rules and provisions which are applicable in the social field shall apply during the performance of a public procurement contract following contract award.

16.70 Contracting authorities are reminded that they are already permitted or obliged to identify in contract documents obligations in respect of health and safety, the directive on the transfer of undertakings, the posting of workers and equality of treatment. Tenders can be excluded where tenderers have not taken into account these obligations where it is considered that an abnormally low bid was submitted as a consequence of non compliance with the tender requirements.

CONCLUSION

16.71   Where local authorities wish to include reference to social, environmental or other policy considerations in any stage of the procurement process, this is not impossible. However, careful consideration must be given to the provisions of the Local Government Act 1988, the EC Treaty principles (in particular that of non-discrimination) and, where applicable, the European public procurement rules, in particular ECJ case law.

CHAPTER 17

Procurement in the context of a community strategy

Kath Nicholson

INTRODUCTION

17.01   The context in which local government operates is a complex and ever changing one. The standard of service provision that local people require of their local authority has become higher and more demanding. At the same time, the services about which they are most concerned span the responsibilities of different public agencies. In Lewisham, for example, for the last five years, the top four concerns of the local population as expressed in residents' survey conducted by MORI have consistently been crime, education, health and transport. Yet none of these issues is the exclusive responsibility of the local authority, and in several instances (for example health and transport) the local authority could not be said to be the main provider in any sense of the word. Local authorities cannot provide solutions to such 'wicked issues' alone. They must act in concert with others if they are to improve the quality of life for local people in these areas.

17.02   At the same time, there has been a proliferation of service providers. The advent of bodies such as regional development agencies, the increasing independence of school governing bodies, the establishment of funding bodies such as the Learning and Skills Council, and the maturing market of private sector provision across a broad range of local government services are but a few examples of this diversification. Local government cannot act alone in the face of such fragmentation.

17.03   Yet local authorities are no strangers to partnerships. In many respects local authorities have long-established and well-developed partnership working. Examples such as development agreements, joint provision with the voluntary sector for social care, funding community initiatives and the contracting out of services to the private sector spring to mind as familiar instances of this approach.

17.04   However, throughout the 1990s, many authorities were of the view that the potential for partnership development was inhibited by the law and judicial interpretation, so that opportunities could not be maximised with confidence. The extent to which these concerns have been addressed or otherwise, whether by the power contained in the Local Government Act 2000, s 2 or otherwise, is more fully explored in chapter 10 but they are summarised here to show the restrictive backdrop against which local authorities were striving throughout recent years to enhance their collaborative working. The major concerns of many local government commentators throughout this period included the following matters.

The doctrine of ultra vires and the limitations of the Local Government Act 1972, s 111

17.05   Although apparently broad and facilitative, providing for local authorities to be able to do that which is calculated to facilitate, be conducive or incidental to their powers and duties, the section was restrictively interpreted by the courts and its application limited. Examples of limitations include:

(1)   s 111 could only be relied on in relation to an authority's own powers and duties. An authority seeking to use it must first identify the function to which the proposed exercise of s 111 power related. It could not be used in support of activities where there was no such function to which it could be related. Consequently the advice of the lawyer advising the local authority on the use of s 111 became 'First find your function';

(2)   s 111 could only be used if the action to be justified by it was calculated to facilitate, be conducive or incidental to a function. A local authority could not rely on it to justify an activity that was 'incidental to the incidental'[1];

(3)   the power is subject to the limits set out in other legislation, both primary and secondary. It could not be relied on to circumvent those limitations[2];

(4)   an impermissible delegation of the local authority's own powers could not be authorised by s 111[3].

1   *McCarthy & Stone (Developments) Ltd v Richmond upon Thames London Borough of Council* [1992] 2 AC 48.
2   *Allsop v North Tyneside Metropolitan Borough Council* (1992) 90 LGR 462.
3   *Credit Suisse v Allerdale Borough Council* [1997] QB 305.

Concerns about powers to participate in partnership vehicles

17.06   There are several methods by which a partnership might be given expression. Many take the form of straightforward contracting arrangements. Yet often, a local authority and a potential partner will seek to use an independent vehicle such as a company to give a partnership an existence. Prior to the introduction of the Local Government Act 2000, the local authority needed to identify the relevant power to participate in a company at all. While those specific powers existed in some cases— for example waste disposal companies and economic development companies—there was no such specific provision in other cases, for example for social care purposes. The ability to participate in companies depended very much on what the purpose of the company was.

Controls over local authority participation in companies

17.07   Part V of the Local Government and Housing Act 1989 and the Local Government (Companies) Order 1995[1] control regulated companies very tightly. Regulated companies are those which are effectively controlled by an authority, or which are influenced companies which are public-sector led. The most significant impact of these controls is that the capital transactions of the regulated company are deemed to be those of the authority for capital control purposes, and with the consequence that their borrowing counts against the limits of the participating authority.

1   SI 1995/849.

Uncertainty about the ability to trade

17.08   Often in partnership arrangements it would be beneficial for local authorities to be able to provide services to the partnership vehicle but that remains impossible unless there is specific statutory provision allowing the authority to do so. The authority would need to identify a power to charge for services rendered. The Local Authorities (Goods and Services) Act 1970 allows such trading activity with public bodies defined in the Act or by statutory instrument, but other than that, the authority would be in difficulty to find a power to justify trading in most circumstances. See also chapter 14 on trading and profit.

A lack of confidence

17.09   The cumulative impact of the issues summarised above was to reduce the confidence of both local authorities and potential partners in the ability to establish effective partnership relationships, particularly through independent vehicles. Financial backers worried about authorities' powers, for example to give guarantees, or even to participate in an arrangement at all, and were wary of participation if their investment looked at risk. Partners were justifiably concerned given the litigation that unpicked arrangements to their detriment. Safe harbour was provided to contractors by the provisions of the Local Government (Contracts) Act 1997, which provided for certification of contracts by authorities to the effect that they were within the powers of the contracting authority. However, whilst providing a much needed boost to the confidence of the independent contractor, the Act did little to provide more certainty about local authority vires, for the certificating officer in the local authority.

THE GOVERNMENT AGENDA

17.10   The commitment of the incoming government in 1997 to the continuation of partnership development for public services could never have been in doubt. Even before it came to power manifesto commitments were made to enhancing the potential for public/private partnership. However, its agenda for public sector reform was much broader. The government's intention was to introduce a whole range of measures aimed at democratic renewal. This included:
(i)   changes in the political governance of local authorities in an attempt to make local government decision making more transparent (as now seen in the Local Government Act 2000, Pt II);
(ii)   a requirement to improve the efficiency and quality of service provision, and a move towards a mixed economy of service provision (as finds expression in the duty of best value under the Local Government Act 1999);
(iii)   a requirement to actively involve and engage local people in decisions (for example the involvement of the community in local strategic partnerships as a vehicle for neighbourhood renewal and developing community strategy);
(iv)   a new power for local authorities to promote the economic, social and environmental well-being of their area (Local Government Act 2000, s 2).

THE COMMUNITY STRATEGY

17.11   Section 4 of the Local Government Act 2000 established a new statutory duty for every local authority to prepare a strategy (known as the community strategy) for promoting or improving the economic, social and environmental well-being of their area and contributing to the achievement of sustainable development in the United Kingdom[1]. In preparing or modifying the strategy, local authorities must consult and seek the participation of such persons as they consider appropriate and have regard to guidance issued by the Secretary of State (the National Assembly in Wales)[2].

1   Section 4(1).
2   Section 4(3).

17.12   In deciding whether, or how, to exercise the power to promote the economic, social and environmental well-being of the area, by virtue of the LGA 2000, s 2(3), local authorities must have regard to their strategy under s 4. This is a mandatory provision. Statutory guidance[1] on the use of the s 2 power declares that this duty is not meant to make a straightjacket out of the community strategy, so long as the authority has regard to its contents when considering whether to use the power. Perhaps more surprisingly however, the same guidance states that authorities who have yet to put a community strategy in place may still rely on the s 2 power notwithstanding the absence of the strategy. Some commentators find this guidance difficult to reconcile with the mandatory nature of s 2(3), as it is difficult to understand how an authority can have regard (as it is compelled to do) to a non-existent strategy. Whether the courts would endorse the approach taken by the guidance or take a stricter approach in relation to s 2(3) remains to be seen in the context of a potential challenge on this specific point.

1   *Power to Promote or Improve Economic, Social or Environmental Wellbeing—Guidance to Local Authorities* (DoETR, March 2001).

17.13   Guidance about the preparation of community strategies was issued by the Secretary of State on 8 December 2000, following consultation with local government associations and representatives[1]. The statutory guidance requires a community strategy to have four elements:
(i)   a long-term vision for the area, focusing on the outcomes to be achieved;
(ii)   an action plan with short-term priorities and actions to contribute to the longer term goals;
(iii) a shared commitment to implementing the action plan as well as proposals to do so;
(iv)   arrangements for monitoring, review and reporting back to local communities on progress.

1   Preparing Community Strategies—Government Guidance to Local Authorities (DETR).

17.14   The way in which these elements are put together is seen as dependent on local circumstances and likely to vary from area to area. However the guidance sets out the principles which must underpin all community strategies. They will need to:
(i)   engage and involve local communities;
(ii)   have active participation from authorities, from within their executive and outside;

(iii) be prepared and implemented through a broad local strategic partnership by which the local authority can work with other bodies; and

(iv) be based on a proper assessment of need and resources.

17.15 Emphasis is placed on the process of developing the community strategy. The government believes that it should be 'bottom up' and not imposed by the local authority from the 'top down'. There is an exhortation to promote effective partnership working and keep the community involved at all stages in the process. Because of this emphasis on community development and involvement the government is not prescriptive in the guidance on the timing of the introduction of the first community strategy. Instead, local authorities are urged to concentrate on building effective partnerships and embedding the community participation approach into their management style.

17.16 Neither is the guidance prescriptive about the level at which the strategy is drawn up, nor about the geographical area to be covered by it. Rather the emphasis is on effective collaboration to draw up a strategy that reflects national, regional and local priorities. For areas which have several tiers of government, authorities are urged to work together so that the functions of the different authorities—education, social services, air quality, leisure etc, are all addressed. So for example, a broad vision for the area is encouraged at county level with the strategies of the smaller authorities being 'nested' within it. Similarly, there must be a close tie-in between the other plans which partners are required to produce or observe. For example, work on the NHS plan in any area should not be delayed by the need to establish a community strategy. Instead, partners must strive to ensure that all individual plans fit the overarching framework of the community strategy. All authorities are encouraged not to duplicate work at the planning level and to avoid 'consultation fatigue'.

17.17 A long-term vision must be put in place taking account of regional and notional priorities. Participating stakeholders should ask 'What should the area look like in 10 to 15 years time?' The aim is to build a consensus around issues such as education, crime, transport and health. In doing this it will be important to draw together the views of the local community. The strategy should concentrate on outcomes (not inputs or efficiency measures) with specific targets. To do this there will need to be an analysis and evaluation of the performance of the local authority and partner organisations to identify whether there are any gaps.

17.18 On the basis of this evaluation, there will then need to be some broad priorities established by consensus. The Guidance suggests that it will be for local authorities to mediate different interests in drawing up the strategy and to resolve conflicts. It is the statutory duty of the authority to establish the community strategy, and so it is seen as the most appropriate partner to try to achieve this agreement.

17.19 The strategy must contain a key action plan to deliver approximately 12 key outcomes reflecting a mix of national and local priorities, including targets for areas or groups at risk of social exclusion. It must be drawn up with the support of the partners. The community planning process is intended to give a forum, the local strategic partnership, in which community and partners have the opportunity to agree action and to deliver. As the agencies responsible for delivery are among the partners involved in drawing up the strategy, the government expects them to have the community strategy at the heart of their planning and resource allocation decisions.

17.20   Once the community strategy is in place, then the key local priorities from it should find their way into the overall approach of local authorities and other partners. The priorities should appear for example in the Best Value Performance Plan and best value reviews should examine how existing services meet community priorities. There should be a smooth co-ordination and close fit of community and authority objectives and actions

17.21   So the intention is for a high level community strategy, with central aims and a broad outline of how these broad aims are expected to be achieved. Working below that, different coalitions of agencies are to work together on specific issues, for example health and social care and the local education authority on children's services, with streamlined consultation to avoid 'partnership fatigue'.

17.22   Performance against the community strategy outcome targets must be monitored, and the government says that data should be collected by a range of bodies and collated into a single accessible summary. The indicators which are considered appropriate, according to the statutory guidance, are some or all of the 29 indicators of social deprivation/quality of life devised by the Central/Local Information Taskforce on Social Deprivation for use in the Local Agenda 21 process. Also the Audit Commission quality of life indicators and cross cutting indicators[1] may be useful. However, whichever indicators are chosen, they must be relevant to the particular strategy and may need to be supplemented locally.

1   See foe example *Voluntary Quality of Life and Cross Cutting Indicators April 2001–March 2002 Indicators Hhandbook* (Audit Commission) and *Quality of Life: Using Quality of Life Indicators* (Audit Commission feedback paper, 26 September 2002).

17.23   The timescale for review of the strategy will depend on its timeframe. Interim reviews may be required if there are long periods between full-blown reviews. The important thing is to keep communities informed of progress, without duplication, using only the main indicators of progress.

17.24   It would be difficult to try to gainsay an initiative which seeks to engender greater community involvement and concerted collaborative action by agencies involved in improving the quality of life for local citizens. Yet the relatively small number of community strategies in place almost two years after the implementation of the Local Government Act 2000 is testimony to the difficulty encountered in setting them up.

17.25   It is clear from the guidance that the strategy must be based on an evaluation of needs and supply, and data about the performance of providers. Yet the co-ordination of this data, and the evaluation of it may be unfamiliar territory to some of those participating in the partnership. Local community representatives may find this requirement difficult to grapple with, particularly as it may well be available in different formats from different agencies, be based on performance indicators that are not user-friendly and they may be unused to handling such material. The participating agencies themselves have experienced different degrees of success in managing the performance regimes to which they are subject, so the issue is all the more significant for those who are uninitiated, and perhaps largely disinterested in them.

17.26 Further, it may be that with such a broad divergence of interests involved in developing the community strategy, strong leadership and new skills are needed to bring the first strategy into being. Local authorities are told by government guidance that they must mediate, and resolve conflict and are encouraged to provide strong leadership, which may run into conflict with the bottom up approach advocated by government. Yet with a plethora of divergent viewpoints, some authorities have found that the incipient community strategy has progressed through a very large number of drafts without yet being finalised. Encouragement to mediate and compromise does not necessarily translate easily into an agreed strategy. It demands great effort from all parties and new skills from local authority participants

LOCAL STRATEGIC PARTNERSHIPS

17.27 The local strategic partnership (LSP) is central to the development of the community strategy. Yet it plays a wider role than that. This section explores the purpose and role of the LSP in a little more depth.

17.28 The LSP is a single non-statutory, non-executive body which brings together agencies of the public sector, private sector, businesses, community and voluntary organisations, as well as local people. Its aim is to involve the community in strategic decisions and allow action to be decided on at a community level. It is also intended that different interests and service providers can work together and support each other through participation in the LSP.

17.29 To get an LSP started the local authority is most likely to play a central role. The community strategy, though developed in concert with others, remains the responsibility of the local authority. So the authority will have an interest in getting the LSP off the ground. Advice from central government[1] is that existing partnerships may be a springboard for the development of the LSP, and that once they are up and running the question of who leads it will be a matter for the LSP itself.

1   *Preparing Community Strategies—Government Guidance to Local Authorities* (DoETR, December 2000), para 26.

17.30 There is no prescription about membership of the LSP as this is expected to reflect local circumstances, but it is anticipated that a range of public sector bodies covering those service areas included in the strategy, as well as community and voluntary organisations, businesses and the private sector and local people will be included. Elected members from within and outside an authority's executive are expected to play a major part.

17.31 A key plank of the neighbourhood renewal strategy, the government sees the LSP as the forum for partnership to sustain regeneration economically, socially and physically in deprived areas and to improve public service delivery to meet locally expressed needs. Local people are intended to influence decisions in this forum and businesses, community and voluntary organisations should play a full part.

17.32 The key tasks of a local strategic partnership are:

(i)   to prepare a community strategy for the area, identify and deliver the most important things which need to be done, keep track of progress, and keep it up to date;

(ii)   to develop and deliver a local neighbourhood renewal strategy to secure more jobs, better education, improved health, reduced crime and better housing, narrowing the gap between deprived neighbourhoods and the rest, and contributing to the national targets to tackle deprivation;

(iii) to bring together local plans, partnerships and initiatives to provide a forum through which mainstream service providers (local authorities, the police, health services, central government agencies) and bodies outside the public sector may work effectively together to meet local needs and priorities;

(iv)   to work with local authorities that are developing a local public service agreement (PSA) to help devise and then meet sustainable targets[1].

1   *Local Strategic Partnerships—Government Guidance* (DoETR, March 2001), para 5.

THE NEIGHBOURHOOD RENEWAL FUND

17.33   In 2001, the Neighbourhood Renewal Fund was established. Access to the fund is available to the 88 most deprived authorities in the country and is designed to assist those authorities improve services and so to narrow the gap between the most deprived areas and the rest of the country. £900 million pounds is available to those 88 authorities over a three-year period. The fund can be spent in any way that tackles deprivation in the most deprived neighbourhoods, though in practice the government supports funding for mainstream services such as schools so long as it tackles deprivation. The grant can be used to support services provided by local authorities or other service providers.

17.34   Though not a condition of receipt of support from the fund in the first year that authorities consult emergent local strategic partnerships, they were encouraged to do so on the ground that it would make sense to avoid any change of focus in future years. In 2002/03 and thereafter it is a condition that the authority and the local strategic partnership agree a Local Neighbourhood Renewal Strategy to include plans for the spend of Neighbourhood Renewal Funds.

17.35   In 2001/02 each authority in receipt of support from Neighbourhood Renewal Fund was required to produce a statement of use by the end of October 2001. That statement outlined previous and planned use of NRF money for that year. It also had to set out how the expenditure would contribute to achievement of the following five key floor targets on crime, employment, housing, health and education.

17.36   For 2002, an accreditation process for local strategic partnerships was introduced. Each LSP in an NRF funded area must be assessed against six key criteria. Whilst it is acknowledged that LSPs start from different points and operate in different conditions, to be accredited they must demonstrate that they are:

(i)   **strategic**: that they are effective and capable of playing a strategic role;

(ii)   **inclusive**: that they actively involve all key players, including public, private, community and voluntary sectors;

(iii) **action-focused**: that they have common priorities and targets, and agreed actions and milestones leading to demonstrable improvements against measurable baselines;

(iv) **performance managed**: member organisations have aligned their performance management systems, aims and objectives, criteria and process to the aims and objectives of the LSP;

(v) **efficient**: that they reduce, not add to, the bureaucratic burden;

(vi) **committed to learning and development**: they build on best practice from successful partnerships by drawing on experiences of local and regional structures and national agencies.

17.37   In April 2002 it was announced that 87 of the 88 areas in receipt of NRF monies have been accredited for 2002/03. Failure to be accredited means that a proportion of the NRF allocation due to be paid this year will be withheld until accreditation has been achieved. LSPs will be accredited on an annual basis. However there is no certainty whether NRF will continue beyond 2004/05.

LOCAL PUBLIC SERVICE AGREEMENTS

17.38   A local public service agreement is an agreement between an individual local authority and the government, setting out the local authority's commitment to deliver service improvements and the government's commitment to reward the improvement achieved.

17.39   The scheme was developed out of the Local Government Association's proposals 'Local Challenge'[1] and the government own public service agreements with its individual departments. A pilot involving 20 local authorities was run in 2000/01. Then in the two years following that the government intends to roll out the scheme to all county councils, shire unitary authorities, metropolitan districts and London boroughs who wish to participate. A further 16 authorities entered into agreements in 2001.

1   *Futureswork—The Local Challenge* (Local Government Association, September 1999).

17.40   Local public service agreements are seen by the government as complementing other initiatives aimed at improving outcomes. Paragraph 7 of *Local Public Service Agreements—New Challenges*[1] states:

'The government sees Local PSAs as complementing other policies that seek to improve outcomes.

— Each authority has a Best Value Performance Plan which is the product of local consultation and the authority's response to national performance indicators and targets for important services.

— Each authority conducts Best Value Reviews to help it rethink its priorities and find the best way jt to secure continuous improvement in the quality of services at an affordable cost.

— These provide a foundation for the authority's choice of the aspects of performance on which the Local PSA should focus; and Best Value gives assurances that improvements highlighted in the Local PSA will not be won at the expense of improvement on services as a whole.

— Authorities will also be setting up Local Strategic Partnerships as part of their role as community leaders. These will concentrate on specific issues, cutting across the usual boundaries of responsibility and involve a number of organisations. There may be a focus on poor neighbourhoods as part of the government's national strategy on neighbourhood renewal. The need to collaborate to improve outcomes is reflected in national PSAs. Each authority decides how far it seeks the support of others to deliver the targets in its Local PSA. It has scope for sharing rewards with partners that have helped them secure the achievement of these targets.

— The Neighbourhood Renewal Fund focuses on tackling deprivation in the 88 most deprived areas. It requires the Local PSAs of these authorities to include targets that support this work.'

This paragraph neatly encapsulates the interplay between the authority's responsibilities and the role envisaged for the LSP in neighbourhood renewal initiatives.

1   Published in July 2001 and endorsed by the Secretary of State for Transport, Local Government and the Regions, the Chief Secretary to the Treasury and the Chairman of the Local Government Association.

Outline

17.41   The nub of the agreement between the government and local authority is the willingness of the authority to commit to about a dozen targets which are very specific and require performance beyond that which would otherwise have been expected in the absence of a local public service agreement. If the authority succeeds then the government will reward that success. There is an initial pump priming grant and scope for extra borrowing in the form of unsupported credit approvals, as well as possible relaxations in statutory and administrative requirements where an authority believes that such relaxation will help achieve the higher target set out in the PSA.

17.42   It is for the authority to choose the targets to be included in the local PSA in the light of local circumstance. However the 12 issues chosen must reflect both national and local priority. The authority must choose the majority from the specific issues incorporated in individual national PSA targets that relate to local government services. They may be supplemented by local issues reflecting local concerns.

17.43   The targets chosen by the authority in relation to each issue must be 'stretching', ie they must show a measurable and specific improvement in outcomes compared to that which would be expected if there were no PSA in place. In return the government offers authorities who succeed in achieving their stretching targets in full a sum equal to 2.5 per cent of a year's net budget. A reduced grant will be given for achievement of a large part of the improvement. The use to which the reward grant is to be put is a matter for the authority to decide. In addition, the guidance suggests that there is flexibility on removing red tape obstacles on the part of government to help local government secure better outcomes.

17.44   The 'agreement' that is a local PSA is not, in effect, a legally binding agreement between central and local government. It is expressly stated that it is not to be a legal agreement and there is no intention that either party should be entitled to be able to enforce the agreement through the courts. Nonetheless it is clearly an expression of intent on the part of the parties to negotiate a position which should increase service performance levels and secure financial rewards for the successful authority.

17.45   *Local Public Service Agreements—New Challenges* sets out the elements that must be present if negotiations are likely to result in agreement:
(i)   there must be high level commitment. There must be high level involvement from leading members and the Chief Executive and senior staff in the authority concerned. The government recognises the need to respond creatively and at a high level. It has established a cabinet sub-committee dealing solely with PSAs consisting of ministers from all the departments concerned;
(ii)   a clear strategic vision is necessary. The PSA is most likely to be successful if it is part of a concerted plan to meet the priorities identified by the local community dovetailing with the authority's plans to secure continuous improvement in accordance with its best value duty;
(iii) local PSAs must concentrate on what people can recognise as results, ie not just process or input, but clear outputs;
(iv)   negotiations must jointly seek solutions;
(v)   the authority must work in partnership with others and the local PSA must say how the authority will do so to improve performance.

Process

17.46   The process for negotiating a local PSA has a number of stages. First there must be agreement on the timing of the negotiations. This becomes all the more important as the programme is rolled out and there are increasing numbers of authorities seeking to negotiate with a few central government officials. The LGA will broker discussions with DTLR on issues of interest to a number of authorities to streamline individual negotiations. There then follows an introductory meeting, before negotiations begin. This involves at least the chief executive and possibly several leading members as well as the senior official leading negotiations for the government the Regional Director and members of the central team working on PSAs. Once these contacts have been established it is for the authority to submit a draft agreement by way of proposal with supporting arguments. Direct negotiation ensues for approximately six weeks and then the matter is submitted to ministers for agreement.

17.47   The local authority's proposals for a PSA must consist of the authority's proposals for the agreement it would like to conclude (which is likely to change in the course of negotiation) and a separate paper setting out the arguments to support what is being sought in the draft, and the strategic context for the proposal. A DTLR pro forma agreement is available on its website.

17.48   From the beginning the draft agreement must be sufficiently precise about the performance levels with and without the PSA and about how performance would be measured. It must also be specific about the obstacles that it wishes the government to remove to facilitate the service improvement

17.49   The PSA must cover a peiod ending with the end of a financial year and usually be for a period of around three years.

Targets

17.50   The targets for improved outcomes must relate to about a dozen issues reflecting national and local priorities. A majority must relate to national priorities. There must be:
— at least one relating to education;
— at least one relating to social services;
— at least one further relating to either education or social services;
— at least one relating to transport; and
— one measure of improved cost-effectiveness.

17.51   The other issues should relate to local priorities and cover issues of substance which have been identified in consultation as important local concerns. They should focus on areas or groups at risk of social exclusion, aiming to reduce the differences in outcomes compared with other people in the authority's area, and complementing work done under the Neighbourhood Renewal Strategy.

17.52   The national priorities are expressed as targets and there are a small group of targets for each issue. The target used in a local PSA in relation to a national priority should be the national target. The issues covered by the national priorities are listed below, alongside an example of the targets associated with them nationally:
— **Education**: eg reduce truancy by 10 per cent from 2002 levels;
— **Employment**: eg by 2004 increase the employment rates of defined disadvantaged groups;
— **Health and social services**: eg improve the level of education, training and employment outcomes for care leavers aged 19 years to at least 75 per cent of that achieved by all young people by March 2004;
— **Drug misuse and treatment**: eg reduce the number of people under 25 years reporting the use of Class A drugs by 25 per cent by 2005;
— **Crime reduction**: eg reduce vehicle crime by 30 per cent by 2004;
— **Waste recycling**: eg enable 17 per cent of household waste to be recycled or composted by 2004;
— **Transport and road safety**: eg double light rail use in England by 2010 from 2000 levels;
— **Housing and planning**: eg ensure all social housing meets set standards of decency by 2010;
— **Fire safety**: eg reduce the incidence of accidental fire related deaths in the home by 25 per cent averaged over five years to march 2004, compared to the five years to March 1999;
— **Council-wide**: eg ensure continuous improvement in economy, efficiency and effectiveness of local services through 100 per cent capability in electronic service delivery by 2005;
— **Supplementary transport targets**: eg triple the number of cycling trips by 2010 against a 2000 baseline.

17.53   For every issue identified in the PSA, the local authority must define how performance is to be measured. It must be outcomes that are measured. The measure must be unambiguous, using existing indicators if at all possible and the data must be available at the end of the PSA period. The target must show the performance level expected were a PSA not in place and the stretching target under the PSA. The supplementary information supplied with the draft agreement must show what level of performance is currently being achieved.

17.54   Before any reward grant is paid to the authority who achieves the PSA target, the performance must be verified. Local authorities are to make their own arrangements during the PSA period for monitoring, and at the end the government will subject the authorities to a verification process. Local authorities will also have to show that they have worked with others to achieve improved performance. If they cannot show that they have done so, then they will need compelling arguments to show why not.

17.55   Much then is expected of local authorities under a local PSA, but in return the government offers the incentives of financial support and potential relaxations in administrative procedures and/or law to facilitate improvements.

17.56   Performance reward grant, made up half in capital and half in revenue, is paid if the stretching performance targets are met. The maximum payable is 2.5 per cent of net budget, scaled down where the targets are for the most part but not completely met. However, where the success rate is less than 60 per cent, no performance reward grant will be paid. Any grant to be paid will be paid in two equal instalments in the two financial years after the expiry of the PSA period, though there is provision for up to 20 per cent to be paid in the final year of the PSA period if interim targets have been met in full.

17.57   In addition pump priming funds may be paid at the beginning of the PSA period to assist authorities to make the service improvements. This is calculated by reference to a formula of £1 per head of population plus £750,000. This is paid by way of capital grant pursuant to a direction under the Local Government and Housing Act 1989, s 40(6). The average paid to the PSA authorities is £1.05 million.

17.58   Local authorities may also have access to additional borrowing capacity in the form of unsupported credit approvals, if they can show that there is a strong link between the need to borrow and the achievement of their stretching targets. However, there must be a particularly noteable improvement flowing from the extra borrowing requirement and a convincing demonstration of cutting across organisational boundaries before any such credit approval will be contemplated.

17.59   Authorities who participated in the pilot and those who signed up to PSAs in the course of 2001 are now in the process of trying to deliver against their stretching targets. The level of success they achieve will only be known at the end of their PSA period.

THE IMPACT OF NEW POLITICAL GOVERNANCE ARRANGEMENTS

17.60   So far, this chapter has concentrated on the general background, the shifting local context against which local authorities are making procurement decisions. As set out above, it is understandable that in making decisions about commissioning, authorities will constantly be driven by their own best value performance plan, the targets they have signed up to in a PSA, the neighbourhood renewal strategy and their own community strategy. They should be inextricable linked.

17.61   Yet the modernisation agenda for local government has focused to a large part on a commitment to making local government more relevant to local people; more transparent and accountable. To this end, the Local Government Act 2000, Pt II amended the political governance arrangements in local government significantly. This section focuses on those changes and the impact on an authority's procurement practice.

17.62   For the first time, by virtue of the LGA 2000, s 10 local authorities have had to put in place arrangements for a separate executive, with responsibility for performing certain functions. The form of the executive can be one of three models set out in s 11 of the Act—a directly-elected mayor and cabinet, a leader and cabinet or a directly elected mayor and council manager. Alternatively, the executive may take a form permitted by regulations made by the Secretary of State and there are specific provisions relating to small authorities with a population of less than 85,000. However it is fair to say that most councils have opted for the leader and cabinet model, with a handful, seven in all, having a directly-elected mayor returned for the first time in elections in May 2002.

17.63   The principle underlying the new political management arrangements is that the full council, and not the executive, sets the budget and a policy framework consisting of eleven statutory plans which must be agreed by council and six others where the council is urged to consider reserving them to council. Within that framework, the executive is responsible for making all decisions that are not forbidden to it by virtue of regulations, but it must act within the scope of the budget and policy framework. An executive which purports to make a decision which is:
(i)   contrary to any plan or strategy approved by full council; or
(ii)   contrary to or not wholly in accordance with the budget or standing orders or regulations applying to the budget; or
(iii)   contrary to or not wholly in accordance with the plan or strategy for controlling the authority's capital expenditure or borrowing
acts beyond its powers and unlawfully. However, so long as it does not do so, the powers of the executive to make decisions are very wide.

17.64   The executive must give account by at least one overview and scrutiny committee which the council is legally bound to appoint to assist in the development of policy and to oversee and scrutinise the performance of the executive and senior management of the council.

17.65   The regulations which determine those decisions which can and cannot be made by the executive are the Local Authorities (Functions and Responsibilities) (England) Regulations 2000[1]. It is these regulations which determine that the budget and policy framework are the responsibility of the council. They also provide that certain functions, mostly of a quasi-judicial nature, such as licensing and development control, health and safety, as well as elections, pensions and appointments are not to be the responsibility of the executive. Whether a short list of matters are to be the responsibility of the executive or not is a matter of local choice, as set out in the regulations. However, subject to the exceptions set out in the regulations, the responsibility for all decision-making rests with the executive, subject to the scrutiny of the overview and scrutiny committee.

1   SI 2000/2853.

17.66   This approach is consistent with the encouragement from the government for decisions to be joined up across the public sector. With one executive making decisions on a very broad range of matters, there is less likelihood that decision-making in an authority will be fragmented. Authorities who have experimented with new interim structures pending the implementation of the LGA 2000 have found that the establishment of a single executive with a very broad remit has led to a more corporate approach which is not characterised by the 'silo' thinking of former single function committees.

17.67   Where then are procurement decisions to be taken? Prior to the LGA 2000, the answer would be found in the terms of reference of the authority's committees, established under the Local Government Act 1972, s 101. These would usually be set out in the authority's standing orders. In those terms of reference would be found the extent of delegation from the council in relation to the matter concerned. Yet now, the first question must be whether the decision is the responsibility of the executive. If it is (and in most cases it is likely to be so), then by operation of law, only the executive can make the decision (unless delegated by the executive in accordance with the LGA 2000, ss 14–16). The council does not have any power to make a decision in relation to it, and by definition cannot delegate the exercise of the function to a committee. It is not the council's function to delegate.

17.68   The next step then will be to turn to the scheme of delegation of executive functions, to establish the identity of the decision maker. It may be the directly elected mayor, or the leader, who is entitled to make the decision, or it may have been delegated to the executive as a whole, to an individual member, to a committee of the executive, to an officer, to an area committee or to joint arrangements—for example to a joint committee. The scheme of delegation must appear in the constitution which the council is required to keep up to date and make publicly available[1] at all reasonable times.

1   Local Government Act 2000, s 37.

17.69   As the power to enter into a contract is incidental to the function being contracted, it follows that the decision to let a contract follows the function. This will generally not create any problem at all. Decisions relating to the contracting out, for example, of a housing management function would be an executive responsibility. However in some, possibly infrequent, circumstances, the position may not be so clear. Imagine that an authority is in the process of letting an information and communication technology contract. It is letting the contract because it is keen to meet its e-government targets. Much of the contract will relate to ICT systems for, say, customer relations management and general ICT support. However, if the contract also relates to non-executive functions, say the implementation of electronic voting procedures at elections, then in that respect the executive would appear not to have power to make the procurement decision. It may be that two decisions would be needed: one from the executive in accordance with the executive scheme of delegation, and one from the appropriate non-executive committee to ensure that all aspects of the contract are covered. It is therefore essential to be clear about the subject matter of the contract and whether there are any aspects of it which would not be an executive responsibility so that appropriate decisions can be taken in the correct forum.

17.70   Similarly it will be of the utmost importance to check that a proposed decision to let a contract is not 'contrary to or not wholly in accordance with the budget and provisions in standing orders or financial rules/regulations in respect of the budget' or 'contrary to any plan or strategy approved by the council'[1]. If it is, then the decision cannot be taken by the executive, and it will be for the authority's Chief Finance Officer or Monitoring Officer to bring the fact to the attention of the executive. A referral to council would be necessary for a decision as to whether to amend the budget or policy framework to accommodate the proposed decision. Authorities which do not want to fetter the activity of the executive in this way will doubtless draw up their policy framework flexibly to facilitate discretion. However, in those authorities where there is a preference for a strong council/weak executive approach, they may prefer the scope of the executive to be limited by tightly drawn policy. The same will apply to the budget which is set by the authority. To avoid the need for referral back to the council where a decision has not been fully accommodated within the budget, there will need to be discretion on virement levels. Again this is a matter of choice about the relative position of the executive as opposed to the full council.

1   SI 2000/2853, reg 4 and *New Council Constitutions—Local Government Act 2000 Guidance to English Local Authorities*, para 2.48.

17.71   Let us assume then that the procurement decision is an executive responsibility and that it is entirely consistent with the budget and policy framework. Authorities will need to address the process by which the decision is to be made. They must next address whether the decision to be made is a key decision. This notion is introduced by the Local Authorities (Executive Arrangements) (Access to Information) (England) Regulations 2000[1]. A decision will be key if it is an executive decision and has a significant impact, by reference to either of two tests. A decision will be key if it will have an impact in two or more wards. It will also be key if the financial impact of making the decision will be more than a limit fixed by the authority and appearing in its constitution. The limit is the level at which the authority considers the financial impact significant by reference to the budget for the function or service concerned. Authorities may also define other decisions as key in addition to those meeting either of the statutory tests.

1   SI 2000/3272.

17.72   The impact of a decision being classified as a key decision is that there is a requirement for it to be inserted in the authority's forward plan. This is a document which must be prepared and updated on a monthly basis. It must cover a period of four months and be made available to the public 14 days before the start of the period it covers. It must contain details of the key decisions likely to be taken in that period. It must contain details of the matter to be decided, the date or period within which the decision is likely to be taken, the identity of the decision maker, including if the decision maker is a body, all the members of the decision-making body, details of consultation that is to be undertaken and how, including the groups to be consulted, how and to whom to respond, by when, and details of any background papers.

17.73   Statutory guidance on the LGA 2000, Pt II acknowledges[1] that authorities will not be able to foresee all of the decisions that it will need to take over a four-month period. Consequently there will be more detail in the plan over the first few weeks than towards the end. It is to be seen as a planning tool. Items may be added as the plan is updated on a monthly basis. However, where a key decision does not appear in the forward plan the decision may only be taken if the criteria in reg 15 (general urgency) or reg 16 (special urgency) of the Access to Information Regulations are met. Key decisions taken at meetings must generally be taken in publi,c save that confidential or exempt information as defined in the Local Government Act 1972, Sch 12A need not be disclosed.

1   *New Council Constitutions—Local Government Act 2000 Guidance to English Local Authorities*, para 7.23.

17.74   Regulation 15 provides that even if a key decision has not been included in the forward plan, a decision may nonetheless be made if three clear days' notice is given and the chairman (or if there is no chairman, then every member) of the relevant overview and scrutiny committee has been informed by the proper officer. However this exception only applies where it is impracticable for the matter to be included in the next forward plan.

17.75   If compliance with reg 15 is impracticable because of the date by which a key decision must be made, the decision may only be taken where the decision-maker has obtained the agreement of the chairman of the relevant overview and scrutiny committee that the decision is urgent and cannot reasonably be deferred. If there is no chairman of a relevant overview and scrutiny committee or they are unable to act, the chairman of the authority may consent. The Vice Chairman of council may also consent if there is neither a chair of a relevant overview and scrutiny committee nor a chairman.

17.76   Authorities should note, however, that if they cannot rely upon either reg 15 or 16, then there would appear to be no basis for taking key decisions as a matter of urgency. It is worthy of note also that with effect from 1 October 2002 the three-day notice period for meetings and for the availability of papers so familiar to local government practitioners for access to information purposes has been increased to five[1].

1   SIs 2002/715 and 2002/716.

17.77   Another new feature of the Local Government Act 2000 is the requirement set out in s 21 for executive arrangements to provide a right of 'call in' for an overview and scrutiny committee. This right of 'call in' is a right to recommend that an executive decision which has been made but not implemented be reconsidered by the person who made it. This right can be exercised by an overview and scrutiny committee, or the council may be requested to do so. The way in which the 'call in' procedure works and the timescales which apply will vary from authority to authority. However the effect of the 'call in' is to suspend implementation of the decision until the decision-maker has reconsidered. In the end the decision will be for the executive decision-maker to make, so the overview and scrutiny committee cannot interfere with the nature of the decision. However, it does seem likely that executive decisions may be delayed by the 'call in' process, and authorities will need to build this into timescales for completion of contractual arrangements and manage the expectations of all parties concerned.

17.78　It is possible for the call in procedure to be set aside in cases of urgency. Indeed the statutory guidance[1] urges authorities to put in place provisions which prevent urgent decisions under reg 16 being called in or delayed in any way. How authorities deal with this depends upon the contents of their constitution. If authorities seek to rely on it, not only must reg 16 apply, but they must closely follow the provisions for doing so or risk challenge for procedural irregularity.

1　*New Council Constitutions—Local Government Act 2000 Guidance to English Local Authorities.*

17.79　Executive decisions once made have to be recorded in accordance with regs 3 and 4 of the Access to Information Regulations. This is a new departure for local authorities, whose minutes of decisions in the past have tended to be a note of the actual decision and little more. In future not only will the decision have to be recorded, but so will the reasons and details of any objections considered and rejected. Conflicts of interest and any dispensation granted by the authority's standards committee must also be recorded. The record then is to be publicly available.

17.80　Authorities also need to be aware of new provisions in relation to contracts standing orders[1]. Local authority contracts above a value or of a description set out in the authority's standing orders must be in writing. That value or description must be fixed by the full council and cannot be delegated under the Local Government Act 1972, s 101.

1　Local Authorities (Executive Arrangments) (Modification of Enactments and Further Provisions) (England) Order 2001, SI 2001/1517.

17.81　The statutory guidance[1] states that it may be that individual members of the executive may seek to be involved in negotiating contracts and may be responsible for making the decision to award if power to do so is delegated to them. However an authority's standing orders must provide that where a contract is made under the authority's seal, it must be attested by at least one officer whether or not it is also attested by any member of the authority (or a council manager where there is one). If it is not made under seal, it must be signed by at least two officers of the authority whether or not signed also by any member of the authority.

1　*New Council Constitutions—Local Government Act 2000 Guidance to English Local Authorities.*

17.82　One further issue which is likely to arise out of the new political management arrangements in relation to the procurement practices of local authorities is the role of the overview and scrutiny committees. Experience to date has shown that the overview and scrutiny committee will be keen to be involved in scrutinising the performance of external providers of services to the authority. It may well be seen as central to their new inquisitive duties. By definition, the role of overview and scrutiny entails a holding to account, and accountability of the executive and its agents to the council as a whole. The overview and scrutiny members may want to question the contractor about its performance and to put any concerns to them in the overview and scrutiny forum. However, there may be a wish for these meetings to take place in public, and it is perhaps not difficult to understand the contradiction that would seem to emerge by conducting overview and scrutiny meetings in private. Yet though there is usually a standard clause requiring the contractor to attend member meetings and report on performance, there is also often a clause protecting the confidentiality of commercially sensitive information about the contract. Meetings held in public in an overview and scrutiny forum may sometimes create tensions around this latter requirement.

17.83   To achieve a workable solution it is suggested that a protocol be adopted by council governing the conduct of such meetings and the reporting of them which would contain the following basic principles, namely the need to:

(a)   examine the contractual framework within which the performance of the contract is being scrutinised. The starting point should be the contract. Most service contracts will provide for a performance regime and a related payment mechanism tying in the contractor's performance with payment and other default remedies. The monitoring scheme is agreed between the parties as a mechanism to measure objectively contractor performance and it is therefore reasonable for it to be taken into consideration when the performance of the contract is being scrutinised. A report of the authority officer authorised to monitor the contractor's performance should form part of the evidence before the committee. It may deal with, for example, defective service notices, rectifications, a summary of any customer surveys and complaints, any agreement to improve performance or any dispute resolution process and details of any variation or suspension of part of the service;

(b)   consider whether confidential and commercially sensitive information is being disclosed in breach of the contract. First an overview and scrutiny committee will need to consider whether any information which will be disclosed contains exempt information as defined under the Local Government Act 1972, s 101A and Sch 12A and, if so, whether it should exclude members of the public from the meeting whilst this information is being discussed. The relevant provision is information relating to the financial or business affairs of any particular person unless it is information which is required to be registered under legislation, eg the Companies Act 1985 (company accounts and Director's Reports etc would not be exempt). This statutory right of exclusion is permissive, not mandatory and it is for the committee to decide whether to exclude. If there is any uncertainty, legal advice should be sought.

Apart from this statutory right which is within the discretion of the committee, it will be necessary to consider any contractual constraint. Normally a contractor will require a term inserted into the contract to place an obligation upon an authority not to disclose confidential or commercially sensitive information to any third party without its consent. The confidential information is usually defined to mean information relating to the business affairs, product development, trade secrets, know how and personnel of the company. It is usual to provide that this would not apply to performance monitoring information.

Any disclosure of such confidential information, which is subject to contractual obligations placed upon the authority, could result in a claim for breach of contract if the contractor could show loss and a causal connection with the disclosure. There is a secondary issue of maintaining a good working relationship with the contractor and of obtaining the trust and confidence of the private sector with whom the council may wish to do business. A balance needs to be struck between public accountability and the need to protect commercially sensitive information relating to third parties.

It would be possible for the meeting to be held in two parts, and for the commercially sensitive information to be dealt with in private. Equally the exempt information in any report (and minutes) should not be disclosed and should be placed in a separate section.

(c)   ensure fairness. The LGA 2000 and government guidance provides that an overview and scrutiny committee may invite other persons to attend meetings. Where the contract provides the contractor can be required to attend or, if not, invited. Part of the scrutiny role may entail obtaining evidence from invitees who are stakeholders, residents, and users of the service as to the contractor's performance. The protocol should emphasise the importance of objectivity and the need to ensure that such invitees are representative, to avoid the accusation of unfairness. As far as possible, invitees should be encouraged to provide sufficient evidence to support their statements. The contractor should be given a right of reply. If the result of the scrutiny points to an inconsistency between the views of the users/invitees and the monitoring information, then this may form part of the recommendation to executive to review the monitoring.

17.84   In conclusion, in relation to the new political arrangements under the LGA 2000, Pt II there may well be a significant impact on local authority's procurement activity, perhaps not least as local authorities across the country grapple to come to terms with the new regime. Practitioners who have never had to give a second thought to their decision-making processes because they were almost second nature are now feeling their way through a new and highly regulated field of administrative law. They are bound to be hesitant at least until the new regime becomes more familiar.

17.85   So if it is new and difficult for the experienced local authority practitioner, then the same is likely to be the case for the external partner. Yet in due diligence tests on process, authorities will have to inspire confidence and be able to demonstrate that their constitutional arrangements have been followed to the letter. It seems that there is likely to be a steep learning curve for all concerned.

PART IV
CASE STUDIES

CHAPTER 18

Case study: construction

Michael Conroy Harris

BACKGROUND AND CONTEXT

The circumstances of this case study

18.01 This case study is based on an LEA having identified the need to provide additional school facilities by building a new secondary school in its borough on a suitable site of which the LEA already has ownership. When completed, the secondary school will be a community school, that is, it will be owned by the LEA. The secondary school is to be designed in such a way that it allows:
— the flexibility of layout to meet the changing demands of the school users;
— the provision of facilities for third party use; and
— linkage to the ICT network of the LEA.

Primary factors which influence the way in which the construction of the secondary school is carried out

18.02 The most critical factor in any case study of this type will be the way in which the development of the school facilities can be funded. Typically, funds are made available by the use of capital resources or via the Private Finance Initiative (PFI). For illustrative purposes, approximately £800 million was made available for schools through the PFI in 2000/2001, whereas approximately £2 billion was made available for schools facilities through the School Building Capital programme (which includes funds made available through New Deals for Schools).

18.03 If the LEA had been confronted with the need, for example, to reorganise its school facilities radically on a borough wide basis, such as the move from a three tier system of education (first school, middle school and high school) to a two tier system (primary school and secondary school), it would have been unlikely that the LEA would have had sufficient capital resources to procure the required school facilities without resorting to the PFI. For more details of schemes procured under the PFI see chapter 13.

18.04 However, for the construction of the new secondary school in this case study, it is assumed that there are sufficient capital funds available to proceed by way of a construction contract. It should be remembered that, when the new school has been built, the LEA or the school, as the case may be, will have to make separate arrangements for the ongoing management of the secondary school (to deal with such matters as cleaning, security, planned maintenance and periodic maintenance) either by the use of its own directly employed staff or by the letting of one or more facilities management contracts.

DESCRIPTION OF THE PARTIES INVOLVED

Main parties to the contract

18.05   The government's green paper *Modernising Local Government Finance*[1] sets out the principle that the proportion of the schools' budget which should be passed directly to the schools themselves should be increased on a continuing basis. The target proportion under this principle, known as fair funding, was 85 per cent for 2001–02, with the target increasing to 90 per cent for 2002–03. In many circumstances, therefore, it will be the school itself, acting through the school governors, which will place the construction contract. However, for the purposes of this case study, it is the LEA that will enter into the construction contract. Formally, this will be through the offices of the director of education or the chief education officer as the case may be. The other party to the construction contract will be the building contractor which submits the best tender to the LEA and with whom the LEA can subsequently conclude negotiation of satisfactory contract terms.

1   19 September 2000, available at www.local.detr.gov.uk/greenpap/.

Other parties

18.06   Having established that the two parties to the construction contract will be the LEA and the building contractor, it should be borne in mind that other parties will be involved with or interested in the construction contract. This would include the school governors in this case study and in other circumstances could include, for example, a Diocesan Authority.

18.07   Such parties may themselves enter into contractual relationships with the LEA (and would include, for example, the architect who designs the secondary school) or with the building contractor (including, for example, the sub-contractors the building contractor engages to carry out the construction works).

18.08   There may also be other parties involved on a non-contractual, advisory basis such as the Commission for Architecture and the Built Environment ('CABE'), a public body which is presently limited by guarantee but which is intended to become a statutory body, or the Royal Institute of British Architects ('RIBA') Schools Client Forum which has published guidance for school governors.

Diagram outlining the contractual relationship

18.09

Note – this shows primary contracts by use of solid lines and indicates
non-contractual relationships (by use of dotted lines). There are
also a number of collateral documents (such as bonds,
guarantees and warranties) which are omitted from this
diagram for the sake of clarity.

OBJECTIVES OF THE CONTRACT

18.10   The LEA will have to balance a whole host of competing factors that will
determine the procurement method used for the construction works. Such factors will
include price, time and risk.

Price

18.11   Ensuring that best value is obtained will require the LEA to give due
consideration and draw an appropriate balance between the sum of the construction
contract and the ongoing costs of maintaining the school when it is in use. For further
details of best value see chapter 11. Once this balance has been drawn and in
circumstances where the LEA wishes to ensure that there is certainty of the sum of
the construction contract, options available to it include:
(i)   initially ensuring that there are as few variables as possible at the time the
       tendering building contractors submit their tenders for the school; and
(ii)   subsequently avoiding variations to the construction works once the successful
       tenderer has been appointed as the building contractor.

One means of achieving this is to complete the design of the majority, if not all, of the construction works before the construction contract is placed.

Time

18.12   Clearly it is important that the school is completed by reference to the academic year. In most cases, completion of construction works under the construction contract will have to occur in July to allow the school to be furnished etc, to be ready for the intake of new pupils in September. Points to consider here include:
(i)   if it is possible to programme the construction works so that completion of them by July is readily achievable, the method of procurement will not have to be structured to accommodate a shorter programme for the construction works; but
(ii)   in most cases there will not be the luxury of a lengthy construction programme as it is likely that the requirement to bring the new school into use will be pressing.

18.13   Where a shorter period of time between the decision to proceed with the construction of the school and its completion is required, such earlier completion can be achieved when the construction works are commenced on site before the design of all elements of the construction works is completed. One method of achieving this, discussed at para **18.41**, is by letting different elements of the construction works in separate packages. This, though, creates tensions between the desire to obtain certainty of price for the construction works and the desire to achieve completion of them within the constraints of the academic year.

Risk

18.14   It may be important to the LEA to attempt to transfer as much risk as possible to the building contractor, in recognition of best value (as mentioned above). However, in transferring significant risk (such as the risk for dealing with any pollution, contamination or other adverse conditions encountered in the ground) to the building contractor, the LEA will be presented with a greater sum for the construction contract. This creates tensions, therefore between the desire to obtain the best price for the construction works and the desire to transfer as much risk as possible for their carrying out.

18.15   From the above, it can clearly be seen that none of the factors considered (and there will, of course, be others) which influence the choice of procurement method for the construction works can be viewed in isolation. Further, it is clear that careful consideration should be given to the factors which are given pre-eminence when settling the form of procurement of the construction works, as incorrect decisions at this point will affect successful completion of the school. In this case study, each of these key factors is given equal weighting and the form of procurement is selected on that basis.

LEGAL AND COMMERCIAL ISSUES

18.16   There are many procurement methods available to the LEA, but the types which would be sensibly considered for this case study are traditional procurement, design and build procurement and procurement by management methods (either management contracting or construction management).

Traditional procurement

18.17 'Traditional procurement' is the term used to describe the procurement mechanism that has been implemented by forms of contract, that have been used in largely the same form since the nineteenth century. If the LEA were to adopt traditional procurement, it would proceed on the basis that it separately engaged:

— a team of professional consultants ('the professional team') to design the construction works necessary for the school. In so doing, the professional team will usually be required to exercise the reasonable skill and care to be expected of competent members of their respective professions; and

— the building contractor to carry out and complete the construction works necessary for the school. In so doing, the building contractor will usually be required to complete them in accordance with the construction contract, using materials and workmanship of and to the standards and quality specified in the construction contract.

18.18 This division of responsibility for design, materials and workmanship is maintained except in the following circumstances:

— the building contractor is responsible for the design of those construction works which do not form part of the completed school ('temporary works'), examples of which include scaffolding and the formwork which supports unset concrete; and

— the building contractor may be responsible for the design of some elements of the construction works if the construction contract expressly provides for this (typically used where those elements of the construction works are in fact designed and carried out by a specialist sub-contractor—an example of which might be the ICT installation).

18.19 The implications of dividing responsibility for design, materials and workmanship are that:

— the members of the professional team are liable to the LEA (to the extent that each of them have not used the reasonable skill and care to be expected by competent members of their respective professions) for any defects in the design of the construction works, such as the failure to specify adequate fire protection to any steel frame used in the school; and

— the building contractor is liable to the LEA (to the extent that it has not complied with the terms of the contract) for any shortcomings in workmanship or in quality of materials (either improperly applying the right material or the wrong material properly applied or a combination of both).

18.20 When a problem occurs, it is often difficult to establish in practice the underlying defect, be it design, workmanship or materials. Often, the underlying defect will be caused by a combination of causes and the division of responsibilities identified above may not be as distinct as they first seemed to be. This may present the LEA with difficulties in establishing which party or parties to pursue for breach of their respective obligations. For further details of breach of contract see para **18.25**

18.21   The LEA may also find itself in the situation where the school is not reasonably fit for the purpose for which it was intended (considered further under design and build contracts at para **18.24**), but not be in a position to seek redress from either the professional team or the building contractor.

18.22   Traditional forms of contract fall into three basic types:
(1)   'lump sum contracts', where the price for the construction works is entered into the construction contract. The price is only then altered as contemplated by the form of contract (eg due to variations, alterations to rates of tax, fluctuations in price);
(2)   'measurement (or remeasurement) contracts', where the price for the construction works is not entered into the construction contract (although a tender total/ estimate of the construction contract sum will be ascertained). The contract price is then ascertained (and paid) in accordance with the provisions of the construction contract; and
(3)   'cost reimbursement contracts', where the building contractor is reimbursed the cost of carrying out the construction works together with a fee (which is calculated on a predetermined basis).

18.23   It should be noted that if the school has any civil engineering works associated with it, such as alterations to the public highway to provide access to the school, the same construction contract may be used for the construction works to the school and the civil engineering works to the public highway.

Design and build procurement

18.24   Design and build procurement is the term used to describe the method of procurement regulated by design and build contracts where the building contractor is responsible for all elements of the construction works: design, workmanship and materials. This is the key distinction between a design and build contract and a traditional contract. It raises two key concepts:
—   the 'single point responsibility' of the building contractor to the LEA; and
—   whether the completed construction works should be 'fit for their purpose'.
The implications of each of these should be carefully considered by the LEA.

Single point responsibility

18.25   As the building contractor is ultimately responsible for design, workmanship and materials (even though it may sub-contract significant parts of each of them), the LEA would be in a position such that, should the roof leak, it does not need to determine whether this is due to an inadequacy in the design, in the materials or in the workmanship (or assess whether the defect is a combination of them). The LEA can simply look to the building contractor to put the situation right. Under traditional procurement the defect could be attributable to any or all members of the professional team and/or the building contractor. Clearly there is an attraction to this method of procurement for the LEA. Further, as the building contractor is responsible for all elements of the design and construction of the works, it is better able to contract on the basis that the completed construction works are fit for their purpose.

Fitness for purpose

18.26   Unless a construction contract expressly provides otherwise, it includes the implied term that the construction works, when completed, will be fit for their purpose. This purpose can either be stated in the documents which constitute the construction contract, for example 'all classrooms will be capable of being upgraded to receive a particular form of ICT', or it may reasonably be inferred from those documents that the classrooms should be upgradeable in such a way (on the basis that such developments in ICT would be well known to both parties to the construction contract). The fitness for purpose obligation is excluded from some construction contracts[1] while others have the facility to select it as an option[2].

1   For example, the JCT Standard Form of Building Contract With Contractor's Design, 1998 edn ('CD 98').
2   For example, the GC/Works contracts which are the government's suite of construction contracts prepared by the OGC's Property and Construction Directorate, formerly the Property Advisors to the Civil Estate.

18.27   The corollary to this is that the building contractor will not want to accept the obligation of fitness for purpose as it imposes a higher obligation on the building contractor which:
—   it will be difficult for the building contractor to put back to back with its own professional team, who will expect to be under an obligation to use reasonable skill and care, as though they had been appointed directly by the LEA and to their sub-contractors; and
—   is extremely difficult, if not impossible, for the building contractor to insure under the terms of its professional indemnity insurance policy (although this must be distinguished from the liability which the building contractor owes to the LEA, which is not usually limited to the extent of what is covered by the relevant policy of insurance).

18.28   A position that is relatively common in the construction market is that the construction works will be reasonably fit for the purposes which have been set out in the client's requirements (known as 'employer's requirements') which form part of the construction contract. In simple terms, the building contractor is liable only to the extent that the construction works are not fit for any purpose which is made known to it by the LEA. In most situations, the purposes will be reasonably apparent to the building contractor, but the ever changing user needs of schools and the ways in which they may be increasingly used for extra-curricular activities tend to blur the boundaries somewhat. For this reason, it is in the LEA's interests to make the intended purpose of the school expressly known to the building contractor

Management contracting procurement

18.29   Management contracting procurement is the method of procurement whereby the LEA would appoint a management contractor, who will provide services which would include the following:
—   the benefit of its construction expertise (management contractors tend to be highly specialised);
—   the setting up of the construction site;

— the obtaining of tenders for the various packages of construction works to be carried out (known as 'works contracts'); and
— the management of the various sub-contractors (known as 'works contractors') appointed under the works contracts who are to provide the workmanship and materials for the construction works.

18.30   The management contractor is appointed for its management input and it must be appreciated that it does not:
— perform the traditional role of a building contractor;
— carry out any of the construction works; and
— become liable to the LEA for the quality of the finished construction works unless any defect in them is due to the management contractor's inadequate management of them.

18.31   The professional team is engaged in largely the same way that it would be on a traditional contract, but the services each perform would reflect the differing nature of management contracting. Responsibility for design is separate to that for workmanship and materials in the same way as it is under traditional procurement.

18.32   It is the works contractors who are primarily liable to the client for the quality of the workmanship and materials used on the development although they are not appointed directly by the client. This is dealt with in the JCT Management Form of Contract, 1998 edn by the use of direct employer/works contractor agreements (similar to collateral warranties, discussed at para 18.42). The LEA would need a complete set of these agreements for all the construction works to put it in the same position as it would be under either a traditional contract or a design and build contract. This is the main reason why, although there are clear advantages to the LEA in terms of programme, management contracting is not used in this case study.

18.33   Construction management procurement is similar to management contracting as a form of procurement in that:
— the professional team is appointed in the same way; and
— the construction works are divided into packages for the various elements.

18.34   However there are some notable differences:
— the LEA would enter into direct contract with each of the trade contractors under a form of trade contract. This avoids the need for the separate employer/works contractor agreements which are necessary in management contracts; and
— a construction manager is appointed, rather than a management contractor. The construction manager is more akin to a member of the professional team (and it may indeed also be appointed as the project manager) rather than acting as a building contractor.

18.35   The primary disadvantage to the LEA in using construction management is the same as that which discounts management contracting, namely that the LEA would not have the single point responsibility that it would get under a design and build contract, nor even the limited points of responsibility it would have under a traditional contract.

18.36   The management methods of procurement have already been discounted above and so the choice is between traditional procurement and design and build procurement. Each of these procurement methods would lead to the same degree of certainty of the sum of the construction contract. However, the construction contract could be placed marginally more quickly under design and build procurement (as the building contractor would finalise the design during the construction process) and this would also give the advantage of single point responsibility to the LEA. For these reasons, design and build is the chosen method of procurement for this case study.

18.37   In this case study the LEA needs to consider, comply with and/or make arrangements for the following:
—   an OJEC Notice—this can be issued by the open procedure (inviting all interested organisations to submit tenders) or, preferably here, by the restricted procedure (restricting numbers by a selection process in advance of the tender invitation). The selection criteria should[1] 'be aimed at selecting the most suitable organisations, capable of carrying out the required work whilst taking account of the need to achieve VFM';
—   a suitable tendering method (bearing in mind the OJEC requirements) from open tendering, single stage selective tendering, two stage selective tendering or selective tendering for design and build;
—   follow established good practice guidance such as those published by the National Joint Consultative Committee and by the Construction Industry Board. Both these bodies have ceased to exist, but their codes remain as a benchmark;
—   at common law, the LEA would not be obliged to reimburse the costs of tendering, nor to award the construction contract to any particular tenderer (as the tender is simply an invitation to treat). However, this position would change if the parties agree otherwise; the tenderer does work that goes beyond the normal tender process; the LEA acts in bad faith, or some contractual arrangement is found to exist. Care should, therefore, be exercised by the LEA in these circumstances.

1   According to Procurement Guidance No 3 (OGC).

18.38   With design and build procurement the primary (and possibly only) document is the employer's requirements. This will set out its requirements for the school by reference to outline drawings, performance specifications and relevant guidance (of which there is much for schools). It should also include, amongst other things, the:
—   ground investigation report (if one has been carried out);
—   pre-tender health and safety plan (which has to be prepared to comply with the Construction (Design and Management) Regulations 1994[1]; and
—   proposed terms and conditions of the construction contract (which should itself include any schedule of amendments, bonds, guarantees, warranties and sub-contract documents, all of which are discussed below).

1   SI 1994/3140.

18.39   It should be noted that, in other procurement situations, the tender documents would include different materials such as full architectural and structural drawings, detailed specifications and bills of quantities.

18.40   The LEA will receive the tenderers' proposals for carrying out and completing the construction works (known as the 'contractor's proposals'). This will include, amongst other things:

— details of any site investigations carried out by the tenderer;
— method statements for carrying out the construction works;
— the tender price;
— a response to the pre-tender health and safety plan; and
— any qualifications: usually these are received in relation to the terms and conditions proposed by the LEA. It is important to review these carefully and consider whether they are acceptable in the circumstances.

18.41   In some situations, usually where the programme time is tight, the LEA (or, more likely, the professional team acting on its behalf) may not be in position to amass all the relevant documents to put together the formal construction contract quickly enough, or there may be one or two points which are not yet agreed with the building contractor. However, in order to ensure the earliest possible start on site (with a view to achieving completion by the required date), the LEA may issue a limited letter of authority ('a letter of intent') to enable the building contractor to put certain of the construction works in hand (usually progressing the design works and putting on order any materials which have a long delivery period) whilst the construction contract is finally agreed and compiled. Whilst this is a helpful mechanism, care should be taken that the letter of intent is superseded by the formal contract as soon as possible, otherwise there is a risk that it becomes the construction contract which binds the parties.

18.42   Having established that the construction contract is to be based on CD 98, it will typically be comprised of the following:
(1)   the employer's requirements and the contractor's proposals, as described above;
(2)   the contract sum analysis, which is the tenderer's breakdown of the proposed contract sum. Although this is usually incorporated into the contractor's proposals, it exists in its own right as part of the overall construction contract;
(3)   Standard Form of Building Contract (CD 98): like most other contract drafters, the Joints Contract Tribunal ('JCT') republished its forms in 1998 as a result of the Construction Act. That said the basic form (with which CD 98 has many parallels) has been existence in substantially the same recognisable form for more than a hundred years (which is why some consider the language and style to be old fashioned). Consequently, it deals with most of the eventualities encountered on a development. Usually, JCT contracts will successfully regulate the relationship between the developer and the building contractor. Only when this relationship breaks down does the selected tribunal have to determine what those parties agreed. Therefore, a body of case law exists which can assist interpretation of what the parties to the contract are construed to have agreed;
(4)   schedule of amendments to CD 98: a standard form of contract is just that— standard. It will require amendment to tailor it to meet the LEA's particular requirements for this secondary school (which might include an amendment for fitness for purpose as outlined above). This is common practice, now recognised by the JCT by the issue of some of their forms of contract on CD-ROM in a format which allows manipulation of the text. Care should be taken, however, to ensure that the amendments are done correctly otherwise it may be difficult to establish what the LEA and the building contractor have, in fact, agreed (and the contra proferentem rule would operate against the LEA);
(5)   supplements: the Sectional Completion Supplement published by the JCT would allow the construction works to be completed in sections. This may be of assistance if one construction contract were to govern the construction works

being carried out on a number of different school sites, but would not probably be of assistance in this case study. Other variables in the construction contract include an optional clause by which the building contractor arranges for a retention bond instead of the LEA deducting retention moneys. Increasingly this is seen as best practice and the LEA should consider its use;

(6) bonds: if there is a question mark over the financial strength of the building contractor, the LEA should consider if it wants the protection afforded by a performance bond. The bond is an instrument, which is independent of the construction contract, by which the bondsman undertakes to pay up to a certain amount (usually 10% of the construction contract sum). There will be a cost to the building contractor in providing the performance bond which it will include in its tender to the LEA. The performance bond is usually one of two types:

— on demand, where the LEA would make a request to the bondsman to pay a specified sum (this type is more advantageous to the LEA as it is easier to obtain the bonded amount); or

— default, where, if a specified default occurs, the LEA can request the bondsman to pay the specified sum (this type is more advantageous to the building contractor as it presents a lower risk to it).

The LEA may decide not to proceed with a performance bond as it has a direct cost effect, particularly if another security mechanism, such as a parent company guarantee is available to it. Some construction contracts (for example, GC/ Works) now contain forms of bond; and forms of bond have been agreed with the British Bankers Association and/or the Association of British Insurers. Consequently, there is a greater degree of consistency in the bond market than has previously been the case;

(7) parent company guarantee: if the building contractor has a parent company, the parent company will probably have more significant assets against which the LEA could satisfy any claim against building contractor company (and there is a theoretical risk that the subsidiary company could be wound up to prevent any claims being made against it). The LEA can protect itself against this happening by considering the use of a parent company guarantee. This is an agreement which is separate from the construction contract under which the parent company guarantees the performance of the building contractor. The parent company guarantee sets out the nature of the guarantee given, the time when a claim may be may under it and the time at which it is to cease. As with performance bonds, forms of parent company guarantee are now included in some standard forms (and GC/Works again provides an example) and such guarantees are becoming more consistent across the market.

(8) collateral warranties: were developed in the 1980s following a series of cases which made it clear that, in most cases, building contractors and consultants would not be responsible in tort to third parties such as funds, purchasers and tenants ('beneficiaries') who acquired an interest in a development in the absence of a special relationship. The use of collateral warranties does away with the problems of establishing a duty in tort by creating a direct contractual relationship between the building contractor and any beneficiaries. Collateral warranties exist independently of the underlying construction contract and their primary purpose is to create a direct contractual responsibility for any breach of the obligation in the underlying contract. In addition to this primary purpose, collateral warranties often restate certain of the obligations contained in the underlying contract in direct favour of the beneficiary including the obligations to:

— not use deleterious materials;

—   maintain professional indemnity insurance;

—   grant a copyright licence to the beneficiary.

In this case study, collateral warranties could be used to create direct contractual relationship with, for example, the school governors who may have the long-term responsibility for maintaining the secondary school.

(9)   sub-contract documents: the building contractor will have to select the form of sub-contract to regulate the contractual relationship between it and the sub-contractors it intends to appoint. This will need to incorporate those provisions specifically required by CD 98 (for example those relating to the ownership of materials) and such others as are appropriate in the circumstance (for example the provision of collateral warranties in favour of the school governors). However, as the building contractor is entirely liable for its domestic sub-contractors the local education does not need to become overly embroiled in regulating the detailed terms of any sub-contract.

CHAPTER 19

Case study: education partnerships

Malcolm Iley & James Snape

BACKGROUND AND CONTEXT

What is an education partnership?

19.01   There are many forms of education partnership. In its simplest sense it can involve partnership arrangements between individual bodies and the LEA, between groups of schools (perhaps as co-purchasers)[1] or indeed between the private sector and the public sector in terms of the provision of specific services, capital investment, back office functions, and accelerating capital investment through the PFI programme.

1   See the new provisions in the Education Act 2002, Pts 2 and 3 in relation to the powers for schools and governing bodies to form companies and create federations of schools.

19.02   Recently, however, there have been some main streams of partnership, some imposed by the intervention of the Secretary of State for Education, and others emerging out of legislation or voluntarily on the basis of co-operation between both public and private sectors. They could be summarised as follows:
(i)   **PFI**: PFI is dealt with extensively elsewhere in this publication, so the standard structure is not set out in detail here. However, there have been a number of completed projects for the design, build, finance and operation of new schools, and also in terms of schools support services, eg PFI Catering Project for the London Borough of Lewisham;
(ii)   **Connexions partnerships**: The Connexions Service provides a range of services to young people, and creates a new structure for a national youth support service through new legal entities formed in each Connexions area. They are mainly limited companies by guarantee, who will contract with the Connexions Service National Unit or a regional Connexions Partnership (eg the Greater Manchester Connexions Partnership) and provide all services required for Connexions and sub-contract the individual parts of those services to individual entities. They are primarily involved in the encouragement and support of the personal development of young people, particularly in relationship to learning and skills and are part of the overall strategy implemented by the Learning and Skills Council under the Learning and Skills Act 2000;
(iii)   **Intervention contracts**: The name 'partnership' is perhaps something of a misnomer in certain cases which fall within this category. These partnerships arise where an LEA is failing in its LEA functions and therefore is required by virtue of the intervention of the Secretary of State for Education to make significant and rapid improvements in all or a specific range of educational services to its schools and their pupils. This will probably be because there has been an adverse and critical OFSTED Report, and the LEA is required to establish a partnership to deliver better and higher quality services, and achieve value for

money against specified output terms set out in a performance-based contract. That contract will involve regular service reviews and improvement processes, the allocation of risk to the private sector operator, and will involve the normal procurement process. The statutory duty to secure best value and the objectives of the LEA's Educational Development Plan (EDP) will obviously be considered carefully in terms of setting outputs and achievement measures. The delivery mechanism may involve a corporate structure to underpin the partnership, but will normally involve a performance-based service contract, perhaps linked to a 'partnership charter' or other stakeholder/consultative processes;

(iv) **Voluntary partnerships**: In more recent times, LEAs have been considering entering into voluntary private partnerships with the private sector in terms of support for specific schools support services, or in connection with the outsourcing of all of its LEA back office functions. This is no doubt anticipating the government's intention to direct central government support to 'front line' services and to allow greater freedom to both schools and LEAs in terms of how resources are used, greater capital investment attracted, and the attainment of higher standards. The provisions of the Education Act 2002 and the recent contracting out order[1] have anticipated these partnerships and will allow greater freedom in terms of delegation of functions, resources and partnership structures.

This case study concentrates on the latter form of partnership.

1   The Contracting Out (Local Education Authority Functions) (England) Order 2002, SI 2002/928.

19.03   In creating these forms of voluntary partnership the parties will need to consider a range of statutory provisions, regulations and guidance, including:
(a)   the Local Government and Housing Act 1989, Pt V;
(b)   the Local Authorities (Companies) Order 1995[1];
(c)   the Local Government Act 2000, s 2 and the Policy Guidance issued by DETR[1];
(d)   the Education Act 1996, ss 13,13A, 14 and Pt V and the Education Act 1997 generally;
(e)   the School Standards and Framework Act 1998, ss 45–50 and generally;
(f)   the Education Act 2002, particularly Pts 1 and 3 (and the explanatory notes);
(g)   the Local Authorities (Capital Finance) Regulations 1997[3], particularly reg 16;
(h)   the Local Government Act 1972 (particularly s 111) and generally;
(i)   the Local Government Act 1999 (particularly ss 3 and 16) and generally; and
(j)   the Local Government (Contracts) Act 1997.

1   SI 1995/849.
2   Now the DTLR, for example December 2000–March 2001.
3   SI 1997/319.

19.04   LEAs will need to consider the implications of the Education Act 2002, and in particular the powers granted to Education Forums to increase delegation to schools, and the powers vested in school governing bodies to form companies to procure services and how these may interact with the voluntary partnership.

Why is there a need for an education partnership in relation to schools support services?

19.05   County council X has traditionally received positive OFSTED Reports, has performed to a high standard and maintained good relationships with most of the 400 schools in its area. Currently schools support services are provided by county council X to maintained and independent schools, schools across its region, and a number of other education organisations. Schools support services within the LEA have had a separate identity as part of the Schools Branch of the Education Department, but have increasingly worked together as an integral unit. The level of collaboration within those services has prompted a move to integration as a natural progression in terms of developing successful services to county council X and schools within its area.

19.06 Both schools and staff have seen the benefit of closer working, and proposals were drawn up for the structure of the organisation designed to be innovative, encourage flexible working and project working across various professional and consultancy disciplines.

19.07 Central government offers county council X the opportunity to respond to the feasibility study to act as a 'pathfinder' in the establishment of a partnership with the private sector to provide the schools support services. The constituent services in the case of county council X are schools inspection and advice (curriculum and management consultancy), technology support for learning, governor support, commissioning and contract management, financial consultancy and personnel advice. The integrated service will be one of the largest group of services in the country and will build on the excellent reputation for quality. There is therefore no negative reason for this proposal (eg an LEA intervention), but the partnership with the private sector will be used to enhance and develop positively existing relationships and opportunities. The range of integrated services is typically as is shown in the diagram at para **19.08**.

Integrated service—range of support schemes

19.08

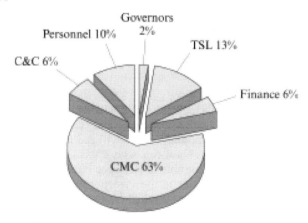

Key:
C&C = Commissioning and Contract Management
Personnel = Personnel Services
Governors = Governor Services
TSL = Technology Support for Learning
Finance = Financial Services
CMC = Curriculum and Management Consultancy

What are the advantages of an education partnership in this case?

19.09   County council X hopes to attract a partner who will pay a capital sum to 'acquire' this business unit, bring forward proposals to encourage and accelerate capital investment, establish the business as a market leader and equip it to be able to bid for other contracts in due course, concentrating on the delivery of services within the area of county council X, but in due course to be able to trade outside that area.

19.10   The business will effectively deliver 'traded services' to both schools and the county council, and also take the benefit of third party contracts which currently exist. The business will expand those services in due course, both within and outside county council X's administrative area.

19.11   Traded services are defined as those functions for which a governing body of a maintained school has a delegated budget under the School Standards and Framework Act 1998, Pt II.

Description of the parties involved

19.12   The parties involved will be county council X as the LEA, who will be a contracting party to a main service provision contract, but also in this case take upto 19.9 per cent equity stake of a joint venture which is also to be formed with the selected private sector partner. The joint venture company (JV Co) will be the other contracting party to the service contract, and the private sector partner will be the majority shareholder in that JV Co. There will be a TUPE transfer of county council staff involved in the delivery of the constituent services. Trade union consultation, therefore, is important and to that extent the trade union, and representations of both head teachers and teaching staff generally, and governors and governing bodies as stakeholders, is an important consideration.

19.13   Within the main service contract there will be a provision for a partnership board to meet as a consultative body on a regular basis. It will not be an express party to the contract, where the principal obligations between county council X and JV Co will be subject to privity between them, and neither will the partnership board intervene or subsume on the relationships between county council X and the private sector partner as an investor in JV Co or be able to intervene directly in rights to be set out in a shareholders' agreement prior to the incorporation of JV Co. The partnership board, however, will be an important vehicle where both the stakeholders and other parties can express their views and bring forward matters for county council X (who will remain the statutory LEA) and its private sector partner to consider.

19.14   The other 'parties' to bear in mind, although not party to the contractual and corporate structures, are of course the Secretary of State for Education who retains reserve powers in relation to county council X, as LEA, and OFSTED, the Audit Commission, etc.

Figure 2

19.15

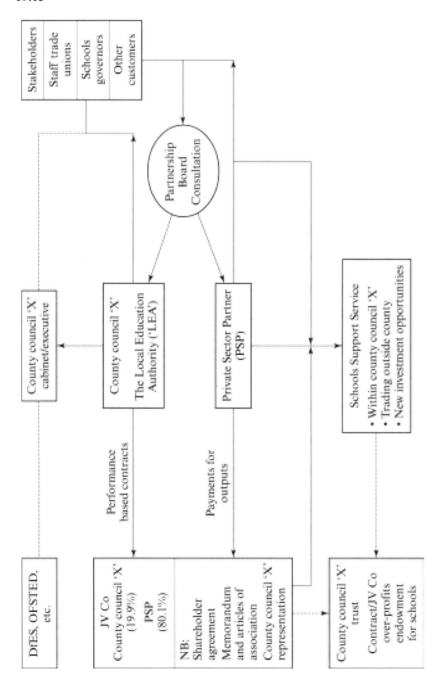

Objectives of the contract in the short term

19.16   The contract will be underpinned by public private partnership principles. It will not be a 'co-sourcing' arrangement (ie staff will not be seconded under the management of JV Co), but will be subject to a full TUPE transfer to JV Co. The contract will be a 'services' contract to provide the services to the county council and schools. JV Co will take a volume risk in this case, derived from the fact that the governing bodies of the schools will determine independently how long and with whom they spend their allocated budget (governing bodies have had freedom to use their budgets under delegated arrangements for some time). The contract could be for a term of seven years, or possibly longer, with options to extend subject to performance and the achievement of key performance indicators. These will be measured in relation not only to securing the duty of 'continuous improvement' (ie best value), but also the objectives of the Education Development Plan.

19.17   The structure of the contract will be intended to reflect the statutory framework, which requires the county council to exercise duties as the LEA as well as the provision of future service expansion and delivery, and also to take over a range of contracts or leases in order to operate the contract. The contract will be operated on the basis of open book accounting/disclosure principles unless expressly prohibited by law, and will also provide for consultation obligations monitored by the 'Partnership Board' as well as monitoring the success of the relationship between JV Co schools and other customers. The contract will set out a consultation protocol as to how the county council's consultation requirements, based in a statutory and non-statutory context, are managed and effectively delivered by JV Co.

19.18   The contract will set out clear performance measures and outputs required, but will also have provisions dealing with:
— the transfer of risk to JV Co;
— change of law/change of policy provisions;
— definition of 'relief' and 'compensation' events;
— payment mechanisms related to performance and indexation and review provisions;
— termination provisions;
— analogies to PFI/PPP contracts elsewhere;
— parent company guarantees and performance bonds, and
— provisions dealing with the incorporation of obligations under the shareholders' agreement underpinning the corporate arrangements, exit plan provisions, and appended agreements dealing with pensions, employment, confidentiality and insurance.

19.19   The county council needs to ensure, as it retains its duties as the LEA, that the contract sufficiently sets out a basis to achieve its statutory duties and objectives, provides sufficient flexibility to respond to future service improvement requirements, and that there is sufficient accountability within the provisions to enable it to act and exercise its fiduciary duties. These should at all times be distinguished both within the main service contract and JV Co structure. The county council also needs to ensure that its position in these respects is not compromised should it need to respond to future requirements.

Legal and commercial Issues

19.20 The county council has a wide range of education powers which are relevant to this proposal including:
(i)   the Education Act 1996, ss 13,13A, 14 and Pt V and the Education Act 1997 generally;
(ii) the School Standards and Framework Act 1998, ss 45–50 and generally; and
(iii) the Education Act 2002, particularly Pts 1, 2 and 3.

However, it is important to consider certain specific matters carefully in relation to the constituent elements of both the contract and corporate structure of the partnership.

19.21 Regard has to be paid to, and an audit undertaken of, all of the county council's education powers and also the powers of governing bodies. Consideration also needs to be given to the *Wednesbury* principles[1], the fiduciary duty of the county council (both as a local authority and as an LEA), the powers contained in the Local Government Acts 1999 and 2000 (the best value duty and the 'well-being' powers), the Local Government and Housing Act 1989 (Pt V), and the Local Authorities (Companies) Order 1995[2], and also the Local Authorities (Capital Finance) Regulations 1997[3].

1   For more detail on *Wednesbury* unreasonableness, see para **10.25**.
2   SI 1995/849.
3   SI 1997/319.

19.22 The corporate structure will need to be flexible enough to adapt and fulfil the county council's proposals, not only to deliver the services within the county council's area but to be able to trade outside its geographical boundary. There are important issues here in terms of the selection of vires (statutory powers) and in terms of the authority being able to trade outside its area. A decision needs to be made as to whether the county council will be exercising powers to trade outside the administrative area, or whether that will be left to the JV Co to decide. Consideration therefore needs to be given to the Local Authorities (Goods and Services) Act 1970, and policy guidelines which have been set out for local authorities to consider before they trade outside their areas.

19.23 The county council, as a minority shareholder within JV Co, will wish to consider the inclusion within the corporate structure of 'a golden share' or similar mechanism and certainly minority protection rights, to give the county council a right of veto, or at least weighted voting rights, on certain policy/future service delivery priorities. A shareholders' agreement and a memorandum and articles of association of JV Co will need to reflect entrenched minority protection provisions. At the same time it must not create 'dominant influence' or trigger the provisions of the Local Authorities Companies Order, ie create a regulated company, but at the same time provide sufficient flexibility for JV Co to be successful and commercially viable and attractive to the private sector partner. This is a difficult balance to achieve and great care needs to be taken in the structuring of the proposal as well as in the drafting of the memorandum and articles of association, the shareholders' agreement, and related documentation.

Power to form JV Co

19.24   Subject to certain processes and steps being undertaken, and establishing the necessary linkage to the county council's community strategy, the power that could be used to form JV Co are those contained within the Local Government Act 2000, s 2. That, in summary, would be in relation to the promotion and improvement of both the economic and social well-being of the county council's area. The *Wednesbury* standards of decision-making/reasonableness referred to above would continue to apply, both as to the exercise of the power and other powers quoted below.

Acquisition of shares in JV Co

19.25   A separate analysis is required to condsider the power that should be relied upon but generally, subject to certain processes being put in place, the 'well-being' power contained in the Local Government Act 2000, s 2 is a principal power which can be primarily considered. In certain cases there may be additional powers, depending on the specific services being transferred.

The power to enter into the contract

19.26   There are various powers upon which the county council can rely for these purposes, including the Local Government (Contracts) Act 1997, s 1 and possibly the Local Government Act 1972, s 111, but a careful review of other powers is necessary prior to the exercise of this particular provision and, in addition, the powers of governing bodies of schools to contract with the JV Co for the provision of supplies and services falling within their delegated and devolved budgets.

Power for JV Co to trade outside the area

19.27   Consideration should here be given to the provisions of the Local Authorities (Goods and Services) Act 1970, and also the Local Government Act 2000, s 2(5), which relates to the possibility of trading outside a local authority's area.

19.28   There are particular considerations relating to a local authority's power to trade outside its area, for example vires, the question of whether the business unit has 'surplus capacity' and also the real objectives of the partnership. For certain services, therefore, this is probably an issue which is best dealt with in the drafting of the memorandum and articles of association of JV Co. The JV Co can therefore, as a normal commercial issue, consider whether and when it is likely to want to trade outside the council's area, particularly in the early years of the partnership.

Powers for schools to participate in JV Co

19.29   It is probably not appropriate for the governing body of a school to consider spending any part of its delegated budget on making a specific investment in such a venture. At this stage it is uncertain as to whether there is a clear express power for that purpose. It is not a matter which needs to be considered so far as it relates to the structures for the partnership. It is a matter for the governing body of a particular school to take advice on. However, providing that partnership structures are set out (eg the Partnership Board) and stakeholder liaison is provided for within the both the contract and the corporate structure, individual schools should have sufficient means to exercise both influence and consultation as customers and as 'clients' of the new venture.

Powers to form a trust

19.30   Consideration could be given to the setting up of a trust to receive an 'endowment' derived from an element of profit, perhaps referred to as 'super-profit' prior to dividend distribution, or perhaps a provision in the main service contract to direct a financial endowment into the trust for the benefit of the schools within the area of county council X.

19.31   The trust does not need to be the centrepiece of the proposed partnership, but could be attractive to certain schools in terms of ensuring that a proportion of profits is 'ploughed back' to the benefit of education in the area of county council X.

19.32   The 'well-being' powers could also be used to form the trust, subject to similar issues being considered and having regard to its community strategy, and subject to the objects and structure of the trust being properly framed and related to its educational and statutory objectives. Alternatively. JV Co could provide for a trust within the shareholders' agreement, so as to create the contractual obligation at that stage.

Delegation of functions

19.33   Delegation of functions needs to be considered both in the context of the Deregulation Contracting Out Act 1994, Pt II but also in relation to the Contracting Out (Local Education Authority Functions) (England) Order 2002[1]. This should not be a risk issue or problematic, as the 2002 order has provided for the delegation of a range of functions to private sector partners and therefore an order under the 1994 Act should not be needed in most cases. However, the individual service elements being transferred within the partnership need to be reviewed on a case-by-case basis before deciding whether the order applies. If it does not, the use of other powers could be considered, possibly an order under the 1994 Act. For example, if related services at the corporate centre of the county council are also to be transferred, which do not come within the 2002 order and there is no other order delegating the function, the 1994 Act may still be relevant.

1   SI 2002/928.

Human rights legislation

19.34   Human rights legislation needs to be monitored and kept continuously under review as the public/private partnership evolves through the procurement process, the setting up of the contract in terms of delivery of functions, and the passing of obligations from county council X to JV Co. The county council will expect, as a minimum, that JV Co indemnifies them and agrees to take all reasonable steps to assist county council X to comply with its obligations under the Human Rights Act 1998. Recent decisions in the *Leonard Cheshire* case[1] and the *Partnerships in Care* case[2] highlight the need for careful consideration. The definition of 'public authority' for the purposes of the Human Rights Act 1998 continues to evolve with each case before the courts, and particular note should be taken of the Court of Appeal's comments in the *Leonard Cheshire* case that local authorities should consider including in their service contracts provision to safeguard individuals' rights under the Act.

1   *R (Heather) v Leonard Cheshire Foundation* (2002) Times, 8 April.
2   *R (A) v Partnerships in Care Ltd* [2002] EWHC 529 (Admin), [2002] 1 WLR 2610.

TUPE and pensions

19.35   As with any other outsourcing/co-sourcing/PPP, the Acquired Rights Directive will apply to certain employees who are transferred. County council X has considered whether it would enter into a 'co-sourcing' of staff as opposed to a full TUPE transfer. In this case, it had decided that it would be a full TUPE transfer and the appropriate consultations undertaken both during the procurement process, in relation to the contract and in terms of protecting certain rights post-transfer.

1   Directive 77/187 implemented by the Transfer of Undertaking (Protection of Employment) Regulations 1981 (TUPE).

Pensions

19.36   The service contract will provide that JV Co will obtain 'admitted body' status with the Local Government Pension Scheme, but also in this case will have to consider achieving 'function provider' status for those members of staff who are technically 'teachers' under the Teachers' Superannuation Scheme. This is a highly specialist area and is an additional dimension to the normal pension provisions which need to be accommodated within both the contract and consultative requirements.

Procurement

19.37   The partnership was procured by using the negotiated procedure following a full OJEC notice, initial ITN (although an ISOP could have been used earlier), moving to a full ITN, a BAFO stage, with a selection of preferred and possibly reserved bidders, and negotiations with the preferred bidder to contract close.

19.38   It is important to consider at an earlier stage the extent of services involved and the distinction between the core services which will form part of the partnership, and the support services corporately managed within the county council (ie ICT, financial property and other central services and support). This is important both at the OJEC stage in order that the services are properly specified and throughout the procurement process to contract close.

Standardisation of contracts

19.39 The contract is based on public/private partnership principles and there are analogous provisions dealing with the transfer of risk, payment mechanism, output specifications, relief and compensation events, change of law and risk management. However, the emerging form of education partnerships do not fit entirely within the PFI contract guidance. The definition of services is materially different, and the payment mechanism provisions have to be constructed around the requirements to achieve outputs, and also the performance measures set out in the Education Development Plan, to secure best value, and may be materially different depending upon the range of services which are comprised in the partnership. If a wide range of LEA back office functions are to be transferred, as opposed to only the schools support services, the contractual provision will vary and, at times, require original drafting and structuring well outside standard guidance.

19.40 The JV Co structures are relatively innovative and need considerable care in terms of the selection of vires and also in the drafting of the memorandum and articles of association, the shareholders' agreement, as matters of company law, public law and local government finance law are inextricably linked. This is probably so to a greater extent than would normally be the case in a standard PFI structure. Therefore, to that extent the guidance issued by TTF and OGC will not necessarily be applicable at material stages.

CHAPTER 20

Case study: e-government

Rosemary Mulley

BACKGROUND AND CONTEXT

What are e-government projects?

20.01   E-government projects in local authorities are initiated for two main reasons:
(i)   to meet the government's target for the delivery of services electronically by local authorities, in compliance with the requirements of Best Value Performance Indicator 157. The current target is for 100% of services capable of electronic delivery to be available to the public in such a form by 2005. 'Electronic' delivery is not confined to websites and email contact with users of services: delivery of services using the telephone counts towards achievement of the target, provided the telephone service is software-enabled;
(ii)   as a means of securing continuous improvements in accordance with the council's general best value obligations.

20.02   In order to qualify for e-government funding, the Local Government Online Initiative (LGOL) required all local authorities to produce implementing electronic government (IEG) statements setting out how they planned to achieve the government targets and, in particular defining:
—   locally defined service targets;
—   corporate measures within the council to support implementation.

Further guidance being produced by the Office of the Deputy Prime Minister will provide guidance on IEG statements for the next round of LGOL funding.

E-government and business change

20.03   Information communications and technology (ICT) has been used in private industry for many years now to reduce operating costs, improve services to customers, provide new services, and find new ways of providing existing services in ways which are convenient to customers.

20.04   Private industry has learned the lesson that computer systems on their own will not achieve any of these benefits. It is only the change to services that is enabled by ICT and information systems, that will bring about benefits. When the Public Accounts Committee in 2000 reviewed IT projects in the public sector it adopted this conclusion. The committee strongly recommended that the public sector should provide for the management of change and organisational development within all ICT projects and that, furthermore, every large IT project should be treated as first and foremost a business change project, not merely a technical project. These recommendations were reflected in the McCartney report *Successful IT Projects* in 2001 and are further being developed in OGC guidance. The purpose of every e-government project is to bring about improvement in services and therefore, by definition, to change the organisation of the local council. It is vitally important to ensure not only that projects are conceived and run primarily as projects to implement organisational and service changes, but that the procurement is conducted as a procurement of organisational change. Furthermore, the contract with the private sector partner must adequately address requirements for process redesign and organisational development and clearly allocate contractual responsibility.

The main types of e-government projects

20.05   The main types of e-government procurement projects can be characterised as follows:
(i)   infrastructure implementation, such as broadband access and data networks;
(ii)   website development and hosting, together with the eventual implementation of transactional websites and integration of back-end and front-end systems;
(iii) procurement of the implementation of a major software package, such as Enterprise Resource Planning (ERP), Customer Relationship Management (CRM), or Knowledge Management applications, together with associated business process re-engineering services;
(iv)   geographic information systems and digital mapping applications to support conveyancing, planning and consultation processes;
(v)   implementation of alternative digital channels, such as digital television, mobile computing and public internet kiosks.

20.06   Each type of project and each type procurement is different and raises different issues. In order to illustrate the general principles, this case study considers one of the most popular e-government projects: the implementation of a CRM system. Figure 1 illustrates the contractual relationships in a prime contracting CRM systems integration.

Figure 1 Contractual relationships between council, prime contractor and subcontractors

20.07

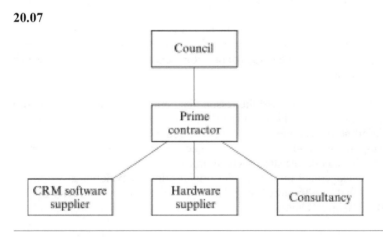

20.08 Councils are often content to contract separately for each of the components of the CRM implementation, although a prime contract relationship is recommended as effecting a greater transfer of commercial and technical integration risks.

CUSTOMER RELATIONSHIP MANAGEMENT (CRM) SYSTEMS

Importance of CRM to e-government

20.09 CRM Pathfinder implementations have been funded as part of the LGOL initiative and their use is encouraged by the Office of the Deputy Prime Minister to ensure continuity and effective management of all contacts with council customers.

20.10 Many electronic contacts are made through websites, but not all. In addition to websites, many councils are creating contact centres, telephone points of contact for users of council services, walk-in centres and internet kiosks in public places as a means of delivering services electronically. These front-line points of contact can concentrate public contact and release resources within 'line of business' departments.

20.11 CRM software is used to make this front-line contact more effective. CRM software can keep track of customers and their enquiries, ensuring continuity of responses and that all necessary follow-up takes place. Implemented correctly, a CRM system will manage contacts across all contact channels, through the internet and telephone contact centres. However, they are most commonly installed in order to manage telephone contact centre enquiries.

A typical CRM procurement

20.12 A CRM procurement will typically consist not only of a CRM software product, but of services to assist with the configuration of the software, the 're-engineering' of processes to make use of the new software, training and organisational development in order to realise the benefits of successful implementation.

Configuration of CRM software packages

20.13 CRM software products have been used in the private sector for many years, and the products now on the market have been designed to embody best current practice in the private sector. Experience has shown that extensive modification of such software products is rarely cost-effective: it greatly increases costs and the risk of time and cost overruns. The most advantageous approach is, as far as is feasible, to change organisational processes to accord with the best practice embodied in the software product.

20.14 Software suppliers recognise that there is no 'one size' that fits all. Well designed products are 'configurable': that is to say, they are capable of being set up so as to provide for each individual implementation. It is this process of setting up which is called configuration. Configuration does not involve changing or adding to the software programming: configuration is one of the inherent functions of the software.

Local government and site-specific CRM configurations

20.15 IT services companies provide consultancy to configure systems to meet the needs of specific clients. Such consultancies can be part of the software supplier's organisation or, perhaps more often, a consultancy company which is an implementation 'partner' of the software supplier—that is to say, there is a more or less formal, more or less exclusive, arrangement between the two companies to work together on customer projects.

20.16 Experience of implementing and configuring CRM software enables consultancies to create standard configurations which reflect the needs and preferences of particular industries. Many CRM suppliers and their consultancy partners are now developing configurations for local government use.

Implementation consultancy

20.17 CRM consultants work with clients to design new business processes to take the best possible advantage of the CRM software. They will also advise on benefits realisation. A typical consultancy engagement will cover the following:
— analysis of existing processes and documenting them in the form of process maps;
— analysis and mapping of desired processes;
— detailed design of new processes;
— specification of necessary configuration;
— training council staff to carry out configuration;
— supervising configuration;
— development of new procedural manuals;
— strategic advice on organisational development;
— training and communications.
Training users in the CRM software product itself is usually provided by the CRM software supplier.

CRM pathfinders

20.18 Some first-wave LGOL Pathfinders have involved the creation of CRM solutions and in particular of solutions which are capable of being reused by other councils. An example is London Borough of Brent's CRM project, which was procured as a framework agreement on preferential commercial terms, taking into account the public sector investment in the creation of processes and configurations. Other councils may call off the following against the framework:
— a licence to use the CRM software product;
— a licence to use a local government-specific configuration of the software;
— consultancy, against a prescribed schedule of rates, to implement CRM.

COMMERCIAL CONSIDERATIONS

Specification of the system and services

20.19 Specifications of CRM systems are crucially important contractual documents. They should ideally receive as much legal and specialist procurement scrutiny as contract terms and conditions. Although interpreting system specifications requires specialist skills, procurement and legal colleagues can be greatly assisted in this task by working closely with those with technical knowledge of the business and technical requirements. Such team-working will enable a clear written expression of the scope of the procurement, which should reduce the risk of debilitating post-contract conflicts.

20.20 Specifications should, as far as possible, be defined in terms of business outcomes rather than by reference to specific system functions. A prescriptive 'input-based' technical description will limit the ability of the private sector to respond to the procurement: there is often more than one approach to meeting a particular business requirement and the different CRM products on the market reflect this fact. An overly prescriptive system requirement will render certain products automatically non-compliant with the specification and potentially exclude them from the competition.

20.21 It is often said that output-based specifications should not be 'too detailed' as this will constrain the ability of the private sector to respond to the procurement. If the specified outputs are genuinely of business requirements, and not of system functions, this is less likely to be the case. Within reason, more detail in output-based specifications will assist with a clear definition of contractual scope. It is recommended that output-based specifications may be specified at a very high level at the invitation to negotiate stage, but that negotiations should lead to a relatively detailed contractual specification.

Post-contract requirements specification

20.22 The continuation of requirements definition post-contract should be treated with great caution and should not be used as an opportunity to increase the overall scope of the development.

Responsibility for system integration

20.23 Councils must decide whether they wish to procure the individual elements of a CRM solution separately, or whether they wish to procure an integrated solution from a single supplier. Most councils will need, as well as software and consultancy, additional server and network capacity to run a new CRM system. The consultants to the project will normally advise about sizing and configuration of hardware components. Councils may take responsibility themselves for purchasing and implementing such hardware and interfaces to existing systems, or alternatively procure the whole system from a single supplier as prime contractor.

20.24   Procuring a prime contract relationship can transfer the following risks:
— overall system design;
— capacity;
— integration.

The prime contractor will, however, normally wish to charge a risk premium, typically of about 15 per cent. The overall cost will therefore be higher than procuring the elements of the system separately.

Procuring the system as a service

20.25   An integrated CRM system can be purchased in return for a capital sum, which will typically be paid on successful completion of acceptance tests. Alternatively, the system can be purchased in the form of a managed service. Monthly or quarterly revenue payments are made against an output based specification and service level agreement, for a typical duration of between five and seven years. It is usual to reserve the right to acquire on expiry the assets used to provide the service for their residual value. When such an arrangement is made, careful attention must be paid to the treatment of assets on expiry in order to ensure compliance with Local Authorities (Capital Finance) Regulations 1997[1].

1   SI 1997/319.

Procuring benefits realisation

20.26   CRM consultants will provide advice on how to ensure that the benefits anticipated in the business case for the system are realised. Some projects in which the system is purchased as a managed service take this a step further, by agreeing a risk/reward arrangement with their prime contractor. The output-based specification will set out not only business outcomes in the form of new processes, but will also specify business benefits. The payment mechanism will typically provide for additional payments to the contractor for over-achievement on benefits realisation targets. There may be service credits for under-achievement, but contractors are reluctant to share a great deal of risk in this regard. That is because, although the contractor can advise on the necessary organisational development measures to realise financial benefits (typically through redeployment of staff), the contractor has relatively little control over the thoroughness of their implementation, which is to a very large extent in the hands of the council.

Change control

20.27   Four main areas of change need to be controlled in a CRM procurement:
(i)   changes to contract terms and conditions that may be agreed at any time. These may have no impact on timescales or cost;
(ii)   changes to the specification that are agreed in the course of the project. These are likely to impact on the implementation date for the system and are also likely to have an impact on development costs and ongoing running costs;
(iii)   changes to the specification of the new CRM system once it is up and running. Such changes are likely to require initial investment and have an impact on ongoing running costs;

(iv) provisions allowing additional or optional services to be called off during the course of the contract, for instance training or assistance with the preparation of a business case for enhancements of the system. Such services may have a cost but no impact on the system itself.

Change control provisions need to be able to accommodate, and where necessary distinguish between, all four.

Visibility of development process

20.28   Councils can protect themselves against some of the risks by including step-in rights in their contracts. These enable the client to assume direct control of the whole or any part of a project if the contractor fails to meet any specified objective, for example to achieve important development milestones. These rights normally provide for clients to recover their step-in costs.

20.29   To support the operation of step-in rights, councils should reserve the right to inspect work in progress and the contractor's project plans to ensure visibility of any problems in the development process at an early enough stage to take effective action.

Framework agreements

20.30   These are agreements which contain the terms on which contractors will provide services which clients may call off in the future. They are particularly useful for joint CRM procurements, to make some types of hardware, software or consultancy services available to purchasing authorities in a consortium.

LEGAL CONSIDERATIONS

Intellectual property

20.31   Councils must procure CRM software licences which are sufficiently extensive to enable use of the software by all of those who may need to do so. The following should be considered:
(i)   council departments;
(ii)   third party contractors, such as temps, other consultants or outsourcing service providers;
(iii) members of the public.

20.32   Ownership of configurations can be the subject of controversy. A council may have contributed substantially to the development of a local government-specific configuration and as a result may expect to own the copyright in that configuration. This view however does not take into account the fact that the consultants which co-developed the configuration are also likely to have contributed substantial background material in which it owns the copyright. Consultants are therefore unlikely to agree to a transfer of copyright outright. A reasonable compromise is to negotiate a discount on the implementation price, or to share the proceeds of commercial exploitation of the standard configuration.

20.33 Standard configurations, even local government-specific standard configurations, will almost certainly require further configuration to meet the needs of an individual customer organisation. The ownership of such configurations is also subject to background rights of the consultants assisting with the configuration, and it is unlikely that consultants will agree to a transfer of copyright to the council. The commercial reasoning behind this is that the cost of configuration is relatively low because of the consultant's ability to use background material.

20.34 The council will therefore require a licence to use and change the configurations. This licence should be extensive, and not subject to the restrictions of the proprietary CRM software product. The licence in the council-specific aspect of the configuration should be perpetual and irrevocable.

Ownership of interfaces and software modifications

20.35 Interfaces to existing systems are likely to be developed as part of a CRM implementation. Ownership of such interfaces, and of any modifications to the CRM software itself, should be agreed with the contractor. Similar arguments will apply as for configurations, and although an outright assignment of copyright from the contractor may not be reaslistic in commercial terms, the proceeds of any commercial exploitation may be shared.

Legal status of process maps and configurations

20.36 Process maps are valuable materials which are used to inform the configuration of the CRM software and organisational development measures to make use of the CRM software. There seems little doubt that process maps are capable of copyright protection in their own right. If it is correct that configurations are 'software', then process maps should correctly be characterised as documentation of the software.

20.37 A CRM configuration is not software in the traditional sense in which a computer program is described as 'software'. It can be characterised as 'data' rather than software, as it frequently consists of little more than the selection of options or input of parameters. However, it is likely that a particular set of options, parameters or both are capable of protection by copyright, subject to the normal rules that the subject matter of copyright must not be trivial and have the requisite degree of originality. They are also likely to be protected by database rights.

20.38 The conclusion is that it is advisable to ensure that licences to use software extend to the use of process maps and configurations. The suggested definition of 'software' below gives effect to this recommendation.

Technology refresh

20.39 A managed service procurement will need to assign contractual responsibility for the replacement of obsolete hardware and software licences during the contract period and for growth in capacity requirements.

Acceptance

20.40   In a CRM project, acceptance is a continuing process of review and approval of process maps and designs, training and implementation plans, configured software modules, migrated data and the eventual integrated CRM system, ready to use. Acceptance provisions should ensure that 'acceptance' of any deliverable by the council does not absolve the contractor of responsibility for meeting the contractual specifications.

Escrow

20.41   Escrow agreements protect customers against the risks of software suppliers becoming insolvent, or for some other reason ceasing to perform their contractual obligations to maintain software. A trusted third party (usually the National Computing Centre) will hold copies of source code on behalf of customers and subject to the terms of the licence, which will typically enable customers to use the source code to generate corrected or updated version of the executable software. CRM suppliers are often based in the United States, and may insist on using a US escrow depository and form of escrow agreement.

20.42   The extent to which CRM suppliers are willing or able to enter into substantial negotiations on their standard licence terms and conditions is limited. Warranties are often confined to compliance with the software supplier's published manuals and it can be difficult to obtain agreement to a warranty that the software will comply with the council's particular CRM specification.

20.43   The council may require its prime contractor to absorb the contractual risk of such non-compliance. On the basis that the prime contractor will also be unable to obtain a sufficiently extensive warranty from the software supplier, such an assumption of risk by a prime contractor will inevitably be associated with a financial premium.

Limitations on liability

20.44   Software suppliers often seek to limit their financial liability for non-compliance of their software products with their own published specifications to the fees paid under the software maintenance contract.

Data protection

20.45   CRM systems, by their very nature, involve members of the public and access by contact centre agents to personal information about callers. A fully integrated CRM system may allow agents to access other council databases, such as social services information, in order to provide a more responsive service. Such access means that issues are likely to arise concerning the Data Protection Act 1998 and the common law of confidence

20.46   The following principles of the Data Protection Act 1998 are particularly relevant to CRM, that:

(i)   personal data must be processed lawfully. Councils must ensure that they have the powers to use data for a purpose other than that for which it was originally obtained;

(ii)   personal data processed for any purpose cannot be kept (even in archive or back-up form) for longer than is necessary for that purpose. The Information Commissioner recommends a schedule of review and destruction of records to make a regular determination as to whether personal records continue to be needed;

(iii)   personal data must be kept secure. Security of data applies not only to the IT systems which process the data, but also to manual parts of the process. Both systems and people dealing with personal data must ensure that there is no unauthorised loss or processing of personal data;

(iv)   data subjects must be told (including applicants for benefits and grants) when decisions about them are being taken on the sole basis of an automatic process.

20.47   Councils should be aware that their statutory obligations as 'data controllers' cannot be transferred contractually. Contracts should ensure that contractors are obliged to take the necessary technical measures to ensure the council's compliance with the Data Protection Act 1998, and should also provide indemnities to the council for any failure to take such action.

Freedom of information

20.48   Freedom of information legislation has not yet been implemented in the United Kingdom, but for the time being it is advisable to provide that contractors will service requests for information to the council in accordance with the requirements of any eventual legislation.

Employment and TUPE

20.49   To the extent that a CRM project will almost certainly change people's roles and job descriptions, there is likely to be a human resources dimension to such projects and the council will need to ensure that all such changes are carried out in compliance with employment legislation and employees' terms and conditions of employment.

20.50   Contracting for a managed CRM service may involve the replacement of an existing system or systems with an external service which is being provided by the contractor. Such a situation can potentially bring about a transfer in TUPE terms and this must be considered at the earliest stages of the project to allow all necessary preparation and consultation.

MANAGING RISK TO ENSURE A SUCCESSFUL PROJECT

20.51   CRM projects are subject to the same risks of time and cost overruns as conventional engineering and construction projects. They are also subject to more specific risks, primarily concerned with difficulties of requirements definition, scope of the contractor's obligations and the management of business change. The Public Accounts Committee in 2000 observed that ICT systems development and integration projects are inherently high risk and identified several reasons for the problems that have beset many large-scale public sector IT procurements and projects. (It should be noted that the private sector has experienced many of the same problems, which however have attracted lower profiles, giving what is probably an unfair perception of the relative success rate of public sector projects.)

20.52   Local authorities have historically been required to make relatively few large, complex procurements of ICT and it is recommended that OGC best practice guidance on risk management for ICT projects[1] is consulted in order to benefit from the experience of central government. Such guidance is not mandatory for local authorities, but provides extremely useful advice on best practice on how to avoid and manage the undoubted risks of ICT projects.

1   Available at www.orc.gov.uk.

20.53   E-government projects are in themselves no more or less risky than any other ICT projects. In general, projects to implement infrastructure consist largely of engineering challenges, which should not present high risks in the implementation of tried and tested technology. Projects which have as their only objective the externalisation of ICT services are time-consuming to implement, but are not in general high risk when the definition of the service to be transferred is known at the outset with a reasonable degree of certainty. Projects for the development or integration of new applications systems are the highest risk e-government projects, principally because of the difficulties of defining requirements in sufficient detail to fix the scope of the project, without constraining the technical solutions to be procured from suppliers.

20.54   CRM projects have high-risk characteristics as they involve organisational change. However, this risk can be mitigated by avoiding modification of the CRM software, making use of standard configurations of the software product and documenting clearly in specifications of consultancy services the respective change management responsibilities of the council and the contractor.

STANDARDISATION OF CONTRACTS

20.55   Model forms of IT contract for conventional supply of systems or of services are available from the OGC. These have wide acceptance among IT suppliers and are suitable for relatively simple software procurements. OGC is expected to make more complex IT contract precedents available shortly. None of these will be specific to CRM, but complex systems integration and managed service precedents are expected to be made available. The OGC guidance on the Standardisation of PFI Contracts—Information Technology[1] provides general guidance and some individual clauses, but not a precedent IT services contract. For a relatively complex procurement of a managed service, the OGC model form of contract for services can be used, augmented as necessary with adapted PFI terms and conditions.

1   Published by Butterworths.

CRM draft clauses

20.56   The following are draft clauses which address the specific needs of a CRM system procurement in respect of ownership of intellectual property, licensing and data protection.

Definitions

'CRM software' means the software which is listed as such in Schedule [   ] to be supplied for use in the provision of the services whether such software is owned by the Contractor or by a third party;

'Deposited software' means the software specified in Schedule [   ] as being subject to Source Code escrow arrangements;

'Object code' means machine code generated by the compiling or assembling of source code;

'Software' means computer programs, configurations and interfaces, any preparatory materials relating to the foregoing (including user requirements, functional specifications, programming specifications, ideas, principles, programming languages, process maps and algorithms to the extent recorded), and any manuals or other documentation relating to any of the foregoing;

'Source code' means software in eye-readable form and in such form that it can be compiled or interpreted into equivalent object code together with all technical information and documentation necessary for the use, reproduction, modification and enhancement of such software.

Licences to use software

1.1   The Council shall not acquire title to the Intellectual Property Rights in any CRM Software.

1.2   The Contractor shall by the Commencement Date either:

1.2.1   grant to the Council a sub-licence to Use the CRM Software; or

1.2.2   if the Contractor is unable to procure the right to grant the sub-licence referred to in Clause 1.2.1, the Contractor shall have procured that [the software supplier] will within seven days after the Commencement Date grant to the Council a licence to Use the CRM Software.

1.3   Any sub-licence to Use the CRM Software granted pursuant to Clause 1.2.1, or licence procured by the Contractor pursuant to Clause 1.2.2, shall:

1.3.1   grant upon delivery of the CRM Software, a non-exclusive licence to Use the CRM Software to the extent required for the proper installation, testing, trialing and conduct of the relevant Acceptance Procedures; and

1.3.2 grant to the Council [and any others who will have direct access to use the system, for example members of the public. The detailed definition of such access may be complex and may best be dealt with in a schedule] upon the successful Acceptance of the System a licence to Use, reproduce, modify, adapt and enhance the CRM Software in the form set out at [   ] with a non-exclusive licence to reproduce any Documentation provided in machine-readable format relating to the same;

1.3.3   include the rights of the Council under Clauses 1.4 and 1.5; and

1.3.4   without prejudice to the foregoing provisions of this Clause, the Contractor shall use all reasonable endeavours to ensure that any third party licences procured pursuant to Clause 1.2.2 are transferable with this Agreement without the further consent of the relevant third party licensor. All third party licences in respect of which the Contractor is unable to obtain such rights shall be expressly listed as requiring the consent of the third party licensor.

In all other respects any sub-licence or licence shall be subject to any express licence terms specified as pertaining to the relevant item of CRM Software set out in the form of licence at Schedule [   ]. All licensing charges relating to the Use of the CRM Software shall be included in the Charges payable by the Council to the Contractor under this Agreement.

1.4   The Council shall be entitled to engage a third party to Use the CRM Software subject to and in accordance with this Agreement on behalf of the Council provided that such third party shall have entered into a confidentiality undertaking in accordance with the terms of this Agreement.

1.5   The Council shall be entitled to copy the CRM Software in order to create an archival copy and a back-up copy of the same. When copying the CRM Software the Council shall include the original machine readable copyright notice and, when copying the Software onto tangible media, affix a label to the media identifying the Software and stating: 'This medium contains an authorised copy of copyrighted software which is the property of (*the Contractor or the CRM Software owner).'

1.6   The Contractor shall place the Source Code of the Deposited Software in escrow with the National Computing Centre ('NCC') on the basis of the appropriate standard agreement or on such other terms as the Council, the Contractor and the NCC shall agree such escrow agreement to be entered into within thirty (30) days of the date of this Agreement.

1.7   The Contractor and the Council hereby agree that both parties shall each pay their respective fees as set out in any escrow agreement entered into pursuant to Clause 1.8.

1.8   The Contractor hereby grants to the Council a perpetual, non-transferable and non-exclusive licence to Use, reproduce, modify, adapt and enhance (and to authorise a third party to Use, reproduce, modify, adapt and enhance) the Source Code and Object Code versions of the Deposited Software. However, the foregoing licence shall only become effective if the Council becomes entitled to obtain access to the Source Code version of the Deposited Software pursuant to the source code escrow agreement referred to in Clause 1.6 and the licence shall be subject to any restrictions contained herein in respect of the object code version of the Deposited Software provided that such restrictions shall not detract from the rights granted hereunder.

2   Intellectual Property Rights

2.1   The Council shall not acquire title to the Intellectual Property Rights in the CRM Software, the Services or any Deliverables which are supplied hereunder.

2.2   In relation to any items of CRM Software which are supplied hereunder the Contractor hereby grants, or shall procure that the owner of the Intellectual Property Rights in the CRM Software grants, to the Council:

2.2.1   upon delivery of the CRM Software, a non-exclusive licence to the Council [and any others who will have direct access to use the system, for example members of the public. The detailed definition of such access may be complex and may best be dealt with in a schedule] to Use the CRM Software to the extent required for the proper installation, testing, trialling and conduct of the relevant Acceptance Procedures; and

2.2.2   upon the successful acceptance of the CRM Software, a non-exclusive licence to Use, reproduce, modify, adapt and enhance the CRM Software together, with a non-exclusive licence to reproduce, modify, adapt and enhance any Deliverables relating to the same. Such licence shall be perpetual and irrevocable.

2.3   Upon the successful acceptance of the CRM Software in accordance with the provisions of Clause 6, the Contractor shall supply the Council with a copy of the Source Code of the CRM Software and any Deliverables relating to the same.

2.4   In relation to any Deliverables that have not been licensed to the Council pursuant to Clause 2.2 the Contractor hereby grants, or shall procure that the owner of the Intellectual Property Rights in such Deliverable grants, to the Council:

2.4.1   upon delivery of the Deliverable, a non-exclusive licence to use and reproduce the Deliverable to the extent required for the proper conduct of the relevant Acceptance Procedures; and

2.4.2   upon the successful Acceptance of the Deliverable, a non-exclusive, perpetual and irrevocable licence to use, reproduce, modify, adapt and enhance the Deliverable in the furtherance of the Council's normal business.

2.5   The Council shall be entitled to engage a third party to use, reproduce, modify, adapt and enhance any Deliverable subject to and in accordance with this Agreement on behalf of the Council provided that such third party shall have entered into a confidentiality undertaking in accordance with the terms of this Agreement.

3   Protection of Personal Data

3.1   Each party shall comply with its respective obligations under the provisions of the Data Protection Act 1984 and the Data Protection Act 1998.

3.2   Where the Contractor or any of its sub-contractors processes personal data as a data processor on behalf of the Council in accordance with the Agreement, the Contractor shall, and shall procure its sub-contractors to:

3.2.1   act only on instructions from the Council as data controller; and

3.2.2   comply with the Council's instructions in relation to the processing of personal data as such instructions are given and varied from time to time by the Council; and

3.2.3 at all times take all appropriate technical and organisational measures against unauthorised or unlawful processing of personal data and against accidental loss or destruction of, or damage to, personal data.

3.3 The Council may from time to time serve on the Contractor an information notice requiring the Contractor, within such time and in such form as is specified in the information notice, to furnish to the Council such information as the Council may reasonably require relating to:

3.3.1 compliance by the Contractor or by its sub-contractors with the Contractor's obligations to the Council under this Agreement in connection with the processing of personal data; and/or

3.3.2 the rights of data subjects, including but not limited to subject access rights.

CHAPTER 21

Case study: district energy

David Lyon

BACKGROUND AND CONTEXT

What is a district energy scheme?

21.01   There is no legal or statutory definition of a district energy scheme. However, all such schemes (also known as district heating, community heating or community energy schemes) share a number of characteristics. They involve the construction and operation of a plant to provide heat, and sometimes electricity, to specified buildings in the vicinity. Most commonly, these buildings will be homes owned by a local authority or social landlord, but they can also include buildings such as schools, hospitals and leisure facilities. The comments in this case study assume that a housing-based scheme is involved, except where otherwise stated.

21.02   The district energy scheme will normally comprise an electricity generation plant, the heat from which is converted into hot water for supply to the buildings linked to the scheme. The electricity is then sold into the local distribution network or, sometimes, directly to the occupants of the building. Some useful additional guidance as to the meaning of a district energy scheme is provided by the Energy Saving Trust Community Energy Programme as follows:

> 'Community energy schemes serve more than one dwelling or building, and can supply a single tower block, or a range of customers across a city. They can be served by conventional fuelled boilers, CHP, renewables-fired boilers or a combination of these sources.'

21.03   A recently completed example is the 'pathfinder' PFI scheme at the Barkantine Estate in Tower Hamlets, East London. In that scheme, a three megawatt gas-fired electricity generation plant produces electricity for sale and consumption at some 200 homes, as well as a local school and leisure centre. The waste heat from this generator is converted into hot water, then carried by insulated pipes under the adjacent streets to the buildings served by the system. Inside the buildings, the hot water is supplied to heat exchangers which make it useable in the buildings, supplying all the needs of the occupiers for hot water and heating.

Parties to a district energy scheme

21.04   There are two main parties to any district energy scheme. The first is the promoter of the scheme, which is usually a local authority or social landlord ('the authority'). The second is the energy company ('the supplier') which is responsible for the construction and operation of the scheme and for the making available of heat and hot water (and, where applicable, electricity) to the occupants of the relevant buildings. This model, almost always involving a partnership between the public and private sectors, reflects the fact that the authority is unlikely to have experience of constructing and operating such schemes itself and therefore needs to involve specialist external expertise.

21.05   The supplier will normally form a separate energy supply company ('ESCO'), specifically for the purposes of constructing and operating a particular scheme. The ESCO will, however, need to have a close relationship with the authority. For example, a local authority will have statutory obligations relating to the residents of its housing stock and will be anxious to ensure that the scheme is managed in such a way that these obligations are carried out and the interests of residents protected. The authority may have certain controls over the ESCO in order to address these issues, such as the right to attend ESCO board meetings and to impose restrictions on the ESCO carrying out any other activities.

21.06   There are a number of other interested parties in a district energy scheme. Where the scheme involves providing energy to homes, the residents of those homes would be an important consideration. The authority and the ESCO will wish to ensure that the residents are consulted as fully and as quickly as possible, to ensure the maximum degree of support for the scheme. The contract documentation will usually provide for a forum for regular consultation with residents (often through a residents' association) throughout the life of the contract and mechanisms such as a helpdesk facility and codes of practice governing the relationship between the supplier and the residents. Other consumers of energy to be provided by a particular scheme (such as the operators of schools, hospitals etc) will also have an important ongoing role. The other main parties will usually be sub-contractors responsible for particular aspects of the scheme. In the great majority of cases, the supplier will sub-contract the design, construction and commissioning of the plant and, sometimes, there will also be a separate facilities management company, responsible for ongoing operation and maintenance. More detail as to the interrelationships between the various parties involved and the contractual documentation reflecting these is set out at paras **21.09–21.17**.

The advantages of district energy

The advantages for the authority

21.07   The advantages for the authority over traditional heating technology can be summarised as follows:
(1)   affordable heat: the underlying purpose for the authority in promoting a district energy scheme will be to secure the provision of reliable, affordable heat. A district energy scheme should offer substantially greater fuel efficiency compared with individual heating systems within housing units and may also generate revenue from electricity sales, which will further benefit the economics of the scheme;
(2)   predictable cost and value for money: the ESCO will agree to construct and commission the plant for a fixed price, subject to very limited exceptions which will be specified in the contract. In addition, the risks relating to the ongoing

operation and maintenance of the plant will be largely with the ESCO, which will be contractually obliged to provide the energy service to the previously agreed standard and at the previously agreed price. The ESCO will be subject to deductions from the payment it receives where the required standard is not met. These factors, together with the technical advantages of well-designed district energy schemes, should combine to ensure that the costs to the authority of the scheme are predictable and that better value for money is obtained. The latter issue will be particularly relevant to local authorities, which will be subject to the best value obligation described in paras **21.23–21.25**;

(3) environmental: the fuel efficiency gains which can be achieved from well-designed district energy plants significantly reduce CO_2 and other emissions and thereby make a contribution towards ensuring that the authority complies with its energy saving and environmental obligations;

(4) other benefits: a range of other benefits can also arise from district energy schemes. For example, more reliable heating sources can reduce damp and the maintenance costs associated with it and the replacement of individual heating systems by a district energy scheme can reduce noise levels and improve safety.

The advantages for the supplier

21.08 The ESCO will commonly be owned and financed by a private sector energy company. The energy company will wish to ensure that any proposed district energy scheme will allow it to make what it regards as an acceptable return on the capital employed in designing and constructing the scheme and on the operation and maintenance services it provides. The ESCO will create a financial model for the scheme, which will enable it to predict the cash flows and costs throughout the term of the contract and from which the internal rate of return ('IRR') is calculated. Once it has established that the IRR is acceptable to it, the advantage for the supplier is that, given that contracts for district energy schemes will commonly last for between 15 and 30 years, it can rely on receiving the IRR throughout that period, provided that it complies with its obligations under the contract. From the authority's viewpoint, it will wish to verify the IRR calculation to ensure that the charges being proposed by the supplier represent value for money.

THE CONTRACTUAL RELATIONSHIPS

The parties' objectives

21.09 As explained above, the authority will wish to ensure a secure and economic energy supply in the context of its wider social and political priorities. The supplier will wish to ensure an acceptable return on its investment and will look for the freedom to operate the scheme on a commercial and efficient basis, in order to maximise the chance of obtaining the desired return. The contractual documents which are negotiated and signed by the parties will need to address these potentially divergent interests. The diagram at para **21.38** represents a typical contract structure for district energy schemes.

The energy supply contract or concession agreement

21.10   This agreement will be entered into between the authority and the ESCO and will contain all the provisions relating to the construction, commissioning, operation and maintenance of the scheme. In summary, the ESCO will contract to provide an energy service to a given standard, for a given length of time and for a given price. The contract will give detailed legal effect to the commercial deal struck between the authority and the ESCO. A number of the major issues which most frequently arise in the negotiation of the concession agreement are discussed in paras **21.18–21.35**.

Heat agreements

21.11   As well as the contract between the authority and the ESCO, there will need to be a contractual relationship between the ESCO and the residents of the relevant buildings, to govern the terms upon which they receive and pay for heat produced by the scheme. Where a scheme provides heat to homes, the concession agreement will usually have annexed to it a standard form of heat agreement which will be entered into between the ESCO and each of the residents wishing to take the heat service. Unlike the supply of electricity, the supply of heat or hot water is not a regulated activity. Therefore, whilst the terms and conditions upon which electricity is supplied by an ESCO to residents are regulated by the ESCO's electricity supply licence, this regulatory framework does not apply to heat and hot water and therefore heat agreements are required to be prepared and entered into, although they would normally be in a fairly simple form. Normally, the authority would expect to have a right of approval of the form of heat agreement, to ensure the interests of residents are protected.

21.12   Where the scheme also involves the provision of electricity to residents, a separate electricity supply agreement will be required. The ESCO may not wish to be licensed as a supplier, so in that event the ESCO would procure supply through a third party licensed supplier. If the ESCO is the supply licensee, the supply of heat cannot be made a condition of the supply of electricity, as this would constitute a breach of its supply licence.

Codes of practice

21.13   The fact that the supply of heat and hot water is not a regulated activity means that the only legal protections available to consumers of heat and hot water are those applicable under the general law, in contrast to the position of electricity consumers who enjoy specific protections under the requirements placed on suppliers under the Electricity Act 1989 and the terms of their electricity supply licences. In order to protect the residents, and in addition to any right of approval over the forms of heat agreement themselves, the authority will wish to ensure as far as possible that the rights of the residents as against the ESCO, for example in relation to matters such as rights of entry and enforcement of payment, are consistent with those applicable to regulated industries, particularly given the essential nature of the provision of heat and hot water. Codes of practice will therefore usually address these issues, forming part of the individual heat and hot water agreements. Such codes of practice are already provided for under the regulatory regime for electricity supply, so it is sensible for the codes prepared for heat and hot water supply to follow this model as far as possible.

Other agreements

21.14   In the majority of district energy schemes, the design, construction and commissioning of the plant will be sub-contracted by the ESCO to a specialist construction contractor, by means of a construction sub-contract. There will sometimes also be a separate operation and maintenance contract, under which the operation and maintenance of the scheme is sub-contracted to a facilities management company. Neither of these sub-contracts will reduce or negate the ESCO's primary contractual responsibility for the scheme. Rather, they provide a means by which the ESCO can 'step down' certain specified responsibilities so that, for example, if there is a delay in the construction of the plant, any remedy which the authority has against the ESCO will be replicated by an equivalent remedy for the ESCO against the construction contractor under the construction sub-contract.

21.15   A lease or licence will be entered into between the authority and the ESCO. This gives the ESCO the right to occupy the land on which the plant is built, and also enables the ESCO to pass wires and pipes through land owned by the authority.

21.16   Other agreements to be entered into may include a guarantee of the ESCO's obligations and liabilities under the concession agreement by the ESCO's parent company. The thinking behind this requirement is generally that the ESCO is a specially formed vehicle with a very limited share capital and that it may not therefore have the resources to meet claims arising under the concession agreement. On occasions, the authority may also require direct agreements between itself and the sub-contractors, giving the authority the right to pursue the sub-contractors for any breaches of their sub-contract with the ESCO.

21.17   Because of their relatively small size compared to other infrastructure projects, district energy schemes are normally financed on the balance sheet of the supplier without the need for third party finance. In schemes where external funding is required, the appropriate financing documentation will also need to be entered into.

LEGAL AND COMMERCIAL ISSUES

21.18   As mentioned above[1], the concession agreement between the authority and the ESCO will reflect the commercial deal between the parties. Central to that commercial deal is how the risks involved in the project are identified and then apportioned between the parties and this will be a major driver of the drafting and negotiation of the contract. The general rule is that the party best placed to manage a particular risk should take it. The practical position, however, is usually more complicated. Regardless of who, in theory, might be in the best position to manage a particular risk, either party would be reluctant to accept a risk which is inconsistent with its expectations from the scheme. Prior to the commencement of contract negotiations, it is strongly recommended that the parties address together the identification of the major commercial risks involved in the project and how those risks are to be allocated. The production of a risk matrix is a useful tool in carrying out this exercise. This should at least make it clear to the parties where any major differences of principle exist and enable them to address these as quickly and efficiently as possible. Although any district energy scheme will throw up its own issues, some of those which most commonly arise in negotiations (and suggestions as to how they might be addressed) are set out below.

1   See para **21.10**.

Payment and security of supply

21.19   This underpins all the other issues set out below. In order to incentivise the ESCO to provide the agreed service to the agreed specification, the authority will wish to ensure that deductions from the payments made to the ESCO arise where the ESCO fails to comply with its obligations. In that way, the risk of sub-standard provision of the energy service is transferred from the authority to the ESCO. The extent of such deductions and the circumstances in which they arise will, of course, be a matter for negotiation. So will the circumstances in which the ESCO is excused from financial liability for poor performance. These exclusions will normally be strictly limited to circumstances which are either outside the control of either party (such as force majeure) or which arise through some action of the authority. Both these situations are dealt with in more detail below.

Procurement

21.20   Given the typical capital values of district energy schemes, the potential application of the European Procurement Directives should always be considered. The European Commission is currently putting forward proposals for the reform of the public procurement regime into a single consolidated Directive. At present, the complexity of the procurement regime is such that, depending on its precise nature and scope, a district energy scheme could be categorised as falling within the European Works Directive, the Utilities Directive or even the Services Directive.

21.21   This is important because of the increasing number of referrals to the European Commission and cases proceeding to the European Court of Justice challenging authorities which have committed what might be regarded as merely technical breaches of the Procurement Directives. Therefore, selecting the correct Directive under which to advertise and tender the contract is essential to avoid this risk. In addition, the choice of Directive will dictate whether the authority can safely use the negotiated procedure. This procedure is centred around a process of negotiation with contractors, based on the premise that the authority can demonstrate that it is unable to establish comparison as to price, value and scope of the project without negotiation with individual tenderers. The difficulty with the alternative, and more rigid, restrictive procedure is that this prohibits dialogue between the authority and tenderers outside the strict parameters of clarification queries. This lack of dialogue can stifle innovation and may well not be suitable for authorities wishing to tender on the basis of an output specification and seeking continuous improvement under best value.

Construction risks

21.22   Construction risk is a prime example of a risk that the authority would wish the ESCO to take; much of the advantage of outsourcing the provision of the district energy scheme would be lost if such risks were retained by the public sector. Even here, however, the solution is unlikely to be a simple as the ESCO taking all construction risks. For example, the ESCO is unlikely to be willing to accept all the risk relating to unforeseen ground conditions, bearing in mind the relevant land will previously have been occupied by the authority rather than the ESCO. The end result would normally be that there would be some sharing of this risk. For instance, the ESCO may be invited to undertake ground condition surveys and other relevant tests on the land and to take responsibility for geological conditions (which can normally be tested for), but not other ground conditions such as archaeological remains or pre-existing contamination to the extent that these cannot be tested for in advance.

Best value

21.23   Both social landlords and local authorities are now obliged to pursue continuous improvement under best value. Inherent within this obligation is the requirement to consult 'stakeholders', in particular service users and potential service users. This goes hand in hand with requirements under the Housing Act 1985 for local housing authorities to consult tenants in relation to proposed changes in the management and maintenance of dwellings. Both the output specification and the contractual terms for a district energy scheme will, therefore, need to be compatible with these duties of consultation and continuous improvement.

21.24   For consultation to be meaningful, it will need to be carried out before the output specification for a proposed district energy scheme is finalised, and certainly before the scheme is put out to tender. Consultation will also need to be carried out throughout the procurement process. Tenants will need to be kept informed at key stages such as drawing up the select list of tenderers, bid evaluation and preferred bidders. To comply with best value, tenants and other users of the scheme should also be consulted throughout the life of the contract, usually at annual or at least five yearly intervals, to co-ordinate with the authority's best value performance plan and best value review. Often, this can take the form of a tenant satisfaction survey but it may also involve the supplier liaising with local tenants' groups.

21.25   Authorities frequently perceive a tension between the requirement to achieve continuous improvement under best value and long term contracts for, say, 25 or 30 years. However, long term contracts need not sacrifice compliance with best value. A long term contract can be the most effective means of securing the capital investment in plant and equipment which is vital to bring about service improvements. Although suppliers will be justifiably nervous about entering into open-ended obligations to achieve continuous improvement, provided there are sufficiently certain and objective mechanisms in the contract relating to the making of changes to the specification and response to best value reviews, the contract can be drafted in such a way as to make the risk profile acceptable to the supplier.

Powers

21.26   Any authority entering into a district energy scheme will need to be satisfied that it has the requisite powers or vires. This is a matter which will also be of crucial importance to the supplier and (where external finance is involved) to the funders, as it can affect the validity of the contract. After a series of decisions in the 1990s, there was doubt as to whether local authorities had the power to enter into schemes of this nature.

21.27   This problem has partly been cured by the Local Government (Contracts) Act 1997, which reassures the private sector that even if a contract with a local authority is challenged and held by a court to be outside the authority's powers and thereby void, the private sector contractor's right to compensation under the contract will be preserved. However, what the Act does not do is prevent aggrieved parties (whether they be rival contractors or disgruntled residents' groups) from challenging an authority's decision to enter into a particular contract. The challenge may be brought on the basis that the authority does not have sufficient powers to enter into a contract for a district energy scheme or, more commonly, that the authority's consultation with local residents was inadequate. In addition, the District Auditor has the power to challenge contracts, which has already been exercised in a number of cases.

21.28   There is now a new power for local authorities to promote or improve the economic, social or environmental well-being of their area under the Local Government Act 2000. This power is undoubtedly useful, but not a cure all and, as yet, should be used with caution, in particular where it has been relied upon by the authority to take shares in the ESCO, which does give rise to particular powers difficulties.

It will be evident from the above that it is extremely important that potential powers issues are investigated at the very early stages of any proposed scheme.

Force majeure and change of law

21.29   These are separate issues but are addressed together as they share two major characteristics. First, they are both risks which could have a significant effect on the economics of the project for either party and which are outside the parties' control. Second, the long-term nature of district energy scheme contracts (up to 25 or 30 years) means not only that there is more chance of a force majeure event or change of law occurring during the term of the contract, but also that the risks of one of the parties being saddled with a potentially uneconomic project for a long period of time are increased accordingly.

21.30   Force majeure is an obvious example of a situation where the ESCO is (at least partly) excused for failure to perform. Force majeure events will be events which are outside the control of either party and which affect one of the parties' ability to perform the contract. While a force majeure event is existing, the supplier will usually be excused from any deductions from its payment. Although this is a simple enough concept, there is considerable scope for negotiation as to how wide the definition of force majeure should be and, thereby, how wide the circumstances are in which the supplier is excused from payment. How this issue is resolved will depend, amongst other things, on whether the scheme is a PFI scheme. The Treasury (now OGC) Guidelines applicable to PFI were not framed with these somewhat specialised schemes in mind, and provide a definition of force majeure which is much narrower than that which is normally found in commercial contracts. This, of course, has the effect that the circumstances in which the ESCO is protected from the consequences of its failure to perform are much narrower and the commercial risks borne by the ESCO are commensurately higher. In practice, a district energy PFI scheme would normally have a definition of force majeure which is somewhere between that set out in the OGC Guidelines and those which are more commonly found in other commercial contracts.

21.31   One of the issues which is likely to give rise to intense negotiation in a district energy scheme is change of law. As explained above, a change of law, particularly in the earlier stages of the project, could have a major effect on the economics of the project for either party. Again, the risk of change of law will be shared, but it is how this risk is to be shared which is the real issue. A number of criteria will determine how negotiations on this issue are concluded, some of which may be specific to the project itself. However, as a rule of thumb, it would be expected that general changes of law (for example those not specific to energy services provision to social housing) would normally be a risk taken by the ESCO, on the basis that the ESCO (or certainly, its parent company) would be dealing with general change of law risk on a daily basis in its normal course of business. However, the risk of a specific or 'qualifying' change of law will usually be taken by the authority. A 'qualifying change' is a change which is specific to the provision of energy services in the particular context in which the authority requires it. However, the meaning of 'qualifying change' will vary according to the scheme. For example, the scope may be different where the scheme serves buildings other than local authority housing. The important rule for the supplier is to ensure that the scope of the definition covers the areas where legislation may be put in place regarding the provision of energy, on a basis which is specific to the authority in question or to the buildings for which that authority is responsible. In addition to these general principles, there are other ways in which the particular characteristics of a scheme could influence how change of law risk is shared. For example, the authority will think carefully before accepting risks for general changes in environmental law affecting heat and electricity generation plant. Depending upon the pricing arrangements between the ESCO and the consumers of the heat or electricity, the ESCO may be able to recover all or a proportion of such change of law costs by increasing the price at which the energy is sold. If that is the case, then the authority may regard its acceptance of such risk as providing for a 'double payment' to the ESCO and therefore decide that this is a risk which should be managed by the ESCO.

Action by supplier or authority

21.32   There are a number of ways in which actions or omissions by the supplier or the authority could have a serious adverse effect on the project from the point of view of the other party. For example, the authority will have chosen the energy supplier with care; its identity is likely to have been made known to residents from an early stage in the consultation process and, in many cases, the reputation of the supplier which is to take the controlling interest in the ESCO will be crucial to obtaining residents' support. Therefore, any disposal by the energy supplier of its interest in the ESCO, or assignment of the energy supply contract as a whole, is likely to be a sensitive issue with the authority, whose attitude may therefore be more restrictive than is commonly found in other outsourcing deals. The authority is likely therefore to wish to impose restrictions on any assignment or sale by the supplier of its interest in the ESCO or the scheme itself and on any change of control of the ESCO.

21.33   Equally, actions by the authority can adversely affect the economics of the scheme for the supplier. One risk from which the ESCO would expect to be protected is any act of the authority which either hinders the supplier's ability to perform the contract or, equally importantly, has the effect of reducing the revenues received by the supplier from performing the contract. For example, in a scheme to which local authority homes are connected, if the authority is negligent in the maintenance of the relevant property, this could eventually lead to technical difficulties for the ESCO in providing the service to the agreed standard. Likewise, anything done by the authority which reduces the occupancy levels of these properties is likely to affect the ESCO's revenues from the scheme if the supplier is taking an element of volume risk, which is likely to be the case. One way in which the interest of the ESCO could be protected in these circumstances is to identify a number of authority actions which would have a detrimental effect on the revenues from the scheme and to prohibit the authority from carrying out any such actions in the contract. The problem is that this is likely to constitute an attempt by the authority to fetter its discretion as to how it carries out its statutory obligations and as such lead to serious powers issues. The safer option is to provide for the authority to compensate the ESCO for any loss of revenue attributable to such authority action, although clearly how this is quantified will be a matter for negotiation.

Grounds for and financial consequences of termination of contract

21.34   Most of the issues relevant to termination in district energy schemes will mirror those in other long-term infrastructure projects. For example, the sunk costs invested in the construction of the plant will mean that the ESCO will wish to ensure that a termination sum reflecting this is paid out. The need for the authority to comply with its statutory obligations will, however, impact on the termination provisions. For example, if residents were without heat for a week, this would represent a serious breach of a local authority's statutory duties and the authority might well insist that this constitutes a termination event in itself. In other types of project, it is unlikely that this would be acceptable to the private sector party, but this is an area where the authority is likely to feel it has little room for manoeuvre.

Electricity export/regulatory

21.35 As mentioned above, the sale of electricity can often be an important part of a scheme, since in many schemes the principal source of the heat delivered to residents will have been produced in heat recovery boilers and the heat produced by electricity generation equipment. The supply of electricity is regulated under the Electricity Act 1989. Depending on the size of the scheme, the ESCO may be able to sell the electricity direct to residents without the requirement for a licence, although to do so may involve private distribution wires, not forming part of the local electricity distribution system. Alternatively, the ESCO could export the electricity direct to a licensed electricity supplier, seeing the electricity sales simply as revenue supporting the economics of the heat provision. At an early stage, the authority will need to decide whether, depending upon the size and configuration of the scheme, including the supply of electricity to residents is practical and whether it could offer those consumers a price advantage.

CONTRACT CLAUSES

21.36 Although the principles set out in the OGC Guidlines will have relevance to district energy schemes procured under the PFI, there is no specific equivalent guidance for such schemes. This is no doubt because district energy is a relatively new and somewhat specialised area. Equally, there are no standard form contracts that have evolved as yet, given that only two major district energy schemes have to date been completed under PPP/PFI. Additional reasons for a lack of standardisation are that each scheme is likely to raise new legal and commercial issues and, inevitably, different individuals and organisations will have differing views as to how the legal issues common to all district energy schemes are addressed.

21.37 However, it is undeniable that experience of how particular issues have been addressed in past district energy schemes enables those negotiating and drafting the contracts for new schemes to do so as efficiently and economically as possible and so avoid 'reinventing the wheel' with each new scheme. This means that time and resources can be directed at those areas where there are genuine commercial differences between the parties which need to be resolved for the project to be completed. It is both inevitable and desirable that as more district energy deals are completed, more precedents will emerge which lead to more standardised solutions being adopted in particular areas. With the above in mind, there is limited value in any attempt to present any specimen clauses as in any way 'standardised'. However, para **21.39** gives some examples of draft clauses which might be used to address some of the issues which commonly arise in district energy schemes. Although for obvious client confidentiality reasons these draft clauses do not represent solutions found for a particular project, the principles contained in them reflect our experience of drafting and negotiating contract solutions for these schemes. They are intended to be 'neutral' as between the interests of the authority and the ESCO, although clearly it will be a matter of opinion as to whether such objectivity has been achieved.

Typical contract structure

21.38

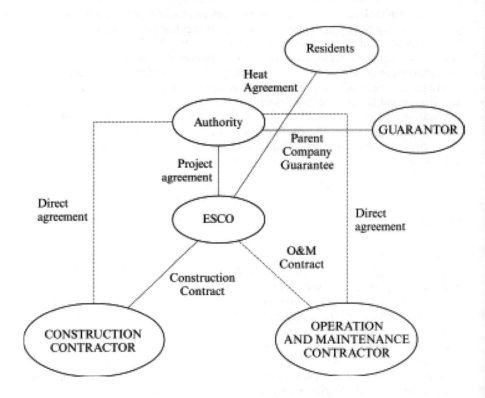

Specimen clauses

21.39

1   Restrictions in relation to ESCO

The Supplier undertakes to the Council that it will exercise its vote as shareholder and procure that its nominee directors on the board of directors of ESCO exercise their voting rights on the board of directors of ESCO to procure so far as it lies within the power of the Supplier or nominee directors (as the case may be) that during the Contract Period ESCO will not, except with the prior written approval of the Council:

1.1   carry on any activities other than those relating solely to the provision of the Energy Services in accordance with this Agreement;

1.2   assign any of its rights or sub-contract any of its obligations under this Agreement;

1.3   sell, transfer, lease, licence or in any way dispose of any part of ESCO; or

1.4 make or permit any material alteration (including cessation) to the provision of the Energy Services or engage in any business other than the provision of the Energy Services.

2 Operating Committee and Residents' Committee

2.1 The Council has the right to establish an operating committee (the 'Operating Committee') which will consist of no more than three named representatives from each party and which shall make recommendations to the board of directors of ESCO and within the authority given to it by the board of directors shall co-ordinate all activities relating to matching the availability of the Energy Services to the Council's requirements as set out in this Agreement including without limitation:

(a) management of any variations in the Council's requirements for the availability of the Energy Services;

(b) discussing and reviewing all aspects of overall performance, annual maintenance and forward planning; and

(c) liaison with the Residents and the operating parameters of the Residents' Committee described in clause 2.2 below.

2.2 The Council will establish a residents' committee (the 'Residents' Committee') to consult with the Residents, on terms to be established and agreed between the parties. Four times in each year ESCO will be required to make available representatives outside normal working hours to attend such meetings and to implement, where reasonable (based upon such factors as cost, resources, time and any other relevant criteria), the suggestions or requests of the Residents. A member of the board of directors of ESCO will attend meetings of the Residents' Committee if so requested.

3 Payment Deduction

3.1 The Council may make deductions from the Availability Charge (an 'Availability Deduction') in accordance with this clause and Schedule [   ] (Deduction from Availability Charge).

3.2 Liability to an Availability Deduction will arise where there is a failure in the Energy Services where such failure is not the result of:

(a) any Force Majeure event;

(b) any breach by the Council of its obligations under this Agreement;

(c) any negligent or deliberate act or omission by any Resident; or

(d) any Planned Outage.

3.3 Where the Council believes there has been a failure in the Energy Services by ESCO, the Council shall serve on ESCO a written notice (a 'Failure Notice') which sets out:

(a) particularised details of the alleged failure; and

(b) the time and date of service of the notice and a reference number for identification purposes.

3.4 Following the service of a Failure Notice pursuant to clause 2.3, no liability to Availability Deductions shall arise until the expiry of the relevant response or remedy period (as appropriate) set out in Schedule [   ] (Deduction from Availability Charge), which period shall run from the time ESCO receives such notice.

3.5   For each failure in the Energy Services where the relevant response or remedy period is not complied with, Availability Deductions shall be calculated in accordance with Schedule [ ] (Deduction from Availability Charge).

4   Change in Legal Requirements

4.1   In the event that any Change in Legal Requirements occurs after the date of this Agreement, ESCO will be responsible for meeting any costs incurred in complying with such change, and will not be entitled to revise the Availability Charge as a result of such change, unless it is a Qualifying Change.

4.2   If the Change in Legal Requirements is a Qualifying Change, and provided that the provisions of clauses 4.3 to 4.5 are complied with, ESCO can require that the Availability Charge be revised upwards; and to the extent that the change causes the costs of providing the Energy Services to fall (or the revenues to rise) the Council can require that the Availability Charge be revised downwards; in either case such revision to be calculated and implemented after having been agreed or determined pursuant to clauses 4.3 and 4.4.

4.3   If an event or circumstance occurs or a public announcement is made of an event or circumstance which if occurred, would constitute a Qualifying Change, the Council and ESCO shall consult together regarding the likely effect of such change occurring. ESCO shall also give the Council written notice of any event or circumstance which constitutes a Qualifying Change within 28 days of it becoming aware of the occurrence of such event or circumstance. ESCO shall within 28 days of the occurrence of any Qualifying Change:
  (a)   specify the relevant event or circumstance that has occurred;
  (b)   identify the effects that the relevant event or circumstance has had or is likely to have upon the performance of ESCO's obligations;
  (c)   provide details of any additional costs and/or loss of revenue that ESCO has incurred or is likely to incur as a result of the relevant event or circumstance; and
  (d)   put forward proposals for any compensation payments payable by the Council under this Agreement in respect of the relevant event or circumstance, for the purpose of ensuring that ESCO shall be held harmless to the extent that the Qualifying Change has a direct material adverse effect on ESCO's costs or revenues.

4.4   The parties shall meet as soon as practicable to discuss and attempt to agree ESCO's proposals put forward pursuant to clause 4.3(d) above. If no such agreement is reached within 28 days of the proposals being put forward, the matter shall be referred to the dispute resolution procedure set out in clause [ ].

4.5   ESCO shall take all reasonable steps which are required in order to mitigate and minimise any detrimental effect caused, or likely to be caused, by any Qualifying Change.

Definitions

'Availability Charge' means the payment specified in Schedule [ ] (Financial Model) for the Energy Services;

'Change in Legal Requirements' means any Legal Requirement coming into effect during the Contract Period or any amendment, replacement or re-enactment of any Legal Requirement at any time during the Contract Period but excluding any proposed change in a Legal Requirement which has been published prior to the Contract Period and subsequently comes into force substantially in the form so published;

'Contract Period' means the period of [25 years] from the date of this Agreement;

'Energy Services' means the making available by ESCO of the heat [and electricity] supply in accordance with the terms of this Agreement;

'Force Majeure' means any event or circumstance which is beyond the reasonable control of either party and which results in or causes the failure of that party to perform any of its obligations under this Agreement, including, but not necessarily limited to, an act of God, strike, lockout or other industrial disturbance, act of the public enemy, war declared or undeclared, threat of war, terrorist act, blockade, revolution, riot, insurrection, civil commotion, public demonstration, sabotage, act of vandalism, lightning, fire, storm, earthquake, accumulation of snow or ice, lack of water arising from weather or environmental problems, explosion, governmental restraint, Act of Parliament, other legislation by law or Directive or the failure of any energy supplier to supply the ESCO with energy or any deficiency in such supply to the extent that such failure or deficiency or the consequences thereof could not have been prevented by the exercise of prudent operating practices by the ESCO;

'Legal Requirement' means any law, proclamation, decision, rule, regulation, order, resolution, notice, rule of court, bye-law, directive, statute, statutory instrument, standard, code of conduct or other instrument or requirement having the force of law made, issued, declared, passed or otherwise enacted, created or given effect by HM Parliament, the Council, Commission or Parliament of the European Union, and court or other judicial forum, any coroner or commission of inquiry, any local authority other competent authority;

'Planned Outage' means an outage of the Energy Services in accordance with the annual maintenance plan for no longer than the appropriate period of time identified by such plan;

'Premises' means [*identify premises served by the scheme*];

'Qualifying Change' means a Change in Legal Requirements specific to the provision of heat on behalf of local authorities to residential accommodation or other premises owned or managed by local authorities or to the provision of private finance for the funding of energy services by local authorities and which in each case has a direct material adverse effect on ESCO's costs of or revenues from providing the Energy Services under this Agreement;

'Residents' means the persons from time to time occupying the Premises.

CHAPTER 22

Case study: housing

Paul McDermott

BACKGROUND AND CONTEXT

Housing options—decent home standards

22.01 Government policy requires United Kingdom social housing stock to be brought up to a 'decent standard' by 2010. This policy has encouraged local authorities to evaluate their options for securing investment in social housing stock and strategies for ensuring effective management of that stock. The options available to local authorities to attract investment for social housing in their area include large scale voluntary transfer ('LSVT'), stock or site disposals to a registered social landlord ('RSL'), housing PFI, best value outsourcing of housing management (with or without maintenance services) and an arm's length management organisation ('ALMO').

22.02 The option or options any individual local authority may choose is likely to be influenced by a number of factors including the likelihood of tenants voting for an LSVT, the success of the local authority in gaining a place either on an LSVT programme or the housing PFI programme and the effect of any decision upon the housing revenue account ('HRA'). The presumption that the future of social housing is LSVTs to RSLs has to an extent been tempered by the development of the housing PFI programme, the development of ALMOs and in certain areas the rejection of LSVT by tenants.

22.03 An increasing number of local authorities are adopting a combination of non-LSVT options to secure much needed investment into social housing and also as part of a range of diverse strategies to ensure a more holistic regeneration and development of local communities, for example:
(i)   Manchester city council's imaginative scheme, which combines housing PFI with land disposals, the building of dwellings for outright sale, low-cost home ownership dwellings, the construction of key worker accommodation and the renovation of a community power scheme;
(ii) London Borough of Newham's housing PFI scheme, which includes the refurbishment of a housing estate, land disposal and the construction of non-council social housing. These are being developed in conjunction with a community and housing regeneration scheme in neighbouring districts.

Housing contracts arrangement

22.04 Local authority X is a housing authority which, for the reasons set out below, intends to work with partners to secure improvements to a housing estate and to outsource its housing management and repair services.

22.05   The local authority has chosen the Eastside estate on the basis of a stock conditions survey which indicated that the majority of the 1950s-built dwellings require investment to achieve a decent homes standard and, further, that the minority 1960s buildings at Eastside are effectively uneconomical to repair. The Eastside estate, like many other estates in the United Kingdom, is showing the signs of chronic under-investment in council housing which has occurred in the previous 20 years. The local authority also wants to combine any improvement in the housing stock in Eastside with wider regeneration and community empowerment programmes. On a previous occasion the tenants of Eastside decisively rejected a stock transfer, though in consultation with the local authority the tenants expressed support for the local authority working in partnership with others provided that the local authority remained the landlord. The local authority was unsuccessful in its application to be admitted to the housing PFI programme and it has opted to undertake a best value outsourcing of housing management and maintenance in Eastside combined with the disposal of the unviable 1960s dwellings.

The advantages of this approach?

22.06   As part of the local authority's decision to outsource its management and maintenance of the Eastside housing stock, it will have undertaken a best value review and found that this option offered better value than retaining those services in-house. The local authority will have also undertaken a housing options appraisal and due to the previous rejection of the stock transfer by the tenants and the authority's failure to achieve a place on the current housing PFI programme it has limited choices. The decision to best value outsource housing management does not prevent the local authority from reapplying for a place on the housing PFI programme, providing the best value contract has termination provisions which enable the local authority to exit in the event that the Eastside estate is either transferred to a RSL and/or the local authority in due course awards a PFI contract to another contractor. The disposal of the 1960s properties will entail the decanting of residents who live there. The local authority would, however, require consent under the Housing Act 1985, s 32 from the Secretary of State for this disposal. The advantage for the local authority in disposing of some dwellings is that the RSL with the aid of social housing grant should be able to invest in new units at Eastside. This will enable the local authority to develop a multi-tenure community at Eastside.

DESCRIPTION OF PARTIES INVOLVED

22.07   The three main parties involved are the local authority in its capacity as the housing authority, the contractor selected to deliver the best value outsourcing of housing management (the 'manager') and an RSL selected to develop the housing land which is being disposed of.

22.08   Another relevant party is the Secretary of State at the Office of the Deputy Prime Minister who grants consent for the best value housing management agreement, consent under the Housing Act 1985, s 34 and also where the disposal constitutes financial assistance also consent under the Local Government Act 1988, s 25.

22.09   A local authority must be careful in setting its criteria for selecting a manager to provide management services under the Housing Act 1985, s 27. The Secretary of State is likely to refuse any proposed transfer of housing management where only RSLs have been invited to tender for the contract. In *R v Secretary of State for the Environment, ex p Harrow London Borough Council*[1], the court upheld the decision of the Secretary of State to refuse consent for the transfer of housing management where only registered social landlords were invited to tender. This decision was on the basis that this was in breach of an EC Directive on public procurement, as implemented through the Public Services Contracts Regulations 1993[2].

1   (1996) 29 HLR 1.
2   SI 1993/3228.

22.10   Other parties involved in the Eastside estate project will include a developer to work with the RSL in respect of the disposed housing land and possibly other service providers such as repairs and maintenance companies who may act as sub-contractors to the manager.

OBJECTIVES OF THE HOUSING CONTRACTS

22.11   As discussed above[1], the local authority in this instance has adopted a combination of a best value outsourcing scheme with a disposal largely because other options are not available to it. The local authority's aim is to introduce best value within its housing management and maintenance services at Eastside and through the disposal of some housing land procure new social housing accommodation.

1   See para **22.05**.

22.12   The procurement of the two schemes will be undertaken separately and the procurement procedures described in Part I are relevant. In this example the legal and commercial issues will also be treated separately for the two types of housing arrangement.

DISPOSAL OF SURPLUS HOUSING LAND

Legal and commercial issues

22.13   In addition to securing social housing for its local residents the local authority will also want to ensure that the RSL develops the units to the specification which it has agreed with the local authority, that persons from its waiting list are nominated to the rented accommodation (and any low cost home ownership units) and that the local authority enjoys a fair share of any surplus generated by the sale of dwellings on the open market ('overage').

22.14   The local authority will enter into a principal development agreement ('PDA') with the RSL which will govern the number and specifications of the units to be developed, set the time limit in which those units must be constructed and deal with issues such as overage. The authority will also enter into a building lease or licence which will enable the RSL and its development partner to undertake the construction of the dwellings. Nomination agreements which will govern rights of the council to nominate persons to the dwellings and a planning agreement of a similar nature to that which the local authority would insist upon for any other type of housing development in its area.

Principal development agreement

22.15   The PDA governs the relationship between the local authority and the RSL in respect of the construction and development of the new dwellings. The local authority will want to give thought to the impact of this development on other residents of the Eastside housing estate. This agreement will also incorporate provisions for site safety and security, the environmental impact of the development, any training or other socio-economic spin-offs from the development which may be of benefit to local residents and such matters as the times of the day when work will be permitted.

Specification provisions

22.16   The PDA will contain provisions for the types of dwellings which will be constructed, the specifications for those dwellings and the designation of dwellings for either social rent, supported accommodation, low cost home ownership or for sale on the open market. These provisions should be based on the specification adopted by the local authority when it procured the scheme. The PDA should also contain a means of allowing the local authority to veto any alterations to buildings or their designation during the construction period and in some cases thereafter and it will also provide a remedy for the local authority in the event that the RSL and its development partner are unable to complete the development within a reasonable period of time. The local authority should bear in mind that unforeseen circumstances do arise which can delay any construction project. Such a remedy should not be onerous but genuinely be a one which enables the local authority to ensure that the site is not left derelict or uncompleted due to lack of funds or other circumstances.

Overage

22.17   The use of an overage or 'clawback' provision is to protect the interests of the local authority and ensure that it gains in any windfall from activities such as the lease of any retail units within the housing development or more probably from the sale of some of the dwellings on the open market. The financial package which the RSL will use to develop the housing units is likely to be based on a combination of income streams including social housing grant, raising funds using its current housing stock for security and, providing there is a market, the disposal of a proportion of the dwellings on the open market. Local authorities are likely to welcome a combination of tenures on such housing developments as this promotes balanced communities and also assists in making such developments financially viable. In a period of rising housing prices in certain areas of the country there is also a need to ensure that the local authority gains a share of any surplus which the RSL and its development partner may make beyond that allowed for in their business plan. The overage provisions contained in the PDA will at their most basic provide for a estimated or projected valuation of units for sale, deal with the marketing and minimum price at which those units may be sold, contain a formula for deducting the legitimate cost and expenses of the RSL and set out the portions which any excess income should be divided between the local authority and the RSL. The local authority should be aware that calculating expenses which might be reasonable for an RSL to deduct from any surplus of sale proceeds will need thought and possibly professional advice from a chartered surveyor and/or project manager.

22.18 In order for the local authority to properly assess its entitlement to overage, the PDA will also have to assess issues such as open book accounting and the local authority's ability to demand information and have access to records during the construction period. The overage provisions will also have to state when and how the local authority is to be paid any surplus. The local authority should bear in mind that overage provisions are useful even in a depressed housing market as values may increase during the construction period. In the Trowbridge Scheme in the London Borough of Hackney, the local authority has received surplus income which it is able to reinvest in social housing elsewhere in its district.

Nomination agreements

22.19 The PDA will also contain provisions which require the RSL to enter into nomination agreements in respect of social rented accommodation and low cost home ownership units at the development. These nomination agreements should be attached as schedules to the PDA. The local authority should reasonably expect 100 per cent of nominations the first time that the dwellings are let or sold and thereafter up to 75 per cent of subsequent nominations to any vacancies. The Housing Corporation and the then Department of Local Government, Transport and the Regions issued joint guidance on nomination agreements which is still current and should where possible be adhered to.

Limited duration

22.20 The PDA's term is limited to the completion of the dwellings, the granting of the lease or transfer of the land, the calculation of overage and the entering into of the nomination agreements. The local authority should bear this in mind in the event it includes any additional provisions within the PDA.

TRANSFER OF HOUSING MANAGEMENT

Legal and commercial considerations

22.21 The transfer of the management of the Eastside estate will be procured in a similar manner to other local authority outsourcing of services. The provisions relating to issues such as best value service specifications and other contractual topics touched on elsewhere[1] are relevant here.

1   See Part II.

22.22 This example concentrates on those aspects of the housing management agreement which are distinct from other types of outsourcing contracts. Section 27 of the Housing Act 1985 enables a local authority to seek the consent of the Secretary of State to appoint a manager to manage part or all of its social housing stock. In July 2002 the Office of the Deputy Prime Minister commenced consultation with local authorities and other interested parties in respect of this section with the aim of providing housing authorities with more options for housing management arrangements. Whatever the final outcome of that consultation, the local authority must bear in mind that it is required by the Housing Act 1985, s 105 to consult with its tenants in respect of the appointment of any external housing manager. Many local authorities have moved to a position where their tenants form part of the panel which evaluates bids from potential managers.

The position of the tenants

22.23 The tenants at Eastside retain their status and rights as either introductory or secure tenants of the local authority. This has a number of implications in the context of the management agreement. Possibly the most important is that the tenants retain the right to establish a tenant management organisation under the Housing Act 1985, s 27AB. The local authority must therefore ensure that it is able to terminate a management agreement with the contractor without incurring penalties in the event that the tenants exercise this right. This is a risk for the private sector, and local authorities should be robust in making the proposition that if the private sector contractor is successful in managing the dwellings there is less likelihood that the tenants would want to create a tenant management organisation. Determination provisions should also encompass the possibility that the local authority may opt to enter into a housing PFI agreement for the Eastside estate or reconsider a stock transfer to a RSL. The policy of tenant empowerment and involvement in the delivery of housing services also raises commercial and legal issues which the local authority will need to consider in the management agreement for management services at Eastside. Some of these are set out below.

Rent collection and enforcement

22.24 The income from rents along with other housing revenue account monies will enable the council to pay the manager and also undertake maintenance and repair works at Eastside. The collection of rent and enforcing court orders against those tenants with rent arrears is an important issue for consideration. If a local authority operates a successful service it may not want to delegate this function. If rent collection figures could be improved then a management agreement could transfer these functions to the manager. The management agreement should also deal with issues such as the relationship between the manager and those operating the housing benefit system, any requirement for the manager to be pro-active in assisting tenants completing and renewing housing benefit applications and management agreement other pro-active methods of assisting tenants pay their rent.

22.25 The manager may also be required to issue rent arrears proceedings in the local county court. If the management agreement is to include such an enforcement provision then the local authority must give careful thought to ensuring that the manager at Eastside does not treat tenants differently from how the local authority treats tenants in other parts of its district. Enforcement provisions therefore may contain rather prescriptive instructions on ensuring that the manager is neither over or under enthusiastic in issuing court actions or seeking evictions for rent arrears compared with the local authority.

Tenant involvement and empowerment

22.26   The management agreement must ensure that tenants at Eastside are not disadvantaged compared with the local authority's other tenants. A provision will be required so that the manager engages with any Eastside tenants' and residents' organisation as the local authority itself would have done. The manager's role in the local tenant compact should also be addressed.

22.27   The council may also want to give consideration to a contractual requirement for the manager to communicate in plain English and where appropriate provide documents in other languages on a similar basis. The Canadian Law Commission has provided a workable definition of plain English and this is set out at para **22.37** as an example definition.

Human rights and diversity

22.28   The Human Rights Act 1998 has not impacted upon housing services to the extent which was envisaged immediately after the legislation came into effect. The management agreement should acknowledge that the local authority is a public authority under the terms of the Human Rights Act 1998 and is required in its dealings with its tenants and others to comply with that legislation. To date the courts are still working towards a definitive decision on the status of contractors in public private partnership and in particular in what circumstances and to what extent they can be deemed public. In this period of uncertainty the local authority should be aware that it may still be liable for the acts of its contractors and should seek contractual protection. As a minimum the local authority should require the manager in its dealings with tenants and leaseholders to act as if it *were* a public authority. In the event there is an investigation or trial in respect of any alleged breaches of the Human Rights Act 1998 the manager must co-operate with the local authority in defending those proceedings and make available its records and personnel for any investigation or court hearing. The local authority may also want to construct a provision whereby a manager indemnifies it in the event that the local authority is required to pay compensation for breaches of the Human Rights Act 1998 which are mainly or wholly due to the actions or abuses of the manager.

22.29   The legislation and regulations which deal with non-commercial considerations has made local authorities careful when stipulating equal opportunity or diversity provisions either within the procurement process or contracts. The management agreement should, however, contain provisions which require the manager to implement and apply the local authority's equal opportunities and diversity policies in its dealings with tenants, leaseholders, members of the general public and the local authority's own staff. Most contractors involved in housing management are generally aware of and embrace equal opportunities and diversity. The management agreement should not, however, rely upon this goodwill.

22.30   The management agreement should also contain provisions requiring the manager to liaise and co-operate with the Local Government Ombudsmen. This will include providing records and information promptly to either the local authority or the Ombudsmen and ensuring its staff members are available for interview or other proceedings. Again the manager should indemnify the local authority for any compensation paid to tenants or leaseholders due mainly or wholly to maladministration caused through its actions or inactions.

Community safety and anti-social behaviour

22.31   The Crime and Disorder Act 1998 places a number of duties upon local authorities. These duties do not disappear with the transfer of housing responsibilities to other organisations. Any contract the housing authority enters into in respect of social housing, whether it is a management agreement, PFI agreement or a transfer of the housing stock, should contain provisions which require the contractor or new landlord to co-operate fully with both the local authority and the police in respect of formulating, implementing and analysing strategies and to reduce anti-social behaviour and nuisance. Police services are generally more comfortable dealing with local authorities than with RSLs or private contractors, not least because there are fewer local authorities and therefore it is easier for them to maintain proper points of contact. Community safety provisions should also ensure that any policies that the local authority has in respect of its tenants and leaseholders concerning anti-social behaviour are offered to the tenants and leaseholders at Eastside. Consideration should be given as to whether any existing specialist anti-social behaviour units are maintained or whether the new manager is required to implement legal and other action against anti-social behaviour.

Disrepair and right to buy

22.32   The tenants at Eastside retain their rights and status as mentioned at para **22.23**. This means that they have the right either to seek an injunction under their tenancies for disrepair or to seek compensation or other remedies under the Landlord and Tenant Act 1985, s 11. In formulating provisions for dealing with both instances of disrepair and legal proceedings it is necessary to analyse the condition of the properties and the volume of legal actions at the time the management agreement is procured. The local authority may want to retain control of legal proceedings for disrepair, though it should be aware that many claims arise in response to rent arrears proceedings which if the agreement allows may have been issued by the manager. The local authority should ensure that it is realistic in its expectations and that if it has neglected repairs and maintenance it might not be economic to place the financial burden for disrepair claims with the manager. On the other hand if the estate had been generally well maintained and there are sufficient funds for the manager to properly repair the housing stock it may be reasonable for the manager to bear the risk of proceedings. The management agreement should require the manager to co-operate in the right to buy process and provide information such as rent arrears and/or other relevant information in a timely and proactive manner to enable the local authority to meet its statutory deadlines.

Leaseholders

22.33   The rights of leaseholders are also affected by the appointment of a manager. In particular the Commonhold and Leasehold Reform Act 2002, s 151 is applicable. In procuring the management agreement the local authority may take advantage of the reforms which enable it to consult with leaseholders about the appointment of a manager (for 12 months or more) rather than in respect of individual works undertaken by the manager.

22.34   It will also be necessary for the existing leases to be reviewed. Many local authorities have a variety of right to buy leases and these can vary in their requirements as to recovery of service charges for works undertaken. Some leases only permit recovery of monies for actual works rather than improvements whilst others only allow recovery of monies where the local authority *itself* has undertaken the works. The manager should be fully advised of the various leases which the local authority may have with its leaseholders.

Disposal and development

22.35

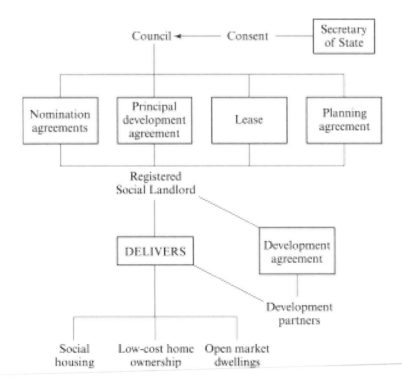

Management structure

22.36

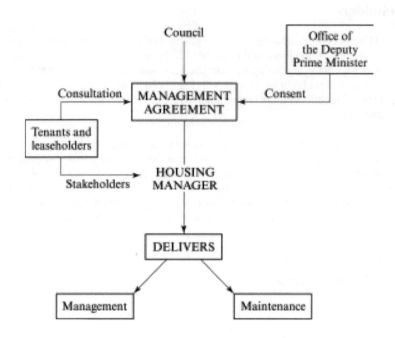

Specimen clauses

22.37

1   Defined terms

'Plain English' means language which is written or set out simply, clearly and concisely with the required degree of precision and as much as possible in ordinary language.

2   Consultation and empowerment

The manager shall during the service period:

2.1   consult on a regular basis with the tenants and residents about the delivery of services;

2.2   support, encourage and foster the development of tenant and resident associations as a forum for tenant and resident involvement in the delivery of the services;

2.3   comply with policies and guidance (including that on tenant participation compacts) issued in connection with tenant and resident involvement in social housing or other housing issues;

2.4   undertake other consultations with the tenants and residents at the reasonable direction of the local authority;

2.5   work with the local authority to better enable the residents to be directly involved in the operation, delivery and monitoring of the services;

2.6   ensure that documents and written materials (including legal documents and contracts) produced by it or on its behalf and which also relate to the services are written in Plain English; and

2.7   fully co-operate with, provide information to and otherwise assist the local authority to comply with any requirements or regulations issued by the Secretary of State pursuant to the Housing Act 1985, s 27BA or pursuant to any similar legislation enacted from time to time.

3   Human rights, equal opportunities and diversity

3.1   In the performance of the services and in its dealings with tenants, residents, local authority employees and members of the general public the manager shall comply and shall ensure that its employees, agents and associate-managers comply with the Human Rights Act 1998 as if it and its sub-managers were public authorities (within the meaning of that Act) and the best professional practice in relation to equal opportunities and diversity as if it and its sub-managers were public authorities and in particular (but without limitation) shall comply with:

3.1.1   all relevant legislation as well as statutory and other official guidance and codes of practice; and

3.1.2   the local authority's own equal opportunities policies and procedures as the same may be adopted and amended from time to time and as notified to the manager.

3.2   The manager shall provide such information as the local authority may reasonably require for the purpose of assessing the manager's compliance with clause 3.1 above.

3.3   The manager shall comply with codes of practice issued pursuant to the Disability Discrimination Act 1995: including the 'Code of practice: Rights of access: Goods, facilities, services and premises'.

3.4   The manager shall at the request of the Authorised Officer provide the local authority with a breakdown of its workforce by race and grade as the Authorised Officer may reasonably require in order to satisfy herself or himself as to the manager's compliance with this clause.

3.5   The manager shall monitor the representation within its workforce of employees of different racial groups (meaning groups of persons defined by reference to colour, race, nationality, or ethnic or national origins).

3.6   The manager shall inform the Authorised Officer as soon as becoming aware of any legal proceedings or complaint brought or likely to be brought against the manager under legislation set out in this clause 3.

3.7   Where any investigation is undertaken by a person or body empowered to conduct such investigation and/or proceedings are either threatened or instituted in connection with the delivery of the services being in contravention of the Human Rights Act 1998, and/or the Disability Discrimination Act 1995, and/or the Race Relations (Amendment) Act 2000, and/or the Sex Discrimination Act 1975 and/or similar legislation enacted from time to time, the manager shall:

3.7.1   provide any information requested in the timescale allotted;

3.7.2   attend any meetings as required and permit its personnel so to attend;

3.7.3   promptly allow access to and investigation of any documents deemed to be relevant;

3.7.4   allow itself and any employee deemed to be relevant to be interviewed;

3.7.5 allow itself and any employee to appear as witness in any ensuing proceedings; and

3.7.6 co-operate fully and promptly in every way required by body conduction such investigations during the course of that investigation.

For the avoidance of doubt, no additional payment shall be made to the manager for performing the requirements set out in this clause 3.

For the further avoidance of doubt, where any investigation is conducted or proceedings are brought and either of them arise directly or indirectly out of the provision of the Services or any other action by the manager or its personnel, then the local authority shall be entitled to recover from the manager the full cost it may have incurred in such investigation or proceedings and such other financial redress to cover any payment the local authority may have been ordered or required to pay to a third party.

4   Community safety

4.1   The manager acknowledges that under the Crime and Disorder Act 1998 the local authority has a duty to:

4.1.1 formulate and implement a strategy for the reduction of crime and disorder within the area of the District of [*insert name of the Local Authority district*]; and

4.1.2 review, analyse and publish levels and patterns of crime within the area of the District of [*insert name of the Local Authority district*]; and

4.1.3 co-operate with the relevant police authority, probation service and other responsible bodies in undertaking its duties as set out in this clause 4.

The manager shall co-operate with the local authority to ensure that the local authority is able to implement the provisions of the Crime and Disorder Act 1998 within the [*name of area which is being managed*] area.

4.2   The manager shall co-operate and work with the [*insert name*] Police Service to reduce crime and disorder within the [*name of area which is being managed*].

4.3   The manager shall on a monthly basis collate and provide information to the local authority concerning incidents of crime and disorder occurring within the [*name of area which is being managed*] (which shall include but not be limited to: anti-social behaviour, 'domestic' violence, criminal damage, crimes of hate/violence) as are reported to it.

5   Legal appointment

5.1   The manager may appoint such legal advisors as it deems appropriate to assist it in delivering the legal services providing the manager obtains the written consent of the local authority's head of legal services (which shall not be unreasonably withheld or delayed) prior to the appointment of any such legal advisor.

5.2   The manager shall notify the local authority's head of legal services of any legal action which is issued in connection with this clause 5 or any other provision of the management agreement.

5.3   During the services period the local authority may at any time assume temporary or permanent responsibility from the manager for the conduct of either all legal proceedings involving tenants or residents or any one or more particular matters providing always the local authority gives the manager 28 days' written notice of its intention to do so.

CHAPTER 23

Case study: leisure trusts

Stephen Ravenscroft

BACKGROUND AND CONTEXT

23.01   Leisure has seen a period of sustained growth in the last few years. The market has ballooned from a predominately local authority dominated market to include many private sector leisure operators. The total fitness market is worth many millions of pounds, of which the private sector will enjoy the lion's share. Changes in demography and working patterns and a greater exposure to different leisure activities mean that providers increasingly have to be flexible and responsive to people's needs.

23.02   Many local authority leisure facilities are ageing and, as a result, find it increasingly difficult to attract a viable number of users. To compound matters, local authorities do not have the capital available to invest in these non-core facilities.

23.03   Against this background, Sport England, the Department for Education and Skills (DfES) and the Department for Culture, Media and Sport (DCMS) are becoming increasingly involved in the issue of leisure provision within the local authority sector. New initiatives encouraging equality of access to sport and recreational facilities are also adding to the pressure for authorities to ensure that there is a suitable level of provision in their area.

23.04   One way of securing improvements to these facilities is to outsource the facility management to a third party operator. In recent years, many leisure operators have come into the market and have been very successful in delivering a high quality, specialist service with improvements to the facilities. Many of these operators are private for-profit limited companies. However, in the last few years, charitable 'leisure trusts' have emerged as a popular means of providing services for local authorities.

This case study will look at the main features of leisure trusts and will explore the contractual background against which leisure trusts operate.

WHAT IS A LEISURE TRUST?

A charity

23.05   The typical model for a leisure trust is that of a charitable company limited by guarantee, although a number adopt the structure of an Industrial and Provident Society (IPS). With such status come various rules and regulations which need to be followed, including compliance with, in the case of a charity, not only company and charity law but also Charity Commission guidelines on the operations of the charity, in addition to usual companies' regulations.

Essential characteristics of a charity

23.06   The traditional form for a charity undertaking the provision of leisure facilities is for it to be a charity conforming with the Recreational Charities Act 1958. The required characteristics of any such body are as follows:

(i)   the charity must provide facilities for recreation or other leisure-time occupation. This has been construed widely and will include facilities such as multi-purpose sports centres but does not include facilities such as theatres;

(ii)   the facilities must be provided in the interests of 'social welfare'. The Recreational Charities Act 1958 goes on to explain that social welfare will require the facilities to be provided with the object of improving the conditions of life for persons for whom the facilities are primarily intended and that those persons have the need for such facilities;

(iii) the charity must also satisfy a 'public benefit' test, which requires that the facilities must be open to members of the public at large with any private benefit being no more than incidental. If there is a membership structure in place, this must only be for reasons of administrative convenience for the best delivery of benefit, rather than to restrict the provision of such benefit. In practice, membership must be open to all those who wish to join;

(iv)   above all, it is essential that the purpose for the creation of the charity is to further the provision of charitable leisure facilities and not to provide the local authority concerned with a more cost efficient way of providing the facilities. Further, it is not the function of charities merely to act as vehicles to relieve local authorities or other for-profit leisure contractors of their duties to provide leisure facilities.

Non-charitable activities

23.07   In a large number of leisure facilities, there is often a broad mix of services provided including, frequently, bars and catering facilities. Such facilities are not of themselves charitable but can be run by a charity if they are ancillary to the activities of the facilities concerned—ie if the facilities can only be used by those attending the facility to participate in the leisure facilities, such as a sports centre. Otherwise, if there is a significant conference suite or a popular local bar contained within the facility, then the suite or bar cannot be operated by the charity and will typically require the creation of a wholly owned non-charitable trading subsidiary of the charity. The only circumstances in which such facilities could be run within the charity itself are if the gross receipts from the activities fall within the Inland Revenue's charitable trading exemption. Broadly, this means trading where the reasonable expectation is of income of no more than £50,000 in any one financial year.

23.08   Additionally, there may be certain sports facilities which will not satisfy the public benefit test: typically, activities such as golf lessons have been rejected by the Charity Commission as being non-charitable, together with activities which promote 'excellence' in certain sports.

23.09   These two types of activities could be undertaken by a wholly owned trading subsidiary which would be set up by the charity. The trading subsidiary would gift aid its profits each financial year to the charity to save the payment of corporation tax on the profits made.

THE ADVANTAGES AND DISADVANTAGES OF LEISURE TRUSTS

Why choose a leisure trust as operator?

23.10 There are three principal reasons to use a leisure trust to operate leisure facilities:
(i) a leisure trust can engender a sense of public ownership in the facilities. It is arguably appropriate that such facilities are provided by a charitable, non-profit distributing body rather than by a profit-making leisure operator;
(ii) a leisure trust ensures that there is an independent body responsible for the provision of leisure facilities. Although the charity and the local authority concerned will have negotiated a detailed management agreement, any leisure trust must be operationally independent from local authority control. This gives it a degree of extra freedom to act in the best interests of the facilities. The trust should have a board of trustees (the directors) of the charity comprised largely of non-local authority connected individuals, giving fresh thinking and ideas to the service provision;
(iii) use of a leisure trust gives reassurance of independent scrutiny of the charity's activities by the Charity Commission. The Charity Commission holds a register of charities and monitors the activities of those charities. The Commission's powers of investigation into a charity's activities are designed to give reassurance to members of the public that charitable funds are being applied effectively and for the correct charitable purposes.

The financial benefits

23.11 Leisure facilities are facing increasing pressures on funding. Local authorities are not required to provide the facilities by virtue of the Local Government (Miscellaneous Provisions) Act 1976, s 19 and thus the temptation can be to reduce spending in this area. Leisure trusts do have certain key financial benefits which can be attractive for the local authority concerned:
(i) relief from National Non-Domestic Rates (NNDR). Pursuant to the provisions of the Local Government Act 1988, s 43, where a building is wholly or mainly used for charitable purposes, the charity concerned is entitled to mandatory 80 per cent NNDR relief, with the remaining 20 per cent relief being discretionary. Discretionary relief is not generally granted to bodies operating local leisure facilities;
(ii) exemption from VAT on admission charges pursuant to the Value Added Tax Act 1994, Sch 9, Group 10. Whilst the fees charged to visiting members of the public would no doubt remain the same, the exemption from the need to charge VAT on admission fees would effectively mean that the net receipts from the gate are 17.5 per cent higher than when operated by a local authority or other profit-distributing organisation;
(iii) relief from corporation tax on profits arising from charitable activities. Additionally, the profit from any activities of a trading subsidiary created to operate part of the portfolio of leisure facilities could be paid to the charity on an annual basis by way of a gift aid payment. Any such gift aided profit would be exempt from corporation tax.

23.12   Local authorities often view these financial advantages as significant in enabling capital investment in their leisure facilities. Dependent on the terms of the agreement reached with the charity, the capital investment may be undertaken either by the local authority or the charity concerned.

Disadvantages of a leisure trust

23.13   The Charity Commission has recently produced a publication[1] dealing with Recreational Charities Act charities and, it is fair to say, is concerned to see that charities are not simply used as tax effective vehicles for the provision of local authority services. For this reason, it is likely that any application to register a new charity will be subject to detailed scrutiny by the Charity Commission and may take some time (we would anticipate anywhere between three and six months for registration, although it is not uncommon for applications to take longer). In addition, the Charity Commission is adopting a 'gateway' approach to new charity registrations which see even the most straightforward applications for registration being subject to an unprecedented level of scrutiny leading to further delay and costs for the applicant charity.

1   RR4: The Recreational Charities Act 1958.

23.14   A charity is operated by its trustees in accordance with its objects for the benefit of its beneficiaries. It is essential that any charity is independent of outside influence, but it is also important to recognise the commercial reality that charities need to contract with outside bodies to enable them to fulfil their objectives. The Charity Commission generally scrutinises such arrangements in significant detail at the point of registration and is concerned to ensure that charities retain independence and discretion where it is reasonable to do so.

23.15   Moving on from this is the requirement for management agreements and other contractual documentation to be negotiated on arms' length terms. Documentation needs to be carefully drafted and negotiated to ensure that it respects the capabilities of the charity concerned, but in a way which achieves as far as possible the local authority's objectives.

23.16   Finally, care will need to be taken to ensure that the charitable and trading activities of any leisure portfolio are allocated correctly to the charity and its trading subsidiary respectively. The management agreement will need to reflect this and any leases etc will need to grant rights to each entity.

CORPORATE STRUCTURES AVAILABLE

23.17   A company limited by guarantee is the preferred option for new, service-providing charities as it has the benefit of limited liability (in most situations) for its directors, contracts can be entered into in the name of the company rather than the individual trustees and people are generally familiar with the corporate format. By way of contrast, trusts and unincorporated associations are unincorporated bodies where contracts are entered into in the names of the trustees and where personal liability could, potentially, attach, although generally the trustees would be entitled to receive an indemnity from the charity's funds.

23.18 A company limited by guarantee is particularly suited to non-profit-distributing companies. It has a board of directors (often referred to as 'trustees' in the voluntary sector) and these directors would be responsible for ensuring that the objects of the charity are fulfilled. There would be a separate membership of the charity (members are akin to shareholders in a for-profit company) and these members would be entitled to attend AGMs and vote on the appointment and removal of trustees. It is important to understand, however, that membership does not give any right to receive payments by way of dividend distributions and all 'profits' from the charity's activities must be kept within the charity or applied for its charitable purposes.

23.19 It would be normal for the membership of the charity to be the same as the trustees; there are no particular reasons why the composition of the membership should be any different to that of the trustee body. The real benefits of membership come from charities such as The National Trust where the existence of a separate membership allows other people to have a full right to participate in the charity's activities.

23.20 An alternative structure might be a non-charitable company limited by guarantee, often referred to as a not for profit organisation (NFPO). This would have the same overall format as a charitable company limited by guarantee but its objects would be non-charitable (eg, could provide for the promotion of sport, which is not a charitable activity). However, the mandatory 80 per cent national non-domestic rates relief enjoyed by charities is discretionary for NFPOs, while there is no exemption from corporation tax on any profits earned by the company.

RELATIONSHIP OF PARTIES INVOLVED

General considerations

23.21 A charity is an independent vehicle which exists for the benefit of its charitable objects only and not for the benefit of any other people or organisations. This includes local authorities. What this means in practical terms is that the charity would need to be operated independently with separate management boards etc.

23.22 It clearly makes sense for the charity and the local authority to work closely together but, when doing so, the charity must be careful to ensure that it is dealing on arm's length terms with the local authority. For example, it might be appropriate for the charity to share certain facilities and services: this could extend from sharing photocopiers to the use of certain members of staff for either managerial or administrative functions. Ideally the charity would have access to its own staff and facilities but, certainly in its early years, this might not be appropriate given the size of the charity.

23.23 If facilities are to be shared, this will need to be evidenced by way of facilities and/or secondment (in the case of staff) agreements. These will need to include clear provisions setting out how the fees for the use of these facilities are to be calculated. It is essential that the charity must be able to justify objectively its use of any facilities provided by the local authority and must in particular ensure that it is paying no more than market rate for these facilities.

Treatment of profits

23.24   As is illustrated by the examples set out below, all profits or surpluses made by the charity must be kept for application in furtherance of the charity's objects and cannot be distributed to other third parties. This is an important point for local authorities to understand at an early stage.

Capital funding issues

23.25   Frequently there are issues about how leisure trusts would be able to raise capital funding. As is clearly shown by the examples set out below, the charity may well require capital funding support from the local authority in the early years but there is no reason why the charity could not seek funding on its own account once the charity has established a track record. It certainly would have the power to do so within the terms of its memorandum of association.

23.26   As a practical issue, leasing companies may well be similarly wary of funding the charity or may not offer as favourable terms as they might offer to more established companies. This is very much a matter for commercial negotiation.

CONTRACTUAL RELATIONSHIPS

Introduction

23.27   Charities can become involved in out-sourced leisure provision either by responding to expressions of interest from leisure providers who are in a current contractual relationship with local authorities for a charity to be involved (on a sub-contract or an assignment basis) or, more commonly, in considering the future leisure provision following a best value review, a local authority may invite a charity to become involved in the provision of the leisure facilities in conjunction with another leisure operator. This might typically see the local authority concerned 'sponsoring' (that is, assisting in the incorporation of) the new charity.

Contract direct with local authority

23.28   Many local authorities are actively considering sponsoring a local leisure trust to operate their leisure facilities. The typical vehicle would see the authority creating a new charity as a company limited by guarantee. The local authority would then enter into a direct relationship with the charity. It may also be necessary to involve the charity's trading subsidiary in the event of the facilities including a large catering or other non charitable facility. This type of arrangement is shown at para **23.35**.

23.29 Alternatively, for those local authorities which feel that the option of creating their own leisure trust is fraught with too many difficulties, the authority may wish to enter into a relationship with an established charity operating in this field. The contractual structure is the same.

Charity involved by way of a sub-contract or assignment from existing for profit leisure operator

23.30 The diagram at para **23.36** shows how relations may appear in the case of a subcontract or assignment structure.

Sub-contract

23.31 A for-profit leisure operator and the local authority have previously entered into an agreement for provision of the leisure facilities. The local authority subsequently wishes to secure cost savings or permit capital works to be undertaken at the facilities. Whilst there may not be the ability to fund such works or make such savings within the existing contract, this objective could be achieved by the involvement of a charitable leisure trust.

23.32 The existing leisure operator, accordingly, approaches the charity with a proposal for the charity to run the facilities as a sub-contractor. The trust would consider the request (for example, review the nature of the facilities and assess whether these fall within the charity's objects) and might agree to submit proposals which will include the financial proposals by the charity for this contract. The local authority would no doubt require either a reduced level of unitary charge to be paid by it to the head contractor or for there to be obligations introduced for the facility management (FM) provider to undertake additional capital works.

23.33 In the event that the agreement with the local authority and the leisure operator includes income share provisions which are activated once the facilities reach a certain level of turnover, these would continue to apply to the head contractor notwithstanding the grant of the subcontract. The agreement with the charity would need to require it to pay a share of its income to the head contractor to enable it to fulfil its payment obligations to the authority.

Assignment

23.34 As above, but the parties agree that the leisure operator shall assign the benefit of and its duties under the contract to the leisure charity. This will, effectively, see the operator drop out of the picture although it may be envisaged that the operator may continue to be involved as the local authority may well require, at least in the leisure trust's early years, a guarantee or bond from the contractor guaranteeing the future provision of services by the leisure trust.

Figure 1: Contract direct with local authority

23.35

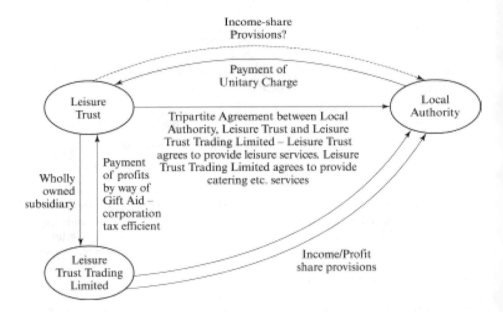

Figure 2: Sub-contract with existing leisure operator

23.36

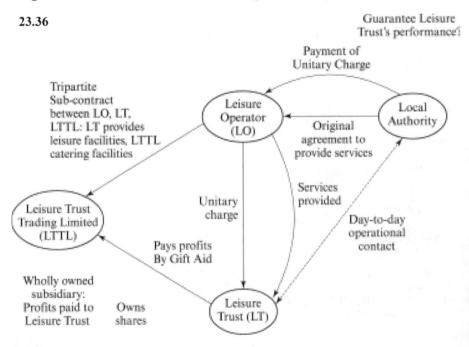

Objectives of the contract

23.37   Clearly, the aim of the contract has to be to transfer the responsibility for the day-to-day running of the leisure centres concerned to the leisure trust. However, the local authority must bear in mind the restrictions placed upon charities, both under the terms of their constitution and under guidelines issued by the Charity Commission. In particular, local authorities should be bearing in mind Charity Commission guidance papers produced in connection with relationships between *Charities and Local Authorities*[1] and *Charities and Contracts*[2].

1   Leaflet CC29.
2   Leaflet CC37. Both of these can be obtained either from the Charity Commission or by visiting the Charity Commission's website (www.charity-commission.gov.uk).

23.38   Whilst on the one hand, the local authority will wish to retain as much control as possible over the activities of the leisure trust, it will need to respect at all times the leisure trust's need to remain independent in the fulfilment of its charitable objectives. As mentioned above, it is important that local authorities appreciate that charities cannot simply be used as tax efficient vehicles to fulfil the local authority's plans.

23.39   Having said this, the commercial reality is that the leisure trust, in order to fulfil its charitable objectives, is required to enter into a contract with the local authority and it is to be expected that the local authority will wish to exert a certain degree of residual, operational control. The key point is to ensure that the level of control is appropriate in all the circumstances. It is important to recognise that these issues are more difficult to get right when dealing with charities than when dealing with other entities.

COMMERCIAL CONTRACT ISSUES

23.40   The contracting out of leisure facilities is nothing new within the public sector. However, there are certain key points which will be different when dealing with leisure trusts than when dealing with for-profit leisure operators.

Demand risk

23.41   The local authority leisure market is unlike many others: most customers pay for using the service and, accordingly, the level of income to be received by an operator will be at a direct correlation to the number of people using the facilities.

23.42   Income from users of the facilities may well be supplemented by the payment of a unitary charge by the local authority. However, in certain circumstances, the facilities themselves are profitable in their own right and the local authority may seek to share the income from those facilities.

23.43   Further, even where a unitary charge is paid by the local authority to the leisure trust, the leisure trust may well be required to share the income generated from the facilities once the income or profit on those facilities reaches a certain trigger level.

23.44   Clearly, it is for the leisure trust and the local authority concerned to negotiate a suitable unitary charge. From the leisure trust's point of view, it is essential that the unitary charge is pitched at a level which enables it to operate the facilities, yet also (and this point is frequently misunderstood as far as charities are concerned) allow it to build up reserves against future expenditure. It is not necessary for charities to pay out all of their income in any one financial year, so long as any money retained is held back pursuant to the terms of a reserves policy agreed by the charity's trustees. As a guide, charities may wish to retain a reserve of up to six months of central administration costs. However, it is for each leisure trust to decide on the appropriate level for its activities. Relevant factors will include the level of risk involved in pursuing responsibility for the facilities.

23.45   It is important to retain the ability for the unitary charge payment to be reviewed, not only to ensure that this remains in line with inflation, but also to reflect the fact that competing facilities may well be opened during the time of the contract. Clearly, such competing facilities will have an impact on the level of monies received from users of the facilities and may well undermine the viability of the leisure trust's business case. The following is a clause contained within a leisure contract:

> 'The annual contract fee shall be reviewed on each anniversary of the commencement date ('the review date') and shall be increased or reduced by a percentage calculated in accordance with the approved index. Such increase or reduction (if any) shall take effect in respect of the 12 month period commencing on the relevant review date'.

23.46   This clause on its own is inadequate to deal with potential variations to the likely demand for the use of the facilities and would require a further review provision taking into account external market conditions (effectively a form of benchmarking exercise) to ensure that the leisure trust can be comfortable in assuming responsibility for the management of the facilities over a medium term period.

Unitary charge—income share/profit share distinction

23.47   Following on from the above, a distinction needs to be made between income and profit share. A key feature of all charities is that their profits cannot be distributed among the members of the charity. Rather, it is essential that any surpluses made by a charity are retained for that charity's use. The only exemption to this is where the charity is subject to an agreement otherwise, but even then the provision can only allow a share of *income* and not of *profit*. An agreement to share profit would be ultra vires the charity.

23.48   Accordingly, in any 'profit' share provision agreed between a local authority and a leisure trust, either because the centre is anticipated to return a surplus each year, or in the event of the total income from the centre exceeding a certain threshold, it is essential to ensure that the revenue sharing clause refers to a share of *revenue or income* and *not of profit*. We are aware that this point has been taken by the Charity Commission previously: it is fundamental to ensure that this key point is correctly dealt with to avoid potential problems in the future.

Maintenance/development of facilities/equipment

23.49 It is generally the case that the contractor will be responsible for the maintenance, repair and replacement of plant and equipment used within the facilities (the soft FM), while the local authority will retain responsibility for the repair, maintenance and, if necessary, renewal of the structure of the building and redecoration etc of the exterior of the building (the hard FM).

23.50 Care clearly needs to be taken when dealing with existing leisure facilities and the state of repair and condition of key aspects of the centres, including the swimming pool itself, plant and equipment used in connection with the swimming pool and changing facilities etc. Schedules of condition should be drawn up at the commencement of the contract to deal with these points. Any schedules would need to be agreed between the parties at the time. Thought will also need to be given to the requirement to repair during the term of the agreement, and the state of the facilities on termination. In particular, if the leisure trust is assuming responsibility for the provision of facilities at an older, 1960s centre, it will be unrealistic to set a too-high delivery up requirement.

23.51 Provision will also need to be made within the contract to deal with the responsibility for any developments to the facilities and the purchase of new equipment. This is a key issue given the dynamic nature of the leisure market, particularly for longer term facility management contracts. In certain cases, leisure trusts agree to fund certain capital works out of their annual income surplus, whilst major capital work would be the responsibility of the local authority concerned. It is important that the respective parties' obligations in this connection are set out clearly within the contract documentation. Whilst ultimately it is in the interests of all concerned to ensure that the facilities are kept up to date and developed in accordance with consumer demand, it is also important for the prospective liabilities of the parties in this connection to be dealt with at an early stage.

23.52 A typical clause may read as follows:

'When considering any investments or expansions to the service after commencement date which are additional to the service required under the contract, the contractors' proposals will be expected to reflect its desire to utilise the assets of the centre in a manner which maintains and enhances their value.

Any proposals from the contractor to enhance the service shall relate to the primary function of providing a quality community sports and leisure service.

The cost of any improvements shall be agreed in writing, between the contractor and the council, and may be borne by the council and the contractor in such proportion and on such a basis as may be agreed.'

23.53 This is essentially no more than an agreement to agree, and may be the best that can be agreed at the outset of the contract. However, it might be possible to require this clause to provide that the costs incurred in effecting any changes of use to the facilities should be borne by the local authority while, say, refurbishment works to, for example, the changing rooms should be borne by the leisure trust. Between these two extremes, there should be a duty on the parties to co-operate in good faith to agree responsibilities for the works.

QUEST accreditation

23.54   Many local authorities are keen to ensure that their leisure centres achieve QUEST accreditation[1] and this is frequently—and increasingly—a requirement built in to leisure contracts. The typical requirement will be for the centre to achieve QUEST accreditation within a fixed period from commencement of the contract, generally between 12 and 24 months. Accreditation is granted in respect of the centre and the systems used at the centre so is not necessarily dependent on the identity of the operator. However, care will need to be taken to ensure any new systems will not impact on any existing QUEST accreditation. Accordingly, on the basis that the leisure trust continues to adopt QUEST accredited systems, then there should be no difficulty for the leisure trust in agreeing to the QUEST accreditation. However, in the case of a new build centre or where QUEST has not been obtained previously, it will be necessary for the local authority concerned to grant a period of grace to enable QUEST to be obtained. Experience suggests that a time period of around 18 months is generally acceptable to leisure operators in this connection.

1   The QUEST accreditation scheme is a scheme which sets out to define leisure industry standards and good practice. Local authorities will require accreditation for 'QUEST Facility Management'. The scheme is operated by PMP Consultancy (www.pmpconsult.com) and is supported by four sports councils, the Local Government Association, the Chief Leisure Officers' Association and the Institute of Leisure and Amenity Management, among others.

National non-domestic rates

23.55   As indicated above, key financial savings can be made by taking advantage of the charity's 80 per cent mandatory exemption from national non-domestic rates. It is essential that a clause along the following lines is included in the contract to achieve this:

'The contractor will be responsible for payment of all national non domestic rates or successor taxes for the centre.'

23.56   It is a matter for the leisure trust subsequently to make an application for exemption from the remaining 20 per cent national non-domestic rates liability. Experience shows that leisure trusts are generally unsuccessful in achieving this further discretionary relief, although much depends on the approach of the local authority concerned.

Role of trading subsidiary

23.57   As explained above, it is essential that a survey is undertaken of the facilities, in conjunction with the local authority's and leisure trusts' professional advisers, to determine whether any parts of the facility may need to be operated by a trading subsidiary, which would be wholly owned by the charity.

23.58   Charities may only agree to provide services which fall within their charitable objects. Developments since the introduction of the Recreational Charities Act 1958 and under charity law generally provide that multi-use sports centres themselves are charitable but that certain aspects of these facilities may give rise to non-charitable trading. Examples of non-charitable trading include the provision of bar and catering facilities which can be accessed by both users and non-users of the facility, and facilities such as golf courses and function suites. In the case of bar and catering facilities, the general guide is that if the facilities are used generally by non-user members of the public, then these facilities cannot be operated by a charity.

23.59   However, there is now an exception to this which provides that, where the leisure trust concerned has a reasonable expectation that its income from non-charitable trading activities will, in any one financial year, not exceed £50,000 (which would cover most leisure trusts), then these facilities can be operated through the charity itself. However, given the potential duration of the contract to provide the leisure services, it would be prudent to ensure that, where any non-charitable trading will be taking place, the leisure trust ensures that another entity is responsible for the provision of those services.

23.60   A key further point to note in this connection is that the contract to provide the leisure services must be a tripartite contract including both the charity and a trading company, with the trading company itself assuming responsibility for the provision of the catering or other trading activities. This can lead to complex drafting of the contract to reflect the fact that certain elements of the unitary charge or any income share provisions must recognise the fact that the catering or other trading activities are run by a separate trading subsidiary.

23.61   It is important to note—and is frequently misunderstood—that the leisure trust cannot generally enter into the contract with the local authority and subsequently sub-contract the provision of the services to its trading subsidiary. A charity cannot agree to be responsible for undertaking activities which are ultra vires its objects. Accordingly, the main contract could not require the leisure trust to provide non-charitable catering etc facilities. However, if as part of the development of the facilities the leisure trust subsequently decides to set up a café facility, it can do so but could only do so on wholly arm's length terms (ie that the catering space within the facilities would need to be rented out on a commercial basis ensuring that a full market rent is charged).

Lease/licence of site

23.62   It goes without saying that the leisure trust concerned must be entitled to occupy the leisure facilities. It is preferable for there to be a lease (which should be contracted out of the Landlord and Tenant Act 1954) entitling the charity (and its trading subsidiary if relevant) to occupy the facilities. However, many contracts simply refer to a licence to occupy the facilities for the purposes of the facility management contracts.

23.63   Whichever route is adopted, if the centre includes facilities which can only be operated through a trading subsidiary of the leisure trust, it will be necessary for the lease or licence to separate out the areas to be occupied by the charity from those to be occupied by the trading subsidiary.

23.64   If this split does not occur, and the charity is required to grant a sub-lease to the trading subsidiary, it would also need to comply with restrictions within the

Charities Act 1993, s 36 in connection with the disposal of charity land. This will be particularly relevant where the lease is for a period in excess of seven years where it would be necessary to obtain a surveyors' report confirming that the disposal of the part of the lease to the trading subsidiary is on the best terms reasonably obtainable. In any event, it will be necessary to ensure that the lease or licence were granted on arm's length terms.

However, these problems can be avoided if it is the local authority concerned which grants separate leases or licences to the charity and its trading subsidiary.

23.65   A standard clause within the contract could read as follows:

'1   The Authority agrees to grant leases of the parts of the properties required to be used by the Charity to discharge its obligations under this Agreement to the Charity subject to and with the benefit of the lease granted under sub-clause 2 in a form satisfactory to the Parties.

2   The Authority agrees to grant leases as appropriate to the Trading Subsidiary over the parts of the Properties required to be used by the Trading Subsidiary (principally covering catering and vending facilities) to enable it to discharge its obligations under this Agreement in advance of granting leases to the Charity in a form satisfactory to the Parties.'

Consequences on termination

23.66   A leisure trust as a charitable company must act prudently when considering what will happen on termination of the contract. It will have secured investment in the facilities: generally, there is no requirement for a charity to secure repayment of the investments made, although, in exceptional circumstances, it may be appropriate to require repayment of certain of those items of investment in the event of early termination by the local authority without fault on the part of the leisure trust. Clearly, in the event of early termination with outstanding equipment, etc leases, the local authority will be required to assume responsibility for the payment of the remaining instalments on any such leases.

23.67   However, the issue of what happens to the employees on termination can be a cause of concern and has prompted the Charity Commission to provide guidance in this area. Specifically, the Charity Commission, in *Charities and Contracts*[1] states as follows:

'We advise charities to bear in mind that they might have future liabilities to their employees, such as payments to those who have to be made redundant if and when a public body terminates its contract with the charity. Liabilities like this could have serious financial consequences particularly for smaller charities without any reserves, if they arise and have to be met when they were not anticipated.'

1   Leaflet CC37.

23.68   Of course, the Transfer of Undertakings (Protection of Employment) Regulations 1981[1] will apply where charities assume responsibility for the provision of the leisure services. It is generally anticipated that, on termination of the contract term and in the event that charities are unsuccessful in securing a further contract to run the facilities, a future contractor will assume responsibility for the employment of the employees, again pursuant to the operation of TUPE.

1   SI 1981/1794, referred to as 'TUPE'.

23.69   However, operators are exposed to risks in certain circumstances: examples include where the contract is for the operation of an old centre which, at the end of the contract period, is closed by the local authority pending construction of new facilities. In the time between the closure of the old centre and the opening of the new one, the local authority will not wish to retain responsibility for the employment of the members of staff and, accordingly, those contracts of employment will terminate and a redundancy situation will arise. This could have significant costs for the leisure trust concerned. The reality could well be that the leisure trust concerned would not be able to finance the redundancy payments and this could lead to an insolvency position.

23.70   It is an issue for the local authority and the leisure trust concerned to negotiate this point but it is essential that the leisure trust addresses this during the contract negotiations. From the leisure trust's perspective, the local authority would ideally offer an indemnity to cover the leisure trust in the event that staff remained employed by the leisure trust on termination of the contract as a result of the closure of the centre. However, any local authority would be very wary about offering any such indemnity.

23.71   The issue at the end of the day will come down to one of risk: if it is likely that the local authority concerned will want to close the centre at the end of the contract period, leisure trusts should attempt to secure a local authority indemnity to cover staff redundancies. On the other hand, in the case of a new build or newly refurbished centre, it is open for the leisure trust concerned to take a view that it feels comfortable with the low degree of risk of the services terminating and thus redundancy costs accruing.

23.72   One solution might be to prepare a detailed termination clause which grants an indemnity in the case of the local authority deciding at the end of the term to no longer provide a leisure service from the centre: otherwise, the leisure trust would be expected to bear the TUPE risk. An alternative might simply be for the leisure trust to built up a Trust reserve fund to ensure that, on termination of the contract, it has sufficient funding to meet any possible redundancies. Clearly, any such reserve would need to be financed, probably by way of an increased unitary charge from the local authority.

THE FUTURE

23.73   As mentioned above, the leisure market is dynamic and continually changing. Recent developments include the availability of PFI credits for the development and refurbishment of leisure facilities. Several key private sector leisure operators are active in this area.

23.74   Where does this leave the leisure trust? On the one level, there is nothing to stop leisure trusts having a role in the provision of facility management services within PFI schemes. Whilst this has yet to be tested, the same advantages which apply to the use of a leisure trust in a normal contracting-out arrangement will continue to apply to PFI schemes. However, if this is to be developed, the particular requirements and restrictions of leisure trusts will need to be borne in mind by the parties concerned. Key points will include the inability for a leisure trust to pay profits to the SPV and the inability of the SPV to 'control' (other than through the contract) the leisure trust. Both of these points may be causes of concern for both the local authorities and funders concerned.

23.75   Outside of PFI, leisure trusts will have an increasing role to play in the provision of leisure facilities. The perception of 'public ownership' of leisure trusts is attractive to local authorities, as are the financial benefits. There is also an increasing understanding among both local authorities and trustees of leisure trusts of the restrictions under which leisure trusts must operate in recognition of their charitable status and, in particular, the requirement for charities to be truly independent of their funding and contracting partners.

CHAPTER 24

Case study: library

Helen Randall

BACKGROUND AND CONTEXT

What is a library PFI scheme?

24.01 Local authority B is a library authority which, for the reasons set out below, wishes to procure a new library. The main options are to procure the construction or refurbishment of an existing building to accommodate a library and to procure the related facilities management services (eg cleaning and maintenance) separately. Alternatively, if the local authority has insufficient capital resources to procure the new library, to seek approval from the Projects Review Group (which is the inter-departmental group in central government which approves the funding of contracts under the PFI) for PFI credits, which are a form of government subsidy used to support schemes procured under the Private Finance Initiative (for more details see chapter 13).

24.02 Nowadays, local authorities often wish to integrate libraries with other services delivered directly to the community and this has certainly been the case in relation to the early PFI library projects. For example:
— Sedgeley PFI Scheme, involving Dudley Metropolitan Borough Council and Dudley Primary Health Trust, who procured a library under the PFI as part of a community healthcare facility which also included the NHS Trust's local mental health unit with day care facilities, out-patients' department, clinical and therapy rooms and Dudley Metropolitan Borough Council's social services office. All the services are provided in one location for the fully-managed accommodation and maintenance through a contract between the council, the NHS Trust and Norwich Union's PPP Fund, as private sector service provider;
— Bournemouth Borough Council's library PFI, which combines a library ICT network to other branch libraries and community access to the internet, provided through a contract between the council and a consortium consisting of Kier, Caxton and Allied Worldwide financed by Helaba Bank;
— London Borough of Hackney's library, procured under the PFI from a consortium headed by Rotch which forms part of a technology and learning centre for the community;
— Brighton and Hove City Council's Library PFI Scheme, which is part of a wider, city centre mixed use redevelopment scheme consisting of café, hotel, shops, social and private housing and new public square to be provided by Norwich Union PPP Fund in conjunction with Walter Llewelyn (building contractor), Caxton (facilities management) and Cypher (bibliographics).

Why is there a need for a library PFI scheme?

24.03   Often library services are accommodated in out-dated buildings which do not allow disabled access, or the raised floors or suspended ceilings required to accommodate cabling and air-conditioning needed for the ICT equipment which is now regarded as an essential component of a public library service.

24.04   The local authority may hold valuable special collections of books or local history archives which cannot be accessed by members of the public within the constraints of existing accommodation.

24.05   A poor maintenance history where schools and residential homes have been prioritised above libraries by the local authorities may mean that addressing the maintenance backlog would be more expensive than procuring an entirely new facility. The present library may be poorly served by public transport and have an ICT system which is inadequate for a modern library service. For example, there may be no online public access to the library catalogue or community information and the existing ICT system may be unable to interact with the internet or with modern ICT systems.

What are the advantages of a library PFI?

24.06   As part of its application for a PFI credit, the local authority will have to demonstrate that pursuing a new library under the PFI would offer better value for money than a traditional procurement. In particular, the scheme will need to achieve significant risk transfer. The private sector consortium usually bears the risk of finding and acquiring a suitable site, obtaining full planning permission and securing design and construction. The private sector consortium will bear other risks, including life cycle maintenance costs, facilities management and administration costs, costs of providing a bibliographic and reprographics service and the risk of costs of general changes in law. As with other PFI projects, the authority can make deductions from the unitary payment where either the space or the ICT fails to meet performance standards.

24.07   The private sector consortium may contribute to the purchase of new book stock and a significant upfront investment in the ICT systems, which will achieve better catalogue and stock control.

DESCRIPTION OF PARTIES INVOLVED

24.08   The two main parties involved are the local authority in its capacity as library authority and a special purpose company in which the main private sector parties in the consortium hold shares. The shareholders could include a construction company, the land owner and equity providers.

24.09   The other relevant parties are the government's Department of Culture, Media and Sport, who grants the PFI credits but who are not party to the contractual arrangements, the ICT system supplier and suppliers of bibliographic, facilities management and other services who sub-contract with the special purpose company.

24.10 Diagram outlining contractual relationships

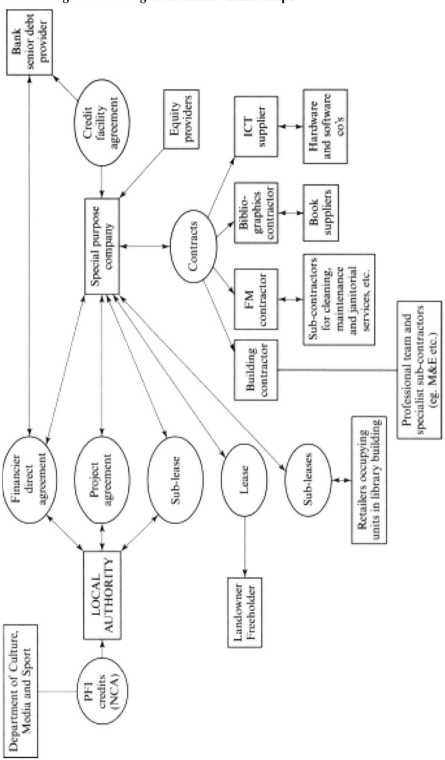

OBJECTIVES OF THE CONTRACT

24.11   In procuring a new library, it is likely that the local authority's members will want a landmark building in the town centre which will make a bold architectural statement. The building will need to attract users and provide a focal point for the community so that the library can be used out of hours for special events and community functions. The Hackney, Bournemouth and Brighton Library schemes have also been at the centre of wider economic regeneration and redevelopment of the area, and in several cases the construction of the new library has been subsidised by commercial development of retail units and other commercial uses such as restaurants, cafes and housing.

24.12   Most librarians are of the view that despite increasing use of ICT and new media, members of the public are likely to continue to use books for recreational and educational purposes. However, the design of the library will need to allow flexibility of layout to meet changing demands of library users. Some of these needs may conflict. For example, a modern library needs to contain quite a quiet reference and study area and audio facilities for a music library. There may need to be a secure archive store for special collection books, a children's library (including baby changing facilities), a separate teenage section and an adult library with a browsing area. There may also need to be facilities for public internet access, a local information inquiry point, meeting rooms for community groups, a café suitable for families and staff facilities.

24.13   If the library contract is to include the provision of ICT systems as well as accommodation, the new library ICT system may also need to link into the authority's other branch libraries and to give public access to the catalogue and community information, the internet, email, word processing, spreadsheet and other applications. Time will also need to be set aside to allow for training of library staff to use new ICT system and for cataloguing of the books on to the system. ICT may be provided at a different date to the main accommodation either beforehand or afterwards and its installation will need to be carried out at an appropriate phase in order not to disrupt the construction and fitting out of the library.

24.14   The authority should consider carefully whether better value for money will be obtained by transferring or retaining demand risk for ICT. Our expectations of what an ICT system should deliver change quickly as new products come on the market. Therefore it is usually appropriate to cater for the refreshment of ICT at frequent intervals of say 3–5 years throughout the life of the contract.

LEGAL AND COMMERCIAL ISSUES

24.15   A local authority's powers to provide library facilities are contained in the Public Libraries and Museums Act 1964, s 4 which provides:

'(2) The functions of a library authority as such shall be exercisable within an area (in this Act referred to as a 'library area') consisting of the administrative area of the authority, or... in the case of a joint board established under section 5 below, consisting of the areas which, if the authorities constituting the board were library authorities, would form their library areas, and may also be exercised elsewhere than within its library area if the authority thinks fit.

(3) In Wales, county councils and county borough councils shall ... be library authorities for the purposes of this Act',

and s 7 which provides:

'(1) It shall be the duty of every library authority to provide a comprehensive and efficient library service for all persons desiring to make use thereof...:

Provided that although a library authority shall have power to make facilities for the borrowing of books and other materials available to any persons it shall not by virtue of this subsection be under a duty to make such facilities available to persons other than those whose residence or place of work is within the library area of the authority or who are undergoing full-time education within that area.

(2) In fulfilling its duty under the preceding subsection, a library authority shall in particular have regard to the desirability—

(a) of securing, by the keeping of adequate stocks, by arrangements with other library authorities, and by any other appropriate means, that facilities are available for the borrowing of, or reference to, books and other printed matter, and pictures, gramophone records, films and other materials, sufficient in number, range and quality to meet the general requirements and any special requirements both of adults and children; and

(b) of encouraging both adults and children to make full use of the library service, and of providing advice as to its use and of making available such bibliographical and other information as may be required by persons using it; and

(c) of securing, in relation to any matter concerning the functions both of the library authority as such and other authority whose functions are exercisable within the library area, that there is full co-operation between the persons engaged in carrying out those functions.'

These are supplemented by the council's well-being powers in the Local Government Act 2000, s 2.

Procurement

24.16   The contract for the provision of a library including ICT will contain elements of works (the building), services (facilities management and bibliographics) and supplies (the ICT systems and books). In preparing the OJEC notice advertising the contract, the local authority will need to consider the predominant purpose of the contract before determining whether it should be advertised as a works, services or supplies contract.

24.17   It should be borne in mind that at present there are only a relatively limited number of suppliers of specialist library ICT systems and bibliographic services and careful consideration should be given as to whether better value for money can be obtained by letting separate contracts for the ICT systems and bibliographic services.

Best value

24.18   The usual provisions allowing for benchmarking, market testing and periodic best value reviews will need to be incorporated within the contract. Given the nature of a library service, public consultation in particular, provisions requiring for user satisfaction surveys will need to be incorporated within the contract. To date, library PFI projects have not involved the transfer of the specialist library staff to the private sector and therefore careful delineation will need to be made in the user satisfaction survey between the quality of the library service consisting of supply of books and information by the library staff, and the quality of the facilities (eg cleanliness, accessibility) and where internet facilities are to be provided careful thought will need to be given both in relation to designing a user satisfaction survey, and to the operation of the performance payment mechanism to build where failure or delay in connecting to the internet is attributable to a cause outside the private sector service provider's control).

BVPIs

24.19   At the time of writing the best value performance indicators ('BVPIs') for library services are as set out below:

Cost/efficiency		
BV code	Indicator	Definition
BV115	The cost per physical visit to public libraries	N/A
BV116	Spending per head of population on cultural and recreational facilities and activities	N/A
BV117	The number of physical visits per 1,000 population to public library premises	An estimate of the total number of visits by members of the public to libraries for whatever purpose during the financial year. Based on a one week sample during the year using the definitions and procedure set out in CIPFA's Activity Sampling Guidance Note, or using a more accurate method of estimation. Authorities may, if they wish, base their figures on a larger statistical sample than the one suggested by CIPFA.

These may be supplemented by local performance indicators and revision to the performance indicators may need to be addressed as a change in law.

24.20   Demographic changes in the local authority's area or increasing demands of service users may require the library opening hours to be fundamentally changed. Careful consideration needs to be given to achieving a balance which is commercially fair on the private sector service provider and which represents value for money for the local authority. Any change in hours may also affect projections of third party income, which would otherwise have been available by letting the library space for special functions.

Security

24.21   Responsibility for security in procurement of a library needs careful thought— it is likely that the local authority will be primarily responsible for maintaining security of the library and its contents (ie preventing theft and vandalism) inside the library during its main hours of operation, with the private sector provider being responsible for the security of the premises out of hours.

New stock

24.22   The private sector may be asked by the local authority to make a contribution to the purchase of new stock. If this is to be the case, discussion will need to take place as to how the funds for the purchase of bookstock are to be held, the advance notice required for purchase of books, how monies will be held when books to be purchased are out of print or are difficult to obtain, how the VAT on purchase of library materials other than books (for example, compact disks) should be treated and accounted for and whether the private sector will be able to take advantage of bulk discounts that would otherwise be available to the local authority. Particular care will need to be given to structuring the arrangement for contribution to the book fund so as to ensure that the transaction does not fall outside the definition of a 'private finance transaction' under the Local Authorities (Capital Finance) Regulations 1997, reg 16[1].

1   SI 1997/319 (as subsequently amended—see para **13.57**).

ICT

24.23   Where the accommodation and ICT elements are to be provided in separate phases, the performance payment mechanism for the contract will need to provide for staggered payments of unitary charge and the contract will need to address the consequences of termination of the ICT component of the contract without the accommodation or vice versa and provide for appropriate compensation provisions in either event.

Decant

24.24   Mobilisation and decanting will be issues where stock held in existing libraries needs to be transferred to the new library. The local authority will need to decide who is to be responsible for carrying out removal and to discuss with its private sector partner what period needs to be allowed after practical completion of the building works has taken place but before the library is open to members of the public. If valuable special collections are to be moved, an appropriate specialist removal contractor with sufficient levels of insurance cover may need to be involved.

Disability Discrimination Act 1995

24.25   As with any accommodation scheme, the library will need to be accessible to disabled users and the private sector contractor will be required to provide a building which complies with the requirements of the Disability Discrimination Act 1995 and current Building Regulations. Although incorporation of disabled access into the design of a newly built library should not be problematic, more difficulties will arise where the local authority is simply requiring the private sector partner to refurbish an existing building which may require substantial work to accommodate lifts, ramps and wider doorways. In that case the cost of those works will need to be factored into the local authority's affordability calculation and public sector comparator.

STANDARDISATION OF CONTRACTS

24.26   Where the library is to be procured under the PFI, the contract will be based on OGC Guidance. No standard form contract has yet been published for libraries.

24.27   Departures from the relevant standard guidance will need to include specific drafting provisions relating to decanting of library stock and mobilisation, supply of bibliographic services, provision of funds to purchase library stock and change of library opening hours. Suggested draft clauses addressing some of these issues are set out below.

Specimen clauses

24.28

1   Definitions

'**Acceptance Certificate**' means the certificate to be issued by the Independent Certifier on the Service Commencement Date;
'**Bibliographic Output Specification**' means the specification for the provision of bibliographic services by the Contractor;
'**Library Materials**' means the library materials including books, audio visual materials and other publications to be supplied as part of the Bibliographic Services during the Service Period;
'**Library Materials Fund**' means the fund established in accordance with the provision of clause [ ] for the purpose of funding the provision of Library Materials throughout the Service Period;
'**New Library Stock**' means the library materials including books, audio visual materials and other publications provided to the Council prior to the Service Commencement Date in accordance with the Bibliographic Output Specification.

2 New library stock

2.1 The Contractor shall supply the New Library Stock to the Council in accordance with the Bibliographic Output Specification.

2.2 The New Library Stock shall be supplied to the Council free from all liens, charges and encumbrances.

2.3 The Contractor warrants to the Council that the New Library Stock shall be of satisfactory quality (within the meaning of the Sale of Goods Act 1979) and fit for purpose.

2.4 [Notwithstanding the issue of the Acceptance Certificate,] the Council shall be entitled to reject any New Library Stock delivered which is not in accordance with this Agreement and shall not be deemed to have accepted any of the New Library Stock until the Council has had a reasonable opportunity to inspect them following delivery or, if later, within a reasonable time after any latent defect in the New Library Stock has become apparent.

2.5 The Contractor shall replace free of charge any items of New Library Stock lost or damaged in transit upon receiving written notice to that effect from the Council.

2.6 The Contractor shall [not] be required to maintain insurance cover in relation to the New Library Stock once the New Library Stock has been delivered to the Library in accordance with Bibliographic Output Specification.

2.7 The Council shall be entitled to visit the Bibliographic Service Provider's storage facility on reasonable notice for the purposes of inspecting and auditing the New Library Stock.

2.8 In the event that the New Library Stock Sum is unspent, the Contractor shall on the Service Commencement Date place the unspent sum into the Library Materials Fund.

3 Engagement of bibliographic service provider

3.1 The Contractor shall engage the services of the Bibliographic Service Provider to supply the Library Materials in accordance with the terms of the Bibliographic Output Specification.

3.2 The Contractor shall at all times comply with its obligations under the Bibliographic Services Supply Agreement and shall not terminate or vary in any material respect the Bibliographic Services Supply Agreement without the prior written consent of the Council.

CHAPTER 25

Case study: property outsourcing

Alan Corcoran

BACKGROUND AND CONTEXT

25.01   There has been a fundamental shift in real estate. The demand to increase shareholder value has led several types of organisation, from government and local authorities to the private sector, to refocus on their core business activities. Real estate outsourcing addresses this directly. In refocusing, organisations have sought (amongst other things) to pass the risk of property ownership and management to a specialist real estate outsourcing organisation, giving the outsourcer the maximum flexibility for its real estate needs.

What is a property outsourcing project?

25.02   Property outsourcing is a generic term covering a large number of potential situations. At its most basic, it is the transfer of ownership of property owned and/or occupied by the 'outsourcer' (for example, a local authority) to the private sector (commonly referred to as the 'service provider') for a cash sum. In return, the outsourcer is provided with flexible serviced accommodation (for an annual fee) by the service provider.

25.03   The outsourcer's estate can constitute (and typically has, to date, constituted) a range of properties from the small and specialised, to major office developments. Indeed, properties that can be outsourced range from town halls, civic accommodation, operational buildings, depots, fire and police stations, to residential houses and major developments. A diverse portfolio can often be an added advantage; the skill is identifying the development opportunities within the portfolio and exploiting the same.

25.04   Under the terms of the outsourcing contract, the property portfolios are transferred to an external organisation (the successful tenderer) and the local authority is provided with flexible serviced accommodation at an annual charge, for the duration of the contract.

25.05   The service provider provides or procures (by way of sub-contractor) the provision of the services required by the local authority, for instance, facilities management including cleaning and maintenance, health and safety, catering and childcare. The contract will provide for the use of performance measurement systems that ensure the outsourcer's issues and problems are resolved quickly, ie if targets are not met in the provision of services, a financial penalty is incurred by the service provider.

In what context could property outsourcing be a viable proposal?

25.06   The principal benefit of outsourcing is that the local authority can focus on its core businesses ie providing services to the public whilst allowing a third party to provide asset and liability management, facilities management and other property related services. Greater flexibility in terms of working practice and resulting cost savings can readily be seen during the life of the contract. For example, a more flexible working environment is a typical result of the outsourcing project with (perhaps) hot desking being introduced. Such a change may be particularly attractive to local authorities who want to introduce flexible working practices to encourage staff retention and recruitment.

25.07   In addition, the outsourcer will enjoy 'flexible' occupation (ie it will be able to vacate premises at short notice and require new premises to be provided by the service provider on short notice), accommodation will be properly maintained by the service provider and occupation costs will be transparent.

25.08   Potential conflicts and disputes can be readily identified with a mechanism built into the contract dealing with resolution of the same. The service provider can step down these obligations to its subcontractors, thus ensuring a high level of service at all time.

25.09   Some local authorities may have a concern that a property subsidiary is 'selling off the family silver', but commentators would argue that the savings to be gained over the life of the contract and inherent benefits gained in the process countermine this view.

Overview of recent outsourcing deals

Prime

25.10   PRIME (Private Sector Resource Initiative for Management of the Estate), was the groundbreaking outsourcing of the Department of Social Security portfolio in April 1998. The estate covers 1.64 million square metres of office accommodation comprising over 700 offices (being 16 per cent of the government civil estate) in 350 town and cities across the UK. The price paid by the service provider was £250 million. The DSS benefits financially by efficiency savings, allowing the benefit agents to concentrate on administering the social security system. The DSS may vacate without charge up to 35 per cent of the estate during the 20 year term of the contract and its service payments are reduced in the event of poor performance or buildings becoming unavailable. The National Audit Office estimates that the PRIME contract will save the government (and therefore the tax payer) £560 million over the contract term.

Abbey

25.11   This was a PFI-style deal which completed in October 2000 in respect of properties worth around £457 million and which involved Mapeley. Abbey National transferred its 6.5 million sq ft property portfolio to the service provider. To achieve the optimal combination of flexibility of tenure and cost certainty, the contract enabled Abbey National to vacate properties early or extend leases using a cost formula unaffected by market conditions. The idea was to match Abbey's business plans including the effect that e-commerce would have on business, the need for fewer branches, or a need for a greater number of smaller branches offering different services. Commentators estimate the deal is worth in the region of £200 million to Mapeley over the life of the 20 year contract.

Steps

25.12   Mapeley acquired 1.5 million sq ft (comprising 723 properties and 90,000 occupiers throughout England, Wales, Scotland and Ireland) from the Inland Revenue and Customs & Excise under a project called STEPS (Strategic Transfer of Estates to the Private Sector) in March 2001. Under the terms of the STEPS contract, the property portfolios were transferred to the successful tenderer and the departments are provided with flexible serviced accommodation (at an annual fee of up to £100 million) for the 20 year term of the contract.

Warren

25.13   The BBC entered into a property partnership with Land Securities Trillium in September 2001 (making this the most recent large scale outsourcing project) which combines property development, financing and facilities management over a 30 year contract. The property portfolio consists of around 500 properties totalling 700,000 sq m, of which two-thirds is in London and 70 per cent held freehold.

DESCRIPTION OF PARTIES INVOLVED

25.14   The two main parties are the outsourcer and the occupier, ie the local authority and the service provider. The service provider will typically either be a consortium of investors who establish a bespoke company or an established property outsourcing business. Emerging from the procurement process has been a new type of company, set up to transform legacy estates into flexible space for their clients by integrating capital, property management and facilities management into a single cost effective package, with investment banks shouldering the risk. Since the PRIME and STEPS contracts, these companies have responded to a new market for total property solutions, now expanding into approaching local authorities and major corporates offering the provision of high-tech services.

25.15   Involvement of the guarantor to the service provider's obligations and funder of the service provider from the initial stages right through to completion is an essential and integral part of the whole outsourcing progress.

Diagram outlining contractual relationships

25.16

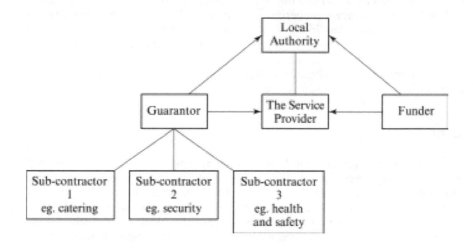

Contractual relationships

25.17   Finance will be provided to facilitate the scheme as a whole, by the funder who will typically be brought into the transaction at an early stage to ensure the structuring elements of the deal are acceptable to it. The service provider is then responsible for the provision of services. Services will typically include:
— management of services and the property portfolio (including (typically) a call centre);
— designated contact point (help desk);
— health and safety;
— facilities maintenance;
— security;
— cleaning;
— catering;
— childcare;
— energy and environment;
— management of removals; and
— additional services, eg insurance.

The service provider will usually put in place service contracts itself (ie by way of sub-contractors) for the provision of these services, or continue those already existing (if any) with the outsourcer.

Diagram outlining real estate structure

25.18

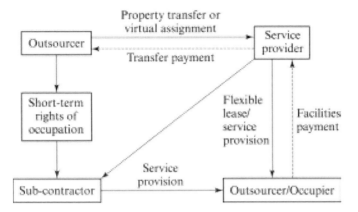

25.19 The scope of the structure is intended to:
(i) transfer the existing freehold properties and a large number of leasehold properties to the service provider in return for a transfer payment (thus realising the value of the property);
(ii) transfer to the service provider the economic burden of the outsourcer's remaining leasehold properties and licensed accommodation;
(iii) require the service provider to provide business space required by the outsourcer (in a specified location and satisfying the outsourcer's requirements, ie short term and probably standard form flexible leases); and
(iv) require the outsourcer to provide services at specified locations for the length of the contract (typically 20 years) in return for a facilities payment. This obligation to provide services is typically sub-contracted to third parties.

25.20 The contract may also provide that the service provider will, in addition to the above, be required to comply with statutory requirements, meet the business needs of the outsourcer and provide a safe and comfortable working environment for the occupying outsourcer, whilst minimising adverse environmental impact. The contract will also typically provide for the provision of any further business space or new services required by the outsourcer. The facilities payment is adjustable to reflect the performance by the service provider of specified services and additional services.

Transfer of properties to the service provider

25.21 At the commencement of the contract, the outsourcer transfers to the service provider the freehold properties in the estate. It also assigns to the outsourcer those leasehold properties which are capable of assignment, either where third party landlord consent is not required or where such third party consent has been obtained. Consideration (the transfer payment) is paid by the outsourcer to the service provider at this point.

Virtual assignments

25.22   Where third party landlord consent is required but has not been, or cannot be, obtained at the date of the commencement of the contract, the outsourcer will typically enter into virtual assignments. Here the outsourcer will continue to occupy the premises under the provisions of their existing leases with the third party landlords but the benefits and burdens of the leases will be transferred to the service provider pursuant to the virtual assignments. As far as the service provider is concerned, the virtual assignment will place the service provider in the same position with the landlord as if the properties had been transferred to it.

25.23   Fundamentally the virtual assignment mechanism is designed for any leasehold property where a third party consent is required for the transfer of the interest. This will generally be the case in respect of most of the leases within a diverse portfolio. The virtual assignment is, in essence, a form of indemnity from the service provider to the outsourcer.

25.24   The virtual assignment is helpful in terms of:
(a)   mechanics; and
(b)   preserving concessions (eg statutory protection, favourable lease terms and the benefit of personal side letters),
which the outsourcer benefits from, for so long as the leases remain vested in the outsourcer. A precedent form of virtual assignment is set out at para **25.36**.

25.25   The key paragraphs in the virtual assignment are paras 2 (economic benefit) para 3 (indemnity) and para 4 (dealings with the rack rent property). Under para 2 all monies received in respect of the property by the outsourcer, other than from any specified parties are payable to the service provider. Under para 3 the service provider must observe, perform and pay all rent due under the leases and indemnify the outsourcer. This is a full indemnity for all the liabilities under the leases which effectively become the entire responsibility of the service provider.

25.26   There is a slight VAT hedge on this. This is because while the outsourcer remains the tenant, services rendered to the outsourcer by the third party landlords will continue to be provided in that way. The supply for VAT purposes remains between the third party landlords and the outsourcer. While the virtual assignment remains in place the service provider would not be able to recover VAT paid to third party landlords if the service provider paid that liability directly. As a result the outsourcer may agree that in respect of VAT on the rents, while a virtual assignment remains in place, the outsourcer will itself pay that VAT. The outsourcer will then be able to recover the VAT paid directly so this is a pass through.

25.27   Under para 4 the service provider is irrevocably appointed as the outsourcer's sole agent and has full discretion to conduct any dealings, discussions or negotiations with third parties including litigating in the name of the outsourcer if necessary.

Flexible leases

25.28   The outsourcer will enter into leases under which they will occupy the premises. These will typically be in standard form, negotiated as between the parties and will usually be contracted out of the security of tenure provisions of the Landlord and Tenant Act 1954.

MATERIAL ISSUES

Provisions allowing occupation and flexibility to outsourcer

25.29 The outsourcer will typically have identified certain properties which must be retained (ie core properties) and those which are no longer required (ie surplus properties). Typically, the core properties will be required for the duration of the contract and may not be sold by the service provider. Surplus properties on the other hand, will be clearly available to the service provider to sell, let, develop etc with effect from the commencement of the contract. The surplus properties provide a key area whereby enhancement of profits by the service provider during the term of the contract can be made.

25.30 It is not unusual to find that there are certain properties which do not fall within the 'core' and 'surplus' categories. For example, there may be properties which are required only for the first five years of the life of the contract and thereafter become surplus properties.

25.31 By identifying the various properties in this way, the outsourcer and service provider are better able to manage the portfolio and provide opportunities to the service provider to enhance value. Further, by identifying properties which will become surplus at a fixed point in the future, the service provider is better able to manage the expectations of the outsourcer and accordingly provide a more streamlined and cost efficient service.

Hand back and grant of long lease at end of term

25.32 Consideration needs to be given to the way in which the parties will deal with the properties on expiration of the contractual term. Where an interest has been granted to the outsourcer by the service provider, what will happen when the contractual term expires? A solution to this issue can be found by the granting of long leasehold interests which will extend beyond the life of the contract and accordingly protect the parties involved. To date it has not yet been seen how these issues are resolved in practice in relation to the large property based outsourcing projects, eg STEPS, Prime etc.

Share in the future profits

25.33 An outsourcer will typically require a share in the future gains realised by the service provider. The size of the share will be determined by the negotiating strengths of the parties at the time of completion of the contract. Similarly, the duration of time for which the potential share in future profits will subsist will largely depend on negotiating strengths at the relevant time.

25.34   The outsourcer must appreciate, however, that whilst sharing future profits can bring great benefit, if this is structured in a way whereby the share is either too great or the duration of time is too long, then the provisions will have the opposite effect to that intended. If there is no incentive for the service provider to put in place deals with the existing portfolio, then none will be done and accordingly neither party will benefit from any profit share. It is suggested that it is both unrealistic and non-commercial to seek to impose profit share on future owners of the property in the event of their disposal. There have been certain outsourcers who require third parties that acquire an interest in the existing portfolio to pay overage in the event of their disposal. This is an excellent example of how 'not to do it'.

Best value

25.35   To ensure compliance with local authorities duty to obtain 'best value' under LGA 1999 the contract may contain market territory, benchmarking and user consultation requirements.

VIRTUAL ASSIGNMENT FOR USE IN ENGLAND AND WALES

25.36
Terms of virtual asignment

*Items marked with an asterisk to be deleted or amended if a freehold Virtual Assignment is required.

THIS DEED is made the   day of   20[ ]
BETWEEN:
(1)   [   ] (the 'Outsourcer');
       and
(2)   [   ] Limited a company registered and incorporated in accordance with
       the laws of England and Wales registered under number [   ] and having its
       registered office at [   ] (the 'Contractor').

WHEREAS:
(a)   The parties have entered into the [Project Agreement] (as hereinafter defined).
(b)   Pursuant to the Project Agreement, the Service Provider has agreed to procure
       that the Service Provider grants a lease of the Property or part thereof in the
       form of the [Lease] (as so defined) to the Outsourcer and further the Service
       Provider has agreed to provide certain services to the Outsourcer at such
       Property.
(c)   As the transfer and lease of the Property have not yet been completed, the parties
       have agreed to enter into this Deed the better to regulate the position and
       arrangements between them pending such completion.
(d)   The intention of this Deed is to enable the Service Provider to have the equivalent
       of all of the economic benefits and burdens of the Property as if the Property
       had been transferred to the Service Provider but without creating, vesting or

granting any legal or equitable estate or interest in the Property (other than that already created by the [Project Agreement]) in or to the Service Provider, together with the appointment of the Service Provider to manage all dealings with third parties, including any landlord and tenant.

(e) To enable the Service Provider better to exercise its rights and to carry out its functions under the [Project Agreement] and this Deed, the Outsourcer has granted to the Service Provider a power of attorney.

THIS DEED WITNESSES:

1 Definitions

In this Deed, unless there is anything indicating to the contrary all words and expressions shall have the same meaning as given to them in the Project Agreement.

In this Deed the following words and expressions have the meanings set opposite them:

'Assurances' a transfer or an assignment of all or part of the Property by the [the Outsourcer] at the direction of the Service Provider to any one or more third parties;

*['Expiry'   the expiry of the Lease (other than a Surrender or Forfeiture) where there is no renewal of the Lease (whether or not under the provisions of the Landlord and Tenant Act 1954);]

*['Forfeiture' the termination of the Lease by the Landlord by re-entering the Property in circumstances where the Service Provider (as appropriate) has obtained relief from forfeiture;]

*['Landlord' the person for the time being and from time to time entitled to the reversion immediately expectant upon the expiry of the Lease;]

*['Lease'   the lease, underlease, sublease, tenancy, subtenancy or licence or an agreement for the creation of any lease, underlease, sublease, tenancy, subtenancy or licence (including any renewal of any of them, whether or not under the provisions of the Landlord and Tenant Act 1954), under or through which the [Outsourcer] at any time holds legal or equitable title to the Property together with any documents ancillary or supplemental to or any licences, consents or agreements given under such lease, underlease, sublease, tenancy, licence or agreement;]

'Project Agreement' The Project Agreement dated [   ] 20[ ] made between the Outsourcer (1), and the Service Provider (2);

'Property'   the property or properties more particularly described in the Schedule to this Deed;

'Rent' all and any rent, reviewed rent, service charge, insurance rent, costs, fees, charges, and any other monies, whether or not reserved as rent, at any time and from time to time due under or payable in accordance with *[the Lease or] an Underlease together with any Value Added Tax on any such items;

'the Service Provider'   includes its successors in title;

*['Surrender' the surrender of the whole or part of the Property to the Landlord;]

'Underlease' any underlease, sublease, subtenancy or licence created out of the Property or any agreement to create any such underlease, sublease, subtenancy or licence, whether created before or after this Deed, together with any documents ancillary or supplemental to, or any licences, consents or agreements given under, such underlease, sublease, subtenancy, licence or agreement;

'Third Party Tenant' any tenant, subtenant or licensee under an Underlease.

Where the context so requires:
the singular includes the plural and vice versa;
the masculine includes the feminine and vice versa, and the neuter includes the
masculine or the feminine and vice versa;
references to persons shall include individuals, bodies corporate, unincorporated
associations, partnerships, governments, governmental bodies, authorities and
agencies and any other person having legal capacity;
references to any Law are to be construed as references to that Law as from time to
time amended or to any Law for the time being replacing, extending,
consolidating or amending the same; and
any right to enter the Property conferred by this Deed shall be exercisable also by
the employees, agents and workpeople of the person on whom the right is
conferred and any others authorised by that person and with all necessary
equipment, tools and materials.
The headings in this Deed shall be deemed not to be part of this Deed and shall not
be taken into consideration in the interpretation of this Deed.

2   Economic benefit
Immediately upon receipt of any monies (including but not limited to Rent, rates,
insurance proceeds, tenant's or other compensation or any money, whether revenue
or capital, resulting from a disposal of, or grant of an interest in, the Property or part
thereof but excluding any sums received in compensation for disruption or disturbance
to, or which are damages to make good any loss sustained by the business carried on
by the Outsourcer) from any person in respect of, or relating to, the Property, the
Outsourcer shall pay an amount which is the equivalent thereof to the Service Provider
without any deduction or set off save as required by law.

3   Indemnity
The Service Provider hereby covenants with the Outsourcer that the Service Provider
will from the [Commencement Date][date hereof] at all times *[duly pay to the
Landlord in full all Rent on the relevant dates for payment in accordance with the
Lease, if relevant, and will] observe and perform, but by way of indemnity only, all
covenants, agreements and conditions (including any for the payment of monies other
than Rent) contained:
  *[in the Lease and on the part of the tenant to be observed and performed except
    to the extent that either this would be the responsibility of the Outsourcer
    had a sub-lease been granted out of the Lease or the Outsourcer had caused
    the breach by its conduct;] in the Underleases and on the part of the landlord
    to be observed and performed;
  *[in any variation of the Lease except to the extent that this would be the
    responsibility of the Outsourcer had a sub-lease been granted out of the
    Lease:];
  *[in any Surrender; and]
  in any other deed, agreement or document of title affecting the Property other
    than the obligations on the part of the Outsourcer contained in the Project
    Agreement and on the part of the Outsourcer to be observed and performed.
  and also at all times keep the Outsourcer indemnified against all proceedings,
    costs, claims, damages and expenses on account of any omission after the
    date hereof to pay or late payment of the Rent or any breach after the date
    hereof of such covenants, agreements and conditions contained in the Lease,
    the Underleases, and any other deeds, agreements and documents affecting
    the Property other than as aforesaid.

4   Dealings with the rack rent property

The Outsourcer hereby irrevocably appoints the Service Provider to be its sole agent to act on its behalf and in the name of the Outsourcer in all dealings connected with the Property, including:

*[paying all Rent and other sums due under the Lease and negotiating and settling any rent reviews under the Lease;]

collecting and getting in all Rent and other sums due under the Underleases and negotiating and settling any rent reviews under the Underlease;

*[applying for all permissions, licences and consents necessary under the Lease;]

granting any new Underleases and negotiating and completing any variations thereto and dealing with any applications for any permissions, licences and consents under any Underleases;

all correspondence and other dealings with *[the Landlord] and any Third Party Tenants;

*[negotiating and completing any Surrender];

dealing with any renewal of *[the Lease or] any Underlease, whether or not under the Landlord and Tenant Act 1954;

negotiating and completing any Assurance;

*[negotiating and completing any variations of the Lease];

exercising any options in the *[Lease or] Underleases;

making any applications to HM Land Registry or the Land Charges Department or any other statutory or non-statutory registry;

paying promptly all rates or charges in lieu of rates due in respect of the Property (subject to reimbursement in accordance with the Project Agreement);

receiving and issuing any notices of whatever nature in respect of the Property and taking part in any proceedings;

applying for all planning permissions or other regulatory approvals necessary for the intended operation of the Property and effective trustees for the Service Provider; and

any other matter whatsoever arising from the rights and/or obligations of the Outsourcer as legal owner of the Property, but not further or otherwise;

and the Outsourcer agrees that (subject to any relevant provision of the Project Agreement) the Service Provider will have full discretion in the conduct and settling of any dealings, discussions or negotiations with third parties.

The Outsourcer will, to enable the Service Provider to carry out its functions better:

confirm to any third party *[, including any Landlord] at the request and cost of the Service Provider that the Service Provider has the authority to act on behalf of the Outsourcer;

provide to the Service Provider at the cost of the Service Provider such information as the Service Provider reasonably requires in relation to the previous dealings of the Outsourcer with the Landlord;

not, save with the prior written agreement of the Service Provider, appoint any other agent to act on behalf of the Outsourcer in relation to any of the matters referred to in clause [   ];

not, save either in case of default by the Service Provider of its obligations pursuant to clause [   ] or as contemplated by the Project Agreement, itself carry out any of the matters referred to in clause [   ] and in the event of any third party, including any Landlord, endeavouring to deal with the Outsourcer in relation to any such matter will immediately refer such third party to the Service Provider; and

forthwith upon receipt (and in any event within such period as may be necessary to enable a timely response to be made) forward to the Service Provider the original of every notice, demand, order, request, consent or other written communication received from any Third Party Landlord or any agent thereof or any other third party relating to the Property.

To the extent that either the Outsourcer is not legally entitled to grant a power of attorney to the Service Provider in accordance with the Project Agreement or in any circumstances where such power of attorney is ineffective (for whatever reason) the Outsourcer hereby covenants with the Service Provider that it will, within 10 working days of the Service Provider submitting any leases, Underleases, transfers, or any other agreements, deeds, documents, assurances, instruments or acts which the Service Provider certifies in an accompanying certificate are properly necessary or required for or to give effect to any of the purposes contemplated by this Deed, execute such documents and return them to the Service Provider.

The Service Provider hereby covenants with the Outsourcer that the Service Provider will at all times duly pay on time and in full all monies due from the Outsourcer under any documents executed by the Service Provider under such powers of attorney executed pursuant to the Project Agreement or under any document executed by the Outsourcer pursuant to clause [ ] and will observe and perform all covenants, agreements and conditions contained in such documents and on the part of the Outsourcer to be observed and performed and shall also at all times keep the Outsourcer indemnified against all proceedings, costs, claims, damages and expenses on account of any omission after the date hereof to pay or late payment of any such monies or any breach of the covenants, agreements and conditions contained in such documents.

The Service Provider shall be entitled to use the name of the Outsourcer in any litigation, court proceedings or other dispute resolution procedure which is necessary or required in connection with any of the powers granted by the Outsourcer under this Deed Provided it keeps the Outsourcer (as the case may be) fully informed as to each step in such proceedings. All pleadings, advice and other documents in such proceedings will be made fully available to the Outsourcer at all times. The Service Provider shall at all times keep the Outsourcer or indemnified against all damages, losses, costs, claims, liability and expenses incurred by the Service Provider or the Outsourcer in connection with or as a result of such proceedings.

Notwithstanding any other provision of this Deed the Outsourcer shall be entitled to grant any underlease, sublease, subtenancy or licence of any part of the Property occupied by the Outsourcer to an Outsourcer's Contractor, or to permit such Outsourcer Contractor, to share possession of or take occupation of all or any part of the Property provided that such arrangement would be permitted to the sub-lease had the same been granted and otherwise in accordance with the terms of the Project Agreement.

The Outsourcer covenants that they will occupy the Property (or such part of the Property which would have been comprised in the sub-lease had the Property been the subject of a completed Transfer of Assignment as the case may be) on the basis as if they were the tenant's under a sub-lease thereof and not in any other way and will comply with the terms of such Lease as if the same had been granted.

The Outsourcer covenants with the Service Provider that it will not exercise any right or benefit whatsoever in relation to the Property other than any that they would have had and will perform all obligations and covenants it would be obliged to perform had the Assurance of the Property to the Service

Provider been completed and the grant of the sub-lease to the Outsourcer been completed and other than as reserved to the Outsourcer pursuant to the terms of this Deed and the Outsourcer shall at all times keep the Service Provider indemnified against all damages, costs, claims, liability and expenses incurred by the Service Provider in connection with, or as a result of, any breach of this clause [ ].

5 End of liability

The Service Provider's liability under this Deed shall cease and determine on the later of:

the earlier of:
  the Expiry or earlier termination of the Lease;
  the Surrender of the Lease;
  the Forfeiture of the Lease;
  the express release, of the Outsourcer's liability under the Lease; and
the payment or satisfaction in full by the Service Provider of all monies and liabilities owed as a result of such Expiry, Surrender, Forfeiture or release which shall include any claim by the Landlord for any dilapidations or other works.
The Outsourcer hereby agrees upon written request by the Service Provider to execute a release of the Service Provider from liability under this Deed in respect of the Property when the events specified in clause [ ] have happened. The Service Provider agrees upon written request from the Outsourcer to surrender the power of attorney so far as it relates to the Property when the events specified in clause [ ] have happened.
*[For the avoidance of doubt, it is hereby agreed that the liability of the Service Provider under this Deed arising from or in relation to the Lease will continue in full force and effect notwithstanding the Assurances of that Lease and will continue until the Expiry or earlier termination of that Lease unless either the Landlord releases the Outsourcer from all future claims and liability under that Lease or the Outsourcer's liability under the Lease (and under any authorised guarantee agreement given to the Landlord in accordance with the terms of the Lease and the provisions of the Landlord and Tenant (Covenants) Act 1995) determines in accordance with the provisions of the Landlord and Tenant (Covenants) Act 1995.]

6 Disputes procedure

In the event of there being any dispute between any of the parties to this Deed as to the effect of this Deed then any relevant party may refer the dispute to the Dispute Resolution Procedures under the Project Agreement.

7 Monies paid and received under this deed

All monies paid and received by the Service Provider under this Deed (whether or not by way of Rent) will be to the account of the Service Provider and the Outsourcer will not have any obligation to pay monies (except pursuant to clause [ ])or any right to receive monies (other than by reason of an indemnity given to either of them by the Service Provider in this Deed) under or by virtue of this Deed or under any Underleases, Assurances or Surrenders. However, the Outsourcer will be entitled to receive and keep all monies paid by [   ] in respect of their respective occupations of the Property.

8   Severability
The invalidity in whole or in part of any of these terms shall not affect the validity of any other provision and all remedies available to either party for breach of contract are cumulative and may be exercised concurrently or separately.

9   Effect of deed
This document shall be treated as having been executed and delivered as a deed only upon being dated.

IN WITNESS whereof this Deed has been duly executed and delivered as a deed the day and year first before written.

THE SCHEDULE

The property

CHAPTER 26

Case study: social services and health

Valda Brooks

BACKGROUND

Introduction

26.01   Over the past 18 months there have been significant legislative changes affecting social services and healthcare. The purpose of this case study is to consider the impact of these changes on the procurement and contractual process of local authorities and health bodies discharging their obligations to provide such services. The focus of this case study is therefore upon the legislative changes. The procurement and contractual process are based on a PPP arrangement for the supply of services under the principles discussed in chapter 13.

The division of responsibility for the provision of health and social care

Responsibility for community care services

26.02   Section 21 of the National Assistance Act 1948 places the duty on local authorities to make arrangements for providing residential accommodation for persons aged 18 or over who, by reason of age, illness, disability or any other circumstances, are in need of care and attention which is not otherwise available to them (including some nursing services)[1]. Section 26 of the National Assistance Act 1948 enables the local authority to make arrangements with independent providers of the services in discharge of the local authority's responsibilities under s 21.

---

1   *R v North and East Devon Health Authority, ex p Coughlan* [2002] QB 213, CA. The Secretary of State can exclude some nursing services from the services provided by the NHS. Such services can then be provided as a social or care service rather than a health service. The nursing services which can be provided as part of the care services are limited to those which can legitimately be regarded as being provided in connection with accommodation which is being provided to the classes of persons referred in s 21, who are in need of care and attention; in other words as part of a social services care package. As a result of the judgment in this case the Department of Health has issued guidance on continuing care: NHS and Local Councils' responsibilities: HSC 200/015: LAC (2001)18.

Responsibility for health and nursing services

26.03   The Health Body may delegate this responsibility to the local authority. As from 1 October 2001 local authorities are not required to provide services by a registered nurse in discharging its community care services duties. See the National

Health Service (Nursing Care in Residential Accommodation (England) Directions 2001 which provides that as from 1 October 2001, a relevant NHS body shall provide a qualifying person for whom it has responsibility with such nursing care as appears to be appropriate having regard to the nursing care provided to that person in the premises immediately before that date. People entering residential care after 1 October 2001 shall be subject to an assessment by the NHS body to determine their need for nursing care, and having regard to the result of the assessment, shall provide such nursing care.

26.04   A qualifying person for nursing care in residential care is defined as someone:
(a)   who, on the date he becomes a resident in the relevant premises, is a person who is provided with accommodation by the local authority under the National Assistance Act 1948, s 21(1); and
(b)   who, if the local authority were to provide nursing care in connection with that accommodation, would be liable to make a payment under the National Assistance Act 1948, s 22(3) or s 26(3) at either the standard rate or a lower rate which is not less than the standard rate minus £110; or
(c)   whose accommodation is not provided by a local authority or a relevant NHS body[1].

1   See also Guidance on Continuing Care Responsibilities of the NHS and Local Authorities Circular HSC 2001/015 and LAC (2001)18.

Recent legislative changes affecting the provision of health and social care

Health Act 1999

26.05   The Health Act 1999 amends the law relating to the national health service:
—   makes provision in relation to arrangements and payments between health service bodies and local authorities regarding the health and health-related functions;
—   confers power to regulate any professions concerned with the physical or mental health of individuals; and for connected purposes.

26.06   Section 27 provides for a formal duty of partnership between health bodies and local authorities. Section 28 provides for a pooled fund arrangement, s 29 provides for the transference of funds to the partnership arrangement.

26.07   Section 31 (which is reproduced in full below) provides that:
(1)   The Secretary of State may by regulations make provision for or in connection with enabling prescribed NHS bodies (on the one hand) and prescribed local authorities (on the other) to enter into prescribed arrangements in relation to the exercise of—
    (a)   prescribed functions of the NHS bodies, and
    (b)   prescribed health-related functions of the local authorities,
    if arrangements are likely to lead to an improvement in the way in which those functions are exercised.
(2)   The arrangements, which may be prescribed include arrangements—
    (a)   for or in connection with the establishment and maintenance of a fund—

     (i) which is made up of contributions by one or more NHS bodies and one or more local authorities, and

     (ii) out of which payments may be made towards expenditure incurred in the exercise of both prescribed functions of the NHS body or bodies and prescribed health-related functions of the authority or authorities,

  (b) for or in connection with the exercise by an NHS body on behalf of a local authority of prescribed health-related functions of the authority in conjunction with the exercise by the NHS body of prescribed functions of theirs,

  (c) for or in connection with the exercise of a local authority on behalf of an NHS body of prescribed functions of the NHS body in conjunction with the exercise by the authority of prescribed health-related functions of theirs,

  (d) as to the provision of staff, goods, services or accommodation in connection with any arrangements mentioned in paragraph (a), (b) or (c),

  (e) as to the making of payments by a local authority to an NHS body in connection with any arrangements mentioned in paragraph (b),

  (f) as to the making of payments by a NHS body to a local authority in connection with any arrangements mentioned in paragraph (c).

(3) Regulations under this section may make provision—

  (a) as to the cases in which NHS bodies and local authorities may enter into prescribed arrangements,

  (b) as to the conditions which must be satisfied in relation to prescribed arrangements (including conditions in relation to consultation),

  (c) for or in connection with requiring the consent of the Secretary of State to the operation of prescribed arrangements (including provision in relation to applications for consent, the approval or refusal of such applications and the variation of withdrawal of approval),

  (d) in relation to the duration of prescribed arrangements,

  (e) for or in connection with the variation or termination of prescribed arrangements,

  (f) as to the responsibility for, and the operation and management of, prescribed arrangements,

  (g) as to the sharing of information between NHS bodies and local authorities.

(4) The provision, which may be made by virtue of subsection (3)(f), includes provision in relation to—

  (a) the formation and operation of joint committees of the NHS bodies and local authorities,

  (b) the exercise of functions which are the subject of prescribed arrangements (including provision in relation to the exercise of such functions by joint committees or employees of the NHS bodies and local authorities),

  (c) the drawing up and implementation of plans in respect of prescribed arrangements,

  (d) the monitoring of prescribed arrangements,

  (e) the provision of reports on, and information about, prescribed arrangements,

  (f) complaints and disputes about prescribed arrangements,

  (g) accounts and audits in respect of prescribed arrangements.

(5) Any arrangements made by virtue of this section shall not affect:

  (a) the liability of NHS bodies for the exercise of any of their functions,

  (b) the liability of local authorities for the exercise of any of their functions, or

  (c) any power or duty to recover charges in respect of services provided in the exercise of any local authority functions.

(6)   The Secretary of State may issue guidance to NHS bodies and local authorities in relation to consultation or applications for consent in respect of prescribed arrangements.

(7)   The reference in subsection (1) to an improvement in the way in which functions are exercised includes an improvement in the provision to any individuals of any services to which those functions relate.

(8)   In this section –

'health related functions', in relation to a local authority, means functions of the authority which, in the opinion of the Secretary of State—

(i)   have an effect on the health of any individuals,

(ii)   have an effect on, or are affected by, any functions of NHS bodies, or

(iii)   are connected with any functions of NHS bodies,

'local authority' means a district council, county council, county borough council, London borough council or Common Council of the City of London,

'NHS body' means a Health Authority, Primary Care Trust or NHS Trust,

'prescribed' means prescribed to any extent by regulations made by the Secretary of State

(9)   Schedule 2A makes provision with respect to the transfer of staff in connection with the arrangements by virtue of this section.

Regulations

26.08   The NHS Bodies and Local Authorities Partnership Arrangements Regulations 2000[1] came into force on 1 April 2000. These regulations identify the prescribed NHS bodies as being:
— a Health Authority;
— a Primary Care Trust; and
— an NHS trust.

1   SI 2000/617.

26.09   The prescribed local authorities are:
— a district council;
— a county council;
— a county borough council; and
— the Common Council of the City of London[1].

1   Regulation 3.

26.10   The partners are prohibited from entering into any partnership arrangement unless they have consulted jointly with such persons as appear to them to be affected by such arrangements; and may not enter into any partnership arrangements which do not fulfil the objectives in the health improvement plan for the health authority in whose area the arrangements are to operate[1].

1   Regulation 4.

Pooled fund arrangements

26.11 The regulations contain detailed terms for the pooled fund arrangement including:

'such arrangement may not be entered into by an NHS trust and a local authority unless the NHS trust obtains the consent of the Health Authority with which it has an NHS contract for the provision of services for persons in respect of whom the functions which are the subject of the pooled fund arrangements may be exercised[1].'

1   Regulation 7(2).

26.12   The partners must agree terms in writing as to:
1   the agreed aims and outcomes of the pooled fund arrangements;
2   the contributions and variation of contributions of the partners;
3   the NHS and health-related functions;
4   identification of the service users who will benefit and the services to be provided;
5   staff, goods and accommodation to be provided;
6   duration and provision for review of the arrangements;
7   how the pooled fund is to be managed[1].

1   Regulation 7.

Local Government Act 2000

26.13   The Local Government Act 2000 makes provision for the Secretary of State to pay grants to local authorities in England towards the expenditure incurred by them in providing, or contributing to the provision of, such welfare services as may be determined by the Secretary of State[1].

1   Local Government Act 2000, s 93.

Care Standards Act 2000

26.14   The Care Standards Act 2000 makes sweeping and wide ranging changes to all aspects of the provision and regulation of social care and private and voluntary health care services in England and Wales including:
—   the establishment of the National Care Standards Commission ('NCSC') for regulating of care homes, children's homes, private and voluntary healthcare services;
—   bringing local authority care homes within the regulatory scheme;
—   repealing the Registered Homes Act 1984.

26.15   A 'care home', as defined under s 3, is an establishment which provides accommodation, together with nursing or personal care, for any of the following persons:
(a)   persons who are or have been ill;
(b)   persons who have had a mental disorder;

(c)   persons who are disabled or infirm;

(d)   persons who are or have been dependent on alcohol or drugs.

For the purpose of regulating the establishment, there is now no distinction between a residential care home and a nursing home as existed under the Registered Homes Act 1984.

26.16   One body is now responsible for the registration, inspection and regulation of care homes (including cancellation of registration resulting in closure of the home). This body is the NCSC. Local authority homes provided under the National Assistance Act 1948, Pt III are no longer exempt from the regulatory regime. The fundamental effect of the new Act on local authority homes is that they are now required to meet the same standards as privately run homes, and local authorities are subject to the same regime of satisfying the conditions for registration in respect of each of their homes and are subject to inspections and cancellation. Under regulations made under the Act which came into force on 1 April 2002[1] all the elements of fitness of the registered owner and (where one is appointed), the manager are required to be satisfied to the standards laid down under the Act and the regulations, before registration will be granted by the NCSC. The requirements are broadly similar to those laid down in the Residential Care Homes Regulations 1984 and the Nursing Homes and Mental Nursing Homes Regulations 1984, which were in force under the Registered Homes Act 1984. The difference now is that local authorities are not permitted to carry on care homes unless they are registered with the NCSC.

1   Care Homes Regulations 2001, SI 2001/3965.

26.17   The Department of Health has issued guidance to health bodies and local authorities on transitional arrangements for obtaining registration under the Act in respect of their current care homes[1]. In respect of current homes, local authorities will not have to strictly meet the new standards when seeking to be registered. However, any new homes will be required to meet the required standards. Under the guidance local authorities are required to apply to the NCSC to be registered in respect of each care home run by them by 1 April 2002. From then they will be subject to regulation under the Care Standards Act through the NCSC.

1   Guidance on Continuing Responsibilities of Local Authorities and Health Authorities following the Transfer of Registration and Inspection to the National Care Standards Commission on 1 April 2002HSC 2001/125: LAC (2001)31.

26.18   The guidance requires local authorities and the relevant health bodies to agree a local procedure for action to be taken in the event of a cancellation of registration, including urgent cancellation. The local authority within whose area the service is operated is required to co-ordinate the assessment and placement of future or alternative service users receiving services from the registered provider.

26.19   Many local authority care homes have been operating below the standards to which privately run care homes have been subjected to, for a number of years, as they were not regulated under the Registered Homes Act 1984. To meet the exacting standards of the new Act and regulations, local authorities, in conjunction with health bodies, are turning to PPP arrangements, contracting with established private providers of care homes to meet the new standards and provide the high standards of facilities, equipment and care required by the NCSC.

26.20 The basis of this case study is on such a relationship. The identity of the parties involved will be anonymous since the transaction has not yet reached completion.

Health and Social Care Act 2001

Exclusion of nursing care from community care services

26.21 Section 49 of the HSCA 2001 deals with the exclusion of the provision of nursing care by a registered nurse from community care services provided by a local authority. Under this section, as from 1 October 2001, the NHS became responsible for providing nursing care, free of charge, to persons in residential accommodation. This therefore represents an equalisation of the positions of persons in care homes with those in NHS hospitals and other NHS facilities. Prior to the coming in force of this provision, persons in care homes were, subject to their means, liable to contribute towards the nursing care they received[1].

1 See para **26.03**.

26.22 This is an important provision to bear in mind when considering the costing submitted by bidders. Although there will still be an element of nursing care provided in care homes on a day to day basis which will not be recoverable from the NHS, a significant element will be recoverable. This will allow a substantial reduction to the value of the care element of the services to be provided by the contractor. Tenders should be reviewed carefully to ensure that best value is achieved, and avoid the overvaluing of beds allocated for nursing care residents.

Preserved rights

26.23 Sections 50–55 deal with the transfer to local authorities of responsibility for providing accommodation to persons on preserved rights.

26.24 Section 26A of the National Assistance Act 1948 prevented local authorities from providing residential accommodation for persons who were in such accommodation on 31 March 1993. Such persons had their long-term care funded through income support and jobseeker's allowance and their right to do so was 'preserved'[1]. Section 26A was repealed by the HSCA 2001, s 50 as from 1 April 2002 and new provisions under ss 50–55 allow the local authority to provide the accommodation charging more commercial rates than allowed for by income support and jobseeker's allowance.

1 As defined under the Income Support (General) Regulations 1987, SI 1987/1967.

26.25 Local authorities are obliged, under the HSCA 2001, s 50, to:
— use their best endeavours to identify every person ordinarily resident in relevant premises in their area who is a qualifying person; and
— carry out such a programme of assessment under the National Health Service and Community Care Act 1948, s 47(1)(a) in respect of persons so identified as appears to the authority to be required for the purpose of enabling them to discharge their duty in relation to such persons[1].

1 HSCA, s 50(4)(a), (b).

26.26   Section 51 provides for disclosure of information in respect of qualifying persons. Section 53 amends the National Assistance Act 1948, s 21(2A) and (2B) and provides that the local authority shall disregard so much of the person's resources, as may be determined from time to time by regulations, when determining whether community care services in otherwise available to him.

26.27   By s 54, the resident seek accommodation in a more expensive care home than that provided by the local authority under the National Assistance Act 1948, Pt 3 provided that the resident contributes to the funding of such accommodation.

26.28   Section 55 allows the local authority to take a charge over land owned by the resident as a deferred payment of contributions due from the resident.

26.29   Since persons who are qualifying persons for preserved rights will make up a significant number of service users of the accommodation to be provided by the contractor, the costing of this element of the services will also require attention. The contractor is now able to charge a higher rate for such residents. Careful attention should be given to valuing this element of the services to ensure optimum best value is achieved.

POLICY CONTEXT

Social care partnership arrangement

26.30   Section 27 of the Health Act 1999 encourages a formal duty of partnership between health bodies and councils.

Advantages as between the public bodies

26.31   The joint commissioning by partnership between the health body and the council enhances the making of changes in policies and strategies, and in the management and commissioning of service delivery.

26.32   Joint commissioning allows for:
— pooled funds[1];
— transfer of additional money to the partnership arrangement[2];
— delegation of health service functions to the council by the health body (including nursing services);
— consultation under the Health Act 1999, s 31;
— monitoring of the partnership arrangement.

1   Health Act 1999, s 31.
2   National Health Service Act 1977, s 28A and s 28BB.

Advantages as between the contractor and the public bodies

26.33   Advantages include:
— the contractual document will provide for penalties and abatements where the contractor fails to meet the specification;
— the public body will relinquish control of the care homes to the contractor for the period granted whilst maintaining control in terms of monitoring of performance, and the ability to 'step in' in the event of default by or the insolvency of the contractor.

Health issues

Clinical governance

26.34   The health body is accountable for continuously improving the quality of its services and safeguarding high standards of care. The components will include:
(a)   clear lines of responsibility and accountability for overall quality of clinical care;
(b)   a comprehensive quality of clinical care.

Best value

26.35   The council is subject to best value under the Local Government Act 1999. To meet this requirement service provision will be subject to:
— challenge;
— consultation;
— comparison;
— competition;
— complaint;
— clear policies and procedures aimed at risk management;
— clear procedure and policy for identifying and remedying poor performance.

These issues are more fully discussed in chapters 3, 4, 6 and 9.

DESCRIPTION OF PARTIES INVOLVED

26.36   The arrangements being considered are based upon the principles of PPP. The main parties are:
— the health body with responsibility for health care in the area (the 'health body');
— the local authority with responsibility for the provision and funding of community care services (the 'council').
— the private contractor appointed to provide the services (the 'contractor').

Other relevant parties will include the building contractor, sub-contractors and service users. See para **26.38**.

26.37

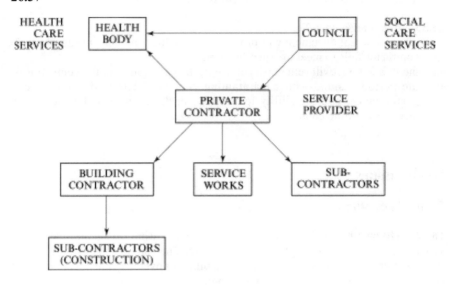

CONTRACTUAL RELATIONSHIP

26.38   These will include the following:
—   agreement between the health body and the council;
—   contract between the council and the contractor;
—   construction contract between the contractor and the building contractor;
—   agreement for lease between the council and the contractor;
—   lease between the council and the contractor;
—   financing agreements between the contractor and the funder;
—   warranty agreements between the council and the building contractor;
—   sub-contracts;
—   care facilities and management contracts

OBJECTIVES

26.39   The council and the health body, by entering into the arrangement, indicate their commitment to furthering the development of partnership working for the joint commissioning of health and social care services for people in their area.

26.40   The council will procure services for service users which are user centred and provide:
—   flexibility;
—   cost effectiveness best value;

— quality of standards whilst maintaining the right of the service users to dignity, privacy and self respect, enhance their independence and complies with the output specification.

26.41   This will entail the bidders demonstrating to the satisfaction of the council that they not only have the experience in caring for the class of service users for whom the facilities are proposed, but that the level and experience of the staff, the facilities in the building and the services are of a standard which will meet these objectives. The services will be provided for the local community. There will be the provision of residential care home care as well as respite care and day care facilities. The contractor will always require a realistic prospect of making a return on its investment, with the ability to extend the term of the contract, or hand back the facility to the council or a new contractor.

26.42   The health body will require user centred services that enhance independence, dignity, privacy and the self-respect of the service users, provide value for money, are compliant with legislative requirements, are transparent and meet all the Department of Health's policied on long-term care.

The objectives of all parties will be addressed in the contractual documents.

LEGAL AND COMMERCIAL ISSUES

Legal

Powers

26.43   As with any public procurement contract, the council and the health body must demonstrate that they have the necessary vires to enter into the PPP agreement. The relevant powers are to be found in the Health Act 1999, which is discussed further in chapter 9.

Force majeure and change of law

26.44   The ability to terminate the contract if either party is rendered unable to continue to perform its obligations under the contract by reason of events beyond its control is a legal issue, which needs to be addressed in the contract with appropriate terms as to compensation.

Insolvency

26.45   An insolvent provider was not deemed fit to be registered in respect of a care home under the Registered Homes Act 1984. This position is maintained under the Care Standards Act 2000. The contractor's funder will wish to ensure that it has the ability to step in and run the home in the event of the contractor's insolvency. Provisions in this regard will be contained in the charge deed between the contractor and his funder. Similarly, the council will require to have the right to step in and run the home in the event of insolvency of the contractor and the contractual document should contain relevant clauses to enable them to do so.

Miscellaneous

26.46   Other legal issues might include:
(i)   TUPE: this subject is discussed in detail in chapter 15;
(ii)   consultation: this is dealt with more fully at para **26.64**;
(iii) registration/licence: see the Care Standards Act 2000 discussed at para **26.16**;
(iv)   cancellation of registration: see the Care Standards Act 2000 discussed at para **26.64**.

Commercial

26.47   The commercial issues will include issues discussed in chapters 5–8. Additional issues will include
—   ability to step-in: it would be imprudent of the council not to retain the ability to step-in and provide the services should the contractor be rendered unable to do so by reason of insolvency. The step-in clause should be drawn wide enough to enable the council to appoint a third party (another independent contractor) to provide the services. The contractor's funder (if any) may also require the right to step-in in place of the contractor to enforce its charge. Although the funder's right to step-in will form part of the security documentation between the contractor and the funder, the council should also be made a party to this agreement. This ensures that notice is given to the council if it becomes necessary for the funder to step-in;
—   monitoring: to ensure that the contractor complies with obligations to provide the services, underpinned by the Care Standards Act 2000, as well as the monitoring of the building works;
—   compensation: the contractors will wish to ensure that they are appropriately compensated for the losses incurred for early termination of the contract for whatever reason. The level of compensation will relate to the costs of providing the building, plus damages for the period remaining in the lease. The council will wish to ensure that the contractual provisions deal with the methodology for calculation of the compensation.

Public private partnership arrangement

26.48   Once the health body and the council have entered into the joint commissioning partnership arrangement, the council may then embark upon the task of procuring the services. The recommended means of doing so is by a PPP arrangement with private independent provider. The benefits of this to the council and the health body are numerous, particularly in the provision of residential care home services since the implementation of the Care Standards Act 2000. Local authorities now find that, in discharging their duties under the National Assistance Act 1948, they are no longer exempt from the statutory regulation and inspection regime of care homes run by them. Under the CSA 2000, councils are required to meet the same standards of care provision as applies to independent providers. A substantial input of funds will be needed to raise homes to the requisite standards. This can be best achieved by a PPP arrangement. The mechanics of such an arrangement for the provision of care homes are considered at para **26.07**.

Documents

As between the public bodies

26.49 The health body and the council will enter into a formal agreement—the partnership agreement—as approved by the boards of the health body and the council. The partnership agreement will contain terms as to financial arrangements detailing how much each body will contribute for the purpose of providing the jointly commissioned services. The ratio will depend on the level of responsibility for the services of the relevant body.

Duration

26.50 The duration of the partnership arrangement between the health body and the council will incorporate:
— provisions for the parties to terminate the arrangement on any subsequent anniversary of the term or on written notice in the event of change in the law or guidance which materially affects the arrangements under the agreement;
— a provision for either party to terminate if the partnership arrangement places either party in breach of their statutory obligations.

The partnership arrangements

26.51 This clause should detail in full the arrangements for which the partnership has been formed.

Consultation under the Health Act 1999, s 31

26.52 This clause should set out the parties and bodies who must be consulted in order to comply with the statutory provisions.

Structure

26.53 This clause should set out the requirement for the health body and the council to establish a partnership board to deal with the working of the partnership. It should also include:
— details as to terms of reference;
— membership; composition of the board;
— scheme of delegation;
— the conduct of business of the partnership board; and
— appointment of a Joint Commissioning Officer.

Finances

26.54 This clause should deal with all aspects of the financial arrangements between the council and the health body, as provided for under the Health Act 1999, ss 28 and 29, including:
— how much each of the statutory partners will contribute to provision of services;
— terms as to review of the level of human resources each partner will contribute;
— provisions for variation of the level of financial and human resources;
— methods of keeping to the budget;

— dealing with underspends and overspends;
— financial management of information;
— exploring possibilities for additional spending;
— VAT implications;
— all aspects of charging service users for the service being provided and recovery of funds. This may require a tri-partite agreement between the council, the health body and the service user.

Operational issues

26.55   This clause should set out the issues which:
— require the parties to ensure the partnership complies with all statutory requirements and guidance (both national and local) on conduct and probity;
— require that contracts for services are entered into in the names of the respective health body and the council;
— deal with governance.

Performance management

26.56   This clause should deal with the requirement of the health body and the council to demonstrate:
— how far the aims and objectives of the partnership arrangement are being met;
— the extent to which outputs are being met;
— the extent to which agreed outcomes are being fulfilled and targets met;
— financial inputs and outputs.

Best value

26.57   This clause should set out the requirement for the council to comply with the duty of best value under the Local Government Act 1999.

Information sharing

26.58   This clause should set out the requirement for the parties to comply with all legislation, regulations and guidance on information sharing between public bodies.

Work force issues

26.59   This clause should deal with any staffing issues, including TUPE issues.

Complaints

26.60   This should set out the procedure for dealing with complaints and the requirement to comply with statutory requirements on the handling of complaints.

Review, disputes, termination

26.61   This clause should:
— set out the period for reviewing the operation of the partnership, including provision for such review to take place on the coming into force of relevant statutory or other legislation or guidance affecting the working arrangements;
— deal with variation and succession;

—   include a dispute resolution clause, and
—   include a clause entitling the parties to deal with issues of staffing, notice period, asset allocation, responsibility for debts on the termination of the arrangement.

Assignments

26.62   Assignment should not be permitted. The ability of the contractor to transfer its contractual obligations and liabilities as a result of corporate changes to its business structure or relinquish the contract, is covered by the right to vary or terminate.

As between the public bodies and the contractor

Project agreement

26.63   The standard draft will not allow for significant changes by the contractor. In the light of recent legislative changes discussed at para **26.05**, the following clauses will require expanding upon:
—   pre-conditions: it would be sensible to include a pre-condition placing the onus on the contractor to ensure that it fulfils the statutory criteria of 'fitness' to be registered under the Care Standards Act 2000 in respect of the home;
—   warranties: consider inserting appropriate warranties on the part of the contractor as to its ability to provide the services in accordance with the standards required by the legislation;
—   design matters: the design of the building as well as the facilities within the building are subject to the approval of the NCSC. Therefore a requirement that the contractor liaise with the NCSC and obtains such approval during the construction stage would be sensible;
—   certification of the building by the independent certifier: consideration should be given to including a provision for approval of the building by the NCSC;
—   best value: the council will require the contractor's full co-operation in ensuring that the services provided under the PPP arrangement deliver best value. Correct valuation of the services, taking into account the issues discussed in paras **26.35** and **26.40** should be a requirement;
—   step-in: the council will wish to ensure that it has the ability to step-in and operate the care home, or nominate an alternative operator, in the event of the contractor's irremediable breach, urgent closure or cancellation of contractor's registration in respect of the home by the NCSC, or the insolvency of the contractor. The contractor should be required to give a sufficient period of notice to the council of the anticipated happening of an event rendering the contractor unable to operate the home. The period allowed should be sufficient to enable the council and the health body to put in place the contingency arrangements made pursuant to the guidelines of the Department of Health discussed above.

Important legal issues for the council

Consulation

26.64   Where the local authority is proposing to close a residential care home provided under the National Assistance Act 1948, Pt III, consultation is an important legal issue. In the *Coughlan* case, the Court of Appeal held that the local authority owed the residents of the home a duty to act fairly. This duty includes a requirement to consult with the residents about the proposed closure. The following elements should be satisfied in the consultation process:

— the residents should have known that the closure of the home was under consideration well before the final decision to close it was made;
— the residents should have had a reasonable opportunity to put to the local authority their objections to the closure;
— the residents' objections should have been considered by the local authority.

26.65   Proper consultation is particularly important where there is a legitimate expectation on the part of the residents that they would remain the establishment for the rest of their lives. Such legitimate expectation may be borne out of an assurance on the part of the local authority[1].

1   See the line of recent cases on this topic: *R v North Devon Health Authority, ex p Coughlan* [2001] QB 213, CA; *Rowe v Walsall Metropolitan Borough Council* (26 April 2001, unreported); *Frank Cowl v Plymouth City Council* [2001] EWHC Admin 734, [2001] All ER (D) 29 (Sep).

Human rights

26.66   Article 8 of the European Convention on Human Rights guarantees the right to respect for private and family life, home and correspondence. This includes a right not to be removed from a residential home occupied by the resident[1]. The council must therefore bear this in mind when contemplating closure of residential homes provided under the National Assistance Act 1948, Pt III and transferring residents to homes provided under the PPP arrangement.

1   This was held in the *Coughlan* case discussed above.

Dispute resolution

26.67   Dispute resolution[1] is a topical and important issue for the public bodies as well as the contractor. The contractual documents contain an informal procedure for determining minor disputes and a more formal procedure for determining major issues of disputes such as those concerning building works, services and payment of the unitary charge.

1   See chapter 7.

Statutory provisions: closure of the home

26.68   The procedure for cancellation and closure of a care home by the NCSC is provided for under the Care Homes Regulations 2001[1]. The cancellation of registration and the closure of the home goes to the very heart of the matter for which the PPP arrangement has been entered into. The particular method of resolving these issues is by way of representation to the NCSC and, if that fails, by an appeal to the tribunal established pursuant to the Protection of Children Act 1999, s 99. The procedure for an urgent closure is more draconian whereby the NCSC will be able to proceed direct to the magistrates' court and obtain an order for closure with or without prior notice[2].

In order to maintain its ability to continue to operate the home where there is a proposal by the NCSC to cancel the registration of the home, the contractor will need to take steps by serving the relevant notices required under the Care Standards Act 2000, making appropriate representation and appealing to the tribunal within the requisite time scale. The council will, in the meantime, put in place contingency plans under the 'step-in' provisions as appropriate. In the event of on 'urgent cancellation' neither the council nor the contractor will have very much input in terms of the application to the magistrates' court, unless prior notice is given by the NCSC.

1   SI 2001/3965.
2   Care Standards Act 2000, ss 17–21.

Contractual issues

26.69   The conventional method of resolving contractual disputes by means of litigation through the civil courts is now regarded as a last resort. Instead, parties are required to consider alternative methods of dispute resolution at all stages[1]. Failure to consider and propose alternative dispute resolution by a party may be penalised by costs orders in the proceedings (including high rates of interest and indemnity costs against the defaulting party, even if he is the winning party). In the recent case of *Cowl v Plymouth City Council*[2] the court emphasised that disputes between public authorities and members of the public should be resolved by alternative methods of dispute resolution outside of the courts.

1   The overriding objective, Civil Procedure Rules 1998, r 1.4(2)(e).
2   [2001] EWHC Admin 734, [2001] All ER (D) 29 (Sep).

CONCLUSION

26.70   The particular PPP arrangement considered above has proceeded at a relatively slow pace due to the nature of the services and potential service users involved. In addition, there have been significant changes in the law (both at legislative level and the common law) during the course of the transaction, which has necessitated an element of rethinking and regrouping. Consultation has not been a straightforward process. Issues as to the right to remain in the existing care provision earmarked for closure has been raised and litigated.

26.71   The procurement process has been relatively straightforward with the appointed contractor demonstrating all the elements required by the council, including best value. The documents are not standardised but the points raised at para **26.63** gives an indication of some of the clauses which are considered to be of importance in a transaction of this nature.

CHAPTER 27

Case study: transport

Mary Bonar

BUS QUALITY PARTNERSHIP SCHEMES AND BUS QUALITY CONTRACTS SCHEMES

Scope

27.01   The Transport Act 2000 (TA 2000) partially implemented the transport policy outlined in the integrated transport White Paper published in 1998. Local transport authorities (LTAs) became subject to a statutory requirement to draw up and keep under review a five year local transport plan for their areas which were to include a bus strategy.

27.02   In addition they were given powers in relation to local bus services which recognised that, since the general deregulation of bus services outside Greater London from 1986, local authorities had little ability to implement integrated transport policies involving bus services.

27.03   The new powers are for a single LTA or two or more LTAs together :
(i)   to make a quality partnership scheme;
(ii)   to make a bus quality contracts scheme followed by a tender for the provision of the bus services specified in the scheme.

27.04   For the purpose of both types of scheme LTAs are:
(1)   English county councils;
(2)   some English non-metropolitan councils;
(3)   English Passenger Transport Authorities;
(4)   Welsh County Councils or County Borough Councils.

27.05   For quality partnership schemes relating to traffic regulation facilities, the traffic regulations authority (ie a metropolitan district council or the Secretary of State for Transport (in England) or the National Assembly for Wales (in Wales)) will also have a role.

27.06   Quality partnership schemes involve the LTA or LTAs providing facilities, and bus operators who wish to use those facilities undertaking to provide a specified level of local services when using those facilities.

27.07   Quality contracts schemes permit the LTA to specify the local services to be provided exclusively in specific areas and any additional facilities or services to be provided in those areas. The services are then provided under contract, which may contain terms covering such matters as frequency, fares and standard of service.

27.08   The TA 2000 gives the national authority, that is the Secretary of State for Transport, in respect of England, or the National Assembly for Wales in respect of Wales, power to make regulations relating to each type of scheme. In the case of bus quality contracts approval of the national authority is required before a scheme can be made: in the case of bus quality partnership schemes, no such approval is required for the making of schemes. However, there is an overriding requirement for the LTAs and Metropolitan District Councils to have regard to any guidance issued by the national authority concerning the carrying out of their functions in making quality partnership schemes. At the time of writing no such regulations have been made in relation to bus quality contracts schemes.

27.09   The Quality Partnership Schemes (Existing Facilities) Regulations 2001[1] deal with the specifying in quality partnership schemes of facilities which were already provided by the relevant LTA or LTAs before the statutory scheme was proposed. No general regulations have been made to date under the TA 2000, s 122 relating to quality partnership schemes. In addition no guidance has been issued.

1   SI 2001/3317.

27.10   The Department for Transport has noted that LTAs have not shown much interest in using the TA 2000 to make statutory quality partnership schemes. The Department is aware that LTAs are interested in making quality contracts schemes, under which they are able to stipulate fares and frequency of services, although no formal applications have been made for approval of such schemes. The lengthy process for making the schemes, which involves obtaining the Secretary of State's approval, as well as the 21-month period before a scheme can start to operate, is seen as a deterrent.

27.11   The purpose of these case studies is therefore to outline the process set out in the TA 2000 for making each type of scheme. It should be borne in mind that, in addition, there may be regulations applying to quality contracts, whilst in the case of quality partnerships there may be regulations and if formal guidance is issued it will need to be taken into account.

27.12   Useful guidance on non-statutory quality partnerships, of which there are a number in operation, can be found in the TAS *Quality Bus Partners Good Practice Guide*, which has been approved by the Department for Transport.

BUS QUALITY PARTNERSHIP SCHEMES

Parties

27.13   A Quality Partnership Scheme (QP Scheme) can be made by a single LTA or two or more LTAs together. Where the provision of facilities under the scheme requires a traffic regulation order to be made relating to a road or other place in a metropolitan district (where the Secretary of State or the National Assembly for Wales is not the traffic authority) the scheme must be made by the LTA or LTAs and the relevant metropolitan district council.

27.14   Where a traffic regulation order will be required for a road for which the Secretary of State or the National Assembly for Wales is the traffic authority the scheme must be made by the LTA or LTAs and the traffic authority.

27.15 The operator or operators of local bus services who intend to make use of the facilities to be provided under the scheme must give a written undertaking to the traffic commissioner for each traffic area to which the scheme relates to provide the services to the required standard when using the facilities.

Objective of case study scheme

27.16 An English LTA plans to make a bus quality partnership scheme in order to implement elements of the bus strategy which is set out in its local transport plan. The LTA plans to install a combined vehicle location, real time passenger information and communication system. This will provide real time information on monitors at bus stops and the potential to link into a new urban traffic control system giving buses priority at signalled junctions. It will also provide driver to police communications, driver to depot communications and for the ability to locate each vehicle, vehicle tracking.

27.17 Bus operators wishing to make use of the new system would need to install a particular type of communication system in vehicles and depots to be able to carry out the different functions referred to above.

Process

27.18 In order to make a bus quality partnership scheme the LTA will need to make a decision in principle to proceed, having first reviewed the bus strategy in its local transport plan. It will then need to define:
— the area to be covered by the QP scheme;
— the facilities which it intends to provide—in the case study the new system including equipment at bus stops;
— the standard of services to be provided by operators who make use of the facilities—in the case study the requirement for vehicles and depots to be equipped to use the system;
— any local services or class of local services to be excluded.

27.19 The LTA will need to consider whether it would be appropriate to make the scheme jointly with any other LTAs, in which case arrangements will need to be made amongst the authorities as to how to take the process forward. It will also be necessary to consider whether any traffic regulation orders will be required. If they are, the traffic authority will also need to join in making the scheme.

27.20 At this stage the LTA should also consider how it intends to carry out consultation. To take the decision to proceed the LTA needs to be satisfied that:
(a) the QP scheme will implement or continue to implement the policies in the bus strategies for the area;
(b) the provision of the facilities and the provision of local bus services to the standard contemplated will:
  (i) improve the quality of local services in the relevant area by bringing benefits to users; or
  (ii) reduce or limit traffic congestion, noise or air pollution.
The LTA or LTAs may need to carry out a consultation exercise and a feasibility study to satisfy (b).

The LTA should also take advice and if necessary obtain informal guidance from the OFT as to whether it should satisfy the competition test for QP schemes contained in the Act. There is a procedure for the LTA or an operator of local services to apply formally for a decision of the Director General of Fair Trading.

Establishing a scheme

27.21   Having taken the decision in principle the following steps need to be taken (subject to any further requirements to be set out in the regulations or guidance from the national authority):

— prepare the draft scheme (see para **27.23** below);
— publish a notice in a newspaper circulating in the area which gives full details of the facilities and the standards of service, or states where the details can be inspected. It is recommended that the notice includes the reasons for wishing to make the service and details of the consultation process;
— consult a range of stakeholders likely to be affected, including local bus operators, other affected local authorities, user groups, the police, the Traffic Commissioners and others as the LTA thinks fit;
— review the results of the consultation.

The draft scheme should then be made as proposed or modified as appropriate in light of the response to the consultation.

Key steps to making a bus quality partnership scheme

27.22

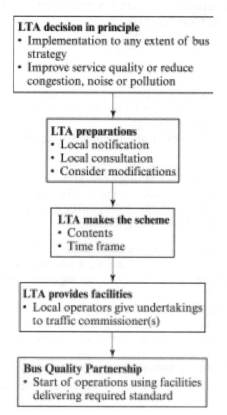

Contents of a scheme

27.23　The formal QP scheme must state:
(i)　the facilities to be provided by the LTA or LTAs including the traffic authority;
(ii)　where appropriate, the standard of services to be provided by local service operators making use of the facilities to be provided by the LTA or LTAs;
(iii)　the date of start of operation: this must not be earlier than three months after the date of the scheme or the last traffic regulation order required to be made under it. Note that the date should be one by which it is practicable for both the facilities and the services to be provided;
(iv)　the period for which the scheme is to be in operation, which must be a minimum of five years;
(v)　any local services or classes of local services excluded and any applicable conditions.

Publication

27.24　Within 14 days of making the QP scheme the LTA must publish a notice that the scheme has been made in a newspaper circulating in the area and notify all affected operators and the Traffic Commissioners. The notice must contain full details of the scheme or state where it can be inspected.

The TA 2000 provides powers for the start date to be postponed by the LTAs by up to 12 months, following consultation.

Effect of scheme

27.25　The relevant authority is obliged to provide the facilities by the date of start of operations and to continue to provide them for the operating period, except where temporarily unable to provide due to circumstances beyond its control. The national authority (party to the scheme as a traffic authority) is not liable if it cannot provide the facilities owing to the variation or revocation of a traffic regulation order.

27.26　No operator of a local service is entitled to use the facilities unless:
(a)　it has given a written undertaking to the relevant Traffic Commissioner[s] to provide the service to the standard specified in the scheme when using the facilities; and
(b)　it actually provides the service to that standard, except when temporarily unable to do so due to circumstances beyond its control.

Legal and commercial issues

27.27　The LTA will need to consider carefully the description of the facilities to be provided and the specification of the standard of services. LTAs are best value authorities under the Local Government Act 1999. The arrangement for the provision of the facilities will therefore be subject to the best value regime.

27.28   In the absence of regulations or guidance it is recommended that the form of undertaking to be given by operators using the facilities should be specified as part of the scheme and a process established for notifying this to the Traffic Commissioners, and receiving notice from the Traffic Commissioners.

27.29   In the case study it is likely that a traffic regulation order or orders will be required in order to implement bus priority at signalled junctions once the relevant part of the system is in operation. Therefore, in making the scheme the LTA will need to decide whether to include the traffic authority and how to enforce the undertaking to cover the bus priority aspects once in operation.

27.30   The TA 2000 does not specify the legal consequences of failure either by the LTA to provide and maintain the facilities or of the operator to fail to give or to abide by its undertaking. The LTA or LTAs will also need to take into account the impact of the Competition Act 1998. The TA 2000 contains a competition test which applies to the making and varying of quality partnership schemes. This case study does not focus on the competition aspects but alerts LTAs to the need to consider the provisions in the context of in principle decisions to make or vary such schemes. The OFT has issued a consultation paper, in which it sets out its proposed guidance in relation to the competition test contained in the TA 2000. Following the consultation, the OFT will issue formal guidance. The proposed guidance states:

> 'The main competition concern that is likely to arise from quality partnerships is that they will raise barriers to entry or force the exit of existing competitors. For example, those operators that do not fulfil the standard of service conditions required by a quality partnership may be prevented from using the facilities provided by the local transport authority, and an operator may consider that without access to the facilities provided under the scheme it would not be able to compete in the market.'

27.31   The details set out in this case study will need to be reviewed if regulations are made, and once guidance is issued by the national authority. Some provisions of the TA 2000 are not yet in force in Wales.

BUS QUALITY CONTRACT SCHEMES

Background

27.32   As explained at para **27.03** the provisions for LTAs to make statutory bus quality contracts schemes were introduced by the TA 2000. The TA 2000 provides for regulations to be made by the national authority, that is the Secretary of State for Transport or the National Assembly for Wales (or both). No regulations have been made at the time of writing (October 2002).

27.33   Bus quality contracts schemes effectively provide a form of regulated bus services which, outside the Greater London Authority area, have been unregulated since 1986. In return for exclusivity the bus operators may be required to commit to terms covering such matters as frequency, fares and standard of service.

27.34   After establishing a bus quality contracts scheme the LTA is required to issue a tender for the provision of the local bus services specified in the scheme. This case study deals with the process of establishing a scheme, not the tender process.

Parties

27.35 The scheme can be made by a single LTA, or two or more LTAs. A scheme cannot be made until approved by the national authority. Having made a scheme the LTA or LTAs must issue a tender for the provision of the local bus services specified in the scheme. The successful tenderer must be the holder of a PSV operator's licence or a community bus permit.

Objective of case study scheme

27.36 An English LTA plans to make a bus quality contracts scheme and to enter into quality contracts, in order to implement the bus strategy which is set out in its statutory local transport plan. The LTA is in the course of conducting a competition for the construction and operation, under a long-term concession, of a new tram scheme and a number of bidders for that scheme have indicated that the existence of bus quality contracts will assist the robustness of the revenue stream and therefore contribute to the value for money of the tram scheme.

27.37 To meet the bidders' concerns bus operations on the term of bus quality contracts would need to start when the tram service begins following construction of the tramway. However there is no precedent for the Secretary of State to approve a scheme in such circumstances and the LTA will therefore need to prepare carefully, involving its stakeholders at an early stage.

Process

27.38 In order to make a bus quality contracts scheme the LTA will need to make a decision in principle to proceed having first reviewed the bus strategy in its local transport plan. It will then need to define:
(a) the area to be covered by the scheme;
(b) the local services to be provided;
(c) any additional facilities or services which should be provided in the areas.

27.39 In this exercise it will be necessary to consider whether it would be appropriate to make the scheme jointly with any other LTA, in which case arrangements will need to be made amongst the authorities as to how to take the process forward. At this stage the LTA should also consider how it intends to carry out consultation.

27.40 To take the decision to proceed the LTA needs to be satisfied that
(a) a quality contracts scheme is the only practicable way of implementing the policies in the bus strategies for the area;
(b) the scheme will provide an economic, efficient and effective way of implementing the services.
Note that the LTAs may need to carry out a consultation exercise and a feasibility study to satisfy (a) and (b).

Establishing a scheme

27.41 Having taken the decision in principle the following steps need to be taken (subject to any further requirements to be set out in the regulations)
(a) prepare the draft scheme (see para **27.46**);

(b)   publish, in a newspaper circulating in the area, a notice which describes the scheme, the reasons for wishing to make it and details of the consultation process;

(c)   consult a range of stakeholders including local bus operators, other PSV licence or community bus permit holders, user groups, the police, the Traffic Commissions and, in this case, the bidders for the tram scheme;

(d)   review the results of the consultation.

The draft scheme should then be modified as appropriate in light of the response to the consultation.

27.42   The LTA must then prepare and submit an application to the Department for Transport as national authority supported by the reasons for wishing to make the scheme and other information reasonably required by the national authority. If the Department proposes any modifications to the scheme the LTA will need to consult on these (consistently with the consultation process applied to the draft scheme) and notify the outcome.

27.43   The Department for Transport will need to be satisfied that a quality contracts scheme is the only practicable way of implementing the policies in the bus strategies for the area, that the scheme provides an economic, efficient and effective way of implementing the services and that the making of the scheme is in the public interests.

Key steps to making a bus quality contract

27.44

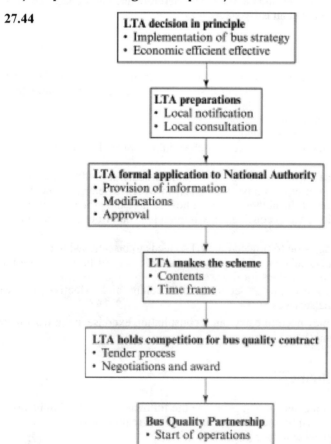

27.45 On receiving formal approval from the Department the LTA will wish to publicise this in the locality, as well as holding meetings with the stakeholders.

Making the scheme

27.46 The scheme must be made within six months following national authority approval. Formal notice has to be given within 14 days of the scheme being made (the details are expected to be set out in the regulations). The time periods referred to above can be varied by an order of the national authority.

Contents of a scheme

27.47 The formal scheme must state:
(a) the date of start of operation: this must not be earlier than 21 months after the date of the scheme;
(b) the duration, which cannot be more than 10 years—although it should be noted that a bus quality contract under the scheme cannot exceed five years;
(c) the geographical area to which it relates;
(d) a description of the local bus services to be provided under quality contracts and the features of the proposed invitations to tender for those contracts—note that this should include any terms relating to such matters as frequencies, fares and standard of service;
(e) any local services or classes of local services excluded,

and may set out provisions varying any existing quality partnership scheme.

Legal and commercial issues

27.48 The maximum duration of a scheme, once made, is 10 years. The maximum period for which the local services may be tendered is five years. Neither period will be long enough to provide certainty to the operator of the tram services. The LTA will need to take advice on any requirements proposed by the bidders for the tram project that the LTA should commit to applying to make further schemes in the future.

27.49 LTAs are best value authorities under the Local Government Act 1999. The contract for the provision of the local services will therefore be subject to the best value regime.

27.50 The Competition Act 1998 contains no relevant exemptions to benefit integrated transport schemes. There is, therefore, a risk that the operator of the tram scheme would be restricted from being the operator of the local service and this is an area on which the LTA may wish to seek informal guidance from the Competition Commission.

27.51 Given the current need for the new local services to start operation at the same time as the tram scheme, considerable care will be required to time the process for making the bus quality contracts scheme and tendering the contract for the local services so that there will be time to install any facilities required under the bus quality contracts scheme. The time limit for making the scheme is six months from national authority approval, and the scheme needs to come into operation no earlier than 21 months after the date of the making of the scheme.

27.52   The LTA will also need to take into account the impact of the Competition Act 1998. The competition test in the Transport Act 2000 does not apply to bus quality contracts. The OFT has recently published informal guidelines on the application of competition law in the bus industry. These indicate that it is important that, when the LTA puts the service out to tender, the tender criteria are 'open, clear and transparent', so that competition is not significantly affected. The OFT's requirements reflect the LTA's general duties under EU law (transparency, non-discrimination, etc). Any restrictions in the tender process would need to be objectively justified. The OFT is in the course of consultation and expected to issue guidance on the competition test in the TA 2000 in early 2003. The OFT welcomes informal discussions with authorities with regard to individual schemes, and can provide guidance, for example whether the operator of the tram scheme is restricted from being the operator of the local service.

The details set out in this case study will need to be reviewed following the making of the regulations. Some provisions of the TA 2000 are not yet in force in Wales.

APPENDIX 1 STATUTES

LOCAL GOVERNMENT AND HOUSING ACT 1989

1989 c 42

PART V
COMPANIES IN WHICH LOCAL AUTHORITIES HAVE
INTERESTS

[App.01]
67 Application of, and orders under, Part V

(1)   Any reference in this Part to a company is a reference to a body corporate of one of the following descriptions—

(a)   a company limited by shares;

(b)   a company limited by guarantee and not having a share capital;

(c)   a company limited by guarantee and having a share capital;

(d)   an unlimited company; and

(e)   a society registered or deemed to be registered under the Industrial and Provident Societies Act 1965 or under the Industrial and Provident Societies Act (Northern Ireland) 1969.

(2)   Expressions used in paragraphs (a) to (d) of subsection (1) above have the same meaning as in Chapter I of Part I of the Companies Act 1985 or the corresponding enactment for the time being in force in Northern Ireland.

(3)   Any reference in this Part to a local authority is a reference to a body of one of the following descriptions—

(a)   a county council;

[(aa) a county borough council;]

(b)   a district council;

[(bb) the Greater London Authority;

(bc)   a functional body, within the meaning of the Greater London Authority Act 1999;]

(c)   a London borough council;

(d)   the Common Council of the City of London in its capacity as a local authority, police authority or port health authority;

(e)   the Council of the Isles of Scilly;

(f)   a parish council;

(g)   a community council;

[(ga) the Greater London Magistrates' Courts Authority;]

(h)   a fire authority constituted by a combination scheme under the Fire Services Act 1947;

[(i)   a police authority established under [section 3 of the Police Act 1996] [. . .];]

(j)   an authority established under section 10 of the Local Government Act 1985 (waste disposal authorities);

(k)   a joint authority established by Part IV of that Act (. . ., fire services, civil defence and transport);

(l)   any body established pursuant to an order under section 67 of that Act (successors to residuary bodies);

(m)   the Broads Authority;

[(ma) a National Park authority;]

(n)   any joint board the constituent members of which consist of any of the bodies specified above;

(o)   ...

[(oo) a joint planning board constituted for an area in Wales outside a National Park by an order under section 2(1B) of the Town and Country Planning Act 1990; and]

(p)   a Passenger Transport Executive.

(4)   Any power to make an order under this Part shall be exercisable by statutory instrument subject to annulment in pursuance of a resolution of either House of Parliament; and under any such power different provision may be made for different cases and different descriptions of cases (including different provision for different areas).

Amendment
Sub-s (3): para (aa) inserted by SI 1996/3071, art 2, Schedule, para 3(6); paras (bb), (bc) inserted by the Greater London Authority Act 1999, s 393; para (ga) inserted by the Access to Justice Act 1999, s 83(3), Sch 12, paras 4, 6; para (i) substituted by the Police and Magistrates' Courts Act 1994, ss 43, 93, Sch 4, Pt I, para 39, Sch 9, Pt I; in para (i) words 'section 3 of the Police Act 1996' in square brackets substituted by the Police Act 1996, s 103, Sch 7, para 1(2)(zd); in para (i) words omitted inserted by the Police Act 1997, s 88, Sch 6, para 30; in para (i) words omitted repealed by the Criminal Justice and Police Act 2001, ss 128(1), 137, Sch 6, Pt 2, paras 49, 52, Sch 7, Pt 5(1); in para (k) word omitted repealed by the Police and Magistrates' Courts Act 1994, ss 43, 93, Sch 4, Pt I, para 39, Sch 9, Pt I; para (ma) inserted by the Environment Act 1995, s 65, Sch 8, para 10; para (o) repealed by the Environment Act 1995, ss 78, 120, Sch 10, para 31(3), Sch 24; para (oo) inserted by the Environment Act 1995, s 78, Sch 10, para 31(3).

[App.02]

68 Companies controlled by local authorities and arm's length companies

(1)   For the purposes of this Part, unless the Secretary of State otherwise directs, a company is for the time being under the control of a local authority if—

(a)   by virtue of section 736 of the Companies Act 1985 the company is at that time a subsidiary of the local authority for the purposes of that Act; or

(b)   paragraph (a) above does not apply but the local authority have at that time power to control a majority of the votes at a general meeting of the company as mentioned in subsection (3) below; or

(c)   paragraph (a) above does not apply but the local authority have at that time power to appoint or remove a majority of the board of directors of the company; or

(d)   the company is under the control of another company which, by virtue of this subsection, is itself under the control of the local authority;

and, for the purposes of paragraph (d) above, any question whether one company is under the control of another shall be determined by applying the preceding provisions of this subsection, substituting a reference to the other company for any reference to the local authority.

(2)   A direction under subsection (1) above—

(a)   may be limited in time and may be made conditional upon such matters as appear to the Secretary of State to be appropriate; and

(b)   may be made with respect to a particular company or a description of companies specified in the direction.

(3)   The reference in subsection (1)(b) above to a power to control a majority of votes at a general meeting of the company is a reference to a power which is exercisable—
(a)   in the case of a company limited by shares, through the holding of equity share capital in any one or more of the following ways, namely, by the local authority, by nominees of the local authority and by persons whose shareholding is under the control of the local authority; or
(b)   in the case of any company, through the holding of votes at a general meeting of the company in any one or more of the following ways, namely, by the local authority, by a group of members of the company the composition of which is controlled by the local authority and by persons who have contractually bound themselves to vote in accordance with the instructions of the local authority; or
(c)   partly in one of those ways and partly in the other.

(4)   Subsection (3) of section 736A of the Companies Act 1985 (right to appoint or remove a majority of a company's board of directors) and the following provisions of that section as they have effect in relation to subsection (3) apply for the purposes of subsection (1)(c) above with the substitution for the word 'right', wherever it occurs, of the word 'power'.

(5)   For the purposes of subsection (3)(a) above, a person's shareholding is under the control of a local authority if—
(a)   his right to hold the shares arose because of some action which the authority took, or refrained from taking, in order to enable him to have the right; and
(b)   the local authority, alone or jointly with one or more other persons can require him to transfer his shareholding (or any part of it) to another person.

(6)   Notwithstanding that, by virtue of the preceding provisions of this section, a company is for the time being under the control of a local authority, the company is for the purposes of this Part an 'arm's length company', in relation to any financial year if, at a time before the beginning of that year, the authority resolved that the company should be an arm's length company and, at all times from the passing of that resolution up to the end of the financial year in question, the following conditions have applied while the company has been under the control of the local authority,—
(a)   that each of the directors of the company was appointed for a fixed term of at least two years;
(b)   that, subject to subsection (7) below, no director of the company has been removed by resolution under section 303 of the Companies Act 1985;
(c)   that not more than one-fifth of the directors of the company have been members or officers of the authority;
(d)   that the company has not occupied (as tenant or otherwise) any land in which the authority have an interest, otherwise than for the best consideration reasonably obtainable;
(e)   that the company has entered into an agreement with the authority that the company will use its best endeavours to produce a specified positive return on its assets;
(f)   that, except for the purpose of enabling the company to acquire fixed assets or to provide it with working capital, the authority have not lent money to the company or guaranteed any sum borrowed by it or subscribed for any securities in the company;
(g)   that the authority have not made any grant to the company except in pursuance of an agreement or undertaking entered into before the financial year (within

the meaning of the Companies Act 1985) of the company in which the grant was made; and

(h)   that the authority have not made any grant to the company the amount of which is in any way related to the financial results of the company in any period.

(7)   If the Secretary of State so directs, the removal of a director shall be disregarded for the purposes of subsection (6)(b) above; but the Secretary of State shall not give such a direction if it appears to him that the director was removed with a view to influencing the management of the company for other than commercial reasons.

[App.03]

69 Companies subject to local authority influence

(1)   For the purposes of this Part, unless the Secretary of State otherwise directs, a company which is not at the time under the control of a local authority is for the time being subject to the influence of a local authority if it is not a banking or insurance company or a member of a banking or insurance group and at that time there is such a business relationship between the company and the authority as is referred to in subsection (3) below and either—

(a)   at least 20 per cent of the total voting rights of all the members having the right to vote at a general meeting of the company are held by persons who are associated with the authority as mentioned in subsection (5) below; or

(b)   at least 20 per cent of the directors of the company are persons who are so associated; or

(c)   at least 20 per cent of the total voting rights at a meeting of the directors of the company are held by persons who are so associated.

(2)   A direction under subsection (1) above—

(a)   may be limited in time and may be made conditional upon such matters as appear to the Secretary of State to be appropriate; and

(b)   may be made with respect to a particular company or a description of companies specified in the direction.

(3)   For the purposes of this section there is a business relationship between a company and a local authority at any time if the condition in any one or more of the following paragraphs is fulfilled—

(a)   within a period of twelve months which includes that time the aggregate of the payments to the company by the authority or by another company which is under the control of the authority represents more than one-half of the company's turnover, as shown in its profit and loss account for the most recent financial year for which the company's auditors have made a report on the accounts or, if there is no such account, as estimated by the authority for the period of twelve months preceding the date of the estimate or for such part of that period as follows the formation of the company;

(b)   more than one-half of the company's turnover referred to in paragraph (a) above is derived from the exploitation of assets of any description in which the local authority or a company under the control of the authority has an interest (disregarding an interest in land which is in reversion on a lease granted for more than 7 years);

(c)   the aggregate of—

(i)   grants made either by the authority and being expenditure for capital purposes or by a company under the control of the authority, and

(ii)   the nominal value of shares or stock in the company which is owned by the authority or by a company under the control of the authority,

exceeds one-half of the net assets of the company;

(d)   the aggregate of—
    (i)   grants falling within paragraph (c)(i) above,
    (ii)   loans or other advances made or guaranteed by the authority or by a company under the control of the authority, and
    (iii) the nominal value referred to in paragraph (c)(ii) above,
    exceeds one-half of the fixed and current assets of the company;
(e)   the company at that time occupies land by virtue of an interest which it obtained from the local authority or a company under the control of the authority and which it so obtained at less than the best consideration reasonably obtainable; and
(f)   the company intends at that time to enter into (or complete) a transaction and, when that is done, there will then be a business relationship between the company and the authority by virtue of any of paragraphs (a) to (e) above.

(4)   In subsection (3) above—
(a)   the reference in paragraph (c) to the net assets of the company shall be construed in accordance with section 152(2) of the Companies Act 1985; and
(b)   the reference in paragraph (d) to the fixed and current assets of the company shall be construed in accordance with paragraph 77 of Schedule 4 to that Act;

and in either case, the reference is a reference to those assets as shown in the most recent balance sheet of the company on which, at the time in question, the auditors have made a report or, if there is no such balance sheet, as estimated by the local authority for the time in question.

(5)   For the purposes of this section, a person is at any time associated with a local authority if—
(a)   he is at that time a member of the authority;
(b)   he is at that time an officer of the authority;
(c)   he is at that time both an employee and either a director, manager, secretary or other similar officer of a company which is under the control of the authority; or
(d)   at any time within the preceding four years he has been associated with the authority by virtue of paragraph (a) above.

(6)   If and to the extent that the Secretary of State by order so provides, a person is at any time associated with a local authority if—
(a)   at that time he is, or is employed by or by a subsidiary of, a person who for the time being has a contractual relationship with the authority to provide—
    (i)   advice with regard to the authority's interest in any company (whether existing or proposed to be formed), or
    (ii)   advice with regard to the management of an undertaking or the development of land by a company (whether existing or proposed to be formed) with which it is proposed that the authority should enter into any lease, licence or other contract or to which it is proposed that the authority should make any grant or loan, or
    (iii) services which facilitate the exercise of the authority's rights in any company (whether by acting as the authority's representative at a meeting of the company or as a director appointed by the authority or otherwise);
(b)   at any time within the preceding four years, he has been associated with the authority by virtue of paragraph (b) or paragraph (c) of subsection (5) above;
(c)   he is at that time the spouse of, or carries on business in partnership with, a person who is associated with the authority by virtue of subsection (5)(a) above; or

(d)   he holds a relevant office in a political association or other body which, in the nomination paper of a person who is an elected member of the authority, formed part of that person's description.

(7)   For the purposes of subsection (6)(d) above, an office in a political association or body is relevant to a local authority in the following circumstances—

(a)   if the association or body is active only in the area of the local authority, any office in it is relevant; and

(b)   in any other case, an office is relevant only if it is in a branch or other part of the association or body which is active in the area of the local authority.

(8)   In relation to a company which is an industrial and provident society, any reference in this section to the directors of the company is a reference to the members of the committee of management.

(9)   Subject to subsections (4) and (8) and section 67 above, expressions used in this section have the same meaning as in the Companies Act 1985.

[App.04]
70 Requirements for companies under control or subject to influence of local authorities

(1)   In relation to companies under the control of local authorities and companies subject to the influence of local authorities, the Secretary of State may by order make provision regulating, forbidding or requiring the taking of certain actions or courses of action; and an order under this subsection may—

(a)   make provision in relation to those companies which are arm's length companies different from that applicable to companies which are not; and

(b)   make provision in relation to companies under the control of local authorities different from that applicable in relation to companies under the influence of local authorities.

(2)   It shall be the duty of every local authority to ensure, so far as practicable, that any company under its control complies with the provisions for the time being made by order under subsection (1) above; and if a local authority fails to perform that duty in relation to any company, any payment made by the authority to that company and any other expenditure incurred by the authority in contravention of any such provisions shall be deemed for the purposes of [the Audit Commission Act 1998] to be expenditure which is unlawful.

(3)   In order to secure compliance, in relation to companies subject to the influence of local authorities, with provisions made by virtue of subsection (1) above, an order under that subsection may prescribe requirements to be complied with by any local authority in relation to conditions to be included in such leases, licences, contracts, gifts, grants or loans as may be so prescribed which are made with or to a company subject to the influence of the local authority.

(4)   It shall be the duty of every local authority to comply with any requirements for the time being prescribed under subsection (3) above; and if a local authority fails to perform that duty, any expenditure which is incurred by the local authority under the lease, licence, contract, gift, grant or loan in question shall be deemed for the purposes of [the Audit Commission Act 1998] to be expenditure which is unlawful.

(5)   Without prejudice to the generality of the power conferred by subsection (1) above, an order under that subsection may make provision requiring a company or local authority to obtain the consent of the Secretary of State, or of the Audit

Commission for Local Authorities in England and Wales, before taking any particular action or course of action.

Amendment
Sub-s (2): words 'the Audit Commission Act 1998' in square brackets substituted by the Audit Commission Act 1998, s 54(1), Sch 3, para 18(3)(a).
Sub-s (4): words 'the Audit Commission Act 1998' in square brackets substituted by the Audit Commission Act 1998, s 54(1), Sch 3, para 18(3)(b).

[App.05]
71 Controls of minority interests etc in certain companies

(1)   In relation to a local authority, subsection (2) below applies to any company other than—

(a)   a company which is or, if the action referred to in that subsection is taken, will be under the control of the local authority; and

(b)   a company of a description specified for the purposes of this section by an order made by the Secretary of State;

and in this section an 'authorised company' means a company falling within paragraph (b) above.

(2)   Except with the approval of the Secretary of State, in relation to a company to which this subsection applies, a local authority may not—

(a)   subscribe for, or acquire, whether in their own name or in the name of a nominee, any shares or share warrants in the company;

(b)   become or remain a member of the company if it is limited by guarantee;

(c)   exercise any power, however arising, to nominate any person to become a member of the company;

(d)   exercise any power to appoint directors of the company;

(e)   permit any officer of the authority, in the course of his employment, to make any such nomination or appointment as is referred to in paragraph (c) or paragraph (d) above; or

(f)   permit an officer of the authority, in the course of his employment, to become or remain a member or director of the company.

(3)   Any approval of the Secretary of State under subsection (2) above may be general or relate to any specific matter or company.

(4)   A local authority may not take any action, or refrain from exercising any right, which would have the result that a person who is disqualified from membership of the authority (otherwise than by being employed by that or any other local authority or by a company which is under the control of a local authority) becomes a member or director of an authorised company or is authorised, in accordance with section 375 of the Companies Act 1985, to act as the authority's representative at a general meeting of an authorised company (or at meetings of an authorised company which include a general meeting).

(5)   In any case where,—

(a)   in accordance with section 375 of the Companies Act 1985, a local authority have authorised a member or officer of the authority to act as mentioned in subsection (4) above, or

(b)   a member or officer of a local authority has become a member or director of an authorised company as mentioned in subsection (7) below,

the authority shall make arrangements (whether by standing orders or otherwise) for enabling members of the authority, in the course of proceedings of the authority (or of any committee or sub-committee thereof), [or, where a local authority is operating executive arrangements under Part II of the Local Government Act 2000, for enabling members of the executive, in the course of proceedings of the executive (or of any committee of the executive),] to put to the member or officer concerned questions about the activities of the company.

(6)   Nothing in subsection (5) above shall require the member or officer referred to in that subsection to disclose any information about the company which has been communicated to him in confidence.

(7)   Any member or officer of a local authority who has become a member or director of an authorised company by virtue of—

(a)   a nomination made by the authority, or

(b)   election at a meeting of the company at which voting rights were exercisable (whether or not exercised) by the authority or by a person bound to vote in accordance with the instructions of the authority, or

(c)   an appointment made by the directors of another company, the majority of whom became directors of that company by virtue of a nomination made by the authority or election at a meeting of the company at which voting rights were exercisable as mentioned in paragraph (b) above,

shall make a declaration to the authority, in such form as they may require, of any remuneration or re-imbursement of expenses which he receives from the company as a member or director or in respect of anything done on behalf of the company.

(8)   Subject to section 67 above, expressions used in this section have the same meaning as in the Companies Act 1985.

Amendment
Sub-s (5): words from 'or, where a local authority' to 'any committee of the executive),' in square brackets inserted in relation to England by SI 2001/2237, arts 1(2), 2(l), 26(1), and in relation to Wales by SI 2002/808, arts 2(k), 25(1).

[App.06]
72 Trusts influenced by local authorities

(1)   The Secretary of State may by order made by statutory instrument adapt the provisions of section 69 above so as to make them applicable to trusts which are not charitable; and, subject to subsection (2) below, this Part shall apply in relation to trusts which are subject to local authority influence by virtue of that section as so adapted as it applies in relation to companies which are subject to local authority influence.

(2)   In the exercise of the power conferred by section 70 above, as applied in relation to trusts by subsection (1) above, the Secretary of State may make different provision for trusts as compared with companies.

[App.07]
73 Authorities acting jointly and by committees

(1)   In any case where—

(a)   apart from this section a company would not be under the control of any one local authority, but

(b)   if the actions, powers and interests of two or more local authorities were treated as those of one authority alone, the company would be under the control of that one authority, the company shall be treated for the purposes of this Part as under the control of each of the two or more local authorities mentioned in paragraph (b) above.

(2)   In any case where, apart from this section, a company would not be treated as being subject to the influence of any one local authority, it shall be treated as being subject to the influence of each of a number of local authorities (in this section referred to as a 'group') if the conditions in subsection (3) below are fulfilled with respect to the company and the group of authorities.

(3)   The conditions referred to in subsection (2) above are—

(a)   that at least one of the conditions in paragraphs (a) to (e) of subsection (3) of section 69 above would be fulfilled—

  (i)   if any reference therein to the company being under the control of a local authority were a reference to its being under the control of any one of the authorities in the group or of any two or more of them taken together; and

  (ii)   if any other reference therein to the local authority were a reference to any two or more of the authorities in the group taken together; and

(b)   that at least one of the conditions in paragraphs (a) to (c) of subsection (1) of section 69 above would be fulfilled if any reference therein to the local authority were a reference to those local authorities who are taken into account under sub-paragraph (i) or sub-paragraph (ii) of paragraph (a) above taken together; and

(c)   that if the condition (or one of the conditions) which would be fulfilled as mentioned in paragraph (b) above is that in subsection (1)(a) of section 69 above, then, so far as concerns each local authority in the group, at least one person who, in terms of subsection (5) of that section, is associated with that authority has the right to vote at a general meeting of the company; and

(d)   that, if paragraph (c) above does not apply, then, so far as concerns each local authority in the group, a person who, in terms of section 69(5) above, is associated with the authority is a director of the company.

(4)   For the purposes of this Part, anything done, and any power exercisable, by a committee or sub-committee of a local authority, or by any of the authority's officers [or, where a local authority is operating executive arrangements under Part II of the Local Government Act 2000, by the authority's executive, any committee of the executive, or any member of the executive], shall be treated as done or, as the case may be, exercisable by the authority.

(5)   For the purposes of this Part, anything done, and any power exercisable, by a joint committee of two or more local authorities or by a sub-committee of such a joint committee shall be treated as done or, as the case may be, exercisable by each of the local authorities concerned.

Amendment
Sub-s (4): words from 'or, where a local authority' to 'any member of the executive' in square brackets inserted in relation to England by SI 2001/2237, arts 1(2), 2(l), 26(2), and in relation to Wales by SI 2002/808, arts 2(k), 25(2).

LOCAL GOVERNMENT (CONTRACTS) ACT 1997

1997 c 65

Contracts for provision of assets or services

[App.08]
1 Functions to include power to enter into contracts

(1)   Every statutory provision conferring or imposing a function on a local authority confers power on the local authority to enter into a contract with another person for the provision or making available of assets or services, or both, (whether or not together with goods) for the purposes of, or in connection with, the discharge of the function by the local authority.

(2)   Where—
(a)   a local authority enters into a contract such as is mentioned in subsection (1) ('the provision contract') under any statutory provision, and
(b)   in connection with the provision contract, a person ('the financier') makes a loan to, or provides any other form of finance for, a party to the provision contract other than the local authority,

the statutory provision also confers power on the local authority to enter into a contract with the financier, or any insurer of or trustee for the financier, in connection with the provision contract.

(3)   The following are local authorities for the purposes of this Act—
(a)   any authority with respect to the finances of which Part IV of the Local Government and Housing Act 1989 has effect at the time in question,
(b)   any probation committee,
(c)   the Receiver for the Metropolitan Police District, and
(d)   any local authority or joint board as defined in section 235(1) of the Local Government (Scotland) Act 1973.

(4)   In this Act 'assets' means assets of any description (whether tangible or intangible), including (in particular) land, buildings, roads, works, plant, machinery, vehicles, vessels, apparatus, equipment and computer software.

(5)   Regulations may be made amending subsection (4).

Certified contracts

[App.09]
2 Certified contracts to be intra vires

(1)   Where a local authority has entered into a contract, the contract shall, if it is a certified contract, have effect (and be deemed always to have had effect) as if the local authority had had power to enter into it (and had exercised that power properly in entering into it).

(2)   For the purposes of this Act a contract entered into by a local authority is a certified contract if (and, subject to subsections (3) and (4), only if) the certification

requirements have been satisfied by the local authority with respect to the contract and they were so satisfied before the end of the certification period.

(3)   A contract entered into by a local authority shall be treated as a certified contract during the certification period if the contract provides that the certification requirements are intended to be satisfied by the local authority with respect to the contract before the end of that period.

(4)   Where a local authority has entered into a contract which is a certified contract ('the existing contract') and the existing contract is replaced by a contract entered into by it with a person or persons not identical with the person or persons with whom it entered into the existing contract, the replacement contract is also a certified contract if—

(a)   the period for which it operates or is intended to operate ends at the same time as the period for which the existing contract was to operate, and

(b)   apart from that, its provisions are the same as those of the existing contract.

(5)   In this Act 'the certification period', in relation to a contract entered into by a local authority, means the period of six weeks beginning with the day on which the local authority entered into the contract.

(6)   Subsection (1) is subject to section 5 (special provisions about judicial reviews and audit reviews).

(7)   The application of subsection (1) in relation to a contract entered into by a local authority does not affect any claim for damages made by a person who is not (and has never been) a party to the contract in respect of a breach by the local authority of any duty to do, or not to do, something before entering into the contract (including, in particular, any such duty imposed by a statutory provision for giving effect to any Community obligation relating to public procurement or by section 17(1) of the Local Government Act 1988).

[App.10]

3 The certification requirements

(1)   In this Act 'the certification requirements', in relation to a contract entered into by a local authority, means the requirements specified in subsections (2) to (4).

(2)   The requirement specified in this subsection is that the local authority must have issued a certificate (whether before or after the contract is entered into)—

(a)   including details of the period for which the contract operates or is to operate,

(b)   describing the purpose of the contract,

(c)   containing a statement that the contract is or is to be a contract falling within section 4(3) or (4),

(d)   stating that the local authority had or has power to enter into the contract and specifying the statutory provision, or each of the statutory provisions, conferring the power,

(e)   stating that a copy of the certificate has been or is to be given to each person to whom a copy is required to be given by regulations,

(f)   dealing in a manner prescribed by regulations with any matters required by regulations to be dealt with in certificates under this section, and

(g)   confirming that the local authority has complied with or is to comply with any requirement imposed by regulations with respect to the issue of certificates under this section.

(3)   The requirement specified in this subsection is that the local authority must have secured that the certificate is signed by any person who is required by regulations to sign it.

(4)   The requirement specified in this subsection is that the local authority must have obtained consent to the issue of a certificate under this section from each of the persons with whom the local authority has entered, or is to enter, into the contract.

[App.11]
4 Certified contracts: supplementary

(1)   Where the certification requirements have been satisfied in relation to a contract by a local authority, the certificate which has been issued shall have effect (and be deemed always to have had effect) as if the local authority had had power to issue it (and had exercised that power properly in issuing it); and a certificate which has been so issued is not invalidated by reason that anything in the certificate is inaccurate or untrue.

(2)   Where the certification requirements have been satisfied in relation to a contract by a local authority within section 1(3)(a) or (d), the local authority shall secure that throughout the period for which the contract operates—
(a)   a copy of the certificate which has been issued is open to inspection by members of the public at all reasonable times without payment, and
(b)   members of the public are afforded facilities for obtaining copies of that certificate on payment of a reasonable fee.

(3)   A contract entered into by a local authority falls within this subsection if—
(a)   it is entered into with another person for the provision or making available of services (whether or not together with assets or goods) for the purposes of or in connection with, the discharge by the local authority of any of its functions, and
(b)   it operates, or is intended to operate, for a period of at least five years.

(4)   A contract entered into by a local authority falls within this subsection if it is entered into, in connection with a contract falling within subsection (3), with—
(a)   a person who, in connection with that contract, makes a loan to, or provides any other form of finance for, a party to that contract other than the local authority, or
(b)   any insurer of or trustee for such a person.

(5)   Regulations may be made amending subsection (3) or (4).

[App.12]
5 Special provision for judicial reviews and audit reviews

(1)   Section 2(1) does not apply for the purposes of determining any question arising on—
(a)   an application for judicial review, or
(b)   an audit review,

as to whether a local authority had power to enter into a contract (or exercised any power properly in entering into a contract).

(2)   Section 2(1) has effect subject to any determination or order made in relation to a certified contract on—
(a)   an application for judicial review, or
(b)   an audit review.

(3)   Where, on an application for judicial review or an audit review relating to a certified contract entered into by a local authority, a court—
(a)   is of the opinion that the local authority did not have power to enter into the contract (or exercised any power improperly in entering into it), but

(b)   (having regard in particular to the likely consequences for the financial position of the local authority, and for the provision of services to the public, of a decision that the contract should not have effect) considers that the contract should have effect,

the court may determine that the contract has (and always has had) effect as if the local authority had had power to enter into it (and had exercised that power properly in entering into it).

(4)   In this section and sections 6 and 7 references to an application for judicial review include any appeal (or further appeal) against a determination or order made on such an application.

[App.13]
6 Relevant discharge terms

(1)   No determination or order made in relation to a certified contract on—
(a)   an application for judicial review, or
(b)   an audit review,
shall affect the enforceability of any relevant discharge terms relating to the contract.

(2)   In this section and section 7 'relevant discharge terms', in relation to a contract entered into by a local authority, means terms—
(a)   which have been agreed by the local authority and any person with whom the local authority entered into the contract,
(b)   which either form part of the contract or constitute or form part of another agreement entered into by them not later than the day on which the contract was entered into, and
(c)   which provide for a consequence mentioned in subsection (3) to ensue in the event of the making of a determination or order in relation to the contract on an application for judicial review or an audit review.

(3)   Those consequences are—
(a)   the payment of compensatory damages (measured by reference to loss incurred or loss of profits or to any other circumstances) by one of the parties to the other,
(b)   the adjustment between the parties of rights and liabilities relating to any assets or goods provided or made available under the contract, or
(c)   both of those things.

(4)   Where a local authority has agreed relevant discharge terms with any person with whom it has entered into a contract and the contract is a certified contract, the relevant discharge terms shall have effect (and be deemed always to have had effect) as if the local authority had had power to agree them (and had exercised that power properly in agreeing them).

[App.14]
7 Absence of relevant discharge terms

(1)   Subsection (2) applies where—
(a)   the result of a determination or order made by a court on an application for judicial review or an audit review is that a certified contract does not have effect, and
(b)   there are no relevant discharge terms having effect between the local authority and a person who is a party to the contract.

(2)   That person shall be entitled to be paid by the local authority such sums (if any) as he would have been entitled to be paid by the local authority if the contract—

(a)   had had effect until the time when the determination or order was made, but

(b)   had been terminated at that time by acceptance by him of a repudiatory breach by the local authority.

(3)   For the purposes of this section the circumstances in which there are no relevant discharge terms having effect between the local authority and a person who is a party to the contract include (as well as circumstances in which no such terms have been agreed) circumstances in which the result of a determination or order of a court, made (despite section 6(4)) on an application for judicial review or an audit review, is that such terms do not have effect.

[App.15]

8 Audit reviews

(1)   In this Act 'an audit review' means—

(a)   an application or appeal under [section 17 of the Audit Commission Act 1998] (application by auditor, or appeal by person objecting to accounts, for declaration as to unlawful item of account),

(b)   consideration by an auditor of whether to give a certificate under [section 18] of that Act (certificate about sum not accounted for or loss or deficiency caused by wilful misconduct) or an appeal under that section,

(c)   consideration by an auditor of whether to issue a prohibition order under [section 20] of that Act (unlawful expenditure etc) or an appeal under [section 22] of that Act (appeals against a prohibition order),

(d)   consideration by the Controller of Audit of whether to make a special report to the Accounts Commission for Scotland under section 102(3) of the Local Government (Scotland) Act 1973 (reports to Commission by Controller of Audit),

(e)   consideration by the Accounts Commission for Scotland of whether to send a special report to the Secretary of State under section 103(3) of that Act (action by Commission on reports by Controller of Audit), or

(f)   consideration by the Court of Session of a case stated under section 103(2)(c) of that Act (Commission may state case on a question of law for opinion of Court of Session),

or any appeal (or further appeal) against a decision made on an application referred to in paragraph (a) or on an appeal referred to in any of paragraphs (a) to (c).

(2)   A prohibition order issued under [section 20 of the Audit Commission Act 1998] shall not make it unlawful to—

(a)   make or implement any decision,

(b)   take or continue to take any course of action, or

(c)   enter any item of account,

relating to a certified contract before the determination or withdrawal of any appeal against the order under [section 22(3)] of that Act or, if no appeal is brought during the period within which it is permitted to bring any such appeal, before the end of that period.

Amendment

Sub-s (1): in para (a) words 'section 17 of the Audit Commission Act 1998' in square brackets substituted by the Audit Commission Act 1998, s 54(1), Sch 3, para 34(2); in para (b) words 'section 18' in square brackets substituted by the Audit Commission Act 1998, s 54(1), Sch 3, para 34(3); in para (c) words 'section 20' in square brackets substituted by the Audit Commission Act 1998, s 54(1), Sch 3, para 34(4);

in para (c) words 'section 22' in square brackets substituted by the Audit Commission Act 1998, s 54(1), Sch 3, para 34(4).
Sub-s (2): words 'section 20 of the Audit Commission Act 1998' in square brackets substituted by the Audit Commission Act 1998, s 54(1), Sch 3, para 34(5)(a); words 'section 22(3)' in square brackets substituted by the Audit Commission Act 1998, s 54(1), Sch 3, para 34(5)(b).

[App.16]
9 Contracting out of functions in connection with certified contracts

(1)   An authorisation given by virtue of an order under section 70 of the Deregulation and Contracting Out Act 1994 (authorisation by local authority of exercise by another person of functions of authority for period not exceeding ten years) may specify that it is to be for a period exceeding ten years if it is given in connection with a certified contract.

(2)   But an authorisation given in connection with a certified contract may not by virtue of subsection (1) specify that it is to be for a period exceeding the shorter of—
(a)   the period for which the contract is to operate, and
(b)   forty years.

(3)   For the purposes of this section an authorisation is given in connection with a certified contract if—
(a)   the authority by which it is given is a local authority for the purposes of this Act,
(b)   the authority and the authorised person are parties to the contract, and
(c)   the authorisation is given to enable the authorised person to perform or better perform his obligations under the contract.

Grants relating to expenditure in respect of magistrates' courts

[App.17]
10 Power to treat expenditure as not being capital expenditure

In section 57 of the Justices of the Peace Act 1997 (grants by the Lord Chancellor towards the capital and other expenditure of authorities responsible for providing accommodation etc for magistrates' courts), after subsection (4) insert—

'(4A)   The Lord Chancellor, with the concurrence of the Treasury, may by statutory instrument make regulations providing that any expenditure of responsible authorities in pursuance of their functions under this Part of this Act which is of a description specified in the regulations shall be taken not to be capital expenditure for the purposes of section 55(3) or (7) above or this section.

(4B)   A statutory instrument containing (whether alone or with other provisions) regulations made by virtue of subsection (4A) above shall be subject to annulment in pursuance of a resolution of either House of Parliament.'

Supplementary

[App.18]
11 Regulations

(1)   Any power to make regulations under this Act is exercisable by the Secretary of State by statutory instrument and may be exercised so as to make different provision

for different purposes or for different cases (including different provision for different areas).

(2)   No regulations shall be made under section 4(5) unless a draft of the statutory instrument containing them has been laid before and approved by a resolution of each House of Parliament.

(3)   Subject to that, a statutory instrument containing regulations under this Act shall be subject to annulment in pursuance of a resolution of either House of Parliament.

[App.19]

12 Short title, commencement and extent

(1)   This Act may be cited as the Local Government (Contracts) Act 1997.

(2)   Sections 2 to 9 shall not come into force until a day appointed by the Secretary of State by order made by statutory instrument; and different days may be appointed for different provisions or purposes.

(3)   Sections 1 to 9 apply to any contract which a local authority enters into after 12th June 1997; but in relation to a contract entered into before the day on which section 2 comes into force 'the certification period' means the period of six weeks beginning with that day.

(4)   Section 10 does not extend to Scotland.

(5)   This Act does not extend to Northern Ireland.

LOCAL GOVERNMENT ACT 2000

2000 c 22

PART I
PROMOTION OF ECONOMIC, SOCIAL OR ENVIRONMENTAL
WELL-BEING ETC

Interpretation

[App.20]
1 Meaning of 'local authority' in Part I

In this Part 'local authority' means—
(a)   in relation to England—
        (i)   a county council,
        (ii)   a district council,
        (iii)   a London borough council,
        (iv)   the Common Council of the City of London in its capacity as a local
                 authority,
        (v)   the Council of the Isles of Scilly,
(b)   in relation to Wales, a county council or a county borough council.

Promotion of well-being

[App.21]
2 Promotion of well-being

(1)   Every local authority are to have power to do anything which they consider is
likely to achieve any one or more of the following objects—
(a)   the promotion or improvement of the economic well-being of their area;
(b)   the promotion or improvement of the social well-being of their area, and
(c)   the promotion or improvement of the environmental well-being of their area.

(2)   The power under subsection (1) may be exercised in relation to or for the benefit
of—
(a)   the whole or any part of a local authority's area, or
(b)   all or any persons resident or present in a local authority's area.

(3)   In determining whether or how to exercise the power under subsection (1), a
local authority must have regard to their strategy under section 4.

(4)   The power under subsection (1) includes power for a local authority to—
(a)   incur expenditure,
(b)   give financial assistance to any person,
(c)   enter into arrangements or agreements with any person,
(d)   co-operate with, or facilitate or co-ordinate the activities of, any person,
(e)   exercise on behalf of any person any functions of that person, and
(f)   provide staff, goods, services or accommodation to any person.

(5)   The power under subsection (1) includes power for a local authority to do
anything in relation to, or for the benefit of, any person or area situated outside their

area if they consider that it is likely to achieve any one or more of the objects in that subsection.

(6)   Nothing in subsection (4) or (5) affects the generality of the power under subsection (1).

[*Sections 3–8 are not reproduced.*]

Procedure for orders under section 5 or 6

[App.22]
9 Procedure for orders under section 5 or 6

(1)   Before the Secretary of State makes an order under section 5 or 6 he must consult—
(a)   such local authorities,
(b)   such representatives of local government, and
(c)   such other persons (if any),
as appear to him to be likely to be affected by his proposals.

(2)   Where those proposals affect any local authorities in Wales, the Secretary of State must also consult the National Assembly for Wales.

(3)   If, following consultation under the preceding provisions of this section, the Secretary of State proposes to make an order under section 5 or 6 he must lay before each House of Parliament a document which—
(a)   explains his proposals,
(b)   sets them out in the form of a draft order,
(c)   gives details of consultation under subsection (1), and
(d)   where consultation has taken place under subsection (2), sets out the views of the National Assembly for Wales.

(4)   Where a document relating to proposals is laid before Parliament under subsection (3), no draft of an order under section 5 or 6 to give effect to the proposals (with or without modifications) is to be laid before Parliament in accordance with section 105(6) until after the expiry of the period of sixty days beginning with the day on which the document was laid.

(5)   In calculating the period mentioned in subsection (4) no account is to be taken of any time during which—
(a)   Parliament is dissolved or prorogued, or
(b)   either House is adjourned for more than four days.

(6)   In preparing a draft order under section 5 or 6 the Secretary of State must consider any representations made during the period mentioned in subsection (4).

(7)   A draft order under section 5 or 6 which is laid before Parliament in accordance with section 105(6) must be accompanied by a statement of the Secretary of State giving details of—
(a)   any representations considered in accordance with subsection (6), and
(b)   any changes made to the proposals contained in the document laid before Parliament under subsection (3).

APPENDIX 2 STATUTORY INSTRUMENTS

PUBLIC WORKS CONTRACTS REGULATIONS 1991

SI 1991/2680

PART I
GENERAL

[App.23]
1 Title and commencement
These Regulations may be cited as the Public Works Contracts Regulations 1991 and shall come into force on 21st December 1991.

[App.24]
2 Interpretation
(1)   In these Regulations—
'to award' means to accept an offer made in relation to a proposed contract;
'carrying out', in relation to a work or works, means the construction or the design and construction of that work or those works;
'the Commission' means the Commission of the Communities;
'concessionaire' means a person who has entered into a public works concession contract with a contracting authority;
'contract documents' means the invitation to tender for or negotiate the contract, the proposed conditions of contract, the specifications or description of the work or works required by the contracting authority and of the materials or goods to be used in or for it or them, and all documents supplementary thereto;
'contract notice' means a notice sent to the Official Journal in accordance with regulation 11(2), 12(2), 13(2), 25(2) or 26(3);
'contracting authority' has the meaning ascribed to it by regulation 3;
'contractor' has the meaning ascribed to it by regulation 4;
. . .
'established' means the same as it does for the purposes of the Community Treaties;
'financial year' means the period of 12 months ending on 31st March in any year or, in relation to any person whose accounts are prepared in respect of a different 12 month period, that period of 12 months;
'government department' includes a Northern Ireland department or the head of such department [and any part of the Scottish Administration];
['Government Procurement Agreement' means the Agreement on Government Procurement between certain parties to the World Trade Organisation (WTO) Agreement signed in Marrakesh on 15 April 1994;
'GPA' means the Government Procurement Agreement;]
'Minister of the Crown' means the holder of an office in Her Majesty's Government in the United Kingdom, and includes the Treasury [and a reference to a Minister of the Crown shall be read as including a reference to the Scottish Ministers];
'national of a [relevant State]' means, in the case of a person who is not an individual, a person formed in accordance with the laws of a [relevant State] and which

has its registered office, central administration or principal place of business in a [relevant State];

'negotiated procedure' means a procedure leading to the award of a public works contract whereby the contracting authority negotiates the terms of the contract with one or more persons selected by it;

'Official Journal' means the Official Journal of the Communities;

'open procedure' means a procedure leading to the award of a public works contract whereby all interested persons may tender for the contract;

'public housing scheme works contract' means a public works contract relating to the design and construction of a public housing scheme;

'public works concession contract' means a public works contract under which the consideration given by the contracting authority consists of or includes the grant of a right to exploit the work or works to be carried out under the contract;

'public works contract' means a contract in writing for consideration (whatever the nature of the consideration)—

(a)   for the carrying out of a work or works for a contracting authority, or

(b)   under which a contracting authority engages a person to procure by any means the carrying out for the contracting authority of a work corresponding to specified requirements;

['relevant State' means a member State or a State for the time being specified in Schedule 3;]

'restricted procedure' means a procedure leading to the award of a public works contract whereby only persons selected by the contracting authority may submit tenders for the contract;

'work' means the outcome of any works which is sufficient of itself to fulfil an economic and technical function;

'working day' means a day other than a Saturday, Sunday or Bank Holiday within the meaning of the Banking and Financial Dealings Act 1971;

'works' means any of the activities specified in Schedule 1, being activities contained in the general industrial classification of economic activities within the Communities; and

'year' means a calendar year.

(2)   . . .

(3)   Where a thing is required to be done under these Regulations—

(a)   within a period after an action is taken, the day on which that action was taken shall not be counted in the calculation of that period;

(b)   within a certain period, that period must include 2 working days;

(c)   within a period and the last day of that period is not a working day, the period shall be extended to include the following working day.

(4)   References in these Regulations to a regulation are references to a regulation in these Regulations and references to a Schedule are references to a Schedule to these Regulations.

Amendment

Para (1): definition 'ECU' (omitted) revoked by SI 2000/2009, reg 3(1)(a)(ii); in definition 'government department' words 'and any part of the Scottish Administration' in square brackets inserted by SI 1999/1042, art 3, Sch 1, para 20(1), (2)(a); definitions 'Government Procurement Agreement' and 'GPA' inserted by SI 2000/2009, reg 3(1)(a)(i); in definition 'Minister of the Crown' words from 'and a reference' to 'the Scottish Ministers' in square brackets inserted by SI 1999/1042, art 3, Sch 1, para 20(1), (2)(b); in definition 'national of a relevant State' words 'relevant State' in square brackets in each place they occur substituted by SI 1995/201, reg 31(1)(a), (b); definition 'relevant State' substituted by SI 2000/2009, reg 3(1)(a)(iii).

Para (2): revoked by SI 2000/2009, reg 3(1)(b).

[App.25]

[3 Contracting authorities]

[(1)   For the purposes of these Regulations each of the following is a 'contracting authority'—
(a)   a Minister of the Crown,
(b)   a government department,
(c)   the House of Commons,
(d)   the House of Lords,
(e)   the Northern Ireland Assembly Commission,
(f)   the Scottish Parliamentary Body Corporate,
(g)   the National Assembly for Wales,
(h)   a local authority,
(i)   a fire authority constituted by a combination scheme under the Fire Services Act 1947,
(j)   the Fire Authority for Northern Ireland,
(k)   a police authority established under section 3 of the Police Act 1996,
(l)   a police authority established under section 2 of the Police (Scotland) Act 1967,
(m)   [the Northern Ireland Policing Board],
(n)   an authority established under section 10 of the Local Government Act 1985,
(o)   a joint authority established by Part IV of that Act,
(p)   any body established pursuant to an order under section 67 of that Act,
(q)   the Broads Authority,
(r)   any joint board the constituent members of which consist of any of the bodies specified in paragraphs (h), (i), (k), (l), (n), (o), (p) and (q), above,
(s)   a National Park authority established by an Order under section 63 of the Environment Act 1995,
(t)   the Receiver for the Metropolitan Police District,
(u)   a corporation established, or a group of individuals appointed to act together, for the specific purpose of meeting needs in the general interest, not having an industrial or commercial character, and—
    (i)   financed wholly or mainly by another contracting authority, or
    (ii)   subject to management supervision by another contracting authority, or
    (iii)   more than half of the board of directors or members of which, or, in the case of a group of individuals, more than half of those individuals, being appointed by another contracting authority,
(v)   an association of or formed by one or more of the above, and
(w)   to the extent not specified in sub-paragraphs (a) to (t) above, an entity specified in Schedule 1 to the Public Supply Contracts Regulations 1995.

(2)   In the application of these Regulations to England, 'local authority' in paragraph (1) above means—
(a)   a county council, a district council, a London borough council, a parish council, a community council or the Council of the Isles of Scilly;
(b)   the Common Council of the City of London in its capacity as local authority or police authority.

(3)   In the application of these Regulations to Wales, 'local authority' in paragraph (1) above means a county council, county borough council or community council.

(4)   In the application of these Regulations to Scotland, 'local authority' in paragraph (1) above has the same meaning as in section 235(1) of the Local Government

(Scotland) Act 1973 and also includes joint board or joint committee within the meaning of section 235(1).

(5)   In the application of these Regulations to Northern Ireland, 'local authority' in paragraph (1) above means a district council within the meaning of the Local Government Act (Northern Ireland) 1972.

(6)   Where an entity specified in paragraph (1) above does not have the capacity to enter into a contract, the contracting authority in relation to that entity is a person whose function it is to enter into contracts for that entity.]

Amendment
Substituted by SI 2000/2009, reg 3(2).
Para (1): in sub-para (m) words 'the Northern Ireland Policing Board' in square brackets substituted by the Police (Northern Ireland) Act 2000, s 2(4), Sch 2, para 6(1).

[App.26]

4 Contractors

(1)   For the purposes of these Regulations a 'contractor' means a person—
(a)   who sought, or who seeks, or would have wished, to be the person to whom a public works contract is awarded, and
[(b)   who is a national of and established in a relevant State].

(2)   When these Regulations apply a contracting authority shall not treat a person who is not a national of and established in a [relevant State] more favourably than one who is.

Amendment
Para (1): sub-para (b) substituted by SI 2000/2009, reg 3(3).
Para (2): words in square brackets substituted by SI 1995/201, reg 31(1)(b).

[App.27]

5 Application of the Regulations

These Regulations apply whenever a contracting authority seeks offers in relation to a proposed public works contract other than public works contracts excluded from the operation of these Regulations by regulations 6 and 7; except that in Parts II, III, IV and V of these Regulations and in regulations 24, 27 and 28 references to a 'public works contract' shall not include a public works concession contract.

[App.28]

6 General exclusions

These Regulations shall not apply to the seeking of offers in relation to a proposed public works contract—
[(a)   where the contracting authority is a utility within the meaning of regulation 3 of the Utilities Contracts Regulations 1996 and the services to be provided under it are for the purposes of carrying out an activity specified in any Part of Schedule 1 to those Regulations in which the utility is specified;]
(d)   which is classified as secret or where the carrying out of the work or works under it must be accompanied by special security measures in accordance with the laws, regulations or administrative provisions of any part of the United Kingdom or when the protection of the basic interests of the security of the United Kingdom require it;
(e)   where different procedures govern the procedures leading to the award of the contract and it is to be entered into—

(i)   pursuant to an international agreement to which the United Kingdom and a State which is not a [relevant State] are parties and it provides for the carrying out of works intended for the joint implementation or exploitation of a project pursuant to that agreement;

(ii)   pursuant to an international agreement relating to the stationing of troops; or

(iii) in accordance with the contract award procedures of an organisation of which only States are members (an 'international organisation') or of which only States or international organisations are members.

Amendment
Para (a): substituted, together with para (b) for paras (a)–(c) as originally enacted, by SI 1992/3279, reg 32(1)(a); further substituted, for original paras (a), (b), by SI 1996/2911, reg 35(1)(c); para (e): in sub-para (i) words in square brackets substituted by SI 1995/201, reg 31(1)(b).

[App.29]

7 Thresholds

[(1)   These Regulations shall not apply to the seeking of offers in relation to—

(a)   a proposed public works contract where the estimated value of the contract (net of value added tax) at the relevant time is less than the euro equivalent of 5,000,000 special drawing rights;

(b)   a proposed public works concession contract or a proposed subsidised works contract under regulation 23 where the estimated value of the contract (net of value added tax) at the relevant time is less than 5,000,000 euro.]

[(1A)   The value in pounds sterling of any amount expressed in this regulation in euro or in the euro equivalent of special drawing rights shall be calculated by reference to the rate for the time being applying for the purposes of Council Directive 93/37/ EEC as published from time to time in the Official Journal.]

(2)   Subject to paragraphs (3), (5) and (6) below, the estimated value for the purposes of paragraph (1) above of a public works contract shall be the value of the consideration which the contracting authority expects to give under the contract.

(3)   Subject to paragraphs (4) and (6) below, the estimated value for the purposes of paragraph (1) above of a public works contract which is one of a number of contracts entered into or to be entered into for the carrying out of a work shall be the aggregate of the value of the consideration which the contracting authority has paid or expects to give under all the contracts for the carrying out of the work.

(4)   Paragraph (3) above shall not apply to any public works contract (unless the contracting authority chooses to apply that paragraph to that contract) if that contract has an estimated value (calculated in accordance with paragraph (2) above) of less than 1,000,000 ECU, and the aggregate value of that contract and of any other public works contract for the carrying out of the work in respect of which the contracting authority takes advantage of the disapplication of paragraph (3) above by virtue of this paragraph is less than 20 per cent of the aggregate of the value of the consideration which the contracting authority has paid or expects to pay under all the contracts for the carrying out of the work.

(5)   Subject to paragraph (6) below, the estimated value for the purposes of paragraph (1) above of a public works concession contract shall be the value of the consideration which the contracting authority would expect to give for the carrying out of the work or works if it did not propose to grant a concession.

(6)   Where a contracting authority intends to provide any goods to the person awarded a public works contract for the purpose of carrying out that contract, the value of the consideration for the purposes of paragraphs (2) and (3) above shall be taken to include the estimated value at the relevant time of those goods.

(7)   The relevant time for the purposes of paragraphs (1) and (6) above means, in relation to a public works contract, the date on which a contract notice would be sent to the Official Journal if the requirement to send such a notice applied to that contract in accordance with these Regulations.

(8)   A contracting authority shall not enter into separate public works contracts with the intention of avoiding the application of these Regulations to those contracts.

Amendment
Para (1): substituted by SI 2000/2009, reg 3(4).
Para (1A): inserted by SI 2000/2009, reg 3(5).

PART II
TECHNICAL SPECIFICATIONS

[App.30]
8 Technical specifications in the contract documents
(1)   In this regulation—
'common technical specification' means a technical specification drawn up in accordance with a procedure recognised by the member States with a view to uniform application in all member States and which has been published in the Official Journal;
'essential requirements' means requirements relating to safety, health and certain other aspects in the general interest which the works must meet;
'European specification' means a common technical specification, a British standard implementing a European standard or a European technical approval;
'European standard' means a standard approved by the European Committee for Standardisation ('CEN') or by the European Committee for Electrotechnical Standardisation ('CENELEC') as a 'European Standard ('EN')' or a 'Harmonisation Document ('HD')' according to the Common Rules of those organisations;
'European technical approval' means an approval of the fitness for use of a product, issued by an approval body designated for the purpose by a member State, following a technical assessment of whether the product fulfils the essential requirements for building works, having regard to the inherent characteristics of the product and the defined conditions of application and use;
'standard' means a technical specification approved by a recognised standardising body for repeated and continuous application, compliance with which is in principle not compulsory;
'technical specifications' means the technical requirements defining the characteristics required of the work or works and of the materials and goods used in or for it or them (such as quality, performance, safety or dimensions) so that the works, work, materials and goods are described objectively in a manner which will ensure that they fulfil the use for which they are intended by the contracting authority. In relation to materials and goods, 'technical specifications' include requirements in respect of quality assurance, terminology, symbols, tests and

testing methods, packaging, marking and labelling. In relation to a work or works, they include requirements relating to design and costing, the testing, inspection and acceptance of a work or works, and the methods or techniques of construction.

(2)   If a contracting authority wishes to lay down technical specifications which the work or works to be carried out under a public works contract and which the materials and goods used in or for it or them must meet it shall specify all such technical specifications in the contract documents.

(3)   Subject to paragraph (4) below, the technical specifications in the contract documents relating to a public works contract shall be defined by reference to any European specifications which are relevant.

(4)   A contracting authority may define the technical specifications referred to in paragraph (3) above other than by reference to relevant European specifications if—

(a)   the contracting authority is under an obligation to define the technical specifications by reference to technical requirements which are mandatory in the United Kingdom for the work or works to be carried out under the contract or for the materials or goods to be used in or for it or them, (but only to the extent that such an obligation is compatible with Community obligations);

(b)   the relevant European specifications do not include provision for establishing conformity to, or it is technically impossible to establish satisfactorily that the work or works or the materials or goods do conform to, the relevant European specifications;

(c)   subject to paragraph (5) below, application of the relevant European specifications would oblige the contracting authority to acquire a work, works, material or goods incompatible with equipment already in use or would entail disproportionate costs or disproportionate technical difficulties; or

(d)   the work or works are of a genuinely innovative nature for which use of existing relevant European specifications would be inappropriate.

(5)   A contracting authority may only define the technical specifications other than by reference to relevant European specifications on the grounds specified in paragraph (4)(c) above where the contracting authority has a clearly defined and recorded strategy for changing over, within a set period, to European specifications.

(6)   A contracting authority shall state in the contract notice which of the circumstances specified in paragraph (4) above was the ground for defining the technical specifications other than by reference to European specifications or, if it is impossible to include this information in the contract notice, the contracting authority shall specify it in the contract documents and shall in any event keep a record of this information which, if the Commission or any [relevant State] requests it, it shall send to the Treasury for onward transmission to the Commission or [relevant State] which requested it.

(7)   In the absence of European specifications relevant to the work or works to be carried out under a public works contract or to the materials or goods to be used in or for it or them, the technical specifications in the contract documents—

(a)   shall be defined by reference to the British technical specifications recognised as complying with the basic requirements specified in any Council Directives on technical harmonisation in accordance with the procedures laid down in those directives and, in particular, in accordance with the procedures laid down in Council Directive 89/106/EEC on the approximation of laws, regulations and administrative procedures in the member States relating to construction products;

(b)   may be defined by reference to British technical specifications relating to design and method of calculation and execution of a work or works and use of materials and goods;

(c)   may be defined by reference to the following standards (and, if they are so defined, preference shall be given to the following standards in the order in which they are listed)—

(i)   British standards implementing international standards;

(ii)   other British standards and technical approvals; or

(iii) any other standards.

(8)   Subject to paragraph (10) below, the contract documents relating to a public works contract shall not include technical specifications which refer to materials or goods of a specific make or source or to a particular process and which have the effect of favouring or eliminating particular contractors.

(9)   Without prejudice to the generality of paragraph (8) above, references to trademarks, patents, types, origin or means of production shall not be incorporated into the technical specifications in the contract documents.

(10)   Notwithstanding paragraph (8) and (9) above, a contracting authority may incorporate the references referred to in paragraphs (8) and (9) above into the technical specifications in the contract documents if—

(a)   such references are justified by the subject of the contract, or

(b)   the work or works to be carried out under the contract cannot otherwise be described by reference to technical specifications which are sufficiently precise and intelligible to all contractors, provided that the references are accompanied by the words 'or equivalent'.

Amendment
Para (6): words in square brackets substituted by SI 1995/201, reg 31(1)(b).

PART III
PROCEDURES LEADING TO THE AWARD OF A PUBLIC WORKS CONTRACT

[App.31]
9 Prior information notices

A contracting authority intending to seek offers in relation to a public works contract shall, as soon as possible after the decision approving the planning of the work or works, send to the Official Journal a notice, in a form substantially corresponding to that set out in Part A of Schedule 2, and containing the information therein specified in relation to the contract.

[App.32]
10 Selection of contract award procedure

(1)   For the purpose of seeking offers in relation to a proposed public works contract (but, in the case of a public housing scheme works contract, subject to regulation 24) a contracting authority shall use the open procedure, the restricted procedure or the negotiated procedure and shall decide which of those procedures to use in accordance with the following paragraphs of this regulation.

(2)   A contracting authority may use the negotiated procedure in the following circumstances—

(a)   subject to paragraph [(3)] below, in the event that the procedure leading to the award of a public works contract by the contracting authority using the open or [restricted] procedure was discontinued—
   (i)   because of irregular tenders, or
   (ii)   following an evaluation made in accordance with regulation 11(7) or 12(4);
   and without prejudice to the generality of the meaning of the words 'irregular tenders' a tender may be considered irregular if the contractor fails to meet the requirements of, or the tender offers variations on the requirements specified in, the contract documents where this is not permitted under the terms of the invitation to tender, or the work, works, materials or goods offered do not meet the technical specifications (within the meaning of regulation 8(1)) of the contracting authority;

(b)   when the work or works are to be carried out under the contract purely for the purpose of research, experiment or development but not where the works are to be carried out to establish commercial viability or to recover research and development costs;

(c)   exceptionally, when the nature of the work or works to be carried out under the contract is such, or the risks attaching thereto are such, as not to permit prior overall pricing;

(d)   subject to paragraph [(3)] below, in the absence of tenders or of appropriate tenders in response to an invitation to tender by the contracting authority using the open or restricted procedure;

(e)   when, for technical or artistic reasons, or for reasons connected with the protection of exclusive rights, the work or works to be carried out under the contract may only be carried out by a particular person;

(f)   when (but only if it is strictly necessary) for reasons of extreme urgency brought about by events unforeseeable by, and not attributable to, the contracting authority, the time limits specified in regulations 11, 12 and 13 if the open or restricted procedures or the negotiated procedure pursuant to paragraphs (2)(a) to (c) are used cannot be met;

(g)   subject to paragraph [(4)] below, when a contracting authority wants a person who has entered into a public works contract with the contracting authority to carry out additional works which through unforeseen circumstances were not included in the project initially considered or in the original public works contract and—
   (i)   such works cannot for technical or economic reasons be carried out separately from the works carried out under the original public works contract without great inconvenience to the contracting authority, or
   (ii)   such works can be carried out separately from the works carried out under the original public works contract but are strictly necessary to the later stages of that contract; and

(h)   subject to paragraph [(5)] below, when a contracting authority wishes a person who has entered into a public works contract with that contracting authority to carry out new works which are a repetition of works carried out under the original contract and which are in accordance with the project for the purpose of which the first contract was entered into.

(3)   A contracting authority shall not use the negotiated procedure pursuant to paragraphs (2)(a) or (d) above unless the proposed terms of the contract are

substantially unaltered from the proposed terms of the contract in relation to which offers were sought using the open or restricted procedure.

(4)   A contracting authority shall not use the negotiated procedure pursuant to paragraph (2)(g) above where the aggregate value of the consideration to be given under contracts for the additional works exceeds 50 per cent of the value of the consideration payable under the original contract; and, for the purposes of this paragraph, the value of the consideration shall be taken to include the estimated value of any goods which the contracting authority provided to the person awarded the contract for the purpose of carrying out the contract.

(5)   A contracting authority shall not use the negotiated procedure pursuant to paragraph (2)(h) above unless the contract notice relating to the original contract stated that a public works contract for new works which would be a repetition of the works carried out under the original contract may be awarded using the negotiated procedure pursuant to paragraph (2)(h) above and unless the procedure for the award of the new contract is commenced within three years of the original contract being entered into.

(6)   In all other circumstances the contracting authority shall use the open procedure or the restricted procedure.

(7)   A contracting authority using the negotiated procedure pursuant to paragraph (2)(d) above shall, if the Commission requests it, submit a report recording the fact that it has done so to the Treasury for onward transmission to the Commission.

Amendment
Para (2): in sub-para (a) figure and word in square brackets, and in sub-paras (d), (g), (h), figures in square brackets, substituted by SI 1992/3279, reg 32(1)(b).

[App.33]

11 The open procedure

(1)   A contracting authority using the open procedure shall comply with the following paragraphs of this regulation.

(2)   The contracting authority shall publicise its intention to seek offers in relation to the public works contract by sending to the Official Journal as soon as possible after forming the intention a notice, in a form substantially corresponding to that set out in Part B of Schedule 2, inviting tenders and containing the information therein specified in relation to the contract.

(3)   Subject to paragraph (4) below, the date which the contracting authority shall fix as the last date for the receipt by it of tenders made in response to the contract notice shall be specified in the notice and shall be not less than 52 days from the date of despatch of the notice but, if the contract documents are too bulky to be supplied within this time or it is necessary that contractors be given the opportunity to inspect the site on which the work or works under the contract is or are to be carried out or documents relating to the contract documents, then that minimum period shall be extended to allow for such supply or inspection.

[(4)   Where—
(a)   the contracting authority has published a prior information notice in accordance with regulation 9 above;
(b)   the prior information notice contained as much of the information referred to in Part B of Schedule 2 as was available at the time of publication; and

(c)   the prior information notice was sent to the Official Journal at least 52 days and no more than 12 months before the date on which the contract notice provided for in regulation 11(2) is despatched;

the contracting authority may substitute for the period of not less than 52 days specified in paragraph (3) above a shorter period of generally no less than 36 days and in any event no less than 22 days, provided in each case that the period is sufficient to allow for effective tendering.]

(5)   The contracting authority shall send the contract documents within 6 days of the receipt of a request from any contractor provided that the documents are requested in good time and any fee specified in the contract notice has accompanied the request.

(6)   The contracting authority shall supply such further information relating to the contract documents as may reasonably be requested by a contractor provided that the request is received in sufficient time to enable the contracting authority to supply the information no later than 6 days before the date specified in the contract notice as the final date for the receipt of tenders.

(7)   The contracting authority may exclude a tender from the evaluation of offers made in accordance with regulation 20 only if the contractor may be treated as ineligible to tender on a ground specified in regulation 14 or if the contractor fails to satisfy the minimum standards of economic and financial standing and technical capacity required of contractors by the contracting authority; for this purpose the contracting authority shall make its evaluation in accordance with regulations 14, 15, 16 and 17.

[(8)   Tenders shall be submitted in writing either in person or by post, except that a contracting authority may authorise another means of submission provided that the chosen means enables—
(a)   each tender to contain all the information necessary for its evaluation;
(b)   the confidentiality of tenders to be maintained pending their evaluation; and
(c)   tenders to be opened only after the time limit for their submission has expired.

(9)   Where a contracting authority has authorised another means of submission in accordance with paragraph (8) above, it may require either that the submission of the tender is confirmed in writing or that a copy of the tender is delivered to it in person or by post in either case as soon as possible after the submission of the tender by another means.]

Amendment
Para (4): substituted by SI 2000/2009, reg 3(6).
Paras (8), (9): inserted by SI 2000/2009, reg 3(7).

[App.34]
12 The restricted procedure
(1)   A contracting authority using the restricted procedure shall comply with the following paragraphs of this regulation.

(2)   The contracting authority shall publicise its intention to seek offers in relation to the public works contract by sending to the Official Journal as soon as possible after forming the intention a notice, in a form substantially corresponding to that set out in Part C of Schedule 2, inviting requests to be selected to tender and containing the information therein specified in relation to the contract.

(3)   Subject to paragraph (14) below, the date which the contracting authority shall fix as the last date for the receipt by it of requests to be selected to tender shall be

specified in the contract notice and shall be not less than 37 days from the date of the despatch of the notice.

(4)   The contracting authority may exclude a contractor from those persons from whom it will make the selection of persons to be invited to tender only if the [contractor] may be treated as ineligible on a ground specified in regulation 14 or if the contractor fails to satisfy the minimum standards of economic and financial standing and technical capacity required of contractors by the contracting authority; for this purpose the contracting authority shall make its evaluation in accordance with regulations 14, 15, 16 and 17.

(5)   The contracting authority shall make the selection of the contractors to be invited to tender in accordance with regulations 14, 15, 16 and 17; and in making the selection and in issuing invitations the contracting authority shall not discriminate between contractors on the grounds of their nationality or the [relevant State] in which they are established.

(6)   The contracting authority may predetermine the range within which the number of persons which it intends to invite to tender for the contract shall be fixed but only if—

(a)   the lower number of the range is not less than 5 and the higher number not more than 20,

(b)   the range is determined in the light of the nature of the work to be carried out under the contract, and

(c)   the range is specified in the contract notice.

(7)   The number of persons invited to tender shall be sufficient to ensure genuine competition.

(8)   The contracting authority shall send invitations to each of the contractors selected to tender and the invitation shall be accompanied by the contract documents, or the invitation shall state the address for requesting them.

(9)   The invitation shall be sent in writing simultaneously to each contractor selected to tender.

(10)   The following information shall be included in the invitation—

(a)   the address to which requests for the contract documents (if not accompanying the invitation) and further information relating to those documents should be sent, the final date for making such a request and the amount and terms of the fee which may be charged for supplying that material;

(b)   the final date for the receipt of tenders, the address to which they must be sent and the language or languages in which they must be drawn up;

(c)   a reference to the contract notice published in accordance with paragraph (2) above;

(d)   an indication of the information to be included with the tender which the contracting authority may require to be provided in accordance with regulations 15, 16 and 17; and

(e)   the criteria for the award of the contract if this information was not specified in the contract notice published in accordance with paragraph (2) above.

(11)   Subject to paragraphs (12) and (14) below, the date which the contracting authority shall fix as the last date for the receipt by it of tenders made in response to the invitation to tender which shall be specified in the invitation to tender in accordance with paragraph (10)(b) above shall not be less than 40 days from the date of the despatch of the invitation but, if it is necessary that contractors should be given the opportunity to inspect the premises on which the works under the contract are to be

carried out or documents relating to the contract documents, then that minimum period shall be extended to allow for such inspection.

[(12) Subject to paragraph (14) below, where—

(a) the contracting authority has published a prior information notice in accordance with regulation 9 above;

(b) the prior information notice contained as much of the information referred to in Part C (or, if appropriate, Part D) of Schedule 2 as was available at the time of publication; and

(c) the prior information notice was sent to the Official Journal at least 52 days and no more than 12 months before the date on which the contract notice provided for in regulation 12(2) is despatched;

the contracting authority may substitute for the period of not less than 40 days in paragraph (11) above, a period of not less than 26 days.]

(13) Subject to paragraph (14) below, the contracting authority shall supply such further information relating to the contract documents as may reasonably be requested by a contractor selected to tender provided that the request for such information is received in sufficient time to enable the contracting authority to supply it not less than 6 days before the date specified in the invitation to tender as the final date for the receipt of tenders.

(14) Where compliance with the minimum periods referred to in paragraphs (3), (11), (12) and (13) above is rendered impracticable for reasons of urgency, the contracting authority may substitute for the period specified in paragraph (3) a period of not less than 15 days and for the periods specified in (11) and (12) periods of not less than 10 days and for the period specified in paragraph (13) a period of not less than 4 days and, in those circumstances, the contracting authority must send the invitation to tender by the most rapid means possible.

(15) A contracting authority shall not refuse to consider an application to be invited to tender if it is made by letter, telegram, telex, facsimile or telephone provided that, in the last 4 cases, it is confirmed by letter before the date fixed by the contracting authority as the last date for the receipt of requests to be selected to tender.

[(16) Tenders shall be submitted in writing either in person or by post, except that a contracting authority may authorise another means of submission provided that the chosen means enables—

(a) each tender to contain all the information necessary for its evaluation;

(b) the confidentiality of tenders to be maintained pending their evaluation; and

(c) tenders to be opened only after the time limit for their submission has expired.

(17) Where a contracting authority has authorised another means of submission in accordance with paragraph (16) above, it may require either that the submission of the tender is confirmed in writing or that a copy of the tender is delivered to it in person or by post, in either case as soon as possible after the submission of the tender by another means.]

Amendment
Para (4): word in square brackets substituted by SI 1992/3279, reg 32(1)(c).
Para (5): words in square brackets substituted by SI 1995/201, reg 31(1)(b).
Para (12): substituted by SI 2000/2009, reg 3(8).
Paras (16), (17): inserted by SI 2000/2009, reg 3(9).

[App.35]

13 The negotiated procedure

(1)   A contracting authority using the negotiated procedure shall comply with the following provisions of this regulation except that—

(a)   a contracting authority using the negotiated procedure pursuant to regulation 10(2)(d), (e), (f), (g) or (h), and

(b)   a contracting authority using the negotiated procedure pursuant to regulation 10(2)(a) who invites to negotiate the contract every contractor who submitted a tender following an invitation made during the course of the discontinued open or restricted procedure (not being a tender which was excluded pursuant to regulation [11(7)]),

need not comply with paragraphs (2) to (6) below.

(2)   The contracting authority shall publicise its intention to seek offers in relation to the public works contract by sending to the Official Journal as soon as possible after forming the intention a notice, in a form substantially corresponding to that set out in Part D of Schedule [2], inviting requests to be selected to negotiate and containing the information therein specified in relation to the contract.

(3)   Subject to paragraph (4) below, the date which the contracting authority shall fix as the last date for the receipt by it of requests to be selected to negotiate shall be specified in paragraph 6(a) of the contract notice and shall be not less than 37 days from the date of despatch of the notice.

(4)   Where compliance with the minimum period of 37 days in paragraph (3) above is rendered impracticable for reasons of urgency, the contracting authority may substitute a period of not less than 15 days and, in those circumstances, the contracting authority must send the invitation to negotiate the contract by the most rapid means possible.

(5)   Where there is a sufficient number of persons who are suitable to be selected to negotiate the contract, the number selected to negotiate shall be not less than 3.

(6)   A contracting authority shall not refuse to consider an application to be selected to negotiate if it is made by letter, telegram, telex, facsimile or by telephone provided that, in the last 4 cases, it is confirmed by letter before the date fixed by the contracting authority as the last date for the receipt of requests to be selected to negotiate.

(7)   The contracting authority may exclude a contractor from those persons from whom it will make the selection of persons to be invited to negotiate the contract only if the supplier may be treated as ineligible on a ground specified in regulation 14 or if the contractor fails to satisfy the minimum standards of economic and financial standing and technical capacity required of contractors by the contracting authority; for this purpose the contracting authority shall make its evaluation in accordance with regulations 14, 15, 16 and 17.

(8)   The contracting authority shall make the selection of the contractors to be invited to negotiate in accordance with regulations 14, 15, 16 and 17; and in making the selection and in issuing the invitations to negotiate the contracting authority shall not discriminate between contractors on the grounds of their nationality or the [relevant State] in which they are established.

Amendment

Paras (1), (2): figures in square brackets substituted by SI 1992/3279, reg 32(1)(d).
Para (8): words in square brackets substituted by SI 1995/201, reg 31(1)(b).

PART IV
SELECTION OF CONTRACTORS

[App.36]
14 Criteria for rejection of contractors

(1) A contracting authority may treat a contractor as ineligible to tender for, or to be included amongst those persons from whom it will make the selection of persons to be invited to tender for or to negotiate a public works contract in accordance with regulations 11(7), 12(4), and 13(7), or decide not to select a contractor to tender for or to negotiate a public works contract in accordance with regulations 12(5) and 13(8) on one of the following grounds, namely that the contractor—

(a) being an individual is bankrupt or has had a receiving order or administration order made against him or has made any composition or arrangement with or for the benefit of his creditors or has made any conveyance or assignment for the benefit of his creditors or appears unable to pay, or to have no reasonable prospect of being able to pay, a debt within the meaning of section 268 of the Insolvency Act 1968, or article 242 of the Insolvency (Northern Ireland) Order 1989, or in Scotland has granted a trust deed for creditors or become otherwise apparently insolvent, or is the subject of a petition presented for sequestration of his estate, or is the subject of any similar procedure under the law of any other state;

(b) being a partnership constituted under Scots law has granted a trust deed or become otherwise apparently insolvent, or is the subject of a petition presented for sequestration of its estate;

(c) being a company has passed a resolution or is the subject of an order by the court for the company's winding up otherwise than for the purposes of bona fide reconstruction or amalgamation, or has had a receiver, manager or administrator on behalf of a creditor appointed in respect of the company's business or any part thereof or is the subject of proceedings for any of the above procedures or is the subject of similar procedures under the law of any other state;

(d) has been convicted of a criminal offence relating to the conduct of his business or profession;

(e) has committed an act of grave misconduct in the course of his business or profession;

(f) has not fulfilled obligations relating to the payment of social security contributions under the law of any part of the United Kingdom or of the [relevant State] in which the contractor is established;

(g) has not fulfilled obligations relating to the payment of taxes under the law of any part of the United Kingdom;

(h) is guilty of serious misrepresentation in providing any information required of him under this regulation and regulation 15, 16 and 17; or

(i) subject to paragraphs (5) and (6) below, is not registered on the professional or trade register of the [relevant State] in which the contractor is established under the conditions laid down by that State.

(2) Subject to regulation 18, the contracting authority may require a contractor to provide such information as it considers it needs to make the evaluation in accordance with paragraph (1) above except that it shall accept as conclusive evidence that a contractor does not fall within the grounds specified in paragraphs (1)(a), (b), (c), (d), (f), or (g) above if that contractor provides to the contracting authority—

(a)   in relation to the grounds specified in paragraphs (1)(a), (b), (c) or (d) above,
    (i)   an extract from the judicial record, or
    (ii)   in a [relevant State] which does not maintain such a judicial record, a document issued by the relevant judicial or administrative authority;
(b)   in relation to the grounds specified in paragraph (1)(f) or (g) above, a certificate issued by the relevant competent authority;
(c)   in a [relevant State] where the documentary evidence specified in paragraphs (2)(a) and (b) above is not issued in relation to one of the grounds specified in paragraph (1)(a), (b), (c), (d), (f) or (g) above, a declaration on oath made by the contractor before the relevant judicial, administrative or competent authority or a relevant notary public or commissioner for oaths.

(3)   In this regulation, 'relevant' in relation to a judicial, administrative or competent authority, notary public or commissioner for oaths means an authority designated by, or a notary public or commissioner for oaths in, the [relevant State] in which the contractor is established.

(4)   The following are the appropriate professional or trade registers for the purposes of paragraph (1)(i) above—

    [in Austria, the Firmenbuch, Gewerberegister or Mitgliederverzeichnisse der Landeskammern;]
    in Belgium, the registre du commerce/Handelsregister;
    in Denmark, [the Handelsregistret, Aktieselskabesregistret or Erhvervsregistret];
    [in Finland, the Kaupparekisteri or Handelsregistret;]
    in France, the registre du commerce or the répertoire des métiers;
    in Germany, the Handelsregister or the Handwerksrolle;
    [in Greece, the registrar of contractors' enterprises '(Mhtrwo Ergolhptikwn Epiceirhsewn)' of the Ministry for Environment, Town and Country Planning and Public Works;]
    [in Iceland, the Firmaskra;]
    in Italy, the Registro della Camera di commercio, industria, agricultura e artigianato;
    in Luxembourg, the registre aux firmes and the rôle de la Chambre des métiers;
    in the Netherlands, the Handelsregister;
    [in Norway, the Foretaksregisteret;]
    in Portugal, the Commissão de Alvarás de Empresas de Obras Públicas e Particulares ('CAEOPP'); and
    in Spain, the Registro Oficial de Contratistas del Ministerio de Industria y Energia.
    [in Sweden, the Aktiebolagsregistret, Handelsregistret or Föreningsregistret;]

(5)   A contractor established in the United Kingdom or Ireland shall be treated as registered on the professional or trade register for the purposes of paragraph (1)(i) above if the contractor—
(a)   is established in Ireland and is certified as registered with the Registrar of Friendly Societies, or
(b)   is established in either State and is either—
    (i)   certified as incorporated by the Registrar of Companies, or
    (ii)   is certified as having declared on oath that he is carrying on business in the trade in question in the State in which he is established at a specific place of business and under a specific trading name.

[(6)   A contractor established in a relevant State, other than the United Kingdom or Ireland, which either has an equivalent professional or trade register which is not listed in paragraph (4) above or which does not have an equivalent professional or trade register shall be treated as registered on a professional or trade register for the purposes of paragraph 1(i) above on production of either a certificate that he is registered on the equivalent professional or trade register or where no such register exists, a declaration on oath, or in a relevant State which does not provide for a declaration on oath a solemn declaration, made by the contractor before the relevant judicial, administrative or competent authority or a relevant notary public or Commissioner for oaths, that he exercises the particular profession or trade.]

Amendment
Paras (1)–(3): words in square brackets substituted by SI 1995/201, reg 31(1)(b).
Para (4): entries in square brackets inserted, and in entry relating to Denmark words in square brackets substituted, by SI 1995/201, reg 31(1)(c).
Para (6): substituted by SI 1995/201, reg 31(1)(d).

[App.37]
15 Information as to economic and financial standing

(1)   Subject to regulation 18 and paragraph (2) below, in assessing whether a contractor meets any minimum standards of economic and financial standing required of contractors by the contracting authority for the purposes of regulations 11(7), 12(4) and 13(7), and selecting the contractors to be invited to tender for or to negotiate the contract in accordance with regulations 12(5) and 13(8), a contracting authority shall only take into account any of the following information (and it may require a contractor to provide such of that information as it considers it needs to make the assessment or selection)—

(a)   appropriate statements from the contractor's bankers;
(b)   statement of accounts or extracts therefrom relating to the business of the contractor where publication of the statement is required under the law of the [relevant State] in which the contractor is established;
(c)   a statement of the overall turnover of the business of the contractor and the turnover in respect of works in the 3 previous financial years of the contractor.

(2)   Where the information specified in paragraph (1) above is not appropriate in a particular case a contracting authority may require a contractor to provide other information to demonstrate the contractor's economic and financial standing.

(3)   A contracting authority which requires information to be provided in accordance with paragraphs (1) and (2) above, shall specify in the contract notice or in the invitation to tender the information which the contractor must provide.

(4)   Where a contractor is unable for a valid reason to provide the information which the contracting authority has required, the contracting authority shall accept such other information provided by the contractor as the contracting authority considers appropriate.

Amendment
Para (1): words in square brackets substituted by SI 1995/201, reg 31(1)(b).

[App.38]
16 Information as to technical capacity

(1)   Subject to regulation 18, in assessing whether a contractor meets any minimum standards of technical capacity required of contractors by the contracting authority

for the purposes of regulations 11(7), 12(4) and 13(7), and in selecting the contractors to be invited to tender for or to negotiate the contract in accordance with regulations 12(5) and 13(8), a contracting authority shall only take into account any of the following information (and it may require a contractor to provide such of that information as it considers it needs to make the assessment or selection)—

(a)   a list of the contractor's educational and professional qualifications where the contractor is an individual and a list of such qualifications of the contractor's managerial staff if any and those of the person or persons who would be responsible for carrying out the works under the contract;

(b)   a list of works carried out over the past 5 years together with (unless the contracting authority specifies that the following certificate should be submitted direct to the contracting authority by the person certifying) certificates of satisfactory completion for the most important of those works indicating in each case the value of the consideration received, when and where the works were carried out and specifying whether they were carried out according to the rules of the trade or profession and properly completed;

(c)   a statement of the tools, plant and technical equipment available to the contractor for carrying out the work under the contract;

(d)   a statement of the contractor's average annual manpower and the number of managerial staff over the previous 3 years;

(e)   a statement of the technicians or technical services which the contractor may call upon for the carrying out of the work under the contract, whether or not the technicians or persons providing the technical services are independent of the contractor.

(2)   The contracting authority shall specify in the contract notice which of the information specified in paragraph (1) above it requires to be provided.

[App.39]
17 Supplementary information

Subject to regulation 18, the contracting authority may require a contractor to provide information supplementing the information provided in accordance with regulations 14, 15 and 16 or to clarify that information, provided that the information so required relates to the matters specified in regulations 14, 15 and 16.

[App.40]
18 Official lists of recognised contractors

Where a contractor is registered on the official list of recognised contractors in a [relevant State] which maintains such lists and in which the contractor is established and the contractor submits to the contracting authority a certificate of registration issued by the authority administering the official list which specifies the information submitted to that authority which enabled the contractor to be registered and which states the classification given, the contracting authority, to the extent that the certificate deals with the grounds referred to in regulation 14(1)(a) to (e), (h), and (i), 15(1)(b) and (c) and [16(1)(b)] and (d)—

(a)   shall accept the certificate as evidence that the contractor does not fall within the grounds specified in regulation 14(1)(a) to (e), (h) and (i) and shall not be entitled to require the contractor to submit such information relating to those grounds as is specified in regulation 14,

(b)   shall not be entitled to require the contractor to provide information specified in regulations 15(1)(b) and (c) and 16(1)(b) and (d), and

(c)   shall not be entitled to seek any supplementary information in accordance with regulation 17 in relation to the matters specified in paragraphs (a) and (b) above.

Amendment
Words in square brackets substituted by SI 1995/201, reg 31(1)(b); figure in square brackets substituted by SI 1992/3279, reg 32(1)(e).

[App.41]
19 Consortium

(1)   In this regulation a 'consortium' means 2 or more persons, at least one of whom is a contractor, acting jointly for the purpose of being awarded a public works contract.

(2)   A contracting authority shall not treat the tender of a consortium as ineligible nor decide not to include a consortium amongst those persons from whom it will make the selection of persons to be invited to tender for or to negotiate a public works contract on the grounds that the consortium has not formed a legal entity for the purposes of tendering for or negotiating the contract; but where a contracting authority awards a public works contract to a consortium it may require the consortium to form a legal entity before entering into, or as a term of, the contract.

(3)   In these Regulations references to a contractor or to a concessionaire where the contractor or concessionaire is a consortium includes a reference to each person who is a member of that consortium.

PART V
THE AWARD OF A PUBLIC WORKS CONTRACT

[App.42]
20 Criteria for the award of a public works contract

(1)   Subject to paragraphs (6) and (7) below, a contracting authority shall award a public works contract on the basis of the offer which—
(a)   offers the lowest price, or
(b)   is the most economically advantageous to the contracting authority.

(2)   The criteria which a contracting authority may use to determine that an offer is the most economically advantageous include price, period for completion, running costs, profitability and technical merit.

(3)   Where a contracting authority intends to award a public works contract on the basis of the offer which is the most economically advantageous it shall state the criteria on which it intends to base its decision, where possible in descending order of importance, in the contract notice or in the contract documents.

(4)   Where a contracting authority awards a public works contract on the basis of the offer which is the most economically advantageous, it may take account of offers which offer variations on the requirements specified in the contract documents if the offer meets the minimum requirements of the contracting authority and it has indicated in the contract notice that offers offering variations will be considered and has stated in the contract documents the minimum requirements which the offer must meet and any specific requirements for the presentation of an offer offering variations.

(5)   A contracting authority may not reject a tender on the ground that the technical specifications in the tender have been defined by reference to European specifications

(within the meaning of regulation 8(1)) or to the national technical specifications specified in regulation 8(7)(a) and (b).

(6)   If an offer for a public works contract is abnormally low the contracting authority may reject that offer but only if it has requested in writing an explanation of the offer or of those parts which it considers contribute to the offer being abnormally low and has—

(a)   if awarding the contract on the basis of the offer which offers the lowest price, examined the details of all the offers made, taking into account any explanation given to it of the abnormally low tender, before awarding the contract, or

(b)   if awarding the contract on the basis of the offer which is the most economically advantageous, taken any such explanation into account in assessing which is the most economically advantageous offer,

and, in considering that explanation, the contracting authority may take into account explanations which justify the offer on objective grounds including the economy of the construction method, the technical solutions suggested by the contractor or the exceptionally favourable conditions available to the contractor for the carrying out of the works or the originality of the works proposed by the contractor.

(7)   If a contracting authority which rejects an abnormally low offer is awarding the contract on the basis of the offer which offers the lowest price, it shall send a report justifying the rejection to the Treasury for onward transmission to the Commission.

(8)   For the purposes of this regulation an 'offer' includes a bid by one part of a contracting authority to carry out work or works for another part of the contracting authority when the former part is invited by the latter part to compete with the offers sought from other persons.

[App.43]

21 Contract award notice

(1)   A contracting authority which has awarded a public works contract shall, no later than 48 days after the award, send to the Official Journal a notice, substantially corresponding to the form set out in Part E of Schedule 2 and, subject to paragraph (2) below, including the information therein specified in relation to the contract.

(2)   Any of the information specified in Part E of Schedule 2 to be included in the contract award notice may be omitted in a particular case where to publish such information would impede law enforcement, would otherwise be contrary to the public interest, would prejudice the legitimate commercial interests of any person or might prejudice fair competition between contractors.

[App.44]

[22 Information about contract award procedures]

[(1)   Where a contracting authority decides either to abandon or to recommence an award procedure in respect of which a contract notice has been published it shall inform the Office for Official Publications of the European Communities and shall inform promptly any contractor who submitted an offer or who applied to be included amongst the persons to be selected to tender for or to negotiate the contract of the reasons for its decision and shall do so in writing if so requested.

(2)   Subject to paragraph (3) below, a contracting authority shall, within 15 days of the date on which it receives a request in writing from any contractor who was unsuccessful (whether pursuant to regulation 11(7), 12(4), 12(5), 13(7), 13(8) or 20),

inform that contractor of the reasons why he was unsuccessful and, if the contractor submitted an admissible tender, the contracting authority shall inform him of the characteristics and relative advantages of the successful tender as well as the name of the person awarded the contract.

(3)   A contracting authority may withhold any information to be provided in accordance with paragraph (2) above where the disclosure of such information would impede law enforcement or otherwise be contrary to the public interest or would prejudice the legitimate commercial interests of any person or might prejudice fair competition between contractors.

(4)   A contracting authority shall prepare a record in relation to each public works contract awarded by it specifying—

(a)   the name and address of the contracting authority;

(b)   the work or works to be carried out under the contract and the value of the consideration to be given under it;

(c)   the names of the persons whose offers were evaluated in accordance with regulation 20 and, where the contracting authority has used the restricted or negotiated procedure, the reasons why those persons were selected;

(d)   the names of the persons who were unsuccessful pursuant to regulation 11(7), 12(4), 12(5), 13(7) or 13(8) and the reasons why they were unsuccessful;

(e)   the name of the person to whom the public works contract was awarded and the reasons for having awarded the contract to him;

(f)   if known to the contracting authority, the works under the contract which the person to whom the contract has been awarded intends to sub-contract to another person; and

(g)   in the case of a contracting authority which used the negotiated procedure, which of the circumstances specified in regulation 10(2) constituted grounds for using that procedure.

(5)   If the Commission requests a report containing the information specified in paragraph (4) above, the contracting authority shall send a written report containing that information, or the main features of it, to the Treasury for onward transmission to the Commission.]

Amendment
Substituted by SI 2000/2009, reg 3(10).

PART VI
MISCELLANEOUS

[App.45]
23 Subsidised works contracts

(1)   Where a contracting authority undertakes to contribute more than half of the consideration to be or expected to be paid under a contract to which this paragraph applies by virtue of paragraph (2) below which has been or is to be entered into by a person other than another contracting authority (in this paragraph referred to as 'the subsidised body'), that contracting authority shall—

(a)   make it a condition of the making of such contribution that the subsidised body complies with the provisions of these Regulations in relation to that contract as if it were a contracting authority, and

(b)   ensure that the subsidised body does so comply or recover the contribution.

(2)   Paragraph (1) above applies to a contract which would be a public works contract if the subsidised body were a contracting authority and which is for the carrying out of any of the activities specified in Schedule 1 as are included in Group 502 or for the carrying out of building work for hospitals, facilities intended for sports, recreation and leisure, school and university building or buildings for administrative purposes.

[App.46]

24 Public housing scheme works contracts

(1)   For the purpose of seeking offers in relation to a public housing scheme works contract, where the size and complexity of the scheme and the estimated duration of the works involved require that the planning of the scheme be based from the outset on a close collaboration of a team comprising representatives of the contracting authority, experts and the contractor, a contracting authority may, except as indicated in the following paragraphs, depart from the provisions of these Regulations insofar as it is necessary to do so to select the contractor who is most suitable for integration into the team.

(2)   The contracting authority shall comply with the provisions of regulation 12(1) to (5).

(3)   The contracting authority shall include in the contract notice a job description which is as accurate as possible so as to enable contractors to form a valid idea of the scheme and of the minimum standards relating to the business or professional status, the economic and financial standing and the technical capacity which the person awarded the contract will be expected to fulfil.

[App.47]

25 Public works concession contracts

(1)   A contracting authority seeking offers in relation to a public works concession contract shall comply with the following paragraphs of this regulation.

(2)   The contracting authority shall publicise its intention to seek offers in relation to the concession contract by sending to the Official Journal as soon as possible after forming the intention a notice in a form substantially corresponding to that set out in Part F of Schedule 2 and containing the information therein specified in relation to the concession contract.

(3)   The date which the contracting authority shall fix as the last date for the receipt by it of tenders or of requests to be selected to tender for or negotiate the contract, as the case may be, shall be specified in paragraph 3(a) of the notice and shall be not less than 52 days from the date of despatch of the notice.

[App.48]

26 Sub-contracting the work or works to be carried out under a public works concession contract

(1)   A contracting authority seeking offers in relation to a public works concession contract shall either—

(a)   include in the invitation to tender for, or to apply to be selected to tender for or to negotiate, the concession contract a request that the applicant specify whether he would intend, if awarded the concession contract, to sub-contract to persons who are not affiliated to him any of the work or works to be carried out under the concession contract and, if so, how much as a proportion of the value of such work or works would be so sub-contracted, or

(b) require as a term of the concession contract—
  (i) that the concessionaire sub-contract to persons who are not affiliated to the concessionaire some or all of the work or works to be carried out under the concession contract, and
  (ii) that the amount of the works so sub-contracted be not less than 30%, or such higher percentage as may be specified in the contract at the option of the contracting authority or the concessionaire, of the value of the consideration which the contracting authority would expect to give for the carrying out of the work or works if it did not grant a concession.

(2) Where the concessionaire is a contracting authority that contracting authority shall comply with the provisions of these Regulations in respect of public works contracts it seeks offers in relation to for the purpose of sub-contracting the work or works to be carried out under the public works concession contract.

(3) Where the concessionaire is not a contracting authority the concessionaire shall—
(a) publicise his intention to seek offers in relation to any contract to which this paragraph applies by virtue of paragraph (4) below by sending to the Official Journal as soon as possible after forming the intention a notice in a form substantially corresponding to that set out in Part G of Schedule 2 and containing the information therein specified in relation to the contract;
(b) comply with regulation 30 in relation to that notice as if the concessionaire were a contracting authority;
(c) if that notice invites tenders, fix as the last date for the receipt by the concessionaire of tenders a date of not less than 40 days from the date of the despatch of the notice and specify that date in paragraph 4(a) of the notice; and
(d) if the notice invites applications to be selected to tender for or negotiate the contract—
  (i) fix as the last date for the receipt of such applications a date not less than 37 days from the date of despatch of the notice and specify that date in paragraph 4(a) of the notice; and
  (ii) fix as the last date for the receipt of tenders following selection of the persons to be invited to tender a date of not less than 40 days from the date of despatch of the invitation and specify that date in the invitation.

(4) Paragraph (3) above applies to a contract—
(a) in relation to which the concessionaire is seeking offers for the purpose of sub-contracting any of the work or works to be carried out under the public works concession contract,
(b) which the concessionaire does not intend to enter into with a person affiliated to him,
(c) which would, if the concessionaire were a contracting authority, be a public works contract other than a public works contract in respect of which a contracting authority would be entitled to use the negotiated procedure pursuant to regulation 10(2)(d) to (h).

(5) For the purposes of this regulation a person is to be treated as affiliated to another person if either exercises, directly or indirectly, a dominant influence over the other or any person exercises, directly or indirectly, a dominant influence over both of them or if they are both members of any consortium formed for the purpose of performing

the public works concession contract; and a person shall be taken to exercise a dominant influence over another person—

(a)   if he possesses the greater part of the issued share capital of that person or controls the voting power attached to such greater part, or

(b)   if he may appoint more than half of the individuals who are ultimately responsible for managing that person's affairs.

(6)   A contracting authority shall require applicants for a public works concession contract to submit a list of all persons affiliated to the applicant with the application and to update that list from time to time to take account of any changes in the persons affiliated to the applicant.

[App.49]

27 Obligations relating to employment protection and working conditions

A contracting authority which includes in the contract documents relating to a public works contract information as to where a contractor may obtain information about obligations relating to employment protection and working conditions which will apply to the works to be carried out under the contract, shall request contractors to indicate that they have taken account of those obligations in preparing their tender or in negotiating the contract.

[App.50]

[28 Statistical and other reports]

[(1)   A contracting authority shall, no later than 31st July in each year, send to the Treasury a report specifying, in relation to each public works contract awarded by it during the reporting period—

(a)   the value (estimated if necessary) of the consideration payable under the contract;

(b)   whether the open, restricted or negotiated procedure was used;

(c)   if the negotiated procedure was used, pursuant to which provision of regulation 10(2) that procedure was used;

(d)   the principal category of work carried out or to be carried out under the contract according to the nomenclature used in Schedule 1; and

(e)   the nationality of the person to whom the contract was awarded.

(2)   Entities specified in Schedule 1 to the Public Supply Contracts Regulations 1995 or any body which is a successor to such an entity and which is a contracting authority shall include in the report referred to in paragraph (1) above the aggregate value (estimated if necessary) of all public works contracts awarded by it during the reporting period which were below the relevant threshold specified in regulation 7.

(3)   A contracting authority shall send to the Treasury a report containing such other information as the Treasury may from time to time require in respect of a particular public works contract (including public works contracts excluded from the application of these Regulations by regulations 6 and 7) for the purposes of informing the Commission.

(4)   In this regulation 'the reporting period' means the year preceding the year in which the report referred to in paragraph (1) above is to be made.]

Amendment
Substituted by SI 2000/2009, reg 3(11).

[App.51]
29 Responsibility for obtaining reports

(1)   Where a contracting authority is not a Minister of the Crown or a government department, that contracting authority shall send any report which it is required in accordance with regulations 8(6), 10(7), 20(7), 22(3) and 28 to send to the Treasury instead to the Minister responsible for that contracting authority and that Minister shall be responsible for sending the report to the Treasury.

(2)   The Minister responsible for a contracting authority shall be the Minister of the Crown whose areas of responsibility are most closely connected with the functions of the contracting authority; and any question as to which Minister of the Crown's areas of responsibility are most closely connected with the functions of a contracting authority shall be determined by the Treasury whose determination shall be final.

(3)   The requirement on a contracting authority to send any report in accordance with paragraph (1) above to the Minister of the Crown responsible for that contracting authority shall be enforceable, on the application of the Minister responsible, by mandamus or, in Scotland, for an order for specific performance.

(4)   Proceedings under paragraph (3) above brought in Scotland shall be brought before the Court of Session.

(5)   In the application of this regulation to Northern Ireland references to the Minister shall include references to the head of a Northern Ireland department.

[(6)   In the application of this regulation to Scotland—
(a)   references to—
    (i)   a Minister of the Crown, other than the first reference in paragraph (1); and
    (ii)   the Minister responsible for a contracting authority,
    shall be construed as references to the Scottish Ministers;
(b)   paragraph (2) shall not apply.]

Amendment
Para (6): inserted by SI 1999/1820, art 4, Sch 2, Pt II, para 148.

[App.52]
30 Publication of notices

(1)   Any notice required by these Regulations to be sent to the Official Journal shall be sent by the most appropriate means to the Office for Official Publications of the European Communities and where the contracting authority is applying the restricted procedure or the negotiated procedure and, for reasons of urgency, is applying the provisions of regulations 12(14) and 13(4), the notice shall be sent by telex, telegram or telefax.

(2)   Any such notice shall not contain more than 650 words.

(3)   The contracting authority shall retain evidence of the date of despatch to the Official Journal of each notice.

(4)   The contracting authority shall not place a contract notice in the press or like publications in the United Kingdom before the date on which the notice is despatched in accordance with paragraph (1) above and if it does after that date, so place the notice it shall not add to the notice any information in relation to the contract which was not contained in the notice sent to the Official Journal.

PART VII
APPLICATIONS TO THE COURT

[App.53]
31 Enforcement of obligations relating to a public works contract

(1)   The obligation on a contracting authority to comply with the provisions of these Regulations other than regulations 8(6), 10(7), 20(7), 22(3), 28 and 29(1), and with any enforceable Community obligation in respect of a public works contract (other than one excluded from the application of these Regulations by regulations 6 and 7), and the obligation on a concessionaire to comply with the provisions of regulation 26(3) is a duty owed to contractors.

[(1A)   The duty owed to a contractor pursuant to paragraph (1) above, except in relation to regulations 23, 25 and 26(1) and(2), shall be a duty owed also to a GPA provider.

(1B)   References to a 'contractor' in paragraphs (3), (5) and (6) below shall be construed as including a reference to a GPA provider.]

(2)   In this regulation and notwithstanding regulation 4, references to a 'contractor' include, where the duty owed pursuant to paragraph (1) above is the obligation on a concessionaire to comply with regulation 26(3), any person—
(a)   who sought, or who seeks, or would have wished, to be the person to whom a contract to which regulation 26(3) applies is awarded, and
(b)   who is a national of and established in a [relevant State].

(3)   A breach of the duty owed pursuant to paragraph (1) [or paragraph (1A)] above shall not be a criminal offence but any breach of the duty shall be actionable by any contractor who, in consequence, suffers, or risks suffering, loss or damage.

(4)   Proceedings under this regulation shall be brought in England and Wales and in Northern Ireland in the High Court and, in Scotland, before the Court of Session.

(5)   Proceedings under this regulation may not be brought unless—
(a)   the contractor bringing the proceedings has informed the contracting authority or concessionaire, as the case may be, of the breach or apprehended breach of the duty owed to him pursuant to paragraph (1) [or paragraph (1A)] above by that contracting authority or concessionaire and of his intention to bring proceedings under this regulation in respect of it; and
(b)   they are brought promptly and in any event within 3 months from the date when grounds for the bringing of the proceedings first arose unless the Court considers that there is good reason for extending the period within which proceedings may be brought.

(6)   Subject to [paragraph (7)] below, but otherwise without prejudice to any other powers of the Court, in proceedings brought under this regulation the Court may—
(a)   by interim order suspend the procedure leading to the award of the contract in relation to the award of which the breach of the duty owed pursuant to paragraph (1) [or paragraph (1A)] above is alleged, or suspend the implementation of any decision or action taken by the contracting authority or concessionaire, as the case may be, in the course of following such a procedure; and
(b)   if satisfied that a decision or action taken by a contracting authority was in breach of the duty owed pursuant to paragraph (1) [or paragraph (1A)] above—

(i)   order the setting aside of that decision or action or order the contracting authority to amend any document, or

(ii)   award damages to a contractor who has suffered loss or damage as a consequence of the breach, or

(iii)   do both of those things.

(7) In proceedings under this regulation the Court shall not have power to order any remedy other than an award of damages in respect of a breach of the duty owed pursuant to paragraph (1) [or paragraph (1A)] above if the contract in relation to which the breach occurred has been entered into.

(8) Notwithstanding sections 21 and 42 of the Crown Proceedings Act 1947, in proceedings brought under this regulation against the Crown the court shall have power to grant an injunction or interdict.

[(9) In this regulation—

(a)   a 'GPA provider' shall mean a person from a GPA State who sought, or who seeks, or would have wished, to be the person to whom the contract is awarded;

(b)   a 'GPA State' shall mean any country other than a relevant State which, at the relevant time is a signatory to the GPA and has agreed with the European Community that the GPA shall apply to a contract of the type to be awarded; and

(c)   'relevant time' shall mean the date on which the contracting authority would have sent a contract notice in respect of the contract to the Official Journal if it had been required by these Regulations to do so.]

Amendment
Paras (1A), (1B): inserted by SI 2000/2009, reg 3(12)(a).
Para (2): in sub-para (b) words in square brackets substituted by SI 1995/201, reg 31(1)(b).
Paras (3), (5)–(7): words 'or paragraph (1A)' in square brackets in each place they occur inserted by SI 2000/2009, reg 3(12)(b).
Para (6): words 'paragraph (7)' in square brackets substituted by SI 1992/3279, reg 32(1)(f).
Para (9): inserted by SI 2000/2009, reg 3(12)(c).

SCHEDULE 1
ACTIVITIES CONSTITUTING WORKS

Regulation 2(1)

[App.54]

Classes	Groups	Subgroups and items	Description
50			BUILDING AND CIVIL ENGINEERING
	500		General building and civil engineering work (without any particular specialisation) and demolition work
		500.1	General building and civil engineering work (without any particular specialisation)
		500.2	Demolition work
	501		Construction of flats, office blocks, hospitals and other buildings, both residential and non-residential
		501.1	General building contractors

	501.2	Roofing
	501.3	Construction of chimneys, kilns and furnaces
	501.4	Waterproofing and damp-proofing
	501.5	Restoration and maintenance of outside walls (repainting, cleaning, etc)
	501.6	Erection and dismantlement of scaffolding
	501.7	Other specialised activities relating to construction work (including carpentry)
502		Civil engineering: construction of roads, bridges, railways, etc.
	502.1	General civil engineering work
	502.2	Earth-moving (navvying)
	502.3	Construction of bridges, tunnels and shafts, drilling
	502.4	Hydraulic engineering (rivers, canals, harbours, flows, locks and dams)
	502.5	Road-building (including specialised construction of airports and runways)
	502.6	Specialised construction work relating to water (i.e. to irrigation, land drainage, water supply, sewage disposal, sewerage, etc)
	502.7	Specialised activities in other areas of civil engineering
503		Installation (fittings and fixtures)
	503.1	General installation work
	503.2	Gas fitting and plumbing, and the installation of sanitary equipment
	503.3	Installation of heating and ventilating apparatus (central heating, air conditioning, ventilation)
	503.4	Sound and heat insulation, insulation against vibration
	503.5	Electrical fittings
	503.6	Installation of aerials, lightning conductors, telephones, etc
504		Building completion work
	504.1	General building completion work
	504.2	Plastering
	504.3	Joinery, primarily engaged in on the site assembly and/or installation (including the laying of parquet flooring)
	504.4	Painting, glazing, paper hanging
	504.5	Tiling and otherwise covering floors and walls
	504.6	Other building completion work (putting in fireplaces, etc)

[SCHEDULE 2
FORMS OF NOTICES FOR PUBLICATION IN THE OFFICIAL JOURNAL]

[Regulations 9, 11(2),(8), 12(2), (16), 13(2), 25(2), 26(3)]

[PART A
PRIOR INFORMATION NOTICE]

[App.55]

[1 Name, address, telegraphic address, telephone, telex and facsimile numbers of the contracting authority.

2
(a)   The site;
(b)   Nature and extent of the work(s) to be provided and, where relevant, the main characteristics of any lots by reference to the work;
(c)   If available, an estimate of the cost range of the proposed work(s).

3
(a)   Estimated date for initiating the award procedures in respect of the contract or contracts;
(b)   If known, estimated date for the start of the work;
(c)   If known, estimated timetable for completion of the work.

4 If known, terms of financing of the work and of price revision and/or references to the relevant provisions.

5 Other information.

6 Date of despatch of the notice.

7 Indication of whether the procurement is covered by the GPA.]

Amendment
Substituted by SI 2000/2009, reg 3(13), Sch 1.

[PART B
OPEN PROCEDURE NOTICE]

[App.56]

[1 Name, address, telegraphic address, telephone, telex and facsimile numbers of the contracting authority.

2
(a)   Award procedure chosen.
(b)   Nature of the contract for which tenders are being requested.

3
(a)   The site;
(b)   Nature and extent of the work(s) to be provided and general nature of the work; including any options for further works and if known, an estimate of the timing when such options may be exercised;

(c)   If the work or the contract is subdivided into several lots, the size of the different lots and the possibility of tendering for one, for several or for all of the lots;

(d)   Information concerning the purpose of the work or the contract where the latter also involves the drawing up of projects.

4 Time limit for completion of the works or duration of the works contract and, as far as possible, time limit for starting the works.

5

(a)   Name and address from which the contract documents and additional documents may be requested;

(b)   Where applicable, the amount and terms of payment of the sum to be paid to obtain such documents.

6

(a)   Final date for receipt of tenders;

(b)   Address to which tenders must be sent;

(c)   Language(s) in which tenders must be drawn up.

7

(a)   Where applicable, the persons authorised to be present at the opening of tenders;

(b)   Date, hour and place of opening of tenders.

8 Any deposit and guarantees required.

9 Main terms concerning financing and payment and/or references to the relevant provisions.

10 Where applicable, the legal form to be taken by the grouping of contractors to whom the contract is awarded.

11 Information concerning the contractor's personal position and minimum standards of economic and financial standing and technical capacity required of him.

12 Period during which the tenderer is bound to keep open his tender.

13 Criteria for the award of the contract. Criteria other than that of the lowest price shall be mentioned where they do not appear in the contract documents.

14 Where applicable, prohibition on variants.

15 Other information.

16 Date of publication of the prior information notice in the Official Journal or references to its non-publication.

17 Date of despatch of the notice.

18 Indication of whether the procurement is covered by the GPA.]

Amendment
Substituted by SI 2000/2009, reg 3(13), Sch 1.

[PART C
RESTRICTED PROCEDURE NOTICE]

[App.57]

[**1** Name, address, telegraphic address, telephone, telex and facsimile numbers of the contracting authority.

2

(a)   Award procedure chosen;

(b)   Where applicable, justification for the use of shorter time limits;

(c)   Nature of the contract for which tenders are being requested.

3

(a)   The site;

(b)   Nature and extent of the work(s) to be provided and general nature of the work, including any options for further works and, if known, an estimate of the timing when such options may be exercised;

(c)   If the work or the contract is subdivided into several lots, the size of the different lots and the possibility of tendering for one, for several or for all of the lots;

(d)   Information concerning the purpose of the work or the contract where the latter also involves the drawing up of projects.

4 Time limit for completion of the works or duration of the works contract and, as far as possible, time limit for starting the works.

5 Where applicable, the legal form to be taken by the grouping of contractors to whom the contract is awarded.

6

(a)   Final date for receipt of requests to participate;

(b)   Address to which requests must be sent;

(c)   Language(s) in which requests must be drawn up.

7 Final date for despatch of invitations to tender.

8 Any deposit and guarantees required.

9 Main terms concerning financing and payment and/or the relevant provisions.

10 Information concerning the contractor's personal position and minimum standards of economic and financial standing and technical capacity required of him.

11 Criteria for the award of the contract where they are not mentioned in the invitation to tender.

12 Where applicable, prohibition on variants.

13 Other information.

14 Date of publication of the prior information notice in the Official Journal or references to its non-publication.

15 Date of despatch of the notice.

16 Indication of whether the procurement is covered by the GPA.]

Amendment
Substituted by SI 2000/2009, reg 3(13), Sch 1.

[PART D
NEGOTIATED PROCEDURE NOTICE]

[App.58]
[1 Name, address, telegraphic address, telephone, telex and facsimile nmbers of the contracting authority.

2

(a)   Award procedure chosen;

(b)   Where applicable, justification for the use of shorter time limits;

(c)   Nature of the contract for which tenders are being requested.

3

(a)   The site;

(b)   Nature and extent of the work(s) to be provided and general nature of the work; including any options for further works and, if known, an estimate of the timing when such options may be exercised;

(c)   If the work or the contract is subdivided into several lots, the size of the different lots and the possibility of tendering for one, for several or for all of the lots;

(d)   Information concerning the purpose of the work or the contract where the latter also involves the drawing up of projects.

4 Time limit for completion of the works or duration of the works contract and, as far as possible, time limit for starting the works.

5 Where applicable, the legal form to be taken by the grouping of contractors to whom the contract is awarded.

6

(a)   Final date for receipt of requests to participate;

(b)   Address to which they must be sent;

(c)   Language(s) in which they must be drawn up.

7 Any deposit and guarantees required.

8 Main terms concerning financing and payment and/or the relevant provisions.

9 Information concerning the contractor's personal position and information and formalities necessary in order to evaluate the minimum standards of economic and financial standing and technical capacity required of him.

10 Where applicable, prohibition on variants.

11 Where applicable, name and address of contractors already selected by the awarding authority.

12 Date(s) of previous publications in the Official Journal.

13 Other information.

14 Date of publication of the prior information notice in the Official Journal.

15 Date of despatch of the notice.

16 Indication of whether the procurement is covered by the GPA.]

Amendment
Substituted by SI 2000/2009, reg 3(13), Sch 1.

[PART E
CONTRACT AWARD NOTICE]

[App.59]
[1 Name and address of the contracting authority

2

(a)   Award procedure chosen;

(b)   Where appropriate, justification for use of the negotiated procedure without a prior call for competition.

3 Date of award of contract.

4 Criteria for award of contract.

5 Number of offers received.

6 Name and address of successful contractor(s).

7 Nature and extent/quantity of the works provided, general characteristics of the finished structure.

8 Price or range of prices (minimum/maximum) paid or to be paid.

9 Value of winning award(s) or the highest and lowest offer taken into account in the award of the contract.

10 Where appropriate, value and proportion of contract likely to be subcontracted to third parties.

11 Other information.

12 Date of publication of the contract notice in the Official Journal.

13 Date of despatch of the notice.]

Amendment
Substituted by SI 2000/2009, reg 13(3), Sch 1.

[PART F
PUBLIC WORKS CONCESSION CONTRACT NOTICE]

[App.60]

[**1** The name, address, telegraphic address, telephone, telex and facsimile numbers of the contracting authority.

2

(a)   The site;

(b)   The subject of the concession and extent of the services to be provided.

3

(a)   Final date for receipt of candidatures;

(b)   The address to which they must be sent;

(c)   The language(s) in which they must be drawn up.

4 Personal, technical and financial conditions to be fulfilled by the candidates.

5 The criteria for the award of the contract.

6 Where applicable, the minimum percentage of the works contracts awarded to third parties.

7 Other information.

8 Date of despatch of the notice.]

Amendment
Substituted by SI 2000/2009, reg 3(13), Sch 1.

[PART G
NOTICE OF WORKS CONTRACTS AWARDED BY
CONCESSIONAIRES]

[App.61]

[1

(a)   The site;

(b)   The nature and extent of the service to be provided and the general nature of the work.

2 Any time limit for completion of the works.

3 Name and address from which the contract documents and additional documents may be requested.

4

(a)   The final date for receipt of requests to participate and/or receipt of tenders;

(b)   The address to which they must be sent;

(c)   The language(s) in which they must be drawn up.

5 Any deposit and guarantees required.

6 The minimum standards of economic and financial standing and technical capacity required of the contractor.

7 The criteria for the award of the contract.

8 Other information.

9 Date of despatch of the notice.]

Amendment
Substituted by SI 2000/2009, reg 3(13), Sch 1.

[SCHEDULE 3
EXTENSION TO NON MEMBER STATES

Regulations 2(1) and 4

[App.62]

[Relevant State	Agreement with the European Union which extend the provisions relating to public procurement to the relevant State	Statutory provisions designating the agreements as European Treaties
1 Bulgaria	Europe Agreement (OJ No L358, 31.12.94, p 2)	SI 1994/758
2 The Czech Republic	Europe Agreement (OJ No L360, 31.12.94, p 2)	SI 1994/759
3 Estonia	Europe Agreement (OJ No L68, 9.03.98, p 3)	SI 1997/269
4 Hungary	Europe Agreement (OJ No L347, 31.12.93, p 2)	SI 1992/2871
5 Iceland	European Economic Area Agreement	European Economic Area Act 1993, section 1.

6 Latvia	Europe Agreement (OJ No L26, 2.02.98, p 2)	SI 1997/270
7 Liechtenstein	European Economic Area Agreement	European Economic Area Act 1993, section 1.
8 Lithuania	Europe Agreement (OJ No L51, 20.02.98 p 3)	SI 1997/271
9 Norway	European Economic Area Agreement	European Economic Area Act 1993, section 1.
10 Poland	Europe Agreement (OJ No L348, 31.12.94, p 2)	SI 1992/2872
11 Romania	Europe Agreement (OJ No L357, 31.12.94, p 2)	SI 1994/760
12 Slovakia	Europe Agreement (OJ No L359, 31.12.94, p 2)	SI 1994/761
13 Slovenia	Europe Agreement (OJ No L51, 26.02.99, p 3)	SI 1998/1062

Amendment
Inserted by SI 2000/2009, reg 3(14), Sch 2.

PUBLIC SERVICES CONTRACTS REGULATIONS 1993

SI 1993/3228

PART I
GENERAL

[App.63]
1 Title and commencement
These Regulations may be cited as the Public Services Contracts Regulations 1993 and shall come into force on 13th January 1994.

[App.64]
2 Interpretation
(1)   In these Regulations—
'to award' means to accept an offer made in relation to a proposed contract;
'the Commission' means the Commission of the Communities;
'contract documents' means the invitation to tender for or to negotiate the contract, the proposed conditions of contract, the specifications or descriptions of the services required by the contracting authority and all documents supplementary thereto;
'contracting authority' has the meaning ascribed to it by regulation 3;
'contract notice' means a notice sent to the Official Journal in accordance with regulations 11(2), 12(2) or 13(2);
'design contest' means a competition particularly in the fields of planning, architecture, civil engineering and data processing—
    (a)   which is conducted by a contracting authority and in which it invites the entry of plans and designs;
    (b)   under the rules of which the plans or designs will be judged by a jury;
    (c)   under which prizes may or may not be awarded; and
    (d)   which enables the contracting authority to acquire the use or ownership of plans or designs selected by the jury;
. . .
'established' means the same as it does for the purposes of the Community Treaties;
'financial year' means the period of 12 months ending on 31st March in any year or, in relation to any person whose accounts are prepared in respect of a different 12 month period, that period of 12 months;
'government department' includes a Northern Ireland department or the head of such department [and any part of the Scottish Administration];
['Government Procurement Agreement' means the Agreement on Government Procurement between certain parties to the World Trade Organisation (WTO) Agreement signed in Marrakesh on 15 April 1994;
'GPA' means the Government Procurement Agreement;]
['letter' has the same meaning as in the Postal Services Act 2000;]

'Minister of the Crown' means the holder of an office in Her Majesty's Government in the United Kingdom, and includes the Treasury [and a reference to a Minister of the Crown shall be read as including a reference to the Scottish Ministers];

'national of a [relevant State]' means, in the case of a person who is not an individual, a person formed in accordance with the laws of a [relevant State] and which has its registered office, central administration or principal place of business in a [relevant State];

'negotiated procedure' means a procedure leading to the award of a contract whereby the contracting authority negotiates the terms of the contract with one or more persons selected by it;

'Official Journal' means the Official Journal of the Communities;

'open procedure' means a procedure leading to the award of a contract whereby all interested persons may tender for the contract;

['postal business' means the provision of postal services in relation to letters;]

['postal services' has the same meaning as in the Postal Services Act 2000;]

['the Post Office company' has the same meaning as in Part IV of the Postal Services Act 2000;]

'prior information notice' means a notice sent to the Official Journal in accordance with regulation 9;

'public services contract' means a contract in writing for consideration (whatever the nature of the consideration) under which a contracting authority engages a person to provide services but does not include—

(a)   a contract of employment or other contract of service;

(b)   a public works contract within the meaning of the Public Works Contracts Regulations 1991;

(c)   a public supply contract within the meaning of the Public Supply Contracts Regulations 1991;

[(d)   any contract where the contracting authority is a utility within the meaning of regulation 3 of the Utilities Contracts Regulations 1996 and the services to be provided under it are for the purposes of carrying out an activity specified in any Part of Schedule 1 to those Regulations in which the utility is specified;]

(e)   a contract under which a contracting authority engages a person to provide services to the public lying within its responsibility and under which the consideration given by the contracting authority consists of or includes the right to exploit the provision of the services;

['relevant State' means a member State or a State for the time being specified in Schedule 4 to these Regulations;]

['relevant subsidiary' has the same meaning as in Part IV of the Postal Services Act 2000;]

'restricted procedure' means a procedure leading to the award of a contract whereby only persons selected by the contracting authority may submit tenders for the contract;

['Schedule 3 entity' means an entity specified in Schedule 3 pursuant to its inclusion in the list of central government bodies in Annex I of the GPA, and for which these Regulations make particular provision;]

'services provider' has the meaning ascribed to it by regulation 4;

'working day' means a day other than a Saturday, Sunday or Bank Holiday within the meaning of the Banking and Financial Dealings Act 1971; and

'year' means a calendar year.

(2)   For the purposes of these regulations—

(a)   'a Part A services contract' is a contract under which services specified in Part A of Schedule 1 are to be provided;

(b)   'a Part B services contract' is a contract under which services specified in Part B of Schedule 1 are to be provided,

and, where services specified in both Parts A and B are to be provided under a single contract, then—

    (i)   the contract shall be treated as a Part A services contract if the value of the consideration attributable to the services specified in Part A is greater than that attributable to those specified in Part B; and

    (ii)   the contract shall be treated as a Part B services contract if the value of the consideration attributable to the services specified in Part B is equal to or greater than that attributable to those specified in Part A.

(3) . . .

(4)   Where a thing is required to be done under these Regulations—

(a)   within a period after an action is taken, the day on which that action was taken shall not be counted in the calculation of that period;

(b)   within a certain period, that period must include 2 working days;

(c)   within a period and the last day of that period is not a working day, the period shall be extended to include the following working day.

(5)   References in these Regulations to a regulation are references to a regulation in these Regulations and references to a Schedule are references to a Schedule to these Regulations.

Amendment

Para (1): definition 'ECU' (omitted) revoked by SI 2000/2009, reg 4(1)(a)(ii); in definition 'government department' words 'and any part of the Scottish Administration' in square brackets inserted by SI 1999/1042, art 3, Sch 1, para 21(1), (2)(a); definitions 'Government Procurement Agreement' and 'GPA' inserted by SI 2000/2009, reg 4(1)(a)(i); definition 'letter' inserted by SI 2001/1149, art 3(1), Sch 1, para 100(1), (2); in definition 'Minister of the Crown' words from 'and a reference' to 'the Scottish Ministers' in square brackets inserted by SI 1999/1042, art 3, Sch 1, para 21(1), (2)(b); in definition 'national of a relevant State' words 'relevant State' in square brackets in each place they occur substituted by SI 1995/201, reg 31(2)(b); definition 'postal business' inserted by SI 2001/1149, art 3(1), Sch 1, para 100(1), (2); definition 'postal services' inserted by SI 2001/1149, art 3(1), Sch 1, para 100(1), (2); definition 'the Post Office company' inserted by SI 2001/1149, art 3(1), Sch 1, para 100(1), (2); in definition 'public services contract' para (d) substituted by SI 1996/2911, reg 35(2)(a)(i); definition 'relevant State' inserted by SI 1995/201, reg 31(2)(a); definition 'relevant State' substituted by SI 2000/2009, reg 4(1)(a)(iii); definition 'relevant subsidiary' inserted by SI 2001/1149, art 3(1), Sch 1, para 100(1), (2); definition 'Schedule 3 entity' inserted by SI 2000/2009, reg 4(1)(a)(i).

Para (3): revoked by SI 2000/2009, reg 4(1)(b).

[App.65]

[3 Contracting authorities]

[(1)   For the purposes of these Regulations each of the following is a 'contracting authority'—

(a)   a Minister of the Crown,

(b)   a government department,

(c)   the House of Commons,

(d)   the House of Lords,

(e)   the Northern Ireland Assembly Commission,

(f)   the Scottish Parliamentary Body Corporate,

(g)   the National Assembly for Wales,

(h)   a local authority,

(i)   a fire authority constituted by a combination scheme under the Fire Services Act 1947,

(j)   the Fire Authority for Northern Ireland,

(k)   a police authority established under section 3 of the Police Act 1996,

(l)   a police authority established under section 2 of the Police (Scotland) Act 1967,

(m)   [the Northern Ireland Policing Board],

(n)   an authority established under section 10 of the Local Government Act 1985,

(o)   a joint authority established by Part IV of that Act,

(p)   any body established pursuant to an order under section 67 of that Act,

(q)   the Broads Authority,

(r)   any joint board the constituent members of which consist of any of the bodies specified in paragraphs (h), (i), (k), (l), (n), (o), (p) and (q), above,

(s)   a National Park authority established by an Order under section 63 of the Environment Act 1995,

(t)   the Receiver for the Metropolitan Police District,

(u)   a corporation established, or a group of individuals appointed to act together, for the specific purposes of meeting needs in the general interest, not having an industrial or commercial character, and—

    (i)   financed wholly or mainly by another contracting authority, or

    (ii)   subject to management supervision by another contracting authority, or

    (iii)   more than half of the board of directors or members of which, or, in the case of a group of individuals, more than half of those individuals, being appointed by another contracting authority,

(v)   an association of or formed by one or more of the above, and

(w)   to the extent not specified in sub-paragraphs (a) to (t) above, an entity specified in Schedule 3.

(2)   In the application of these Regulations to England, 'local authority' in paragraph (1) above means—

(a)   a county council, a district council, a London borough council, a parish council, a community council or the Council of the Isles of Scilly;

(b)   the Common Council of the City of London in its capacity as local authority or police authority.

(3)   In the application of these Regulations to Wales, 'local authority' in paragraph (1) above means a county council, county borough council or community council.

(4)   In the application of these Regulations to Scotland, 'local authority' in paragraph (1) above has the same meaning as in section 235(1) of the Local Government (Scotland) Act 1973 and also includes joint board or joint committee within the meaning of section 235(1).

(5)   In the application of these Regulations to Northern Ireland, 'local authority' in paragraph (1) above means a district council within the meaning of the Local Government Act (Northern Ireland) 1972.

(6)   Where an entity specified in paragraph (1) above does not have the capacity to enter into a contract, the contracting authority in relation to that entity is a person whose function it is to enter into contracts for that entity.]

Amendment
Substituted by SI 2000/2009, reg 4(2).
Para (1): in sub-para (m) words 'the Northern Ireland Police Board' in square brackets substituted by the Police (Northern Ireland) Act 2000, s 2(4), Sch 2, para 6(1).

[App.66]

4 Services providers

(1)   For the purposes of these Regulations, a 'services provider' means a person—
(a)   who sought, or who seeks, or who would have wished,
       (i)   to be the person to whom a public services contract is awarded, or
       (ii)   to participate in a design contest, and
[(b)   who is a national of and established in a relevant State].

(2)   When these Regulations apply a contracting authority shall not treat a person who is not a national of and established in a [relevant State] more favourably than one who is.

Amendment
Para (1): sub-para (b) substituted by SI 2000/2009, reg 4(3).

[App.67]

5 Application of the Regulations

(1)   Whenever a contracting authority seeks offers in relation to a proposed Part A services contract other than one excluded by virtue of regulation 6 or 7, these Regulations apply in their entirety.

(2)   Whenever a contracting authority seeks offers in relation to a proposed Part B services contract other than one excluded by virtue of regulation 6 or 7, Part I (General) and Part VII (Applications to the court) apply but only the following provisions in Parts II to VI apply—
       regulation 8 (Technical specifications in contract documents)
       regulation 22 (Contract award notices)
       regulation 27(2) (Statistical and other reports)
       regulation 28 (Responsibility for obtaining reports)
       regulation 29 (Publication of notices).

[App.68]

6 General exclusions

These Regulations shall not apply to the seeking of offers in relation to a proposed public services contract—
(a)   for the acquisition of land, including buildings and other structures, land covered with water, and any estate, interest, easement, servitude or right in or over land;
(b)   for the acquisition, development, production or co-production of programme material for radio or television by a broadcaster or for the purchase of broadcasting time;
(c)   for voice telephony, telex, radiotelephony, paging or satellite services;
(d)   for arbitration or conciliation services;
(e)   for financial services in connection with the issue, purchase, sale or transfer of securities or other financial instruments;
(f)   for central banking services;
(g)   for research and development services unless—
       (i)   the benefits are to accrue exclusively to the contracting authority for its use in the conduct of its own affairs, and
       (ii)   the services are to be wholly paid for by the contracting authority;
(h)   to which the provisions of Article 223 of the EEC Treaty apply;

(i)   which is classified as secret or where the carrying out of the services under it must be accompanied by special security measures in accordance with the laws, regulations or administrative provisions of any part of the United Kingdom or when the protection of the basic interests of the security of the United Kingdom require it;

(j)   where different procedures govern the procedures leading to the award of the contract and it is to be entered into—

    (i)   pursuant to an international agreement to which the United Kingdom and a State which is not a [relevant State] are parties and it provides for the provision of services intended for the joint implementation or exploitation of a project pursuant to that agreement;

    (ii)   pursuant to an international agreement relating to the stationing of troops; or

    (iii)   in accordance with the contract award procedures of an organisation of which only States are members (an 'international organisation') or of which only States or international organisations are members; or

(k)   under which services are to be provided by another contracting authority, or by a person which is a contracting authority in another [relevant State] for the purposes of Council Directive 92/50/EEC, because that contracting authority or person has an exclusive right—

    (i)   to provide the services, or

    (ii)   which is necessary for the provision of the services,

pursuant to any published law, regulation or administrative provision, which is compatible with the EEC Treaty.

Amendment
Paras (j), (k): words in square brackets substituted by SI 1995/201, reg 31(2)(b).

[App.69]

7 Thresholds

[(1)   These Regulations shall not apply to the seeking of offers in relation to a proposed public services contract where the estimated value of the contract (net of value added tax) at the relevant time is less than the relevant threshold, which, in relation to a Part A services contract, other than

(a)   a subsidised services contract under regulation 25,

(b)   a contract for research and development services specified in category 8 of Schedule 1, or

(c)   a contract for telecommunication services specified under CPC references 7524, 7525 and 7526 within category 5 of Schedule 1, Part A,
    shall be—

    (i)   in the case of offers sought by Schedule 3 entities the euro equivalent of 130,000 special drawing rights; and

    (ii)   in the case of offers sought by any other contracting authority the euro equivalent of 200,000 special drawing rights;

and in relation to any other public services contract shall be 200,000 euro.]

[(1A)   The value in pounds sterling of any amount expressed in these Regulations in euro or in the euro equivalent of special drawing rights shall be calculated by reference to the rate for the time being applying for the purposes of Council Directive 92/50/EEC as published from time to time in the Official Journal.]

(2) Subject to paragraphs (3) to (11) below, the estimated value for the purposes of paragraph (1) above of a public services contract shall be the value of the consideration which the contracting authority expects to give under the contract.

(3) In determining the value of the consideration which the contracting authority expects to give under a public services contract it shall, where appropriate, take account of—

(a) the premium payable for insurance services,

(b) the fees, commissions or other remuneration payable for banking and financial services, and

(c) the fees or commissions payable for design services.

(4) Subject to paragraphs (5) and (8) below, where a contracting authority has a single requirement for services and a number of public services contracts have been entered or are to be entered into to fulfil that requirement the estimated value for the purposes of paragraph (1) above of each public services contract shall be the aggregate of the value of the consideration which the contracting authority expects to give under each of those contracts.

(5) Paragraph (4) above shall not apply to any public services contract (unless the contracting authority chooses to apply that paragraph to that contract) if that contract has an estimated value (calculated in accordance with paragraph (2) above) of less than 80,000 ECU and the aggregate value of that contract and of any other contract in respect of which the contracting authority takes advantage of the disapplication of paragraph (4) above by virtue of this paragraph is less than 20 per cent of the aggregate of the value of the consideration which the contracting authority has given or expects to give under all the contracts entered or to be entered into to fulfil the requirement.

(6) Subject to paragraph (8) below, where a contracting authority has a requirement over a period for services of the type to be provided under the public services contract and for that purpose enters into—

(a) a series of contracts, or

(b) a contract which under its terms is renewable,

the estimated value of the contract for the purposes of paragraph (1) above shall be the amount calculated under paragraph (7) below.

(7) The contracting authority shall calculate the amount referred to in paragraph (6) above either—

(a) by taking the aggregate of the value of the consideration given by the contracting authority under public services contracts which have similar characteristics and which were for the provision of services of the type to be provided under the contract, during its last financial year ending before, or during the period of 12 months ending immediately before, the relevant time and by adjusting that amount to take account of any expected changes in the quantity and cost of the services in the period of 12 months commencing with the relevant time, or

(b) by estimating the aggregate of the value of the consideration which the contracting authority expects to give under such contracts which have similar characteristics and which are for the provision of services of the type to be provided under the contract during the period of 12 months from the first date on which the services will be performed or, where the contract is for a definite term of more than 12 months, during the term of the contract.

(8) Notwithstanding paragraphs (4) and (6) above, when the services to be provided under the contract are required the sole purpose of a discrete operational unit within the organisation of the contracting authority and—

(a)   the decision whether to enter the contract has been devolved to such a unit, and

(b)   that decision is taken independently of any other part of the contracting authority,

the valuation methods described in paragraphs (4) and (7) above shall be adapted by aggregating only the value of the consideration which the contracting authority has given or expects to give, as the case may be, under contracts for the provision of services which were or are required for the sole purposes of that unit.

(9)   The estimated value for the purposes of paragraph (1) above of a public services contract under which services are to be provided over a period exceeding 4 years or over an indefinite period shall be the value of the consideration which the contracting authority expects to give in respect of each month of the period multiplied by 48.

(10)   Where a public services contract includes one or more options the estimated value of the contract for the purposes of paragraph (1) above shall be determined by calculating the highest possible consideration which could be given under the contract.

(11)   A contracting authority shall not enter into separate public services contracts nor select nor exercise a choice under a valuation method in accordance with paragraph (7) above with the intention of avoiding the application of these Regulations to those contracts.

(12)   The relevant time for the purposes of paragraphs (1) and (7)(a) above means the date on which a contract notice would be sent to the Official Journal if the requirement to send such a notice applied to that contract in accordance with these Regulations.

Amendment
Para (1): substituted by SI 2000/2009, reg 4(4).
Para (1A): inserted by SI 2000/2009, reg 4(5).

PART II
TECHNICAL SPECIFICATIONS

[App.70]
8 Technical specifications in contract documents

(1)   In this regulation—
'common technical specification' means a technical specification drawn up in accordance with a procedure recognised by the member States with a view to uniform application in all member States and which has been published in the Official Journal;
'essential requirements' means requirements relating to safety, health and certain other aspects in the general interest which the services must meet;
'European specification' means a common technical specification, a British standard implementing a European standard or a European technical approval;
'European standard' means a standard approved by the European Committee for Standardisation ('CEN') or by the European Committee for Electrotechnical Standardisation ('CENELEC') as a 'European Standard ('EN')' or a 'Harmonisation Document ('HD')' according to the Common Rules of those organisations, or by the European Telecommunications Standards Institute ('ETSI') as a 'European Telecommunications Standard ('ETS')';

'European technical approval' means an approval of the fitness for use of a product, issued by an approval body designated for the purpose by a member State, following a technical assessment of whether the product fulfils the essential requirements for building works, having regard to the inherent characteristics of the product and the defined conditions of application and use;

'standard' means a technical specification approved by a recognised standardising body for repeated and continuous application, compliance with which is in principle not compulsory;

'technical specifications' means the technical requirements defining the characteristics required of the work or works and of the materials and goods used in or for it or them (such as quality, performance, safety or dimensions) so that the works, work, materials and goods are described objectively in a manner which will ensure that they fulfil the use for which they are intended by the contracting authority. In relation to materials and goods, 'technical specifications' include requirements in respect of quality assurance, terminology, symbols, tests and testing methods, packaging, marking and labelling. In relation to a work or works, they include requirements relating to design and costing, the testing, inspection and acceptance of a work or works, and the methods or techniques of construction.

(2)   If a contracting authority wishes to lay down technical specifications which the services to be provided under a public services contract and which the materials and goods used in or for it must meet it shall specify all such technical specifications in the contract documents.

(3)   Subject to paragraph (4) below, the technical specifications in the contract documents relating to a public services contract shall be defined by reference to any European specifications which are relevant.

(4)   A contracting authority may define the technical specifications referred to in paragraph (3) above other than by reference to relevant European specifications if—

(a)   the contracting authority is under an obligation to define the technical specifications by reference to technical requirements which are mandatory in the United Kingdom for the services to be provided under the contract or for the materials or goods to be used in or for it (but only to the extent that such an obligation is compatible with Community obligations);

(b)   the relevant European specifications do not include provision for establishing conformity to, or it is technically impossible to establish satisfactorily that the services or the material or goods do conform to, the relevant European specifications;

(c)   definition by reference to European specifications would conflict with the application of—

(i)   Council Directive 86/361/EEC on the initial stage of the mutual recognition of type approval for telecommunications terminal equipment,

(ii)   Council Decision 87/95/EEC on standardisation in the field of information technology and telecommunications, or

(iii)   other Community instruments relating to specific types of services, material or goods;

(d)   subject to paragraph (5) below, application of the relevant European specifications would oblige the contracting authority to use material or goods incompatible with equipment already in use or would entail disproportionate costs or disproportionate technical difficulties; or

(e)   the project is of a genuinely innovative nature for which use of existing relevant European specifications would be inappropriate.

(5)   A contracting authority may only define the technical specifications other than by reference to relevant European specifications on the grounds specified in paragraph (4)(d) above where the contracting authority has a clearly defined and recorded strategy for changing over, within a set period, to European specifications.

(6)   A contracting authority shall state in the contract notice which of the circumstances specified in paragraph (4)(b) to (e) above was the ground for defining the technical specifications other than by reference to European specifications or, if it is impossible to include this information in the contract notice or it is a proposed Part B services contract, the contracting authority shall specify it in the contract documents and shall in any event keep a record of this information which, if the Commission or any [relevant State] requests it, it shall send to the Treasury for onward transmission to the Commission or [relevant State] which requested it.

(7)   In the absence of European specifications relevant to the services to be provided under a public services contract or to the materials or goods to be used in or for it, the technical specifications in the contract documents—

(a)   shall be defined by reference to the British technical specifications recognised as complying with the basic requirements specified in any Council Directive on technical harmonisation in accordance with the procedures laid down in those directives and, in particular, in accordance with the procedures laid down in Council Directive 89/106/EEC on the approximation of laws, regulations and administrative procedures in the member States relating to construction products;

(b)   may be defined by reference to British technical specifications relating to design and method of calculation and execution of a work or works and use of materials and goods;

(c)   may be defined by reference to the following standards (and, if they are so defined, preference shall be given to the following standards in the order in which they are listed)—

    (i)   British standards implementing international standards;

    (ii)   other British standards and technical approvals; or

    (iii)   any other standards.

(8)   Subject to paragraph (10) below, the contract documents shall not include technical specifications which refer to materials or goods of a specific make or source or to a particular process and which have the effect of favouring or eliminating particular services providers.

(9)   Without prejudice to the generality of paragraph (8) above, references to trademarks, patents, types, origin or means of production shall not be incorporated into the technical specifications in the contract documents.

(10)   Notwithstanding paragraph (8) or (9) above, a contracting authority may incorporate the references referred to in paragraphs (8) and (9) above into the technical specifications in the contract documents if—

(a)   such references are justified by the subject of the contract, or

(b)   the subject of the contract cannot otherwise be described by reference to technical specifications which are sufficiently precise and intelligible to all services providers, provided that the references are accompanied by the words 'or equivalent'.

Amendment
Para (6): words in square brackets substituted by SI 1995/201, reg 31(2)(b).

PART III
PROCEDURES LEADING TO THE AWARD OF A PUBLIC SERVICES CONTRACT

[App.71]
9 Prior information notices

(1)   Subject to paragraph (2) below, a contracting authority shall, as soon as possible after the commencement of each of its financial years, send to the Official Journal a notice, in a form substantially corresponding to that set out in Part A of Schedule 2 and containing the information therein specified, in respect of the public services contracts in relation to which it expects to seek offers leading to an award during that financial year and the notice shall be subdivided to give that information separately for each category of services specified in Part A of Schedule 1.

(2)   The obligation under paragraph (1) above shall only apply—
(a)   to proposed Part A services contracts which are not excluded from the application of these Regulations by virtue of regulation 6 or 7; and
(b)   where, at the date of despatch of the notice, the total consideration which the contracting authority expects to give under all the proposed public services contracts for the provision of services falling within the same category specified in Part A of Schedule 1, equals or exceeds 750,000 ECU.

[App.72]
10 Selection of contract award procedure

(1)   For the purposes of seeking offers in relation to a proposed public services contract a contracting authority shall use the open procedure, the restricted procedure or the negotiated procedure and shall decide which of those procedures to use in accordance with the following paragraphs of this regulation.

(2)   A contracting authority may use the negotiated procedure in the following circumstances—
(a)   subject to paragraph (3) below, in the event that the procedure leading to the award of a contract by the contracting authority using the open or restricted procedure was discontinued—
  (i)   because of irregular tenders, or
  (ii)   following an evaluation made in accordance with regulation 11(8) or 12(4),
  and, without prejudice to the generality of the meaning of the words 'irregular tenders', a tender may be considered irregular if the services provider fails to meet the requirements of, or the tender offers variations on the requirements specified in, the contract documents where this is not permitted under the terms of the invitation to tender, or the services, materials or goods offered do not meet the technical specifications (within the meaning of regulation 8(1) above) of the contracting authority;
(b)   exceptionally, when the nature of the services to be provided, or the risks attaching thereto, are such as not to permit prior overall pricing;
(c)   when the nature of the services to be provided, in particular in the case of intellectual services or services specified in category 6 of Part A of Schedule 1, is such that specifications cannot be drawn up with sufficient precision to permit the award of the contract using the open or restricted procedure;

(d)   subject to paragraph (3) below, in the absence of tenders or of appropriate tenders in response to an invitation to tender by the contracting authority using the open or restricted procedure;

(e)   when, for technical or artistic reasons, or for reasons connected with the protection of exclusive rights, the services to be provided may only be provided by a particular person;

(f)   when the rules of a design contest require the contract to be awarded to the successful contestant or to one of the successful contestants, provided that all successful contestants are invited to negotiate the contract;

(g)   when (but only if it is strictly necessary) for reasons of extreme urgency brought about by events unforeseeable by, and not attributable to, the contracting authority, the time limits specified in regulations 11 and 12 if the open or restricted procedure is used, or the time limits specified in regulation 13 if the negotiated procedure is used pursuant to paragraph (2)(a) to (c) above, cannot be met;

(h)   subject to paragraph (4) below, when a contracting authority wants a person who has entered into a public services contract with the contracting authority to provide additional services which were not included in the project initially considered or in the original services contract but which through unforeseen circumstances have become necessary, and—

    (i)   such services cannot for technical or economic reasons be provided separately from the services provided under the original contract without great inconvenience to the contracting authority, or

    (ii)   such services can be provided separately from the services provided under the original contract but are strictly necessary to the performance of that contract; and

(i)   subject to paragraph (5) below, when a contracting authority wishes a person who has entered into a public services contract with it to provide new services which are a repetition of services provided under the original contract and which are in accordance with the project for the purpose of which the first contract was entered into.

(3)   A contracting authority shall not use the negotiated procedure pursuant to paragraph (2)(a) or (d) above unless the proposed terms of the contract are substantially unaltered from the proposed terms of the contract in relation to which offers were sought using the open or restricted procedure.

(4)   A contracting authority shall not use the negotiated procedure pursuant to paragraph (2)(h) above where the aggregate value of the consideration to be given under contracts for the additional services exceeds 50 per cent of the value of the consideration payable under the original contract; and, for the purposes of this paragraph, the value of the consideration shall be taken to include the estimated value of any goods which the contracting authority provided to the person awarded the contract for the purpose of carrying out the contract.

(5)   A contracting authority shall not use the negotiated procedure pursuant to paragraph (2)(i) above unless the contract notice relating to the original contract stated that a services contract for new services which would be a repetition of the services provided under the original contract may be awarded using the negotiated procedure pursuant to paragraph (2)(i) above and unless the procedure for the award of the new contract is commenced within three years of the original contract being entered into.

(6)   In all other circumstances the contracting authority shall use the open procedure or restricted procedure.

(7)   A contracting authority using the negotiated procedure pursuant to paragraph (2)(d) above shall, if the Commission requests it, submit a report recording the fact that it has done so to the Treasury for onward transmission to the Commission.

[App.73]

11 The open procedure

(1)   A contracting authority using the open procedure shall comply with the following paragraphs of this regulation.

(2)   The contracting authority shall publicise its intention to seek offers in relation to the public services contract by sending to the Official Journal as soon as possible after forming the intention a notice, in a form substantially corresponding to that set out in Part B of Schedule 2, inviting tenders and containing the information therein specified.

(3)   Subject to paragraph (4) below, the date which the contracting authority shall fix as the last date for the receipt by it of tenders made in response to the contract notice shall be specified in the contract notice and shall be not less than 52 days from the date of despatch of the notice.

[(4)   Where—
(a)   the contracting authority has published a prior information notice in accordance with regulation 9 above;
(b)   the prior information notice contained as much of the information referred to in Part B of Schedule 2 as was available at the time of publication; and
(c)   the prior information notice was sent to the Official Journal at least 52 days and no more than 12 months before the date on which the contract notice provided for in regulation 11(2) is despatched—

the contracting authority may substitute for the period of not less than 52 days specified in paragraph (3) above, a shorter period of generally no less than 36 days and in any event no less than 22 days, provided in each case that the period is sufficient to allow for effective tendering.]

(5)   The contracting authority shall send the contract documents within 6 days of the receipt of a request from any services provider provided that the documents are requested in good time and any fee specified in the contract notice has accompanied the request.

(6)   The contracting authority shall supply such further information relating to the contract documents as may reasonably be requested by a services provider provided that the request is received in sufficient time to enable the contracting authority to supply the information no later than 6 days before the date specified in the contract notice as the final date for the receipt of tenders.

(7)   If the contract documents are too bulky to be supplied within the periods referred to in paragraphs (5) or (6) above or it is necessary that services providers be given the opportunity to inspect the site in relation to which the services are to be provided or documents relating to the contract documents, then the minimum periods referred to in paragraphs (3) and (4) above shall be extended to allow for such supply or inspection.

(8)   The contracting authority may exclude a tender from the evaluation of offers made in accordance with regulation 21 only if the services provider may be treated as ineligible to tender on a ground specified in regulation 14 or if the services provider fails to satisfy the minimum standards of economic and financial standing, ability and technical capacity required of services providers by the contracting authority;

for this purpose the contracting authority shall make its evaluation in accordance with regulations 14, 15, 16 and 17.

[(9)   Tenders shall be submitted in writing either in person or by post, except that a contracting authority may authorise another means of submission provided that the chosen means enables—

(a)   each tender to contain all the information necessary for its evaluation;

(b)   the confidentiality of tenders to be maintained pending their evaluation; and

(c)   tenders to be opened only after the time limit for their submission has expired.

(10)   Where a contracting authority has authorised another means of submission in accordance with paragraph (9) above, it may require either that the submission of the tender is confirmed in writing or that a copy of the tender is delivered to it in person or by post, in either case as soon as possible after the submission of the tender by another means.]

Amendment
Para (4): substituted by SI 2000/2009, reg 4(6).
Paras (9), (10): inserted by SI 2000/2009, reg 4(7).

[App.74]

12 The restricted procedure

(1)   A contracting authority using the restricted procedure shall comply with the following paragraphs of this regulation.

(2)   The contracting authority shall publicise its intention to seek offers in relation to the public services contract by sending to the Official Journal as soon as possible after forming the intention a notice, in a form substantially corresponding to that set out in Part C of Schedule 2, inviting requests to be selected to tender and containing the information therein specified.

(3)   Subject to paragraph (15) below, the date which the contracting authority shall fix as the last date for the receipt by it of requests to be selected to tender shall be specified in the contract notice and shall not be less than 37 days from the date of the despatch of the notice.

(4)   The contracting authority may exclude a services provider from those persons from whom it will make the selection of persons to be invited to tender only if the services provider may be treated as ineligible on a ground specified in regulation 14 or if the services provider fails to satisfy the minimum standards of economic and financial standing, ability and technical capacity required of services providers by the contracting authority; for this purpose the contracting authority shall make its evaluation in accordance with regulations 14, 15, 16 and 17.

(5)   The contracting authority shall make the selection of the services providers to be invited to tender in accordance with regulations 14, 15, 16 and 17; and in making the selection and in issuing invitations the contracting authority shall not discriminate between services providers on the grounds of their nationality or the [relevant State] in which they are established.

(6)   The contracting authority may predetermine the range within which the number of persons which it intends to invite to tender for the contract shall be fixed but only if—

(a)   the lower number of the range is not less than 5 and the higher number not more than 20,

(b)   the range is determined in the light of the nature of the services to be provided under the contract, and

(c)   the range is specified in the contract notice.

(7)   The number of persons invited to tender shall be sufficient to ensure genuine competition.

(8)   The contracting authority shall send invitations to each of the services providers selected to tender and the invitation shall be accompanied by the contract documents, or the invitation shall state the address for requesting them.

(9)   The invitation shall be sent in writing simultaneously to each services provider selected to tender.

(10)   The following information shall be included in the invitation—

(a)   the address to which requests for the contract documents (if not accompanying the invitation) and further information relating to those documents should be sent, the final date for making such a request and the amount and terms of the fee which may be charged for supplying that material;

(b)   the final date for the receipt of tenders, the address to which they must be sent and the language or languages in which they must be drawn up;

(c)   a reference to the contract notice published in accordance with paragraph (2) above;

(d)   an indication of the information to be included with the tender which the contracting authority may require to be provided in accordance with regulations 15, 16 and 17; and

(e)   the criteria for the award of the contract if this information was not specified in the contract notice published in accordance with paragraph (2) above.

(11)   Subject to paragraphs (12) and (15) below, the date which the contracting authority shall fix as the last date for the receipt by it of tenders made in response to the invitation to tender which shall be specified in the invitation to tender in accordance with paragraph (10)(b) above shall not be less than 40 days from the date of the despatch of the invitation.

[(12)   Subject to paragraph (15) below, where—

(a)   the contracting authority has published a prior information notice in accordance with regulation 9 above;

(b)   the prior information notice contained as much of the information referred to in Part C (or, if appropriate, Part D) of Schedule 2 as was available at the time of publication; and

(c)   the prior information notice was sent to the Official Journal at least 52 days and no more than 12 months before the date on which the contract notice provided for in regulation 12(2) is despatched;

the contracting authority may substitute for the period of not less than 40 days in paragraph (11) above, a period of not less than 26 days.]

(13)   If it is necessary that services providers should be given the opportunity to inspect the site in relation to which the services under the contract are to be provided or documents relating to the contract documents, then the minimum periods referred to in paragraphs (11) and (12) above shall be extended to allow for such inspection.

(14)   Subject to paragraph (15) below, the contracting authority shall supply such further information relating to the contract documents as may reasonably be requested by a services provider selected to tender provided that the request for such information is received in sufficient time to enable the contracting authority to supply it not less than 6 days before the date specified in the invitation to tender as the final date for the receipt of tenders.

(15)   Where compliance with the minimum periods referred to in paragraphs (3), (11), (12) and (14) above is rendered impracticable for reasons of urgency, the contracting authority may substitute for the period specified in paragraph (3) a period of not less than 15 days and for the periods specified in paragraphs (11) and (12) periods of not less than 10 days and for the period specified in paragraph (14) a period of not less than 4 days and, in those circumstances, the contracting authority must send the invitation to tender by the most rapid means possible.

(16)   A contracting authority shall not refuse to consider an application to be invited to tender for a contract if it is made by letter, telegram, telex, facsimile or telephone provided that, in the last 4 cases, it is confirmed by letter despatched before the date fixed by the contracting authority as the last date for the receipt of applications to be invited to tender for the contract.

[(17)   Tenders shall be submitted in writing either in person or by post, except that a contracting authority may authorise another means of submission provided that the chosen means enables—

(a)   each tender to contain all the information necessary for its evaluation;
(b)   the confidentiality of tenders to be maintained pending their evaluation; and
(c)   tenders to be opened only after the time limit for their submission has expired.

(18)   Where a contracting authority has authorised another means of submission in accordance with paragraph (17) above, it may require either that the submission of the tender is confirmed in writing or that a copy of the tender is delivered to it in person or by post, in either case as soon as possible after the submission of the tender by another means.]

Amendment
Para (5): words in square brackets substituted by SI 1995/201, reg 31(2)(b).
Para (12): substituted by SI 2000/2009, reg 4(8).
Paras (17), (18): inserted by SI 2000/2009, reg 4(9).

[App.75]

13 The negotiated procedure

(1)   A contracting authority using the negotiated procedure shall comply with the following provisions of this regulation except that—

(a)   a contracting authority using the negotiated procedure pursuant to regulation 10(2)(d) to (i), and
(b)   a contracting authority using the negotiated procedure pursuant to regulation 10(2)(a) who invites to negotiate the contract every services provider who submitted a tender following an invitation made during the course of the discontinued open or restricted procedure (not being a tender which was excluded pursuant to regulation 11(8) or 12(4)),

need not comply with paragraphs (2) to (6) below.

(2)   The contracting authority shall publicise its intention to seek offers in relation to the contract by sending to the Official Journal as soon as possible after forming the intention a notice, in a form substantially corresponding to that set out in Part D of Schedule 2, inviting requests to be selected to negotiate and containing the information therein specified.

(3)   Subject to paragraph (4) below, the date which the contracting authority shall fix as the last date for the receipt by it of requests to be selected to negotiate shall be specified in the contract notice and shall be not less than 37 days from the date of despatch of the notice.

(4)   Where compliance with the minimum period of 37 days in paragraph (3) above is rendered impracticable for reasons of urgency, the contracting authority may substitute a period of not less than 15 days and, in those circumstances, the contracting authority must send the invitation to negotiate the contract by the most rapid means possible.

(5)   Where there is a sufficient number of persons who are suitable to be selected to negotiate the contract, the number selected to negotiate the contract shall not be less than 3.

(6)   A contracting authority shall not refuse to consider an application to be selected to negotiate if it is made by letter, telegram, telex, facsimile or by telephone provided that, in the last 4 cases, it is confirmed by letter before the date fixed by the contracting authority as the last date for the receipt of requests to be selected to negotiate.

(7)   The contracting authority may exclude a services provider from those persons from whom it will make the selection of persons to be invited to negotiate the contract only if the services provider may be treated as ineligible on a ground specified in regulation 14 or if the services provider fails to satisfy the minimum standards of economic and financial standing, ability and technical capacity required of services providers by the contracting authority; for this purpose the contracting authority shall make its evaluation in accordance with regulations 14, 15, 16 and 17 below.

(8)   The contracting authority shall make the selection of the services providers to be invited to negotiate in accordance with regulations 14, 15, 16 and 17; and in making the selection and in issuing invitations to negotiate the contracting authority shall not discriminate between services providers on the grounds of their nationality or the [relevant State] in which they are established.

Amendment
Para (8): words in square brackets substituted by SI 1995/201, reg 31(2)(b).

PART IV
SELECTION OF SERVICES PROVIDERS

[App.76]
14 Criteria for rejection of services providers
(1)   A contracting authority may treat a services provider as ineligible to tender for, or to be included amongst those persons from whom it will make the selection of persons to be invited to tender for or to negotiate a contract in accordance with regulations 11(8), 12(4), and 13(7) above, or decide not to select a services provider to tender for or to negotiate a contract in accordance with regulations 12(5) and 13(8) above on one of the following grounds, namely that the services provider—
(a)   being an individual is bankrupt or has had a receiving order or administration order made against him or has made any composition or arrangement with or for the benefit of his creditors or has made any conveyance or assignment for the benefit of his creditors or appears unable to pay, or to have no reasonable prospect of being able to pay, a debt within the meaning of section 268 of the Insolvency Act 1986, or article 242 of the Insolvency (Northern Ireland) Order 1989, or in Scotland has granted a trust deed for creditors or become otherwise apparently insolvent, or is the subject of a petition presented for sequestration

of his estate, or is the subject of any similar procedure under the law of any other state;

(b)   being a partnership constituted under Scots law has granted a trust deed or become otherwise apparently insolvent, or is the subject of a petition presented for sequestration of its estate;

(c)   being a company has passed a resolution or is the subject of an order by the court for the company's winding up otherwise than for the purposes of bona fide reconstruction or amalgamation, or has had a receiver, manager or administrator on behalf of a creditor appointed in respect of the company's business or any part thereof or is the subject of proceedings for any of the above procedures or is the subject of similar procedures under the law of any other state;

(d)   has been convicted of a criminal offence relating to the conduct of his business or profession;

(e)   has committed an act of grave misconduct in the course of his business or profession;

(f)   has not fulfilled obligations relating to the payment of social security contributions under the law of any part of the United Kingdom or of the [relevant State] in which the services provider is established;

(g)   has not fulfilled obligations relating to the payment of taxes under the law of any part of the United Kingdom;

(h)   is guilty of serious misrepresentation in providing any information required of him under this regulation and regulations 15, 16 and 17;

(i)   is not licensed in the [relevant State] in which he is established or is not a member of an organisation in that [relevant State] when the law of that [relevant State] prohibits the provision of the services to be provided under the contract by a person who is not so licensed or who is not such a member; or

(j)   subject to paragraphs (5) and (6) below, is not registered on the professional or trade register of the [relevant State] in which he is established under conditions laid down by that State.

(2)   Subject to regulation 18, the contracting authority may require a services provider to provide such information as it considers it needs to make the evaluation in accordance with paragraph (1) above except that it shall accept as conclusive evidence that a services provider does not fall within the grounds specified in paragraph (1)(a), (b), (c), (d), (f) or (g) above if that services provider provides to the contracting authority—

(a)   in relation to the grounds specified in paragraph (1)(a), (b), (c) or (d) above,
      (i)   an extract from the judicial record, or
      (ii)   in a [relevant State] which does not maintain such a judicial record, a document issued by the relevant judicial or administrative authority;

(b)   in relation to the grounds specified in paragraph (1)(f) or (g) above, a certificate issued by the relevant competent authority; and

(c)   in a [relevant State] where the documentary evidence specified in paragraphs (2)(a) and (b) above is not issued in relation to one of the grounds specified in paragraph (1)(a), (b), (c), (d), (f) or (g) above, a declaration on oath made by the services provider before the relevant judicial, administrative or competent authority or a relevant notary public or commissioner for oaths.

(3)   In this regulation, 'relevant' in relation to a judicial, administrative or competent authority, notary public or commissioner for oaths means an authority designated by, or a notary public or commissioner for oaths in, the [relevant State] in which the services provider is established.

(4)   The following are the appropriate professional or trade registers for the purposes of paragraph (1)(j) above—

[in Austria, the Firmenbuch, Gewerberegister or Mitgliederverzeichnisse der Landeskammern;]

in Belgium, the registre du commerce/Handelsregister or the ordres professionels - Beroepsorden;

in Denmark, the Erhvervs- and Selskabstyrelsen;

[in Finland, the Kaupparekisteri or Handelsregistret;]

in France, the registre du commerce or the repertoire des metiers;

in Germany, the Handelsregister, the Handwerksrolle or the Vereinsregister;

[in Iceland, the Firmaskra or Hlutafelagaskra;]

in Italy, the Registro della Camera di commercio, industria, agricultura e artigianato, the Registro delle commissioni provinciali per l'artiginiato or the Consiglio nazionale degli ordini professionali;

in Luxembourg, the registre aux firmes and the role de la Chambre des metiers;

in the Netherlands, the Handelsregister;

[in Norway, the Foretaksregisteret;]

in Portugal, the Registo nacional das Pessoas Colectivas; and

in Spain, the Registro Central de Empresas Consultoras y de Servicios del Ministerio de Economia y Hacienda.

[in Sweden, the Aktiebolagsregistret, Handelsregistret or Föreningsregistret;]

(5)   A services provider established in the United Kingdom or Ireland shall be treated as registered on the professional or trade register for the purposes of paragraph (1)(j) above if the services provider—

(a)   is established in Ireland and is certified as registered with the Registrar of Friendly Societies, or

(b)   is established in either State and is either—

    (i)   certified as incorporated by the Registrar of Companies, or

    (ii)   is certified as having declared on oath that he is carrying on business in the trade in question in the State in which he is established at a specific place of business and under a specific trading name.

(6)   A services provider established in Greece shall be treated as registered on the professional or trade register for the purposes of paragraph (1)(j) above—

(a)   when the services to be provided under the contract are specified in paragraph 8 of Schedule 1 and when Greek legislation requires persons who provide those services to be registered on the professional register 'Mhtrwo Melethtwn' and 'Mhtrwo Grafeiwn Meletwn', if he is registered on that register; and

[(b)   in any other case, in accordance with paragraph (7) below].

[(7)   A services provider established in a relevant State, other than the United Kingdom or Ireland, which either has an equivalent professional or trade register which is not listed in paragraph (4) above or which does not have an equivalent professional or trade register shall be treated as registered on a professional or trade register for the purposes of paragraph 1(j) above on production of either a certificate that he is registered on the equivalent professional or trade register or where no such register exists, a declaration on oath, or in a relevant State which does not provide for a declaration on oath a solemn declaration, made by the services provider before the relevant judicial, administrative or competent authority or a relevant notary public or Commissioner for oaths, that he exercises the particular profession or trade.]

Amendment
Paras (1)–(3): words in square brackets substituted by SI 1995/201, reg 31(2)(b).

Para (4): entries in square brackets inserted by SI 1995/201, reg 31(2)(c).
Para (6): sub-para (b) substituted by SI 1995/201, reg 31(2)(d).
Para (7): inserted by SI 1995/201, reg 31(2)(e).

[App.77]
15 Information as to economic and financial standing

(1)   Subject to regulation 18 and paragraph (2) below, in assessing whether a services provider meets any minimum standards of economic and financial standing required of services providers by the contracting authority for the purposes of regulations 11(8), 12(4) and 13(7), and in selecting the services providers to be invited to tender for or to negotiate the contract in accordance with regulations 12(5) and 13(8), a contracting authority shall only take into account any of the following information (and it may require a services provider to provide such of the information as it considers it needs to make the assessment or selection)—

(a)   appropriate statements from the services provider's bankers, or evidence of relevant professional risk indemnity insurance;

(b)   statement of accounts or extracts therefrom relating to the business of the services provider where publication of the statement is required under the law of the [relevant State] in which the services provider is established;

(c)   a statement of the overall turnover of the business of the services provider and the turnover in respect of the provision of services of the type to be provided under the proposed services contract in the 3 previous financial years of the services provider.

(2)   Where the information specified in paragraph (1) above is not appropriate in a particular case a contracting authority may require a services provider to provide other information to demonstrate the services provider's economic and financial standing.

(3)   A contracting authority which requires information to be provided in accordance with paragraphs (1) and (2) above shall specify in the contract notice or in the invitation to tender the information which the services provider must provide.

(4)   Where a services provider is unable for a valid reason to provide the information which the contracting authority has required, the contracting authority shall accept such other information provided by the services provider as the contracting authority considers appropriate.

Amendment
Para (1): words in square brackets in sub-para (b) substituted by SI 1995/201, reg 31(2)(b).

[App.78]
16 Information as to ability and technical capacity

(1)   Subject to regulation 18, in assessing whether or not a services provider meets any minimum standards of ability and technical capacity required of services providers by the contracting authority for the purposes of regulations 11(8), 12(4) and 13(7), and in selecting the services providers to be invited to tender for or to negotiate the contract in accordance with regulations 12(5) and 13(8), a contracting authority may have regard to—

(a)   the services provider's ability, taking into account in particular his skills, efficiency, experience and reliability; and

(b)   his technical capacity, taking into account any of the following—

(i)   the services provider's educational and professional qualifications where the services provider is an individual and the qualifications of the services provider's managerial staff if any and those of the person or persons who would be responsible for providing the services under the contract;

(ii) the principal services provided by the services provider of a similar type to the services to be provided under the contract in the past 3 years, the dates on which the services were provided, the consideration received and the identity of the person to whom the services were provided, any certificate issued or countersigned by that person confirming the details of the services provided or, but only where that person was not a contracting authority, any declaration by the services provider attesting the details of the services provided;

(iii) the technicians or technical bodies who would be involved in the provision of the services under the contract, particularly those responsible for quality control, whether or not they are independent of the services provider;

(iv) the services provider's average annual manpower and the number of managerial staff over the previous 3 years;

(v) the tools, plant and technical equipment available to the services provider for providing the services under the contract;

(vi) the services provider's measures for ensuring quality and his study and research facilities in relation to the services to be provided under the contract;

(vii) where the services to be provided under the contract are complex or are required for a special purpose, any check, carried out by the contracting authority or on its behalf by a competent official body of the [relevant State] in which the services provider is established, on the technical capacity of the services provider in relation to the services to be provided under the contract and, if relevant, on the services provider's study and research facilities and quality control measures;

(viii) any certificate that the services of the services provider to be provided under the contract conform to BS 5750 or any certificate of an independent body established in any [relevant State] conforming to the EN 45 000 European standards series attesting conformity to relevant quality assurance standards based on the EN 29 000 series, or where the services provider has no access to such a certificate, or cannot obtain such a certificate within the relevant time limits, any other evidence of conformity to equivalent quality assurance standards;

(ix) any proportion of the contract which the services provider intends to sub-contract to another person.

(2) The contracting authority shall specify in the contract notice or in the invitation to tender or to negotiate what information, for the purposes of making the assessment or selection for the purposes of paragraph (1) above, it requires to be provided and it may require a services provider to provide such of that information as it considers it needs to make the assessment or selection.

Amendment
Para (1): words in square brackets in sub-para (b) substituted by SI 1995/201, reg 31(2)(b).

[App.79]
17 Supplementary information

The contracting authority may require a services provider to provide information supplementing the information supplied in accordance with regulations 14, 15 and

16 or to clarify that information, provided that the information so required relates to the matters specified in regulations 14, 15 and 16.

[App.80]

18 Official lists of recognised services providers

Where a services provider is registered on the official list of recognised services providers in a [relevant State] which maintains such lists and in which the services provider is established and the services provider submits to the contracting authority a certificate of registration issued by the authority administering the official lists which specifies the information submitted to that authority which enabled the services provider to be registered and which states the classification given, the contracting authority, to the extent that the certificate deals with the grounds referred to in regulations 14(1)(a) to (e) and (h) to (j), 15(1)(b) and (c) and 16(1)(b)(i)—

(a)   shall accept the certificate as evidence that the services provider does not fall within the grounds specified in regulation 14(1)(a) to (e) and (h) to (j) and shall not be entitled to require the services provider to submit such information relating to those grounds as is specified in regulation 14,

(b)   shall not be entitled to require the services provider to provide information specified in regulations 15(1)(b) and (c) and 16(1)(b)(i), and

(c)   shall not be entitled to seek any supplementary information in accordance with regulation 17 above in relation to the matters specified in paragraphs (a) and (b) above.

Amendment
Words in square brackets substituted by SI 1995/201, reg 31(2)(b).

[App.81]

19 Consortia

(1)   In this regulation a 'consortium' means 2 or more persons, at least one of whom is a services provider, acting jointly for the purpose of being awarded a public services contract.

(2)   A contracting authority shall not treat the tender of a consortium as ineligible nor decide not to include a consortium amongst those persons from whom it will make the selection of persons to be invited to tender for or to negotiate a public services contract on the grounds that the consortium has not formed a legal entity for the purposes of tendering for or negotiating the contract; but where a contracting authority awards a public services contract to a consortium it may require the consortium to form a legal entity before entering into, or as a term of, the contract.

(3)   In these Regulations references to a services provider where the services provider is a consortium includes a reference to each person who is a member of that consortium.

[App.82]

20 Corporations

(1)   A contracting authority shall not treat the tender of a services provider as ineligible nor decide not to include a services provider amongst those persons from whom it will make the selection of persons to be invited to tender for or to negotiate a contract on the ground that under the law of any part of the United Kingdom the services provider is required to be an individual, a corporation or other type of body,

if under the law of the [relevant State] in which the services provider is established, he is authorised to provide such services.

(2)   A contracting authority may require a services provider which is not an individual to indicate in the tender or in the request to be selected to tender for or to negotiate the public services contract the names and relevant professional qualifications of the staff who will be responsible for the provision of the services.

Amendment
Para (1): words in square brackets substituted by SI 1995/201, reg 31(2)(b).

PART V
THE AWARD OF A PUBLIC SERVICES CONTRACT

[App.83]
21 Criteria for the award of a public services contract

(1)   Subject to paragraphs (5), (6) and (7) below, a contracting authority shall award a public services contract on the basis of the offer which—
(a)   is the most economically advantageous to the contracting authority, or
(b)   offers the lowest price.

(2)   The criteria which a contracting authority may use to determine that an offer is the most economically advantageous include period for completion or delivery, quality, aesthetic and functional characteristics, technical merit, after sales service, technical assistance and price.

(3)   Where a contracting authority intends to award a public services contract on the basis of the offer which is the most economically advantageous it shall state the criteria on which it intends to base its decision, where possible in descending order of importance, in the contract notice or in the contract documents.

(4)   Where a contracting authority awards a public services contract on the basis of the offer which is the most economically advantageous, it may take account of offers which offer variations on the requirements specified in the contract documents if—
(a)   the offer meets the minimum requirements of the contracting authority, and
(b)   it has stated those minimum requirements and any specific requirements for the presentation of an offer offering variations in the contract documents,

but if the contracting authority will not take account of offers which offer such variations it shall state that fact in the contract notice.

(5)   A contracting authority may not reject an offer which offers variations on the requirements specified in the contract documents on the ground that it would lead to the award of a public supply contract within the meaning of the Public Supply Contracts Regulations 1991.

(6)   A contracting authority may not reject an offer on the ground that the technical specifications in the offer have been defined by reference to European specifications (within the meaning of regulation 8(1)) or to the national technical specifications specified in regulation 8(7)(a) and (b).

(7)   If an offer for a public services contract is abnormally low the contracting authority may reject that offer but only if it has requested in writing an explanation of the offer or of those parts which it considers contribute to the offer being abnormally low and has—

(a)   if awarding the public services contract on the basis of the offer which offers the lowest price, examined the details of all the offers made, taking into account any explanation given to it of the abnormally low tender, before awarding the contract, or

(b)   if awarding the public services contract on the basis of the offer which is the most economically advantageous, taken any such explanation into account in assessing which is the most economically advantageous offer,

and, in considering that explanation, the contracting authority may take into account explanations which justify the offer on objective grounds including the economy of the method of providing the services, the technical solutions suggested by the services provider or the exceptionally favourable conditions available to the services provider for the provision of the services or the originality of the services proposed by the services provider.

(8)   If a contracting authority which rejects an abnormally low offer is awarding the public services contract on the basis of the offer which offers the lowest price, it shall send a report justifying the rejection to the Treasury for onward transmission to the Commission.

(9)   For the purposes of this regulation 'offer' includes a bid by one part of a contracting authority to provide services to another part of the contracting authority when the former part is invited by the latter part to compete with the offers sought from other persons.

[App.84]

22 Contract award notice

(1)   A contracting authority which has awarded a Part A or Part B services contract shall, no later than 48 days after the award, send to the Official Journal a notice, substantially corresponding to the form set out in Part E of Schedule 2 and, subject to paragraph (2) below, including the information therein specified.

(2)   Any of the information specified in Part E of Schedule 2 to be included in the contract award notice may be omitted in a particular case where to publish such information would impede law enforcement, would otherwise be contrary to the public interest, would prejudice the legitimate commercial interest of any person or might prejudice fair competition between services providers.

(3)   A contracting authority which has awarded a Part B services contract shall state in the contract award notice whether or not it agrees to its publication.

[App.85]

[23 Information about contract award procedures]

[(1)   Where a contracting authority decides either to abandon or to recommence an award procedure in respect of which a contract notice has been published it shall inform the Office for Official Publications of the European Communities and shall inform promptly any service provider who submitted an offer or who applied to be included amongst the persons to be selected to tender for or to negotiate the contract of the reasons for its decision and shall do so in writing if so requested.

(2)   Subject to paragraph (3) below, a contracting authority shall, within 15 days of the date on which it receives a request in writing from any service provider who was unsuccessful (whether pursuant to regulation 11(8), 12(4), 12(5), 13(7), 13(8) or 21), inform that service provider of the reasons why he was unsuccessful and, if the service

provider submitted an admissible tender, the contracting authority shall inform him of the characteristics and relative advantages of the successful tender as well as the name of the person awarded the contract.

(3)   A contracting authority may withhold any information to be provided in accordance with paragraph (2) above where the disclosure of such information would impede law enforcement or otherwise be contrary to the public interest or would prejudice the legitimate commercial interests of any person or might prejudice fair competition between service providers.

(4)   A contracting authority shall prepare a record in relation to each public services contract awarded by it specifying—

(a)   the name and address of the contracting authority;

(b)   the services to be provided under the contract and the value of the consideration to be given under it;

(c)   the names of the persons whose offers were evaluated in accordance with regulation 21 and, where the contracting authority has used the restricted or negotiated procedure, the reasons why those persons were selected;

(d)   the names of the persons who were unsuccessful pursuant to regulation 11(8), 12(4), 12(5), 13(7) or 13(8) and the reasons why they were unsuccessful;

(e)   the name of the person to whom the contract was awarded and the reasons for having awarded the contract to him;

(f)   if known to the contracting authority, the services under the contract which the person to whom the contract has been awarded intends to sub-contract to another person; and

(g)   in the case of a contracting authority which used the negotiated procedure, which of the circumstances specified in regulation 10(2) constituted grounds for using that procedure.

(5)   If the Commission requests a report containing the information specified in paragraph (4) above, the contracting authority shall send a written report containing that information, or the main features of it, to the Treasury for onward transmission to the Commission.]

Amendment
Substituted by SI 2000/2009, reg 4(10).

PART VI
MISCELLANEOUS

[App.86]
24 Design contests

[(1)   This regulation shall apply to a design contest if it is organised as part of a procedure intended to lead to the award of a public services contract whose estimated value (net of value added tax) is not less than the relevant threshold, which, in relation to a Part A services contract other than—

(a)   a contract for research and development specified in category 8 of Schedule 1, Part A; or

(b)   a contract for telecommunications services specified under CPC references 7524, 7525 and 7526 within category 5 of Schedule 1, Part A,

shall be—

(i)   in the case of offers sought by Schedule 3 entities the euro equivalent of 130,000 special drawing rights;

(ii)   in the case of offers sought by any other contracting authority the euro equivalent of 200,000 special drawing rights;

and in relation to any other public services contract shall be 200,000 euro.

(1A)   This regulation shall apply to a design contest whether or not it is organised as part of a procedure leading to the award of a public services contract, if the aggregate value of the prizes or payments for the contest is not less than 200,000 euro.]

(2)   The contracting authority shall publicise its intention to hold a design contest by sending to the Official Journal a notice in a form substantially corresponding to that set out in Part F of Schedule 2 and containing the information therein specified.

(3)   The contracting authority shall make the rules of the design contest available to services providers who wish to participate in the contest.

(4)   The contracting authority may restrict the number of persons invited to participate in the design contest, but it shall make the selection on the basis of clear and non discriminatory criteria.

(5)   The contracting authority shall take account of the need to ensure adequate competition in determining the number of persons invited to participate in the design contest.

(6)   Regulation 20 applies to design contests as it applies to the seeking of offers in relation to a proposed public services contract.

(7)   The contracting authority shall provide for the participants' proposals to be submitted to the jury without any indication as to the authorship of each proposal.

(8)   The contracting authority shall ensure that the members of the jury are all individuals who are independent of participants in the design contest and, when the participants are required to possess a particular professional qualification, that at least one third of the members of the jury also possess that qualification or an equivalent qualification.

(9)   The contracting authority shall ensure that the jury makes its decision independently and solely on the basis of the criteria set out in the notice referred to in paragraph (2) above.

(10)   The contracting authority shall, no later than 48 days after the date the jury has made its selection, publicise the results of the design contest by sending to the Official Journal a notice substantially corresponding to the form set out in Part G of Schedule 2 and including the information therein specified.

Amendment
Paras (1), (1A): substituted, for para (1) as originally enacted, by SI 2000/2009, reg 4(11).

[App.87]

25 Subsidised public services contracts

(1)   Where a contracting authority undertakes to contribute more than half of the consideration to be or expected to be paid under a public services contract to which this paragraph applies by virtue of paragraph (2) below which has been or is to be entered into by a person other than a contracting authority (in this paragraph referred to as 'the subsidised body'), that contracting authority shall—

(a)   make it a condition of the making of such contribution that the subsidised body complies with the provisions of these Regulations in relation to that public services contract as if it were a contracting authority, and

(b)   ensure that the subsidised body does so comply or recover the contribution.

(2)   Paragraph (1) above applies to a contract which would be a public services contract if the subsidised body were a contracting authority and which is for the carrying out of services in connection with the carrying out of any of the activities specified in Schedule 1 of the Public Works Contracts Regulations 1991 as are included in Group 502 or for the carrying out of building work for hospitals, facilities intended for sports, recreation and leisure, school and university building or buildings for administrative purposes.

[App.88]
26 Obligations relating to employment protection and working conditions

A contracting authority which includes in the contract documents information as to where a services provider may obtain information about obligations relating to employment protection and working conditions which will apply to the services to be provided under the public services contract shall request services providers to indicate that they have taken account of those obligations in preparing their tender or in negotiating the contract.

[App.89]
[27 Statistical and other reports]

[(1)   A contracting authority shall, no later than 31st July in each year, send to the Treasury a report specifying, in relation to each public services contract awarded by it during the reporting period—

(a)   the value (estimated if necessary) of the consideration payable under the contract;

(b)   whether the open, restricted or negotiated procedure was used;

(c)   if the negotiated procedure was used, pursuant to which provision of regulation 10(2) that procedure was used;

(d)   the principal category of service carried out or to be carried out under the contract according to the nomenclature used in Schedule 1; and

(e)   the nationality of the person to whom the contract was awarded.

(2)   A Schedule 3 entity shall include in the report referred to in paragraph (1) above the aggregate value (estimated if necessary) of all public services contracts awarded by it during the reporting period which were below the relevant threshold specified in regulation 7.

(3)   A contracting authority shall send to the Treasury a report containing such other information as the Treasury may from time to time require in respect of a particular public services contract (including public services contracts excluded from the application of these Regulations by regulations 6 and 7) for the purposes of informing the Commission.

(4)   In this regulation 'the reporting period' means the year preceding the year in which the report referred to in paragraph (1) above is to be made.]

Amendment
Substituted by SI 2000/2009, reg 4(12).

[App.90]

28 Responsibility for obtaining reports

(1)   Where a contracting authority is not a Minister of the Crown or a government department, that contracting authority shall send any report which it is required in accordance with regulations 8(6), 10(7), 21(8), 23(3) and 27 to send to the Treasury instead to the Minister responsible for that contracting authority and that Minister shall be responsible for sending the report to the Treasury.

(2)   The Minister responsible for a contracting authority shall be the Minister of the Crown whose areas of responsibility are most closely connected with the functions of the contracting authority; and any question as to which Minister of the Crown's areas of responsibility are most closely connected with the functions of a contracting authority shall be determined by the Treasury whose determination shall be final.

(3)   The requirement on a contracting authority to send any report in accordance with paragraph (1) above to the Minister of the Crown responsible for that contracting authority shall be enforceable, on the application of the Minister responsible, by mandamus or, in Scotland, for an order for specific performance.

(4)   Proceedings under paragraph (3) above brought in Scotland shall be brought before the Court of Session.

(5)   In the application of this regulation to Northern Ireland references to the Minister shall include references to the head of a Northern Ireland department.

[(6)   In the application of this regulation to Scotland—
(a)   references to—
    (i)   a Minister of the Crown, other than the first reference in paragraph (1); and
    (ii)   the Minister responsible for a contracting authority,
    shall be construed as references to the Scottish Ministers;
(b)   paragraph (2) shall not apply.]

Amendment
Para (6): inserted by SI 1999/1820, art 4, Sch 2, Pt II, para 153.

[App.91]

29 Publication of notices

(1)   Any notice required by these Regulations to be sent to the Official Journal shall be sent by the most appropriate means to the Office for Official Publications of the European Communities and where the contracting authority is applying the restricted procedure or the negotiated procedure and, for reasons of urgency, is applying the provisions of regulation 12(15) or 13(4), the notice shall be sent by telex, telegram or telefax.

(2)   Any such notice shall not contain more than 650 words.

(3)   The contracting authority shall retain evidence of the date of despatch to the Official Journal of each notice.

(4)   The contracting authority shall not place a contract notice [and design contest notice] in the press or like publications in the United Kingdom before the date on which the notice is despatched in accordance with paragraph (1) above and if it does after that date so place the notice it shall not add to the notice any information in relation to the contract which was not contained in the notice sent to the Official Journal [on or after that date].

(5)   When a contracting authority is not required to send a contract notice to the Official Journal in respect of a particular services contract it may nevertheless send such a notice and request that it be published.

Amendment
Para (4): words in square brackets inserted by SI 1996/2911, reg 35(2)(c).

[App.92]
30 Confidentiality of information
A contracting authority shall comply with such requirements as to confidentiality of information provided to it by a services provider as the services provider may reasonably request.

[App.93]
31 Sub-contractors
A contracting authority may require a services provider to indicate in his tender what part of the public services contract he intends to sub-contract to another person.

PART VII
APPLICATIONS TO THE COURT

[App.94]
32 Enforcement of obligations
(1)   The obligation on a contracting authority to comply with the provisions of these Regulations other than regulations 8(6), 10(7), 21(8), 23(3) and 27, and with any enforceable Community obligation in respect of a public services contract (other than one excluded from the application of these Regulations by regulation 6 or 7), is a duty owed to services providers.

[(1A)   The duty owed to a service provider pursuant to paragraph (1) above, except in relation to—
(a)   regulation 25;
(b)   a Part B services contract; and
(c)   a contract for the services referred to in paragraphs (a) to (c) of regulation 7(1) above,
shall be a duty owed also to a GPA provider.

(1B)   References to a 'service provider' in paragraphs (2), (4) and (5) below shall be construed as including a reference to a GPA provider.]

(2)   A breach of the duty owed pursuant to paragraph (1) [or paragraph (1A)] above shall not be a criminal offence but any breach of the duty shall be actionable by any services provider who, in consequence, suffers, or risks suffering, loss or damage.

(3)   Proceedings under this regulation shall be brought in England and Wales and in Northern Ireland in the High Court and, in Scotland, before the Court of Session.

(4)   Proceedings under this regulation may not be brought unless—
(a)   the services provider bringing the proceedings has informed the contracting authority of the breach or apprehended breach of the duty owed to him pursuant to paragraph (1) [or paragraph (1A)] above by the contracting authority and of his intention to bring proceedings under this regulation in respect of it; and
(b)   they are brought promptly and in any event within 3 months from the date when grounds for the bringing of the proceedings first arose unless the Court

considers that there is good reason for extending the period within which proceedings may be brought.

(5)   Subject to paragraph (6) below, but otherwise without prejudice to any other powers of the Court, in proceedings brought under this regulation the Court may—

(a)   by interim order suspend the procedure leading to the award of the contract in relation to which the breach of the duty owed pursuant to paragraph (1) [or paragraph (1A)] above is alleged, or suspend the implementation of any decision or action taken by the contracting authority in the course of following such procedure; and

(b)   if satisfied that a decision or action taken by a contracting authority was in breach of the duty owed pursuant to paragraph (1) [or paragraph (1A)] above—

(i)   order the setting aside of the decision or action or order the contracting authority to amend any documents, or

(ii)   award damages to a services provider who has suffered loss or damage as a consequence of the breach, or

(iii)   do both of those things.

(6)   In any proceedings under this regulation the Court shall not have power to order any remedy other than an award of damages in respect of a breach of the duty owed pursuant to paragraph (1) [or paragraph (1A)] above if the contract in relation to which the breach occurred has been entered into.

(7)   Notwithstanding sections 21 and 42 of the Crown Proceedings Act 1947, in proceedings brought under this regulation against the Crown the Court shall have power to grant an injunction or interdict.

[(8)   In this regulation—

(a)   a 'GPA provider' shall mean a person from a GPA State who sought, or who seeks, or would have wished, to be the person to whom the contract is awarded;

(b)   a 'GPA State' shall mean any country other than a relevant State which, at the relevant time is a signatory to the GPA and has agreed with the European Community that the GPA shall apply to a contract of the type to be awarded; and

(c)   'relevant time' shall mean the date on which the contracting authority would have sent a contract notice in respect of the contract to the Official Journal if it had been required by these Regulations to do so.]

Amendment
Paras (1A), (1B): inserted by SI 2000/2009, reg 4(13)(a).
Paras (2), (4)–(6): words 'or paragraph (1A)' in square brackets in each place they occur inserted by SI 2000/2009, reg 4(13)(b).
Para (8): inserted by SI 2000/2009, reg 4(13)(c).

SCHEDULE 1
CATEGORIES OF SERVICES

Regulation 5

PART A

[App.95]

Category	Services	CPC Reference
1	Maintenance and repair of vehicles and equipment	6112, 6122, 633, 886

2	Transport by land, including armoured car services and courier services but not including transport of mail and transport by rail	712 (except 71235), 7512, 87304
3	Transport by air but not transport of mail	73 (except 7321)
4	Transport of mail by land, other than by rail, and by air	71235, 7321
5	Telecommunications services other than voice telephony, telex, radiotelephony paging and satellite services	752
6	Financial services (a) Insurance services (b) Banking & investment services other than financial services in connection with the issue, sale, purchase or transfer of securities or other financial instruments, and central bank services	81 (Part) 812, 814
7	Computer and related services	84
8	R&D services where the benefits accrue exclusively to the contracting authority for its use in the conduct of its own affairs and the services are to be wholly paid for by the contracting authority	85
9	Accounting, auditing and book-keeping services	862
10	Market research and public opinion polling services	864
11	Management consultancy services and related services, but not arbitration and conciliation services	865, 866
12	Architectural services: engineering services and integrated engineering services: urban planning and landscape architectural services: related scientific and technical consulting services: technical testing and analysis services	867
13	Advertising services	871
14	Building-cleaning services and property management services	874 82201 to 82206
15	Publishing and printing services on a fee or contract basis	88442
16	Sewerage and refuse disposal service: sanitation and similar services	94

PART B

[App.96]

Category	Services	CPC Reference
17	Hotel and restaurant services	64
18	Transport by rail	711
19	Transport by water	72

20	Supporting and auxiliary transport services	74
21	Legal services	861
22	Personnel placement and supply services	872
23	Investigation and security services, other than armoured car services 873 (except 87304)	
24	Education and vocational education services	92
25	Health and social services	93
26	Recreational, cultural and sporting services	96
27	Other services	

[SCHEDULE 2
FORMS OF NOTICES FOR PUBLICATION IN THE OFFICIAL JOURNAL]

[Regulations 9, 11(2), (9), 12(2), (17), 13(2), 22(1), 24(2), (10)]

[PART A
PRIOR INFORMATION NOTICE]

[App.97]

[1 Name, address, telegraphic address, telephone, telex and facsimile numbers of the contracting authority and of the office from which additional information may be obtained.

2 For each category of services in Part A of Schedule 1, the intended total quantity or value to be provided.

3 For each category of services in (2), the estimated date of the commencement of the procedures leading to the award of the contract(s) (if known).

4 Other information.

5 Date of despatch of the notice.

6 Indication of whether the procurement is covered by the GPA.]

Amendment
Substituted by SI 2000/2009, reg 4(14), Sch 3.

[PART B
OPEN PROCEDURE NOTICE]

[App.98]

[1 Name, address, telegraphic address, telephone, telex and facsimile numbers of the contracting authority.

2 Category of service and description. CPC reference number. Quantity or value including, where applicable, any options for further services and, if known, an estimate of the timing when such options may be exercised. In the case of regular or recurring contracts, if known, the expected dates of the subsequent calls for tender.

3 Place of delivery.

4

(a)   Indication of whether the provision of the service is reserved by law, regulation or administrative provision to a particular profession;

(b)   Reference to the law, regulation or administrative provision;

(c)   Indication of whether legal persons should indicate the names and professional qualifications of the staff to be responsible for the provision of the services.

5 Indication of whether service providers can tender for some or all of the services required.

6 Where applicable, prohibition on variants.

7 Time limits for completion of the service or duration of the service contract and, as far as possible, time limit for starting to provide the service.

8

(a)   Name and address of the office from which the contract and additional documents may be requested;

(b)   Final date for making such requests;

(c)   Where applicable, the amount and terms of payment of any sum payable for such documents.

9

(a)   Final date for receipt of tenders;

(b)   Address to which they must be sent;

(c)   Language(s) in which they must be drawn up.

10

(a)   Where applicable, persons authorised to be present at the opening of tenders;

(b)   Date, time and place of such opening.

11 Where applicable, any deposits and guarantees required.

12 Main terms concerning financing and payment and/or references to the relevant provisions.

13 Where applicable, the legal form to be taken by the grouping of service providers to whom the contract is awarded.

14 Information concerning the service provider's own position, and information and formalities necessary for an appraisal of the minimum standards of economic and financial standing, ability and technical capacity required of him.

15 Period during which the tenderer is bound to keep open his tender.

16 Criteria for the award of the contract and, if possible, their order of importance. Criteria other than the lowest price shall be mentioned if they do not appear in the contract documents.

17 Other Information.

18 Date(s) of publication of the prior information notice in the Official Journal or reference to its non-publication.

19 Date of despatch of the notice.

20 Indication of whether the procurement is covered by the GPA.]

Amendment
Substituted by SI 2000/2009, reg 4(14), Sch 3.

[PART C
RESTRICTED PROCEDURE NOTICE]

[App.99]
[1 Name, address, telegraphic address, telephone, telex and facsimile numbers of the contracting authority.

2 Category of service and description. CPC reference number. Quantity or value including, where applicable, any options for further services and, if known, an estimate of the timing when such options may be exercised. In the case of regular or recurring contracts, if known, the estimated date(s) of the subsequent calls for tender.

3 Place of delivery.

4
(a)   Indication of whether the provision of the service is reserved by law, regulation or administrative provision to a particular profession;
(b)   Reference to the law, regulation or administrative provision;
(c)   Indication of whether legal persons should indicate the names and professional qualifications of the staff to be responsible for the provision of the services.

5 Indication of whether service providers can tender for some or all of the services.

6 If known, number of service providers which will be invited to tender or the range within which that number is expected to fall.

7 Where applicable, prohibition on variants.

8 Time limits for completion of the service or duration of the service contract and, as far as possible, time limit for starting to provide the service.

9 Where applicable, the legal form to be taken by the grouping of service providers to whom the contract is awarded.

10
(a)   Where applicable, justification for use of shorter time limits;
(b)   Final date for receipt of requests to participate;
(c)   Address to which requests must be sent;
(d)   Language(s) in which they must be drawn up.

11 Final date for despatch of invitations to tender.

12 Where applicable, any deposits and guarantees required.

13 Information concerning the service provider's own position, and the information and formalities necessary for an appraisal of the minimum standards of economic and financial standing, ability and technical capacity required of him.

14 Criteria for the award of the contract and, if possible, their order of importance. Criteria other than the lowest price shall be mentioned if they do not appear in the contract documents.

15 Other Information.

16 Date(s) of publication of the prior information notice in the Official Journal or reference to its non-publication.

17 Date of despatch of the notice.

18 Indication of whether the procurement is covered by the GPA.]

Amendment
Substituted by SI 2000/2009, reg 4(14), Sch 3.

[PART D
NEGOTIATED PROCEDURE NOTICE]

[App.100]

[1 Name, address, telegraphic address, telephone, telex and facsimile numbers of the contracting authority.

2 Category of service and description. CPC reference number. Quantity or value including, where applicable, any options for further services and, if known, an estimate of the timing when such options may be exercised. In the case of regular or recurring contracts, if known, the estimated date(s) of the subsequent calls for tender.

3 Place of delivery.

4
(a)   Indication of whether the execution of the service is reserved by law, regulation or administrative provision to a particular profession;
(b)   Reference of the law, regulation or administrative provision;
(c)   Indication of whether legal persons should indicate the names and professional qualifications of the staff to be responsible for the execution of the service.

5 Indication of whether the service providers can offer some or all of the services required.

6 If known, the number of service providers which will be invited to tender or the range within which that number is expected to fall.

7 Where applicable, prohibition of variants.

8 Time limit for completion of the service or duration of the service contract and, as far as possible, time limit for starting to provide the service.

9 Where applicable, the legal form to be taken by the grouping of service providers to whom the contract is awarded.

10
(a)   Where applicable, justification for the use of shorter time limits;
(b)   Final date for the receipt of requests to participate;
(c)   Address to which they must be sent;
(d)   Language(s) in which they must be drawn up.

11 Where applicable, any deposits and guarantees required.

12 Information concerning the service provider's own position, and the information and formalities necessary for an appraisal of the minimum economic and technical standards required of him.

13 Where applicable, the names and addresses of service providers already selected by the contracting authority.

14 Other information.

15 Date of despatch of the notice.

16 Date(s) of previous publications in the Official Journal.

17 Indication of whether the procurement is covered by the GPA.]

Amendment
Substituted by SI 2000/2009, reg 4(14), Sch 3

[PART E
CONTRACT AWARD NOTICE]

[App.101]

[1 Name and address of the contracting authority.

2
(a)   Award procedure chosen.
(b)   Where applicable, justification for use of the negotiated procedure without a call for competition.

3 Category of service and description. CPC reference number. Quantity of services procured.

4 Date of award of the contract.

5 Criteria for award of the contract.

6 Number of offers received.

7 Name and address of service provider(s).

8 Price or range of prices (minimum/ maximum) paid or to be paid.

9 Value of winning award(s) or the highest and lowest offer taken into account in the award of the contract.

10 Where appropriate, value and proportion of the contract which may be subcontracted to third parties.

11 Other information.

12 Date of publication of the contract notice in the Official Journal.

13 Date of despatch of the notice.

14 In the case of contracts for services specified in Part B of Schedule 1, agreement by the contracting authority to publication of the notice.]

Amendment
Substituted by SI 2000/2009, reg 4(14), Sch 3.

[PART F
DESIGN CONTEST NOTICE]

[App.102]

[1 Name, address and telegraphic address, telephone, telex and facsimile numbers of the contracting authority and of the office from which additional information may be obtained.

2 Project description.

3 Nature of the contest: open or restricted.

4 In the case of open contests: final date for receipt of plans and designs.

5 In the case of restricted contests:
(a)   the number of participants envisaged;
(b)   where applicable, names of the participants already selected;
(c)   criteria for the selection of participants;
(d)   final date for receipt of requests to participate.

6 Where applicable, an indication of whether participation is reserved to a particular profession.

7 Criteria to be applied in the evaluation of projects.

8 Where applicable, names of the persons selected to be members of the jury.

9 Indication of whether the decision of the jury is binding on the contracting authority.

10 Where applicable, number and value of prizes.

11 Where applicable, details of payments to all participants.

12 Indication of whether follow-up contracts will be awarded to one of the winners.

13 Other information.

14 Date of despatch of the notice.]

Amendment
Substituted by SI 2000/2009, reg 4(14), Sch 3.

[PART G
DESIGN CONTEST RESULT NOTICE]

[App.103]

[**1** Name, address and telegraphic address, telephone, telex and facsimile numbers of the contracting authority.

2 Project description.

3 Number of participants.

4 Number of participants established outside the United Kingdom.

5 Winner(s) of the contest.

6 Where applicable, the prize(s) awarded.

7 Other information.

8 Reference to publication of the design contest notice in the Official Journal.

9 Date of despatch of the notice.]

Amendment
Substituted by SI 2000/2009, reg 4(14), Sch 3.

[SCHEDULE 3
GPA ANNEX I CONTRACTING AUTHORITIES]

[Regulations 2(1), 7(1), 24(1), 27(3)]

[App.104]

[Where an entity listed in this Schedule is succeeded by another entity, which is itself a contracting authority, the successor entity shall be deemed to be included in this Schedule.

Cabinet Office
    Central Commuter and Telecommunications Agency (CCTA)
    Civil Service College
    Office of the Parliamentary Counsel
    The Buying Agency

Central Office of Information
Charity Commission
Crown Prosecution Service
Crown Estate Commissioners (Vote Expenditure Only)
HM Customs and Excise
Department for Culture, Media and Sport
    British Library
    British Museum
    Historic Buildings and Monuments Commission for England (English
        Heritage)
    Imperial War Museum
    Museums and Galleries Commission
    National Gallery
    National Maritime Museum
    National Portrait Gallery
    Natural History Museum
    Royal Commission on Historical Manuscripts
    Royal Commission on Historical Monuments of England
    Royal Fine Art Commission (England)
    Science Museum
    Tate Gallery
    Victoria and Albert Museum
    Wallace Collection
Department for Education and Employment
    Higher Education Funding Council for England
Department of the Environment, Transport and the Regions
    Building Research Establishment Agency
    Commons Commission
    Countryside Agency
    Maritime and Coastguard Agency
    Rent Assessment Panels
    Royal Commission on Environmental Pollution
    Valuation Tribunal
Department of Health
    Central Council for Education and Training in Social Work
    Dental Practice Board
    National Board for Nursing, Midwifery and Health Visiting for England
    National Health Service Authorities and Trusts
    Prescription Pricing Authority
    Public Health Service Laboratory Board
    UK Central Council for Nursing, Midwifery and Health Visiting
Department for International Development
Department for National Savings
Department of Social Security
    Disability Living Allowance Advisory Board
    Independent Tribunal Service
    Medical Boards and Examining Medical Officers (War Pensions)
    Occupational Pensions Regulatory Authority

Regional Medical Service
Social Security Advisory Committee

Department of the Procurator General and Treasury Solicitor
Legal Secretariat to the Law Officers

Department of Trade and Industry
Central Transport Consultative Committees
Competition Commission
Electricity Committees
Employment Appeal Tribunal
Employment Tribunals
Gas Consumers' Council
National Weights and Measures Laboratory
Office of Manpower Economics
Patent Office

Export Credits Guarantee Department

Foreign and Commonwealth Office
Wilton Park Conference Centre

Government Actuary's Department

Government Communications Headquarters

Home Office
Boundary Commission for England
Gaming Board for Great Britain
Inspectors of Constabulary
Parole Board and Local Review Committees

House of Commons

House of Lords

Inland Revenue, Board of

Intervention Board for Agricultural Produce

Lord Chancellor's Department
Circuit Offices and Crown, County and Combined Courts (England and Wales)
Combined Tax Tribunal
Council on Tribunals
Court of Appeal—Criminal
Immigration Appellate Authorities
Immigration Adjudicators
Immigration Appeals Tribunal
Lands Tribunal
Law Commission
Legal Aid Fund (England and Wales)
Office of the Social Security Commissioners
Pensions Appeal Tribunals
Public Trust Office
Supreme Court Group (England and Wales)
Transport Tribunal

Ministry of Agriculture, Fisheries and Food
Agricultural Dwelling House Advisory Committees
Agricultural Land Tribunals
Agricultural Wages Board and Committees

Cattle Breeding Centre
Plant Variety Rights Office
Royal Botanic Gardens, Kew

Ministry of Defence
Meteorological Office
Defence Procurement Agency

National Assembly for Wales
Higher Education Funding Council for Wales
Local Government Boundary Commission for Wales
Royal Commission for Ancient and Historical Monuments in Wales
Valuation Tribunals (Wales)
Welsh National Health Service Authorities and Trusts
Welsh Rent Assessment Panels
Welsh National Board for Nursing, Midwifery and Health Visiting

National Audit Office

National Investment and Loans Office

Northern Ireland Assembly Commission

Northern Ireland Court Service
Coroners Courts
County Courts
Court of Appeal and High Court of Justice in Northern Ireland
Crown Court
Enforcement of Judgements Office
Legal Aid Fund
Magistrates Courts
Pensions Appeals Tribunals

Northern Ireland, Department of Agriculture and Rural Development

Northern Ireland, Department of Culture, Arts and Leisure

Northern Ireland, Department of Education

Northern Ireland, Department of Enterprise, Trade and Investment

Northern Ireland, Department of the Environment

Northern Ireland, Department of Finance and Personnel

Northern Ireland, Department of Health, Social Services and Public Safety

Northern Ireland, Department of Higher and Further Education, Training and Employment

Northern Ireland, Department of Regional Development

Northern Ireland, Department of Social Development

Northern Ireland, Office of the First Minister and deputy First Minister

Northern Ireland, Crown Solicitor's Office
Department of the Director of Public Prosecutions for Northern Ireland
Northern Ireland Forensic Science Laboratory
Office of Chief Electoral Officer for Northern Ireland
[Northern Ireland Policing Board]
Probation Board for Northern Ireland
State Pathologist Service

Office of Fair Trading

Office for National Statistics
    National Health Service Central Register

Office of the Parliamentary Commissioner for Administration and Health Service Commissioners

Paymaster General's Office

[the Post Office company in connection with its postal business or a relevant subsidiary of that company in connection with the subsidiary's postal business]

Privy Council Office

Public Record Office

Registry of Friendly Societies

Royal Commission on Historical Manuscripts

Royal Hospital, Chelsea

Royal Mint

Scotland, Auditor-General

Scotland, Crown Office and Procurator Fiscal Service

Scotland, General Register Office

Scotland, Queen's and Lord Treasurer's Remembrancer

Scotland, Registers of Scotland

The Scotland Office

The Scottish Executive Corporate Services

The Scottish Executive Education Department
    National Galleries of Scotland
    National Library of Scotland
    National Museums of Scotland
    Scottish Higher Education Funding Council

The Scottish Executive Development Department

The Scottish Executive Enterprise and Lifelong Learning Department

The Scottish Executive Finance

The Scottish Executive Health Department
    Local Health Councils
    National Board for Nursing, Midwifery and Health Visiting for Scotland
    Scottish Council for Postgraduate Medical Education
    Scottish National Health Service Authorities and Trusts

The Scottish Executive Justice Department
    Accountant of Court's Office
    High Court of Justiciary
    Court of Session
    HM Inspectorate of Constabulary
    Lands Tribunal for Scotland
    Parole Board for Scotland and Local Review Committees
    Pensions Appeal Tribunals
    Scottish Land Court
    Scottish Law Commission
    Sheriff Courts
    Scottish Criminal Record Office
    Scottish Crime Squad

Scottish Fire Service Training Squad
Scottish Police College
Social Security Commissioners' Office

The Scottish Executive Rural Affairs Department
Crofters Commission
Red Deer Commission
Rent Assessment Panel and Committees
Royal Botanic Garden, Edinburgh
Royal Commission on the Ancient and Historical Monuments of Scotland
Royal Fine Art Commission for Scotland

The Scottish Executive Secretariat

The Scottish Parliamentary Body Corporate

Scottish Record Office

HM Treasury

The Wales Office (Office of the Secretary of State for Wales)]

Amendment
Inserted by SI 2000/2009, reg 4(15), Sch 4.
In entry 'Northern Ireland, Crown Solicitor's Office' words 'Northern Ireland Policing Board' in square brackets substituted by the Police (Northern Ireland) Act 2000, s 2(4), Sch 2, para 6(1).
Entry beginning 'the Post Office company' substituted by SI 2001/1149, art 3(1), Sch 1, para 100(1), (3).

[SCHEDULE 4
EXTENSION TO NON MEMBER STATES]

[Regulations 2(1) and 4]

[App.105]

[Relevant States	Agreement with the European Union which extend the provisions relating to public procurement to the relevant State	Statutory provisions designating the agreements as European Treaties
1 Bulgaria	Europe Agreement (OJ No L358, 31.12.94, p 2)	SI 1994/758
2 The Czech Republic	Europe Agreement (OJ No L360, 31.12.94, p 2)	SI 1994/759
3 Estonia	Europe Agreement (OJ No L68, 9.03.98, p 3)	SI 1997/269
4 Hungary	Europe Agreement (OJ No L347, 31.12.93, p 2)	SI 1992/2871
5 Iceland	European Economic Area Agreement	(a)European Economic Area Act 1993 (b), section 1
6 Latvia	Europe Agreement (OJ No L26, 2.02.98, p 3)	SI 1997/270
7 Liechtenstein	European Economic Area Agreement	(a) European Economic Area Act 1993 (b), section 1

8 Lithuania	Europe Agreement (OJ No L51, 20.02.98 p 3)	SI 1997/271
9 Norway	European Economic Area Agreement	(a) European Economic Area Act 1993 (b), section 1
10 Poland	Europe Agreement (OJ No L348, 31.12.94, p 2)	SI 1992/2872
11 Romania	Europe Agreement (OJ No L357, 31.12.94, p 2)	SI 1994/760
12 Slovakia	Europe Agreement (OJ No L359, 31.12.94, p 2)	SI 1994/761
13 Slovenia	Europe Agreement (OJ No L51, 26.02.99, p 3)	SI 1998/1062

Amendment
Inserted by SI 2000/2009, reg 4(15), Sch 5.

PUBLIC SUPPLY CONTRACTS REGULATIONS 1995

SI 1995/201

PART I
GENERAL

[App.106]
1 Title and commencement

These Regulations may be cited as the Public Supply Contracts Regulations 1995 and shall come into force on 21st February 1995.

[App.107]
2 Interpretation

(1)   In these Regulations—
'to award' means to accept an offer made in relation to a proposed contract;
'the Commission' means the European Commission;
'contract documents' means the invitation to tender for or to negotiate the contract, the proposed conditions of contract, the specifications or description of the goods required by the contracting authority, and all documents supplementary thereto;
'contract notice' means a notice sent to the Official Journal in accordance with regulation 11(2), 12(2) or 13(2);
'contracting authority' has the meaning ascribed to it by regulation 3;
. . .
'established' means the same as it does for the purposes of the Community Treaties;
'financial year' means the period of 12 months ending on 31st March in any year or, in relation to any person whose accounts are prepared in respect of a different 12 month period, that period of 12 months;
. . .
'goods' includes electricity, substances, growing crops and things attached to or forming part of the land which are agreed to be severed before the purchase or hire under the supply contract and any ship, aircraft or vehicle;
'government department' includes a Northern Ireland department or the head of such department [and any part of the Scottish Administration];
['Government Procurement Agreement' means the Agreement on Government Procurement between certain parties to the World Trade Organisation (WTO) Agreement signed in Marrakesh on 15 April 1994,
'GPA' means the Government Procurement Agreement;]
['letter' has the same meaning as in the Postal Services Act 2000;]
'Minister of the Crown' means the holder of an office in Her Majesty's Government in the United Kingdom, and includes the Treasury [and a reference to a Minister of the Crown shall be read as including a reference to the Scottish Ministers];
'national of a relevant State' means, in the case of a person who is not an individual, a person formed in accordance with the laws of a relevant State and which

has its registered office, central administration or principal place of business in a relevant State;

'negotiated procedure' means a procedure leading to the award of a public supply contract whereby a contracting authority negotiates the terms of the contract with one or more persons selected by it;

'Official Journal' means the Official Journal of the European Communities;

'open procedure' means a procedure leading to the award of a public supply contract whereby all interested persons may tender for the contract;

['postal business' means the postal services in relation to letters;]

['postal services' has the same meaning as in the Postal Services Act 2000;]

['the Post Office company' has the same meaning as in Part IV of the Postal Services Act 2000;]

'prior information notice' means a notice sent to the Official Journal in accordance with regulation 9;

'public supply contract' means a contract in writing for consideration (whatever the nature of the consideration)—

(a)   for the purchase of goods by a contracting authority (whether or not the consideration is given in instalments and whether or not the purchase is conditional upon the occurrence of a particular event), or

(b)   for the hire of goods by a contracting authority (both where the contracting authority becomes the owner of the goods after the end of the period of hire and where it does not),

and for any siting or installation of those goods, but where under such a contract services are also to be provided, the contract shall only be a public supply contract where the value of the consideration attributable to the goods and any siting or installation of the goods is equal to or greater than the value attributable to the services;

['relevant State' means a member State or a State for the time being specified in Schedule 4 to these Regulations;]

['relevant subsidiary' has the same meaning as in Part IV of the Postal Services Act 2000;]

'restricted procedure' means a procedure leading to the award of a public supply contract whereby only persons selected by the contracting authority may submit tenders for the contract;

['Schedule 1 entity' means an entity specified in Schedule 1 pursuant to its inclusion in the list of central government bodies in Annex I of the GPA, and for which these Regulations make particular provisions;]

'ship' includes any boat and other description of a vessel used in navigation;

'substance' means any natural or artificial substance, whether in solid, liquid or gaseous form or in the form of a vapour;

'supplier' has the meaning ascribed to it by regulation 4;

'working day' means a day other than a Saturday, Sunday or Bank Holiday (within the meaning of the Banking and Financial Dealings Act 1971); and

'year' means a calendar year.

(2)   . . .

(3)   Where a thing is required to be done under these Regulations—

(a)   within a period after an action is taken, the day on which that action was taken shall not be counted in the calculation of that period;

(b)   within a certain period, that period must include two working days;

(c)   within a period and the last day of that period is not a working day, the period shall be extended to include the following working day.

(4) References in these Regulations to a regulation are references to a regulation in these Regulations and references to a Schedule are references to a Schedule to these Regulations.

Amendment
Para (1): definition 'ECU' (omitted) revoked by SI 2000/2009, reg 5(1)(a)(ii); definition 'a GATT contracting authority' (omitted) revoked by SI 2000/2009, reg 5(1)(a)(iv); in definition 'government department' words 'and any part of the Scottish Administration' in square brackets inserted by SI 1999/1042, art 3, Sch 1, para 22(1), (2)(a); definitions 'Government Procurement Agreement' and 'GPA' inserted by SI 2000/2009, reg 5(1)(a)(i); definition 'letter' inserted by SI 2001/1149, art 3(1), Sch 1, para 106(1), (2); in definition 'Minister of the Crown' words from 'and a reference' to 'the Scottish Ministers' in square brackets inserted by SI 1999/1042, art 3, Sch 1, para 22(1), (2)(b); definition 'postal business' inserted by SI 2001/1149, art 3(1), Sch 1, para 106(1), (2); definition 'postal services' inserted by SI 2001/1149, art 3(1), Sch 1, para 106(1), (2); definition 'the Post Office company' inserted by SI 2001/1149, art 3(1), Sch 1, para 106(1), (2); definition 'relevant State' substituted by SI 2000/2009, reg 5(1)(a)(iii); definition 'relevant subsidiary' inserted by SI 2001/1149, art 3(1), Sch 1, para 106(1), (2); definition 'Schedule 1 entity' inserted by SI 2000/2009, reg 5(1)(a)(i).
Para (2): revoked by SI 2000/2009, reg 5(1)(b).

[App.108]

[3 Contracting authorities]

[(1) For the purposes of these Regulations each of the following is a 'contracting authority'—

(a) a Minister of the Crown,
(b) a government department,
(c) the House of Commons,
(d) the House of Lords,
(e) the Northern Ireland Assembly Commission,
(f) the Scottish Parliamentary Body Corporate,
(g) the National Assembly for Wales,
(h) a local authority,
(i) a fire authority constituted by a combination scheme under the Fire Services Act 1947,
(j) the Fire Authority for Northern Ireland,
(k) a police authority established under section 3 of the Police Act 1996,
(l) a police authority established under section 2 of the Police (Scotland) Act 1967,
(m) [the Northern Ireland Policing Board],
(n) an authority established under section 10 of the Local Government Act 1985,
(o) a joint authority established by Part IV of that Act,
(p) any body established pursuant to an order under section 67 of that Act,
(q) the Broads Authority,
(r) any joint board the constituent members of which consist of any of the bodies specified in paragraphs (h), (i), (k), (l), (n), (o), (p) and (q) above,
(s) a National Park authority established by an Order under section 63 of the Environment Act 1995,
(t) the Receiver for the Metropolitan Police District,
(u) a corporation established, or a group of individuals appointed to act together, for the specific purposes of meeting needs in the general interest, not having an industrial or commercial character, and—
    (i) financed wholly or mainly by another contracting authority, or
    (ii) subject to management supervision by another contracting authority, or

(iii)   more than half of the board of directors or members of which, or, in the case of a group of individuals, more than half of those individuals, being appointed by another contracting authority,

(v)   an association of or formed by one or more of the above, and

(w)   to the extent not specified in sub-paragraphs (a) to (t) above, an entity specified in Schedule 1.

(2)   In the application of the Regulations to England, 'local authority' in paragraph (1) above means—

(a)   a county council, a district council, a London borough council, a parish council, a community council or the Council of the Isles of Scilly;

(b)   the Common Council of the City of London in its capacity as local authority or police authority.

(3)   In the application of these Regulations to Wales, 'local authority' in paragraph (1) above means a county council, county borough council or community council.

(4)   In the application of these Regulations to Scotland, 'local authority' in paragraph (1) above has the same meaning as in section 235(1) of the Local Government (Scotland) Act 1973 and also includes joint board or joint committee within the meaning of section 235(1).

(5)   In the application of these Regulations to Northern Ireland, 'local authority' in paragraph (1) above means a district council within the meaning of the Local Government Act (Northern Ireland) 1972.

(6)   Where an entity specified in paragraph (1) above does not have the capacity to enter into a contract, the contracting authority in relation to that entity is a person whose function it is to enter into contracts for that entity.]

Amendment
Substituted by SI 2000/2009, reg 5(2).
Para (1): in para (m) words 'the Northern Ireland Policing Board' in square brackets substituted by the Police (Northern Ireland) Act 2000, s 2(4), Sch 2, para 6(1).

[App.109]

4 Suppliers

(1)   For the purposes of these Regulations a 'supplier' means a person—

(a)   who sought, or who seeks, or who would have wished, to be the person to whom a public supply contract is awarded, and

[(b)   who is a national of and established in a relevant State].

(2)   Where these Regulations apply a contracting authority shall not treat a person who is not a national of and established in a relevant State more favourably than one who is.

Amendment
Para (1): sub-para (b) substituted by SI 2000/2009, reg 5(3).

[App.110]

5 Application of the Regulations

These Regulations apply whenever a contracting authority seeks offers in relation to a proposed public supply contract other than a public supply contract excluded from the application of these Regulations by virtue of regulation 6 or 7.

[App.111]

6 General exclusions

These Regulations shall not apply to the seeking of offers in relation to a proposed public supply contract—

[(a)   where the contracting authority is a utility within the meaning of regulation 3 of the Utilities Contracts Regulations 1996 and the services to be provided under it are for the purposes of carrying out an activity specified in any Part of Schedule 1 to those Regulations in which the utility is specified;]

(c)   which is classified as secret or where the delivery of the goods under it must be accompanied by special security measures in accordance with the laws, regulations or administrative provisions of any part of the United Kingdom or when the protection of the basic interests of the security of the United Kingdom require it;

(d)   where goods to be purchased or hired under the contract are goods to which the provisions of Article 223.1(b) of the EEC Treaty apply; or

(e)   where different procedures govern the procedures leading to the award of the contract and it is to be entered into—

    (i)   pursuant to an international agreement to which the United Kingdom and a State which is not a relevant State are parties and it relates to goods intended for the joint implementation or exploitation of a project pursuant to that agreement;

    (ii)   pursuant to an international agreement relating to the stationing of troops; or

    (iii)   in accordance with the contract award procedures of an organisation of which only States are members (an 'international organisation') or of which only States or international organisations are members.

Amendment
Para (a): substituted, for original paras (a), (b), by SI 1996/2911, reg 35(3)(c).

[App.112]

7 Thresholds

(1)   These Regulations shall not apply to the seeking of offers in relation to a proposed public supply contract where the estimated value of the contract (net of value added tax) at the relevant time is less than the relevant threshold.

[(2)   The relevant threshold for the purposes of paragraph (1) above—

(a)   is the euro equivalent of 130,000 special drawing rights where a Schedule 1 entity seeks offers for a public supply contract, but in the case of a public supply contract in relation to which offers are sought by the Secretary of State for Defence, only if the contract is for the purchase or hire of goods specified in Schedule 2; and

(b)   is the euro equivalent of 200,000 special drawing rights in relation to all other public supply contracts.]

[(2A)   The value in pounds sterling of any amount expressed in these Regulations in euro or in the euro equivalent of special drawing rights shall be calculated by reference to the rate for the time being applying for the purposes of Council Directive 93/36/EEC as published from time to time in the Official Journal.]

(3)   Subject to paragraphs (4) to (10) below, the estimated value for the purposes of paragraph (1) above of a public supply contract shall be the value of the consideration which the contracting authority expects to give under the contract.

(4)   Subject to paragraph (7) below, where a contracting authority has a single requirement for goods and a number of public supply contracts has been entered or is to be entered into to fulfil that requirement, the estimated value for the purposes of paragraph (1) above of each public supply contract shall be the aggregate of the value of the consideration which the contracting authority expects to give under each of those contracts.

(5)   Subject to paragraph (7) below, where a contracting authority has a requirement over a period for goods of the type to be purchased or hired under the public supply contract and for that purpose enters into—

(a)   a series of contracts; or

(b)   a contract which under its terms is renewable,

the estimated value for the purposes of paragraph (1) above of the contract shall be the amount calculated under paragraph (6) below.

(6)   The contracting authority shall calculate the amount referred to in paragraph (5) above either—

(a)   by taking the aggregate of the value of the consideration given by the contracting authority under such public supply contracts which have similar characteristics and which were for the purchase or hire of goods of the type to be purchased or hired under the contract, during its last financial year ending before, or during the period of 12 months ending immediately before, the relevant time, and by adjusting that amount to take account of any expected changes in quantity and cost of the goods of that type in the period of 12 months commencing with the relevant time, or

(b)   by estimating the aggregate of the value of the consideration which the contracting authority expects to give under such public supply contracts which have similar characteristics and which are for the purchase or hire of goods of the type to be purchased or hired under the contract during the period of 12 months from the first date of delivery of the goods to be purchased or hired or, where the contract is for a definite term of more than 12 months, during the term of the contract.

(7)   Notwithstanding paragraphs (4) and (5) above, when the goods to be purchased or hired under the contract are required for the sole purposes of a discrete operational unit within the organisation of the contracting authority and—

(a)   the decision whether to purchase or hire goods of that type has been devolved to such a unit, and

(b)   that decision is taken independently of any other part of the contracting authority,

the valuation methods described in paragraphs (4) and (6) above shall be adapted by aggregating only the value of the consideration which the contracting authority has given or expects to give, as the case may be, for goods of the type to be purchased or hired under the contract which were or are required for the sole purposes of that unit.

(8)   The estimated value for the purposes of paragraph (1) above of a public supply contract for the hire of goods for an indefinite period, or for a period which is uncertain at the time the contract is entered into, shall be the value of the consideration which the contracting authority expects to give in respect of each month of the hire multiplied by 48.

(9)   Where a public supply contract includes one or more options the estimated value of the contract for the purposes of paragraph (1) above shall be determined by calculating the highest possible amount which could be payable under the contract.

(10)   A contracting authority shall not enter into separate public supply contracts nor select nor exercise a choice under a valuation method in accordance with paragraph (6) above with the intention of avoiding the application of these Regulations to those contracts.

(11)   The relevant time for the purposes of paragraphs (1) and (6)(a) above means, in relation to a public supply contract, the date on which a contract notice would be sent to the Official Journal if the requirement to send such a notice applied to that contract in accordance with these Regulations.

Amendment
Para (2): substituted by SI 2000/2009, reg 5(4).
Para (2A): inserted by SI 2000/2009, reg 5(5).

PART II
TECHNICAL SPECIFICATIONS

[App.113]
8 Technical Specifications in the Contract Documents
(1)   In this regulation—
'common technical specification' means a technical specification drawn up in accordance with a procedure recognised by the member States with a view to uniform application in all member States and which has been published in the Official Journal;
'European specification' means a common technical specification, a British standard implementing a European standard or a European technical approval;
'European standard' means a standard approved by the European Committee for Standardisation ('CEN') or by the European Committee for Electrotechnical Standardisation ('CENELEC') as a 'European Standard ('EN')' or a 'Harmonisation Document ('HD')' according to the Common Rules of those organisations;
'European technical approval' means an approval of the fitness for use of a product, issued by an approval body, designated for the purpose by a member State following a technical assessment of whether the product fulfils the essential requirements for building works, having regard to the inherent characteristics of the product and the defined conditions of application and use;
'standard' means a technical specification approved by a recognised standardising body for repeated and continuous application, compliance with which is in principle not compulsory; and
'technical specifications' means the technical requirements defining the characteristics required of goods (such as quality, performance, safety or dimensions and requirements in respect of quality assurance, terminology, symbols, tests and testing methods, packaging, marking and labelling) so that the goods are described objectively in a manner which will ensure that they fulfil the use for which they are intended by the contracting authority.

(2)   If a contracting authority wishes to lay down technical specifications which the goods to be purchased or hired under a public supply contract must meet it shall specify all such technical specifications in the contract documents.

(3)   Subject to paragraph (4) below, the technical specifications in the contract documents relating to a public supply contract shall be defined by reference to any European specifications which are relevant.

(4)   A contracting authority may define the technical specifications referred to in paragraph (3) above other than by reference to relevant European specifications if—

(a)   the contracting authority is under an obligation to define the technical specifications by reference to technical requirements which are mandatory in the United Kingdom for the goods to be purchased or hired under the contract (but only to the extent that such an obligation is compatible with Community obligations);

(b)   the relevant European specifications do not include provision for establishing conformity to, or it is technically impossible to establish satisfactorily that the goods to be purchased or hired under the contract do conform to, the relevant European specifications;

(c)   definition by reference to the relevant European specifications would conflict with the application of—

   (i)   Council Directive 86/361/EEC on the initial stage of mutual recognition of type approval for telecommunication terminal equipment;

   (ii)   Council Decision 87/95/EEC on standardisation in the field of information technology and telecommunications; or

   (iii)   other Community obligations in specific service or goods areas;

(d)   subject to paragraph (5) below, application of the relevant European specifications would oblige the contracting authority to acquire goods incompatible with equipment already in use or would entail disproportionate costs or disproportionate technical difficulties; or

(e)   the project for which the goods to be purchased or hired under the contract are required is of a genuinely innovative nature for which use of existing relevant European specifications would be inappropriate.

(5)   A contracting authority may only define the technical specifications other than by reference to relevant European specifications on the grounds specified in paragraph 4(d) above where the contracting authority has a clearly defined and recorded strategy for changing over, within a set period, to European specifications.

(6)   A contracting authority shall state in the contract notice which of the circumstances specified in paragraph (4)(b) to (e) above was the ground for defining the technical specifications other than by reference to European specifications, or, if it is impossible to include this information in the contract notice, the contracting authority shall specify it in the contract documents and shall in any event keep a record of this information which, if the Commission or any relevant State requests it, it shall send to the Treasury for onward transmission to the Commission or relevant State which requested it.

(7)   In the absence of European specifications relevant to the supplies to be provided under a public supply contract, the technical specifications in the contract documents—

(a)   shall be defined by reference to British technical specifications recognised as complying with the basic requirements specified in any Council Directives on technical harmonisation in accordance with the procedures laid down in those directives and, in particular, in accordance with the procedures laid down in Council Directive 89/106/EEC on the approximation of laws, regulations and administrative procedures in the member States relating to construction products;

(b)   may be defined by reference to British technical specifications relating to design and method of calculation and execution of a work or works and use of materials and goods;

(c)   may be defined by reference to the following standards (and, if they are so defined, preference shall be given to the following standards in the order in which they are listed)—

    (i)   British standards implementing international standards;

    (ii)   other British standards and technical approvals; or

    (iii)   any other standards.

(8)   Subject to paragraph (10) below, the contract documents shall not include technical specifications which refer to goods of a specific make or source or to a particular process and which have the effect of favouring or eliminating particular goods or suppliers.

(9)   Without prejudice to the generality of paragraph (8) above but subject to paragraph (10) references to trademarks, patents, types, origin or means of production shall not be incorporated into the technical specifications in the contract documents.

(10)   Notwithstanding paragraphs (8) and (9) above, a contracting authority may incorporate the references referred to in paragraphs (8) and (9) above into the technical specifications in the contract documents if—

(a)   such references are justified by the subject of the contract, or

(b)   the goods to be purchased or hired under the contract cannot otherwise be described by reference to technical specifications which are sufficiently precise and intelligible to all suppliers, provided that the references are accompanied by the words 'or equivalent'.

PART III
PROCEDURES LEADING TO THE AWARD OF A PUBLIC SUPPLY CONTRACT

[App.114]

9 Prior Information Notices

(1)   Subject to paragraph (2) below, a contracting authority shall, as soon as possible after the commencement of each of its financial years, send to the Official Journal a notice, in a form substantially corresponding to that set out in Part A of Schedule 3 and containing the information therein specified, in respect of the public supply contracts in relation to which it expects to seek offers leading to an award during that financial year and the notice shall be subdivided to give that information separately for each product area.

(2)   The obligation under paragraph (1) above shall only apply—

(a)   to proposed public supply contracts which are not excluded from the application of these Regulations by virtue of regulation 6 or 7; and

(b)   where, at the date of despatch of the notice, the total consideration which the contracting authority expects to give under all the proposed public supply contracts which are for the purchase or hire of goods falling within the same product area equals or exceeds 750,000 ECU.

[App.115]

10 Selection of contract award procedure

(1)   For the purposes of seeking offers in relation to a proposed public supply contract a contracting authority shall use the open procedure, the restricted procedure or the negotiated procedure and shall decide which of those procedures to use in accordance with the following paragraphs of this regulation.

(2)   A contracting authority may use the negotiated procedure in the following circumstances—

(a)   subject to paragraph (3) below, in the event that the procedure leading to the award of a public supply contract by the contracting authority using the open or restricted procedure was discontinued—
   (i)   because of irregular tenders, or
   (ii)   following an evaluation made in accordance with regulation 11(7) or 12(4);
   and, without prejudice to the generality of the meaning of the words 'irregular tenders', a tender may be considered irregular if the supplier fails to meet the requirements of, or the tender offers variations on the requirements specified in, the contract documents where this is not permitted under the terms of the invitation to tender, or the goods offered do not meet the technical specifications (within the meaning of regulation 8(1)) of the contracting authority;

(b)   subject to paragraphs (3) and (6) below, in the absence of tenders or of appropriate tenders in response to an invitation to tender by the contracting authority using the open or restricted procedure;

(c)   when the goods to be purchased or hired under the contract are to be manufactured purely for the purpose of research, experiment, study or development but not when the goods are to be purchased or hired to establish their commercial viability or to recover their research and development costs;

(d)   when, for technical or artistic reasons, or for reasons connected with the protection of exclusive rights, the goods to be purchased or hired under the contract may only be manufactured or supplied by a particular person;

(e)   when (but only if it is strictly necessary), for reasons of extreme urgency brought about by events unforeseeable by, and not attributable to, the contracting authority, the time limits specified in regulations 11 and 12 if the open or restricted procedure is used, or the time limits specified in regulation 13 if the negotiated procedure is used pursuant to sub-paragraph (a) above, cannot be met; and

(f)   subject to paragraph (4) below, when the goods to be purchased or hired under the contract are required by the contracting authority as a partial replacement for, or addition to, existing goods or an installation and when to obtain the goods from a person other than the person who supplied the existing goods or the installation would oblige the contracting authority to acquire goods having different technical characteristics which would result in—
   (i)   incompatibility between the existing goods or the installation and the goods to be purchased or hired under the contract, or
   (ii)   disproportionate technical difficulties in the operation and maintenance of the existing goods or the installation.

(3)   A contracting authority shall not use the negotiated procedure pursuant to paragraphs (2)(a) or (b) above unless the proposed terms of the contract are

substantially unaltered from the proposed terms of the contract in relation to which offers were sought using the open or restricted procedure.

(4) A contracting authority shall not use the negotiated procedure pursuant to paragraph (2)(f) above if the term of the proposed contract, or the term of that contract and of any other contract entered into for the same purpose, is more than three years unless there are reasons why it is unavoidable that this period should be exceeded.

(5) In all other circumstances the contracting authority shall use the open or restricted procedure.

(6) A contracting authority using the negotiated procedure pursuant to paragraph (2)(b) above shall submit a report recording the fact that it has done so to the Treasury for onward transmission to the Commission.

[App.116]

11 The open procedure

(1) A contracting authority using the open procedure shall comply with the following paragraphs of this regulation.

(2) The contracting authority shall publicise its intention to seek offers in relation to the public supply contract by sending to the Official Journal as soon as possible after forming the intention a notice, in a form substantially corresponding to that set out in Part B of Schedule 3, inviting tenders and containing the information therein specified.

[(3) Subject to paragraphs (3A) and (6) below, the date which the contracting authority shall fix as the last date for the receipt by it of tenders made in response to the contract notice shall be specified in the notice and shall be not less than 52 days from the date of despatch of the notice.]

[(3A) Where—
(a) the contracting authority has published a prior information notice in accordance with regulation 9 above;
(b) the prior information notice contained as much of the information referred to in Part B of Schedule 3 as was available at the time of publication; and
(c) the prior information notice was sent to the Official Journal at least 52 days and no more than 12 months before the date on which the contract notice provided for in regulation 11(2) is despatched,

the contracting authority may substitute for the period of not less than 52 days specified in paragraph (3) above a shorter period of generally no less than 36 days and in any event no less than 22 days, provided in each case that the period is sufficient to allow for effective tendering.]

(4) The contracting authority shall send the contract documents within 6 days of the receipt of a request from any supplier provided that the documents are requested by the date specified in the contract notice and any fee specified in the notice has accompanied the request.

(5) The contracting authority shall supply such further information relating to the contract documents as may reasonably be requested by a supplier provided that the request is received in sufficient time to enable the contracting authority to supply the information no later than 6 days before the date specified in the contract notice as the final date for the receipt of tenders.

(6) If the contract documents are too bulky to be supplied within the periods referred to in paragraphs (4) and (5) above or it is necessary that suppliers be given the

opportunity to inspect the premises at which the goods are to be used or documents relating to the contract documents, then the minimum period laid down in paragraph (3) above shall be extended to allow for such supply or inspection.

(7)   The contracting authority may exclude a tender from the evaluation of offers made in accordance with regulation 21 only if the supplier may be treated as ineligible on a ground specified in regulation 14 or if the supplier fails to satisfy the minimum standards of economic and financial standing and technical capacity required of suppliers by the contracting authority; for this purpose the contracting authority shall make its evaluation in accordance with regulations 14, 15, 16 and 17.

[(8)   Tenders shall be submitted in writing either in person or by post, except that a contracting authority may authorise another means of submission provided that the chosen means enables—

(a)   each tender to contain all the information necessary for its evaluation;

(b)   the confidentiality of tenders to be maintained pending their evaluation; and

(c)   tenders to be opened only after the time limit for their submission has expired.

(9)   Where a contracting authority has authorised another means of submission in accordance with paragraph (8) above, it may require either that the submission of the tender is confirmed in writing or that a copy of the tender is delivered to it in person or by post, in either case as soon as possible thereafter.]

Amendment
Para (3): substituted by SI 2000/2009, reg 5(6)(a).
Para (3A): inserted by SI 2000/2009, reg 5(6)(b).
Paras (8), (9): inserted by SI 2000/2009, reg 5(7).

[App.117]
12 The restricted procedure

(1)   A contracting authority using the restricted procedure shall comply with the following paragraphs of this regulation.

(2)   The contracting authority shall publicise its intention to seek offers in relation to the public supply contract by sending to the Official Journal as soon as possible after forming the intention a notice, in a form substantially corresponding to that set out in Part C of Schedule 3, inviting requests to be selected to tender and containing the information therein specified.

(3)   Subject to paragraph (14) below, the date which the contracting authority shall fix as the last date for the receipt by it of requests to be selected to tender shall be specified in the contract notice and shall not be less than 37 days from the date of the despatch of the notice.

(4)   The contracting authority may exclude a supplier from those persons from whom it will make the selection of the persons to be invited to tender only if the supplier may be treated as ineligible on a ground specified in regulation 14 or if the supplier fails to satisfy the minimum standards of economic and financial standing and technical capacity required of suppliers by the contracting authority; for this purpose the contracting authority shall make its evaluation in accordance with regulations 14, 15, 16 and 17.

(5)   The contracting authority shall make the selection of the suppliers to be invited to tender in accordance with regulations 14, 15, 16 and 17; and in making the selection and in issuing invitations the contracting authority shall not discriminate between suppliers on the grounds of their nationality or the relevant State in which they are established.

(6)   The contracting authority may predetermine the range within which the number of persons which it intends to invite to tender for the contract shall be fixed but only if—

(a)   the lower number of the range is not less than 5 and the higher number not more than 20;

(b)   the range is determined in the light of the nature of the goods to be purchased or hired under the contract, and

(c)   the range is specified in the contract notice.

(7)   In any event, the number of persons invited to tender shall be sufficient to ensure genuine competition.

(8)   The contracting authority shall send invitations to each of the suppliers selected to tender and the invitation shall be accompanied by the contract documents, or the invitation shall state the address for requesting them.

(9)   The invitation to tender shall be sent in writing simultaneously to each supplier selected to tender.

(10)   The following information shall be included in the invitation—

(a)   the address to which requests for the contract documents (if not accompanying the invitation) and further information relating to those documents should be sent, the final date for making such a request and the amount and terms of the fee which may be charged for supplying that material;

(b)   the final date for the receipt of tenders, the address to which they must be sent and the language or languages in which they must be drawn up;

(c)   a reference to the contract notice published in accordance with paragraph (2) above;

(d)   an indication of the information to be included with the tender which the contracting authority may require to be provided in accordance with regulations 15, 16 and 17; and

(e)   the criteria for the award of the contract if this information was not specified in the contract notice published in accordance with paragraph (2) above.

[(11)   Subject to paragraphs (11A) and (14) below, the date which the contracting authority shall fix as the last date for the receipt by it of tenders made in response to the invitation to tender which shall be specified in the invitation to tender in accordance with paragraph 10(b) above shall be not less than 40 days from the despatch of the invitation.]

[(11A)   Where—

(a)   the contracting authority has published a prior information notice in accordance with regulation 9 above;

(b)   the prior information notice contained as much of the information referred to in Part B of Schedule 3 as was available at the time of publication; and

(c)   the prior information notice was sent to the Official Journal at least 52 days and no more than 12 months before the date on which the contract notice provided for in regulation 12(2) is despatched,

the contracting authority may substitute for the period of not less than 40 days specified in paragraph (11) above, a period of not less than 26 days.]

(12)   If it is necessary that suppliers should be given the opportunity to inspect the premises at which the goods are to be used or documents relating to the contract documents, then the minimum period referred to in paragraph (11) above shall be extended to allow for such inspection.

(13)   Subject to paragraph (14) below, the contracting authority shall supply such further information relating to the contract documents as may reasonably be requested by a supplier selected to tender provided that the request for such information is received in sufficient time to enable the contracting authority to supply it not less than 6 days before the date specified in the invitation to tender as the final date for the receipt of tenders.

(14)   Where compliance with the minimum periods referred to in paragraphs (3), (11) and (13) above is rendered impracticable for reasons of urgency, the contracting authority may substitute for the periods specified in those paragraphs periods of not less than 15 days, 10 days and 4 days respectively and, in those circumstances, the contracting authority shall send the invitation to tender by the most rapid means possible.

(15)   A contracting authority shall not refuse to consider an application to be invited to tender if it is made by letter, telegram, telex, facsimile or telephone provided that, in the last four cases, it is confirmed by letter despatched before the date fixed by the contracting authority as the last date for the receipt of applications to be invited to tender for the contract.

[(16)   Tenders shall be submitted in writing either in person or by post, except that a contracting authority may authorise another means of submission provided that the chosen means enables—
(a)   each tender to contain all the information necessary for its evaluation;
(b)   the confidentiality of tenders to be maintained pending their evaluation; and
(c)   tenders to be opened only after the time limit for their submission has expired.

(17)   Where a contracting authority has authorised another means of submission in accordance with paragraph (16) above, it may require either that the submission of the tender is confirmed in writing or that a copy of the tender is delivered to it in person or by post, in either case as soon as possible thereafter.]

Amendment
Para (11): substituted by SI 2000/2009, reg 5(8)(a).
Para (11A): inserted by SI 2000/2009, reg 5(8)(b).
Paras (16), (17): inserted by SI 2000/2009, reg 5(9).

[App.118]

13 The negotiated procedure

(1)   A contracting authority using the negotiated procedure shall comply with the following paragraphs of this regulation except that—
(a)   a contracting authority using the negotiated procedure pursuant to regulation 10(2)(b), (c), (d), (e) or (f), and
(b)   a contracting authority using the negotiated procedure pursuant to regulation 10(2)(a) who invites to negotiate the contract every supplier who submitted a tender following an invitation made during the course of the discontinued open or restricted procedure (not being a tender which was excluded pursuant to regulation 11(7) or 12(4)),
need not comply with paragraphs (2) to (6) below.

(2)   The contracting authority shall publicise its intention to seek offers in relation to the public supply contract by sending to the Official Journal as soon as possible after forming the intention a notice, in a form substantially corresponding to that set out in Part D of Schedule 3, inviting requests to be selected to negotiate and containing the information therein specified.

(3)   Subject to paragraph (4) below, the date which the contracting authority shall fix as the last date for the receipt by it of requests to be selected to negotiate shall be specified in the contract notice and shall be not less than 37 days from the date of despatch of the notice.

(4)   Where compliance with the minimum period of 37 days in paragraph (3) above is rendered impracticable for reasons of urgency, the contracting authority may substitute a period of not less than 15 days and, in those circumstances, the contracting authority shall send the invitation to negotiate the contract by the most rapid means possible.

(5)   A contracting authority shall not refuse to consider an application to be selected to negotiate if it is made by letter, telegram, telex, facsimile or telephone provided that, in the last four cases, it is confirmed by letter despatched before the date fixed by the contracting authority as the last date for the receipt of applications to be invited to tender for the contract.

(6)   Where there is a sufficient number of persons who are suitable to be selected to negotiate the contract, the number selected to negotiate shall not be less than 3.

(7)   The contracting authority may exclude a supplier from those persons from whom it will make the selection of persons to be invited to negotiate the contract only if the supplier may be treated as ineligible on a ground specified in regulation 14 or if the supplier fails to satisfy the minimum standards of economic and financial standing and technical capacity required of suppliers by the contracting authority; for this purpose the contracting authority shall make its evaluation in accordance with regulations 14, 15, 16 and 17.

(8)   The contracting authority shall make the selection of the suppliers to be invited to negotiate in accordance with regulations 14, 15, 16 and 17; and in making the selection and in issuing invitations to negotiate the contracting authority shall not discriminate between suppliers on the grounds of their nationality or the relevant State in which they are established.

PART IV
SELECTION OF SUPPLIERS

[App.119]
14 Criteria for rejection of suppliers

(1)   A contracting authority may treat a supplier as ineligible to tender for or to be included amongst those persons from whom it will make the selection of persons to be invited to tender for or to negotiate a contract in accordance with regulations 11(7), 12(4) and 13(7) above, or decide not to select a supplier to tender for or to negotiate a contract in accordance with regulations 12(5) and 13(8), on one of the following grounds, namely that the supplier—

(a)   being an individual is bankrupt or has had a receiving order or administration order made against him or has made any composition or arrangement with or for the benefit of his creditors or has made any conveyance or assignment for the benefit of his creditors or appears unable to pay, or to have no reasonable prospect of being able to pay, a debt within the meaning of section 268 of the Insolvency Act 1986, or article 242 of the Insolvency (Northern Ireland) Order 1989, or in Scotland has granted a trust deed for creditors or become otherwise apparently insolvent, or is the subject of a petition presented for sequestration of his estate, or is the subject of any similar procedure under the law of any other state;

(b)   being a partnership constituted under Scots law has granted a trust deed or become otherwise apparently insolvent, or is the subject of a petition presented for sequestration of its estate;

(c)   being a company has passed a resolution or is the subject of an order by the court for the company's winding up otherwise than for the purposes of bona fide reconstruction or amalgamation, or has had a receiver, manager or administrator on behalf of a creditor appointed in respect of the company's business or any part thereof or is the subject of proceedings for any of the above procedures or is the subject of similar procedures under the law of any other state;

(d)   has been convicted of a criminal offence relating to the conduct of his business or profession;

(e)   has committed an act of grave misconduct in the course of his business or profession;

(f)   has not fulfilled obligations relating to the payment of social security contributions under the law of any part of the United Kingdom or of the relevant State in which the supplier is established;

(g)   has not fulfilled obligations relating to the payment of taxes under the law of any part of the United Kingdom or the relevant State in which the supplier is established;

(h)   is guilty of serious misrepresentation in supplying any information required of him under this regulation and regulations 15, 16 and 17; or

(i)   subject to paragraphs (5) and (6) below, is not registered on the professional or trade register of the relevant State in which the supplier is established under the conditions laid down by that State.

(2)   Subject to regulation 19, the contracting authority may require a supplier to provide such information as it considers it needs to make the evaluation in accordance with paragraph (1) above except that it shall accept as conclusive evidence that a supplier does not fall within the grounds specified in paragraphs (1)(a), (b), (c), (d), (f) or (g) above if that supplier provides to the contracting authority—

(a)   in relation to the grounds specified in paragraphs (1)(a), (b), (c) or (d) above,
   (i)   an extract from the judicial record, or
   (ii)   in a relevant State which does not maintain such a judicial record, a document issued by the relevant judicial or administrative authority;

(b)   in relation to the grounds specified in paragraph (1)(f) or (g) above, a certificate issued by the relevant competent authority;

(c)   in a relevant State where the documentary evidence specified in paragraphs 2(a) and (b) above is not issued or where it is issued but does not extend to all of the grounds specified in paragraph (1)(a), (b), (c) or (d) above, a declaration on oath, or in a relevant State which does not provide for a declaration on oath a solemn declaration, made by the supplier before the relevant judicial, administrative or competent authority or a relevant notary public or commissioner for oaths.

(3)   In this regulation, 'relevant' in relation to a judicial, administrative or competent authority, notary public or commissioner for oaths means such an authority designated by, or a notary public or commissioner of oaths in, the relevant State in which the supplier is established.

(4)   The following are the appropriate professional or trade registers for the purposes of paragraph (1)(i) above—

in Austria, the Firmenbuch, the Gewerberegister or the Mitgliederverzeichnisse der Landeskammen;

in Belgium, the Registre du commerce/Handelsregister;

in Denmark, the Aktieselskabsregistret, Foreningsregistret or Handelsregistret;

in Finland, the Kaupparekisteri or Handelsregistret;

in France, the Registre du commerce or répertoire des métiers;

in Germany, the Handelsregister or Handwerksrolle;

in Greece, the BioTeCniKo h BiomhCaniKo h EmporiKo EpimelhThrio;

in Iceland, the Firmaskra;

in Italy, the Registro della Camera di commercio, industria, agricoltura e artigianato or Registro delle Commissioni provinciali per l'artigianato;

in Liechtenstein, the Gewerberegister;

in Luxembourg, the Registre aux firmes or Role de la chambre des metiers;

in Norway, the Foretaksregisteret;

in the Netherlands, the Handelsregister;

in Portugal, the Registo Nacional das Pessoas Colectivas;

in Spain, the Registro Mercantil; and

in Sweden, the Aktiebolagsregistret or the Handelsregistret.

(5) A supplier established in the United Kingdom or Ireland shall be treated as registered on the professional or trade register for the purposes of paragraph (1)(i) above if the supplier—

(a) is established in Ireland and is certified as registered with the Registrar of Friendly Societies, or

(b) is established in either State and is either—

    (i) certified as incorporated by the Registrar of Companies, or

    (ii) is certified as having declared on oath that he is carrying on business in the trade in question in the State in which he is established at a specific place of business and under a specific trading name.

(6) An individual who is established in Spain shall be treated as registered on the professional or trade register for the purposes of paragraph (1)(i) above if he is certified as having declared an oath that he exercises the particular profession or trade.

(7) A supplier established in a relevant State, other than the United Kingdom or Ireland, which either has an equivalent professional or trade register which is not listed in paragraph (4) above or which does not have an equivalent professional or trade register shall be treated as registered on a professional or trade register for the purposes of paragraph 1(i) above on production of either a certificate that he is registered on the equivalent professional or trade register or where no such register exists, a declaration on oath, or in a relevant State which does not provide for a declaration on oath a solemn declaration, made by the supplier before the relevant judicial, administrative or competent authority or a relevant notary public or Commissioner for oaths, that he exercises the particular profession or trade.

[App.120]

15 Information as to economic and financial standing

(1) Subject to regulation 19 and paragraph (2) below, in assessing whether a supplier meets any minimum standards of economic and financial standing required of suppliers by the contracting authority for the purposes of regulations 11(7), 12(4) and 13(7), and in selecting the suppliers to be invited to tender for or to negotiate the contract in accordance with regulations 12(5) and 13(8), a contracting authority may take into account any of the following information—

(a)   appropriate statements from the supplier's bankers;

(b)   statements of accounts or extracts therefrom relating to the business of the supplier where publication of the statement is required under the law of the relevant State in which the supplier is established;

(c)   a statement of the overall turnover of the business of the supplier and the turnover in respect of goods of a similar type to the goods to be purchased or hired under the public supply contract in the 3 previous financial years of the supplier.

(2)   Where the information specified in paragraph (1) above is not appropriate in a particular case, a contracting authority may require a supplier to provide other information to demonstrate the supplier's economic and financial standing.

(3)   A contracting authority which requires information to be provided in accordance with paragraphs (1) and (2) above shall specify in the contract notice or in the invitation to tender the information which the supplier must provide and it may require a supplier to provide only such of that information as it considers it needs to make the assessment or selection.

(4)   Where a supplier is unable for a valid reason to provide the information which the contracting authority has required, the contracting authority shall accept such other information provided by the supplier as the contracting authority considers appropriate.

[App.121]

16 Information as to technical capacity

(1)   Subject to regulation 19, in assessing whether a supplier meets any minimum standards of technical capacity required of suppliers by the contracting authority for the purposes of regulations 11(7), 12(4) and 13(7), and in selecting the suppliers to be invited to tender for or to negotiate the contract in accordance with regulations 12(5) and 13(8), a contracting authority may take into account any of the following information—

(a)   the principal deliveries by the supplier of goods of a similar type to the goods to be purchased or hired under the public supply contract in the past 3 years, specifying in each case the date of delivery, the consideration received and the identity of the purchaser accompanied by a certificate issued or countersigned by the purchaser confirming the details of the purchase or hire or, but only where the purchaser was not a contracting authority, a declaration by the supplier attesting the details of the purchase or hire;

(b)   the supplier's technical facilities, measures for ensuring quality and study and research facilities in relation to the goods to be purchased or hired under the public supply contract;

(c)   the technicians or technical bodies who would be involved with the production of the goods to be purchased or hired under the public supply contract, particularly those responsible for quality control, whether or not they are independent of the supplier;

(d)   samples, descriptions and photographs of the goods to be purchased or hired under the public supply contract and certification of the authenticity of such samples, descriptions or photographs;

(e)   certification by official quality control institutes or agencies of recognised competence attesting that the goods to be purchased or hired under the public supply contract conform to standards and technical specifications (within the meaning of regulation 8(1)) identified by the contracting authority;

(f)   where the goods to be sold or hired under the public supply contract are complex or are required for a special purpose, a check, carried out by the contracting authority or on its behalf by a competent official body of the relevant State in which the supplier is established, on the production capacity of the supplier in respect of the goods to be purchased or hired under the contract and, if relevant, on the supplier's study and research facilities and quality control measures.

(2)   The contracting authority may only require a supplier to provide information specified in paragraph (1) above and only such of that information as it considers it needs to make the assessment or selection and it shall specify in the contract notice or in the invitation to tender which of that information it requires to be provided.

[App.122]
17 Supplementary information

The contracting authority may require a supplier to provide information supplementing the information supplied in accordance with regulations 14, 15 and 16 or to clarify that information, provided that the information so required relates to the matters specified in regulations 14, 15 and 16.

[App.123]
18 Confidentiality of information

A contracting authority shall comply with such requirements as to the confidentiality of information provided to it by a supplier as the supplier may reasonably request.

[App.124]
19 Official lists of recognised suppliers

Where a supplier is registered on the official list of recognised suppliers in a relevant State which maintains such lists and in which the supplier is established and the supplier submits to the contracting authority a certificate of registration issued by the authority administering the official lists which specifies the information submitted to that authority which enabled the supplier to be registered and which states the classification given, the contracting authority, to the extent that the certificate deals with the grounds referred to in regulations 14(1)(a) to (e), (h) and (i), 15(1)(b) and (c) and 16(1)(a)—

(a)   shall accept the certificate as evidence that the supplier does not fall within the grounds specified in regulations 14(1)(a) to (e), (h) and (i) and shall not be entitled to require the supplier to submit such information relating to those grounds as is specified in regulation 14,

(b)   shall not be entitled to require the supplier to provide information specified in regulations 15(1)(b) and (c) and 16(1)(a), and

(c)   shall not be entitled to seek any supplementary information in accordance with regulation 17 above in relation to the matters specified in subparagraphs (a) and (b) above.

[App.125]
20 Consortia

(1)   In this regulation a 'consortium' means 2 or more persons, at least one of whom is a supplier, acting jointly for the purpose of being awarded a public supply contract.

(2)   A contracting authority shall not treat the tender of a consortium as ineligible nor decide not to include a consortium amongst those persons from whom it will make the selection of persons to be invited to tender for or to negotiate a public supply contract on the grounds that that consortium has not formed a legal entity for the purpose of tendering for or negotiating the contract; but where a contracting authority awards a public supply contract to a consortium it may, if to do so is justified for the satisfactory performance of the contract, require the consortium to form a legal entity before entering into, or as a term of, the contract.

(3)   In this part of these Regulations references to a supplier where the supplier is a consortium includes a reference to each person who is a member of that consortium.

PART V
THE AWARD OF A PUBLIC SUPPLY CONTRACT

[App.126]
21 Criteria for the Award of a Public Supply Contract

(1)   Subject to paragraphs (5), (6) and (7) below, a contracting authority shall award a public supply contract on the basis of the offer which—
(a)   is the most economically advantageous to the contracting authority, or
(b)   offers the lowest price.

(2)   The criteria which a contracting authority may use to determine that an offer is the most economically advantageous include delivery date, running costs, cost effectiveness, quality, aesthetic and functional characteristics, technical merit, after sales service, technical assistance and price.

(3)   Where a contracting authority intends to award a public supply contract on the basis of the offer which is the most economically advantageous it shall state the criteria on which it intends to base its decision, where possible in descending order of importance, in the contract notice or in the contract documents.

(4)   Where a contracting authority awards a public supply contract on the basis of the offer which is the most economically advantageous, it may take account of offers which offer variations on the requirements specified in the contract documents if—
(a)   the offer meets the minimum requirements of the contracting authority, and
(b)   it has stated those minimum requirements and any specific requirements for the presentation of an offer offering variations in the contract documents,

but if the contracting authority shall not take account of offers which offer such variations it shall state that fact in the contract notice.

(5)   A contracting authority may not reject an offer which offers variations on the requirements specified in the contract documents on the ground that it would lead to the award of a public services contract within the meaning of the Public Services Contracts Regulations 1993.

(6)   A contracting authority may not reject an offer on the ground that the technical specifications in the offer have been defined by reference to European specifications (within the meaning of regulation 8(1)) or to the British technical specifications specified in regulation 8(7)(a) and (b).

(7)   If an offer for a public supply contract is abnormally low the contracting authority may reject that offer but only if it has requested in writing an explanation

of the offer, or of those parts which it considers contribute to the offer being abnormally low, and has—

(a)   if awarding the public supply contract on the basis of the offer which offers the lowest price, examined the details of all the offers made, taking into account any explanation given to it of the abnormally low tender, before awarding the contract, or

(b)   if awarding the public supply contract on the basis of the offer which is the most economically advantageous, taken any such explanation into account in assessing which is the most economically advantageous offer,

and, in considering that explanation, the contracting authority may take into account explanations relating to the economics of the manufacturing process, or to the technical solutions suggested by the supplier or the exceptionally favourable conditions available to the supplier for the provision of the supply of goods or the originality of the supplies proposed by the supplier.

(8)   If a contracting authority which rejects an abnormally low offer is awarding the public supply contract on the basis of the offer which offers the lowest price, it shall send a report justifying the rejection to the Treasury for onward transmission to the Commission.

(9)   For the purposes of this regulation an 'offer' includes a bid by one part of a contracting authority to make available to another part of the contracting authority the goods required by it when the former part is invited by the latter part to compete with the offers sought from other persons.

[App.127]

22 Contract award notice

(1)   A contracting authority which has awarded a public supply contract shall, no later than 48 days after the award, send to the Official Journal a notice, substantially corresponding to the form set out in Part E of Schedule 3 and, subject to paragraph (2) below, including the information therein specified.

(2)   Any of the information specified in Part E of Schedule 3 to be included in the contract award notice may be omitted in a particular case where to publish such information would impede law enforcement, would otherwise be contrary to the public interest, would prejudice the legitimate commercial interests of any person or might prejudice fair competition between suppliers.

[App.128]

[23 Information about contract award procedures]

[(1)   Where a contracting authority decides either to abandon or to recommence an award procedure in respect of which a contract notice has been published it shall inform the Office for Official Publications of the European Communities and shall inform promptly any supplier who submitted an offer or who applied to be included amongst the persons to be selected to tender for or to negotiate the contract of the reasons for its decision and shall do so in writing if so requested.

(2)   Subject to paragraph (3) below, a contracting authority shall, within 15 days of the date on which it receives a request in writing from any supplier who was unsuccessful (whether pursuant to regulation 11(7), 12(4), 12(5), 13(7), 13(8) or 21), inform that supplier of the reasons why he was unsuccessful and, if the supplier submitted an admissible tender, the contracting authority shall inform him of the

characteristics and relative advantages of the successful tender as well as the name of the person awarded the contract.

(3)   A contracting authority may withhold any information to be provided in accordance with paragraph (2) above where the disclosure of such information would impede law enforcement or otherwise be contrary to the public interest or would prejudice the legitimate commercial interests of any person or might prejudice fair competition between suppliers.

(4)   A contracting authority shall prepare a record in relation to each public supply contract awarded by it specifying—
(a)   the name and address of the contracting authority;
(b)   the type of goods purchased or hired or to be purchased or hired under the contract and the value of the consideration to be given under it;
(c)   the names of the persons whose offers were evaluated in accordance with regulation 21 and, where the contracting authority has used the restricted or negotiated procedure, the reasons why those persons were selected;
(d)   the names of the persons who were unsuccessful pursuant to regulation 11(7), 12(4), 12(5), 13(7) or 13(8) and the reasons why they were unsuccessful;
(e)   the name of the person to whom the public supply contract was awarded and the reasons for having awarded the contract to him;
(f)   if known to the contracting authority, which parts of the contract the person to whom the contract has been awarded intends to sub-contract to another person; and
(g)   in the case of a contracting authority which used the negotiated procedure, which of the circumstances specified in regulation 10(2) constituted grounds for using that procedure.

(5)   If the Commission requests a report containing the information specified in paragraph (4) above, the contracting authority shall send a written report containing that information, or the main features of it, to the Treasury for onward transmission to the Commission.]

Amendment
Substituted by SI 2000/2009, reg 5(10).

PART VI
MISCELLANEOUS

[App.129]
24 Public service bodies

Where a contracting authority, other than one which is a contracting authority only by reason of being a [Schedule 1 entity], grants to a person other than a contracting authority special or exclusive rights to carry on a service for the benefit of the public, it shall impose an express duty on that person not to discriminate in seeking offers in relation to, or in awarding, a contract for the purchase or hire of goods on the grounds of nationality against a person who is a national of and established in a relevant State or on the grounds that the goods to be supplied under the contract originate in another relevant State.

Amendment
Words 'Schedule 1 entity' in square brackets substituted by SI 2000/2009, reg 5(11).

[App.130]

[25 Statistical and other reports]

[(1)   A contracting authority shall, no later than 31st July in each year, send to the Treasury a report specifying, in relation to each public supply contract awarded by it during the reporting period—

(a)   the value (estimated if necessary) of the consideration payable under the contract;

(b)   whether the open, restricted or negotiated procedure was used;

(c)   if the negotiated procedure was used, pursuant to which provision of regulation 10(2) that procedure was used;

(d)   the type of goods purchased or hired or to be purchased or hired under the contract; and

(e)   the nationality of the person to whom the contract was awarded.

(2)   A Schedule 1 entity shall include in the report referred to in paragraph (1) above the aggregate value (estimated if necessary) of all public supply contracts awarded by it during the reporting period which were below the relevant threshold specified in regulation 7.

(3)   A contracting authority shall send to the Treasury a report containing such other information as the Treasury may from time to time require in respect of a particular public supply contract (including public supply contracts excluded from the application of these Regulations by regulations 6 and 7) for the purposes of informing the Commission.

(4)   In this regulation 'the reporting period' means the year preceding the year in which the reports referred to in paragraph (1) are to be made.]

Amendment
Substituted by SI 2000/2009, reg 5(12).

[App.131]

26 Responsibility for obtaining reports

(1)   Where a contracting authority is not a Minister of the Crown or a government department, that contracting authority shall send any report which it is required in accordance with regulations 8(6), 10(6), 21(8), 23(3) and 25 to send to the Treasury instead to the Minister responsible for that contracting authority and that Minister shall be responsible for sending the report to the Treasury.

(2)   The Minister responsible for a contracting authority shall be the Minister of the Crown whose areas of responsibility are most closely connected with the functions of the contracting authority; and any question as to which Minister of the Crown's areas of responsibility are most closely connected with the functions of a contracting authority shall be determined by the Treasury whose determination shall be final.

(3)   The requirement on a contracting authority to send any report in accordance with paragraph (1) above to the Minister of the Crown responsible for that contracting authority shall be enforceable, on the application of the Minister responsible, by mandamus or, in Scotland, for an order for specific performance.

(4)   Proceedings under paragraph (3) above brought in Scotland shall be brought before the Court of Session.

(5)   In the application of this regulation to Northern Ireland references to the Minister shall include references to the head of a Northern Ireland department.

[(6)   In the application of this regulation to Scotland—

(a)   references to—
    (i)   a Minister of the Crown, other than the first reference in paragraph (1); and
    (ii)   the Minister responsible for a contracting authority,
    shall be construed as references to the Scottish Ministers;
(b)   paragraph (2) shall not apply.]

Amendment
Para (6): inserted by SI 1999/1820, art 4, Sch 2, Pt II, para 156.

[App.132]
27 Publication of notices

(1)   Any notice required by these Regulations to be sent to the Official Journal shall be sent by the most appropriate means to the Office for Official Publications of the European Communities and where the contracting authority is applying the restricted procedure or the negotiated procedure and, for reasons of urgency, is applying the provisions of regulations 12(14) and 13(4), the notice shall be sent by telex, telegram or facsimile.

(2)   Any such notice shall not contain more than 650 words.

(3)   The contracting authority shall retain evidence of the date of despatch to the Official Journal of each notice.

(4)   The contracting authority shall not place a contract notice in the press or like publications in the United Kingdom before the date on which the notice is despatched in accordance with paragraph (1) above and if it does, after that date, so place the notice it shall not add to the notice any information in relation to the public supply contract which was not contained in the notice sent to the Official Journal except that it shall mention the date on which that notice was despatched.

[App.133]
28 Sub-contractors

A contracting authority may require a supplier to indicate in his tender what part of the contract he intends to sub-contract to another person.

PART VII
APPLICATIONS TO THE COURT

[App.134]
29 Enforcement of obligations

(1)   The obligation on a contracting authority to comply with the provisions of these Regulations other than regulations 8(6), 10(6), 21(8), 23(3) and 25, and with any enforceable Community obligation in respect of a public supply contract (other than one excluded from the application of these Regulations by regulations 6 and 7), is a duty owed to suppliers.

[(1A)   The duty owed to a supplier pursuant to paragraph (1) above shall be a duty owed also to a GPA provider, but such a duty to a GPA provider shall only be owed by the Secretary of State for Defence in relation to public supply contracts for the purchase or hire of goods specified in Schedule 2.

(1B) References to a 'supplier' in paragraphs (2), (4) and (5) below shall be construed as including a reference to a GPA provider.]

(2) A breach of the duty owed pursuant to paragraph (1) [or paragraph (1A)] above shall not be a criminal offence but any breach of the duty shall be actionable by any supplier who, in consequence, suffers, or risks suffering, loss or damage.

(3) Proceedings under this regulation shall be brought in England and Wales and in Northern Ireland in the High Court and, in Scotland, before the Court of Session.

(4) Proceedings under this regulation may not be brought unless—

(a) the supplier bringing the proceedings has informed the contracting authority of the breach or apprehended breach of the duty owed to him pursuant to paragraph (1) [or paragraph (1A)] above by the contracting authority and of his intention to bring proceedings under this regulation in respect of it; and

(b) they are brought promptly and in any event within 3 months from the date when grounds for the bringing of the proceedings first arose unless the Court considers that there is good reason for extending the period within which proceedings may be brought.

(5) Subject to paragraph (6) below, but otherwise without prejudice to any other powers of the Court, in proceedings brought under this regulation the Court may—

(a) by interim order suspend the procedure leading to the award of the contract in relation to which the breach of the duty owed pursuant to paragraph (1) [or paragraph (1A)] above is alleged, or suspend the implementation of any decision or action taken by the contracting authority in the course of following such procedure; and

(b) if satisfied that a decision or action taken by a contracting authority was in breach of the duty owed pursuant to paragraph (1) [or paragraph (1A)] above—

  (i) order the setting aside of that decision or action or order the contracting authority to amend any document, or

  (ii) award damages to a supplier who has suffered loss or damage as a consequence of the breach, or

  (iii) do both of those things.

(6) In proceedings under this regulation the Court shall not have power to order any remedy other than an award of damages in respect of a breach of the duty owed pursuant to paragraph (1) [or paragraph (1A)] above if the contract in relation to which the breach occurred has been entered into.

(7) Notwithstanding sections 21 and 42 of the Crown Proceedings Act 1947, in proceedings brought under this regulation against the Crown the court shall have power to grant an injunction or interdict.

[(8) In this regulation—

(a) a 'GPA provider' shall mean a person from a GPA State who sought, or who seeks, or would have wished, to be the person to whom the contract is awarded;

(b) a 'GPA State' shall mean any country other than a relevant State which, at the relevant time is a signatory to the GPA and has agreed with the European Community that the GPA shall apply to a contract of the type to be awarded; and

(c) 'relevant time' shall mean the date on which the contracting authority would have sent a contract notice in respect of the contract to the Official Journal if it had been required by these Regulations to do so.]

Amendment

Paras (1A), (1B): inserted by SI 2000/2009, reg 5(13)(a).

Paras (2), (4)–(6): words 'or paragraph (1A)' in square brackets in each place they occur inserted by SI 2000/2009, reg 5(13)(b).
Para (8): inserted by SI 2000/2009, reg 5(13)(c).

PART VIII
REVOCATION AND AMENDMENT

[App.135]

30 [*This regulation revokes SI 1991/2679, SI 1992/3279, reg 32(2) and SI 1993/3228, reg 33.*]

[App.136]

31 [*This regulation amends SI 1991/2680, regs 2, 4, 6, 8, 12–15, 18, 31 and SI 1993/3228, regs 2, 4, 6, 8, 12–16, 18, 20, 23.*]

[SCHEDULE 1
GPA ANNEX I CONTRACTING AUTHORITIES]

[Regulations 2(1), 7(1), 24, 25(3)]

[App.137]

[Where an entity listed in this Schedule is succeeded by another entity, which is itself a contracting authority, the successor entity shall be deemed to be included in this Schedule.

Cabinet Office
 Central Computer and Telecommunications Agency (CCTA)
 Civil Service College
 Office of the Parliamentary Counsel
 The Buying Agency

Central Office of Information

Charity Commission

Crown Prosecution Service

Crown Estate Commissioners (Vote Expenditure Only)

HM Customs and Excise

Department for Culture, Media and Sport
 British Library
 British Museum
 Historic Buildings and Monuments Commission for England (English Heritage)
 Imperial War Museum
 Museums and Galleries Commission
 National Gallery
 National Maritime Museum
 National Portrait Gallery
 Natural History Museum
 Royal Commission on Historical Manuscripts

Royal Commission on Historical Monuments of England
Royal Fine Art Commission (England)
Science Museum
Tate Gallery
Victoria and Albert Museum
Wallace Collection

Department for Education and Employment
Higher Education Funding Council for England

Department of the Environment, Transport and the Regions
Building Research Establishment Agency
Commons Commission
Countryside Agency
Maritime and Coastguard Agency
Rent Assessment Panels
Royal Commission on Environmental Pollution
Valuation Tribunal

Department of Health
Central Council for Education and Training in Social Work
Dental Practice Board
. . .
National Health Service Authorities and Trusts
Prescription Pricing Authority
Public Health Service Laboratory Board
. . .

Department for International Development

Department for National Savings

Department of Social Security
Disability Living Allowance Advisory Board
Independent Tribunal Service
Medical Boards and Examining Medical Officers (War Pensions)
Occupational Pensions Regulatory Authority
Regional Medical Service
Social Security Advisory Committee

Department of the Procurator General and Treasury Solicitor
Legal Secretariat to the Law Officers

Department of Trade and Industry
Central Transport Consultative Committees
Competition Commission
Electricity Committees
Employment Appeal Tribunal
Employment Tribunals
Gas Consumers' Council
National Weights and Measures Laboratory
Office of Manpower Economics
Patent Office

Export Credits Guarantee Department

Foreign and Commonwealth Office
Wilton Park Conference Centre

Government Actuary's Department

Government Communications Headquarters

Home Office
    Boundary Commission for England
    Gaming Board for Great Britain
    Inspectors of Constabulary
    Parole Board and Local Review Committees

House of Commons

House of Lords

Inland Revenue, Board of

Intervention Board for Agricultural Produce

Lord Chancellor's Department
    Circuit Offices and Crown, County and Combined Courts (England and Wales)
    Combined Tax Tribunal
    Council on Tribunals
    Court of Appeal—Criminal
    Immigration Appellate Authorities
    Immigration Adjudicators
    Immigration Appeals Tribunal
    Lands Tribunal
    Law Commission
    Legal Aid Fund (England and Wales)
    Office of the Social Security Commissioners
    Pensions Appeal Tribunals
    Public Trust Office
    Supreme Court Group (England and Wales)
    Transport Tribunal

Ministry of Agriculture, Fisheries and Food
    Agricultural Dwelling House Advisory Committees
    Agricultural Land Tribunals
    Agricultural Wages Board and Committees
    Cattle Breeding Centre
    Plant Variety Rights Office
    Royal Botanic Gardens, Kew

Ministry of Defence
    Meteorological Office
    Defence Procurement Agency

National Assembly for Wales
    Higher Education Funding Council for Wales
    Local Government Boundary Commission for Wales
    Royal Commission for Ancient and Historical Monuments in Wales
    Valuation Tribunals (Wales)
    Welsh National Health Service Authorities and Trusts
    Welsh Rent Assessment Panels
    . . .

National Audit Office

National Investment and Loans Office

Northern Ireland Assembly Commission

Northern Ireland Court Service

        Coroners Courts
        County Courts
        Court of Appeal and High Court of Justice in Northern Ireland
        Crown Court
        Enforcement of Judgements Office
        Legal Aid Fund
        Magistrates Courts
        Pensions Appeals Tribunals

Northern Ireland, Department of Agriculture and Rural Development

Northern Ireland, Department of Culture, Arts and Leisure

Northern Ireland, Department of Education

Northern Ireland, Department of Enterprise, Trade and Investment

Northern Ireland, Department of the Environment

Northern Ireland, Department of Finance and Personnel

Northern Ireland, Department of Health, Social Services and Public Safety

Northern Ireland, Department of Higher and Further Education, Training and Employment

Northern Ireland, Department of Regional Development

Northern Ireland, Department of Social Development

Northern Ireland, Office of the First Minister and deputy First Minister

Northern Ireland, Crown Solicitor's Office
        Department of the Director of Public Prosecutions for Northern Ireland
        Northern Ireland Forensic Science Laboratory
        Office of Chief Electoral Officer for Northern Ireland
        [Northern Ireland Policing Board]
        Probation Board for Northern Ireland
        State Pathologist Service

Office of Fair Trading

Office for National Statistics
        National Health Service Central Register

Office of the Parliamentary Commissioner for Administration and Health Service Commissioners

Paymaster General's Office

[the Post Office company in connection with its postal business or a relevant subsidiary of that company in connection with the subsidiary's postal business]

Privy Council Office

Public Record Office

Registry of Friendly Societies

Royal Commission on Historical Manuscripts

Royal Hospital, Chelsea

Royal Mint

Scotland, Auditor-General

Scotland, Crown Office and Procurator Fiscal Service

Scotland, General Register Office

Scotland, Queen's and Lord Treasurer's Remembrancer

Scotland, Registers of Scotland

The Scotland Office

The Scottish Executive Corporate Services

The Scottish Executive Development Department

The Scottish Executive Education Department
     National Galleries of Scotland
     National Library of Scotland
     National Museums of Scotland
     Scottish Higher Education Funding Council

The Scottish Executive Enterprise and Lifelong Learning Department

The Scottish Executive Finance

The Scottish Executive Health Department
     Local Health Councils
     . . .
     Scottish Council for Postgraduate Medical Education
     Scottish National Health Service Authorities and Trusts

The Scottish Executive Justice Department
     Accountant of Court's Office
     High Court of Justiciary
     Court of Session
     HM Inspectorate of Constabulary
     Lands Tribunal for Scotland
     Parole Board for Scotland and Local Review Committees
     Pensions Appeal Tribunals
     Scottish Land Court
     Scottish Law Commission
     Sheriff Courts
     Scottish Criminal Record Office
     Scottish Crime Squad
     Scottish Fire Service Training Squad
     Scottish Police College
     Social Security Commissioners' Office

The Scottish Executive Rural Affairs Department
     Crofters Commission
     Red Deer Commission
     Rent Assessment Panel and Committees
     Royal Botanic Garden, Edinburgh
     Royal Commission on the Ancient and Historical Monuments of Scotland
     Royal Fine Art Commission for Scotland

The Scottish Executive Secretariat

The Scottish Parliamentary Body Corporate

Scottish Record Office

HM Treasury

Wales Office (Office of the Secretary of State for Wales)]

Amendment
Substituted by SI 2000/2009, reg 5(14), Sch 6.
In entry relating to 'Department of Health' first words omitted revoked by SI 2002/881, art 2, Schedule, para 11(a); in entry relating to 'Department of Health' second words omitted revoked by SI 2002/881, art

2, Schedule, para 11(d); in entry relating to 'National Assembly for Wales' words omitted revoked by SI 2002/881, art 2, Schedule, para 11(b); in entry relating to 'Northern Ireland, Crown Solicitor's Office' words 'Northern Ireland Policing Board' in square brackets substituted by the Police (Northern Ireland) Act 2000, s 2(4), Sch 2, para 6(1); entry beginning 'the Post Office company' substituted by SI 2001/1149, art 3(1), Sch 1, para 106(1), (3); in entry relating to 'The Scottish Executive Health Department' words omitted revoked by SI 2002/881, art 2, Schedule, para 11(c).

SCHEDULE 2
GOODS FOR THE PURPOSES OF THE THRESHOLDS

Regulation 7(2)(a)

[App.138]

The goods for the purpose of regulation 7(2)(a) are those specified in the following chapters of the CCCN (Customs Co-operation Council Nomenclature).

Chapter 25: Salt; sulphur; earths and stone; platering materials, lime and cement

Chapter 26: Metallic ores, slag and ash

Chapter 27: Mineral fuels, mineral oils and products of their distillation; bituminous substances; mineral waxes
except:
ex 27.10: special engine fuels

Chapter 28: Inorganic chemicals; organic and inorganic compounds of precious metals, of rare-earth metals, of radio-active elements and of isotapes
except:
ex 28.09: explosives
ex 28.13: explosives
ex 28.14: tear gas
ex 28.28: explosives
ex 28.32: explosives
ex 28.39: explosives
ex 28.50: toxic products
ex 28.51: toxic products
ex 28.54: explosives

Chapter 29: Organic chemicals
except:
ex 29.03: explosives
ex 29.04: explosives
ex 29.07: explosives
ex 29.08: explosives
ex 29.11: explosives
ex 29.12: explosives
ex 29.13: toxic products
ex 29.14: toxic products
ex 29.15: toxic products
ex 29.21: toxic products
ex 29.22: toxic products
ex 29.23: toxic products
ex 29.26: explosives
ex 29.27: toxic products
ex 29.29: explosives

Chapter 30: Pharmaceutical products

Chapter 31: Fertilizers

Chapter 32: Tanning and dyeing extracts; tannins and their derivatives; dyes, colours, paints and varnishes; putty, fillers and stoppings; inks

Chapter 33: Essential oils and resinoids; perfumery, cosmetic or toilet preparations

Chapter 34: Soap, organic surface-active agents, washing preparations, lubricating preparations, artificial waxes, prepared waxes, polishing and scouring preparations, candles and similar articles, modelling pastes and 'dental waxes'

Chapter 35: Al++buminoidal substances; glues; enzymes

Chapter 37: Photographs and cinematographic goods

Chapter 38: Miscellaneous chemical products
   except:
   ex 38.19: toxic products

Chapter 39: Artificial resins and plastic materials, cellulose esters and ethers; articles thereof
   except:
   ex 39.03: explosives

Chapter 40: Rubber, synthetic rubber, factice, and articles thereof
   except:
   ex 40.11: bullet-proof tyres

Chapter 41: Raw hides and skins (other than furskins) and leather

Chapter 42: Articles of leather; saddlery and harness; travel goods, handbags and similar containers; articles of animal gut (other than silk-worm gut)

Chapter 43: Furskins and artificial fur; manufactures thereof

Chapter 44: Wood and articles of wood; wood charcoal

Chapter 45: Cork and articles of cork

Chapter 46: Manufactures of straw of esparto and of other plaiting materials; basketware and wickerwork

Chapter 47: Paper-making material

Chapter 48: Paper and paperboard; articles of paper pulp, of paper or of paperboard

Chapter 49: Printed books, newspapers, pictures and other products of the printing industry; manuscripts, typescripts and plans

Chapter 65: Headgear and parts thereof

Chapter 66: Umbrellas, sunshades, walking-sticks, whips, riding-crops and parts thereof

Chapter 67: Prepared feathers and down and articles made of feathers or of down; artificial flowers; articles of human hair

Chapter 68: Articles of stone, of plaster, of cement, of asbestos, of mica and of similar materials

Chapter 69: Ceramic products

Chapter 70: Glass and glassware

Chapter 71: Pearls, precious and semi-precious stones, precious metals, rolled precious metals, and articles thereof, imitation jewellery

Chapter 73: Iron and steel and articles thereof

Chapter 74: Copper and articles thereof

Chapter 75: Nickel and articles thereof

Chapter 76: Aluminium and articles thereof

Chapter 77: Magnesium and beryllium and articles thereof

Chapter 78: Lead and articles thereof

Chapter 79: Zinc and articles thereof

Chapter 80: Tin and articles thereof

Chapter 81: Other base metals employed in metallurgy and articles thereof

Chapter 82: Tools, implements, cutlery, spoons and forks, of base metal; parts thereof
    except:
    ex 82.05: tools
    ex 82.07: tools, parts

Chapter 83: Miscellaneous articles of base metal

Chapter 84: Boilers, machinery and mechanical appliances; parts thereof
    except:
    ex 84.06: engines
    ex 84.08: other engines
    ex 84.45: machinery
    ex 84.53: automatic data-processing machines
    ex 84.55: parts of machines under heading No 84.53
    ex 84.59: nuclear reactors

Chapter 85: Electrical machinery and equipment; parts thereof
    except:
    ex 85.13: telecommunications equipment
    ex 85.15: transmission apparatus

Chapter 86: Railway and tramway locomotives, rolling-stock and parts thereof; railway and tramway tracks fixtures and fittings; traffic signalling equipment of all kinds (not electrically powered)
    except:
    ex 86.02: armoured locomotives, electric
    ex 86.03: other armoured locomotives
    ex 86.05: armoured wagons
    ex 86.06: repair wagons
    ex 86.07: wagons

Chapter 87: Vehicles, other than railway or tramway rolling-stock, and parts thereof
    except:
    87.08 tanks and other armoured vehicles
    ex 87.01: tractors
    ex 87.02: military vehicles
    ex 87.03: breakdown lorries
    ex 87.09: motorcycles
    ex 87.14: trailers

Chapter 89: Ships, boats and floating structures
    except:
    89.01 A: warships

Chapter 90: Optical, photographic, cinematographic, measuring, checking, precision, medical and surgical instruments and apparatus; parts thereof
    except:
    ex 90.05: binoculars

ex 90.13: miscellaneous instruments, lasers
ex 90.14: telemeters
ex 90.28: electrical and electronic measuring instruments
ex 90.11: microscopes
ex 90.17: medical instruments
ex 90.18: mechano-therapy appliances
ex 90.19: orthopaedic appliances
ex 90.20: X-ray apparatus

Chapter 91: Clocks and watches and parts thereof

Chapter 92: Musical instruments; sound recorders or reproducers; television image and sound recorders or reproducers; parts and accessories or such articles

Chapter 94: Furniture and parts thereof; bedding, mattresses, mattress supports, cushions and similar stuffed furnishings

> *except:*
> ex 94.01 A: aircraft seats

Chapter 95: Articles and manufactures of carving or moulding material

Chapter 96: Brooms, brushes, powder-puffs and sieves

Chapter 98: Miscellaneous manufactured articles

[SCHEDULE 3
FORMS OF NOTICES FOR PUBLICATION IN THE OFFICIAL JOURNAL]

[Regulations 9(1), 11(2), (8), 12(2), (16), 13(2) and 22(1)]

[PART A
PRIOR INFORMATION NOTICE]

[App.139]

[**1** Name, address, telegraphic address, telephone, telex and facsimile numbers of the contracting authority or the office from which additional information may be obtained.

2 Nature and quantity or value of the goods to be supplied. CPA reference number.

3 Estimated date of the commencement of the procedures leading to the award of the contract(s) (if known).

4 Other information.

5 Date of despatch of the notice.

6 Indication of whether the procurement is covered by the GPA.]

Amendment
Substituted by SI 2000/2009, reg 5(15), Sch 7.

[PART B
OPEN PROCEDURE NOTICE]

[App.140]

[**1** Name, address, telegraphic address, telephone, telex and facsimile numbers of the contracting authority.

2
(a)   Award procedure chosen;
(b)   Form of contract for which offers are invited.

3
(a)   Place of delivery.
(b)   Nature and quantity of the goods to be supplied, including CPA reference number and where applicable any options for further supplies and, if known, the expected date(s) when such options may be exercised. In the case of regular or recurring contracts, an estimate of the timing of the subsequent calls for tenders;
(c)   Indication of whether the suppliers can tender for some and/or all of the goods required.
(d)   Whether offers are invited for purchase, lease, rental, hire purchase or a combination of these.

4 Time limit for delivery or duration of the contract and, as far as possible, the date on which delivery should commence.

5
(a)   Name and address from which the contract documents and additional documents may be requested;
(b)   Final date for making such requests;
(c)   Where applicable, the amount and terms of payment of any sum payable for such documents.

6
(a)   Final date for receipt of tenders;
(b)   Address to which they must be sent;
(c)   Language(s) in which they must be drawn up.

7
(a)   Person(s) authorised to be present at the opening of tenders;
(b)   Date, time and place of opening.

8 Where applicable, any deposits and guarantees required.

9 The main terms concerning financing and payment and/or references to the relevant provisions.

10 Where applicable, the legal form to be taken by a grouping of suppliers to whom the contract is awarded.

11 Information concerning the supplier's own position, and information and formalities necessary for an appraisal of the minimum standards of economic and financial standing and technical capacity required of him.

12 Period during which the tenderer is bound to keep open his tender.

13 Criteria for the award of the contract. Criteria other than that of the lowest price shall be mentioned if they do not appear in the contract documents.

14 Where applicable, prohibition on variations.

15 Other information.

16 Date of publication of the prior information notice in the Official Journal or references to its non-publication.

17 Date of despatch of the notice

18 Indication of whether the procurement is covered by the GPA.]

Amendment
Substituted by SI 2000/2009, reg 5(15), Sch 7.

[PART C
RESTRICTED PROCEDURE NOTICE]

[App.141]

[1 Name, address, telegraphic address, telephone, telex and facsimile numbers of the contracting authority.

2

(a)   Award procedure chosen;

(b)   Where applicable, justification for use of the shorter time limits;

(c)   Form of contract for which offers are invited.

3

(a)   Place of delivery;

(b)   Nature and quantity of goods to be delivered, including CPA reference number; and, where applicable, any options for further supplies and, if known, an estimate of the timing when such options may be exercised. In the case of regular or recurring contracts, the estimated date(s) of the subsequent calls for tender;

(c)   Indication of whether the supplier can tender for some and/or all of the goods required;

(d)   Whether offers are invited for purchase, lease, rental, hire purchase or a combination of these.

4 Time limit for delivery, or duration of the contract and as far as possible, the date on which delivery should commence.

5 Where applicable, the legal form to be assumed by a grouping of suppliers to whom the contract is awarded.

6

(a)   Final date for the receipt of requests to participate;

(b)   Address to which they must be sent;

(c)   Language(s) in which they must be drawn up.

7 Final date for the dispatch of invitations to tender.

8 Any deposits and guarantees required.

9 Information concerning the supplier's own position, and the information and formalities necessary for an appraisal of the minimum standards of economic and financial standing and technical capacity required of him.

10 Criteria for the award of the contract if these are not stated in the invitation to tender.

11 If known, the number of suppliers which will be invited to tender or the range within which that number is expected to fall.

12 Where applicable, prohibition on variations.

13 Other information.

14 Date of publication of the prior information notice in the Official Journal or references to its non-publication.

15 Date of despatch of the notice.

16 Indication of whether the procurement is covered by the GPA.]

Amendment
Substituted by SI 2000/2009, reg 5(15), Sch 7.

[PART D
NEGOTIATED PROCEDURE NOTICE]

[App.142]

[**1** Name, address, telegraphic address, telephone, telex and facsimile number of the contracting authority.

2

(a)   Award procedure chosen;

(b)   Where applicable, justification for use of shorter time limits;

(c)   Where applicable, form of contract for which offers are invited.

3

(a)   Place of delivery.

(b)   Nature and quantity of goods to be delivered, including CPA reference number; and, where applicable, any options for further supplies and, if known, the estimated date(s) when such options may be exercised. In the case of regular or recurring contracts, the estimated date(s) of the subsequent calls for tender.

(c)   Indication of whether the suppliers can tender for some and/or all of the goods required;

(d)   Whether offers are invited for purchase, lease, rental, hire purchase or a combination of these.

4 Where applicable, the legal form to be taken by a grouping of suppliers to whom the contract is awarded.

5

(a)   Final date for the receipt of request to participate;

(b)   Address to which they must be sent;

(c)   Language(s) in which they must be drawn up.

6 Any deposits or guarantee required.

7 Information concerning the supplier's own position, and the information and formalities necessary for an appraisal of the minimum standards of economic and financial standing and technical capacity required of him.

8 If known, the number of suppliers which will be invited to tender or the range within which that number is expected to fall.

9 Where applicable, prohibition on variations.

10 Where applicable, the names and addresses of suppliers already selected by the awarding authority.

11 Date(s) of previous publications in the Official Journal.

12 Other information.

13 Date of despatch of the notice.

14 Indication of whether the procurement is covered by the GPA.]

Amendment
Substituted by SI 2000/2009, reg 5(15), Sch 7.

[PART E
CONTRACT AWARD NOTICE]

[App.143]

[**1** Name and address of contracting authority.

2
(a)   Award procedure chosen;
(b)   where appropriate, justification for the use of the negotiated procedure without a call for competition.

3 Date of award of contract.

4 Criteria for award of contract.

5 Number of offers received.

6 Name(s) and address(es) of supplier(s).

7 Nature and quantity of goods supplied, where applicable, by supplier: CPA reference number.

8 Price or range of prices paid or to be paid.

9 Value of winning award(s) or the highest and lowest offer taken into account in the award of the contract.

10 Where appropriate, value and proportion of the contract which may be subcontracted to third parties.

11 Other information.

12 Date of publication of the tender notice in the Official Journal.

13 Date of despatch of the notice.]

Amendment
Substituted by SI 2000/2009, reg 5(15), Sch 7.

[SCHEDULE 4
EXTENSION TO NON MEMBER STATES]

[Regulations 2(1) and 4]

[App.144]

[Relevant States	Agreement with the European Union which extend the provisions relating to public procurement to the relevant State	Statutory provisions designating the agreements as European Treaties
1 Bulgaria	Europe Agreement (OJ No L358, 31.12.94, p 2)	SI 1994/758
2 The Czech Republic	Europe Agreement (OJ No L360, 31.12.94, p 2)	SI 1994/759
3 Estonia	Europe Agreement (OJ No L68, 9.03.98, p 3)	SI 1997/269
4 Hungary	Europe Agreement (OJ No L347, 31.12.93, p 2)	SI 1992/2871

5 Iceland	European Economic Area Agreement	(a)European Economic Area Act 1993 (b), section 1
6 Latvia	Europe Agreement (OJ No L26, 2.02.98, p 3)	SI 1997/270
7 Liechtenstein	European Economic Area Agreement	(a) European Economic Area Act 1993 (b), section 1
8 Lithuania	Europe Agreement (OJ No L51, 20.02.98 p 3)	SI 1997/271
9 Norway	European Economic Area Agreement	(a) European Economic Area Act 1993 (b), section 1
10 Poland	Europe Agreement (OJ No L348, 31.12.94, p 2)	SI 1992/2872
11 Romania	Europe Agreement (OJ No L357, 31.12.94, p 2)	SI 1994/760
12 Slovakia	Europe Agreement (OJ No L359, 31.12.94, p 2)	SI 1994/761
13 Slovenia	Europe Agreement (OJ No L51, 26.02.99, p 3)	SI 1998/1062

Amendment
Inserted by SI 2000/2009, reg 5(15), Sch 8.

LOCAL AUTHORITIES (COMPANIES) ORDER 1995

SI 1995/849

PART I
GENERAL

[App.145]
1 Citation, commencement and interpretation

(1)   This Order may be cited as the Local Authorities (Companies) Order 1995 and shall come into force as provided in paragraph (2) below.

(2)   This Order shall come into force—

(a)   for the purposes of article 4, on 1st July 1995;

(b)   for the purposes of articles 5 to 10 in so far as they relate to companies formed on or before 31st March 1995, on 1st July 1995; and

(c)   for all other purposes on 1st April 1995.

(3)   Except where the context otherwise requires, any reference in this Order to a section or Part is to a section or Part of the 1989 Act.

(4)   In this Order—

'the 1985 Act' means the Companies Act 1985;

'the 1989 Act' means the Local Government and Housing Act 1989;

'the Audit Commission' means the Audit Commission for Local Authorities and the National Health Service in England and Wales;

'controlled company' means a company (other than a company within a description set out in the Schedule to this Order) which for the purposes of Part V is under the control of a local authority or is treated as being under the control of each of two or more local authorities;

'director', except in so far as the context otherwise requires, includes, in relation to a company which is an industrial and provident society, a member of the committee of management of the society and its chief officer;

'relevant authority', in relation to a regulated company, means any local authority having control of that company or to whose influence the company is subject, or which is, by virtue of section 73 (authorities acting jointly, etc) treated as having such control or influence;

and any reference to a regulated company is a reference to a company which is for the time being either—

(a)   a controlled company, or

(b)   a company which for the purposes of Part V is, or is treated as, subject to the influence of a local authority (the 'relevant authority') and which—

(i)   is an unlimited company or a society registered or deemed to be registered under the Industrial and Provident Societies Act 1965 or under the Industrial and Provident Societies Act (Northern Ireland) 1969; or

(ii)   satisfies either or both of the first and second conditions set out in paragraphs (5) and (7) below,

but is not within any description set out in the Schedule to this Order.

(5)   The first condition mentioned in paragraph (4)(b)(ii) above is that the relevant authority would, if it were a company registered under the 1985 Act, be treated by virtue of section 258 of that Act as having the right to exercise, or as having, during the relevant period, actually exercised, a dominant influence over the company in question.

(6)   For the purposes of paragraph (5) above 'the relevant period', in relation to any duty or any action referred to in Part II of this Order, means the financial year of the relevant authority which ended immediately before the financial year in which, if the company in question were a regulated company, that duty would fall to be fulfilled, or in which that action is performed.

(7)   The second condition mentioned in paragraph (4)(b)(ii) above is that if the authority were a company registered under the 1985 Act it would be required, by virtue of section 227 of that Act, or of accounting standards such as would, by virtue of that Act, be applicable in the circumstances, to prepare group accounts in respect of the company in question.

(8)   For the purposes of paragraph (7) above, in determining whether a local authority would be required to prepare group accounts it shall be assumed that no exclusion of or exemption from such requirement, other than those referred to in section 229(3)(a) and (c) of the 1985 Act, would be applicable by virtue of that Act.

[App.146]
2 Companies subject to the influence of local authorities

In determining for the purposes of this Order whether a company is subject to the influence of a local authority no account shall be taken of any condition specified in any paragraph of subsection (1) or (3) of section 69, in so far as that condition is fulfilled by reference only to another company which is of a description mentioned in the Schedule to this Order, or to a person who is both an employee and either a director, manager, secretary or similar officer of such a company.

[App.147]
3 Application of the Order

No provision in this Order shall be construed as requiring a company to act (or refrain from acting) in breach of any provision made by or under any enactment, or any obligation subsisting on the day on which such provision comes into force.

PART II
REGULATION OF CONTROLLED AND INFLUENCED COMPANIES

[App.148]
4 Identification of companies

(1)   A regulated company shall have mentioned on all relevant documents the fact that it is a company controlled, or, as the case may be, influenced, by a local authority, within the meaning of Part V; and naming the relevant authority or authorities.

(2)   In this article 'relevant documents' means business letters, notices and other documents of the company, being of any kind mentioned in paragraphs (a) to (d) of section 349(1) of the 1985 Act.

[App.149]

5 Requirements applicable to regulated companies

(1)   A regulated company shall not—

(a)   in respect of the carrying out of any relevant duty, pay to a regulated director remuneration in excess of the maximum amount;

(b)   in respect of expenditure on travelling or subsistence in connection with the carrying out of a relevant duty, pay to a regulated director an allowance, or reimburse expenses, in excess of the maximum amount;

(c)   publish any material which the relevant authority would be prohibited from publishing by section 2 of the Local Government Act 1986.

(2)   Where a director becomes disqualified for membership of a local authority otherwise than by being employed by a local authority or a controlled company, the company shall make such arrangements as may be necessary for a resolution to be moved for his removal in accordance with section 303 of the 1985 Act.

(3)   In this article—

(a)   for the purposes of paragraph (1)(a), the maximum amount is the greatest amount which would for the time being be payable by the relevant authority in respect of a comparable duty performed on behalf of that authority, less any amount paid by that authority in respect of the relevant duty to the regulated director in question;

(b)   for the purposes of paragraph (1)(b), the maximum amount in relation to a director is the maximum amount of travelling or subsistence allowance which would for the time being be payable to that director by the local authority of which he is a member if the relevant duty were an approved duty for the purposes of section 174 of the Local Government Act 1972;

(c)   'regulated director' means a director of the company who is also a member of a relevant authority; and

(d)   'relevant duty' means a duty carried out on behalf of the company.

[App.150]

6 Provision of information to authority's auditor

A regulated company shall provide, and authorise or instruct its auditors to provide—

(a)   to the person who is for the time being the auditor in relation to the accounts of the relevant authority, such information and explanation about the affairs of the company as that person may require for the purposes of the audit of the local authority's accounts; and

(b)   to any person authorised by the Audit Commission, such information as that person or the Commission may require for the discharge of any function under Part III of the Local Government Finance Act 1982.

[App.151]

7 Provision of information to members of local authority

(1)   Subject to paragraph (2), a regulated company shall provide to a member of a relevant authority such information about the affairs of the company as the member reasonably requires for the proper discharge of his duties.

(2)   Nothing in this article shall require a company to provide information in breach of any enactment, or of an obligation owed to any person.

[App.152]
8 Provision of financial information to authority

(1)   A regulated company shall, on the request of any relevant authority, provide to that authority, within such reasonable time as may be specified by the authority, such information about the affairs of the company as that authority may require for the purposes of any order for the time being in force under section 39 (revenue accounts and capital finance) of the 1989 Act.

(2)   Information required under paragraph (1) shall be supplied in such form as the relevant authority may reasonably require.

[App.153]
9 Appointment of auditor

A controlled company shall, before it first appoints any person as auditor of the company, obtain the Audit Commission's consent to the appointment of that person.

PART III
CONTROLLED COMPANIES WHICH ARE NOT ARM'S LENGTH COMPANIES

[App.154]
10 Public inspection of minutes

(1)   A controlled company which is not an arm's length company shall, until the expiry of the period of four years beginning with the date of the meeting, make available for inspection by any member of the public a copy of the minutes of any general meeting of the company.

(2)   Nothing in paragraph (1) requires any copy to be made available which includes any matter the disclosure of which would be in breach of any enactment, or of an obligation owed to any person.

(3)   Nothing in this article shall require a company to make available for inspection the minutes of any meeting held before the date on which this Order comes into force.

PART IV
MINORITY INTERESTS

[App.155]
11 Authorised companies

There are hereby specified for the purposes of section 71 (control of minority interests) companies, other than regulated companies and companies within any description set out in the Schedule to this Order, in which any person associated with a local authority (within the meaning of section 69(5)) has a right to vote at a general meeting or of which any such person is a director.

PART V
CAPITAL FINANCE

[App.156]
12 Interpretation

(1)   A local authority together with any companies in relation to which that authority is the relevant authority are for the purposes of section 39 and this Part of the Order referred to as members of a local authority group, and any reference in relation to a particular company to the same local authority group is a reference to the local authority group of which that company is a member.

(2)   In this Part—
'called-up share capital' has the same meaning as in section 737(1) of the 1985 Act, and 'share' has the same meaning as in section 744 of that Act;
'credit transaction' means a lease or a single contract or two or more contracts taken together which, if a local authority became lessees under the lease or entered into the contract or contracts, would constitute a credit arrangement, but does not include—
  (a)   any lease granted or assigned to a regulated company under which the lessor is a member of the same local authority group; or
  (b)   any contract entered into by a regulated company with a member of the same local authority group.
['relevant lender' means—
  (a)   the Public Works Loan Board,
  (b)   the Bank of England,
  (c)   the European Investment Bank,
  (d)   a body mentioned in any of paragraphs 1 to 17, or in paragraph 28 or 29, of Part II of the Schedule to the Local Authorities (Capital Finance) (Approved Investments) Regulations 1990,
  (e)   a person who has permission under Part 4 of the Financial Services and Markets Act 2000 to accept deposits, or
  (f)   an EEA firm or the kind mentioned in paragraph 5(b) of Schedule 3 to that Act which has permission under paragraph 15 of that Schedule (as a result of qualifying for authorisation under paragraph 12 of that Schedule) to accept deposits.]

[(3)   Sub-paragraphs (e) and (f) of the definition of 'relevant lender' in paragraph (2) must be read with—
(a)   section 22 of the Financial Services and Markets Act 2000;
(b)   any relevant order under that section; and
(c)   Schedule 2 to that Act.]

Amendment
Para (2): definition 'relevant lender' inserted by SI 1996/621, art 3; definition 'relevant lender' substituted by SI 2001/3649, art 489(1), (2).
Para (3): inserted by SI 2001/3649, art 489(1), (3).

[App.157]
13 Receipts, contracts and liabilities of regulated companies

(1)   Subject to the following provisions of this article, where a regulated company on or after 1st April 1995—
(a)   receives a sum which, if it were a local authority, would be a capital receipt,

(b)   receives consideration to which, if it were a local authority, section 61 would apply,

(c)   receives a sum by way of grant from a Community institution to which, if it were a local authority, section 63(4) would apply,

(d)   enters into a credit transaction,

(e)   with respect to a credit transaction, agrees to a variation of terms which, if it were a local authority, would be a variation within the meaning of section 51(1),

(f)   incurs additional liabilities within the meaning of article 16, or

(g)   reduces its liabilities within the meaning of article 16,

the sum, consideration, credit transaction, variation, liabilities or reduction in question shall be treated for the purposes of the application of Part IV as having been received, entered into, agreed, incurred or, as the case may be, made by the relevant authority.

(2)   Paragraph (1) does not apply to any sum or consideration which, apart from this paragraph, would fall within paragraph (1) if it is received by the company—

(a)   from a person who is a member of the same local authority group;

(b)   in respect of the disposal of assets held for charitable purposes.

(3)   Where a company is a regulated company on 1st April 1995 and is no longer a regulated company on 31st March 1996, any sum, consideration, credit transaction, variation, liabilities or reduction in liabilities which is or are treated by virtue of paragraph (1) above as having been received, entered into, agreed, incurred or, as the case may be, made by the relevant authority during the financial year beginning on 1st April 1995 shall cease on 31st March 1996 to be so treated.

(4)   Where a company falling within paragraph (3) above becomes a regulated company at any time on or before 31st March 1997, any sum, consideration, credit transaction, variation, liabilities or reduction in liabilities which ceased by virtue of paragraph (3) above to be treated as having been received, entered into, agreed, incurred or, as the case may be, made by the relevant authority shall be so treated as if the company had not ceased to be a regulated company on or before 31st March 1996.

[App.158]
14 Application of Part IV: requirement for credit cover

(1)   Where in relation to things done by or to a regulated company in a financial year (in this article referred to as the 'current year') a relevant authority are treated by virtue of article 13(1) as having—

(a)   received a sum such as mentioned in article 13(1)(a),

(b)   received any consideration such as mentioned in article 13(1)(b),

(c)   received a sum such as mentioned in article 13(1)(c),

(d)   entered into a credit transaction,

(e)   agreed to a variation of the terms of a credit transaction,

(f)   incurred additional liabilities, or

(g)   made a reduction in liabilities,

the provisions of Part IV shall apply to the members of the local authority group to the extent and subject to the modifications referred to in the following provisions of this article and in articles 15 to 18.

(2)   Subject to paragraph (4), with respect to each regulated company in the local authority group [the requirement for credit cover in section 50(2) shall apply as if, but only as if,] there is required to be available to the relevant authority in the financial

year following the current year an amount of credit cover which is equal to the aggregate of—

(a)　the amount which, if the company were a local authority, other than an authority to whom paragraph (3) below applies, the company would have been required to set aside as provision for credit liabilities in accordance with section 59 or section 61(4) with respect to sums or consideration falling within paragraph (1)(a) or (b) above;

(b)　an amount equal to the total receipts by the company of sums falling within paragraph (1)(c) above;

(c)　the amount which, if the company were a local authority, would be the initial cost of any credit transaction entered into by the company; and

(d)　the amount of credit cover which, if the company were a local authority, would be required to be available to it in accordance with section 51(4) with respect to any variation of the terms of a credit transaction;

(e)　where in the current year the company incurs additional liabilities within the meaning of article 16, the amount of the excess referred to in article 16(3).

[(3)　This paragraph applies to a local authority whose credit ceiling, as determined under Part III of Schedule 3 to the Act, is nil or a negative amount at the beginning of the current year, and who have no money outstanding by way of borrowing other than—

(a)　short-term borrowing (within the meaning of section 45(6));

(b)　borrowing undertaken under section 5 of the City of London (Various Powers) Act 1924; or

(c)　borrowing undertaken before 24th August 1995, other than borrowing by the issue of stock on or after 15th December 1993, from a person who is not a relevant lender.]

(4)　For the purposes of paragraph (2), an amount of credit cover shall only be required by virtue of sub-paragraphs (c), (d) and (e) where the aggregate of the amounts referred to in those sub-paragraphs exceeds £10,000.

[(5)　For the purposes of this article, in relation to any financial year beginning on or after 1st April 2001, one or more of the following amounts, in any combination, constitutes an amount of credit cover—

(a)　an amount which the authority determine to set aside from the usable part of the authority's capital receipts or from a revenue account as provision to meet credit liabilities (being an amount over and above amounts required to be set aside by virtue of any other provision of Part IV);

(b)　an amount by which the authority determine to treat as reduced the balance of a credit approval;

(c)　an amount by which the authority determine to treat as reduced any credit cover provision designated in accordance with paragraph (8).]

(6)　In paragraph (5)(b)—

(a)　the reference to a credit approval is a reference to a basic credit approval or a supplementary credit approval issued or transferred to the authority and having effect for the financial year following the current year;

(b)　the balance of a credit approval is that part of the approval with respect to which a determination has not been made under section 56(1).

(7)　A determination by a local authority under paragraph (5) shall take effect at the time it is made, and shall be made not later than six months after the end of the financial year following the current year.

[(8)   Where, in relation to any financial year ending on or after 31st March 2001, a basic credit approval having effect for that year is, pursuant to article 15, treated as increased by any amount, the authority may—

(a)   where a determination under section 56(1) is made in respect of part only of that amount, designate all or part of the residue of that amount as credit cover provision; or

(b)   where no determination under section 56(1) is made in respect of any part of that amount, designate all or part of that amount as credit cover provision.]

Amendment
Para (2): words 'the requirement for credit cover' to 'but only as if,' in square brackets substituted in relation to local authorities in England by SI 2001/3042, art 2(1), (2), and in relation to local authorities in Wales by SI 2002/2118, art 2(1), (2)(a).
Para (3): substituted by SI 1996/621, art 4.
Para (5): substituted in relation to local authorities in England by SI 2001/722, art 2(1), (2)(a); a corresponding amendment has been made in relation to local authorities in Wales by SI 2002/2118, art 2(1), (2)(b).
Para (8): inserted in relation to local authorities in England by SI 2001/722, art 2(1), (2)(b); a corresponding amendment has been made in relation to local authorites in Wales by SI 2002/2118, art 2(1), (2)(c).

[App.159]
15 Application of Part IV: increase in the basic credit approval

(1)   Where in a financial year (in this article referred to as the 'current year') a regulated company reduces its liabilities within the meaning of article 16, [the provisions in Part IV as to basic credit approvals shall apply] subject to the modification that the relevant authority may treat a relevant credit approval as increased by the amount relating to that company of the excess referred to in article 16(4).

(2)   In paragraph (1), the reference to a relevant credit approval is a reference to a basic credit approval issued or transferred to the authority and having effect for the financial year following the current year.

(3)   A basic credit approval may be treated as increased under paragraph (1) notwithstanding that a determination has been made under section 56(1) with respect to the whole or any part of the amount of the approval, and, where the amount of a basic credit approval is nil, the amount of the increase shall be treated as the amount of the approval.

Amendment
Para (1): words 'the provisions in Part IV as to basic credit approvals shall apply' in square brackets substituted in relation to local authorities in England by SI 2001/3042, art 2(1), (3), and in relation to local authorities in Wales by SI 2002/2118, art 2(1), (3).

[App.160]
16 Liabilities of regulated companies

(1)   [Subject to paragraph (6),] any reference in this article to the relevant liabilities of a regulated company is a reference to the total of the company's liabilities less its current assets (and the total so calculated may, accordingly, be a negative amount); and for this purpose, . . .—

(a)   'current assets' shall be construed in accordance with section 262(1) of the 1985 Act, but do not include—

(i)   land in which the company has any interest, or

(ii)   any liability owed to the company by a member of the same local authority group unless the liability was incurred before the date on

which the company became a regulated company ('the relevant date');
(b)   where the company's current assets in a financial year are reduced by any payments made by the company under—
    (i)   any credit transaction treated as having been entered into by the relevant authority by virtue of article 13(1)(d) above, or
    (ii)   any variation of the terms of a credit transaction treated as having been agreed by the relevant authority by virtue of article 13(1)(e) above, they shall be treated as if those payments had not been made;
[(bb)   the company's assets shall not be treated as reduced by the defraying, after the relevant date, of expenditure for any purpose, where that expenditure is defrayed from monies accumulated before the relevant date;]
(c)   'liabilities' do not include—
    [(i)   any liability under a credit transaction (whether entered into by the company before, on or after the relevant date),]
    (ii)   any liabilities under an agreement entered into by the company after the relevant date to a variation of the terms of a credit transaction entered into before the relevant date, or
    (iii)   any liability which is owed by the company to a person who is a member of the same local authority group, unless the liability was incurred before the relevant date; and
(d)   subject to paragraph (2), the sum of the called-up share capital of a regulated company with respect to shares held by persons who are not members of the same local authority group, and any premium paid to the company for such shares, is to be treated as a liability of the company.

(2)   Where any shares in a regulated company are transferred by the relevant authority to a person who is not a member of the same local authority group, the liabilities of the company on and at any time after the date on which the shares are transferred shall not include the amount which is on that date the called-up share capital of the company with respect to those shares.

(3)   A regulated company incurs additional liabilities where in any financial year (in this article referred to as 'year two') its relevant liabilities exceed its relevant liabilities in the financial year immediately preceding year two (in this article referred to as 'year one').

(4)   A regulated company reduces its liabilities where its relevant liabilities in year one exceed its relevant liabilities in year two.

[(5)   In a financial year other than the last year, the relevant authority shall determine the relevant liabilities of a regulated company by reference to—
(a)   amounts shown for assets and liabilities in the company's balance sheet prepared as at a date in that year, or, if there is more than one such balance sheet, in the last such balance sheet to have been prepared, or, if there is no such balance sheet,
(b)   amounts which they determine to be assets and liabilities of the company on the last day of that year.

(5A)   In the last year, the relevant authority shall determine the relevant liabilities of a regulated company by reference to amounts which they determine to be assets and liabilities of the company on the day immediately before the day on which the company ceases to be a member of the same local authority group.

(5B)   In [paragraphs (5) and (5A)] above, 'the last year' means the financial year in which the company concerned ceases to be a regulated company or becomes a regulated company of a different local authority.]

(6)   Where year two is the financial year in which by virtue of the coming into force of this Part or otherwise the company becomes a regulated company, [the amount determined] by the relevant authority in accordance with paragraph (7) shall be treated for the purposes of paragraphs (3) and (4) as the company's relevant liabilities in year one.

[(7)   The relevant authority shall determine the amount by which the total of the company's liabilities as at the date immediately before the day on which the company became a regulated company exceeded the company's current assets as at that date (and the total so calculated may, accordingly, be a negative amount); and for this purpose—

(a)   'current assets' shall be construed in accordance with section 262(1) of the 1985 Act, but do not include land in which the company had any interest on that date; and

(b)   the sum of the called-up share capital of the company with respect to shares held on that date by persons who were not, on the following day, members of the same local authority group, and any premium paid to the company for such shares, is to be treated as a liability of the company.]

(8)   Where two companies are members of the same local authority group, and the relevant liabilities of the companies in a particular financial year fall to be calculated as at different dates, if as a result of a transaction or a group of transactions between those companies—

(a)   the relevant liabilities in that year of one company would, apart from this paragraph, be reduced,

(b)   the relevant liabilities in that year of the other company would, if the relevant liabilities of the two companies fell to be calculated as at the same date, be increased, and

(c)   the relevant liabilities in that year of the other company are not increased or are increased by an amount which is less than the amount of the reduction referred to in sub-paragraph (a),

no account shall be taken of the amount of that reduction in calculating the relevant liabilities in that year of the company mentioned in sub-paragraph (a).

Amendment
Para (1): words 'Subject to paragraph (6),' in square brackets inserted by SI 1996/621, art 5(a); words omitted revoked by SI 1996/621, art 5(a); sub-para (bb) (as originally inserted by SI 1996/621, art 5(a)) substituted in relation to local authorities in England by SI 2001/722, art 2(1), (3)(a), and in relation to local authorities in Wales by SI 2002/2118, art 2(1), (4)(a); sub-para (c)(i) substituted in relation to local authorities in England by SI 2001/722, art 2(1), (3)(b), and in relation to local authorities in Wales by SI 2002/2118, art 2(1), (4)(b).
Paras (5), (5A), (5B): substituted, for para (5) as originally enacted, by SI 1996/621, art 5(b)
Para (5B): words 'paragraphs (5A) and (5B)' in italics revoked and subsequent words in square brackets substituted in relation to local authorities in England by SI 2001/722, art 2(1), (4), and in relation to local authorities in Wales by SI 2002/2188, art 2(1), (5).
Para (6): words 'the amount determined' in square brackets substituted by SI 1996/621, art 5(c).
Para (7): substituted by SI 1996/621, art 5(d).

[App.161]

17 Dealings between members of a local authority group

(1)   This paragraph applies where a local authority—

(a)   become the lessees under a lease of any property, and the lessor under the lease and the authority are members of the same local authority group; or

(b)   enter into a contract for the supply of any property, and the other party to the contract and the authority are members of the same local authority group; and

(c)   in either case, the property in question was acquired by the company after it became a regulated company.

(2)   Where paragraph (1) applies, the lease or the contract in question shall not be treated as a credit arrangement for the purposes of Part IV, and any variation of such a lease or contract shall not be treated as the variation of such an arrangement for those purposes.

(3)   Where a local authority receive from a regulated company a sum which, apart from this paragraph, would be a capital receipt for the purposes of Part IV, the sum shall not be treated as a capital receipt for those purposes if the authority and the company are members of the same local authority group.

(4)   Where a local authority receive from a regulated company any consideration which, apart from this paragraph, would fall within section 61(1), section 61 shall not apply to the consideration if the authority and the company are members of the same local authority group.

[App.162]

18 Provisions where there are two or more relevant authorities

(1)   Paragraphs (2) and (3) apply where a regulated company ('a relevant company') is treated as being under the control, or subject to the influence of, each of two or more local authorities.

(2)   Where under any provision in this Part anything done by or to a regulated company is treated as done by or to the relevant authority in relation to that company, that thing shall be treated as having been done by or to each of the relevant authorities to the extent of their involvement in the relevant company.

(3)   Where under any provision in this Part any requirement is imposed, or any entitlement is conferred, on the relevant authority in relation to a regulated company, that requirement or entitlement shall be treated as having been imposed or conferred on each of the relevant authorities to the extent of their involvement in the relevant company.

(4)   For the purposes of this article, the extent of an authority's involvement in a relevant company shall be determined by agreement with the other relevant authorities in relation to that company or, in default of agreement, by a person nominated jointly by all such authorities or, where no such nomination can be agreed, by a person appointed by the Secretary of State.

(5)   Section 31 of the Arbitration Act 1950 shall have effect for the purposes of the determination of any question by a person nominated or appointed under paragraph (4) as if the determination were an arbitration under any other Act within the meaning of that section.

SCHEDULE
COMPANIES NOT SUBJECT TO THE ORDER

Article 1(2), 11

[App.163]

1 A public transport company within the meaning of section 72 of the Transport Act 1985.

2 A public airport company within the meaning of Part II of the Airports Act 1986.

3 A company which is under the control or subject to the influence of a Passenger Transport Executive.

4 A company which by virtue of section 73 of the 1989 Act is treated as under the control or subject to the influence of two or more authorities, where each of those authorities is a Passenger Transport Executive.

5 A company which, in relation to a company ('the holding company') within any description in paragraphs 1 to 4, would, if the holding company were a local authority within the meaning of Part V, be under the control of that authority.

LOCAL AUTHORITIES (CONTRACTS) REGULATIONS 1997

SI 1997/2862

[App.164]

1 Citation and commencement

These Regulations may be cited as the Local Authorities (Contracts) Regulations 1997 and shall come into force on 30th December 1997.

[App.165]

2 Interpretation

In these Regulations—

'the 1989 Act' means the Local Government and Housing Act 1989;

'the auditor', in relation to a local authority, means the auditor appointed under [section 3 of the Audit Commission Act 1998] to audit the accounts of the authority in accordance with . . . that Act; and

'certificate' means a certificate issued by a local authority in satisfying the certification requirements in relation to a contract.

Amendment

In definition 'the auditor' words 'section 3 of the Audit Commission Act 1998' in square brackets substituted by virtue of the Audit Commission Act 1998, s 54(2), Sch 4, para 4(1); in definition 'the auditor' words omitted revoked by virtue of the Audit Commission Act 1998, s 54(2), Sch 4, para 4(1).

[App.166]

3 Copies of certificates—all local authorities

A local authority shall ensure that a copy of every certificate issued by it is given to each of the persons with whom the authority has entered, or is to enter, into the contract in relation to which the certificate is issued.

[App.167]

4 Copies of certificates—authorities with a monitoring officer

A local authority which is under the duty imposed by section 5(1) of the 1989 Act to designate one of its officers as the monitoring officer shall ensure that a copy of every certificate issued by it is given to the officer designated by it under that section and to the auditor.

[App.168]

5 Copies of certificates—other authorities

(1)   Each of the following authorities shall ensure that a copy of every certificate issued by it is given to the auditor—

(a)   the Broads Authority;

(b)   the London Pensions Fund Authority;

(c)   the South Yorkshire Pensions Authority;

(d)   the Lee Valley Regional Park Authority;

(e)   the Residuary Body for Wales or Corff Gweddilliol Cymru; . . .

(f)   a probation committee, except the inner London probation committee;

[(g)   Transport for London; . . .

(h)   the London Development Agency][; and

(i)   the Greater London Magistrates' Courts Authority].

(2)   The inner London probation committee shall ensure that a copy of every certificate issued by it is given to the Receiver for the Metropolitan Police District and the Comptroller and Auditor General.

(3)   The Receiver for the Metropolitan Police District shall ensure that a copy of every certificate issued by him is given to the Comptroller and Auditor General.

Amendment
Para (1): in sub-para (e) word omitted revoked by SI 2000/1033, reg 4(1), (2); sub-paras (g), (h) inserted, in relation to England, by SI 2000/1033, reg 4(1), (2); in sub-para (g) word omitted revoked, in relation to England, by SI 2001/723, regs 2, 10(1), (2); sub-para (i) and word 'and' immediately preceding it inserted, in relation to England, by SI 2001/723, regs 2, 10(1), (2).

[App.169]

6 Matters to be dealt with in a manner prescribed by regulations

(1)   Where, in relation to a contract, a local authority on which there is conferred the power in section 111 of the Local Government Act 1972 (subsidiary powers of local authorities) [or, in the case of the Greater London Authority, in section 34(1) of the Greater London Authority Act 1999 or, in the case of Transport for London, in paragraph 1(3) of Schedule 10 to the Greater London Authority Act] [1999 or, in the case of the Greater London Magistrates' Courts Authority, section 59A(2) of the Justices of the Peace Act 1997]—

(a)   states in a certificate that it had or has power to enter into the contract, and

(b)   specifies that the statutory provision, or one of the statutory provisions, conferring the power is section 111 of the Local Government Act 1972 [or, in the case of the Greater London Authority, section 34(1) of the Greater London Authority Act 1999 or, in the case of Transport for London, paragraph 1(3) of Schedule 10 to the Greater London Authority Act] [1999 or, in the case of the Greater London Magistrates' Courts Authority, section 59A(2) of the Justices of the Peace Act 1997],

the authority shall specify in the certificate each statutory provision conferring a relevant function, or, where there are two or more relevant functions, the statutory provisions conferring the main relevant functions.

(2)   For the purposes of this regulation, in relation to a contract, a function is a relevant function if the contract is calculated to facilitate, or is conducive or incidental to, the discharge of the function.

Amendment
Para (1): words from 'or, in the' to 'London Authority Act' in square brackets inserted, in relation to England, by SI 2000/1033, reg 4(1), (3)(a); words from '1999 or, in' to 'Justices of the Peace Act 1997' in square brackets inserted, in relation to England, by SI 2001/723, regs 2, 10(1), (3)(a); in sub-para (b) words from 'or, in the' to 'London Authority Act' in square brackets inserted, in relation to England, by SI 2000/1033, reg 4(1), (3)(b); in sub-para (b) words from '1999 or, in' to 'Justices of the Peace Act 1997' in square brackets inserted, in relation to England, by SI 2001/723, regs 2, 10(1), (3)(b).

[App.170]

7 Signature of certificates—authorities with a chief finance officer

(1)   In this regulation—

'chief finance officer' means an officer of a local authority who, for the purposes of section 151 of the Local Government Act 1972, section 73 of the Local

Government Act 1985, section 112 of the Local Government Finance Act 1988[, section 6 of the 1989 Act or section 127 of the Greater London Authority Act 1999], has responsibility for the administration of the authority's financial affairs; and

'relevant authority' means a local authority which is required by any of those enactments to have a chief finance officer (that is every local authority other than an authority mentioned in regulation 8).

(2)   A relevant authority which is under the duty imposed by section 4(1) of the 1989 Act to designate one of its officers as the head of its paid service shall ensure that a certificate issued by it is signed by one of the following officers of the authority—

(a)   one of the statutory chief officers within the meaning given to that expression in section 2(6) of the 1989 Act [or, in the case of the Greater London Authority, its chief finance officer];

(b)   a non-statutory chief officer within the meaning given to that expression in section 2(7) of the 1989 Act; or

(c)   a deputy chief officer within the meaning given to that expression in section 2(8) of the 1989 Act.

(3)   A relevant authority which is not under a duty to designate one of its officers under section 4(1) of the 1989 Act shall ensure that a certificate issued by it is signed by the chief finance officer of the authority, or a person who, as respects all or most of the duties of his post, is required to report directly or is directly accountable to the chief finance officer.

Amendment
Para (1): in definition 'chief finance officer' words in square brackets substituted by SI 2000/1033, reg 4(1), (4)(a).
Para (2): in sub-para (a) words from 'or, in the' to 'chief finance officer' in square brackets inserted, in relation to England, by SI 2000/1033, reg 4(1), (4)(b).

[App.171]

8 Signature of certificates—other authorities

(1)   The Broads Authority shall ensure that every certificate issued by it is signed by the chairman, vice-chairman or chief officer of the authority.

(2)   The Lee Valley Regional Park Authority shall ensure that every certificate issued by it is signed by the chairman or vice-chairman of the authority.

(3)   The Residuary Body for Wales or Corff Gweddilliol Cymru shall ensure that every certificate issued by it is signed by its chairman.

(4)   A probation committee, except the inner London probation committee, shall ensure that every certificate issued by it is signed by the secretary to the committee, by the treasurer of the committee or by the Chief Probation Officer appointed by the committee.

(5)   The inner London probation committee shall ensure that every certificate issued by it is signed—

(a)   by the secretary to the committee;

(b)   by the Receiver for the Metropolitan Police District or a person who, as respects all or most of the duties of his post, is required to report directly or is directly accountable to him; or

(c)   by the Chief Probation Officer appointed by the committee.

(6)   The Receiver for the Metropolitan Police District shall ensure that every certificate issued by him is signed by him or by a person who, as respects all or most of the duties of his post, is required to report directly or is directly accountable to him.

INDEX